KISS, BOW, OR SHAKE HANDS

Second Edition

The Bestselling Guide to Doing Business in More Than 60 Countries

Terri Morrison
and
Wayne A. Conaway

Adams Media
New York London Toronto Sydney New Delhi

To Nica, Brendan, and Alex
Forever Wise, Forever True, Forever Loved
And to Tony
Forever
—*Terri M.*

To my Parents
I hope I was a good long-term investment.
—*Wayne A. Conaway*

And to the late George A. Borden, Ph.D., a gifted friend.

Aadamsmedia

Adams Media
An Imprint of Simon & Schuster, Inc.
57 Littlefield Street
Avon, Massachusetts 02322

For information about special discounts for bulk purchases, please contact Simon & Schuster Special Sales at 1-866-506-1949 or business@simonandschuster.com.

The Simon & Schuster Speakers Bureau can bring authors to your live event. For more information or to book an event contact the Simon & Schuster Speakers Bureau at 1-866-248-3049 or visit our website at www.simonspeakers.com.

Interior design and composition by Electronic Publishing Services, Inc. Tennessee

Maps © Map Resources

Manufactured in the United States of America

20 19 18

Library of Congress Cataloging-in-Publication Data has been applied for.

ISBN 978-1-59337-368-9

"In this global economy, ANYONE who leaves the United States is a fool if they don't read up on their destination's customs. *Kiss, Bow, or Shake Hands* is THE definitive authority on how to conduct yourself around the world. You can easily offend your prospects and there is no faster way to kill the most lucrative business deal. *Kiss, Bow, or Shake Hands* has been immeasurably helpful over the years."

—Louis Altman, President, New Hampshire International Trade Association (NHITA), and President, GlobaFone

"Kiss, Bow, or Shake Hands is the one book on international culture and customs that our students couldn't do without. And the new edition is even more impressive."

—Kris Swank, Pima Community College, Librarian and International Business instructor

"Kiss, Bow, or Shake Hands is recommended reading in each of our six international real estate education courses. This book has helped REALTORS˚ throughout the world understand how to serve their international clients."

—Heidi Hennig, Manager, International Education and Membership, National Association of REALTORS˚

"Kiss, Bow, or Shake Hands is a great resource of cultural and business-related information. The material is concise and easy to read. The cultural information is unique, educational, and fun! It's a book that can be enjoyed by a great number of people, from a student, to a leisure traveler, to the most sophisticated business person."

—Joanna Savvides, President, World Trade Center of Greater Philadelphia

"In my work, I train employees of multinational corporations on how to manage the inter-cultural aspects of an international assignment. *Kiss, Bow, or Shake Hands* is a tremendous resource for the growing number of individuals in today's global workforce who find them-selves working across international borders and on assignment outside their home country."

—Carolyn Ryffel, Senior Manager of Intercultural Services, Cartus, Chicago, IL

"Kiss, Bow, or Shake Hands is a smart, authoritative source of good, useful information. Over the years I've had the pleasure of recommending this treasure to students, business travel-ers, and friends who love travel. They've all emerged with a better understanding of how to interact with other citizens of our varied and wonderful planet."

—Joanne St. John, President, International Academy at Santa Barbara and the University Club of Santa Barbara

"Terri Morrison's book *Kiss, Bow, or Shake Hands* has been an invaluable asset over the years when used by our transferees and travelers. The expertly written chapters give our business people an edge when dealing with people in other countries, helping them gain insight into such topics as negotiation strategies, cognitive styles, country history, and even what to bring as a gift. I highly recommend this book to anyone visiting a new country on business."

—Nancy Linwood, Staff Information Specialist, DuPont Central Research and Development Information and Computing Technologies

Contents

Preface

In the dozen years since *Kiss, Bow, or Shake Hands* was originally published, the world has changed in remarkable ways. Several countries have dissolved (such as the Soviet Union), others have been absorbed (East Germany), and some have emerged (Azerbaijan). Trade barriers have been lifted (note the addition of South Africa and Vietnam to this edition) and economies have shifted (Ireland and India).

The interesting thing is that over twelve years—throughout all of the massive political and economic changes—the cultures, values, and belief systems of major ethnic groups have remained constant.

For example, many Hong Kong executives relocated to Vancouver prior to the return of Hong Kong (a former British Crown Colony) to China in 1997. These senior Chinese managers have successfully adapted to North American business practices, yet they clearly appreciate some knowledge of their negotiating styles and cultural values. Just understanding Chinese name order and titles will give you an advantage over other executives who do no research. As Johann Wolfgang von Goethe said, "There is nothing more terrible than ignorance in action" *(Es ist nichts schrecklicher als eine tätige Unwissenheit).*

During my life, I have seen World War, reconstruction, terrorism, and tremendous advances in technology. On this increasingly interconnected planet, businesses need to acknowledge that people are not alike all over the world—the more you respect local attitudes toward families, work, and religion, the more successful you will be in those locales. Priorities in Warsaw are not equivalent to those on Wall Street.

Once again, it is a pleasure to introduce you to this important book. Review it before you embark on your international trips. Gain the information you need on business practices, cognitive styles, negotiation techniques, and social customs. Give the right gift; make the right gesture. Read *Kiss, Bow, or Shake Hands.*

—Hans H. B. Koehler, the former
Director of the Wharton Export Network

"There is no conceivable human action which custom has not at one time justified and at another condemned."

—Joseph Wood Crutch (1929)

Introduction

What will you need to know in 2010 or 2020 to work internationally? As Hans Koehler pointed out in the Preface, we live in changing times. But many of the cultural tenets presented in *Kiss, Bow, or Shake Hands* took hundreds of years to develop. These stable precepts help us understand why people behave differently around the world, and they will help you to avoid global marketing faux pas like these:

> McDonald's Corporation settled a group of lawsuits for $10 million in 2002. Why were they sued? Because of their French fries and hash browns. After 1990, McDonald's stated that only pure vegetable oil was used to cook their fries, implying that they were prepared in a "vegetarian" manner. However, the oil contained the essence of beef flavor, which is an anathema to Hindus and vegetarians worldwide. Most of the money from the lawsuit was donated to Hindu and other vegetarian causes.

> Nike was forced to recall thousands of pairs of Air Bakin, Air BBQ, Air Grill, and Air Melt shoes because of a decoration intended to resemble fire on the back of the sneakers. Unfortunately, when viewed from right to left (which is the way Arabic is read), the flames resembled the Arabic word for Allah. Muslims saw this as a desecration on two levels: 1) the name of Allah may not be used on a product, and 2) Arabic tradition deems that the foot is unclean. Facing worldwide protests and boycotts, Nike implemented an enormous recall of the expensive sneakers.

As these examples show, an unintentional misstep can destroy your costly international marketing efforts. *Kiss, Bow, or Shake Hands* is organized to help you easily find the data you need to avoid many of the errors others have made before you.

For this revision, we consulted with over sixty embassies, hundreds of representatives from private and public sectors, and many institutions of higher education. The work resulted in not only this volume, but much additional information that is available on our Web site at *www.kissboworshakehands.com*. The Web site also contains information on official world holidays, foreign language phrases, country histories, gift-giving suggestions, legal data, and hundreds of articles like "Subtle Gestures," and "Lie To Me." *Kiss, Bow* is now part of a larger electronic database as well—*Kiss, Bow, or Shake Hands: Expanded Edition*. Data on all our books, seminars, and electronic products is on our three Web sites: *www.getcustoms.com, www.kissboworshakehands .com*, and *www.TerriMorrison.com*. You are also welcome to contact us at 610-725-1040 or e-mail *TerriMorrison@getcustoms.com* with your questions or comments.

Each chapter in this new edition focuses on a single country, and all are organized into sections, such as in the following example for Ireland:

What's Your Cultural IQ?	Three quick questions to gauge your knowledge
Tips on Doing Business in Ireland	Three business-related highlights
Country Background	History, Type of Government, Language, and The Irish View (perspectives from the country's viewpoint)
Know Before You Go	Natural and human hazards
Cultural Orientation	A cultural anthropologist's view. This section is described in detail in the introductory chapter.
Business Practices	Punctuality, Appointments, and Local Time; Negotiating; Business Entertaining
Protocol	Greetings, Titles/Forms of Address*, Gestures, Gifts, and Dress

And, as in the previous edition, many Cultural Notes are scattered throughout the chapters.

*For more details on Titles/Forms of Address, Mailing Addresses, etc., we also recommend an excellent book called *Merriam-Webster's Guide to International Business Communications*, by Toby D. Atkinson.

Please remember that you will work with individuals, and there are always exceptions to every rule. For example, *Kiss, Bow* suggests that many Japanese executives are reserved, polite, quiet, and rarely display emotion. Somewhere there is probably a loud, boisterous, gesticulating Japanese manager who is as emotional and imperious as any prima donna. Just because we haven't met him (or her) doesn't mean that no such person exists.

The process of communication is fluid, not static. The success of your intercultural interactions depends upon you, and the quality of your information. *Kiss, Bow, or Shake Hands* provides you with the best and most current data possible on what foreign business and social practices to expect in your efforts at globalization.

"The most universal quality is diversity."

—Michel de Montaigne, 1580

Cultural Orientation

For each of the countries in *Kiss, Bow, or Shake Hands* there is a Cultural Orientation section. The study of cultural orientation gives us a model for understanding and predicting the results of intercultural encounters. It is, however, a model—a theory. New discoveries continue to be made about why we act the way we do.

Furthermore, communication always takes place between individuals, not cultures. Few individuals are perfect representations of their culture. Citizens of the United States of America are generally known for addressing one another by first names, a habit that most of the world does not follow. However, there are many U.S. citizens who are more comfortable with formality, and prefer to use last names and titles. This does not make them any less like U.S. citizens. It just makes them individuals.

What can our model of cultural orientation do for you?

It can help you predict how people in certain cultures will speak, act, negotiate, and make decisions. Because we deal with individuals, there is a margin of error. For example, a German who would be addressed by his German colleagues as Herr Doktor Wagner might tell a U.S. consultant, "Just call me Joe." This is not generally standard practice in Germany. However, Dr. Josef Wagner may be very familiar with North American customs and may be attempting to make his Canadian or U.S. associates more comfortable.

Many global executives adopt the manners of their targeted countries, so why do U.S. executives need to study foreign ways? There are a variety of reasons. First of all, many foreign businesspeople often cannot or will not imitate U.S. mannerisms. Can you afford to leave them out of your business plans? Second, you might wish to sell to the general public in a foreign market. The average foreign consumer is certainly not going to have the same habits or tastes as consumers in the United States of America. Third, although our friend Josef may act and sound like an American or Canadian or Australian, he isn't. He probably is not even thinking in English; he is thinking in German. Knowing how Germans tend to arrive at decisions gives you an edge. And don't we all need every business advantage we can get?

Here is a breakdown of the information in the cultural orientation section.

Cognitive Styles: How We Organize and Process Information

The word "cognitive" refers to thought, so "cognitive styles" refers to thought patterns. We take in data every conscious moment. Some of it is just noise, and we ignore it. Some of it is of no interest, and we forget it as soon as we see/hear/feel/smell/taste it. Some data, however, we choose to accept.

Open-minded or Closed-minded?

Studies of cognitive styles suggest that people fall into *open-minded* and *closed-minded* categories. The open-minded person seeks out more information before making a decision. The closed-minded person has tunnel vision—he or she sees only a narrow range of data and ignores the rest.

Something that might surprise you is that most experts in cultural orientation consider the citizens of the United States and Canada to be closed-minded.

Open-minded people are more apt to see the relativity of issues. They admit that they don't have all the answers, and that they need to learn before they can come to a proper conclusion. Frankly, there are not many cultures like that. Most cultures produce closed-minded citizens.

Here's an example: Most theocratic (governed by religious leaders) cultures are closed-minded. That's one of the characteristics of such a culture: God tells you what is important. Anything outside of those parameters can be ignored. From a business point of view, that can be a weakness. For example, Islam prohibits charging interest on a loan. There can be no argument and no appeal: charging interest is wrong. Obviously, running a modern banking system without charging interest is challenging.

So why are Canada and the United States closed-minded?

Assume that someone from an Islamic country tells a North American that the United States of America is evil and should become a theocracy. The North American is likely to scoff. The United States a theocracy? Nonsense! Why, the separation of church and state is one of the most sacred precepts established by the founding fathers of the United States of America.

That North American is being closed-minded. He or she is refusing to even consider the Muslim's reasoning. A truly open-minded person would consider the proposition. He or she might reject the possibility after due thought, but not without a complete evaluation.

In fact, a person who wants to study cultural orientation should consider such questions. Granted, most businesspeople would probably decide that the United States of America should not become a theocracy. But considering the topic can lead to some useful insights. Perhaps most important is the concept that much of the world does not share the United States' predilection for the separation of church and state. This separation is a specifically Western notion, which evolved out of the hundreds of years of European religious wars that followed the Protestant Reformation.

In point of fact, most cultures tend to produce closed-minded citizens as long as things are working fairly well. It often takes a major disaster to make people open-minded. For example, the citizens of many former Communist nations are now becoming open-minded. Their old Communist ideology has fallen apart, and they realize they need new answers.

Associative or Abstractive Thinking?

Another aspect of cognitive styles is how people process information. We divide such processing into *associative* and *abstractive* characteristics.

A person who thinks associatively is filtering new data through the screen of personal experience. New data (we'll call it X) can only be understood in relation to similar past experiences (Is this new X more like A, or maybe B?). What if X is not like anything ever encountered before? The associative thinker is still going to pigeonhole that new data in with something else (X is just another B). On the other hand, the abstractive thinker can deal with something genuinely new. When the abstractive person encounters new data, he or she doesn't have to lump it in with past experiences (It's not A, it's not B or C—it's new! It's X!). The abstractive person is more able to extrapolate data and consider hypothetical situations ("I've never experienced X, but I've read about how such things might occur").

Obviously, no country has more than its share of smart (or dull) people. However, some cultures have come to value abstractive thinking, whereas others encourage associative patterns. Much of this has to do with the educational system. A system that teaches by rote tends to produce associative thinkers. An educational system that teaches problem-solving develops abstractive thinking. The scientific method is very much a product of abstractive thinking. Both northern Europe and North America produce a lot of abstractive thinkers.

Particular or Universal Thinking?

One final category has to do with how thinking and behavior are focused. People are divided into *particular* versus *universal* thinkers. The particularistic person feels that a personal relationship is more important than obeying rules or laws. On the other hand, the universalistic person tends to obey regulations and laws; relationships are less important than an individual's duty to the company, society, and authority in general.

Not surprisingly, the previous categories tend to go together in certain patterns. Abstractive thinkers often display universalistic behavior: It requires abstractive thought to see beyond one's personal relationships and consider "the good of society" (which is a very abstract concept).

Negotiation Strategies: What We Accept as Evidence

In general, let us assume that everyone acts on the basis of his or her own best interests. The question becomes: How do I decide if this is a good deal or not? Or, in a broader sense, what is the truth?

Different cultures arrive at truth in different ways. These ways can be distilled into *faith*, *facts*, and *feelings*.

The person who acts on the basis of faith is using a belief system, which can be a religious or political ideology. For example, many small nations believe in self-sufficiency. They may reject a deal that is overwhelmingly advantageous simply because they want their own people to do it. It doesn't matter that you can provide a better-quality product at a much lower price; they believe it is better that their fellow citizens produce the product, even if they produce an inferior product at a higher cost. Presenting facts to such a person is a waste of time. His or her faith operates independently from facts.

Clearly, people who believe in facts want to see evidence to support your position. They can be the most predictable to work with. If you offer the low bid, you get the job.

People who believe in feelings are the most common throughout the world. These are the people who "go with their gut instincts." They need to like you to do business with you. It can take a long time to build up a relationship with them. However, once that relationship is established, it is very strong. They aren't going to run to the first company that undercuts your offer.

Value Systems: The Basis for Behavior

Each culture has a system for dividing right from wrong, or good from evil. After a general statement concerning the values of the culture, this section identifies the culture's three value systems (Locus of Decision-Making, Sources of Anxiety Reduction, and Issues of Equality/Inequality). These following three sections identify the Value Systems in the predominant culture of each country.

Locus of Decision-Making

This section explores how much a culture prizes individualism as opposed to collectivism. Some countries, such as the United States, are very individualistic, while others, such as China, are very collectivistic. A person in the United States may consider only himself or herself when making a decision, while a person in China must abide by the consensus of the collective group.

Such pure individualism and collectivism is rare. In most countries people consider more than just themselves but are not bound by the desires of the group.

It is possible to consider the loci of decision-making as a series of concentric circles. In the center, in the smallest circle, is the individual. The next circle, slightly larger, is usually the family. Many cultures expect each individual to consider "What is best for my family?" prior to making any decisions. The next circle represents a larger group. It could be an ethnic group, a religion, or even the individual's country. Some cultures expect individuals to consider the best interests of the entire, expansive group.

Of course, when a person is acting as representative for a company, the best interests of the company may be paramount.

Sources of Anxiety Reduction

Every human being on this planet is subject to stress. How do we handle it? How do we reduce anxiety?

We can identify four basic sources of security and stability that people turn to: interpersonal relationships, religion, technology, and the law. Frequently, a combination of sources is used.

A person who must decide on an important business deal is under stress. If this person is your client, it may help you to know where he or she will turn for help and advice. This is especially true when the person turns to interpersonal relationships. If an executive is going to ask his or her spouse for advice, you had better make sure that you have made a good impression on that spouse.

Issues of Equality/Inequality

An important characteristic of all cultures is the division of power. Who controls the government, and who controls the business resources?

"All men are created equal" is a sacred tenet of the United States of America. Despite this, prejudice against many groups still exists in the United States.

All cultures have disadvantaged groups. This section identifies some sectors that have unequal status. These can be defined by economic status as well as by race or gender. Only the most industrialized nations tend to have a large, stable middle class. Many countries have a small, rich elite and a huge, poverty-stricken underclass.

Issues of male-female equality are also analyzed in this section. It is useful for a female business executive to know how women are regarded in a foreign country.

Never forget that this model represents cultural patterns that may or may not apply to each individual you contact and get to know. Utilize this information as a guideline and remain open to the new experiences we all encounter abroad.

> "Vérité en-deca des Pyrénées, erreur au-dela."
>
> —Blaise Pascal, 1623–1662

> "There are truths on this side of the Pyrenees which are falsehoods on the other."
>
> —translation: Geert Hofstede

Argentina

Argentine Republic
Local short form: Argentina
Local long form: República Argentina

Cultural Note

When Spain ruled Argentina, immigration was restricted to Spaniards. However, after Argentina gained independence in 1816, immigration from all over Europe was encouraged. The new Argentinians were not only Spanish but Italian, English, Irish, German, Polish, Jewish, and Ukrainian. By the 1990s, the majority of new immigrants were from the Pacific Rim.

 WHAT'S YOUR CULTURAL IQ?

1. Argentine has produced some extraordinary authors. Match the writer with his work:
    a. Jorge Luis Borges
    b. Manuel Puig
    c. Jacobo Timerman
    1. *Kiss of the Spider Woman*
    2. *Prisoner Without a Name, Cell Without a Number*
    3. *Labyrinths*

    ANSWER: a. 3; b. 1; c. 2

    Jorge Luis Borges wrote a multitude of highly acclaimed poems and short stories and was a strong influence on the development of magic realism.

    Manuel Puig authored novels about popular culture in Argentina, including *Betrayed by Rita Hayworth* and *Kiss of the Spider Woman*. He lived most of his life in Brazil.

    Journalist Jacobo Timerman's works included *Prisoner Without a Name, Cell Without a Number*.

2. When he became an ally of Fidel Castro in 1953, Argentine-born revolutionary Ernesto Guevara Serna became known as "Che" Guevara. Why?
    a. He sneezed a lot.
    b. Latin Americans often call Argentines "che."
    c. He stammered.
    d. C-H-E is an acronym of the Cuban revolution.

    ANSWER: b. Argentines use the interjection "che" so often that has become a nickname for all Argentines.

3. The tango is both the national dance and a national obsession in Argentina. TRUE or FALSE: In 1954, a tango artist named Astor Piazzolla so outraged some Argentine tango fans that he received death threats.

ANSWER: TRUE. For years, Astor Piazzolla had been one of Argentina's top tango musicians, leading tango bands with his bandoneon (a type of accordion). In 1954, Piazzolla performed a radically different "new tango," which broke decades of tango conventions. This brought him many fans—and vociferous protests from traditionalists.

▶ TIPS ON DOING BUSINESS IN ARGENTINA

- Compared with other South Americans, Argentines have a reputation for seriousness and melancholy. To call someone or something "not serious" is one of the most damning accusations an Argentine can make. A formal, sober manner is appropriate.
- On the other hand, when somber Argentines become amused, you know that they have become comfortable with you. Argentine banter is full of putdowns, from comments about your wardrobe to your weight. Don't be offended.
- Appropriate, refined attire is very important—particularly in the capital, Buenos Aires. Businesspeople should bring a conservative wardrobe to be taken seriously.

▶ COUNTRY BACKGROUND

History

The original Amerindian inhabitants of Argentina were nomadic hunters and gatherers more warlike than agricultural. They killed the first Spanish explorers to arrive in 1516 and even forced the abandonment of the first Buenos Aires settlement some twenty years later. Their ultimate fate was similar to that of their North American brethren: they were defeated and hunted down.

Buenos Aires gained importance late during the Spanish reign, when it was designated as the capital of the new viceroyalty of Río de la Plata in 1776. This Spanish viceroyalty lasted for scarcely four decades.

Napoleon's conquest of Spain prompted the Argentines to declare temporary self-rule in 1810. This led to a full declaration of independence in 1816, under the grandiose title of the United Provinces of Río de la Plata.

Fighting quickly broke out, as many provinces refused to be ruled by Buenos Aires. The territory of Río de la Plata divided into modern Argentina, Bolivia, Paraguay, Uruguay, and southern Chile. Even the old, established cities of northern Argentina resisted domination by the upstart port of Buenos Aires. Not until 1880 was Argentina fully united.

Military coups preceded and followed Juan Perón's dictatorship between 1946 and 1955. After Perón's banishment to Spain, Argentina had another thirty years of military rule (there were some short episodes of civilian leadership during those decades). In 1973 he returned briefly to office, and when he died, power was transferred to his wife, Isabel Perón.

In 1976, threatened by terrorism and hyperinflation, most Argentines were relieved when the military seized power. But stability was restored at the cost of human rights. The plight of the *desaparacidos* (the "disappeared") began to be covered in the media when the mothers of thousands of missing Argentine citizens started keeping a public vigil for family members who had become victims of the military. The "Dirty War" lasted until 1983, and up to 30,000 Argentines disappeared—kidnapped, tortured, and illegally executed.

After a few years, brutality, corruption, and bad monetary policy made the junta unpopular. The junta decided to distract the populace by invading the British-held Malvinas (or Falkland) Islands in 1982. To the junta's surprise, the United Kingdom fought to hold the territory. Argentina lost the Falkland War, and the humbled junta ceded power to an elected government in 1983.

The economy of Argentina suffered through a loan default in 2001, which was the largest in history to that point. Riots and resignations followed. After a series of five presidents in two weeks, Eduardo Duhalde became president and made some significant economic decisions to be eligible for aid again from the International Monetary Fund. In May of 2003 Nestor Kirchner was elected president, and he became noteworthy for his decision to persecute those responsible for the human rights abuses between 1976 and 1983.

Type of Government
La República Argentina is a federal republic. Argentina has twenty-three provinces; its capital is Buenos Aires. The president is both the chief of state and head of government. The cabinet is appointed by the president. The legislative branch is a bicameral National Congress. It consists of the Senate and the Chamber of Deputies. In the judicial branch, nine Supreme Court judges are appointed by the president with the Senate's approval. Current information on the government of Argentina can be found with the Embassy of Argentina, at *www.embassyofargentina.us/*.

Cultural Note
Juan Domingo Perón founded a political dynasty. But despite her fame, Eva (Evita) Perón, his second wife, was never president—she died while her husband was in office. Perón's third wife, Isabel, succeeded to the presidency after he died in office in 1974. And Carlos Saul Menem, president from 1989 to 1999, was a member of the Justicialista Party—the modern-day Peronist Party.

Language
Spanish is the official language, although many people speak English, and an estimated 1.5 million people speak Italian. German and French are also commonly spoken. The heavy influence of Italian on Argentine Spanish makes it unique on the continent. Ethnologue, a catalogue of world languages, references twenty-six languages in Argentina—one of which is extinct. For

further data on the various languages of Argentina, visit *www.ethnologue.com*. The site provides well-researched databases and maps of information on the languages of the world.

The Argentine View

Church and state are officially separate, but about 90 percent of the population consider themselves Roman Catholic. Protestants, Muslims, and Jews account for the remainder.

Like the French, Argentines tend to consider themselves more cultured than people from most countries. This can hamper their business dealings with people from nations Argentines have been known to look down upon.

For a country with many European attitudes, the Argentines still may exhibit a substantial amount of machismo. Antiglobalization sentiment has increased in Argentina since the nation's 2001 economic crisis.

☑ Know Before You Go

Most of Argentina is relatively safe from natural disasters. The exceptions are the San Miguel de Tucumán and Mendoza areas in the Andes, which are subject to earthquakes.

Violent windstorms (called pamperos) can strike the Pampas and northeast; heavy flooding may also occur.

The greatest risk to travelers is from street crime, which has often been an issue in Argentine politics. Such crime is not usually violent but often manifests as scams and car theft.

Corrupt officials, especially rural policemen, have been known to extort fines from travelers. This seemed to be on the increase since the economic dislocations of 2001.

In 2005, Argentina ranked ninety-seventh out of 158 countries (they tied with Algeria, Madagascar, Malawi, Mozambique, Serbia, and Montenegro) in Transparency International's Corruption Perception Index. See *www.transparency.org* for further information; for more discussion of Transparency International, see Appendix B.

The convergence of the Argentina-Brazil-Paraguay borders is a locus of money laundering and smuggling. Travelers to this region may find themselves interrogated upon their return to their home country.

▶ CULTURAL ORIENTATION

Cognitive Styles: How Argentines Organize and Process Information

Strong European influences make Argentines less open to discussion of new ideas than the citizens of most other Latin American countries. Those with higher educations are more apt to be abstractive in their thinking, although associative, experiential thinking is the rule of thumb. Strong personal relationships make Argentines more concerned about the consequences of an action than about the action itself.

Negotiation Strategies: What Argentines Accept as Evidence

There is a decided conflict among the forces of feeling, faith, and facts. Argentines look at problems from a subjective perspective, but these feelings are usually influenced by faith in some ideology (primarily the Catholic Church, a political party, or ethnocentrism). Facts are always acceptable as long as they do not contradict either feeling or faith.

Argentines have been evaluated to have a higher-than-average ranking in uncertainty avoidance. This may make Argentines averse to risk and somewhat unwilling to accept change.

Value Systems: The Basis for Behavior

Humanitarian values are strong, but consumerism is resulting in a more materialistic society. The following three sections identify the Value Systems in the predominant culture—their methods of dividing right from wrong, good from evil, and so forth.

Locus of Decision-Making

A single, high-ranking individual usually makes business decisions, but decisions are also made with the best interest of a larger group in mind. The most honored group is the extended family, from which one gains his or her self-identity. Kinships and friendships play significant roles in decision-making. Some cultural anthropologists believe that Argentines are less collectivist than their Latin American neighbors and chart a high individuality index.

Sources of Anxiety Reduction

Although the older generations are still attached to the Church and the extended family for their security, the younger generation is putting more faith in the social structure. This sometimes leads to unrealistic allegiance to a strong political figure or ideology.

Issues of Equality/Inequality

Those who are in power consider themselves entitled to the privileges that come with the office. Argentines have been measured to have a higher-than-average masculinity index. Although machismo is still very strong, it is being challenged on all fronts. There are now more women than men in school, and women are taking a leading role in both politics and business.

▶ BUSINESS PRACTICES

Punctuality, Appointments, and Local Time

- Visitors are expected to be punctual. However, do not be surprised if your Argentine counterpart is late. In general, the more important the person, the more likely it is that he or she will keep you waiting.
- Guidelines for punctuality are different for social occasions. Even North Americans are expected to be thirty minutes late (or more) for dinner or parties; to show up on time would be impolite. But be on time for lunch and for events with a scheduled starting time, such as the theater.

- When it is important to know if your Argentine counterpart expects promptness, you can ask, "*¿En punto?*" (on the dot?).
- Remember that many South Americans and Europeans write the day first, then the month, then the year (e.g., December 3, 2010, is written 3.12.10 or 3/12/10). This is the case in Argentina.
- Your first appointments in Argentina should be with potential representatives (sometimes called *enchufados*)—individuals who have high-level contacts in your industry segment. The person you ultimately select opens the doors and can greatly facilitate the process of doing business in Argentina. Get a list of potential enchufados or local representatives through your embassy or your company's legal or accounting firm.
- Be certain you hire the correct Argentine personnel; it can be very difficult to change or fire your local representative.
- Argentine executives may put in a very long day, often lasting until 10:00 P.M. The ability to keep irregular business hours is the prerogative of an important executive.
- Argentina is three hours behind Greenwich Mean Time (G.M.T. –3), making it two hours ahead of U.S. Eastern Standard Time (E.S.T. +2).

Negotiating

- Visitors are often surprised that, despite its European manners, the pace of business negotiations is much slower than in Europe. Do not be surprised if it takes you several trips to accomplish your goal. One reason business moves slowly is that Argentina is a bureaucratic and litigious country. Even after the top decision-maker has agreed to something, many others must concur.
- Argentine negotiators have a reputation for toughness, yielding very little. Part of their immobility is due to the fact that they are generally averse to risk.
- Personal relationships are far more important than corporate ones. Each time your company changes its representative, you will virtually be starting from scratch. New alliances must be built up before business can proceed.
- Whenever you want to deal with the Argentine government, it is vital to have an Argentine contact to act as an intermediary. Without one, you probably won't even get an appointment.
- Don't assume that each portion of a contract is finalized once agreement on that section has been reached. Until the entire contract is signed, each part is subject to renegotiation.
- Expect the final contract to be long and detailed.

Business Entertaining

- Business meals are popular and are usually held in restaurants; offers to dine in Argentine homes are relatively infrequent.

Argentina

- To summon a waiter, raise your hand with your index finger extended or call out *mozo* (waiter) or *moza* (waitress). Don't adopt the local habit of making a kissing noise to attract a waiter; although common, it is considered impolite.
- Business lunches are less common outside of Buenos Aires; it is still common for people to go home to eat lunch.
- Argentines do not usually discuss business over meals; meals are considered social occasions.
- Since dinner does not begin until 10:00 P.M. (or later on weekends), Argentines have tea or coffee and pastries between 4:00 and 6:00 P.M. If you are in a meeting during that time, you will be offered something. Accept something to drink, even if you don't want it.
- When dining, keep your hands on the table, not in your lap.
- There are several complexities involved with pouring wine, which a foreigner can unknowingly violate. For example, pouring with the left hand may be an insult.
- Taxes on imported liquors are enormous. When you are invited out, your host will be paying, so don't order imported liquors unless your host does so first. Try a local drink instead; most types of liquor are produced in local versions.
- Argentina produces some of the best beef in the world; expect to see a lot of it at meals. Parrillada, a mixed grill of beef, beef, and more beef is very popular. Every variety of cut is included, from the udders on up. Many Argentines eat meat twice a day.

Cultural Note

Try to avoid offering any political opinions. Be especially cautious about praising Argentina's neighbors (notably Chile). Argentina has fought wars with all of them.

Most Argentines are anxious to put the Falkland Islands War behind them, so avoid bringing up the subject. However, if it is discussed, remember to refer to the islands by their Argentine name, the Malvinas Islands.

Argentines are great sports fans. Talking about sports is always a good way to open a conversation. Soccer (called *fútbol*) is the most popular sport. U.S.–style football is *fútbol americano.*

Many older Argentines love opera, so it may be a good topic to discuss. Restaurants and sightseeing are also fine topics.

PROTOCOL

Greetings

- Except when greeting close friends, it is traditional to shake hands briefly and nod to both men and women.
- Close male friends shake hands or embrace upon meeting; men kiss close female friends. Close female friends usually kiss each other. The full embrace (*abrazo*) may entail a hug, a handshake, and several thumps on the shoulder, ending with another handshake.

Titles/Forms of Address

- Travelers should be attentive to Argentina's unique naming conventions; they are different from many other Spanish-speaking cultures.
- Rather than include the surnames of both parents in their full names, Argentines generally use just one surname (or family name). For example, a business card might say: "Señor Alberto Paz," or "Señor Alberto Paz Esteban." In both cases, Paz, or Paz Esteban would be his father's name. His mother's surname will probably not appear.
- The word de may be used in surnames, particularly by women who want to add their husbands' family names to their own.
- While Argentines may have double first names on their business cards (like María Teresa or José Antonio), they might not use both those names in person—or in print. If you have not been told which first name they use, you should address them by their surnames.
- Appendix A contains further data on Titles and Forms of Address.

Gestures

- The Argentine people converse at a closer distance than North Americans or northern Europeans are used to—often with a hand on the other person's lapel or shoulder. Restrain yourself from backing away; an Argentine will probably step forward to close the distance.
- Maintaining eye contact is very important—something that North Americans may find difficult while speaking to a person at such close quarters.
- A pat on the shoulder is a sign of friendship.
- The gesture that some North Americans use to mean "so-so" (twisting the flat, open hand from side to side) is common in Argentina. The meaning is the same.
- A sweeping gesture beginning under the chin and continuing up over the top of the head is used to mean "I don't know" or "I don't care."
- With thumb and middle finger touching (as if holding a pinch of salt), one taps them with the index finger to indicate "hurry up" or "a lot."
- Avoid placing your hands on your hips while speaking.
- Sit only on chairs, not on a ledge, box, or table.
- Eating in the street or on public transportation is considered impolite.

Gifts

- High taxes on imported liquor makes this a highly appreciated gift. Scotch and French champagne are popular. Don't bring wine; the Southern Cone produces an abundance of quality wines.
- As in any country, gifts should be beautifully designed and of superior workmanship. If the item is produced by your corporation, the corporate name or logo should appear discreetly, not be emblazoned over the whole surface.

- Avoid giving knives; they symbolize the severing of a friendship.
- Electronic gadgets like iPods are popular.
- Argentina is a major cattle producer, and thus a major leather producer. Avoid bringing leather gifts.
- If you are invited to an Argentine home, bring a gift of flowers, imported chocolates, or whiskey. Bird of paradise flowers are appreciated.
- Further gift suggestions and guidelines are available at *www.kissboworshakehands.com*.

Dress

- Dress is very important for making a good impression in Argentina. Your entire wardrobe will be scrutinized.
- While Argentines are more in touch with European clothing styles than many Latin Americans, they tend toward the modest and the subdued. The provocative clothing popular in Brazil, for example, is rarely seen in Argentina.
- Business dress in Argentina is fairly conservative: dark suits and ties for men; white blouses and dark suits or skirts for women.
- Men may wear the same dark suit for evening wear. Women should wear a dress or skirt.
- Both men and women wear pants as casualwear. If you are meeting business associates (outdoor barbecues, called *asado*, are popular), avoid jeans and wear a jacket or blazer. Women should not wear shorts, except when invited to a swimming pool.
- Indian clothing is for Indians; don't adopt any native costumes, no matter how attractive. The same goes for gaucho outfits.
- Bring lightweight clothing for the summer, and topcoats and sweaters for the winter (especially since central heating is not universal). Don't forget that the seasons in South America are the reverse of those in the Northern Hemisphere.
- Don't wear anything outside that can be damaged by water during Carnival. Drenching pedestrians is a favorite Carnival pastime of the young.

Cultural Note

A common Argentine saying is that Argentina has always been "blessed by resources but cursed by politics." Despite its turbulent political history, Argentina has remained one of Latin America's most prosperous nations.

Today the Republic of Argentina is once again a democracy. Its military junta stepped down after the country's loss to Great Britain in the 1982 Falkland Islands War. As of 2004, the military has remained in the background, even during the mass protests caused by the economic meltdown of 2001.

Austria

Republic of Austria
Local short form: Oesterreich
Local long form: Republik Oesterreich

Cultural Note
Learn to enjoy Austria's coffeehouses, but don't expect to be able to get a hurried cup of coffee in one. Austrians give specific instructions on how they want their coffee and then may make that single cup last their entire visit.

WHAT'S YOUR CULTURAL IQ?

1. Which of the following Austrian emperors ruled for an astonishing sixty-eight years?
   a. Francis I
   b. Ferdinand I
   c. Francis Joseph I
   d. Charles I

   ANSWER: c. Francis Joseph I—also known as Franz Joseph—ruled from 1848 to 1916. He died during the First World War, to be succeeded by Charles I, the final emperor.

2. Austria has a glorious musical heritage. In addition to Mozart and Haydn, there were multiple composers named Strauss. Which one of the following people was not an Austrian composer?
   a. Oscar Straus
   b. Eduard Strauss
   c. Johann Strauss
   d. Richard Strauss

   ANSWER: d. Richard Strauss was German; his work is unfortunately associated with Nazi Germany, although after the war he was cleared of charges of collaboration with the Nazis. The Austrian Strauss family included two men named Johann (traditionally called "the Elder" and "the Younger"), plus Josef Strauss and Eduard Strauss. Oscar Straus (note the single s at the end of the name) was also Viennese but unrelated to the Strauss family.

3. Literature is also very important to Austrians, although most Austrian writers are not well-known outside the German-speaking world. TRUE or FALSE? The classic Walt Disney cartoon "Bambi" was based on the work of an Austrian writer.

Austria

ANSWER: TRUE. It is from a short 1923 novel written by Felix Salten (real name Siegmund Salzmann) (1869–1954) entitled *Bambi, ein Leben im Walde* ("Bambi, a Life in the Woods"). He coined the name "Bambi" from the Italian word for "baby," *bambino*.

TIPS ON DOING BUSINESS IN AUSTRIA

- Austrian executives are often very charming, relaxed, and unhurried. They do not usually respond positively to high-pressure tactics or limited-time opportunities.
- Austrian management style emphasizes consensus-building and sophisticated "people skills." Confrontation is usually avoided, even if rules must be bent to do so.
- Austrians are animal lovers, and the government has passed one of the toughest animal rights laws in the European Union (EU). Chickens must be free-range (not caged), dog ears cannot be cropped, and "invisible fences" are illegal. Ask about their beloved Lipizzaner stallions.

COUNTRY BACKGROUND

History

The written history of Austria dates back to 14 B.C., when the Romans marched north to the Danube River, conquering a Celtic kingdom known as Noricum. Thereafter, Austria's history paralleled that of Germany and France. Eight centuries later, Austria became part of Charlemagne's empire. Like the French and the Germans, the Austrians consider Charlemagne a forefather of their nation.

Rudolph of Habsburg was elected emperor of the Holy Roman Empire in 1273. He seized Austria (among other territories), marking the beginning of Habsburg rule of Austria.

In a watershed event for all Europe, the Ottoman Turks laid siege to Vienna in 1683. Thanks to help from the Polish and German armies, the Turks were swept back—not just from Austria, but from Hungary as well.

In reaction to Napoleon's annexation of various Habsburg lands, Francis II renounced his title of Holy Roman emperor and declared himself hereditary emperor of Austria (this made him Francis I of Austria). In 1806, the Holy Roman Empire ceased to exist, replaced by Napoleon's Confederation of the Rhine.

Metternich became foreign minister of Austria in 1809, and for the next thirty-nine years, he cleverly manipulated the politics of Europe. Following Napoleon's defeat in 1814, Metternich presided over the Congress of Vienna, a gathering of the victorious powers. Metternich assured Austrian supremacy over Germany by making Austria the president of the new German Confederation.

In 1867, the crowns of Austria and Hungary were granted to a single monarch, who was emperor in Austria and king in Hungary. This empire became known as Austria-Hungary and was popularly referred to as the dual monarchy. They were separate states, each with its own constitution, government, parliament, and language. The Magyars had a privileged position in Hungary while the Germans predominated in Austria.

The First World War was sparked in 1914 by the assassination of Archduke Francis Ferdinand and his wife in the Bosnian capital of Sarajevo.

Austria-Hungary fought as one of the Central Powers alongside Germany and the Ottoman Empire—which was the losing side in the war.

After the war, Austria-Hungary was carved up into separate nations. Austria itself became an independent republic in 1918.

In 1938, German troops entered Austria, and *Anschluss* (annexation) was declared. Austria, renamed the Ostmark (Eastern March), was divided into seven administrative districts under the central authority of the German Third Reich.

The Austrian Republic was restored after World War II. Allied forces—including those of the USSR—remained for ten years. Austria narrowly escaped becoming a Soviet satellite like its Eastern European neighbors. The occupying troops left only after Austria promised to remain neutral, allied with neither East nor West.

Austria became a member of the European Union (EU) on January 1, 1995.

Type of Government

The Republic of Austria is a federal multiparty republic with two legislative houses, the Federal Council and the National Council. The president is the chief of state; the chancellor is the head of the government.

Suffrage is universal at eighteen years of age and is compulsory for presidential elections.

Austria has a high standard of living, but this cannot be maintained as its population ages. The country has two choices: to allow increased immigration or to encourage its elderly to re-enter the work force (probably by cutting social entitlements). Both of these are controversial political issues.

For current government data, check with the Embassy of Austria: *www.austria.org*

Language

The official language of Austria is German. *www.ethnologue.com* has identified nine languages spoken in Austria.

When Austrians study foreign languages, they usually learn those of their neighbors, especially the French and Italians. English speakers can usually be found in major cities and in multinational corporations.

> ### Cultural Note
> Both Austria and Germany have designated *Hochdeutsch* (High German) as their official language. However, there are some vocabulary differences between Austrian and German. For example, the artistic movement called "art nouveau" (the term used in France and the United States of America) is called *Sezessionstil* in Austria and *Jugendstil* in Germany. But, for the most part, Austrians and Germans have little trouble understanding each other.

The Austrian View

The Austro-Hungarian Empire was staunchly Catholic, but modern Austria has no official religion. The majority of Austrians remain Roman Catholic (78 percent). Nonreligious and atheists make up the next largest group at 8.6 percent, followed by Lutherans (4.8 percent), and Muslims (2.0 percent). Today, Jews constitute only 0.2 percent of Austria's population.

Austria's birth and death rates are almost equal. Thanks to immigration, Austria now exhibits a miniscule growth rate of 0.22 percent. Since the immigrants are usually Turkish, this is a concern for Austrians, who see their cultural traditions under siege. Whether or not to limit immigration is a constant political issue.

Almost all Austrians avow a love of nature. In addition to skiing, many Austrians enjoy hiking and camping. They also enjoy long vacations to take advantage of their country's scenic landmarks.

Some Austrians believe that their country's best days are past. Because the twentieth century was not particularly good for Austria, there may be substantial resistance to change and technology.

One exception to this is in the field of medical technology. Austria ranks near the top of countries with the best medical care for its citizens. For example, Austria ranks in the top five for the number of MRI machines per population.

The preoccupation with the Austria's glorious past weighs less heavily upon the younger generation. Some are far more optimistic about Austria's future. Younger executives are also much less likely to be technophobes. However, power is heavily concentrated in the hands of senior executives and politicians.

> ### Cultural Note
> Austria joined the European Union in 1995. This yielded increased trade and prosperity—and forced the Austrian bureaucracy to reduce the regulations that impeded business. (Some might say they simply replaced Austrian red tape with EU red tape.) During this period, Austria was on the periphery of the EU. Only Greece lay further east.

The expansion of the EU in 2004 changed this. With much of eastern Europe now in the European Union, Austria is now strategically placed near the EU center. Austrian investment in central and eastern Europe has been skyrocketing ever since the fall of the Iron Curtain in 1990. This is expected to continue.

If anything can overcome traditional Austrian pessimism, it is the chance to make money in the former Communist countries of Europe.

 Know Before You Go

The greatest hazards to visitors tend to be exposure to cold and sunburn. Because of Austria's high altitude, there is less protection from the sun.

Avalanches and landslides are also hazards. Earthquakes occasionally occur in Austria.

Almost 75 percent of Austria's land surface is more than 1,700 feet above sea level. Altitude sickness is a danger for visitors to the mountains, but not for travelers in the cities. Altitude sickness can strike anyone, even if you have never experienced it before. There is no sure prevention except gradual acclimation to high elevation. Alcohol consumption tends to make the symptoms worse.

Austria has an active Green Party, which believes Austrians are in danger from aging nuclear power plants in neighboring Slovenia and the Czech Republic.

▶ CULTURAL ORIENTATION

Cognitive Styles: How Austrians Organize and Process Information

Austrians traditionally have a structured approach to absorbing and processing information. They are most comfortable with a linear approach to data and feel concern about taking action in a premature manner.

Negotiation Strategies: What Austrians Accept as Evidence

Scientific data, or facts, are the most important component of any decision. Feelings sometimes influence the process, because of the number of people who are usually consulted prior to large decisions. However, if there is a conflict between an individual's feelings, faith, and scientific evidence, the facts will outweigh any other factor.

Value Systems: The Basis for Behavior

The following three sections identify the Value Systems in the predominant culture—their methods of dividing right from wrong, good from evil, and so forth.

Locus of Decision-Making

A desire to seek consensus and a widespread respect for order are Austrian characteristics, as evidenced by the fact that there have been almost no labor strikes in the postwar era. Every Austrian has a responsibility to support the social order. Actions that disrupt this social order are seen as inherently wrong.

Sources of Anxiety Reduction

Some sociologists believe that Austrians have a high index of uncertainty avoidance. As a result, Austrians use laws and morality to give structure to their worldview. Certainly, Austrians tend to be extremely averse to risk.

In 1955, the USSR demanded that Austria adopt permanent neutrality in exchange for agreeing to remove its troops from Austria. Official neutrality (while remaining economically engaged with the West) seems to have suited the Austrian character. The fall of the Iron Curtain and Austria's entry into the European Union has required some redefinition of neutrality.

Issues of Equality/Inequality

Although titles of nobility were abolished after the First World War, Austria still has a rigid class system. Business leaders tend to come from the upper class.

Historically, Austria's ornate Catholic churches were the only place where all citizens, whatever their status, could enjoy the sort of environments found in the palaces of the nobility. Today, church attendance has plummeted, but Austrian laws protect all citizens equally. Even legally employed noncitizens (of any nationality) belong to a legal body designed to protect their interests. For most workers, this is the *Arbeiterkammern* (Workers' Chambers), which provides legal representation without regard for a worker's ability to pay. In fact, when it loses a case, the Arbeitierkammern usually pays the opponent's legal fees.

⏵ BUSINESS PRACTICES

Punctuality, Appointments, and Local Time

- In business meetings between equals, Austrians are very punctual, expecting to begin at the exact time specified. They expect the same from visitors.
- As in every country, rank has its privileges: a higher-ranking person can make a subordinate wait. However, a subordinate who makes his boss wait even five minutes is in trouble.
- Social events in Austria (such as the start time of the opera) also begin on time.
- Lateness is not just impolite in Austria; it is believed that an inability to use time wisely is indicative of deficiencies in other areas. Failure to be prompt will eliminate you from consideration as a prospective business partner.
- Austrian executives have their schedule planned weeks in advance (or longer). Make your appointments as far in advance as possible, and try and give plenty of advance notice if you must reschedule.
- The residents of Austria, like most Europeans, write the day first, then the month, then the year (e.g., December 3, 2010, is written 3.12.10 or 3/12/10).
- Many Austrian businesspeople take just thirty minutes for lunch.
- Do not expect to catch Austrian executives at work after business hours. Many Austrians believe that people who work excessively late are using their time inefficiently.

Austria

- Austrians typically take long summer vacations (often the entire month of August) and long December holidays. Check on Austrian official holidays at *www.kissboworshake hands.com.*
- Austria is one hour ahead of Greenwich Mean Time (G.M.T. +1). This makes it six hours ahead of U.S. Eastern Standard Time (E.S.T. +6).

> **Cultural Note**
> Listen for reports of "good snow" at the many ski resorts. Many Austrians ski, and they may take off from work to take advantage of excellent skiing weather.

Negotiating

- Business meetings typically begin with small talk. Expect to be asked about your journey, what scenic Austrian sights you have visited, and so on. You may also be asked your opinion about current events. Although this conversation seems inconsequential, you are being judged by the Austrians, so be ready with intelligent commentary.
- All meeting attendees are expected to be fully prepared. Facts and figures must be provided— if not in the body of your presentation, then in supplementary materials.
- Unless a presentation is being made, the senior person present sets the agenda. Expect discussions to be linear and to follow the agenda point by point.
- When the final item is addressed, the meeting may end abruptly. Austrian concepts of time management do not call for meetings to "wind down." If additional matters not on the agenda require discussion, those will be dealt with in subsequent meetings.
- Austrians tend to negotiate in a direct, linear fashion. Anything that upsets the natural order of things tends to throw off the entire process.
- Decision-making is generally slow in Austria. Although consensus is sought, the top of the hierarchy, which tends to be very traditional and averse to risk, makes final decisions.
- There are still relatively few female executives at the upper levels of Austrian management. Foreign businesswomen should not be offended if Austrian men are more formal and courteous around them.

Business Entertaining

- Austrians keep a strict division between work and play. While you may invite your Austrian counterparts to a dinner or a party, do not be surprised if they decline. You might never see them outside the office until the close of successful negotiations, when they will invite you to a meal.
- Breakfast is usually eaten at home; business breakfasts are still rather uncommon.

- Midmorning breaks often include a sandwich; midafternoon breaks usually involve coffee and cake.
- While the typical Austrian lunch is often as brief as thirty minutes, it can nevertheless be a heavy meal. A business lunch will probably last longer.
- Invitations to dine will usually be at a restaurant. Austrians rarely entertain business associates at home.
- If you are invited into an Austrian home, consider it an honor. Dress well and bring gifts.
- Keep your hands above the table during the meal.
- Good topics of conversation include Austria's culture, cuisine, history, and beautiful landscape.
- The Austrians take coffee and wine quite seriously.
- Except for traditional winter sports such as skiing, Austrians do not tend to be sports fanatics. Even football (soccer) did not become an important sport in Austria until after the Second World War. Snowboarding has become popular.

▶ PROTOCOL

Greetings
- If possible, find someone to introduce you. Austrians do not feel it is appropriate to introduce yourself to strangers.
- The usual greeting between men is a brief but firm handshake. (Most Austrians will have excellent posture—no hands in your pockets, etc.) While it is not traditional for men to shake hands with women, Austrian men will do so if a woman offers her hand first. Austrian women do not traditionally shake hands with each other but may choose to do so in a business setting.
- Never put your hand in your pocket for longer than it takes to retrieve an object. Austrians find it insulting when someone speaks to them with his hands in his pockets.
- Carry a good supply of business cards. If your company is an old one, include the year it was founded on your card.
- Extended, direct eye contact is expected when conversing. Failure to meet an Austrian's gaze will give the impression that you are untrustworthy.

Titles/Forms of Address
- In business settings, Austrians address each other by titles and surnames. Do not address an Austrian by his or her first name unless requested to do so.
- Even when an adult Austrian is not present, it is considered ill-mannered to refer to him or her by surname alone. The title or honorific must be used at all times.

Gifts

- Gift giving is not traditionally an integral part of doing business in Austria. When given, gifts tend to be well-chosen but modest in value.
- It is wise to carry several small presents with you, so if you are presented with a gift you can reciprocate immediately.
- Preferred gifts are manufactured in your home country. An illustrated book of your home city or region is a good choice. If the recipient drinks alcohol, wine or spirits produced in your home region is also a good choice.
- In business settings, Austrians open gifts immediately.
- Once a close business relationship is established, Austrians give business colleagues gifts at holidays (especially Christmas) and to celebrate the completion of a successful business deal.

Dress

- Conservative, formal dress is expected in Austria. Shoes must be recently shined. Clothes must be clean and recently pressed.
- Dark, sober colors are preferred. Flashy, bright clothing is inappropriate for a business setting.

Cultural Note

Austria has a hierarchical culture, in which age is respected. Your company should send senior executives to important meetings in Austria. If younger people (such as technicians) must be sent, they should be accompanied by an older executive—even if he or she has no real function other than to provide gravitas.

When speaking to Austrian executives, do not make jokes. Austrians do not believe that jokes and humor have any place in business. Never open a speech or presentation with a joke or humorous anecdote.

On the other hand, in social settings, Austrians are great admirers of wit. Many intellectual habitués of Austrian coffeehouses were noted for their cleverness.

Australia

Commonwealth of Australia

Cultural Note

Australians do not appreciate people who go on about their education, qualifications, or achievements. Modesty is considered a virtue, and braggarts are considered fair game for ridicule or criticism. "Cutting down the tall poppy" is a common Australian aphorism for this behavior. The habit may have grown out of the nation's origin as a British penal colony and the Australian prisoners' hatred for their high-class British overseers. The feeling is still so ingrained that Australian politicians sometimes decline an offer of a British knighthood for fear of alienating their constituents.

 WHAT'S YOUR CULTURAL IQ?

1. Aborigines believe they have lived in Australia since the beginning of time—and there is evidence that some people have existed there for over 100,000 years. When Captain Cook arrived in 1770, approximately how many Aborigines were on the continent?
   a. 30,000
   b. 300,000
   c. 3,000,000

   ANSWER: b. The precise numbers are debatable, but the Aborigine population declined quickly because of disease, sterilization, murder, and marginalization.

2. Australia covers a vast area and spans three time zones. Frequent travelers from the Americas know they will cross the International Date Line to get to and from Australia. In which direction do they gain a day?
   a. Flying westward (from the Americas to Australia)
   b. Flying eastward (from Australia to the Americas)

   ANSWER: b. If you fly east, you "earn" a day. If you fly west, you "lose" one.

3. TRUE OR FALSE: Gallipoli was a famous battle in WWII in Australia that cost Australians (and New Zealanders) heavy casualties.

   ANSWER: FALSE. The Gallipoli campaign was in WWI (in 1915), and in Turkey. Their brave efforts generated a strong sense of identity for Australians.

 TIPS ON DOING BUSINESS IN AUSTRALIA

- Less is more among the Australian business community. Australians tend to be laconic; brevity is admirable. Keep your business presentation short and to the point; do not

Australia

digress or go into too much detail. A verbose saleswoman can easily talk herself out of a sale.

- High-pressure sales and hype are counterproductive down under. Australians prefer honesty and directness and tend to fiercely resist pressure tactics. Present your case in a forthright manner, articulating both the good and the bad. Also, price your initial offer realistically, as the final price agreed upon will probably be close.

- Good health and participation in sports are top priorities for Australians. They draw a sharp line between work and play and definitely value their play. Do some research on the local sports, top players, and upcoming matches before you meet your Australian contacts. There is no safer topic of conversation with Australians than their wide variety of sports.

▶ COUNTRY BACKGROUND

History

The original inhabitants of the continent, the Aborigines, were hunters and gatherers who arrived at least 38,000 years ago. Many of them tried to retain their traditional culture and live separately from the rest of the population. In recent decades, efforts have been made by the Australian government to be more responsive to aboriginal rights.

In 1770, Captain Cook took formal control of Australia for Britain. Soon after, Australian penal colonies were established; thus, the first settlers in the country were convicts and soldiers. Free settlers arrived later when word spread of the opportunities available "down under." The numbers greatly increased when gold was discovered in 1851.

Australia became a member of the British Commonwealth in 1901. In 1942, the Statute of Westminster Adoption Act was passed, which officially gave Australia complete autonomy in both internal and external affairs. British authority was finally removed in 1986 when Queen Elizabeth severed the Australian Constitution from Great Britain's.

In 1992, the "Mabo" decision by the Australian High Court determined that Australia had not been an empty land *(terra nullius)* before the British invasion, which led to another act allowing Aborigines and other distinct people to lay claim to government-owned land.

Subsequently, some of these new rights were curtailed by Prime Minister John Howard.

In 2000, Australia hosted a safe and successful Olympics in Sydney.

Cultural Note

Before World War II, most Australians were from Britain or Ireland. With open immigration opportunities, this changed. Australia has now become one of the world's ethnic melting pots, and many of its residents were born outside of its borders.

Type of Government

The Commonwealth of Australia is a democratic federal state system that recognizes the British monarch as the chief of state (represented nationally by a governor-general and in each state by a governor). However, Australia is an independent nation and does not consider itself a constitutional monarchy.

The legislative branch of the government is a federal parliament, composed of the Senate and the House of Representatives. The prime minister heads the executive branch and is the head of the government. An independent high court heads the judicial branch. There are three major political parties: Labor, Liberal, and Australian Democrat.

Australia is known for offering extensive social welfare programs to its citizens. It is active in the United Nations and is particularly involved in assisting its developing neighbors in Asia and the Pacific. Over fifty countries receive aid from Australia.

For current government data, visit the Embassy of Australia *www.austemb.org*.

> **Cultural Note**
>
> If you drive in the outback, be sure to bring plenty of water, your cell phone, and other safety supplies (have a roo-bar on the front of the car). In case of a breakdown or other emergency, never leave your vehicle. The biggest risk is for people who walk away from their cars to look for water or assistance—wandering around until their bodies dehydrate and they become delusional.

Language

English is the official language of Australia; it is spoken by 95 percent of the population. Australian grammar and spelling are a mix of British and American patterns. For example, the Australian majority party is spelled "Labor" (American spelling), not "Labour" (British spelling).The Web site *www.ethnologue.com* lists 268 languages in Australia, and of those, 235 are living languages.

> **Cultural Note**
>
> Although most Australians speak English, communication problems can—and do—exist with foreign English speakers. An extensive accent and slang have developed that make spoken Australian English quite unique. "Aorta" is a good example of how an Aussie makes the words "They ought to..." sound. Some idiomatic differences in "Strine" (Australian) include:
>
> "Full bottle" = fully informed, knowledgeable
>
> "Ringer" = An outstanding performer
>
> "Ripper" = Terrific, fantastic (A ripper game, night, etc.)
>
> "Tucker" = Food
>
> "Barbie" = A barbecue pit, or the quintessential party that goes on all summer in an Australian's yard.

Australians tend to shorten words to one syllable and then add a long e sound to the end. Therefore, a mosquito becomes a "mozzi" and the people are known as "Auzzies" rather than Australians. Avoid the terms "stuffed" (which is said in the United States after one eats too much) and "rooting" (which those in the United States do for their favorite team); both these terms have vulgar connotations in Australia.

The Australian View

Because of their isolation, Australians are comfortable doing business with people they never meet. They may wish to communicate via e-mails, conference calls, Webex, or phone. If face-to-face meetings are possible, Australians are extremely approachable, but even if you cannot fly to Canberra or Sydney, it does not preclude working together.

Australians are creative, curious, and not averse to risk—they generally adopt new technologies as soon as they are available. Their independent, self-reliant viewpoint explains why they will often try major projects themselves, and then ask for help from "professionals" if they find it too difficult.

Christians make up approximately 75 percent of the population, but that percentage does not reflect the actual number of people who attend religious meetings. Jews, Muslims, and Buddhists are also present. A significant proportion of Australians (almost 13 percent) claim no religious affiliation.

☑ Know Before You Go

Driving is on the left in Australia. Remember to wear your seat belt (even in a taxi), and watch out for "road trains," which are trucks with multiple trailers (or carriages) linked together. Try not to drive around dawn or dusk to avoid colliding with a kangaroo in nonurban areas.

Remember that the seasons in the Southern Hemisphere are the reverse of the Northern. The hottest months in Australia are from November through March. But the peak travel seasons are during the midwinter in Australia—June, July, and August.

Australia's climate varies—from severe droughts and forest fires, to cyclones along the coast. In 2003, more than 500 homes were destroyed by bushfire in Canberra, the capital. Fires also spread across Tasmania, Victoria, and New South Wales.

▶ CULTURAL ORIENTATION

Cognitive Styles: How Australians Organize and Process Information

Australians are individually open-minded and trusting of equals until given reason not to be. They are quite analytical and conceptual in their thinking. Rules and laws almost always take precedence over personal or emotional feelings about an issue. Company policy is followed regardless of who is doing the negotiating.

Negotiation Strategies: What Australians Accept as Evidence

Facts are given the highest validity because Australians tend to reason from an objective perspective. Little credence is given to feelings, as personal emotions are untrustworthy. Australians are highly ethnocentric, so a basic faith in their nation may underlie some of their arguments.

Value Systems: The Basis for Behavior

The Judeo-Christian ethic pervades most behavior, but material progress is more important than humanistic progress. The following three sections identify the Value Systems in the predominant culture—their methods of dividing right from wrong, good from evil, and so forth.

Locus of Decision-Making

Individualism is very important in decision-making, but it is subject to company policy. Australians do not find it difficult to say "no." A person's life is private and not to be discussed in business negotiations. True friendships are few and highly valued.

Sources of Anxiety Reduction

There is low anxiety about life, as external structures (democracy, organizations, and scientific method) provide stability and insulation from life. The nuclear family is the rule and is the strongest socializing force. There are established rules for everything. Anxieties sometimes develop over deadlines and expected results.

Issues of Equality/Inequality

Egalitarianism stresses a high minimum standard of well-being for the whole of society and an outward show of equality that minimizes privileges associated with formal rank. Emphasis is on an individual's ability. Traditional sex roles are changing rapidly, but women are still fighting for equality in pay and power.

▶ BUSINESS PRACTICES

Punctuality, Appointments, and Local Time

- Be punctual to meetings. To Australian businesspeople, tardiness signals a careless business attitude.
- As an employer, however, it is not always easy to get punctuality out of traditionally antiauthoritarian Australian employees. It's not enough to request that people arrive on time; you have to prove that their tardiness causes harm.
- Appointments are relatively easy to schedule at all corporate levels. Most executives are friendly and open to discussions. Make arrangements for in-person meetings weeks in advance.

Australia

- The best time to visit is from March through November, as the peak tourist season is December through February. Christmas and Easter are especially hectic; many executives will be on vacation.
- Along with official holidays, each Australian state also celebrates additional holidays. The Queen's Birthday is celebrated—but not on the same day in each state! For the official holidays of Australia, visit *www.kissboworshakehands.com*.
- Australia has three time zones. The westernmost zone, which includes the city of Perth, is eight hours ahead of Greenwich Mean Time (G.M.T. +8). The central zone, which encompasses Adelaide, Alice Springs, and Darwin, is 9½ hours ahead of G.M.T. (G.M.T. +9½). The easternmost zone (the closest to the Americas) is ten hours ahead of G.M.T. (G.M.T. +10). Most of the big cities are in this zone, including Sydney, Melbourne, and Canberra (the national capital). The Australians name these time zones Eastern, Central, and Western Standard Time, respectively.
- All of Australia practices daylight-saving time except Queensland and western Australia, which remain on standard time throughout the year.

Negotiating

- Australians generally do not like skewed negotiations or high-pressure sales. They value directness. Therefore, present your case in a forthright manner, articulating both the good and the bad.
- Modesty and casualness are Australian characteristics. A business presentation filled with hype and excitement will not impress Australians; instead, it will inspire them to deflate the presenter with caustic humor.
- Australians may emphasize profit over market share.
- Do not digress or go into too much detail. As we stated, laconic Australians consider brevity a virtue.
- Decision-making takes place with the consultation of top management. This takes time—be patient.
- Australians are very direct and love to banter. If you are teased, take it in good humor.
- Australians are wary of authority and of those who consider themselves "better" than others. Be modest in interactions, and downplay your knowledge and expertise. Let your accomplishments speak for themselves. More than one Australian has complained that eager young U.S. executives "sound like walking resumes" because they are so quick to list their accomplishments and qualifications.
- Before beginning business meetings, spend a brief period of time in small talk. This social time will be short but will establish a familiar rapport, which is important to Australians.
- If you are invited out for a drink to establish a friendly relationship, do not talk about business unless your host brings it up. Work and play are taken equally seriously in Australia and are not to be confused.

Business Entertaining

- Australians do not make unannounced visits; always call ahead.
- In an Australian pub, it is vital to remember that each person pays for a round of drinks. Missing your turn to "shout for a round" is a sure way to make a bad impression.
- Australians don't invite strangers into their homes right away. They take their time getting to know someone before an invitation is made. Barbecues are a favorite reason for gathering.
- Good conversation topics are sports, which are very popular, and sightseeing, because Australians are very proud of their country. Politics and religion are taken very seriously, so expect some strong opinions if you discuss these topics.
- Remember that Australians respect people with opinions, even if those opinions conflict with their own. Arguments are considered entertaining, so do not be shy about espousing any truly held beliefs. People who are afraid of candor and cannot frankly express themselves are not respected.
- That said, if you bring up inappropriate topics like politics, religion, or Australia's treatment of the Aborigines, you may become engaged in an unpleasant conversation that can be destructive to your business relationship. Pick less volatile topics.
- Allegations exist that U.S. intelligence services intervened covertly in the 1980 Australian national elections. Whether this is true or not, many Australians believe it. It is a tossup, which they resent more: CIA interference in their elections or the implication that Australia is in the same league as so-called banana republics where the United States has toppled governments with impunity.

Cultural Note

Your best approach is to be friendly, relaxed, modest, and unpretentious. Australians find it amusing how hard foreigners (especially North Americans) try to make a good impression. Australians are very difficult to impress . . . and if you did impress them, they would not admit it.

The usual advice is "just be yourself" in dealing with Australians. However, if your usual demeanor is wired, nervous, officious, or self-important, you should downplay those aspects of your personality.

▶ PROTOCOL

Greetings

- Australians are friendly and easy to get to know. They do not have the British reserve of their ancestors. It is acceptable for visitors to introduce themselves in social situations.
- Australians greet each other with "Hello" or "How are you?" The informal "G'day" is not as common as it was, and they tire of hearing tourists overusing it.

Australia

- It is the custom to shake hands at the beginning and end of a meeting. The handshake is usually firm, but not bone-crushing. Women may shake hands with one another, or they may give a kiss on the cheek in greeting.
- Strong eye contact is very important—it implies a clear, honest communication.
- Don't get too close during a conversation—Australians like about two feet of space around them.
- It is appropriate to present a business card at an introduction, but don't be surprised if you do not get one in return.

Titles/Forms of Address
- Full names are used for initial greetings, and "sir" is an address of respect.
- Australians are quick to go to a first-name basis. Wait for them to initiate this as a cue for you to do the same.
- "Mate" will be heard far more often than "sir." It refers to anyone of one's own sex, but when used with the pronoun "my" (e.g., "my mates"), it refers to one's friends. Women also refer to other women as "mate."
- As part of Australia's classless society, academic qualifications are downplayed—in public. Australians will make sport of anyone who sounds like a resume, quoting his or her qualifications and experience.
- Follow the lead of others in using titles. In Australia, a title—whether academic or job-related—does not command respect in and of itself. The individual must still win the respect of others.

Gestures
- Raising one or two fingers up in the air can be considered rude.
- For a man to wink at a woman, even when being friendly, is inappropriate.
- Men should not be too physically demonstrative with other men. Do not put your arm around another man's shoulders, unless you are very good friends.

Gifts
- Australians do not generally give gifts in a business context. If you are invited to a home for dinner, however, you may want to bring a small gift of flowers, wine, chocolates, or folk crafts from home.
- As a foreigner, an illustrated book from your home area makes a good gift. You may also bring a preserved food product from your home area, but it will be confiscated by Australian customs unless it is in a can or bottle. MP3 players, handheld satellite locators, and other electronics that can used outside on trails, etc., are very nice gifts.

Dress

- Australia is in the Southern Hemisphere, so the seasons are opposite to those of North America. Most of the country is tropical, but with Australia's great size, this varies. Southern Australia has warm summers and mild winters, so light clothing is best. During winter months, warmer clothes and rain gear are needed.
- Casual dress is very informal. Shorts are quite common (sometimes, even at work).
- Business dress for visiting executives is conservative. Men may wear a high-quality dark suit and tie. Businesswomen wear suits, dresses, or pantsuits.

Cultural Note

The theology of Aborigines is found in their Dreamtime stories and their artwork. The Spirits from the Dreamtime created everything and reside in Australia's Sacred Sites. When Aborigines re-enact Dreamtime stories, or practice certain ceremonies, or create certain art, they feel a deep spiritual connection with the Dreamtime spirits.

Belarus

Republic of Belarus

Local long form: Respublika Byelarus
Former: Belorussian (Byelorussian)
Soviet Socialist Republic

Cultural Note

This nation has been known in the West under several different names: White Russia, Byelorussia, Belorussia, and others. Historians sometimes use the term "Ruthenia," although the Ruthenians are both Belarusians and Ukrainians. Its current official name is the Republic of Belarus.

There is still dispute on the spelling of the adjectival form in English. Both Belarusan (without the i) and Belarusian (with the i) are currently in use. Some even use Belarussian (two s's and an i, as in Russian).

▶ WHAT'S YOUR CULTURAL IQ?

1. TRUE or FALSE? When the United Nations was formed, the Byelorussian Soviet Socialist Republic had a vote in the UN, separate from that of Russia.

   ANSWER: TRUE. The price for the USSR to join the United Nations was that they received three votes in the general assembly, not just one. Russia, Ukraine, and Byelorussia all had a vote. Of course, all three voted the same way.

2. The Radzivil family was the most famous and accomplished house of Belarusian nobles. Match the individual with his or her accomplishments.

   a. Mikalaj Radzivil Corny (1515–1565)   1. Fought Calvinism; wrote travelogues
   b. Mikalaj Radzivil Sirotka (1549–1616)   2. Established first secular Slavic theater
   c. Franciska Ursula Radzivil (1705–1753)   3. Governor of Vilnius

   ANSWERS: a. 3; b. 1; c. 2

3. TRUE or FALSE? The Pahonia—a symbol featuring an armored knight astride a charging horse—is now the national symbol of the Republic of Belarus.

   ANSWER: FALSE. The Pahonia (which can be translated as "the chase") was often used as the national symbol of Belarus, including immediately after the collapse of the USSR in 1991. However, it was banned as an official symbol in 1995 because it is also associated with the Nazi-occupied state of Belarus during the Second World War.

Cultural Note

Belarus has a variety of instruments for folk music, which includes familiar items like the mandolin (*mandalina*) and button accordion (*harmonik*) and the hammer dulcimer (*cymbaly*). They also have more unusual instruments, such as the double pipes (*parnyia dudki*); a musician playing the double pipes looks as if he has stuck two wooden pipes of different lengths in his mouths at the same time. Another odd-looking instrument is the Belarus bagpipe (*duda*), which sports three different pipes.

TIPS ON DOING BUSINESS IN BELARUS

- While many Russians will assure you that reunification between Russia and Belarus is only a matter of time, you should take Belarusian nationalism seriously. Many Belarusians consider themselves ethnically separate from Russians and believe they are fully entitled to a separate state. Stating a different opinion may invite a lecture on the complex, interlocking history of Ruthenians, Poles, Lithuanians, Ukrainians, and Russians.
- On the other hand, there are many citizens of Belarus who would welcome reunification with Russia. These are not limited to ethnic Russians.
- Western governments have accused Belarus of all manner of crimes, from money laundering to weapons trafficking with Iran to human rights violations. Of interest to foreign businessmen is Belarus's habit of confiscating entire shipments and the vehicles they came in on if there is the slightest irregularity. A 2005 World Bank report lists Belarus as one of the most difficult countries in the world in which to do business.
- Despite all the drawbacks, Belarus currently has a growing economy and there are business opportunities there. The country reminds some intrepid foreigners of Russia in the lawless years after the collapse of the USSR.
- Belarus is almost completely dependent upon Russia for its supplies of petroleum and natural gas. Consequently, events in Russia can have a major effect upon Belarus and its economy.

COUNTRY BACKGROUND

History

Belarus experienced it's first modern independence in 1917 and 1918, after the collapse of Czarist Russia and the Brest-Litovsk Treaty, which divided up the Russian Empire. This Belarusian Peoples Republic was short-lived; it was soon absorbed into the new USSR.

Between the wars, Belarus and neighboring Ukraine suffered famine due to purges and the forced collectivization policies of Stalin. Millions of people died, and thousands more were deported to Siberia.

Belarus was occupied by Nazi Germany from 1941 to 1944. Thousands of Jews were executed and deported to concentration camps. As they did in other occupied areas of the USSR, the Nazis raised local troops to fight Moscow.

In 1986, the Chernobyl nuclear accident in neighboring Ukraine spewed radioactive fallout over much of Belarus.

Belarus declared its independence from the USSR on July 27, 1991. It established itself as a parliamentary republic within the Commonwealth of Independent States (CIS).

In 1994, Alexander Lukashenko was elected the first president of Belarus. Thanks to a constitutional referendum in 1996, he extended his presidential term and concentrated almost all government power in the executive branch.

Belarus signed the Belarus-Russian Union Treaty on April 2, 1997. This provided close coordination of military and economic policies between the two countries. Eventual union of the two nations is considered likely, but no date for that has been set.

Cultural Note

Astonishingly, in October of 2004, President Lukashenko opened a monument outside Minsk commemorating the birthplace of Felix Dzerzhinsky (Feliks Dzerzhinskii) (1877–1926). Dzerzhinsky was the founder of the Soviet secret police known as the Cheka and was the long-time head of the Soviet terror campaign, which caused the torture and execution of thousands! After the collapse of the USSR, Dzerzhinsky's statue outside Moscow's KGB headquarters was torn down, but Lukashenko seems intent on rehabilitating his memory.

Type of Government

The Republic of Belarus is a parliamentary republic. However, since his election in 1994, all power has gravitated to Alexander Lukashenko. Sometimes called "the last European dictator," President Lukashenko has ruled Belarus while maintaining a semblance of democracy. Lukashenko's "market socialism" has effectively isolated his country from Western capitalism and trade. Most of Belarus's trade is with Russia and Ukraine.

Belarus was one of three founding members of the Commonwealth of Independent States, a successor organization to the USSR.

For current government data, check with the Embassy of Belarus, which has a Web site at *www.belarusembassy.org*.

Cultural Note

The Belarusian language has not always been written in Cyrillic script. The Muslim Tatars who immigrated to Belarus once wrote Belarusian in Arabic script. Their books, called kitabs, date back to the fourteenth century. Today, surviving kitabs are prized artifacts, as well as important subjects for linguistic study.

Language

The official language of Belarus is Belarusian, which is understood by some 98 percent of the population. Belarusian is written in Cyrillic script. It is a Slavic language, midway between Russian and Ukrainian. Most dialects of Belarusian are more or less intelligible to speakers of both Russian and Ukrainian.

Because of the dominance of Russia in education and the media, most citizens of Belarus can also speak Russian. In fact, many ethnic Belarusians use Russian in everyday life.

Also spoken in Belarus are Polish, Ukrainian, Yiddish, Tatar, Lithuanian, Latvian, and Roma (Gypsy).

For data on the various languages of Belarus, see *www.ethnologue.com.*

Cultural Note

Now that government repression of religion has abated, old conflicts between the faiths have re-emerged. Some citizens of Belarus see the Roman Catholic Church and the recently revived Uniate Church (a.k.a., the Greek Orthodox Catholic Church) as agents of a foreign power—that is, the Vatican. Because some churches now occupied by the Belarus Orthodox Church were once owned by the Catholics and Uniates, there are issues over disputed property as well.

The Belarusian View

There is no official religion in Belarus, but at least 60 percent of the population identify themselves as Orthodox. (Some reports indicate as high as 80 percent Orthodox.) Formerly this was the Russian Orthodox Church, but in 1990 Belarus was designated an exarchate.

Religion was discouraged under Communism, so church attendance has experienced a substantial revival since independence. Nineteen different religious denominations have been officially registered.

As with other institutions, churches have historically been under the control of outsiders in Belarus. Some three-quarters of Belarusians once belonged to the Uniate Church, which is a Greek rite church that accepts the authority of the Roman Catholic pope. Moscow outlawed the Uniate Church in 1839, replacing it with the Orthodox faith. More recently, Moscow suppressed the Roman Catholic Church, especially when John Paul II of Poland became pope. Recently, various Protestant groups have experienced rapid growth.

Belarus is considered the slowest ethnically Slav republic to make adjustments to capitalism.

Belarusians generally do not feel in control of their own destiny. They have lived under authoritarian governments their entire lives. Also, the radioactive fallout from the Chernobyl accident in neighboring Ukraine has contaminated much of Belarus, causing increased rates of thyroid cancer—another factor over which they have no control.

While many older citizens of Belarus feel nostalgia for the USSR and would welcome reunion with Russia, these feelings are not necessarily shared by the young, who have grown up in an independent Belarus.

The best and brightest of Belarus have often left their homeland. During the days of the USSR, many left for more prestigious positions in Moscow. Today, some also seek success in the West.

☑ **Know Before You Go**

Reciprocity, a common tactic in the Cold War, is alive and well in Belarus. If your nation does something that displeases the leaders of Belarus, you may be caught up in the dispute. For example, if your nation refuses entry to an important citizen of Belarus, you may be refused entry into Belarus—even though you had nothing to do with your government's actions.

As in other former republics of the USSR, street crime is present. Corruption is rife; the police are always willing to demand a few dollars from foreigners for some imaginary infraction.

Although the location of Belarus in eastern Europe should make it an important transit point for trade, many of its roads remain in poor condition.

Street demonstrations against the government occur at times, especially in the capital of Minsk. Foreigners should avoid such demonstrations, which risk the possibility of arrest.

Despite recent claims by the Belarusian minister of health that their health care system "is now reaching the world level in terms of using modern equipment and technologies," the U.S. State Department recommends that foreigners who experience medical emergencies in Belarus opt for medical evacuation and seek treatment elsewhere.

Although the 1986 Chernobyl nuclear accident occurred in Ukraine, the prevailing winds blew much of the fallout into neighboring Belarus. The cleanup of this fallout has been haphazard; vast stretches of southern Belarus remain contaminated. There is also soil pollution from heavy pesticide use.

▶ CULTURAL ORIENTATION

Cognitive Styles: How Belarusians Organize and Process Information

Belarusians have a great desire for independence and autonomy, but they are steeped in tradition and tend to follow powerful leaders without question. Most education is skill-oriented; it is practical rather than conceptual. Belarusians' concerns are generally for the immediate, particular situation.

Negotiation Strategies: What Belarusians Accept as Evidence

Truth is found in the pressing, real-time feelings of the participant. It is often enhanced by faith in an ideology or a strong leader, but not generally by the accumulation of objective facts.

Value Systems: The Basis for Behavior

Although the name of this country means "White Russia," Belarusians are more similar to Ukrainians in their values than they are to Russians. The following three sections identify the Value Systems in the predominant culture—their methods of dividing right from wrong, good from evil, and so forth.

Locus of Decision-Making

There is a continual struggle between individual freedom and obligations to the collective unit. Traditionally the extended family is the basic unit for decision-making, but this unit includes persons other than blood kin who are accepted into the family. Although all members have a strong need to contribute to the welfare of the collective unit, the head of the family or the family unit makes decisions. In general, Belarusians value stability over freedom and are willing to cede decision-making to a strong leader as long as he keeps the peace.

Sources of Anxiety Reduction

Because Belarus has historically been dominated by Poland, Lithuania, and Russia, there is considerable national ambiguity stemming from the controversies over its name, language, traditions, and national heritage. Loyalty to an employer or local leader provides a sense of security. This makes the extended family or collective unit essential in avoiding uncertainty.

Religion has experienced a revival since 1990 and helps provide structure and reassurance into the lives of its adherents. However, even here there is uncertainty, with some smaller religions (such as the Uniates, the Old Believers, and some Protestant sects) claiming that they are the true nationalist Church of Belarus, while the two majority religions (Orthodoxy and Roman Catholicism) are controlled by non-Belarusians.

Issues of Equality/Inequality

There is a strong desire for autonomy, individual freedom, and private property, but both tradition and Communism have taught Belarusians to accept and respect collectivism. Power is vested in the leader, and he or she is responsible for the behavior of subordinates. (For example, disobedience among children is considered the fault of the parents.) Men and women have strict sex roles that are not to be confused, but each has an autonomy that is respected by the other. There is a strong sense of equality between husbands and wives, even though men do not usually share the household chores.

▶ BUSINESS PRACTICES

Punctuality, Appointments, and Local Time

- Belarusians believe that punctuality is a hallmark of foreign business practices. Your image as a business professional depends upon your punctuality.
- Don't be surprised if high-level Belarusians are late. Punctuality is your tradition, not theirs.
- Residents of Belarus write the day first, then the month, then the year (e.g., December 3, 2010, is written 3.12.10 or 3/12/10).
- Before your first meeting, the company's top executive should know who you are, what you are interested in, what your project is, and (most importantly) which other Belarusian bureaucrats have agreed to it or are supportive.
- This data is usually transmitted most effectively through your hired intermediary. Your contact can be a medium-level executive, but he or she should be respected and known by top management.

- At the first meeting, Belarusian managers will appreciate a written, straightforward out-line of the project under discussion. Your intermediary should be prepared to expand on details when necessary.
- The intermediary should not only promote your project but follow up as well. A good intermediary verifies that e-mails and faxes are properly prepared, translated, transmit-ted, and received. Equipment and delivery can be frustratingly inefficient.
- Further meetings should be planned immediately and the dates fixed; the names of people to be involved (plus their contact information) should also be determined. If this meeting is to be a month later, send follow-up messages with copies to your intermedi-ary.
- Belarus is two hours ahead of Greenwich Mean Time (G.M.T. +2). This makes Belarus seven hours ahead of U.S. Eastern Standard Time (E.S.T. +7).
- Belarus undergoes a form of daylight-saving time, with the switch usually occurring around the end of March and October. The exact dates of time changes are announced from year to year and generally differ from the schedule used in western Europe.

Negotiating

- Traditionally, bureaucrats tended to answer "no" to a proposal if they had nothing to gain by agreeing. Indeed, the ability to say "no" was historically their only real power.
- More recently, the higher the executive level, the easier it seems to be able to get a "yes." But this does not guarantee an affirmative on lower levels. Remember that Belarus iso-lated itself from capitalism, so some routine Western business practices may be unfamil-iar. Be prepared to explain every aspect of a deal.
- Getting a positive response at every bureaucratic level requires solid groundwork and help from an intermediary.
- At this time there is a dearth of experts in Belarus's ever-changing business and legal regulations. Belarus executives themselves may not have a full grasp of the legal issues. Hire a local lawyer who is an expert in Belarusian law to monitor the entire business environment and report to you independently.
- Belarusian negotiators may walk out of the talks at some juncture. While this tactic is becoming less common, and can alarm westerners, a deal might not be considered well made if its discussion and details went completely smoothly.
- Your Belarusian partners are expecting concessions, so go to the talks with a private list, made in advance, of items on which you are prepared to bargain. Concede one item at a time, so that your partners feel that such benefits are a result of their efforts. Once a deal is final, Belarusians usually consider renegotiation impossible.
- At the appropriate time, make certain that all sides completely understand any legal regulations from your home country that are involved in the deal.

Business Entertaining

- Breakfast is usually between 7:00 and 8:30 A.M. Business breakfasts are not common.
- Belarusians like to invite business partners to restaurants or to their homes. They have a strong tradition of hospitality that was strictly restrained during the Communist years, when every foreigner was considered a spy.
- Accept all invitations. Be aware that the food will be rich and the drinks strong. In fact, Belarusians feel that business arrangements go more smoothly when their business partner is more relaxed through convivial drinking. Belarusian men are proudly confident of their own drinking ability, and a man may drink half a liter of vodka in an evening without any obvious effect.
- It is gracious to learn a few toasts. The most common are *na zdo ro vie* (your health) and an ancient Polish toast, *sto-lyat* (a hundred years).
- When hosting a meeting, be certain to use china, not plastic, for serving refreshments. Belarusians usually supply a variety of refreshments when conducting meetings and appreciate reciprocity. Also, have a supply of cigarettes, lighters, calculators, and so forth.
- Traditional Belarusian restaurants have tables designed for four or six people. If your party has only two or three, you may be asked to share a table with strangers when you are seated.
- Once you open one, you must pay for an entire bottle; no matter how little of it you drink. Many restaurants and cafés accept only hard currency.
- Bottles are often left on the tables, along with as much food as the guests can possibly consume, because it is traditional to present an atmosphere of comfortable abundance. Choices of sodas, wines, cocktails, brandy, and "the best Belarus vodka in the world" will be served.
- Dinner invitations at a home are usually for Saturdays at six, but guests take up to an hour to gather. In a home, you will probably find that the children are included.
- Good topics of conversation include the cultural and artistic achievements of Belarus, sightseeing, and (especially) sports. For a small country, Belarus has produced more than its share of Olympic winners.
- Bad topics of conversation include anything that might meet with disapproval from the government of Belarus, such as allegations of corruption, money-laundering, or human rights violations.
- Remember that it is usually to your advantage to look and sound like a foreigner because foreigners get preferential treatment and help almost everywhere. (However, this can also make you more of a target for street crime since you presumably have more valuables.)

Belarus

▶ PROTOCOL

Greetings

- Belarusians are not demonstrative in public. Only relatives, very good friends, or well-known business friends of long standing are greeted cheerfully with an embrace and a kiss on each cheek.
- Except at formal or state affairs, Belarusians usually shake hands and state their own last name to a stranger instead of using a phrase like "How do you do?" Respond in the same way.
- Men and women readily shake hands with each other.

> **Cultural Note**
> When written in a foreign alphabet, there may be many ways to write a Belarusian name. For example, in English, the president's surname is alternately written as Lukashenko or Lukashenka. His first name may be Anglicized into Alexander, or the more traditional Alyaksander or even Alyaksandr.
> Since there is no rule to follow, ask your Belarusian associate how he or she would like the name to be transcribed into your language.

Titles/Forms of Address

- Belarusian names are written in the same order as in the West. The middle name is a patronymic (a name derived from the father's first name). In the example of "Svyatoslav Alesevich Bryl," Svyatoslav is the first name, the patronymic means "son of Ales," and the surname is Bryl.
- Women often add an a to their surname.
- Be careful not to confuse the order of names. It is now acceptable to use only the last name for a person of slight acquaintance; for example, Bryl, Gospodin Bryl (the polite method), or even Mr. Bryl is appropriate. His wife would be Gospozha Bryl or Mrs. Bryl.
- The only title of respect traditionally used in Belarus is "Professor." It is used when addressing a doctor of science, an elderly scientist, or a schoolteacher beyond the elementary level.
- There are few variations of first names and surnames. Some are so often used (e.g., Vasil, Vasilievich, and Vasiliev) that confusion is inevitable. Furthermore, if you are invited to address a person by his or her first name, remember that all first names have diminutives, nicknames, and pet names. Which you will use depends on the depth of your acquaintance. The best advice is to ask; he or she will be happy to explain.

Gestures

- Belarusians have their share of obscene gestures. The North American "okay" sign (thumb and forefinger touching in a circle) and any shaken-fist gestures are interpreted as vulgar.

- It is impolite to sit with your legs spread apart or with your feet propped up on a table.
- The thumb between the forefinger and middle finger means "you'll get nothing."
- Whistling is not a sign of approval at a concert or sporting event; instead, it indicates strong disapproval.
- Whistling inside a building is also inappropriate because of a superstition that it will cause one to lose money.
- Sitting a minute before leaving home brings good luck, as does knocking three times on wood.
- "Thumbs-up" means "good" or "okay," as it does in North America.
- *Nyekulturny* is a Russian word that is used the same way in Belarus. It means that something is "just not done," or is ill-mannered. Some nyekulturny behaviors include:
  - Wearing an overcoat in a public building, concert hall, or restaurant, and particularly the theater. Leave your coat in the *garderob* (cloakroom). Many office buildings have them, too
  - Sitting on your coat at a concert or restaurant (but it is acceptable at the cinema)
  - Standing with your hands in your pockets, raising your voice, or laughing loudly in public buildings, subways, or on the street

Gifts
- Belarusians appreciate small gifts—pens, business card holders, rock or country and western CDs, illustrated books, fine bars of soap, American cigarettes, solar calculators, gold or silver jewelry, or electronic gadgets (digital cameras, iPods, etc).
- Note that some visitors may give expensive, prestigious watches, pens, lighters, and so forth. You are not expected to compete in gift giving. Flowers are always proper to give to a hostess.
- Exotic food, especially seafood, can be a good gift, but avoid caviar, salmon, sturgeon, and shrimp, all of which are abundant in the area.

Dress
- Belarusians dress conservatively for the office. Even businesspeople who are familiar with current Western styles rarely wear clothes that draw notice.
- Some buildings may not be well heated in winter, so a layered dress style will be more comfortable.
- Dress for a dinner invitation can be anything from black tie to blue jeans. Hosts may offer slippers, but guests sometimes bring extra footwear, especially in winter, when overshoes are often left at the door.

Belgium

Kingdom of Belgium
Local short form: Belgique/Belgie
Local long form: Royaume de
Belgique/Koninkrijk Belgie

Cultural Note

Belgium has the most complex legislation regarding language in Europe. Three languages are recognized by the constitution: French, Dutch, and German. Brussels is officially bilingual (French and Dutch). The northern part of the country (called Flanders) speaks Dutch, while the southern part (called Wallonia) speaks French. Business is conducted in both. You will hear German most in the eastern part of Belgium

 WHAT'S YOUR CULTURAL IQ?

1. The Benelux countries have a tradition of religious tolerance and took in substantial numbers of Jews who fled from other countries (especially from Spain and Portugal during the Inquisition). But during the Nazi occupation during the Second World War, the Jewish communities were destroyed. TRUE or FALSE? Thanks to the Belgian Resistance Movement, almost half of Belgium's Jews escaped from occupied Europe.

   ANSWER: TRUE. Sadly, most of the remainder were killed in the Nazi death camps.

2. Some familiarity with Belgium's impressive artistic history is expected of visitors. This includes such world famous artists as Peter Paul Rubens, Peter Bruegel (the Elder), Jan van Eyck, and the surrealist painter René Magritte. Magritte's painting "L'Oiseau de Ciel" (Sky Bird) sold for U.S. $3.4 million in 2004. TRUE or FALSE? The money went to charity.

   ANSWER: TRUE. "L'Oiseau de Ciel" was originally commissioned by the former Belgian airline, Sabena (which went bankrupt in 2001). Profits were donated to help the 12,000 ex-Sabena employees.

3. Belgium is often used as a test market. What is the primary reason for this?
   a. Statistically, Belgians reflect the average population of the European Union.
   b. Belgians are notoriously difficult to sell to; if they'll buy a product, most other consumers will.
   c. The Belgians are the wealthiest of the Benelux people—they've got the money to buy products.
   d. All of the above.

ANSWER: a. The Belgians are not a hard sell, nor are they the wealthiest. They simply mirror the average EU member in age, income, and education.

 ## TIPS ON DOING BUSINESS IN BELGIUM

- The majority (over 90 percent) of Belgians are Roman Catholics.
- Belgians value privacy, so open-plan offices are uncommon. Expect high-ranking executives to have traditional offices. Office doors are kept closed—knock and wait to be admitted. When you enter, close the door after you.
- Generally, Belgian executives are willing to listen and compromise, although the process may take a long time.
- Executives who work with both the Dutch and the Belgians usually find the Belgians friendlier and more flexible. Belgians also tend to be more comfortable with multitasking.

 ## COUNTRY BACKGROUND

History

Julius Caesar conquered what is now Belgium in 50 B.C. Roman rule faded, and Belgium came under the domination of the Franks in the fifth century. After Charlemagne's empire fragmented, Belgium was attached to one duchy after another.

In 1516, through marriage and inheritance, Belgium and the Netherlands came under the rule of Spain (the whole area was then called the Spanish Netherlands). The Protestant Dutch resented being ruled by the Catholic Spanish king. With some help from Protestant England, the Dutch successfully broke away and formed the Dutch Republic. Catholic Belgium did not revolt, but it was hard-pressed to survive, trapped between two aggressive nations—the Dutch in the north and the French in the south.

After the War of the Spanish Succession, the Treaty of Utrecht gave control of Belgium to Austria in 1713. Religious repression continued, and Belgium became more Catholic as many of its Protestants emigrated north into the Netherlands.

With France in the grip of the French Revolution, the Austrians and Prussians decided to invade France in 1792. This was a mistake; the French army not only defeated them but also occupied the Austrian Netherlands. Belgium would remain a part of France until the final defeat of Napoleon I in 1815.

When the Congress of Vienna redrew the map of Europe in 1815, control of Belgium was given to the Netherlands. The Belgians successfully broke away from the Netherlands (with help from Britain and France) in 1830. The independent Kingdom of Belgium dates from this revolt.

When, in 1879, the Belgian Parliament declined to establish an African colony, King Leopold II put together a private company to exploit the resources of the Congo. International censure over the treatment of the people of the Congo led to the colony's annexation by the Belgian government in 1908, when the name of the country was changed to the Belgian Congo. After the First World War, Germany's African colonies of Ruanda and Urundi (now called Rwanda and Burundi) were given to Belgium by the League of Nations. This marked the extent of the Belgian Colonial Empire. After the Second World War, Belgium's African colonies gained their independence.

Belgium remained neutral in the Franco-Prussian War of 1870. Unfortunately, for the Belgians, German armies would occupy their country in both world wars, marching through Belgium on the way to invading France.

In 1957, Belgium became a founding member of the European Economic Community, which evolved into today's European Union.

In 1995, Belgium completed a constitutional realignment from a centralist to a federal form of government. This has granted more power to the regions but failed to satisfy demands for regional autonomy. Further devolution of power to the regions was undertaken in 2002.

Cultural Note

The Belgian city of Antwerp has long been one of the world's great diamond trading centers. Lately, Antwerp's preeminence has been threatened by two factors: the discovery and mining of high-grade diamonds in Canada (which are marketed outside the worldwide diamond cartel system) and the production of gem-quality artificial diamonds.

Type of Government

Belgium is a constitutional monarchy with two legislative houses. The king is the chief of state, and the prime minister is the head of the government. Elections to Parliament occur every four years, and voting is compulsory. There is a Senate and a House of Representatives. Local communities and regions have been granted the authority to make decisions regarding education, welfare, public works, and investment.

Brussels is not only the capital of Belgium but is also the headquarters of the European Union and the North Atlantic Treaty Organization (NATO).

Belgium has a high standard of living, supported in part by the politicians of the European Union who meet in Brussels. It also has very high taxes.

For current government data, check with the Embassy of Belgium, at *www.diplobel.us*.

Language

The Kingdom of Belgium recognizes three official languages: French, Dutch, and German.

Linguists have identified eight languages spoken in Belgium. One of them is an artificial language called Europanto; as an invented tongue, it is a second language with no native speakers.

English is the common language of choice for the politicians of the European Union in Brussels.

The Belgian View

Although all the major world religions are represented in Belgium, the country is overwhelmingly Roman Catholic. Holidays and cultural festivals are determined by the Catholic Church calendar.

Belgium's northern region, called Flanders, is populated primarily by Dutch speakers. In the southern region (Wallonia), Belgians usually speak French. The north and the south are almost separate, rival countries. Historically, the economic center of Belgium has fluctuated between the two regions. Before the Second World War, the mines and heavy industry in the south made Wallonia the wealthier region. Since the war, Wallonia's industries proved unable to fight off global competition, but Flanders prospered. Today, the Dutch speakers suggest that the Walloons are an economic drag on the economy.

To foreigners, Belgians can seem extremely private and unwilling to discuss their interests with visitors. One of their saving graces is their absurdist sense of humor—which compliments their important artistic movement—surrealism.

☑ Know Before You Go

Belgium is a very safe and peaceful country. Some wits claim that the greatest hazard to visitors are the high prices in Brussels.

Belgium is one of the "Low Countries." Flooding is always a hazard during long spells of rain. Land has been reclaimed from the sea via dikes (although not as much as in the Netherlands). A failure in the dike system would cause catastrophic property damage and perhaps loss of life.

Belgium (like Luxembourg) is a European banking haven, where illegal funds are sometimes laundered.

In response to high taxation, Belgium has a large underground economy, which may be as large as 20 percent of Belgium's GNP.

▶ CULTURAL ORIENTATION

Cognitive Styles: How Belgians Organize and Process Information

In general, the Belgians are open-minded to outside information and will engage anyone in a discussion of facts, principles, or theories. Information is generally processed from a conceptual perspective. They are proud of their intellectual heritage. The German speakers tend to follow abstract codes of behavior while the Dutch and French speakers are more apt to emphasize interpersonal relationships. In all three groups friendships are particular and deep.

Negotiation Strategies: What Belgians Accept as Evidence

Although facts are the most valid form of evidence, the Belgians' strong humanitarian perspective makes feelings important in any negotiation situation. Belgians also have a strong faith in the perspectives of their religious ideologies.

Value Systems: The Basis for Behavior

There are three major cultural value systems in Belgium: Dutch, French, and German. Knowing the cultural orientations of these three cultures may help someone who goes to Belgium. The following three sections identify the Value Systems in the predominant culture—their methods of dividing right from wrong, good from evil, and so forth.

Locus of Decision-Making

The individual is responsible for his or her decisions. Although ethnocentric values are adhered to, the relationship between the participants is a major variable in the decision-making process. Decision-making is slow and involved, as all peripheral concerns must be taken care of in the process. Belgians hold to the principles of common sense and compromise.

Sources of Anxiety Reduction

Some sociologists believe that the Belgians have an extraordinarily high index of uncertainty avoidance. Presumably, this is the result of being twice occupied by German armies in the twentieth century—not even as a goal in itself, but more as a convenient transit to invading France. As a result, Belgians are highly risk-averse and use laws and morality to give structure to their worldview.

The nuclear family remains the basic unit, but the extended family is the primary focus all through life, bringing structure and stability. One of three social units shapes a person's life: A person is born into the Catholic, socialist, or liberal group. This then supplies the agencies in which the person participates socially. Belgians are usually joiners, so there is an organization for every kind of need.

Issues of Equality/Inequality

Although most Belgians are Catholic and bi- or trilingual, they have not come to terms with their religious and linguistic cleavages. There is still considerable group and ethnic bias. Class distinctions remain.

> **Cultural Note**
> The Belgians often cope with adversity through a self-deprecating sense of humor. Even King Leopold II put down his nation with the comment "petit pays, petites gens" ("small country, small-minded people"). However, such comments are only allowed by the Belgians themselves. Foreigners who make negative comments about Belgium or its people will quickly find themselves on the defensive.

BUSINESS PRACTICES

Punctuality, Appointments, and Local Time

- Always be punctual for business appointments in Belgium.
- Belgians write the day first, then the month, then the year (e.g., December 3, 2010, is written 3.12.10 or 3/12/10).
- Most Belgians take a one-month vacation each year.
- Phone, e-mail, or write for an appointment at least a week in advance.
- The Belgian company will set the time of your appointment. An 11:30 A.M. appointment is a lunch appointment.
- Expect the first appointment to be social. Most Belgians must get to know you before they decide whether they want to do business with you.
- For Belgium's official holidays, visit *www.kissboworshakehands.com.*
- Belgium is one hour ahead of Greenwich Mean Time (G.M.T. +1). This makes it six hours ahead of U.S. Eastern Standard Time (E.S.T. +6).

Negotiating

- With two distinct business cultures, business practices naturally vary. Meetings may begin with socializing or may immediately get down to business. If Belgians want to engage in small talk, do so. Although such conversation may seem inconsequential, your Belgian counterparts are judging you.
- Be modest about talents and about wealth.
- Mutual trust is highly valued by Belgian businesspeople.
- Senior executives arrive at the office later than subordinates do. Don't try to "get in good" with the staff by going early, because Belgians are very aware of status and will feel uncomfortable.
- The Belgians respect privacy; knock and wait for an answer, and keep doors closed in the office.
- It is important to reply promptly to any request from a Belgian office.
- Assure clients that you will be available and will meet all deadlines.
- Exchanging business cards is standard practice.
- It is good to have your business card translated; one side can be in English and the other in French or Dutch, depending on the dominant language in your region.
- Present the card with the language of your colleague facing him or her.
- The cultural and linguistic divisions of the country are sensitive subjects. Do not confuse the major cultural groups and their languages.
- In general, Belgians do not discuss personal subjects. At a social event, the question "What do you do?" is considered too intrusive.

Belgium

- Religion is not a good topic of conversation. Unless they are in the news, it is better not to bring up Belgium's former African colonies. Belgium's colonial era did not reflect well upon its rulers.
- Belgians prize visual stimuli. Your presentation should include high-end graphics.

Cultural Note
Belgium suffered badly in both world wars. Not surprisingly, the Belgians are active in the care of refugees and in international peace movements. Several Belgians have been awarded the Nobel Peace Prize for their efforts.

▶ PROTOCOL

Greetings
- Belgians shake hands with everyone in the room or office upon meeting and departure.
- Among friends, Belgians touch cheeks and kiss the air, alternating cheeks.

Gestures
- Never converse with a Belgian while you have your hand in your pockets—Belgians find this very rude.
- Belgians do not use toothpicks in public.
- It is rude to point with the index finger.
- Snapping the fingers of both hands is ill-mannered in Belgium.

Titles/Forms of Address
- Remember that there are three linguistic groups in Belgium; each has its own customs.
- With German or Dutch speakers, you should use the English terms "Mr." and "Miss," "Mrs.," or "Ms." before the surname.
- With French speakers, use "Monsieur" and "Madame" or "Mademoiselle" before the surname.
- As in much of Europe, the use of first names is inappropriate with the older generation, except among close friends. Younger Belgian executives may invite you to use their first name—but when in doubt, err on the side of formality.
- The order of names is the same as in most of Europe: first name followed by surname. However Belgians often introduce themselves by saying their surname first. If you are unsure as to which is the given name and which is the surname, ask.

Gifts
- Gift giving is not normally a part of business relationships in Belgium.
- When gifts are given, they are opened immediately in the presence of the giver.

- If you wish to give a gift to a close business associate, do not include your business card with it, and do not give a gift that is a vehicle for your company logo.
- If you are invited to a Belgian home, bring flowers (not chrysanthemums, which signify death) or chocolates for the host. Do not bring thirteen of any flower. Red roses are only for lovers.
- Present any gift before, not after, the meal.

Dress

- Conservative, formal dress is expected in Belgium. Clothes must be clean and recently pressed.
- Shoes should be recently shined. Slip-on shoes (such as loafers) are not appropriate for men, except when going through security checkpoints where shoes must be removed.
- Belgians dress in their finest clothes on Sundays, whether they intend to go visiting or just take a stroll.

Cultural Note

In 2003, Belgium passed legislation banning the construction of new nuclear reactors. They also committed to closing their existing seven nuclear reactors by 2025. The government will be exploring and investing in alternative energy resources, such as renewable energy products and gas reserves.

Belize

Former: British Honduras

 WHAT'S YOUR CULTURAL IQ?

1. TRUE or FALSE: The first Europeans to claim Belize were from the United Kingdom.

   ANSWER: FALSE. Actually, the Spanish claimed Belize first, but they never bothered settling it. It was an Englander, Peter Wallace, who established the first European settlement in Belize in 1638. Spaniards expelled the British settlers three times (in 1754, 1759, and 1765), but the British always returned after the Spanish forces left.

2. Many of the first European settlers came to Belize to pursue careers as what?
   a. Farmers
   b. Missionaries
   c. Pirates
   d. Puritans and other religious exiles

   ANSWER: c. Belize, the one area of Central America free of Spanish settlements, had long been a haven for the pirates and privateers who preyed on Spanish ships. Piracy declined in the seventeenth century (in part because the British revoked the charters of its privateers), leading some pirates to settle down.

3. Belizeans are proud of their varied and spectacular wildlife. TRUE or FALSE? The mountain cow is the national animal of Belize.

   ANSWER: TRUE. The mountain cow—better known as the tapir—is the national animal of Belize. Tapirs are protected and are the largest land mammal in the tropics, weighing up to 600 pounds. Belize's national bird is the spectacular keel-billed toucan.

▶ TIPS ON DOING BUSINESS IN BELIZE

- Belize is Central America's youngest independent nation; it was the colony of British Honduras until 1981. There are two political parties: the People's United Party (PUP) and the United Democratic Party (UDP). Whichever party is out of power often tries to inflame public opinion by denouncing the local plans of non-Belizeans. Curiously, once that party achieves power, they tend to be relatively cooperative with outside businesspeople and investors.
- Although Belize's official language is English, visitors may be surprised that the Creole dialect of English spoken by most Belizeans is unintelligible to many foreign speakers of English. However, Belizean businesspeople can converse in conventional English.
- Business in Belize is concentrated in the areas of tourism, agriculture, and forestry. However, Belize has recently become a banking haven.

Cultural Note
Belizeans are as relaxed about street addresses as they are about most other things. Many houses and buildings do not have street numbers, nor do all streets have names. To find a particular address, get directions from a well-known landmark.

▶ COUNTRY BACKGROUND

History
In 1638, the British pirate Peter Wallace established the first European settlement in Belize, near the mouth of the Belize River. Then another British pirate, Bartholomew Sharp, began regular timber exports from Belize in 1660. He shipped valuable logwood, which provided dyes for textiles. His success brought other British loggers to Belize, who collectively became known as the Baymen.

The first African slaves were brought to Belize for the timber-cutting industry sometime between 1700 and 1710. This combination of African and European ethnicity was the origin of Belize's Creole population.

The Spanish drove out the Baymen in 1754, 1759, and 1779. Each time, the Spanish did not stay, and the Baymen soon returned. The beginnings of local government emerged in 1765, when the Baymen established Burnaby's Code. With the discovery of synthetic dyes, mahogany replaced logwood as Belize's most important export.

The 1783 Treaty of Paris confirmed Britain's right to conduct logging in Belize but prohibited the establishment of agriculture. From then on, Belize would not be able to produce enough food to feed itself and became dependent upon outside imports.

Slavery was outlawed in 1838, but the black population of Belize was still subject to restrictions, such as a prohibition against ex-slaves from receiving Crown land grants.

A few white families became wealthy and owned most of Belize's land. In 1853 the country established a local legislative assembly, dominated by the landowners.

In 1862, while the United States of America was embroiled in the Civil War (and unable to enforce the Monroe Doctrine), Belize formally became the British colony of British Honduras, ruled by a lieutenant governor who was subordinate to the governor of Jamaica. The post of British Honduras's highest official, the lieutenant governor, was raised to governor in 1884. This meant Belize was no longer subordinate to the governor of Jamaica.

Creole soldiers, who returned from service overseas in World War I, rioted in 1919. Many date the start of the Belizean independence movement to this incident, known as the Ex-Servicemen's Riot.

Due to the vulnerability of Belize City to hurricanes, the capital was moved fifty miles inland to the new city of Belmopan in 1973.

British Honduras became the independent nation of Belize in 1981.

Cultural Note

The people of Belize have a distinct style of popular music and dance called punta. Of West African origin, Punta dance is unique in that the feet remain stationary. Instead, the rest of the body—especially the hips—moves. It is especially popular among the Garifuna.

Type of Government

Since independence from the United Kingdom in 1981, Belize has been a constitutional monarchy. In the executive branch there is a prime minister and a Cabinet, and there are two legislative houses: the Senate and the House of Representatives.

The monarch of the United Kingdom (currently Queen Elizabeth II) is the chief of state, represented by a governor-general (who is a native of Belize). The prime minister is head of the government.

For current government data, check with the Embassy of Belize at *www.embassyofbelize .org*. An interesting, excellent source for additional information is *www.belize.gov.bz*.

Language

The official language of Belize is English. However, the dialect of English spoken by much of the Creole population is unintelligible to most foreigners. While the speech patterns sound familiar, the overall speech is not generally understood by outside English speakers.

There are a total of nine languages currently spoken in Belize. If English and Creole English are categorized as separate languages, the majority language of Belize is actually Spanish. Also spoken is Plautdietsch, a dialect of German spoken by the 6,000 Mennonite farmers in Belize. Most of the other languages are indigenous Amerindian tongues.

For further data on the various languages of Belize, see *www.ethnologue.com*.

The Belizean View

There is no official religion in Belize, and the constitution guarantees freedom of religion. However, the country has a national prayer, which includes Christian references.

Roman Catholics make up almost exactly 50 percent of the population. Some 27 percent of the remainder are Protestants, divided among Pentecostalists, Anglicans, Seventh-Day Adventists, Mennonites, Methodists, and Jehovah's Witnesses. About 14 percent of Belizeans follow non-Christian religions, and over 9 percent are not members of any organized religion.

Ever since the Anglican Church established the first Belizean school in 1816, most primary schools in Belize have been run and staffed by churches. Traditionally, most schools were supported by Roman Catholics (who ran over half the schools in Belize), the Anglicans, and the Methodists. In recent years, evangelical churches (such as the Assemblies of God) have opened schools. Primary education is free in Belize.

Isolated behind its barrier reef, Belize has been (and continues to be) ignored for the most part by outside forces. Race relations among the wide variety of ethnic groups are relatively good. The Creoles have formed the backbone of Belizean urban society for decades.

Belize is an anomaly in Central America—a new nation with an English-speaking heritage surrounded by Spanish-speaking countries. Belizeans cannot agree on whether they live in a Central American country or a Caribbean country. Certainly, the Caribbean influence (and through that, their heritage from the United Kingdom) is predominant among the business class and along the coast. But in the interior, where the majority of inhabitants are Spanish speakers who have immigrated from Mexico or Guatemala, the heritage is very much Latin American.

Belize has no oil, coal, or hydroelectric resources. The cost of electricity is high, as is the cost of air conditioning. Most Belizeans do without air conditioning.

The people of Belize have come to view their wildlife protectively. Posters showing local animals with the slogan "This Is Their Land Too" abound. Land is constantly being set aside as nature reserves, and many species are protected.

In Belize, the influence of the United States of America has long eclipsed the influence of the United Kingdom. Since World War II, it is estimated that one in every five Belizeans emigrated to the United States, legally or otherwise.

☑ Know Before You Go

The greatest hazard to visitors comes from vehicles. Traffic accidents are the leading cause of accidental death in Belize. Most such accidents occur in Belize City; victims include bicyclists and pedestrians.

Street crime is also a concern—again, primarily in Belize City.

Malaria is present throughout Belize and is a leading cause of hospital admissions.

Road conditions vary in rural areas. Many are unpaved and become muddy during rainstorms. If you drive, be careful not to hit any of Belize's wildlife—especially the tapirs.

Of course, keep alert for weather emergencies while in Belize. Hurricanes and other tropical storms have caused widespread dislocations and destruction.

Marijuana is widely available in Belize. While Belizeans are rarely prosecuted for using marijuana, foreigners may be. In tourist areas, the greatest hazard often comes from rowdy foreigners under the influence of alcohol or drugs.

When you leave Belize, expect a thorough search of your luggage. Belizeans are very protective of their wildlife, and they are determined that none of their endangered exotic birds be smuggled out (either live or in the form of eggs).

▶ CULTURAL ORIENTATION

This information reflects the cultural orientation of the majority of English-speaking businesspeople in Belize. It is not applicable to Belize's other ethnic groups, including the Spanish speakers concentrated in the interior and border areas.

Cognitive Styles: How Belizeans Organize and Process Information

In Belize there is a basic tendency to accept information on any topic for discussion. Their beliefs are arrived at through association and experiential thinking. They look at each particular situation rather than using universal rules or laws to guide their behavior.

Further research needs to be done among the Belizeans.

Negotiation Strategies: What Belizeans Accept as Evidence

An individual's feelings about a topic or situation are the primary source of the truth. Faith in an ideology of class structure may influence that perception as well. Typically, an argument based entirely on quantifiable data is not convincing to the majority of Belizeans.

Value Systems: The Basis for Behavior

Class distinctions are more fluid in Belize than in its neighboring countries. The following three sections identify the Value Systems in the predominant culture—their methods of dividing right from wrong, good from evil, and so forth.

Locus of Decision-Making

Individuals in Belize are responsible for making their own decisions. The majority culture falls somewhere in the middle between individualism and collectivism. The effect of business decisions on one's family must be considered, but ultimately the decision belongs to one individual (almost inevitably a man).

Sources of Anxiety Reduction

Belizeans tend to be a remarkably relaxed people. They typically do not feel the need for strict laws and regulations to give order to their lives. This puts them in direct contrast with most of their Latin American neighbors. Belizeans are often unconcerned about ambiguity; for example, village government currently works without strict delineation of powers and responsibilities by the central government. Belizeans also tend to be willing to take risks, in business and in other aspects of their lives.

Issues of Equality/Inequality

Historically, Belize was a slave society, with a few white landowners bringing slaves from Africa to work in agriculture—from logging to sugar production. While some very wealthy families remain, there is a smaller differential between rich and poor in Belize than in many Latin American nations. Despite relative poverty among many Belizeans, race relations are fairly quiet. However, in regard to gender, Belize is a very masculine society. Gender roles tend to be rigid. As the Political Reform Commission noted, women are rare in government. Except for women who have inherited businesses, Belizean women are infrequently seen in executive roles.

▶ BUSINESS PRACTICES

Punctuality, Appointments, and Local Time

- As a foreigner, you are expected to be punctual to all business appointments. Professionals in Belize's small business community tend to be on time.
- Outside the business community, Belizeans tend to have a casual relationship with time.
- Belizeans, like many Europeans and South Americans, write the day first, then the month, then the year (e.g., December 3, 2010, is written 3/12/10 or 3.12.10).
- Before you arrive in Belize, make appointments at least a week in advance.
- Keep an eye on the weather forecast. Hurricanes and tropical storms can disrupt your entire business schedule.
- Some businesses keep Saturday morning hours—but, to compensate, they usually close early on Wednesday.
- Belize is six hours behind Greenwich Mean Time (G.M.T. -6), which is one hour behind U.S. Eastern Standard Time (E.S.T. -1).

Negotiating

- It will be difficult to conduct business without hiring a local contact, preferably a native of Belize. (Remember, anyone can buy Belizean citizenship; that does not make him or her an expert on Belizean business.)
- Just as many Belizeans vote for political leaders on the basis of their personality rather than their platforms, business decisions are often dependent upon the personality of the individual. A Belizean must like you to do business with you.
- Business is done from the top down in Belize. A company's top executives make the decisions.

- English (not Creole English) is used in business transactions. All materials should be translated into English. Spelling follows the British pattern.
- Your business cards should be printed in your native language on one side, and the translation in English on the other. These should be presented with the English side facing your Belizean colleague.
- Expect delays. Deadlines and completion dates, even when put in writing, are flexible.
- Avoid discussing local politics, religion, or race. Good topics are sports, the natural beauty of Belize, and places you have visited in the UK or in Latin America.
- It is a good idea to be informed about local culture and history, or at least to show curiosity about Belize.

Business Entertaining

- Breakfast is known as "tea" in Belize. It is a light meal eaten around 6:30 or 7:00 A.M.
- Lunch is known as "dinner" in Belize. It is the main meal of the day, and the usual choice for a business meal. It is usually served between noon and 1:00 P.M.
- Confusingly, the evening meal is also called "dinner" in Belize. Another term for eating the evening meal is "drinking tea." Obviously, if you are confused by an invitation to dine, ask what time you should arrive. This meal begins anytime from 6:00 to 8:00 P.M. It is a lighter meal than the noon dinner.
- Traditionally, the meal ends with the main course. There is no dessert, coffee, or after-dinner drink.
- Belizean tradition holds that you accept any food or drink offered to you, and that you eat everything on your plate. Claiming that your doctor prohibits you from eating certain foods is the only acceptable excuse for declining, and you should inform your host of this issue before you arrive.
- Belizeans tend to have large families and small dining tables, so families often eat in shifts. The men are always served first. As an honored guest in a private home, a foreign businesswoman might be allowed to eat with the men.
- In a restaurant, Belizean men may refuse to let a woman pay (unless everyone has agreed in advance to pay for their own food). If a businesswoman wants to pay, she should make arrangements in advance with the waiter or the restaurant.

▶ PROTOCOL

Greetings

- The standard greeting between men is the handshake. Men will shake hands with women, but women rarely shake hands with other women.
- Older women often hug visitors, usually with just one arm.
- The handshake is also used when departing.

Titles/Forms of Address

- Among English-speaking Belizeans, address people by their surnames, prefixed with "Mister," "Mrs.," or "Miss." ("Ms." is not in common use in Belize.)
- The only titles in common use are "Doctor" for anyone with a Ph.D., and "Professor" for college teachers.
- Among Spanish-speaking Belizeans, use the traditional Spanish forms of address that are listed in Appendix A.

Gestures

- Because so many Belizeans have lived in the United States, North American gestures are understood and used in Belize.

Gifts

- Gift giving is not traditionally part of doing business in Belize.
- When invited into a home for a meal, bring wine, liquor, or a dessert.

Dress

- In theory, businessmen should wear a dark suit and tie for business meetings. Women should wear a dress. If you are in a conservative business such as banking, this is appropriate garb.
- The same outfits are appropriate for the most formal of social occasions in Belize.
- When not at business-related events, jeans or other casualwear are standard. However, women should not wear revealing or tight clothes on the street.
- In practice, because of the heat, attire tends to be much more casual. Even the prime minister rarely dons a jacket or tie.

Cultural Note

When Belize achieved independence in 1981, the design of its flag was somewhat controversial because of its strong similarity to the dominant political group—the People's United Party (PUP). Public opinion was divided on the flag, because it was supposed to be a symbol of unification. Therefore, some additions were made in deference to the opposition—the United Democratic Party. Two horizontal red stripes were added at the top and bottom.

Bolivia

Republic of Bolivia
Local long form: Republica de Bolivia

Cultural Note

Bolivia has one of the largest natural gas reserves in South America. It exports some of the gas (e.g., one contract runs through 2019 with Brazil), but the government plans to increase exports. However, the path is precarious. In October of 2003, President Gonzalo Sánchez de Lozada dared to suggest that Bolivia start exporting their natural gas through Chile, and massive protests were staged. The furor ultimately led to his resignation.

 ## WHAT'S YOUR CULTURAL IQ?

1. Why were Bolivians irate about selling natural gas through Chile?
   a. Bolivians want to keep the gas to themselves.
   b. Bolivia lost a war with Chile in 1883 and still resents it.
   c. Peru offered Bolivia more money than Chile, and the Bolivian populace found out.

   ANSWER: b. Bolivia has never forgiven Chile for annexing Bolivia's entire coastline back in 1883. This may sound like ancient history, but those (like former president Gonzalo Sánchez de Lozada) who forget the Bolivian-Chilean animosity do so at their own risk. Bolivian presidents still commemorate an annual "Day of the Sea" with a vow to regain their seacoast, and landlocked Bolivia still maintains a navy that patrols Lake Titicaca.

2. What is the capital of Bolivia?
   a. La Paz
   b. Sucre
   c. Santa Cruz
   d. a and b
   e. b and c

   ANSWER: d. Unique among the Americas, Bolivia has two capital cities. La Paz is the permanent capital, but Sucre is the summer capital. Santa Cruz is the most populous city.

3. TRUE or FALSE? Today Bolivia's Potosí Mine produces tin, but hundreds of years ago it yielded so much silver that the expression "as rich as Potosí" became a popular expression throughout Europe and the Americas.

   ANSWER: TRUE. Unfortunately, the silver in Potosí was exhausted decades ago.

▶ TIPS ON DOING BUSINESS IN BOLIVIA

- The Spanish dialect spoken in Bolivia is very conservative. Unlike the Spanish used in most of Latin America, Bolivians retain the second-person plural (vosotros) form of verbs.
- Business is conducted at a leisurely pace. The best way to break into the market is with a local representative who knows how deals are done. Because business is conducted on a personal level, agreements are made between people, not companies. You will need the right person to introduce you. Be certain to contract with the correct individual—once you sign an agreement, you may not be able to change your representative.
- In 2005 Bolivia elected its first indigenous President, Evo Morales. President Morales supported left-wing policies and politicians in Latin America. Avoid political discussions with your Bolivian associates, but if they do arise, be extremely sensitive to their viewpoints.

▶ COUNTRY BACKGROUND

History

Once part of the powerful Inca empire, Bolivia was conquered by the Spanish in 1538. Naming the area Upper Peru, the Spanish found that Bolivia possessed the mineral wealth they so avidly sought. The huge silver mines at Potosí, discovered in 1545, were the richest in the world. Until the silver was depleted, Potosí was one of the biggest and wealthiest cities in North or South America.

In 1809 Bolivia rebelled against Spanish rule, a revolt that inspired independence movements throughout the entire Southern Cone. But unlike the other countries, Bolivia was known to contain great mineral wealth. The Spanish fought for sixteen years to keep Bolivia a colony. Bolivia finally gained its independence in 1825. The country was named after its liberator, Simón Bolívar.

At the time of its independence, Bolivia was much larger; it even had a seacoast and a port on the Pacific. Unfortunately, a quarter of this land was lost in several wars with neighboring nations. The War of the Pacific (1879–1883) resulted in the loss of Bolivia's seaport of Antofagasta to Chile. Bolivians have never reconciled themselves to this loss, and to this day they maintain a small navy—just in case they ever get the coast back. The loss of its only access to the Pacific has been blamed for many of Bolivia's problems, as the country even lacks large navigable rivers to connect it with the outside world.

Bolivia's territory was further reduced in the Chaco War of 1932 to 1935. For a century, neither Bolivia nor Paraguay felt the need to delineate their borders in the desertlike Chaco region. But in the 1920s, oil was discovered there, and the two countries fought for control of the Chaco. Both countries agreed to a truce in 1935, but Bolivia lost most of the Chaco in the subsequent peace negotiations. The loss of the Chaco also cut off Bolivia from the Paraguay River, its only remaining outlet to the sea.

Despite its mineral wealth, Bolivia has the lowest per capita income of any country in South America. There is a large underground economy, due largely to coca production. The United States has backed coca eradication programs, which generate large anti-American sentiment among poor Bolivians. Recently, Bolivia has begun exporting natural gas to Brazil and other countries.

The past few decades have been turbulent for Bolivia. The violent narco-regime of General Luis García Meza ended in a coup in 1981. Unable to maintain a stable government, the military recalled the Congress, and a civil government was installed in 1982. Since that time the military has eschewed direct political involvement. Bolivia's economy subsequently suffered hyperinflation, which by 1985 had reached 24,000 percent a year. Great sacrifices were made to stabilize the economy. Changes in the political landscape in 2006 under President Evo Morales may include relaxation on restrictions for growing coca leaves, and increased controls over the natural gas industry.

Type of Government

The Republic of Bolivia is a multiparty republic with two legislative houses, the Chamber of Senators and the Chamber of Deputies. The president is both the chief of state and the head of the government.

Bolivian heads of state do not necessarily complete their entire term of office. President Hugo Bánzer Suárez resigned for health reasons in August 2001. In October of 2003, massive protests brought down the government of his successor, President Gonzalo Sánchez de Lozada. Ostensibly, these protests were over the government's plan to export natural gas via a pipeline through Chile (and from there by ship to the United States). However, many of the protest leaders were traditional coca-growers, who were opposed to the government's U.S.–backed coca eradication policy. This resulted in the 2005 election of Chile's first indigenous President, Evo Morales.

For current government data, check with the Embassy of Bolivia at *www.bolivia-usa.org*.

Language

Bolivia has three official languages: Spanish, Aymara, and Quechua. While all business-people speak Spanish, many of the Indians speak their native Aymara or Quechua. These are not the only Amerindian languages; linguists have identified forty-four distinct languages in Bolivia, six of which are now extinct.

Spanish is the language of the business community. The Spanish spoken in Bolivia is linguistically conservative.

The Bolivian View

Although Protestantism has been making some gains, about 93 percent of Bolivians are Roman Catholics. Catholicism is the official religion, but freedom of worship is guaranteed by law. Protestants and Jews each number 2 percent of the population. Seventh Day Adventists and Mennonites are among Bolivia's fastest-growing Protestant religions.

Bolivia is a nation with many factions. Groups are divided by ethnicity, wealth, and language. Amerindians are subdivided by tribe. Unions remain powerful; protests by unions have brought down more than one Bolivian government.

The family remains the single most powerful social unit. Nepotism is considered proper at all levels of society.

There is hostile sentiment toward those countries that took Bolivian land over the past two centuries: Brazil, Paraguay, and especially Chile. Anti-Americanism and antiglobalization protests break out periodically.

☑ Know Before You Go

Foreign visitors to Bolivia are at risk of altitude sickness. Altitude sickness presents a problem in areas over 6,000 feet above sea level. There is no effective predictor of who will succumb and who won't. People of different ages, sexes, and health are struck down.

The best way to avoid altitude sickness is to acclimate yourself. Once you get to 6,000 feet, you should ideally spend at least two nights at that altitude, repeating this acclimation period at each increase of 3,000 feet. La Paz is the highest capital city in the world—at 13,000 feet.

Earthquakes occur with some frequency, and automobile accidents are a major hazard.

Bolivians are generally heavy smokers. Individuals who are sensitive to cigarette smoke may encounter difficulties. Between March and April, flooding occurs in the northeast.

▶ CULTURAL ORIENTATION

Cognitive Styles: How Bolivians Organize and Process Information

The basic tendency of the Bolivians is to be open to discussion of new ideas, but this is tempered by a strong ethnocentrism in each of the several ethnic groups. Those with higher educations have learned to think abstractively, but associative, experiential thinking is the rule. Very strong kinship ties make Bolivians more concerned about the consequences of an action than about the action itself.

Negotiation Strategies: What Bolivians Accept as Evidence

There is much conflict between the forces of feeling, faith, and facts. Basically, Bolivians look at problems from a subjective perspective. The word of a friend or family member (feelings) has the highest validity, but a strong faith in an ideology (e.g., the Catholic Church, a political party, or ethnocentrism) may override an individual's feelings. Facts are always acceptable as long as they do not contradict the other two forces. Note that it is difficult for Bolivians to disagree with someone they like. Their true opinion might not be evident.

Value Systems: The Basis for Behavior

The four ethnic groups—Quechua, Aymara, mestizos, and whites—have very different value systems. The following three sections identify the Value Systems in the economically and politically dominant white culture—their methods of dividing right from wrong, good from evil, and so forth.

Locus of Decision-Making

Decisions are usually made by an individual, but always with the best interests of a larger group in mind. Self-identity is based on the social system and the history of the extended family. Consensus forms the basis of community decision-making, with kinships and friendships playing major roles.

Sources of Anxiety Reduction

The Church has a great moral influence and gives a sense of stability to life. The nuclear family is extremely stable. Kin and family are the core of social structure, and great stress is placed on the bonds of responsibility among kin. There is a laid-back view of life that always allows time to talk with a friend. Deadlines are not a high priority.

Issues of Equality/Inequality

Ethnicity is the focus of much of national life and the white elite holds a strong bias against others. There are extreme contrasts between rich and poor. Machismo is very strong; women are still considered subordinate.

▶ BUSINESS PRACTICES

Punctuality, Appointments, and Local Time

- Punctuality is not a high priority in Bolivia. However, foreigners from North America, Europe, and Asia are expected to be punctual.
- Bolivian business meetings rarely start on time. Expect your Bolivian counterparts to be late; do not get indignant. Some foreign-educated businesspeople or younger executives will be prompt.
- Be aware that social occasions have different rules. Even North Americans are expected to be fifteen to thirty minutes late for dinner or parties; to show up on time would be impolite. But be on time for lunch and for events with a scheduled starting time, such as the theater.
- When it is important to know if your Bolivian counterpart expects promptness, you can ask, "¿En punto?" (on the dot?).

- In Bolivia, as in most of Latin America, the date is written with the day first, then the month, then the year (e.g., October 2, 2011, is written 2/10/11). The U.S. pattern of month-day-year is uncommon in Bolivia.
- Mornings are best for appointments.
- Try to make appointments at least a week in advance.
- Allow yourself to get acclimated to the high altitude by arriving in Bolivia a day early.
- The best months of the year to conduct business in Bolivia are April and May, and September and October. Little business is accomplished in the two weeks before and after Christmas and Easter, during Carnival week (the week before Ash Wednesday) or during Independence Week (the first week in August). January through March is typically vacation time in Bolivia. For further holiday data in Bolivia, visit *www.kissboworshakehands.com*.
- Bolivia is four hours behind Greenwich Mean Time (G.M.T. −4), making it one hour ahead of U.S. Eastern Standard Time (E.S.T. +1).

Negotiating

- The pace of business negotiations in Latin America is usually much slower than it is in western Europe or North America. This is especially true in Bolivia, where trying to rush a deal by applying pressure will probably fail.
- Do not be surprised if it takes you several trips to Bolivia to accomplish your goal. Bolivians respond best to low-key, slow-paced negotiations.
- Vivid presentations that incorporate simulations or models will be well received.
- Personal relationships are far more important than corporate ones in Bolivia. With traditional Bolivians, every time your company changes its representative, you will probably be starting from scratch. Historically, a new relationship must be built up before business can proceed. Younger or foreign-educated Bolivians may put more emphasis on their relationship with your company, not its individual representatives.
- Don't assume that each portion of a contract is settled once an agreement on that portion has been reached. Until the entire contract is signed, each portion is subject to renegotiation.
- Bolivians will doubt your importance unless you stay at the most prestigious international hotels.
- Bolivians converse at a closer distance than do North Americans and northern Europeans. If you instinctively back away, a Bolivian will probably move forward to close up the space. This physical closeness makes maintaining eye contact more difficult for some foreigners.
- While many of the executives you meet will speak English, check beforehand as to whether or not you will need an interpreter.
- All printed material you hand out should be translated into Spanish. This goes for everything from business cards to reports to brochures.

- Sometimes Bolivians have trouble with foreign names, so be ready to hand out your business card when you are introduced.
- Bolivians are great sports fans. Talking about sports is always a good way to open a conversation. Soccer, which is called fútbol (U.S.–style football is fútbol americano), is the most popular sport.
- Families and food are good topics of conversation as well. Bolivians also appreciate visitors who know something about their country.

Business Entertaining

- Business meals are popular in Bolivia. They are usually held in restaurants; offers to dine in a Bolivian home are relatively infrequent.
- While one can discuss business over lunch, dinner is considered a social occasion. Do not bring up business over dinner unless your Bolivian counterpart does so first.
- Lunch is usually the largest meal of the day. Dinner may start anytime from 7:30 to 9:30 P.M. A formal dinner usually begins at 9:00 P.M.
- Be warned that Bolivian food may contain very hot peppers.
- When dining, keep your hands on the table, not in your lap.
- Never eat with your fingers; there are utensils for everything. Even fruits such as bananas are eaten with a fruit knife and fork.
- When eating at a Bolivian home, understand that everyone—including the guest—is expected to eat everything on his or her plate. Your hosts will encourage you to eat, and it is traditional for you to decline the first time your hostess asks if you want more. Wait until they insist, or you may be deluged with food. A compliment is taken as a request for more food, so hold your compliments until after the meal.
- Stay at the table until everyone is finished eating. It is polite to leave a home about thirty minutes after dinner is concluded.
- At a gathering such as a party, you may have to introduce yourself. Only at a formal party (or one hosted by a older person) can you expect that someone else will introduce you.
- Eating in the street is considered improper by older Bolivians.
- Avoid whispering; it is impolite to anyone out of earshot and arouses suspicion. Wait until you can talk to the person in private.

▶ PROTOCOL

Greetings

- Except when greeting close friends, it is traditional to shake hands firmly with both men and women.
- Close male friends shake hands or embrace upon meeting; men kiss close female friends. Close female friends usually kiss each other. The full embrace (abrazo) may entail a hug, a handshake, and several thumps on the shoulder, ending with another handshake.

- Close friends of either sex may walk arm in arm. Women often hold hands.
- Good friends will greet each other at each encounter, even if they have greeted each other already that day.

Titles/Forms of Address

- While the Indian languages of Aymara and Quechua are (along with Spanish) official languages in Bolivia, all the businesspeople you meet will be fluent in Spanish, so Spanish titles may be used.
- Most people you meet should be addressed with a title and their surname. Only children, family members, and close friends address each other by their first names.
- Further data is available in Appendix A.

Gestures

- A pat on the shoulder is a sign of friendship.
- The gesture that some North Americans use to mean "so-so" (twisting the flat, open hand from side to side) indicates "no" in Bolivia. Bus and taxi drivers use this gesture to indicate that their vehicles are full. Street vendors use it to indicate that they have no more of something.
- Another gesture for "no" is a wave of the index finger.
- Beckon using a scooping motion with the palm down. Children can be summoned in this way, but adults may find it demeaning.
- Make sure to cover your mouth when either yawning or coughing.
- Sit only on chairs, not on a ledge, box, or table. Manners dictate an erect sitting posture; don't slump.

Cultural Note

Gifts identified with the United States of America (such as T-shirts and caps) were popular in the past. However, the United States is no longer universally popular in Bolivia, because the U.S. policy of coca eradication has put thousands of coca farmers out of work. As Quechuan activist Leonida Zurita-Vargas pointed out, "because of the American drug problem, we can no longer grow coca, which was part of our life and our culture long before the United States was a country. . . . We (the Quechua) are used to chewing coca leaves every day, much as Americans drink coffee. We sustained ourselves by growing coca for products like shampoo, medicinal teas and toothpaste. We did not turn coca into cocaine; the chemicals needed for that are made in countries like the United States." The international community may have to deal with the coca growers. The head of the coca-growers' federation, Evo Morales, finished second in the election for president of Bolivia in 2002, and may run again.

Gifts

- Bolivians are favorably impressed by gifts. The intention is more important than the gift itself.
- As in any country, a gift should be of high quality. If the item is produced by your corporation, the corporate name or logo should appear discreetly, not be emblazoned over the whole surface.
- Bolivia's vast underground economy provides electronic items (both genuine and counterfeit) at a discount. Be careful to give only high-quality, cutting-edge gifts, with a means to support the product (e.g., iPods with gift certificates, etc.).
- Avoid giving knives; they symbolize the severing of a friendship.
- Popular gifts are fine leather briefcases, well-made chess and backgammon sets, and imported linen items. Kitchen gadgets are popular.
- When invited to a Bolivian home, bring a gift of flowers, chocolates, wine, or whiskey. Avoid purple flowers, which are used at funerals, or yellow flowers, which signify enmity.

Dress

- Business dress in Bolivia is conservative: dark suits and ties for men; light-colored blouses and dark suits or skirts for women. Men should follow their Bolivian colleagues' lead with regard to wearing ties and removing jackets in the summer.
- The formality of dress varies in different cities. La Paz will be very formal (of course, the altitude of La Paz often makes it very chilly). In Cochabamba suits are normal business garments; and in freewheeling, tropical Santa Cruz, businessmen wear lightweight suits or go without a jacket.
- Dress to handle the weather in Bolivia. The lowlands are subject to great heat and humidity in summers. Most local people wear cotton in such weather. Don't forget that the seasons in the Southern Hemisphere are the reverse of those in the Northern Hemisphere.
- Sweaters are recommended during the winter or at night in high-altitude cities.
- Whatever the season, be prepared for sudden changes in weather and temperature.

    Men may wear the same dark suit for formal occasions (such as the theater, a formal dinner party, and so forth), but women are expected to wear different evening attire. The invitation will specify that the affair is formal. Tuxedos are rarely worn.
- Both men and women wear pants as casualwear. If you are meeting business associates, avoid jeans and wear a jacket or blazer. Women should not wear shorts.

Brazil

Federative Republic of Brazil
Local short form: Brasil
Local long form: Republica Federativa do Brasil

Cultural Note

Despite its economic problems, Brazil is often regarded as a potentially rich country with strong industrial sectors, huge possibilities for agricultural production, and massive natural resources. An example of its potential for efficient utilization of resources is its processing of sugar cane into ethyl alcohol for fueling 1.5 million Brazilian cars. Its natural resources include gold, nickel, tin, oil, and timber taken from its tropical rain forest in the Amazon River basin—a practice that is now internationally regarded as controversial.

▶ WHAT IS YOUR CULTURAL IQ?

1. In Brazil, a jeito is:
   a. The national dish
   b. An Afro-Brazilian religion
   c. A way to sidestep a rule

   ANSWER: c. When an obstacle presents itself, Brazilians prefer to go around the rules. Such a maneuver is called a *jeito* or (if the maneuver is small) *jeitinho*. In business, it often consists of calling in a favor to have someone bend a regulation.

2. Many ethnic groups have come to Brazil in search of opportunity. For example, there are more Japanese in Brazil than in any other country except Japan. TRUE or FALSE: Japanese is the second most commonly spoken language in Brazil.

   ANSWER: FALSE. Germans got to Brazil earlier than the Japanese and established entire German-speaking enclaves, making German second to Portuguese as Brazil's leading language.

3. Brazil has had several capitals since the first one was established in 1549. Which of the following cities was created specifically to be the capital of Brazil?
   a. Salvador da Bahia
   b. Rio de Janeiro
   c. Brasília

   ANSWER: c. Brasília was built on undeveloped land in the interior to be the national capital of Brazil. By moving the capital inland, it spurred migration away from the crowded coastal areas. Salvador da Bahia was the nation's capital from 1549 to 1763; Rio de Janeiro was the capital from 1763 to 1960.

▶ TIPS ON DOING BUSINESS IN BRAZIL

- Brazilians do not consider themselves to be Hispanics, and they resent being spoken to in Spanish. Be sure all your documentation—including business cards—is printed in both Portuguese and English.
- Brazil is Latin America's largest and most populous country. Be certain to understand the cultural background of your Brazilian client—it is a hugely diverse nation, and an individual's ethnicity, language, and belief systems can range from Portuguese to Japanese or Egyptian to German.
- Brazilians once had a monopoly on the production of natural rubber. They lost it when British adventurers stole rubber tree seeds and successfully grew rubber in East Asia. Ever since, Brazilians have been sensitive to real or perceived theft of their natural resources. Today there is new emphasis placed on Brazil's proprietorship of the biodiversity of the Amazon.

▶ COUNTRY BACKGROUND

History

Unlike the Mayans or Incas, the Amerindians of Brazil have left few artifacts behind for archaeologists to study. Many tribes disappeared after contact with Europeans, through death or intermarriage with the colonists. Most of the tribes that remain today have adapted to interactions with modern civilization, although a few groups may remain hidden in the Amazon.

To contest occupation by other European powers, King João III of Portugal sent out the first colonizing expedition in 1531. Martim Afonso de Sousa established the settlement of São Vicente. This settlement would eventually become a profitable sugar-producing center, after African slaves were imported to work the plantations.

After nearly two centuries of searching, Portuguese explorers finally found gold in Brazil in the 1690s. Thousands of people poured into the goldfields of Minas Gerais. In the next hundred years, 400,000 Portuguese emigrants would come to Brazil, most of them lured by gold. Two million Africans were also enslaved and imported during the same period.

In 1807, Napoleon occupied Portugal, and members of the Portuguese royal family fled to Brazil. Rio de Janeiro was the seat of the entire Portuguese empire from 1808 to 1821, but the Portuguese emperor became increasingly unpopular. After the emperor returned to Lisbon in 1822, Brazil declared independence. September 7 is Brazil's national holiday, which marks their independence from Portugal.

The new Brazilian empire experienced instability until its second emperor, Dom Pedro II, came of age. Ruling from 1840 to 1889, Dom Pedro II proved to be a dedicated, enlightened, and modest ruler. Industrialization came to Brazil, and coffee replaced sugar as the nation's most important export. Dom Pedro II was also the final emperor; the military overthrew him and proclaimed Brazil a republic in 1889.

Brazil's ill-defined borders were largely established in the nineteenth century. On its southern border, Brazil annexed what is now Uruguay in 1821. From 1825 to 1828, Brazil fought a war with Argentina for control of Uruguay, but neither side managed to win a decisive victory. After British intervention, Uruguay became an independent buffer state, largely separating Brazil and Argentina. Brazil and Argentina would fight another war from 1851 to 1852; this time Brazil was victorious.

On its southwestern border, Brazil fought in the 1864–1870 War of the Triple Alliance. This war pitted Brazil, Argentina, and Uruguay against Paraguay. It ended with Paraguay's defeat, allowing Brazil to annex some Paraguayan territory. In 1903, Brazil also took land from Bolivia.

Brazil's expansion to the north was stopped by the colonies of the United Kingdom, the Netherlands, and France (which today are Guyana, Surinam, and French Guiana).

By 1890, Brazil's sugar and coffee exports were eclipsed by rubber. The market for automobile tires exploded, requiring massive amounts of rubber. Brazil was then the world's sole producer of natural rubber, and the country once again experienced a sudden boom. But Brazil's monopoly on natural rubber was broken when plantations in Southeast Asia (using stolen Brazilian rubber tree seeds) began rubber production in 1910.

Brazil celebrated its modernity by inaugurating the new city of Brasília as the capital in 1960. Fueled by government spending, inflation soared. After several unpopular presidents in a row, the military seized power in 1964. Many Brazilians supported the coup at first, despite rights abuses. Faced with increased protests from the Brazilian people, the military allowed a presidential election to take place in 1985. Brazil has had free elections since then.

Type of Government

Brazil is a multiparty federal republic. The president is both the chief of state and the head of the government. There are two legislative houses: a Senate and a Chamber of Deputies. The ministers in the Supreme Federal Tribunal are appointed for life by the president and confirmed by the Senate.

For current government data, check with the Embassy of Brazil at *www.brasilemb.org*.

Language

Portuguese is the official language. Some segments of the population speak German, Spanish, Italian, French, English, or various Amerindian languages.

An astonishing total of 234 languages have been catalogued in Brazil by *www.ethnologue .com*. Of these, 192 of these are living languages, and 42 are now extinct.

The Brazilian View

There is no official religion in Brazil, but nearly 80 percent of the population identify themselves as Catholic. (Note that this includes syncretic Afro-Catholic groups with spiritualist beliefs; they are sometimes called Spiritist Catholics.) Protestantism is growing in Brazil,

Brazil

now accounting for over 23 percent of the population. The bulk of Brazilian Protestants belong to Pentecostal groups. There are also small numbers of Buddhists, Jews, and Muslims in Brazil. Indeed, virtually every religion on Earth is represented in Brazil.

The African heritage of many Brazilians may account for the large numbers of syncretic Afro-Catholic groups, which puts African gods into the realm of Catholic saints.

It has been speculated that Brazil's diverse, sprawling cultures respond best to strong, authoritarian leadership. This may be reinforced by the historic recollection of the rule of Emperor Dom Pedro II (1840–1889) as a golden age. Certainly, the Brazilian people have often accepted military dictatorships in times of crisis. Whether this has changed remains to be seen.

☑ Know Before You Go

Crime rates continued to spiral in cities like Rio de Janeiro—travelers should utilize precautions when working late or traveling alone in various urban areas. Even police can be a potential hazard for uninformed visitors. Real and suspected criminals have been tortured and killed, primarily from the large number of homeless, and from those who live in the slums (*favelas*) in the big cities. Prisons are hugely overcrowded, and riots over poor conditions break out on a regular basis.

There is still a prolific illegal wildlife trade in the Amazon Basin, and deforestation is a major problem. Air and water pollution are serious issues in Rio de Janeiro, Sao Paulo, and several other large cities.

The Amazon Basin holds many potential hazards for travelers, from mosquito-borne diseases to poisonous insects. Be certain that you consult with your physician for current inoculations and medical precautions before you travel to rural areas. Also, visit the Center for Disease Control Web site for information on outbreaks of virulent infections at *www.cdc.gov.*

The northeastern part of Brazil suffers from recurring droughts, while floods and frost occur in the south.

▶ CULTURAL ORIENTATION

Cognitive Styles: How Brazilians Organize and Process Information

Brazilians are open to discussions of most subjects, but home and family are private topics, and generally not talked about with incidental acquaintances. Brazilians tend to be more analytical and abstractive than other Latin Americans. They look at the particulars of each situation rather than looking to universal rules or laws.

Negotiation Strategies: What Brazilians Accept as Evidence

Brazilians tend to approach problems indirectly, allowing their feelings to dictate the solution. Facts are admissible as evidence, but they may change with the needs of the negotiator, and they seldom overrule subjective feelings.

Value System: The Basis for Behavior

There are large groups of Germans (who kept their own language) and Japanese (who learned Portuguese) that have their own value systems, which differ somewhat from other

Brazilians. The following three sections identify the Value Systems in the predominant culture—their methods of dividing right from wrong, good from evil, and so forth.

Locus of Decision-Making

The individual is responsible for his or her decisions, but family loyalty is the individual's highest duty. Nepotism is the influential family member's first obligation. The family is more important in Brazil than in any other Latin American country. It has been the single most important institution in the formation of Brazilian society.

Sources of Anxiety Reduction

The most significant kin group is the *parentela*—the relatives one recognizes from both families—which may include hundreds of individuals, all related to an illustrious ancestor. This creates a social structure that gives the individual a great sense of stability. The Catholic Church is an essential part of the culture and social life. Although many Brazilians are only nominal Catholics, the Church gives structure to their lives.

Issues of Equality/Inequality

The concepts of class and status are strong and may determine what job a person will have. Class is described in economic terms. There is a strong color bias. There are extreme contrasts between rich and poor, but the concept that powerful people are entitled to special privileges of office is being questioned. The macho male image prevails, and Brazilian men generally continue to expect women to be subordinate.

BUSINESS PRACTICES

Punctuality, Appointments, and Local Time

- The lack of punctuality is a fact of life in Brazil. Become accustomed to waiting for your Brazilian counterpart.
- Avoid any business transactions around Carnival, which is celebrated for up to a week before Lent begins on Ash Wednesday. The most spectacular festivities culminate on Fat Tuesday.
- Make appointments at least one week in advance. Never try to make impromptu calls at business or government offices.
- Try to make your appointments between 10:00 A.M. and noon, so that your business runs into lunch. It is important to host a good meal with a Brazilian prospect; it is a key part of building a relationship.
- Be prepared to commit long-term resources (both in time and money) toward establishing strong relationships in Brazil. Without such commitments, there is no point in attempting to do business there at all.

Brazil

- Brazilians conduct business through personal connections and expect long-term relationships. Before you invest in a trip, hire an appropriate Brazilian contact in your industry to help you meet the right people. Your Brazilian contact (called a *despechante* in Portuguese) will be invaluable.
- A list of Brazil's official holidays is available at *www.kissboworshakehands.com*.
- Most of Brazil is three hours behind Greenwich Mean Time (G.M.T. –3), or two hours ahead of U.S. Eastern Standard Time (E.S.T. +2). Western Brazil is four hours behind G.M.T., or one hour ahead of U.S. Eastern Standard Time.

Negotiating

- Be patient. It will usually require several trips to get through a bargaining process.
- During negotiations, be prepared to discuss all aspects of the contract simultaneously rather than sequentially.
- Seemingly, extraneous data may be reviewed and rereviewed. Try to be as flexible as possible without making definite commitments.
- Sometimes Brazilians find aggressive business attitudes offensive—do not expect to get right to the point. Avoid confrontations, and hide any frustrations.

    If you change your negotiating team, you may undermine the entire contract. Brazilians value the person they do business with more than the firm name.
- Make sure you have a local accountant and notario (similar to a lawyer) or lawyer for contract issues. Brazilians may resent an outside legal presence.
- It is normal for a conversation to be highly animated, with many interruptions, many statements of "no" being interjected, and a great deal of physical contact.
- Brazilians are enthusiastic soccer (called fútbol) fans. Soccer is always a lively topic for conversation.
- Avoid deep discussions of politics and any topics relating to Argentina (Brazil's traditional rival).
- Brazilians use periods to punctuate thousands (e.g., 5.550 = 5,550).
- Be aware that Brazilians consider themselves Americans also. Do not use the phrase "in America" when referring to the United States of America.

Business Entertaining

- Ask your prospect's secretary to recommend a prestigious restaurant.
- Do not expect to discuss business during a meal. You should participate in the conversation, but not try to direct it too much. Wait until coffee is served to broach a work-related topic.
- Stay at a first-class hotel, and entertain there if the hotel has an excellent restaurant.
- If you are invited to a party, it will probably be given at a private club rather than at a home. Arrive at least fifteen minutes late.
- A snack consisting of cookies, cake, and beverages is usually served at 4:00 or 5:00 P.M.

- Brazilian dinners take place anytime from 7:00 to 10:00 P.M. Dinner parties can easily continue until 2:00 A.M., but it is not unheard of for dinner parties to break up as late as 7:00 A.M. the next morning!

PROTOCOL

Greetings

- Greetings can be effusive, with extended handshakes common during the first encounter, progressing to embraces once a friendship has been established. Women often kiss each other on alternating cheeks. Depending upon your location in Brazil, they may kiss you twice if you are married, three times if single. The third kiss is supposed to indicate "good luck" for finding a spouse.
- It is polite to shake hands with everyone present in a group, both upon arrival and upon departure.

Titles/Forms of Address

- When applicable, titles such as "Doctor," "Professor," and so forth are used to address business acquaintances. Or the term Senhor (Mr.) or Senhora (Mrs.) is used to precede the surname. Be aware that people may sometimes introduce themselves using their titles and their first names (e.g., Doctor John).
- Unlike Spanish-speaking countries, the order of names in Portuguese is first name, middle name, last name (from one's father).

Gestures

- Brazilians communicate in extremely close proximity. They may keep in physical contact by touching arms, hands, or shoulders during the entire conversation. They are friendly and outgoing, and physical interaction is simply an extension of the Brazilian persona—do not back away.
- The sign for "okay" in North America (a circle of first finger and thumb) is totally unacceptable in Brazil. It is considered vulgar.
- To signal "come here," extend your palm face down and wave your fingers toward your body.
- Snapping your fingers while whipping your hand up and down adds emphasis to a statement or can indicate "long ago."
- To invoke good luck, place your thumb between your index and middle fingers while making a fist. This is also known as the "fig."
- Flicking the fingertips underneath the chin indicates that you do not know the answer to a question.

Gifts

- Avoid giving anything black or purple, since these are colors of mourning.
- Avoid giving knives, which symbolize cutting off a relationship, or handkerchiefs, which connote grief.
- Giving a gift is not required at the first meeting. Instead, buy lunch or dinner, and then consider the individual's tastes for future gift giving.
- Wait until after the formal meeting is over to present a gift. A relaxed social situation is the best time.
- Small electronic gadgets are appreciated—for example, calculators, iPods or CD players, digital cameras, and so forth. CDs or DVDs of popular movies and entertainers can be expensive in Brazil and make good gifts.
- Name-brand pens are appropriate.
- When invited to a home (an important occurrence), bring candy, champagne, or Scotch. Also bring something for the children—T-shirts or caps from prestigious universities or sports teams in your country, etc.

Dress

- Brazil is a tropical country, so expect the weather to be hot. Clothing made of natural fibers will be cooler and more comfortable. (The seasons in Brazil are the opposite of those in the Northern Hemisphere—July is midwinter, and January is summertime.)
- The colors of the Brazilian flag are green and yellow, so foreigners should avoid wearing this combination in any fashion.
- Conservative attire for women is very important in business. Any misstep in clothing or behavior will reflect upon your firm and may even determine whether or not anyone will do business with you. Also make sure your nails are manicured.
- Only young people wear jeans (always clean and pressed). Men should wear slacks and long-sleeved shirts for casual attire.

Cultural Note

Brazil has a naturally advantageous location on the equator for a space program. Rockets can launch and enter orbit using less propellant, and carrying bigger payloads from the Alcantara rocket base. However, Brazil encountered setbacks with their program, like the explosion on the ground at the Alcantara base that killed twenty-one people in August of 2003. Subsequently, their first successful launch occurred in October of 2004. Other countries have expressed interest in sending their rockets into orbit from Brazil's tropical site.

Canada

Cultural Note

Most Canadians live in the country's southernmost area, within 300 miles of the U.S. border. For marketing purposes, it is possible to think of Canada as a country some 3,500 miles long by 300 miles wide.

 ## WHAT'S YOUR CULTURAL IQ?

1. Canadians are justifiably proud of their famous citizens. What endeavor do all of these men have in common?
   a. Gordie Howe
   b. Bobby Orr
   c. Wayne Gretzky

   ANSWER: They were all world-class hockey players.

2. One of Canada's current provinces was not part of Canada until 1949. Which one was it?
   a. Alberta
   b. British Colombia
   c. Newfoundland
   d. Prince Edward Island

   ANSWER: c. After two referenda, Newfoundlanders voted by a narrow margin to join Canada. The province's preferred current name is Newfoundland and Labrador, recognizing the importance of the province's mainland.

3. TRUE or FALSE: Canada created the Territory of Nunavut on April 1, 1999 as a homeland for the indigenous Inuit people.

   ANSWER: TRUE. "Inuit" is the current preferred term for "Eskimo." Canada's Amerindians generally use the term "First Nations."

 ## TIPS ON DOING BUSINESS IN CANADA

- Canada is a multicultural nation. Although the majority are French or English/Irish/Scottish, there are many Canadians of Amerindian, German, and Ukrainian descent. Many new Canadians in British Columbia were born in Asia. Each ethnic group has its own customs.

- English-speaking Canadians tend to be very polite and rarely interrupt another person's conversation . . . except to point out that someone or something just mentioned is from Canada.
- French-speaking Canadians, on the other hand, often interrupt each other. They tend to find the linear, give-and-take speech of English speakers pedantic.

Cultural Note

While the United States and Canada are now firm allies, Canada's valiant defense against unprovoked U.S. aggression is taught to every schoolchild. The idea that the United States will someday swallow up Canada—if not by military force, than by economic or cultural means—remains deeply embedded in the Canadian psyche.

▶ COUNTRY BACKGROUND

History

The original inhabitants of Canada were Inuits (the preferred term for Eskimos) and the people of the First Nations (Amerindians). French explorers established the first permanent European colony in 1534, with the founding of New France in what is now Quebec. The British followed with a colony in Newfoundland in 1583, and for almost 200 years France and England ruled competing colonies in Canada. Finally, during the course of the European Seven Years' War, the British forces in Canada overwhelmed the French. The French troops abandoned the unprofitable New France colony in 1760, and Canada became a British possession.

Like the original thirteen colonies of the United States, Canada was divided into separate colonies under British rule. After the grievances of the American colonies resulted in the U.S. Revolutionary War and eventual independence, Britain tried to avoid the same mistakes with Canada. The Canadian provinces were given a considerable amount of self-government, and most Canadians generally found Britain's rule acceptable. Canada's population also grew as many U.S. citizens loyal to the British crown moved to Canada.

After the U.S. Civil War, thousands of Irish soldiers were discharged from the Union Army and joined the Fenian Brotherhood, a society dedicated to freeing Ireland from British rule. The Fenians hatched a lunatic scheme: They would invade the Canadian colonies and hold them for ransom, demanding freedom for Ireland. In 1866, Fenian forces invaded Canada at three separate border crossings. Their incursions posed little threat, and the Fenians were soon repulsed. However, they did frighten most of the recalcitrant Canadian colonies into accepting unification.

Under the British North America Act, most of the colonies were united on July 1, 1867. Canada dates its origin as a country from this event. Because the United States objected to the title "Kingdom of Canada," the new country was given the less imperial, biblically inspired name "Dominion of Canada."

Like the United States, Canada expanded westward in the nineteenth century, and new provinces were added. The Canadian frontier expansion is remembered as a fairly peaceful process, unlike the violent American "winning of the West." Rather than gunslingers, outlaws, and Indian fighters, Canadians glorified the builders of their transcontinental railroad, which was completed in 1885.

The 1931 Statute of Westminster granted Canada full independence from the United Kingdom, and the postwar NATO alliance brought the United States and Canada closer together. Canada reached its current configuration in 1949, when the last remaining colony, Newfoundland, finally joined the Canadian confederation.

In recent years, the Canadian Confederation has weathered substantial separatist pressures. In addition to the always-fractious Quebec province, the western provinces have opposed many of the rulings of the national government in Ottawa.

Canada joined the North American Free Trade Agreement (NAFTA) in 1994, creating a free trade zone spanning Canada, the United States of America, and Mexico. In 1999, Canada created a new territory called Nunavut, providing self-government to the Inuit people of the central and eastern Arctic.

Type of Government

Canada is a federal multiparty parliamentary democracy, with the provinces holding more power than do states in the United States.

The titular head of state of Canada is the British monarch, represented by the governor-general. The head of government in Canada is the prime minister. The Canadian Parliament has two houses: a Senate and a House of Commons.

For current government data, check with the Embassy of Canada, *www.ambassadeducanada .org*, which can also provide guides on doing business in Canada.

Language

English and French are the official languages, with French predominating only in Quebec. The approximate breakdown is 60 percent English speakers, 24 percent French speakers. Due to the large numbers of ethnic Chinese who have recently immigrated to Canada (many of whom fled Hong Kong prior to its takeover by the People's Republic of China), Chinese is now the third most common language spoken in Canada.

Language issues can be intensely political in Canada. The Métis people are descended from French and Scottish fur traders who intermarried with Amerindians. They spoke a tongue called Michif, which combined French and Cree. Although almost extinct, some Métis are reviving the language in the hopes of solidifying their claims as a distinct society.

The Inuit language Inuktitut is the language of the new territory of Nunavut. Inuktitut does not use the Roman alphabet but uses its own syllabic form of writing, originally developed by Anglican missionaries.

Linguists count ninety different languages used in Canada, five of which are extinct. All the extinct languages are Amerindian.

The Canadian View

The traditional division of Canada between Roman Catholic (46 percent) and Protestant (41 percent) remains; Jews and Eastern Orthodox each constitute less than 2 percent.

Canada's geography and harsh winters have always isolated its rural population. However, the introduction of computers and the Internet has reduced this isolation for Canadians who use this technology, notably the younger segment of the population.

As in other countries, Canada's churches are weathering serious scandals rising from sexual abuse of children by the clergy. In Canada, various churches ran most of the schools for the Amerindian population. Canada's Inuit, First Nation, and Métis (mixed-blood) populations had already been at odds with church schools over the destruction of indigenous culture and language. (Typically, students at boarding schools were prohibited from speaking their indigenous tongues.) The sexual abuse scandal has exacerbated relations between the Amerindians and the churches. Younger Canadians generally do not consider church as crucial a priority as older generations.

While Canadians appreciate public figures with sophistication and charisma, they also respect frank and honest speech. One of Canada's most respected leaders has been Auditor General Sheila Fraser, who investigated fiscal irregularities in the government and reported them in the straightforward manner of a scolding mother.

As previously mentioned, some linguistic requirements in the provinces affect business, such as Quebec's laws requiring French titles and labeling.

Separatist movements can also affect business. Separatist sentiment can cause people to reject brand names they view as foreign, in favor of local brands.

Canada has benefited from Anti-American sentiments in the last few years. International firms who do not want to do business directly with companies from the United States have sometimes become clients of Canadian companies that can provide similar, or exact products as in the United States. This has contributed to Canada's trade surplus.

☑ Know Before You Go

Canada is a remarkably peaceful country. However, robberies and street violence do occur.

The weather presents the greatest hazard to travelers. Canada's winters are long and cold. Frostbite is a danger.

Canada is relatively free of natural disasters. Tornadoes occur occasionally, as do earthquakes—mostly along the country's Pacific coast.

▶ CULTURAL ORIENTATION

Cognitive Styles: How Canadians Organize and Process Information

Canadians in general are well informed and open to reasonable discussions. The French province of Quebec is less open. Canadians, in general, are quite analytical and prefer objective information over subjective. They act on problems more from the perspective of universal rules than from the particular perspectives of the people involved.

Negotiation Strategies: What Canadians Accept as Evidence

Facts are accepted as the primary evidence in negotiations, with little credence given to feelings. There is a strong ethnocentrism within the provinces, especially in Quebec. This leads to a faith in self-determination that may underlie their behavior in negotiations.

Value Systems: The Basis for Behavior

The French province of Quebec has quite a different value system from the rest of Canada. Consumerism is well developed in all provinces. The following three sections identify the Value Systems in the predominant culture—their methods of dividing right from wrong, good from evil, and so forth.

Locus of Decision-Making

There is extremely high individualism in decision-making, but one must follow company policy. Therefore, one person can be exchanged for another without disrupting negotiations. Canadians do not find it difficult to say "no." A need for privacy prohibits discussing one's family and personal affairs in business negotiations. Friendships are few and specific to needs.

Canadians have been charted by sociologists as having a low long-term orientation. This would indicate that Canadians focus on immediate results, rather than on how decisions will affect future generations.

Sources of Anxiety Reduction

Canadians generally have a relatively low index of uncertainty avoidance. As a result, Canadians do not feel the need to establish strict laws to give structure to their worldview.

An objective approach to life allows the use of social organizations and other external structures to provide stability and insulation from life. Emotion is not to be shown in public. Competitive behavior is expected, because recognition is an individual's greatest reward. Time is money. Experts are relied upon at all levels.

Canadian public services, especially its universal health care, provide a great degree of security. However, with Canada's aging population, it is unknown whether this level of social service can be maintained. As has been observed, Canadians have social services equivalent to those of western Europe—paid for by tax rates similar to those in the United States.

Canada

Issues of Equality/Inequality
Emphasis is on an individual's ability, but considerable tension exists between the provinces, particularly with Quebec. Although there are inequalities in roles, equal rights should be guaranteed to all, as superiors and subordinates are "people like me." Material progress is as important as humanistic progress. Traditional sex roles are changing rapidly.

▶ BUSINESS PRACTICES

Punctuality, Appointments, and Local Time
- Being punctual is important. Be on time for all business-related meetings.
- French-speaking areas of Canada may have a somewhat more casual attitude toward time, but individual businesspeople vary. As a foreigner, you will be expected to be prompt, even if your Canadian counterpart is not.
- In general, it is acceptable to be fifteen minutes late for evening social occasions.
- Canadians usually write the day first, then the month, then the year (e.g., December 3, 2011, is written 3.12.11 or 3/12/11).
- Mornings tend to be preferred for appointments.
- A list of official Canadian holidays is available at *www.kissboworshakehands.com*.
- Canada spans six time zones. Most of Quebec and Ontario are on Eastern Standard Time, which is five hours behind Greenwich Mean Time (G.M.T. –5). Western Ontario, Manitoba, and eastern Saskatchewan (including Regina) are on Central Standard Time. Western Saskatchewan, Alberta, and easternmost British Columbia are on Mountain Standard Time. Most of British Columbia is on Pacific Standard Time (eight hours behind G.M.T.). All of these correspond to time zones in the United States.
- Atlantic Standard Time (four hours behind G.M.T.) is one hour ahead of Eastern Standard Time. All the Maritime Provinces are on Atlantic Standard Time except for Newfoundland Island, which reminds the world of its separate identity by maintaining a separate time zone that is thirty minutes ahead of Atlantic Standard Time (3½ hours behind G.M.T.). Note that this thirty-minute difference applies only to Newfoundland Island; Labrador, which is the mainland part of Newfoundland Province, is on Atlantic Standard Time. Note that the name Newfoundland is pronounced "new-fin-land," not "new-found-land."
- From the end of April through late October, most of Canada is on daylight-saving time.

Negotiating
- Negotiating styles tend to be very similar to those in the United States, although the pace may be slightly slower.
- Canadians associate the United States with self-promotion and "hype." Never inflate a product's benefits; it could generate claims of illegal promotion. Canadians expect to hear the truth.

- When working with French Canadians, it is important to have all material written in French as well as English.

> **Cultural Note**
> In Quebec, there are very stringent French-language requirements for all commercial endeavors. French is the only legal language in which to conduct business, and all signs must be posted in French only. However, English phrases that have no French equivalents (such as "happy hour" or "bargain basement") are permitted.

- English-speaking Canadian businesspeople expect a firm handshake, direct eye contact, and an open, friendly manner.
- Despite these similarities to citizens of the United States, English-speaking Canadians are closer to the reserved traditions of the British. It is important not to come off as an overbearing boor from the United States.
- While many Canadians quickly address others by their first names, it is safest to wait for your Canadian counterpart to suggest it.
- Acknowledge Canadians' desire for a "Canadian identity."
- French Canadians generally exhibit less reserve than English-speaking Canadians. Their gestures will be more expansive, they may stand closer while talking, and they are more likely to touch during a conversation.
- Canada is a multiethnic nation—British, French, Inuit, Indian, German, and so forth—and the etiquette of businesspeople may reflect their ethnic background. For example, many wealthy Hong Kong Chinese have acquired Canadian citizenship; their habits may be significantly different from those of other Canadians.

Business Entertaining
- Business meals are popular in Canada, although the breakfast meetings are not as commonplace as in the United States.
- Traditionally, dinners were considered social occasions—if business was discussed at all, it was at the end of the meal. While this is changing, it is wise to allow your Canadian counterpart to bring up business first.
- Invitations to dine at a Canadian home are relatively infrequent, except in the western provinces, where outdoor barbecues have become popular.

PROTOCOL

Greetings
- The standard greeting is a smile, often accompanied by a nod, wave, and/or verbal greeting.
- In business situations, a handshake is used upon greetings or introductions.

- Among Canadians of British descent, the handshake tends to be firm, and a weak handshake may be taken as a sign of weakness. Men usually wait for women to offer their hand before shaking.
- French Canadians also have a fairly firm handshake. And they shake hands more often: upon greetings, introductions, and departures, even if the person has been greeted earlier that day.
- Good friends and family members sometimes embrace, especially between the French. A kissing of cheeks may occur as well. Note that the French do not finish an embrace with a pat or two on the back, as many U.S. citizens do.
- If you see an acquaintance at a distance, a wave is appropriate.
- The greetings "How are you?" is not an inquiry about your health. The best response is a short one, such as "Fine, thanks."

Titles/Forms of Address
- The order of most Canadian names is first name, middle name, last name.
- To show respect, use a title such as "Dr.," "Ms.," "Miss," "Mrs.," or "Mr." with the last name.
- When you meet someone for the first time, use the person's title and surname until you are told to do otherwise (this may happen immediately).
- Note that although they often use first names over the telephone, French Canadians may revert to using surnames in person.

Gestures
- The standard space between you and your conversation partner should be two feet. British Canadians are uncomfortable standing any closer to another person. French Canadians may stand slightly closer.
- Canadians, especially those of British descent, do not tend toward frequent or expansive gesturing.
- In general, English-speaking friends of the same sex do not link arms or hold hands. However, female French Canadians commonly touch during conversation and may walk arm-in-arm.
- To point, you can use the index finger, although it is not polite to point at a person.
- To beckon someone, wave all the fingers in a scooping motion with the palm facing up.
- To show approval, there are two typical gestures. One is the "okay" sign, done by making a circle of the thumb and index finger. The other is the "thumbs-up" sign, done by making a fist and pointing the thumb upward.
- The "V-for-victory" sign is done with the palm facing out. It can be taken as an insult when done with the palm inward.
- The backslap is a sign of close friendship among British Canadians. It is rarely used among the French.

- To wave good-bye, move your entire hand, facing outward.
- Direct eye contact shows that you are sincere, although it should not be too intense. Some minorities look away to show respect.
- When sitting, Canadians often look very relaxed. They may sit with the ankle of one leg on the knee of the other or prop their feet up on chairs or desks.
- In business situations, maintain good posture and a less casual pose.

Gifts

- Business gifts should be modest. Ostentation tends to be frowned upon by Canadians.
- When you visit a home, it is customary to take a gift. Flowers, candy, or alcohol are common gifts.
- At Christmastime gifts are exchanged. To your business associates, you can give gifts that are helpful at the office, or liquor or wine. Most stores gift-wrap at Christmas.
- A good time to give a gift is when you arrive or when you leave. The best gifts are those that come from your country.
- Business gifts are given after you close a deal. Unless the giver specifies a time at which the gift is to be opened, as may happen with a gift at Christmastime, gifts are usually unwrapped immediately and shown to everyone.
- Taking someone out for a meal or other entertainment is a common gift.

Cultural Note
When visiting a French-Canadian family, be aware that houses are divided into "public" rooms (which visitors may enter) and "private" rooms (which they may enter only when invited). The kitchen is often a private room; do not enter unless asked.

Dress

- In cities, conservative business attire is best.
- In rural areas and small towns, clothing is less formal and less fashionable.
- When not working, Canadians dress casually.
- Canadian winters can be quite cold; dress warmly.

Chile

Republic of Chile
Local short form: Chile
Local long form: Republica de Chile

Cultural Note

Chileans have a renowned reputation for achievement in many cultural fields. Literature, social science, and fine arts are considered prestigious areas of study. Since the 1920s, Chile has challenged Argentina's place as South America's biggest producer of books in the Spanish language.

A Chilean also created Latin America's answer to Mickey Mouse: Condorito, a cartoon condor dressed in a red beret, red shirt, and black soccer (fútbol) shorts. Created by the late cartoonist René Ríos Boettiger, Condorito is one of the most beloved cartoon characters in the world. Syndicated in every Spanish-speaking country, Condorito has been used to sell everything from food to Microsoft Windows.

▶ WHAT IS YOUR CULTURAL IQ?

1. TRUE or FALSE: The date of September 11 is remembered with sadness by many Chileans.

   ANSWER: TRUE. but not because of the terrorist attacks in the United States on September 11, 2001. The Chileans remember September 11, 1973, when the Marxist government of Salvador Allende was overthrown in a military coup backed by the CIA. The subsequent seventeen years of military rule were accompanied by repression, torture, and executions (although they also ushered in economic prosperity).

2. Which of the following is not true about Chile?
   a. If placed in Europe, Chile would stretch from the north of Scotland to the island of Gibraltar in the Mediterranean.
   b. Chile is almost as long as California.
   c. To fit the entire country on a television screen, Chile's weather maps have to divide the country into three parts.
   d. If placed horizontally, Chile would stretch across the Pacific Ocean at its widest point.

   ANSWER: d. Chile is long, but not that long.

3. Which of the following famous Chilean authors have won the Nobel Prize for literature?
   a) Isabel Allende
   b) Gabriela Mistral
   c) Pablo Neruda
   d) None of the above

   ANSWER: b and c. Of the three, only Isabel Allende has never received a Nobel.

> **Cultural Note**
> Many North American gestures have completely different meanings in other countries. In Chile, slapping your right fist
> into your left open palm is obscene, and displaying an open palm with the fingers splayed means "stupid."

▶ COUNTRY BACKGROUND

History

The first European settlers in Chile were Spanish explorers in search of gold and silver, who arrived after the defeat of the Inca empire in 1533. What they found instead was a fertile valley. Chile soon became part of the Spanish empire, governed from Peru.

Bernardo O'Higgins, Chile's renowned patriot, led a struggle for independence against the Spanish from 1810 to 1818. Helped by an army trained by Argentine patriot José de San Martín, Chilean independence was formally declared on February 12, 1818.

During the nineteenth century, Chile expanded its territories. A treaty with Argentina gave Chile control of the Strait of Magellan (although most of Patagonia went to Argentina). Chile twice fought Peru and Bolivia for control of the Pacific coast. In 1883, Chile won the War of the Pacific, expanding the country's territory northward to an area rich in natural resources. Relations with Bolivia remain difficult to this day, as the now-landlocked Bolivia has never reconciled itself to the loss of its entire Pacific seaboard.

In 1964, Eduardo Frei, a Christian Democrat, was elected to the presidency. His program was marked by the slogan "Revolution in Liberty" and consisted of far-reaching social programs. In the next election, in 1970, Dr. Salvador Allende won with 36 percent of the votes over two other candidates, becoming the first freely elected Marxist leader in this hemisphere. But Allende did not have majority support in the Chilean Congress, and discontent grew as a result of shortages of food and consumer goods. On September 11, 1973, a bloody, CIA-backed military coup overthrew Allende, abolished the Congress, and banned political parties. A four-man military junta instituted a repressive regime. The leading general, Augusto Pinochet Ugarte, ruled as president and commander of the army.

In 1980, a new constitution was approved in a national plebiscite. Under it, General Pinochet was elected to an eight-year term, with the military junta acting as the legislature. At the end of that term, Pinochet allowed another plebiscite to decide if he should continue for another eight years. When he lost the plebiscite, he called for free elections in December 1989. As a result of that election, President Patricio Aylwin Azócar took office in March 1990 as the first elected president since 1970. Since then, political power has passed peacefully from one elected government to the next. In 2006, Chile swore in a new President, Michelle Bachelet, who was an unprecedented leader for a traditionally conservative, generally Catholic country. Prior to serving as President she was Secretary of Defense and supervised some of the same military personnel who had overseen her own inprisonment, torture, and her father's murder. One Chilean reporter explained her election thus: When we go into the booth, we vote with our souls, not our wallets.

Type of Government

The Republic of Chile is a multiparty republic with two legislative houses, the Senate and the Chamber of Deputies. The president is the chief of state as well as the head of the government.

Suffrage is universal and compulsory at age eighteen.

The current government is considered stable; however, it must still address continued problems from poverty. For current government data, check with the Embassy of Chile at *www.chile-usa.org*.

Language

The official language of Chile is Spanish, although English is spoken by well-educated businesspeople and in tourist centers. Chileans speak a very conservative form of Spanish. In most of Latin America, the second-person plural of verbs is ignored (the third-person plural is used instead). Chileans, however, continue to use the traditional second-person plural form of the verb.

The Web site *www.ethnologue.com* lists a total of eleven languages, two of which are extinct and several of which are endangered. Aside from Spanish, all the other languages are Amerindian—except for the Polynesian language Rapa Nui, spoken by the 2,500 natives of Easter Island (a Chilean possession).

The Chilean View

There is no official religion in Chile, but over 78 percent of the population identify themselves as Roman Catholics. As in most European countries, relatively few people attend church every Sunday. Protestants account for over 13 percent. There is also a small Jewish population. A sizable number of people consider themselves nonreligious or atheist.

Chile is prone to natural disasters (earthquakes, volcanoes, etc.), and some sociologists believe that this is the source of the traditional Chilean pessimism and fatalistic attitude.

In the past, ostentation was rarely seen in public. However, Chile's recent economic success has made public displays of wealth more common—if not acceptable to traditionalists.

☑ Know Before You Go

Nature has bestowed many things upon Chile, including many dangers. Earthquakes and volcanoes are an ever-present hazard, as are tsunamis (tidal waves) caused by offshore earthquakes.

Some cities in Chile are elevated enough to cause altitude sickness in visitors. Altitude sickness can strike anyone, even if you have never experienced it before. There is no sure prevention except gradual acclimation to high elevation: once you get to 6,000 feet above sea level, spend at least two nights there. Repeat this acclimation period at each increase of 3,000 feet. Alcohol consumption tends to make the symptoms worse. Sunburn is also a danger at high altitudes, because there is less atmosphere to protect you from the sun.

There is a new hazard in the southernmost part of Chile: the Antarctic ozone hole in the atmosphere. As in high altitudes, sunburn can occur quickly. Sunblock and/or protective clothing (including sunglasses) are the best preventatives.

Many Chileans are heavy smokers. It can be difficult to find smoke-free establishments. International hotel chains tend to be the best at enforcing no-smoking rules.

Although Chile has more than its share of natural hazards, the country lacks many of the dangers associated with other Latin American countries. The roads—especially the main highways—are good, and Chileans are relatively safe, polite drivers. Armed robbery and kidnapping are rare. Corruption (aside from tax evasion) is uncommon. Even the Chilean traffic police (the Carabineros) tend to be honest; they make take an attempt to bribe them as an insult.

▶ CULTURAL ORIENTATION

Cognitive Styles: How Chileans Organize and Process Information

In Chile, information is readily accepted for the purpose of discussion. Negotiations may be extensive, with little movement from the initial position. Chileans educated abroad or in foreign business methods may process information conceptually and analytically, but most are associative in their thinking. Typically, Chileans see each problem as having a particular solution rather than looking to a universal rule or law.

Negotiation Strategies: What Chileans Accept as Evidence

In traditional negotiations, Chileans consider feelings more important than facts. The truth is considered to be subjective and personal. In addition, faith in a strong Catholic or Protestant ideology may form the basis for truth.

Value Systems: The Basis for Behavior

This is not a culture of conquerors but of cosmopolitans who assimilated all European cultures into their social strata through marriage. The following three sections identify the Value Systems in the predominant culture—their methods of dividing right from wrong, good from evil, and so forth.

Locus of Decision-Making

Chile has a collectivist culture in which the extended family is a dominating factor in the individual's decision-making process. The prospect that a bad decision could bring dishonor on one's group or family is always a factor in decision-making. Expertise is considered less important than membership in the appropriate group. Thus, kinship and friendship play a major role in a person's business associations. It is essential for a foreigner to become friends with Chileans with whom one wants to do business.

Sources of Anxiety Reduction

Chileans evidently have a high index of uncertainty avoidance. As a result, Chileans use laws and morality to give structure to their worldview. (This can be seen in how Chileans wait in orderly lines, as opposed to how some other Latin Americans crowd and push instead of queue.) Social stratification has traditionally been strong in Chile. Marriage into the right family was considered essential, as family ties are a major determinant of success. Chileans used to accept their social class as destiny. However, the economic boom of the 1990s has made class structure less of a determinant. Although relatively few Chileans have gotten rich, the new entrepreneurs are not all from Chile's upper class.

Issues of Equality/Inequality

On a philosophical level, Chileans consider each individual to have equal rights, and no law needs to be passed to ensure this equality. On a practical level, black and Amerindian Chileans remain discriminated against. There is a small, traditional, class-conscious elite, a bigger middle class than in most other Latin American countries, and a large impoverished underclass. The Chilean masculinity index has been charted as lower than average for Latin America, resulting in more equality for Chilean women, as evidenced by the election of their first female president in 2006.

▶ BUSINESS PRACTICES

Punctuality, Appointments, and Local Time

- Be punctual at meetings. Punctuality is appreciated and expected from North Americans. Do not be offended, however, if your counterpart is up to thirty minutes late.
- On the other hand, everyone (even foreigners) is expected to arrive at social functions late. Be at least fifteen minutes late to a dinner and thirty minutes late to a party.
- Remember that many Europeans and South Americans write the day first, then the month, then the year (e.g., December 3, 2010, is written 3.12.10 or 3/12/10). This is the case in Chile.
- The best times to make appointments are from 10:00 A.M. to 12:00 and 2:30 to 5:00 P.M. Following up a late-morning appointment with a business lunch is also popular.
- Make appointments at least one week in advance of your arrival, and reconfirm them when you get there.
- A popular time for vacations is January and February (summer holidays). This is not the time to try to do business in Chile.
- Chile is four hours behind Greenwich Mean Time (G.M.T. –4). This makes it one hour ahead of U.S. Eastern Standard Time (E.S.T. +1). Chile goes on daylight-saving time from mid-October through mid-March.

> **Cultural Note**
>
> The decision-making process is centralized, residing mostly with the upper-level presidente or gerente general. Next in importance comes the gerente, followed by mid- and low-level managers; all provide support to the upper levels. But all levels usually have input, so business transactions may take place at a slower pace than in North America or Europe. Be patient and expect delays. Several trips may be necessary to conclude a business transaction.

Negotiating

- Personal relationships are paramount in business relations in Chile. The initial visit should be by an upper-level executive, accompanied by midlevel executives. These mid-level executives are the ones who will make subsequent visits to conduct more detailed business negotiations. At a first meeting, spend most of the time establishing a rapport, then gradually steer the conversation toward introducing your firm.

- Attitudes toward trading with North America are positive, despite how Chile's admittance to the North American Free Trade Area has been delayed for years.

- Conservative values in politics, economics, and social attitudes prevail. Honesty and integrity are highly valued. A sense of humor is appreciated, but generally serious, businesslike behavior is expected.

- There is a strong sense of personal honor on the part of Chilean businesspeople. A single accusation of wrongdoing can follow a Chilean for his or her entire life. Consequently, avoid criticizing a person in public or doing anything that would cause him or her embarrassment.

- Chileans are straightforward and take negotiating quite seriously. A hard-sell approach, however, will not work. Have your bottom line and other terms clearly drawn out. Also outline a strong financial package with options such as nontraditional financing terms.

- Many women are professionally advanced in Chile, and a woman will have better success here than in most other Latin American countries.

- Show commitment to the business relationship through a willingness to provide continued service to your client, despite the long distances involved. Remember that Chileans strive to overcome the isolation imposed on them by geography.

- Making a good impression includes staying at one of the finer international hotels while in Chile.

- Chileans generally converse in closer proximity than North Americans or northern Europeans. Do not pull away from a person who is speaking quite close to you, even if you are uncomfortable. This may be interpreted as a personal affront.

- Try to cover any tattoos you may have while in Chile. To older Chileans, only criminals wear tattoos, although this attitude is changing among the young.

- Have business cards printed with English on one side and Spanish on the other. Present cards to everyone in a meeting except secretaries.

- Third parties are very important for making contacts in Chile. Banks and consulting firms can make introductions.
- The business atmosphere tends to be more formal than in other South American countries. Proper etiquette and dress are expected.
- Chileans avoid behavior that may appear aggressive. Kindness and respect for others are valued.
- Learn a little about Chile's history, culture, economy, exports, and so forth, and be prepared to discuss them. Appreciation of Chile's history will impress and please your contacts.

Cultural Note
Chileans do not bargain in either stores or street markets. Note that it is illegal to sell something and fail to give a receipt. When a receipt is not issued, this often means that the merchant is not declaring the sale on tax reports. Both the buyer and the seller can be fined for this infraction; it is the buyer's responsibility to ask for the receipt when making a purchase.

▶ BUSINESS ENTERTAINING

- Breakfast is usually eaten between 7:00 and 9:00 A.M. Breakfast tends to be very light. A substantial number of Chileans eat breakfast in bed (which is possible because even middle-class families can afford a maid and/or cook).
- Lunch, the largest meal of the day, begins anytime from noon to 1:30. Lunch is often a multicourse meal lasting as long as two hours. (The higher-ranking the businessperson, the longer he or she can take for lunch.)
- Between 5:00 and 6:00 P.M., Chileans eat a snack called *once*. This consists of tea or coffee and light food, such as cookies or cheese. Some Chileans also drink alcohol at this time, which is where the "once" got its name. The traditional Chilean spirit is called aguardiente. Once is the Spanish word for "eleven," and there are eleven letters in the word aguardiente.
- Dinner is served between 8:00 and 9:00 P.M. Alcohol, in the form of a mixed drink, often starts the dinner. Wine or beer is served during the meal. Dinner ends with coffee, tea or yerba mate—and more alcohol. (Yerba mate is a caffeinated herb served in a gourd. It is more common in the Chilean south. See the entry under Paraguay on how to drink yerba mate.) Men often drink spirits after dinner and expect foreign businessmen to do the same; businesswomen are exempt from this ritual.
- Chileans are very hospitable and often invite foreigners into their home. If you are invited for drinks in the evening, you will probably be asked to stay for dinner as well.
- It is not customary to send a thank-you gift or note following an invitation to a Chilean home, but flowers or candy sent to the hostess in advance are appreciated. If you wish to convey your thanks, do so by telephone rather than by mail.

- Entertaining is often done in large hotels and restaurants. Make arrangements concerning the bill with the maître d' in advance to avoid competition for paying. If you are a guest, reciprocate the hospitality at a later date.
- Proper table manners are very important in Chile. In general, follow European standards. Make an attempt to try everything that is served to you.
- Superstitious Chileans consider it bad luck to pass a salt shaker directly to another person. Instead, put the salt down on the table within reach of the person.
- There are several traditions concerning the pouring of wine in Chile. If you pour wine in the wrong way, you risk insulting your Chilean hosts. "The wrong way" includes pouring with your left hand, or pouring so that the wine splashes against the opposite side of the glass.
- Good topics of conversation include family, Chilean history, cuisine, wines, and sights that they might recommend—including Easter Island, a Chilean possession. Many Chileans are very interested in world travel, so mention other places you have visited. Skiing and fishing are very popular in Chile. Topics to avoid include local politics, human rights violations, and religion. Do not criticize Chile, even if your host is doing so.

▶ PROTOCOL

Greetings
- Men will shake hands when greeting someone. Women will often pat each other on the right forearm or shoulder instead of shaking hands. If they are close, women may hug or kiss each other on the cheek.
- At a party, greet and shake hands with each person individually. Do not ask a person his or her occupation directly, but wait for the information to be volunteered.

Titles/Forms of Address
- Do not address a Chilean by his or her first name unless invited to do so. Older executives may wish to use their last names at work. Generally, younger Chileans are more comfortable using first names.
- Futher data is available in Appendix A.

Gestures
- The Chilean people converse at a closer distance than many Asians, North Americans, or Northern Europeans are used to—often with a hand on the other person's lapel or shoulder. Restrain yourself from trying to back away; a Chilean will probably step forward and close the distance.
- Maintaining eye contact is necessary to show interest and sincerity—something that North Americans may find difficult when speaking to a person at such close quarters.

- At a meal, keep your hands above the table at all times.
- Do not raise your right fist to head level, as this is a Communist sign.

Gifts

- Gifts are not expected in business until the relationship is a close one.
- When visiting a Chilean home, send flowers in advance (avoid yellow roses, which signify contempt) or bring wine or liquor. Other popular gifts include leather appointment books, quality pens or cigarette lighters, perfume, and local crafts from home.
- If you receive a gift, open it promptly in the presence of the giver and extend thanks.
- Give gold jewelry to a girl on her fifteenth birthday. This birthday (called the *quinceaños*; the party is called a *quinceañera*) is a very important celebration in Chile; to be invited to one is a privilege.

Dress

- *Business:* Dress is generally equivalent to that in Europe (meaning it is more conservative than in the United States). Men may wear a dark blue or gray suit, a light shirt, and a conservative tie. Bright colors and flashy fashions are not appropriate, nor is wearing anything on the lapel. Women should wear a suit and heels.
- *Casual:* When not doing business, pants or good jeans and a shirt are appropriate. Shorts will rarely be seen in public. Chile experiences temperature extremes from the beaches to the mountains. You will need warmer clothes at higher altitudes.

China

People's Republic of China
Local short form: Zhong Guo
Local long form: Zhonghua Renmin Gongheguo
Abbreviation: PRC

Cultural Note

The People's Republic of China is well on its way to becoming the superpower of the twenty-first century. Aside from having the world's largest population and the world's largest army, it is a nuclear and space power. Now it is a global economic power as well. In February of 2005, the government of China lent the government of Russia U.S.$6 billion to help Moscow nationalize the oil company Yukos.

 WHAT'S YOUR CULTURAL IQ?

1. TRUE or FALSE? The Chinese are not interested in most international sports.

   ANSWER: FALSE. While many Chinese have limited experience playing sports, they are often avid fans (and sports gamblers). When Shanghai-born Yao Ming joined the Houston Rockets in 2002, Chinese interest in basketball soared overnight. And the Beijing Olympics has generated massive interest in Olympic sports.

2. Match the following Nobel Prize laureates with the appropriate prize:
   a. Tenzin Gyatso   1. Nobel in physics, 1957
   b. Chen Ning Yang   2. Nobel for literature, 2000
   c. Gao Xingjian   3. Nobel Peace Prize, 1989

   ANSWERS: a. 3; b. 1; c. 2. Tenzin Gyatso is better known as the fourteenth Dalai Lama of Tibet. Tibet, of course, has been occupied by the PRC since 1950. Gao Xingjian was the first Chinese to win the Nobel for literature. There have been many Nobel Prizes awarded to Chinese in the sciences, although most of the recipients (like Chen Ning Yang) have done their most important scientific work in the West.

3. There are many places in Asia where the People's Republic of China finds itself in conflict with other countries. Which of these is not currently an international "hot spot?"
   a. Macao
   b. North Korea
   c. The Spratly Islands
   d. Taiwan

   ANSWER: a. Portugal ceded its colony of Macao to the PRC at the end of 1999, and Macao has been relatively peaceful since then. A traditional site for gambling, Macao is the only place on the Chinese mainland where casinos are permitted.

TIPS ON DOING BUSINESS IN CHINA

China

- Experienced travelers avow that patience is the most important skill needed to do business in China. The Chinese are very good at figuring out when a foreigner is under pressure from a tight deadline, and they turn that to their advantage in negotiations.
- Although the economic boom is changing things, China is still a hierarchical society. Age is respected. When you send more than one representative to China, the oldest person should receive deference from the younger ones. The elder representative should even enter and leave the conference room first.
- While the Chinese have made great strides in using the Internet, they face serious obstacles. For one thing, the thousands of ideographs in Chinese language are not easily adapted to use on a computer keyboard. Also, Internet use in China is hampered by the government, which censors Web sites and periodically shuts down Internet cafés.
- While many urban Chinese are consumers on par with any in the world, even wealthy Chinese may lack credit cards. This is another factor hampering Internet commerce in China.
- If possible, avoid traveling to China during the lunar New Year. Also called Spring Festival, this is China's most important, nationwide weeklong holiday. Tradition demands that every Chinese return to his or her traditional home during the lunar New Year. With so many migrants to the cities, this means that there are millions of trips taken by car, bus, train, or airplane during the festival.

Cultural Note
The lunar New Year puts enormous strains on China's transportation infrastructure. Many people wait for days just to secure standing room on a train or bus. To alleviate this, the Chinese government is considering mandating staggered vacations, in the hope that travel will be eased if not everyone is off work at the same time. This may ease travel during China's other national holidays, but it is doubtful whether it will eliminate the Spring Festival tradition of returning to one's ancestral home.

COUNTRY BACKGROUND

History

The Chinese boast the world's oldest continuous civilization, with more than 4,000 years of recorded history. Beijing (old Peking) has been the capital of China for over 800 years and is the country's political, economic, and cultural hub.

China was ruled by strong dynasties for thousands of years. The first recorded dynasty, the Hsia, existed around 2200 B.C., and the last dynasty, the Ch'ing, ended in 1911. Some of the most important cultural achievements in history were produced during this time, such as papermaking, the compass, gunpowder, and movable-type printing.

China

After the fall of the last dynasty, Sun Yat-sen founded the Republic of China and was succeeded by Chiang Kai-shek in 1927.

Mao Tse-tung's Communist forces took control in 1949 and established the Communist government that still exists, although events—from the massacre in Tiananmen Square in June of 1989 on—have shown an increasingly popular demand for democratic reform.

China has been divided into twenty-two provinces, five autonomous regions, and three municipalities.

Type of Government

The People's Republic of China has a Communist government. There is a single legislative house, the National People's Congress; all members belong to the Communist Party. The National People's Congress elects the Standing Committee, which holds executive power and is made up of the premier and leading ministers. The premier is the head of the government; the president is the chief of state. The position of secretary general of the Central Committee of the Chinese Communist Party is also an office of great power; it is often held by the current president.

The Communist regime is highly centralized and authoritarian and controls many aspects of life in China.

Current government data can be found at the Embassy of China at *www.china-embassy.org.*

Cultural Note

The revolutionary government of the People's Republic of China made changes to the Chinese language. Many complex symbols in written Chinese were simplified. And the direction of written Chinese was changed: instead of being written in vertical columns, it is now primarily written like most Western tongues, from left to right in horizontal rows.

This reformed Chinese has not been universally accepted by the Chinese outside the PRC. Some Taiwanese refuse to reform Chinese, preferring the prerevolutionary forms. When you go to the PRC, make sure your translators use reformed Chinese.

Language

The official national language is standard Chinese, based on the Mandarin dialect. It is spoken by more than 70 percent of the population. Many Chinese speak Cantonese, Shanghainese, and Kejia dialects. Ethnologue, at *www.ethnologue.com*, recognizes 202 languages. Each minority speaks its own dialect or language. English is spoken by many businesspeople.

Although spoken Chinese has many dialects (some of which are as different as English is from German) there is one common written language. This is why many Chinese movies include Chinese subtitles, so that Cantonese-speaking Chinese audiences can understand the Mandarin-speaking actors, or vice versa.

The government of the PRC has begun investing in Chinese language training for foreigners. Contributions to support Chinese language programs are being made to major trade partners worldwide.

The Chinese View

Despite the fact that the government encourages atheism, the Chinese Constitution guarantees religious freedom (within certain constraints). Buddhism, Islam, and Christianity are the three major formal religions practiced in China. However, even larger numbers of Chinese believe in traditional Chinese philosophies, notably Confucianism and Taoism.

Confucianism, although not a religion with a divine deity, has great influence on Chinese society. Confucius was a Chinese scholar and statesman who lived during feudal times over 2,000 years ago. He established a rigid ethical and moral system that governs all relationships.

Confucius taught that the basic unit of society is the family. To preserve harmony in the home, certain reciprocal responsibilities must be preserved in relationships. These relationships are between ruler and subjects, between husband and wife, between father and son, between elder brother and younger brother, and between friends. Since all but the last are hierarchal, rank and age have historically been very important in all interactions. All actions of the individual reflect upon the family, and filial devotion is of utmost importance. The virtues of kindness, propriety, righteousness, intelligence, and faithfulness have also been deeply revered.

☑ Know Before You Go

Most foreign businesspeople in China's major cities will find an environment comparable to that of any city in the industrially developed world. The greatest hazards are from traffic and environmental pollution.

China's less-developed areas present greater challenges. The transportation infrastructure is overloaded, and some foreign goods (including medicines) may not be readily available.

China is thought to be the source for many forms of influenza that eventually infect people all over the world. It is theorized that this happens not just because of China's unsurpassed population density, but because of Chinese farming techniques, which allow animals of different species to come into close contact. This is believed to facilitate viral transfer between species, eventually resulting in a virus, which infects humans. Certainly, anyone who has visited an outdoor Chinese market will see different species of live animals on sale. The Chinese government recently prohibited such markets from selling civet cats, which were suspected to be the source of the SARS virus.

China is a huge nation, subject to all manner of natural hazards. Earthquakes have caused widespread deaths in the past, but China also suffers from typhoons and other dangerous storms, floods, and mudslides.

▶ CULTURAL ORIENTATION

Cognitive Styles: How the Chinese Organize and Process Information

The Chinese are generally circumspect toward outside sources of information. They usually process data through a subjective perspective, derived from experience—unless they have been educated at a Western university. Universalistic behavior that follows the Communist Party line is still required under the Communist government. The favoritism shown to members of the Communist Party is overtly particularistic.

Negotiation Strategies: What the Chinese Accept as Evidence

In general, truth is subjective, and one's feelings, along with a modified belief in the Communist Party line, are primary sources of the truth. Facts are accepted by younger Chinese, particularly within the burgeoning entrepreneurial sector. However, they still strongly consider the other two sources and will not usually accept a proposal if it is in conflict with their personal feelings for the prospect.

Value Systems: The Basis for Behavior

China is still primarily a collectivistic culture dominated by the Communist Party. The following three sections identify the Value Systems in the predominant culture—their methods of dividing right from wrong, good from evil, and so forth.

Locus of Decision-Making

In a centrally controlled economy, responsibility rests with government planners, but individuals are held responsible for their decisions within the system. Local decisions are made by the head of the collective, and members must behave accordingly. Collectives are insular, closed entities in which individual goals are subordinated to those of the collective. In the zones of free enterprise, businesses are experimenting with freedom from party rule but not from the collectivist way of thinking.

Sources of Anxiety Reduction

The family, school, work unit, and local community are the basic social structures that give stability to a person's life. There is a strong commitment to the extended family. The state, rather than religion, traditionally dictated the standards of wisdom, morality, and the common good. Obedience to parents is integral to a sense of security and stability. Maintaining harmony is vital.

Faith in the Communist Party, which rules the PRC, is abating. Some Chinese look to other ideologies for solace. These include native and Western religions, and organizations such as Falun Gong. While most westerners view Falun Gong as a harmless physical-fitness cult, Beijing has labeled it an "ideological threat." The fierce persecution of Falun Gong demonstrates how ruthlessly the government will attack any rival to its power.

Issues of Equality/Inequality

Relative to the general population (over 1 billion), the number of people who are powerful members of the Communist Party is small. There has always been some concern about inequality in a system in which equality is the purpose, but being a member of the party is the only avenue to a position of authority. Free enterprise is purported to breed inequality

China

and uncertainty, but there are rapidly increasing areas where it is allowed to flourish. Age is the only noticeable interpersonal indicator of inequality because it is still revered. Women are purported to be equal to men, but economic and social inequalities continue.

Gender inequality in China also manifests itself in the official "one child" policy. Because a generation of Chinese were only permitted to have one child, many did everything they could to ensure that their child was a boy. Today, China has many more boys than girls, which presents interesting problems when they reach adulthood.

▶ BUSINESS PRACTICES

Punctuality, Appointments, and Local Time

- Punctuality is very important in China, not only for business meetings, but for social occasions as well. Lateness or a cancellation is a serious affront.
- Remember that written Chinese does not have tenses, but there are many words to indicate the passage of time—tomorrow, now, etc.
- Be sure to establish contacts in China before you invest in a trip. Your government's Department of Trade or Commerce can usually assist in arranging appointments with local Chinese business and government officials and can identify importers, buyers, agents, distributors, and joint venture partners.
- The best times to schedule business trips are April to June and September to October.
- The work week has generally run from 8:00 A.M. to 5:00 P.M., Monday through Saturday. However, a five-day work week has been initiated in some large cities.
- Do not plan business trips during the Chinese New Year, since many businesses close for a week before and after the festival. The date of the New Year varies according to the lunar calendar.
- Be cognizant of the fact that the Chinese write the date differently than most North Americans. The year is written first, then the month, then the day (e.g., December 3, 2010, is written 10.12.03 or 10/12/03).
- For a list of the official holidays of China, visit *www.kissboworshakehands.com*.
- China is eight hours ahead of Greenwich Mean Time (G.M.T. +8), or thirteen hours ahead of U.S. Eastern Standard Time (E.S.T. +13). Despite the immense size of the country, it has only one time zone.

Negotiating

- Be prepared for the Chinese to supply an interpreter. If possible, bring your own interpreter as well to help you understand nuances in the discussion.
- Avoid slang or jargon, especially figures of speech from sports. Use short, simple sentences, and pause often to make sure that your exact words are understood.
- Expect to make presentations to many different groups at different levels.

China

- Unless you understand the significance of different colors in China, use black and white for your collateral materials.
- Foreign executives—especially those from the United States—have a reputation for impatience, and the Chinese will drag out negotiations well beyond your deadlines just to gain an advantage. They may try to renegotiate everything on the final day of your visit, and they may continue to try for a better deal even after the contract is signed.
- Never exaggerate your ability to deliver, because the Chinese believe humility is a virtue—and also because they will investigate your claims.
- Chinese may not make any important decisions without first considering whether it is an auspicious day and hour.
- Be patient. Expect to make several trips to China before negotiations are final. The Chinese are cautious in business matters and expect a strong relationship to be built before they close a deal.
- Weights and measures are mainly metric, but several old Chinese measures may still be used.
- Bring business cards with a translation printed (in Mandarin Chinese) on the reverse side. Gold ink is the most prestigious color for the Chinese side. Never place a person's card in your wallet and then put it in your back pocket.
- When entering a business meeting, the highest-ranking member of your group should lead the way.
- The Chinese expect the business conversation to be conducted by the senior officials of each side. Subordinates may speak when they are asked to provide corroborating data, or a comment, but in general, they do not interrupt.
- Familiarize yourself with all aspects of China before you arrive. The Chinese appreciate Western visitors who demonstrate an interest in their culture and history.
- Be patient, expect delays, show little emotion, and do not talk about your deadlines.
- At the end of a meeting, leave before the Chinese.

Cultural Note

One dish you will no longer encounter in China is "dragon, tiger, phoenix"—which was made with the meat of a snake, a civet cat, and a pheasant. In 2003, the Chinese government prohibited the sale and consumption of the civet cat (which is actually not a feline but related to the mongoose). Civet cats were the source of the coronavirus, which causes the potentially lethal form of pneumonia known as SARS. The SARS outbreak ended after the ban, although it left Chinese breeders with thousands of unwanted, unsellable civet cats.

Business Entertaining

- Business lunches have become popular.
- You will probably be treated to at least one evening banquet. You should always return the favor.

- Banquets at restaurants can be ordered in varying degrees of extravagance. Be sure to reciprocate at the same price per person as your Chinese host spent at your banquet—never surpass your host in the degree of lavishness.
- Most banquets start between 6:30 and 7:00 P.M. and last for several hours. You should arrive about thirty minutes before your guests—they will arrive on time.
- If you are the guest, always arrive promptly or even a little early.
- Business is not generally discussed during a meal.
- Never begin to eat or drink before your host does.
- When eating rice, it is customary to hold the bowl close to your mouth.
- At a meal, eat lightly in the beginning, as there could be up to twenty courses served. Expect your host to keep filling your bowl with food whenever you empty it. Finishing all of your food may be an insult to your host, because it can mean he did not provide enough food. Leaving a bowl completely full is also rude.
- The Chinese use chopsticks for eating and a porcelain spoon for soup. Your attempts at using chopsticks will be appreciated. When you are finished, set your chopsticks on the chopstick rest. Placing them parallel on top of your bowl is considered a sign of bad luck.
- Sticking your chopsticks straight up in your rice bowl is rude, as they will resemble the joss sticks used in religious ceremonies.
- Try not to drop your chopsticks; it is considered bad luck.
- Serving dishes are not passed around. Reach for food with your chopsticks, but do not use the end you put in your mouth! It is acceptable to reach in front of others to get to the serving dishes.
- Good topics of conversation include Chinese sights, art, calligraphy, and inquiries about the health of the other's family. Generally, conversation during a meal focuses on the meal itself and is full of compliments to the preparer.
- While the Chinese are not traditionally sports fans, their interest in sport has been increased by the Olympics. U.S. football is called "olive ball" in Mandarin Chinese because the ball is roughly olive-shaped.
- At a banquet, expect to be served rice in an individual bowl by a waiter. In a home, your hostess will serve the rice.
- Toasting is popular in China. At banquets, the host offers the first toast, and the ceremony continues all evening. It is acceptable to toast with a soft drink, but various alcoholic drinks will be available.
- Never take the last bit of food from a serving dish; this can signify that you are still hungry.
- The serving of fruit signals the end of the meal.
- If you do not want refills of tea, leave some in your cup.
- If you smoke, offer your cigarettes to others in your group. Many Chinese are heavy smokers.

- Historically, women did not drink alcoholic beverages. If the business dinner is extremely formal (like a black-tie event), businesswomen should accept a drink if offered, take a sip, and leave it. However, at a less formal affair (like a trade association dinner), women can now be the drinking representative!

> **Cultural Note**
> It is considered polite to sample every dish. The Chinese may even test your fortitude on purpose with exotic delicacies, like thousand-year-old eggs or marinated, deep-fried scorpions (completely intact with their stingers).

▶ PROTOCOL

Greetings
- The Chinese nod or bow slightly when greeting another person, although handshakes are common. Wait for your Chinese associate to extend a hand first.
- Visitors to factories, theaters, or schools may be greeted with applause as a sign of welcome. The usual response is to applaud back.
- Introductions tend to be formal, with courtesy rather than familiarity preferred.

Titles/Forms of Address
- The Chinese are very sensitive to status and titles, so you should use official titles such as "General," "Committee Member," or "Bureau Chief" when possible. Never call anyone "Comrade" unless you are a Communist also.
- Names are listed in a different order from Western names. Each person receives a family name, a middle name (which used to be called a generational name), and a given name at birth—in that order. Middle and given names can be separated by a space or a hyphen, but are often written as one word. For example, President Hu Jintao has the family name of Hu, a middle name of Jin, and a given name of Tao. (His name could also be rendered Hu Chin-t'ao.)
- Most people you meet should be addressed with a title and their name. If a person does not have a professional title (President, Engineer, Doctor), simply use "Mr." or "Madam," "Mrs.," or "Miss," plus the name.
- Chinese wives do not generally take their husband's surnames but instead maintain their maiden names. Although westerners commonly address a married woman as "Mrs." plus her husband's family name, it is more appropriate to call her "Madam" plus her maiden family name. For example, Liu Yongqing (female) is married to Hu Jintao (male). While westerners would probably call her Mrs. Hu, she is properly addressed as Madam Liu.
- Thankfully, many Chinese adopt an English first name so that English speakers can have a familiar-sounding name to identify them. Thus, Chang Wu Jiang may call himself Mr. Tony Chang. Others use their initials (Mr. T. J. Chang).

China

- If many Chinese seem to have similar clan names, it is because there are only about 400 different surnames in China! However, when these surnames are transcribed into English, there are several possible variations. For example, Wong, Wang, and Huang are all English versions of the same Chinese clan name.

Gestures

- Avoid making exaggerated gestures or using dramatic facial expressions. The Chinese do not use their hands when speaking and become distracted by a speaker who does.
- The Chinese do not like to be touched by people they do not know. This is especially important to remember when dealing with older people or people in important positions.
- Members of the same sex may be seen publicly holding hands, but public affection between the opposite sexes is not condoned.
- Use an open hand rather than one finger to point.
- To beckon, turn the palm down and wave the fingers toward the body.
- Do not put your hands in your mouth (biting your nails, dislodging food from your teeth); this is considered disgusting.

Gifts

- Gift giving is a sensitive issue in China. While often in violation of Chinese law, gift giving is widespread.
- Avoid giving anything of value in front of others; it could cause the recipient both embarrassment and trouble.
- A gift from your company to the Chinese organization or factory is acceptable. Make it clear that the gift is on behalf of the whole company you represent and is for the whole group on the receiving end. Be sure to present the gift to the acknowledged leader of the Chinese delegation. Gifts of this sort might include items from your region of the country, like local crafts, historical memorabilia, or an illustrated book.
- A banquet is considered an acceptable gift. Your Chinese hosts will certainly give you one, and you should reciprocate.
- High-quality pens are appreciated. Other good gifts include gourmet food items and expensive liquors, like good cognac.
- Stamps are appreciated gifts if your associate is a collector (stamp collecting is popular in China). Cigarette lighters, T-shirts of well-known foreign sports teams, and electronic gadgets like iPods, electronic toys, etc., are also suitable. However, many of these items are made in China—be certain to check to make sure they are produced in your own home country!
- When giving or receiving a gift, use both hands. The gift is not opened in the presence of the giver.

China

- The Chinese traditionally decline a gift three times before accepting; this prevents them from appearing greedy. Continue to insist; once they accept the gift, say you are pleased that they have done so.
- Gifts of food are always appreciated by Chinese, but avoid bringing food gifts with you to a dinner or party (unless it has been agreed upon beforehand). To bring food may imply that your host cannot provide enough. Instead, send food as a thank-you gift afterward. Candy and fruit baskets are good choices.
- Older Chinese associate all of the following gifts and colors with funerals—avoid them:
  - Straw sandals
  - Clocks
  - A stork or crane (although the Western association of storks with births is known to many young Chinese)
  - Handkerchiefs (often given at funerals, they symbolize sadness and weeping)
  - Gifts (or wrapping paper) in which the predominant color is white, black, or blue.
- Do not wrap a gift before arriving in China; it may be unwrapped in Customs.
- If possible, wrap gifts in red, a lucky color. Pink and yellow are happy, prosperous colors and are also good choices. Do not use white, which is the color for funerals. Ask about appropriate paper at your hotel or at a store that wraps gifts.
- All business negotiations should be concluded before gifts are exchanged.
- At Chinese New Year, it is customary to give a gift of money in a red envelope to children and to the service personnel that help you on a regular basis. This gift is called a hong bao. Give only new bills in even numbers and even amounts. Many employers give each employee a hong bao equivalent to one month's salary.

Dress

- For business, men should wear conservative suits, shirts, and ties. Loud colors are not appropriate. Women should also wear conservative suits, with relatively high-necked blouses and low heels—their colors should be as neutral as possible.
- At formal occasions, evening gowns are not necessary for women unless the event is a formal reception given by a foreign diplomat. Men may wear suits and ties.
- Casualwear is still somewhat conservative. Revealing clothing may be offensive, but jeans are acceptable for both men and women. Shorts are appropriate when exercising.

Cultural Note

Written Chinese does not have a future tense, or any other verb tense. Therefore, the sentence "Wo mai shu" can mean: I bought a book, I buy a book, or I will buy a book. Time frames can only be determined by the context of the sentence, or by time indicators like "tomorrow." Be very specific on times and dates for appointments, contracts, or other transactions.

Hong Kong

Hong Kong Special Administrative Region

▶ COUNTRY BACKGROUND

History

Hong Kong's modern history begins with Imperial China's defeat in the First Opium War (1839–1842). Under the terms of the Treaty of Nanking, China was forced to cede Hong Kong Island to the United Kingdom. British and Scottish traders made Hong Kong their primary outpost for trade with China. The adjacent Kowloon Peninsula was added to Hong Kong after China's loss in the Second Opium War (1856–1858). The final expansion occurred in 1898, when the United Kingdom took a ninety-nine-year lease on what are called the New Territories. Hong Kong remained a British colony for most of the twentieth century. British rule was interrupted only during the Second World War, when the Japanese occupied Hong Kong from 1941 to 1945.

After Mao Tse-tung's Communist forces took control of China in 1949, Hong Kong (along with Portugal's colony of Macao) became one of the only points of contact between China and the West. As the People's Republic of China consolidated its power, it became increasingly clear that the United Kingdom could not keep the People's Liberation Army from overrunning Hong Kong. After long negotiations, the United Kingdom agreed to give Hong Kong back to China. The People's Republic of China promised to respect the laws of Hong Kong, under a policy of "one country, two systems." The United Kingdom handed over its colony of Hong Kong to the People's Republic of China in 1997.

> **Cultural Note**
> Hong Kong packs 6.81 million inhabitants (2003 estimate) into its 1,092 square kilometers, giving it one of the highest population densities on the planet.
> The Hong Kong Special Administrative Region includes Hong Kong Island, Kowloon, the New Territories, and numerous small islands.

Type of Government

It is useful to remember that Hong Kong has never known self-rule. It was a colony of the United Kingdom from 1842 to 1997; only at the end of that period did the British allow the formation of a locally elected body, the Legislative Council (a.k.a., the Legco). The governor of Hong Kong was always appointed by London.

The former British colony is now the Hong Kong Special Administrative Region (SAR), part of the People's Republic of China, which has an authoritarian Communist government. To date, the chief executive of the Hong Kong SAR has been chosen by 800 electors, all of whom have been appointed by Beijing. The term of office of the chief executive is five years.

Current government data can be found at the Embassy of China at *www.china-embassy .org*.

Language

The Cantonese form of Chinese and English are the official languages. Since the takeover of Hong Kong by the PRC, more students are studying Mandarin, which is the official language of China. Many businesspeople speak English.

For data on the various languages of China, see Ethnologue at *www.ethnologue.com*.

Cultural Note

Hong Kong has always been a halfway point between China and the West. Today, it is the home of designers who are helping to brand China's manufactured products. China's emerging middle class wants prestigious names on their consumer goods, and Chinese manufacturers want to create an identity for themselves with Western consumers. Although a distinct Hong Kong style did not develop until the end of the twentieth century, Hong Kong designers are helping to brand products all over China.

The Hong Kong View

The British established the colony as a place to earn money, not as a way to bring Western education, technology, or forms of government to the Chinese. And, although the Chinese of Hong Kong were eventually exposed to all of these, they saw Hong Kong primarily as a means to build wealth.

Hong Kong was also a place of refuge during unsettled times in China, especially during the Communist takeover in 1949. Since then, the PRC has closely guarded its border with Hong Kong. Even today, Beijing determines how many "mainland" Chinese may visit Hong Kong. (When China wants to boost the Hong Kong economy, it allows many visitors to come and spend money.)

Hong Kong has often felt like a transitory home. Of course, many businesspeople from the West are posted in Hong Kong for just a few years. But Hong Kong has sometimes felt temporary to its Chinese residents as well. Before the 1997 handover to China, many residents of Hong Kong sought citizenship in other countries so that they could flee if Beijing's rule became oppressive. Hong Kong's Chinese were angered that the United Kingdom offered passports to relatively few ethnic Chinese (but gave one to virtually all persons of British descent). A substantial number of Hong Kong's wealthier citizens immigrated to Canada.

Hong Kong has its own miniconstitution, known as its Basic Law. According to the Sino-British Joint Declaration (1984) and the Basic Law, Hong Kong will retain its political, economic, and judicial systems for fifty years following the 1997 handover. Furthermore, Hong Kong will continue to participate in international agreements and organizations under the name "Hong Kong, China." Consequently, Hong Kong will keep its own special identity—at least for the next four decades.

Less than 45 percent of Hong Kong citizens participate in some form of religious practice. Of those who do, about 8 percent consider themselves Christians. Most religions are represented in Hong Kong; the city even has four Islamic mosques. However, Confucianism (a philosophy rather than a religion) dominates the culture.

As a trading center, the citizens of Hong Kong have learned to do business with partners from many countries. Perhaps the only country with which they have a problematic relationship is Japan. During the Second World War, Japan occupied Hong Kong on Christmas Day, 1941. The occupation was harsh: Many residents were executed, while others were exiled or interred. Thousands of women were raped. Food was confiscated for Japanese troops, leaving Hong Kong's remaining population to starve. By the end of the war, Hong Kong's population was down by about 1 million people.

There have been occasional anti-Japanese protests in Hong Kong, including one in April of 2005. However, little is taught about the Japanese occupation in Hong Kong schools. If the younger generations have negative viewpoints about the Japanese, it is primarily traced to Beijing's general opposition to Japan.

☑ Know Before You Go

Hong Kong has been a safe destination, except during periodic outbreaks of disease. New strains of influenza (while later spread worldwide) have often first been identified in Hong Kong. The most serious disease outbreak in recent times was that of SARS (severe acute respiratory syndrome), which killed almost 300 people in Hong Kong in 2003.

The residents of Hong Kong pride themselves on their legal system and their free flow of information; in this, they are much freer than their fellow citizens of the People's Republic of China. But Beijing has not given up trying to bring Hong Kong into line. Beijing tried to impose an antisedition statute called Article 23 on Hong Kong in 2003. This would have reduced the city's freedoms, and Hong Kong residents responded with massive protests, forcing an indefinite postponing of the adoption of Article 23.

▶ BUSINESS PRACTICES

Punctuality, Appointments, and Local Time

- The official format for writing dates in Hong Kong follows British tradition: day, month, and year. In this format, December 3, 2010, would be written 03/12/10, or 3.12.10. However, because influence is strong from the United States, some people use the U.S. pattern of month, day, and year. This renders December 3, 2010, as 12/3/10. To make matters even more confusing, the standard in the PRC is year/month/date. In this format, December 3, 2010, is written as 10/12/3. Naturally, if you have any question about a date, ask.

- Hong Kong, like China, is eight hours ahead of Greenwich Mean Time (G.M.T. +8), or thirteen hours ahead of U.S. Eastern Standard Time (E.S.T. +13).

Cultural Note

Chinese names can be rendered different ways in English, so do not be surprised by variations. Chinese normally have three names, and the most common variant is whether or not to hyphenate the final two names.

For example, the first chief executive of Hong Kong was Tung Chee Hwa. His name can also be rendered Tung Chee-hwa, or even Tung Cheehwa. (As with most Chinese, his surname is listed first, so he would be referred to as "Mr. Tung.")

Dress

- Hong Kong residents consider themselves better dressed and more fashionable than most Chinese. While this may be true for much of China, there are residents of Shanghai and Beijing who are equally stylish.

Cultural Note

Many residents of Hong Kong are sports fans. Horseracing is one of the most popular spectator sports. The first horserace was run back in 1846, and the races have been part of Hong Kong life since then. The season runs from September through June, with races held on Wednesday evening and either Saturday or Sunday. Hong Kong has two racetracks, at Sha Tin and Happy Valley.

Colombia

Republic of Colombia
Local short form: Colombia
Local long form: Republica de Colombia

Cultural Note

Colombians have distinctive methods for indicating height and length:

To indicate the height of an animal, Colombians hold one hand horizontally at the appropriate height, as if they were resting their hand on top of the animal's head. However, to describe the height of a person, the hand is held vertically (palm out, thumb on top), as if it were touching the back of the person's head. To describe a person's height using a horizontal hand is to dismiss him or her as an animal.

North Americans often indicate length by holding both hands out with the index fingers extended. This means that the length is the distance between the two fingers. However, two pointing fingers is an obscene gesture in Colombia. Colombians indicate length by extending their right arm and placing their left hand at the point on the arm where the distance from the fingertips on the right hand to the point marked by the left hand is equal to the length being indicated.

▶ WHAT'S YOUR CULTURAL IQ?

1. To date, Gabriel García Márquez is the only Colombian author to win a Nobel Prize for literature. With which of the following Latin literary styles is he associated?
   a. Nueva sensibilidad (new sensibility)
   b. Modernism (modernism)
   c. Nudísts (beat poetry)
   d. Reálism magic (magic realism).

   ANSWER: d. This style, favored by García Márquez and others, intertwines dreams and mythic archetypes with reality.

2. TRUE or FALSE? Although Colombia is named after Christopher Columbus, he never set foot on Colombian soil.

   ANSWER: TRUE. The first Europeans to reach Colombia were led by Alonso de Ojeda in 1499.

3. Believing Colombia to be the site of El Dorado (the lost city of gold), the Spanish quickly explored and conquered the country. While all of the following resources were eventually found in Colombia, the Spanish only discovered one of them in substantial quantities. Which one was it?
   a. Salt
   b. Emeralds
   c. Gold
   d. Silver

   ANSWER: a. The Chibcha Indians led the Spanish to an amazingly productive salt mine at Zipaquirá. This hugely productive mine is so large that it now contains an underground cathedral!

Colombia

▶ TIPS ON DOING BUSINESS IN COLOMBIA

- Colombia has a reputation (which may or may not be deserved) as the most dangerous nation for foreigners to visit in Latin America. The danger to foreigners comes not from narcoterrorists but kidnappers, who hold businesspeople for ransom.
- While foreigners are not usually in danger from narcoterrorists, you must be sure that you are not doing business with a Colombian company that has ties to the narcotraffickers. The United States of America (and other countries) maintains a list of companies with links to narcotics trafficking. It is illegal for U.S. citizens to work with them.
- Colombians are known for having long greeting rituals. Every conversation seems to begin with long inquiries as to the health, welfare, location, and status of the speakers and their relatives. Visitors who attempt to cut this greeting are considered impolite.

▶ COUNTRY BACKGROUND

History

At the time of Christopher Columbus's discovery of the New World, Colombia was home to several Amerindian peoples. None of these native peoples could overcome the Spanish conquistadores, who arrived in the early 1500s.

Colombia became part of the Spanish viceroyalty of New Granada, which encompassed present-day Colombia, Ecuador, Panama, and Venezuela. Bogotá was designated the capital of the entire viceroyalty in 1717. Along with other colonies, Colombia sought independence from Spain at the beginning of the nineteenth century. In 1810, under its first president, Simón Bolívar, Colombia defied Spanish authority, and full independence was proclaimed in 1813.

Bolívar also founded Colombia's Conservative Party; his rivals founded the Liberals. This rivalry contributed to Colombia's eight civil wars. These two parties continue to this day and have frequently alternated as the party in power.

Gran Colombia broke up in 1830 into Ecuador, Venezuela, and Colombia. Panama became Colombia's northernmost province. Panama remained a part of Colombia until 1903, when it broke away with the support of the United States.

After the assassination of a Liberal leader, the most violent of the Colombian civil wars erupted in 1948. Known as La Violencia, 300,000 Colombians died in the fighting. With the country on the verge of breaking apart, members of both the Liberal and Conservative parties supported a military coup by General Gustavo Rojas Pinilla, Colombia's only military junta of the twentieth century. He remained in power from 1953 to 1957.

Elections returned in 1957, although the choice was limited to approved Liberal and Conservative candidates. For the first time, women were allowed to vote in Colombia. Over the next sixteen years, the two major parties shared political power, with the presidency alternating between the Liberals and the Conservatives. All other political parties were suppressed, contributing to the eventual growth of guerrilla movements. This sharing of power is known as the National Front; they renewed their power-sharing agreement in 1974.

During the 1980s, the rise of the narcotraficantes, with their enormous wealth and power, threatened to undermine the authority of the Colombian government. Guerrillas, such as the M-19 group, also fought the government.

In 1984, the narcotraficantes finally went too far when they assassinated Justice Minister Rodrigo Lara Bonilla. In response, the Colombian government finally began to extradite Colombian narcotraficantes wanted for trial by the United States. These drug lords, who become known as Los Extraditables, alternated violence with bribes to avoid being extradited. They even offered to pay off Colombia's entire U.S.$13 billion foreign debt. (The offer was declined.)

In November of 1985, the M-19 guerrillas occupied the Colombian Palace of Justice in Bogotá. Government troops defeated the occupiers, but the fighting caused the death of over 100 people, including eleven justices of the Colombian Supreme Court. Following this event, paramilitary death squads were formed to execute government opponents.

Open elections were finally held in 1990, allowing the participation of candidates from outside the National Front. Some former guerrillas were elected, and violence by many guerrilla organizations ceased. The last of the well-known narcotraficantes, Medellín Cartel leader Pablo Escobar, was killed in 1993. The new Cartel leaders learned to keep a lower profile and were less likely to assassinate government officials.

Type of Government

The Republic of Colombia is a unitary, multiparty republic with two legislative houses: the Senate and the House of Representatives. There is also a judiciary branch. The president is elected to a single four-year term and cannot succeed himself. The president is both chief of state and head of the government.

The rule of government in Bogotá does not reach all of Colombia. For the past few decades, armed guerrilla groups have set up de facto governments in large areas of the Colombian countryside. For current government data, check with the Embassy of Colombia, at *www.colombiaemb.org*.

Language

The official language of Colombia is Spanish (which they call *Castellano*, not *Español*). Colombians have many regional terms, which are collectively known as *colombianismos*.

English is not widely spoken, although some international business executives speak it.

Colombia has a substantial Amerindian population, and the country's rugged geography resulted in the evolution of many isolated linguistic groups, many of whom speak only their indigenous languages. An estimated half-million Colombians speak an Amerindian tongue as their first language.

Counting Spanish, the Amerindian tongues, and various imported languages—such as Creole and Romany, the language of the Rom (Gypsies)—linguists have identified ninety-eight languages in Colombia. Of these, twenty are now considered extinct.

The Colombian View

The vast majority (90 percent) of Colombians are Roman Catholic. The constitution guarantees freedom of religion. Protestant groups are making inroads, especially Pentecostalists.

If geography is destiny, then Colombia's geography accounts for much of the country's uniqueness. Colombia borders Venezuela, Brazil, Peru, Ecuador, and Panama. It is the only South American country to have coasts on both the Caribbean and the Pacific. Furthermore, Colombia's mountainous interior isolates regions from each other. One has to expect diversity in such an environment.

While the United States has a history of intervention throughout Latin America, its effect on Colombia is unique. The United States prompted the removal of Panama from Colombia in 1903 to facilitate the building of the Panama Canal. Today, the United States is increasingly involved in Colombian interior affairs as the central government attempts to regain control of the countryside and reduce narcotics trafficking. Consequently, Colombians see the United States as both a savior and a demon.

As for Colombia's drug trade, smuggling didn't start with marijuana and cocaine. The illegal export of Colombian emeralds and exotic birds has been occurring for decades. Smuggling occurs in the other direction as well. Onerous taxes (as high as 36 percent) on imported goods have made it profitable to smuggle consumer goods into Columbia.

☑ Know Before You Go

As previously noted, the major hazard to foreign visitors is kidnapping. (Many Colombians have been kidnapped and held for ransom as well.) Colombia is one of the countries where you should secure kidnap insurance before your visit.

Street crime, such as pickpocketing, is common in Colombian cities. Such crimes are usually nonviolent, except when an unwary traveler is drugged. Burundanga is a drug derived from a common Colombian tree. A full dose renders a person unconscious. Burundanga has no taste or odor and can be added to almost anything you put in your mouth: candy, chewing gum, drinks, and even cigarettes. To avoid being drugged, avoid accepting anything from someone you do not know.

Volcanic eruptions occur in the highlands. There are also periodic earthquakes and droughts.

Due to vehicle emissions, the air quality in Bogotá is sometimes hazardous.

The highlands of Colombia are elevated enough to cause altitude sickness. Altitude sickness can strike anyone, even if you have never experienced it before. There is no sure prevention except gradual acclimation to high elevation: once you get to 6,000 feet above sea level, spend at least two nights there. Repeat this acclimation period at each increase of 3,000 feet. Alcohol consumption tends to make the symptoms worse. Sunburn is also a danger at high altitudes, because there is less atmosphere to protect you from the sun.

While they are not the pastimes of the upper classes, Colombians have a penchant for diversions that can cause injury or property damage. Urban Colombians like to set aloft hot air balloons made of paper; they often catch fire from the lit candle inside, raining down flaming debris. *Papeletas* are small, triangular bags filled with gunpowder, used in various games; although banned in some cities, they are still omnipresent.

▶ CULTURAL ORIENTATION

Cognitive Styles: How Colombians Organize and Process Information

Colombia is a large and diverse nation with many cultural and linguistic groups. The following information applies to the majority culture.

In Colombia one perceives an openness to discuss any topic, but do not expect attitudes to change based upon these discussions. Colombians process information primarily on a subjective, associative level unless they have extensive higher education. They tend not to abstract to higher principles but rather treat each situation as a unique experience.

Negotiation Strategies: What Colombians Accept as Evidence

Feelings are the primary source of truth. Colombians' interpersonal reality is such that they will give you the "truth" as they think it should be or as you would like it to be. Thus, their use of facts is nebulous. For the majority of Colombians, there are no ideologies strong enough to make faith a source of the truth.

Some sociologists believe that Colombians have a high level of uncertainty avoidance, although it is not out of line with other Latin American countries. This makes Colombians averse to risk and hesitant to accept change.

Value Systems: The Basis for Behavior

The effects of the drug cartels cut across all levels of Colombian society. The following three sections identify the Value Systems in the predominant culture—their methods of dividing right from wrong, good from evil, and so forth.

Locus of Decision-Making

There are informal, yet very powerful decision-making groups called *roscas*. Individuals make their own decisions but are influenced by their need to satisfy their families or groups. Kinship plays a major role in one's business associations because traditional elements of trust and mutual dependence among relatives are very strong, no matter how distant the relationship. The collectivist mindset is very much in evidence.

Sources of Anxiety Reduction

It is an individual's role in the social structure and the presence of the extended family that gives a sense of stability to life. This also brings anxiety, as one must be a success in the eyes of both the extended family and society. There is a strong need for consensus in the group, but values differ with the situation, and the rules are learned only by experience.

Colombia

Issues of Equality/Inequality

The economic and political elite are generally European in heritage. They handle most of the business, commerce, and industry. Society is very class-conscious and is stratified by skin color and class membership, with limited vertical mobility. Colombian women are among the most politically active in Latin America, in spite of cultural restrictions on their social and work behavior. On the other hand, Colombians still have one of the highest masculinity index levels in Latin America, which tends to ossify gender roles.

BUSINESS PRACTICES

Punctuality, Appointments, and Local Time

- As a foreigner, you are expected to be punctual. Be on time for all business appointments.
- Colombians are not known for punctuality. They may arrive at a business meeting fifteen or twenty minutes late, yet feel they are on time. Do not expect them to apologize for being late.
- Even foreigners are expected to be late to social occasions. Arrive fifteen to thirty minutes late for a party; some Colombians will be a full hour late.
- Like many Europeans and South Americans, Colombians write the day first, then the month, then the year (e.g., December 3, 2010, is written 3.12.10 or 3/12/10).
- Schedule appointments at least one week before your arrival in Colombia. Do not depend upon regular mail service to arrange appointments; use the phone, e-mail, fax, or registered mail.
- Unless you are traveling only to the coastal lowlands, it is best to arrive a day early so that you can adjust to the high altitude. This is especially true in the capital, Bogotá, which is 8,600 feet (2,600 meters) above sea level.
- Colombia is five hours behind Greenwich Mean Time (G.M.T. –5), which is the same as U.S. Eastern Standard Time.

Negotiating

- Inland Colombians are among the most formal and traditional of Latin Americans. Only along the coast does a more relaxed attitude prevail.
- It will be difficult, if not impossible, to conduct business without hiring a local contact. This contact not only will introduce you to the Colombians you must deal with, but often will pick you up at the airport and reserve a room for you at a hotel as well.

  In most situations with the government, you will need to speak Spanish or have an interpreter. However, many businesspeople speak English.

Colombia

- Never change the members of your negotiating team. Such a change could bring the negotiations to a halt. Colombians feel that they are negotiating with people, not a corporation.
- Expect delays. You should allocate a week in Colombia to accomplish something that would generally take several days in other countries.
- Avoid discussing politics, terrorism, or illegal drugs.
- Avoid unfavorable comparisons between your native country and Colombia.
- Colombians are very proud of their nation and its achievements. It is a good idea to be informed about Colombian culture, literature, and history, or, at least, to show curiosity about such things.
- Business cards printed in your native language on one side and the translation in Spanish on the other are most effective. These should be presented with the Spanish side facing your Colombian colleague.

Business Entertaining
- Lunch is the main meal of the day and is a popular choice for a business meal.
- Colombians have a tradition of hospitality and frequently invite guests to their homes.
- Let the host be the first to make a toast; then you might wish to make one.
- Theoretically, the person who has initiated the invitation will pay for a meal in a restaurant. In practice, you may have to fight for the check even when you issued the invitation.
- Leave a small amount of food on your plate to demonstrate that you have had enough to eat.

Cultural Note
Dinner is normally eaten between 7:00 and 9:00 P.M., but a dinner party will begin and end later. Guests will not arrive until at least 8:00 P.M., and people will sit down to dinner anytime from 10:00 P.M. to midnight. Many people eat something before going to a dinner party so that they will not starve (or be drunk) by the time dinner begins. A dinner party will end soon after the meal, but a cocktail party (with dancing) may go on until 5:00 A.M. Expect formal dress for either event.

 PROTOCOL

Greetings
- The standard greeting is the handshake. It is also used when departing.
- Among close friends, women may clasp forearms or kiss each other on one cheek. Men embrace and slap each other's back; this manly hug is called the abrazo.
- Colombians often complain that North Americans and Europeans don't know how to greet someone. Colombians take a long time in greetings; they feel that this conveys respect for the other person. After the handshake (or hug), Colombians ask numerous

polite questions. North Americans typically progress beyond the greeting phase after one or two questions. Expect inquiries as to your health, your trip, your relatives, and any friends or acquaintances you have in common. Don't rush! Rushing is interpreted as callousness or disrespect.

Titles/Forms of Address
- Do not address a Colombian by his or her first name unless invited to do so. In general, only children, family members, and close friends address each other by their first names.
- See Appendix A for basic information on titles.
- The only professional title in common use is "Doctor" (Doctora for women). However, it is often applied to any accomplished or educated person, whether or not he or she has a PhD. Indeed, the poor often refer to any upper-class person as "Doctor."

Gestures
- Colombians stand somewhat closer together when conversing than do North Americans. However, Colombians engage in less physical contact during conversations than some South Americans.
- The formality of inland Colombians extends to their mannerisms; they do not engage in expansive gestures and animation. Residents of the coastal regions tend to be more expressive and less formal.
- It is considered impolite to yawn in public.
- Colombians indicate that someone is stingy by tapping their fingers on their elbow.
- The North American "okay" gesture (thumb and forefinger curled into a circle) has a different meaning in Colombia. A Colombian places the circle over his nose to indicate that someone is homosexual.
- Bare feet are acceptable only at the beach. Slippers or sandals should be worn at all other times, even when going to or from the bathroom.
- In a restaurant, some Colombians summon a waiter by raising their hands over their head and clapping. Others use a hissing sound. Neither method is considered courteous, and both should be avoided by foreigners.

Gifts
- If you are given a gift, you should be very effusive in your thanks.
- When invited to a home for a meal, bring flowers, pastries, or chocolates. Avoid lilies and marigolds, which are used at funerals.
- You may give perfume to women.
- If you know you will meet a business associate's family, it is a good idea to bring a gift for the children.

- Although gifts are always appreciated, a wrapped gift is generally not opened in the presence of the giver, because Colombians feel that this would make them appear greedy. Indeed, the gift may never be mentioned again. You can be sure, though, that it was noted and appreciated.
- Other good gifts are fine wines and liquors. Do not bring foreign beer; Colombia brews fine local beers.

Colombia

Dress

- In general, formality increases as you move inland. The coastal resort areas are the most casual, and shorts may be worn in public there.
- On the coast, where it is hot, some men will wear a guayabera shirt to work, and women will wear sleeveless dresses. Foreigners, however, are expected to dress more formally for business meetings.
- Inland, it is important to adopt conservative business attire. Men should wear a jacket and tie even in hot weather. Suits in dark colors are preferred. Expect to wear the jacket and tie to social occasions as well.
- Women should dress conservatively and modestly. A suit or dress is appropriate for business, while a cocktail dress will be required for most social occasions.
- Although Colombia is an equatorial country, the high elevations of some cities result in cool weather. Wool sweaters or jackets are needed in Bogotá and sometimes in Medellín.

Cultural Note

Colombia is divided by three mountain ranges, and this has led to the development of strong regional movements. When these movements fail to find common ground with the government in Bogotá, guerrilla movements (usually left-wing) evolve. Some guerrilla movements accept government amnesty and become political parties, such as the April 19 Movement Democratic Alliance (a.k.a., M-19). Others continue to fight the government. The end of the Cold War also ended foreign subsidies for Marxist guerrillas; therefore, some have increasingly turned to kidnapping and drug smuggling to earn funds. However, there is no mistaking the guerrillas for the drug cartels; the late Pablo Escobar failed to convince anyone that his Medellín drug cartel was a political organization.

Costa Rica

Republic of Costa Rica
Local long form: Republica de Costa Rica

Cultural Note

It has been over a decade since the United States, Canada, and Mexico entered into the North American Free Trade Agreement (NAFTA). In December 2003, the United States negotiated a similar trade pact with Central American nations. The signatories to this deal, tentatively known as CAFTA, include Guatemala, Nicaragua, El Salvador, and Honduras. However, to the surprise of many, Costa Rica decided to opt out of the agreement. It's not that Costa Rica opposes trade (one of their official government slogans is "Exportar es Bueno"); their government actively promotes trade and investment, yet it declined to join a free-trade agreement with the United States. Costa Rica's rejection of the CAFTA agreement illustrates the diversity of Latin America: every Latin American is not alike, and obstacles may appear where you least expect them. On the positive side, Costa Rica allows foreigners to own businesses without taking a Costa Rican citizen as a partner. (A somewhat unusual circumstance in Latin America).

 WHAT'S YOUR CULTURAL IQ?

1. Which of the following is not true about Costa Rica?
   a. Costa Rica is currently the wealthiest country in Central America.
   b. Coast Rica abolished its army in 1948.
   c. The people of Costa Rica are the best educated in Central America.
   d. Costa Rican President Oscar Arias received the 1987 Nobel Peace Prize for his work in negotiating a peace plan in neighboring Central American nations.

   ANSWER: a. Actually, the wealthiest nation in Central America is Panama, where the economy is buoyed by fees from the Panama Canal. Costa Rica comes in second, although its wealth is distributed much more evenly.

2. TRUE or FALSE? *Ticos* (as Costa Ricans are called) worry about losing their sovereignty to foreign influences; some accuse the United States of running a "parallel government" within Costa Rica.

   ANSWER: TRUE. The U.S. Agency for International Development (among other U.S. organizations) is so omnipresent in Costa Rica that it has been accused of being a "parallel government."

3. The name Costa Rica means "Rich Coast." TRUE or FALSE: On his fourth and final expedition to the New World, Christopher Columbus gave Costa Rica its name because of the gold he acquired here.

   ANSWER: TRUE. However, the gold artifacts Columbus got from the local Amerindians were not mined locally. Costa Rica has no gold; the artifacts had been imported, presumably from Mexico. Far from being a prosperous place, the Spanish who settled there found a coast so pestilent that they settled in the central highlands, where agricultural riches finally came their way, centuries later.

Cultural Note

To preserve its unique natural resources, the government of Costa Rica has set aside 21 percent of its land area as protected areas. This is a larger percentage than any other nation in the world and is one reason that Costa Rica is a favorite destination for ecotourists.

TIPS ON DOING BUSINESS IN COSTA RICA

- Even though almost all Costa Rican business executives speak English, all written materials should be translated into Spanish.
- While it is often pointed out that peaceful Costa Rica has no army, it has plenty of other law enforcement personnel. These range from the police to the Civil Guard to the commandos of the Immediate Action Unit.
- Face-to-face contact is preferred over telephone calls. Traditionally, Costa Ricans kept phone calls short. This is changing as cell phones become more common, and upperclass youths utilize them constantly.

COUNTRY BACKGROUND

History

Christopher Columbus led the first European expedition to visit Costa Rica in 1502. He collected several gold decorations from the friendly Amerindians. Believing that the gold was mined locally (it was not), the Spanish named the region Costa Rica (Rich Coast).

After several failed attempts, the first successful Spanish outpost was established under Juan Vásquez de Coronado in 1562. To avoid the disease-ridden coastal regions, he selected the central highlands for the site of his new city, which was named Cartago. The Spanish found few surviving Amerindians to enslave or marry, so Costa Rica never developed a significant mestizo population. In 1821, all of Central America declared its independence from Spain. Costa Ricans were so remote that the news took a month to reach them. The Mexican empire claimed all of Central America, but Costa Rica was too far south—Mexican troops never arrived there. Costa Rica declared its independence from Mexico in 1832 and became the southernmost part of the new Central American Federation.

The Central American Federation collapsed in 1838; Costa Rica became an independent republic and was one of the five successor states. Export of Costa Rican coffee began around this time.

Costa Rica soon established a tradition of democracy and peaceful transition from one government to another. When former president Juan Rafael Mora tried to seize power in 1860, his coup failed and he was executed. The voting franchise was extended from wealthy landowners to poor male farmers in 1889.

Rafael Angel Calderón Guardia, elected president in 1940, ran a reformist administration supported by the Communists and opposed by the Conservative landowners. When he ran for re-election in 1948, Calderón was declared the loser in a disputed election. The Conservative candidate, Otilio Ulate was proclaimed the winner. The dispute escalated into civil war, and some 2,000 Costa Ricans were killed.

Peace was restored in 1949, and Otilio Ulate became president. A new constitution extended the vote to all citizens over eighteen, including blacks and women. The Costa Rican Army was dissolved. Peace is maintained by the Civilian and Rural Guard. Since 1949, Costa Rica has run free and democratic elections.

In 1987, Costa Rican president Oscar Arias received the Nobel Peace Prize for his work in negotiating a peace plan in neighboring Central American nations. Some believe this regional peace plan also had the effect of reducing the influence of the United States in Central America.

Type of Government

The government is a unitary multiparty republic, composed of a president, a unicameral legislative assembly made up of deputies, and the Supreme Court of Justice. The president is both the chief of state and the head of the government. The president and his deputies may only hold one successive four-year term of office. Judges are elected to eight-year terms. A fourth branch of government, the Supreme Electoral Tribunal, oversees the electoral process.

The people of Costa Rica are politically active and proud of their government. Elections, with voting mandatory for anyone over eighteen years old, are likened to a party, with festivities and celebrations lasting many days. Governments swing from moderately conservative to moderately progressive, as the political parties traditionally alternate power with each election.

For current government data, check with the Embassy of Costa Rica at *www.costarica embassy.org*.

Language

Spanish is the official language of Costa Rica. Caribbean Creole English is spoken by about 2 percent of the population, descended from Caribbeans who were imported to work on Costa Rica's railroads. English has become Costa Rica's second language and is widely understood, especially in urban centers and among the young.

Nevertheless, all materials should be translated into Spanish, rather than presented in English.

Linguists have identified eleven languages in Costa Rica, one of which is now extinct. The largest Amerindian language, Bribri, has only 6,000 native speakers.

The Costa Rican View

Costa Rica has retained Roman Catholicism as its national religion. Some 86 percent of Costa Ricans identify themselves as Catholics. As in other Latin American countries, there is rapid growth of Protestant religions. Over 9 percent of Costa Ricans are Protestants, and more than half of them belong to Pentecostal churches.

Costa Ricans welcome all affluent foreigners, although they have an ambivalent relationship with citizens of the United States. Costa Ricans are also convinced (with reason) that they live in the best and most stable country in Central America and do not encourage poor immigrants from neighboring nations. Many social ills, from petty crime to the perceived loss of civility, are attributed to Central American immigrants.

Costa Rica has a tradition of egalitarianism. "Sharing the wealth" is not just a social custom but a government mandate. Costa Rica's relative prosperity and ethnic homogeneity allows such egalitarianism, as does a commitment to widespread education. Nevertheless, there is a Costa Rican upper class, consisting of wealthy landowners. Three-quarters of the pre-1970 presidents descended from just three of the original colonizers of Costa Rica.

☑ Know Before You Go

Costa Rica has four volcanoes, two of them active, which rise near the capital of San Jose in the center of the country. One of the volcanoes, Irazu, erupted between 1963 and 1965.

There are occasional earthquakes, hurricanes along the Atlantic coast, and flooding during the rainy season. Visitors need to be prepared for the hot, humid climate.

 CULTURAL ORIENTATION

Cognitive Styles: How Costa Ricans Organize and Process Information

Costa Ricans love to use language and are open to discussions on any topic. However, they have very strong beliefs and are not easily persuaded to another's point of view. They are primarily associative in their thinking and look at each situation as a unique happening. They are intuitive and use rules only as guidelines.

Negotiation Strategies: What Costa Ricans Accept as Evidence

Facts are usually interpreted through subjective feelings, though Costa Ricans will sometimes use faith in a humanitarian ideology as a source of the truth. Frank criticism is rare because the use of tentative language is much more conducive to saving face. The truth is what is believed at the moment.

Value Systems: The Basis for Behavior

This is a very humanitarian, fiercely democratic culture with a belief in peace through negotiations. The following three sections identify the Value Systems in the predominant culture—their methods of dividing right from wrong, good from evil, and so forth.

Locus of Decision-Making

Costa Rican culture is traditionally collectivist as opposed to individualist. While each individual is independent, there is a strong sense of responsibility to the family or group. Favored treatment is given to kin. Upward mobility often means using the group for individual advancement. A person trusts only those who appreciate his or her uniqueness. Costa Ricans have a strong self-image but loath arrogance and expect people in high places to display humility.

Sources of Anxiety Reduction

Family lineage is important to who you are; it determines your identification and status. Success is in the eyes of the extended family. There is a strong work ethic, but progress toward the goal of the project is not as important as working on the project. Costa Ricans prefer to think small, go slowly, and avoid risks, anxiety, or overwork. They generally try to avoid precise commitments, although they may make them vocally to avoid hurting your feelings.

Sociologists have determined that Costa Ricans typically display what is called a "high uncertainty avoidance." This leads them to establish strict rules and policies, both in their legal system and in societal norms. Such cultures are highly risk-averse and generally resist change.

Issues of Equality/Inequality

Costa Ricans believe strongly in the philosophy of the equality of all people because each one is a unique individual—more so than any other Latin American culture. Wealth and family lineage are the primary determinants of social position. Costa Ricans' "power distance ratio" has been measured as half that typical among Latin cultures. That means that there is a strong emphasis on the equality and dignity of work regardless of your social class.

Machismo, while extant, is also lower in Costa Rica than in its neighbors. The masculinity index of Costa Ricans has been quantified as less than half the amount typical for Latin cultures. This is indicative of low levels of gender discrimination. Women maintain their own identity apart from that of their husband in all legal and business matters.

▶ BUSINESS PRACTICES

Punctuality, Appointments, and Local Time

- Costa Ricans are by far the most punctual people in Central America.
- All foreign businesspeople are expected to be on time for appointments.

- Costa Ricans allow themselves only a limited time for their midday break, so everyone is expected to be on time for a business lunch.
- In Costa Rica, as in many European and South American countries, the date is written day first, then the month, then the year (e.g., December 3, 2010, is written 3.12.10 or 3/12/10).
- Good times to do business in Costa Rica are February to March and September to November. The rainy season runs from May through November (with rain heaviest on the Caribbean coast). The most popular vacation times are December and January and around the Christmas and Easter holidays.
- Make appointments in advance, and reconfirm before arrival.
- In the public sector, the fiscal year is the same as the calendar year.
- Local time is six hours behind Greenwich Mean Time (G.M.T. –6); this is one hour behind U.S. Eastern Standard Time (E.S.T. –1).

Negotiations

- Decision-makers are readily accessible and will be frank and open during discussions. Business takes place on a personal basis in Costa Rica. It is important to establish a relationship with your Costa Rican counterpart before proceeding to business issues.
- There is a strong sense of personal honor and social equality on the part of the Costa Rican businessperson. More so than anywhere else in Central America, every person is assumed to have value and dignity. Therefore, avoid any behavior that would demean another person, especially in public.
- Decisions are made by consensus of all involved, not just by top officials. This may slow the process down; avoid showing impatience. Being impatient lowers your credibility and puts you at a disadvantage.
- Precisely because persons at all levels of a company have input, remember to be polite to everyone you meet.
- Foreign investment—notably from the United States and Mexico—is aggressively competitive in Costa Rica. Contacts are very important to doing business. Remember to treat your business counterparts with the same respect with which you would treat a valued client at home.
- Time estimates and deadlines may not be strictly observed. Also, late payments are very frequent. Be prepared to travel to Costa Rica several times to finalize plans. Be tolerant of delays, and remain flexible by building these factors into your own plans.
- Women in business will meet with greater acceptance in Costa Rica than in many other Latin American countries. Women have been elected to the vice presidency in Costa Rica.
- Costa Ricans are much more formal and serious than their neighbors. Informality, casual dress, and the use of obscenity are negative traits that Costa Ricans associate with other Central Americans.

- Have business cards, proposals, and other material printed in both English and Spanish. While most executives speak English well, technical workers may not.
- While it is not technically necessary for foreigners to offer a partnership to a Costa Rican citizen, you should have local legal representation and use a local advertising agency. Some foreign businesses offer partnerships to Costa Ricans to make use of their local connections.

Business Entertaining

- Most business entertaining takes place in the evening, since lunch is the main meal of the day. Spouses are welcome at business dinners.
- Good topics of conversation are children, families, and the beauty of Costa Rica.
- The Costa Rican people enjoy discussing politics, particularly with foreigners. Costa Rica's history of stable democracy provides a good topic for conversation. Foreigners should have some knowledge of the political history of Central America to speak intelligently on the subject.

▶ PROTOCOL

Greetings

- Men will shake hands with other men in greeting. Women will often pat each other on the right forearm or shoulder instead of shaking hands.
- Women who are close friends may hug or kiss each other on the cheek. However, Costa Rican men do not usually hug other men. The hearty male abrazo (backslapping embrace) seen in other Latin American countries is rare in Costa Rica.
- In rural areas, some men will nod instead of shaking hands.
- Costa Ricans who are used to greeting North Americans may offer a firm handshake, but many handshakes may tend to be gentle. Adjust your grip to the other person's handshake.
- Do not refer to the people as ricans, as this word has a bad connotation. The people of Costa Rica are referred to as ticos.
- At parties, it is customary to be introduced to and shake hands with everyone in the room.

Titles/Forms of Address

- You should address most people you meet by their title and their surname. Only children, family members, and close friends address each other by their first names.
- When a person has a title, it is important to utilize it. Usually the title alone is preferred; no surname is necessary. A Ph.D. or a physician is called "Doctor." Teachers prefer the title Profesor, engineers go by Ingeniero, architects are Arquitecto, and lawyers are Abogado.

Gestures

- Making a fist with the thumb sticking out between the middle and index fingers is obscene. This gesture is known as the "fig."
- Most North American gestures will be understood in Costa Rica.
- Don't rest your feet on any furniture except items expressly designed for that purpose.

Gifts

- Costa Ricans will exchange gifts frequently for all kinds of special occasions.
- Because of the large number of U.S. citizens in Costa Rica and the lack of import restrictions, U.S. goods are freely available there.
- If you are invited to a home for dinner, bring flowers, chocolates, Scotch, or wine.
- Baskets of assorted delicacies are very popular. Do not bring calla lilies; they are associated with funerals.

Dress

- Business: Men should wear a conservative dark suit. During business meetings, expect to keep your jacket on even in the heat. Costa Rican men in the hot coastal areas sometimes do without a jacket, but foreigners should bring a jacket and remove it if their counterpart does not wear one. Women should wear a dress or skirt and blouse.
- Historically, trousers were never worn by businesswomen, but this is changing.
- Casual: Shorts are worn only on the beach. Revealing clothing for women is not acceptable. Bring a sweater or jacket to wear at night in the higher elevations.
- Bring multiple changes of clothes. Because of the heat, people in Costa Rica bathe frequently—often more than once a day.

Cultural Note

Costa Rica's egalitarianism manifests itself in extensive squatters' rights. Squatters cannot be evicted if they are allowed to remain for three months. If they remain for ten years, squatters can even claim title to the land. This makes it difficult for absentee landowners to maintain ownership of their property.

Czech Republic

Local form: Ceska Republika

> **Cultural Note**
> The Czech Republic has undergone two radical but nonviolent changes in recent years: the "Velvet Revolution" that removed the USSR-backed Communists from power and the "Velvet Divorce" that separated Czechoslovakia into two independent nations, the Czech and Slovak Republics. Even at their most angry moment, when protesters jammed Prague's Wenceslas Square demanding the removal of the Communists, the protesters admonished one another not to trample on the flower beds!

WHAT'S YOUR CULTURAL IQ?

1. The Czech Republic has frequently been ruled by outsiders. Which of the following was not a former foreign ruler?
   a. Austro-Hungarian Empire
   b. Kingdom of Bohemia
   c. Holy Roman Empire
   d. Nazi Germany

   ANSWER: b. Bohemia is another name for most of the Czech Republic (the westernmost portion is known as Moravia).

2. TRUE or FALSE: The 1618 Defenestration of Prague refers to an incident that marked the revolt of Bohemia against the Emperor Ferdinand of the Holy Roman Empire.

   ANSWER: TRUE. "Defenestration" is a fancy term for throwing something or someone out of a window. The Bohemian nobility became so angry with Ferdinand's viceroys that they threw them both out of a window of a Prague castle. The viceroys survived the fall, and the incident sparked the Thirty Years' War (1618–1648).

3. Under Communist rule, many of Czechoslovakia's greatest modern writers fled to the west. Which of the following stayed in Czechoslovakia:
   a. Václav Havel
   b. Milan Kundera
   c. Josef Škvorecký

   ANSWER: a. Václav Havel endured years of repression to become the first president of post-Communist Czechoslovakia (and later the Czech Republic). Kundera, author of *The Unbearable Lightness of Being*, fled to Paris; Škvorecký, author of *The Engineer of Human Souls*, immigrated to Canada.

TIPS ON DOING BUSINESS IN THE CZECH REPUBLIC

- Prague has become a magnet for young Western expatriates. Czechs have become used to dealing with English speakers.
- During the Communist era (1945–1989), industrial pollution was seen as a sign of industrial progress. Since then, pollution control and environmental stewardship has become very important to Czechs.
- Even if you do not drink beer, you should express admiration for the breweries of the Czech Republic. Most Czechs can expound on the subtleties of beer for hours.

 COUNTRY BACKGROUND

History

The Czech Republic represents the westernmost migration of Slavic tribes into Europe. During the fifth century A.D., these tribes arrived in what would eventually become Czechoslovakia. Two distinct Slavic groups emerged: the Czechs, who settled in the west, and the Slovaks, who took the east. By 900 A.D. the Slovak tribes were conquered by the Magyars (Hungarians). In the west, the city of Prague was developing into one of the most important cultural and political centers of the Holy Roman Empire.

In the fifteenth century, Prague became a focal point for the Protestant Reformation. Protestant leader Jan Hus, burned at the stake in 1415, is still a national hero to the Czechs. But the Battle on the White Mountain in 1620 put an end to Czech resistance, and both Czechs and Slovaks came to be ruled by the Austrian Hapsburg dynasty until the twentieth century.

While all of Czechoslovakia spent centuries under the control of the Austro-Hungarian Empire, these two ethnic areas developed independently. The western Czech provinces (Bohemia and Moravia) were industrialized; they prospered under direct Austrian control.

After its defeat in World War I, the Austro-Hungarian Empire was broken up into smaller states in accordance with Woodrow Wilson's principles of self-determination. The Czechs and the Slovenes found themselves lumped together in the newly independent state of Czechoslovakia. The aggressive, educated, and more numerous Czechs quickly took charge, and the Slovenes felt excluded from their own government. The existence of other minorities within the Czechoslovakian borders, notably the ethnic Germans in the Sudetenland, also caused friction. Nevertheless, Czechoslovakia managed to remain a democracy until it was overrun by Nazi Germany in 1938–1939.

Liberated by the Red Army in 1945, Czechoslovakia became a Soviet satellite. Despite repressive measures, the Communist leadership in Prague was unable to keep protests from periodically erupting, notably in 1968 and 1977. Finally, the tide of reform that washed over Eastern Europe in 1989 allowed the Czechoslovak people to elect a truly popular, non-Communist government. Dissident writer Václav Havel was elected the country's president.

Czechoslovakia became a parliamentary democracy and remained so until 1992, when political and social events resulted initially in the establishment of a multiparty republic of two equal states, and eventually in two separate countries—the Czech and Slovak Republics.

As an independent state, the new Czech Republic came into being on January 1, 1993. The Czech Republic also joined NATO in 1999 and the European Union in 2004.

Type of Government

The Czech Republic is a multiparty parliamentary democracy. The president is the chief of state—a largely ceremonial office. The prime minister is the head of the government. There are two legislative houses, an upper Senate and a lower Chamber of Deputies.

For current government data, check with the Embassy of the Czech Republic at *www.mzv.cz/washington.*

Cultural Note

Jan Hus (1369–1415) was not only an important religious leader, he also reformed Czech spelling. He adapted the Roman alphabet to Czech sounds by using diacritical marks; many of his innovations are still in use today. Without his spelling reforms, modern Czech might still look like Polish, with double letters like sz or rz—or, for that matter, the cz in Czech. The Czechs do not spell the name of their language that way; the English version came via Polish.

Language

The official language is Czech, which is a West Slavic language related to Polish. Although the Czechs and the Slovaks have gone to great lengths to differentiate their languages, the Czech and Slovak languages are actually quite similar and are mutually intelligible.

Czech is considered a difficult language for English speakers to master. Although it is written in the Latin alphabet (with diacritical marks), its pronunciation includes several sounds that are not present in English.

Ethnologue, at *www.ethnologue.com*, has identified a total of nine languages in the Czech Republic, one of which became extinct in the late Middle Ages.

The Czech View

There is no official religion in the Czech Republic. Religion was actively discouraged under the former Communist regime. More Czechs identify themselves as nondenominational (39.9 percent) than as members of the dominant religion, the Roman Catholic Church (39.0 percent). Most other religions are represented in the Czech Republic. Some local Protestant variations include Czechoslovak Brethren Reformed (2.0 percent), Czechoslovak Hussite (1.7 percent), and Silesian Evangelical (0.3 percent).

Avoidance of violence is an important part of Czech philosophy. Czechs are proud of the way they endured two wrenching changes without violence: the 1989 Velvet Revolution in which the Communist regime gave way to democracy, and the peaceful separation of Czechoslovakia into the separate Czech and Slovak Republics in 1993.

Egalitarianism is a priority in Czech thinking. In fact, one of the disappointments Czechs have with the market economy is that everyone is no longer equal. Under Communism, most Czechs lived under similar conditions.

Czechs tend toward modesty and informality. Ostentation is seen only on old buildings from the days of the Austro-Hungarian Empire. However, some younger Czechs are adopting a more opulent style, at least in matters of dress.

The Czech populace is well educated, with a 99 percent literacy rate. Emphasis has been placed on scientific research, and the educated elite is the equal of any in the world.

☑ Know Before You Go

The greatest hazard to travelers to the Czech Republic is probably vehicular accidents. Czechs tend to be erratic drivers. There is also a substantial amount of petty crime, mostly pickpocketing.

Tobacco smoke is also omnipresent. Czechs even smoke in places meant primarily for children, such as ice-cream parlors. This adds to the heavy pollution in many Czech cities.

The Czech Republic still operates mainly on cash. Credit cards and checks are accepted only in a limited number of venues.

While bribery is not omnipresent, the Czech police have a reputation for needlessly stopping foreign drivers, then accepting small bribes in lieu of a ticket.

▶ CULTURAL ORIENTATION

Cognitive Styles: How Czechs Organize and Process Information

The Czechs have always been open to information on most issues. They tend to be more analytic than associative, but they value relationships more than obedience to abstract rules of behavior.

Negotiation Strategies: What Czechs Accept as Evidence

Czechs find truth through a mixture of subjective feelings and objective facts. Their faith in the ideologies of humanitarianism and democracy will influence the truth in nearly every situation.

Value Systems: The Basis for Behavior

The amicable separation of Czechoslovakia into the Czech and Slovak Republic is an example of the humanitarian value systems of both cultures. The following three sections identify the Value Systems in the predominant culture—their methods of dividing right from wrong, good from evil, and so forth.

Locus of Decision-Making

The responsibility for decision-making rests on the shoulders of the individual. Individualism has always been encouraged, and individual achievement is more important than family in determining status. Czechs feel that they have a right to a private life; their friends are few and specific to their needs. Czechs feel that the same values should apply to all members of their culture.

Sources of Anxiety Reduction

With the demise of Communist rule, the guarantee of full employment ended. This produces considerable day-to-day anxiety. Although the traditional role of the family as the basic educating and socializing unit has been weakened, the family unit is still recognized as a stabilizing force. Religion seems to be regaining its influence on family life and social structure, and with this comes more security for both the individual and the family.

Issues of Equality/Inequality

The homogeneity of the Czech culture has eliminated most of the ethnic bias that existed before the breakup of Czechoslovakia. There is keen competition for status, but when a person is recognized for his or her accomplishments, that individual gains prominence among equals. The desire for power may undercut the humanitarian need for equality. This drive for power can yield strong, hierarchical structures in government, business, and society.

The husband is the titular head of the home. However, because most women work outside the home, husbands take some responsibility for raising the children.

Although women have legal equality with men, sexual harassment is still widespread in the workplace.

Cultural Note

There is a general feeling among Czechs that Communism cheated them out of forty years of profits. Consequently, many Czechs want to earn years of profits in a single business transaction. They may make inordinate financial demands upon foreigners.

 BUSINESS PRACTICES

Punctuality, Appointments, and Local Time

- Punctuality is important; be on time for business and social engagements.
- Czechs, like most Europeans, write the day first, then the month, then the year (e.g., December 3, 2010, is written 3.12.10 or 3/12/10).
- For many years, Russian was the foreign language most frequently studied in schools. Since the Velvet Revolution of 1989, Western languages like English and German have

become the most popular. English speakers should expect to hire a translator, especially if their destination is outside of Prague itself.

- Appointments should be made well in advance. Allow one to two weeks' notice for an appointment made by telephone or e-mail.
- Business letters may be written in English, although your counterpart will be favorably impressed if you take the trouble to translate the letter into Czech.
- As the business day begins early and ends in midafternoon, expect to schedule your appointments between 9:00 A.M. and 12 noon or between 1:00 and 3:00 P.M.
- Most Czechs receive four weeks of vacation per year. The traditional vacation time runs from mid-July to mid-August, so do not expect to be able to conduct business during this period.
- The Czech Republic is one hour ahead of Greenwich Mean Time (G.M.T. +1), or six hours ahead of U.S. Eastern Standard Time (E.S.T. +6).

Negotiating

- Expect the decision-making process to operate at a fairly slow pace. Czechs do not necessarily believe that "time is money."
- Many Czechs have adopted the German propensity for slow, methodical planning. Every aspect of the deal you propose will be pored over. Do not anticipate being able to speed up this process.
- Only a few entrepreneurs are ready to move more quickly. However, you should move cautiously with the ones who offer you a partnership, since you will be the one putting hard currency into the enterprise.
- The change from a communist to a capitalist society has resulted in a tangle of regulation. Don't depend on a Czech joint-venture partner to understand the law. Hire a Czech business lawyer.
- While Czechs are known for their hospitality, they may take a lot of time to establish a close business relationship.
- Executives usually understand enough English to decipher a business card, so it is not necessary to have a card in English translated. However, it is preferable to have promotional materials and instruction manuals translated into Czech.
- Bring plenty of cards; quite a few Czechs may wish to exchange them with you.
- If your company has been around for many years, the date of its founding should be on your card. Education is highly respected, so be sure to include any degree above the bachelor's level as well.
- Do not get down to business too quickly. Czechs typically converse before talking business. Expect to be asked about your flight, your accommodations, where you are from, your impressions of the country, and so forth.

- Your counterparts may not mind asking or being asked personal questions. You may want to ask about an executive's family. Part of establishing a relationship is expressing an interest in each other's family, although it may be a long time before you actually meet any of them.
- While political discussions cannot be avoided, don't ask embarrassing political questions. Many of the people with enough money to conduct business are former Communists or black marketeers. Also do your best to avoid siding with Czechs against Slovaks, or vice versa.
- Czechs tend to be well-informed about politics and to have firm political opinions. They are also honest and may tell you their opinions. While they dislike what Communism has done to their country, they may not be as approving of the West as you might expect.
- Sports are a good topic for conversation; soccer, ice hockey, hiking, and cycling are popular sports. Music is a good topic as well, as are dogs—Czechs are inordinately fond of their dogs.
- Czechs make some excellent beers. The pilsner style of beer was developed here. The town of Budweis (now renamed Ceské Budéjovice), after which "Budweiser" was named, is in the Czech Republic. A beer drinker will be happy to explain about Czech beer.
- Coffee is usually served during business meetings. Taste it before you add sugar; it may already be sweetened. The coffee is Turkish and will probably have grounds at the bottom.

> **Cultural Note**
>
> As in most Christian countries, every day of the calendar year is dedicated to one or more saints. Almost every Czech shares a first name with one of these saints. The day that celebrates their namesake saint is known as their "name day" and is celebrated like a second birthday.
>
> If you are not sure what saint is being celebrated, walk by a flower shop. Many flower shops post the name of that day's saint.

Business Entertaining

- Breakfast meetings are not as common as in North America.
- Historically, business meetings were confined to offices. Business lunches were rare; the only meal people shared with a business associate was a celebratory dinner. However, this segregation was due in part to restrictive government regulations—fraternization with westerners was actively discouraged. Czechs are now accustomed to Western business practices, including business lunches.
- At a lunch, business may be discussed before and (sometimes) after the meal, but rarely during the meal itself. If you are invited out to a luncheon, you may offer to pay, but

expect your host to decline your offer. Insist on paying only when you have made the invitation.

- Restaurants tend to be very busy. Always make a reservation. It may be easier to ask your counterpart to choose a restaurant; just make sure to explain that you intend to pay for the meal.
- Do not anticipate good service in all restaurants. Under the Communists, restaurant workers got the same pay no matter how busy they were. Additional customers were simply an inconvenience. These attitudes take time to change.
- The one category of customer to get immediate attention in restaurants is dogs! Like the French, the Czechs allow people to bring their dogs into their restaurants.
- You may be invited to eat lunch in the company cafeteria.
- Czechs do not often entertain business associates in their homes. If you are invited into a home, consider it a great honor. Do not be surprised if the living quarters are crowded. You may be asked to remove your shoes when you enter a private home.
- A host will invite you to eat additional portions. It is traditional to turn down the first invitation.
- When eating, always use utensils; very few items are eaten with the hands. Place your utensils together on one side of the plate when you have finished eating. If you just wish to pause between courses, cross your utensils on the plate.

 ## PROTOCOL

Greetings

- Always shake hands, firmly but briefly, when introduced. When introduced to a Czech woman or an elderly person, wait to see if he or she extends a hand before offering to shake.
- In both business and social situations, always shake hands upon arriving and upon departing from any meeting.
- When several people are being introduced, take turns shaking hands. It is impolite to reach over someone else's handshake.
- Never keep your left hand in your pocket while shaking hands with your right.
- In formal situations, it is better to be introduced by a third person than to introduce yourself. However, in informal situations, it is appropriate to introduce yourself.
- When you are the third person making an introduction between two parties, give the name of the younger (or lower-ranking) person first.

Titles/Forms of Address

- The order of names is the same as in most of Europe: first name followed by a surname.

- Traditionally, only family members and close friends address each other by their first names. While young people are using first names more frequently, most businesspeople you meet will prefer to be called by their title or surname.
- When speaking to persons who do not have professional titles, use "Mr.," "Mrs.," or "Miss" and the surname:

    Mr. = *Pan* (pronounced "Pahn")

    Mrs. (or Ms.) = *Pani* ("PAH-nee")

    Miss = *Slecna* ("SLEH-chnah")
- It is important to use professional titles. Attorneys, architects, engineers, and other professionals will expect you to address them as "Pan" or "Pani" plus their title. This goes for anyone with a Ph.D. as well.

Gestures
- To get someone's attention, raise your hand, palm facing out, with only the index finger extended. Avoid waving or beckoning.
- When sitting, cross one knee over the other, rather than resting your ankle on the other knee. Do not prop your feet up on anything other than a footstool.
- The eldest or highest-ranking person enters a room first. If their age and status are the same, men enter before women.
- Do not talk to someone with your hands in your pockets or while chewing gum.

Gifts
- Under the Communist regime, the frequent shortages made gift giving simple: You gave whatever was in short supply in Czechoslovakia. Now that consumer items are freely available (albeit expensive), gift giving is more of a problem.
- By and large, businessmen do not give or expect to receive expensive gifts. A gift should be of good quality, but not exorbitant.
- Appropriate gifts include good-quality pens, small electronics (such as MP3 players), cigarette lighters, and imported wine or liquor, especially Scotch, bourbon, or cognac.
- When invited to dinner at a Czech home, bring a bouquet of unwrapped flowers for your hostess. The bouquet should have an uneven number of flowers, but not thirteen. Red roses are reserved for romantic situations, and calla lilies are for funerals.

Dress
- Czech clothing is modest and unassuming; whether in business or casualwear. Ostentation is looked at askance, as are bright clothing or loud patterns.
- Generally, businessmen wear dark suits, ties, and white shirts. Businesswomen also dress conservatively, in dark suits or dresses and white blouses.

- Follow the lead of your colleagues with regard to removing jackets or ties in hot weather.
- There are many social events in the Czech Republic, and Czechs often dress up for them. Business wear is also appropriate for most formal social events: parties, dinners, and the theater.
- Formalwear is expected for the opening night of an opera, concert, or play. Men are expected to wear their best dark suit or tuxedo, and women a long evening gown. Virtually every Czech institution, including business associations and libraries, hosts a formal ball sometime during February, and formalwear is required for them.
- Casualwear is essentially the same as in the United States. Jeans are ubiquitous, but they should not be worn, torn, or dirty.

Cultural Note

Cold, wet weather often keeps Czechs bundled up. When the weather permits, Czechs enjoy wearing light casualwear. Their long-time president, Václav Havel, was known for appearing in public in a T-shirt.

Denimark

Kingdom of Denmark
Local short form: Danmark
Local long form: Kongeriget Danmark

Cultural Note

Alone of all the Scandinavian nations, Denmark has maintained extraterritorial possessions into modern times. Today, Denmark retains Greenland and the Faroe Islands. This requires the Danish government to consider the interests of those citizens and gives Danish artists extra inspiration. Part of Peter Høeg's bestselling 1992 novel *Smilla's Sense of Snow* takes place in Greenland.

▶ WHAT'S YOUR CULTURAL IQ?

1. Which of the following are true about "The Little Mermaid"—the famous statue in Copenhagen's harbor?
   a. She has been blown off her granite stone by explosives.
   b. She has been decapitated.
   c. Her right arm was cut off.
   d. All of the above.

   ANSWER: d. This beautiful statue is one of the most-often photographed pieces of art worldwide. It is also one of the most abused. A Danish brewer, Carl Jacobsen, commissioned the statue after attending a performance of *The Little Mermaid* in 1909. The Danish sculptor was Edward Eriksen.

3. Match these famous Danes with their areas of accomplishment:
   a. Vitus Jonassen Bering (1681–1741)   1. Astronomy
   b. Niels Bohr (1885–1962)   2. Exploration
   c. Tycho Brahe (1546–1601)   3. Quantum physics

   ANSWER: a. 2; b. 3; c. 1. Of the three, only physicist Niels Bohr died in Denmark. Brahe died in Prague, and Bering died on an island in what is now called the Bering Sea.

3. Which of the following Danes did not win the Nobel Prize for literature?
   a. Karen Blixen, writing as Isak Dinesen (1885–1962)
   b. Karl Adolph Gjellerup (1857–1919)
   c. Johannes V. Jensen (1873–1950)
   d. Henrik Pontoppidan (1857–1943)

   ANSWER: a. Ironically, Blixen is the best known of these authors outside of Denmark (in part because of the Hollywood film version of "Out of Africa"). She wrote in English, then translated her work into Danish. Isak Dinesen was just one of her pseudonyms.

> **Cultural Note**
> Denmark gave us one author read by millions all over the world: Hans Christian Andersen (1805–1875). Best known as a children's storyteller, he was also a journalist, novelist, and travel writer. Today, more than 200 years after his birth, he is considered Denmark's national storyteller.

TIPS ON DOING BUSINESS IN DENMARK

- Although Denmark is considered one of the least-corrupt countries in the world, Danes do not tend to regard rules as inflexible. Finding ways to get around regulations is almost considered a sport by many Danes.

- Danes try to maintain a strict divide between their public and private lives. Most do not like working overtime and are unwilling to discuss business matters outside of the office. Similarly, they do not like to discuss their personal lives with casual business acquaintances.

- Danes are very individualistic, and leading a Danish company requires skill at consensus building. There is a great deal of give-and-take among all levels of a Danish company. Strong negative input from even a minor member of a company could sink your proposal.

- Danes are both slow to decide and independent, so a hard sell is the worst technique one can take. Present your pitch, supply all the follow-up data requested (no matter how extraneous this data may seem to you), and wait. The Danes cannot be rushed.

COUNTRY BACKGROUND

History

During the Middle Ages, the Viking raiders and conquerors were largely Danes. For a time the Danish realm included most of Scandinavia and England.

In 1389, the Danish queen Margaret I acquired the vacant crown of Sweden. Denmark and Sweden were formally united under the Union of Kalmar. Denmark already ruled Norway, Iceland, and the Faroe Islands. Sweden did not permanently break away from Danish rule until 1523.

Christian III became king in 1534. During his twenty-five-year reign, he consolidated Danish power and established the Lutheran Church as the official Church of Denmark.

In the eighteenth century, Denmark colonized Greenland. Danish traders sailed to the West Indies and East Asia.

Denmark supported Napoleon during the Napoleonic Wars. As punishment, the Congress of Vienna took Norway away from Denmark in 1814 and gave it to Sweden.

In 1849, Denmark became a constitutional monarchy.

Denmark lost additional territory in 1864, when it fought both Austria and Prussia for control of Schleswig (along the border of present-day Germany). As a result, Denmark lost

40 percent of its land and over a third of its people. However, what was left was an extremely homogenous population. Denmark's borders have been more-or-less stable since then.

Although Denmark has existed since around 750, it became a constitutional monarchy in 1849. By the 1880s, Denmark experienced both economic growth and a population explosion. Many Danes immigrated to North America.

Despite signing a nonaggression pact with Germany in 1939, the Nazis invaded Denmark in 1940. With Denmark under German control, Iceland severed ties with Denmark in 1944. The United States built military bases on both Iceland and Greenland. At the end of the war, Greenland returned to Danish control, but Iceland remained independent.

Denmark became a founding member of NATO in 1949. The country joined the European Community (now known as the European Union) in 1972.

Almost fifty years of Social Democratic Party control changed after September 11, 2001. Since then, a right-wing coalition, which promised tighter controls on immigration, has held power.

> **Cultural Note**
> In 2000, a tunnel and bridge, which connects Denmark with Sweden, was completed.
> The Øresundsbron is approximately 16 kilometers long and features a motorway and railway line. Travelers can go from Copenhagen to Malmo over the Øresund fixed link, the world's largest cable-stayed bridge.

Type of Government

The Kingdom of Denmark is today a constitutional monarchy. The symbolic chief of state is the queen or king. The prime minister is the head of the government and is chosen by the Parliament. The legislative body is called the *Folketing*.

For current government data, check with the Embassy of Denmark at *www.denmark emb.org*.

> **Cultural Note**
> The current sovereign of Denmark, Queen Margrethe II, has a reputation as one of Europe's most modern and progressive monarchs. She makes herself highly accessible to the press. She is also a professional artist who has produced critically acclaimed paintings.

Language

The official language is Danish. English starts to be taught at the elementary level; it is the predominant second language, and a majority of Danes speak it with a high level of competency. Most are eager to use their English with visitors from English-speaking countries.

Ethnologue, at *www.ethnologue.com*, has identified eight languages in Denmark, all of which are extant. The largest of these is Faroese, the language of the Faroe Islands, which has about 47,000 speakers.

> **Cultural Note**
>
> The famous Danish philosopher Søren Kierkegaard (1813–1855) is considered the founder of existentialism. Existential philosophy seems suited to Danes: it posits a world in which humankind is essentially alone and helpless, in a hostile universe, with no universal truths except those we create for ourselves.

The Danish View

The official religion of Denmark is Evangelical Lutheran. The vast majority (around 97 percent) of Danes belong to this religion, although less than 14 percent attend church regularly.

Denmark observes a National Prayer Day, or Common Prayer Day, called Store Bededag, on the fourth Friday after Easter. Most Danes use it as a long weekend to enjoy the spring.

Other Christian denominations account for about 1.6 percent of the overall population; Muslims make up 1.4. percent. Other religions and persons categorized as nonreligious number 9.6 percent.

Danes have been seafarers for centuries—as you would expect in a country made up of 482 islands.

Their maritime tradition remains strong, as does their merchant tradition. But Danes also have a strong agricultural heritage, and the country is a net exporter of food.

☑ Know Before You Go

Denmark is a remarkably safe county, with little violent crime or accidental death.

Flooding is the major hazard in Denmark, especially in those parts protected from the sea by a system of dikes.

Denmark has various territorial disputes with other countries over fishing rights and ownership of some remote islands. Also, the Faroe Islands often debate independence.

▶ CULTURAL ORIENTATION

Cognitive Styles: How Danes Organize and Process Information

The Danes are a proud people who tend to be satisfied with their own accomplishments and thus do not need (and are not open to) information or help from others. Their educational system is moving away from rote learning and toward the application of abstractive, conceptual thinking. They tend to follow universalistic rules of behavior rather than react to particular situations.

Negotiation Strategies: What Danes Accept as Evidence

Truth is centered in a faith in the ideology of social welfare, with objective facts used to prove a point. Subjective feelings do not play a part in negotiation processes.

Value Systems: The Basis for Behavior

Denmark is a social welfare state in which the quality of life and environmental issues are given top priority. The Danes put a high value on individualism and personal freedom.

The following three sections identify the Value Systems in the predominant culture—their methods of dividing right from wrong, good from evil, and so forth.

Locus of Decision-Making

Danes have a strong belief in individual decisions within the social welfare system. There is a strong self-orientation, but with an obligation to help those who are not able to help themselves. There is an emphasis on individual initiative and achievement, with one's ability being more important than his or her station in life. The dignity and worth of the individual is emphasized, along with the right to a private life and opinions.

Sources of Anxiety Reduction

Sociologists have found that Danes have a low index of uncertainty avoidance. This indicates a society with little concern about ambiguity and a high tolerance for divergent opinions. As a result, Danes are not rule-oriented and have a relatively high tolerance for risk.

Danes reduce their anxiety through a strong social welfare system—the government is there to serve the people. Though individualistic, most Danes are resigned to a high-tax social welfare state in which there is little distinction available through individual accomplishment. Danes who wish to become wealthy often seek their fortunes abroad.

Young people are encouraged to mature early and to take risks to develop a strong self-image.

Issues of Equality/Inequality

Denmark has a middle-class society, with family needs as the central issue of social policy and governmental intervention. Danes strive to minimize social differences, so there is very little evidence of poverty or wealth, although they exist.

Danes have been charted as having the lowest power distance index in all of Scandinavia. Such a society minimizes the differences between the power and wealth of each citizen.

A largely homogeneous population minimizes ethnic differences. In this society, upper-class husbands and wives share the responsibilities of child care.

▶ BUSINESS PRACTICES

Punctuality, Appointments, and Local Time

- Punctuality is very important; be exactly on time for all business appointments. Tardiness conveys to Danes an impression of incompetence and poor time management.
- Danes expect punctuality for social engagements as well.
- When writing down the date, Danes first write the day, then the month, then the year (e.g., December 3, 2010, is written 3.12.10 or 3/12/10).
- As in the rest of Scandinavia, summer is a time of leisure. It is both difficult and inconsiderate to try to conduct serious business during July and August. Many firms close for extended periods during these two months to allow their employees to take summer vacations. Danes have five weeks of paid vacation per year.
- There is no designated national holiday in Denmark, but June 5, Constitution Day, is generally viewed as the national day. For further information on official holidays, see *www.kissboworshakehands.com*.
- Local time is one hour ahead of Greenwich Mean Time (G.M.T. +1), or six hours ahead of U.S. Eastern Standard Time (E.S.T. +6).

> **Cultural Note**
> If your firm is an old one, have the date your company was established printed on your business card. Danes respect tradition.

Negotiating

- The Danes tend to get down to business right away, with a minimum of small talk.
- For Scandinavians, Danes are relatively informal. As long as he or she is expecting you, you can introduce yourself to an executive, rather than wait for his secretary to introduce you.
- Be prepared to give detailed briefings, because Danes are rather meticulous.
- Danes are often quite frank in their manner of speaking. Statements are often direct but are not meant to be insulting in any way.
- Avoid making any comments that could be regarded as personal. Even complimenting someone on his or her clothes can be taken as too invasive!
- Like most Scandinavians, Danes have a dry sense of humor that can be opaque to foreigners. Don't expect your jokes to translate well, either. In fact, humor has little place in Danish business.
- Although Danes are not as reserved as most Scandinavians, Danes rarely speak to strangers (except when they are anxious to practice a foreign tongue). Don't be surprised or insulted if an unfamiliar Dane is not responsive if you attempt to make small talk with him or her.
- Danes are very tolerant; it is not advisable to criticize other people or political systems.

Business Entertaining

- Danes prefer to eat breakfast at home; business breakfasts are not common.
- Business lunches are held between noon and 2:00 P.M. A typical lunch fare is an open-faced sandwich called a smorrebord. This is eaten with a knife and fork, not with the hands.
- The main meal of the day is dinner, which is eaten between 6:00 and 8:00 P.M. This meal usually includes alcohol—either beer or wine.
- Do not discuss business during a meal unless your Danish host does so first.
- Good topics of conversation include sports, Danish culture, and your hometown.
- The smorgasbord, a cold buffet, is very popular.
- Toasts in Denmark can be quite formal. Never toast your host or anyone senior to you in rank or age until he or she has toasted you first. Never taste your drink until the host has said the traditional toasting word, skoal.
- If you are toasting someone, or someone is toasting you, be sure to maintain eye contact with that person during the entire toast.
- Toasts are given both standing and sitting. If your host stands when he makes a toast, so should you when you give your toast. Only the person proposing the toast stands.
- A traditional Danish drink, *aquavit* (literally, "water of life"), is quite potent. Be forewarned, as Danes often like to share this alcoholic beverage with their guests.
- In a Danish home, assume very proper manners. For example, your host will suggest where you should sit. (At the table, the host and hostess usually sit at opposite ends, with the guest of honor next to the host.)
- Expect to be at the table for a long time. Danish dinners can take as long as four hours. You should not rise from the table before your hostess does.
- It is impolite to leave a host's home too soon after dinner. Again, cocktails are offered after dinner, not before. These may be at the table or in the main room. It is not unusual for a dinner party to last until 1 A.M., especially in the summer.
- If the weather is pleasant, the dinner party may end with a late-night walk around the neighborhood. This is especially true in the summer, when it stays light very late.
- Danes hold their fork in their left hand, while their knife remains in the right.
- Danes have a traditional way of signaling when they have had enough to eat. To indicate that you have finished eating, place the knife and fork side by side on the plate, pointed away from you. On the other hand, if you want another serving, point the fork's tines down toward you.
- Unlike many Europeans, Danes have a tradition of inviting foreign guests into their homes for a meal. If you are invited to a Danish home for dinner, be prompt. There is often no predinner cocktail, so you may be led straight to the dinner table. Danes usually serve cocktails after the meal, not before.

▶ PROTOCOL

Greetings

- It is common to rise when being introduced to someone, and to shake hands with both men and women. Handshakes are firm but brief. When greeting a couple, it is customary to shake hands with the woman first.
- Your colleague will usually shake your hand when leaving as well.
- Danes like plenty of personal space around them. Stand about two arm's length away from a Dane.
- Danes say the traditional greeting *heij*, which sounds exactly like the English "hi," when both greeting and departing.
- The common North American greeting "Hi, how are you?" will lead a Dane to think you really want to know how he or she is doing. A preferable greeting would be "Hi, it's a pleasure to meet you."

Cultural Note

Danes (and other Scandinavians) sometimes use a person's initials and surname instead of using the entire name. For example, the writer Hans Christian Andersen is known as H. C. Andersen in Denmark. That is how you would search for his name in a Danish database. There is no pattern to this, just the personal preferences of the individual.

Titles/Forms of Address

- The order of Danish names is the same as in most of Europe: first name followed by surname.
- It is appropriate to use a person's title and surname until the use of first names is suggested. The use of first names in business environments is currently in vogue in Denmark.

Gestures

- Danes are rather reserved in public. Avoid talking loudly or gesticulating wildly.
- The gesture North Americans use to indicate that someone is crazy (index finger circling while pointed at one's temple) is used to insult other drivers while on the road.
- The North American "okay" gesture (thumb and forefinger forming a circle) can be taken as an insult in Denmark.
- At the theater, enter a row with your back to the stage (so that you face people seated in the row). It is considered insulting to squeeze past seated people with your backside facing them.

Gifts

- Gifts are not required in a business relationship. If a gift is given, it should be modest so it won't be mistaken for a bribe.
- If and when a gift is given, it can be unwrapped immediately in front of the giver.
- It is quite acceptable to bring a bouquet of flowers or chocolates to a host's home.
- You may bring roses to your hostess in Denmark as long as they are not white (which are associated with mourning). Flowers should be presented wrapped.
- Send your flowers before the dinner, so the hostess does not have to arrange them when you arrive.
- An illustrated book from your home region makes an appropriate gift. So do spirits or wine produced in your home country. Technological gadgets are appreciated as well.

Dress

- Sometimes high-ranking Danish executives host formal dinners. Male executives should consider bringing a tuxedo along; female executives may need an evening gown.
- Conservative dress will generally be expected in business situations.
- Danish casual attire is still conservative, although jeans that are clean and pressed are not uncommon. At the beach, some women wear topless bathing suits.

Cultural Note

The Danish alphabet has three additional letters that are placed at the end of the alphabet. They are:

27 letter: æ/Æ (pronounced like the *e* in "pet")

28 letter: ø/Ø (pronounced like the *e* in "err")

29 letter: å/Å (pronounced like the *o* in "core")

If you have no way of printing these characters, substitute "ae" for æ, "oe" for ø, and "aa" for å.

There are pronunciation differences even in the letters shared by Danish and English. The most notable peculiarity is the Danish "soft *d*," which foreigners—even other Nordics—find difficult to duplicate.

There is also a guttural r sound that English speakers have trouble imitating.

Ecuador
Republic of Ecuador

> ## Cultural Note
> Ecuador is South America's second largest producer of oil. The drop in oil prices since 1982, plus an earthquake in 1987 that crippled the country's main oil line, forced Ecuador to temporarily suspend interest payments on its foreign debt. Ecuador resigned from OPEC in 1992, stating that the cartel failed to benefit smaller oil producers.

▶ WHAT'S YOUR CULTURAL IQ?

1. Which of the following islands are administered by Ecuador?
   a. Easter Island
   b. Galápagos Islands
   c. Malvinas Islands

   ANSWER: b. Ecuador administers the Galápagos Islands. (Chile has Easter Island, and Argentina claims the Malvinas Islands—but they are occupied by the United Kingdom, which calls them the Falkland Islands.)

2. Until the discovery of oil, Ecuador was primarily an agricultural nation.
   TRUE or FALSE: Since the Second World War, coffee has been Ecuador's primary cash crop.

   ANSWER: FALSE. Ecuador has never been one of South America's top coffee producers. Until the 1920s its major agricultural export was cacao (the source of chocolate). But after an infestation of insects damaged cacao production, bananas became Ecuador's most important crop.

3. Which South American country invaded Ecuador in 1941?
   a. Brazil
   b. Colombia
   c. Peru

   ANSWER: c. Peru invaded Ecuador in 1941 and annexed almost half of Ecuador's territory. Ecuador has resented Peru ever since, and these sentiments have boiled over several times at the ill-defined border. Military on both sides of the border attacked each other in 1981 and again in 1995.

> ## Cultural Note
> Dinners at Ecuadorian homes last long into the night. Expect drinks and appetizers around 8:00 P.M., with dinner served around 11:00 P.M. or midnight. Your hosts may be dismayed if you leave as early as 1:00 A.M.
>
> Parties at Ecuadorian homes also begin late and end around 4:00 or 5:00 A.M. Guests may sometimes be served breakfast before they leave.

▶ TIPS ON DOING BUSINESS IN ECUADOR

- Do not discuss other Latin American countries with Ecuadorians. In 1941, Ecuador lost half its land to Peru, (a decision supported by the United States, Argentina, and Brazil). This made Ecuador one of the smallest nations in South America and has resulted in strained relations between Ecuador and Peru ever since. The most recent border war between the two countries flared in 1995 and was resolved in 1999.
- The Galápagos Islands are a major ecotourism site for Ecuador. A visit to the islands—which were claimed by Ecuador in 1832—shows interest in their natural resources (besides oil).
- There are differences between Ecuadorians who live in the interior, and those on the coast. The inhabitants of Quito (known as Quiteños) tend to be formal, conservative, and very Catholic. People on the coastal city of Guayaquíl tend to be more liberal and serene.

▶ COUNTRY BACKGROUND

History

Archaeological evidence indicates that Ecuador has been continuously occupied for some 5,000 years. The powerful Inca empire reached its height in this area just prior to Columbus's discovery of the New World.

The Spanish conquistadores' arrival came at a time when the Incas were weakened by a brutal civil war. The Spanish conquest of Ecuador was complete by 1534. Ecuador became part of the Spanish viceroyalty of Peru. The colony got off to a poor start when the conquistadores began assassinating one another. This precedent for political change accompanied by violence has been repeated many times in Ecuador.

Along with other colonies, Ecuador sought independence from Spain at the beginning of the nineteenth century. Independence was declared in 1809 but was not secured until 1822. At first, Ecuador joined with Colombia, Panama, and Venezuela to form the Republic of Greater Colombia. But this turbulent union soon fell apart, and Ecuador became an independent nation in 1830.

Ecuador suffered through both political unrest and border disputes with both Colombia and Peru. Revolts and dictatorships became common; rarely did one freely elected government succeed another.

Political instability continued throughout the twentieth century. Peru invaded in 1941 and annexed almost half of Ecuador's land. The two countries still dispute their borders.

Ecuador's turbulence is reflected in the leadership of José María Velasco Ibarra, who was elected president five times between 1944 and 1972, yet was allowed to complete only one full term in office!

Despite this instability, Ecuador often managed to be better off than its neighboring countries, both politically and economically.

Ecuador underwent its most recent coup in 2000.

Type of Government

Ecuador has endured frequent civilian and military dictatorships over its history. Ecuadorian political parties have often had difficulties with disorganized platforms (or lack of platforms), charismatic leaders who do not follow specific programs, and small factions within the parties. Ecuador suffered a coup in January 2000, when a huge demonstration in Quito occupied the National Assembly building (the police and the military refused to stop them). President Jamil Mahaud was forced to flee. A military triumvirate, which was running the country, backed Vice President Gustavo Noboa and he succeeded to the presidency.

The Republic of Ecuador is a unitary multiparty republic. It has a single legislative house, the National Congress. The president is both the chief of state and the head of the government, and serves a single four-year term.

According to Ecuador's current constitution, the president may not be re-elected, and legislators must sit out a term before running again for a two-year term. Voting is compulsory in Ecuador from age eighteen to sixty-five for all literate citizens.

For current government data and guidelines for doing business in Ecuador, check with the Embassy of Ecuador at *www.ecuador.org*.

Language

The official language of Ecuador is Spanish. Many businesspeople speak English.

Ecuador has a large Amerindian population, many of whom speak only their indigenous languages. Quichua is the most common Amerindian language, numbering approximately 1.5 million speakers of its various dialects.

Counting all the varieties of Quichua, a total of twenty-three languages have been identified in Ecuador by *www.ethnologue.com*; one of those is now extinct.

The Ecuadorian View

There is no official religion in Ecuador, and the constitution guarantees freedom of religion. The vast majority (93 percent) of Ecuadorians are Roman Catholic; various Protestant groups have made inroads in the past few decades.

Ecuador is subject to the hazards typical of the Andes: earthquakes, volcanoes, and mudslides. Some sociologists believe that this is one source of many Ecuadorians' fatalistic viewpoint.

Ecuador is unusual in that Amerindians form a bloc as large as any other ethnic group. In the past, Amerindians formed the lowest level of Ecuadorian society. In the past few decades, increasing militancy and political activism has raised the prestige of Ecuador's indigenous people.

One reason for increased political activity by Ecuador's poor (Amerindians and mestizo alike) is the perceived failure of Ecuador's oil exports to improve their lives.

 Know Before You Go

Ecuador is subject to earthquakes and volcanoes, as well as severe weather due to fluctuations in the El Niño Current. The latter caused massive flooding and mud slides in 2002.

As a result of Ecuador's wars with Peru, there are as many as 100,000 land mines along the country's border. Since 1995, the mines have caused over sixty casualties (both civilian and military). Persons traveling along the border should use extreme caution.

Rebel groups from Colombia sometimes retreat into Ecuadorian territory. Some of these rebel groups kidnap foreigners and hold them for ransom.

Altitude sickness can strike anyone, even if you have never experienced it before. There is no sure prevention except gradual acclimation to high elevation: once you get to 6,000 feet above sea level, spend at least two nights there. Repeat this acclimation period at each increase of 3,000 feet. Alcohol consumption tends to make the symptoms worse. Sunburn is also a danger at high altitudes, as there is less atmosphere to protect you from the sun.

▶ CULTURAL ORIENTATION

Cognitive Styles: How Ecuadorians Organize and Process Information

In Ecuador there is a basic tendency to accept information on any topic for discussion. However, Ecuadorians are not easily moved from their positions. They arrive at their beliefs through association and experiential thinking. They generally look at each particular situation rather than using universal rules or laws to guide their behavior.

Negotiation Strategies: What Ecuadorians Accept as Evidence

A person's feelings about a topic or situation are the primary source of the truth. Faith in an ideology of class structure may influence the truth. Typically, an argument based entirely on quantifiable data is not convincing to the majority of Ecuadorians.

Value Systems: The Basis for Behavior

Rigid class distinctions are supported by a strong tradition of social distance between the upper class and the common people. The following three sections identify the Value Systems in the predominant culture—their methods of dividing right from wrong, good from evil, and so forth.

Locus of Decision-Making

There is a preoccupation with each individual's status. This lends itself to the belief in *personalismo*—an exaggerated attention to one's own personal position with relatives and society. Self-identity is based on the social system and the history of the extended family. Kinship and friendship play a major role in business associations.

Ecuadorians have been measured to have a low individualism ranking. This indicates a collectivist culture in which a person's group identity is paramount.

Sources of Anxiety Reduction

One's role in the social structure and the presence of the extended family and kinship groups give a sense of stability to life. The Catholic Church has a strong influence on personal and social behavior. There is a strong work ethic, but progress toward the goal of the project is less important than working on the project.

Issues of Equality/Inequality

The Sierra elite (conservative) consider themselves the upper class by birth and intermarriage, so there is a power struggle between the Sierra and Costa (liberal). Ecuadorians have displayed a higher power distance rating than is average for Latin Americans, meaning that there are extreme contrasts between rich and poor. There is still a belief that powerful people are entitled to special privileges that come with an important office—although this is changing among the young. Machismo is widespread. The man is still the head of the household, and the woman is responsible for managing it.

Cultural Note

Individual honor is so highly prized in Ecuador that defamation is a criminal offense punishable by up to three years in prison. This sometimes results in reporters taking a rather nonconfrontational viewpoint on potentially controversial topics.

The media is also required by law to give the government free air time, therefore many government-produced programs that feature the president and top officials are broadcast.

▶ BUSINESS PRACTICES

Punctuality, Appointments, and Local Time

- As a foreigner, you are expected to be punctual to all business appointments.
- Be aware that Ecuadorians do not always stress punctuality among themselves. If Ecuadorians arrive at a meeting fifteen or twenty minutes late, they still feel they are on time. There have been recent government efforts to force Ecuadorians to be more punctual.
- Remember that many Europeans and South Americans write the day first, then the month, then the year (e.g., December 3, 2010, is written 3.12.10 or 3/12/10). This is the case in Ecuador.

Ecuador

- Make appointments about two weeks in advance.
- It is best to arrive in Quito a day before you begin work, because it takes time to adjust to the high altitude.
- Many executives arrive later than 9:00 A.M., so do not schedule appointments earlier than 10:00 A.M..
- Ecuador is five hours behind Greenwich Mean Time (G.M.T. –5), which is the same as U.S. Eastern Standard Time.

Negotiating

- Ecuadorians are more relaxed and informal in business settings than some other Latin Americans.
- It will be difficult to conduct business without hiring a local contact, who can be either a business consultant or an Ecuadorian lawyer.
- When dealing with the government, you will need to speak Spanish or have an interpreter. However, many executives in private industry will speak English.
- Business cards printed with English on one side, and the translation in Spanish on the other are most effective. These should be presented with the Spanish side facing your Ecuadorian colleague.
- Never change the members of your negotiating team. Such a change could bring the negotiations to a halt. Ecuadorians feel they are negotiating with people, not a corporation. Expect delays and many contract iterations.
- Avoid discussing politics, especially Ecuador's relations with Peru. (The two countries have had many disputes.)
- Ecuadorians are sensitive to foreign attitudes of superiority; be careful not to give that impression. Don't compare how things are done in Ecuador to how things are done "back home."
- It is a good idea to be informed about local culture and history, or at least to show curiosity about Ecuador.

Business Entertaining

- Lunch is the main meal of the day and is the most popular for business meetings.
- Let the host be the first to make a toast; then you can follow his or her lead.
- It is considered rude to suggest an ending time for a social gathering.
- It is acceptable to order a cocktail before the meal.
- Wine may be served with the lunch. Keep in mind that Ecuadorians will be accustomed to a heavy meal with alcohol at midday.
- Ecuadorians are very friendly; if you establish a good relationship, you may be invited to your associate's home or farm. Never decline an offer like this—it is an honor.

- Women should note that while it is acceptable to drink wine, Ecuadorians are not accustomed to seeing a woman drink whiskey or other hard liquor.
- If a businesswoman wishes to pay for an Ecuadorian man's meal, she should make arrangements ahead of time. If the check is presented at the end of the meal, the man will probably refuse to let her pay.

▶ PROTOCOL

Greetings

- The standard greeting is the handshake, both for men and women and between the sexes.
- The handshake is also used when departing.
- Among close friends, women kiss each other on one cheek. Men embrace; generally, men only honor elders (of either sex) with a kiss on one cheek.

Titles/Forms of Address

- Do not address an Ecuadorian by his or her first name unless you are invited to do so. Younger executives may move to a first name basis quickly, but it is better to err on the side of formality.
- See Appendix A for general data on titles in Ecuador.
- Be sure to use an Ecuadorian's professional title, if he or she has one.

Gestures

- Ecuadorians stand closer together when conversing than do North Americans and northern Europeans. There is a good deal more contact, including touching on the arm, shoulder, and lapel. Try not to back away; an Ecuadorian is likely to move forward to restore what he or she feels is the proper distance.
- Instead of using head motions to indicate "yes" or "no," it is safest to indicate consent or disagreement verbally. Not all Ecuadorians may be able to interpret your physical signals.
- As in most of the world, it is considered impolite to yawn in public or to point at others.
- Nervous, repetitive movements (toe tapping, knee jiggling, thumb twiddling, and so forth) should be minimized. Ecuadorians find them disturbing.
- In a restaurant, some Ecuadorians summon a waiter by raising their hands over their head and clapping. This is not considered courteous, and it should be avoided by foreigners.

Gifts

- If you are given a gift, you should be effusive in your thanks.
- When invited into a home for a meal, bring flowers, pastries, or chocolates. Avoid lilies and marigolds, which are used at funerals.
- Fine wines and liquors are also good gifts.

- Be sure to select name-brand gifts.
- If you know you will meet a business associate's family, it is a good idea to bring gifts for the children.

Dress

- In general, formality increases as you move inland. The coastal resort areas are the most casual, and shorts may be worn in public there (although bikinis are rarely seen, even on the beach).
- On the coast, where it is hot, some men will wear a guayabera shirt to work, and women will wear sleeveless dresses. Foreigners, however, are expected to dress more formally for business meetings.
- Inland, it is important to adopt conservative business attire. Men should wear a jacket and tie even in hot weather. Suits in dark colors are preferred. Jackets and ties can be worn to social occasions as well.
- Women should dress conservatively and modestly. A suit, dress, or designer pantsuit is appropriate for business. A cocktail dress will be required for most social occasions.

Ecuador

Cultural Note

In an effort to stabilize the economy and slow inflation, Ecuador adopted the U.S. dollar as its national currency in 2000.

Egypt

Arab Republic of Egypt
Local short form: Misr
Local long form: Jumhuriyat Misr al-Arabiyah
Former: United Arab Republic (with Syria)

Egypt

Cultural Note

Arabic is read from right to left, rather than left to right—the direction of writing in English and modern European languages. An Arabic-language magazine or book starts at what would be the last page or back cover in the United States. Businesspeople bringing sales literature to Egypt should make sure that all the materials, even items printed in English, have an impressive back cover.

 WHAT'S YOUR CULTURAL IQ?

1. TRUE or FALSE? Egypt was primarily a Christian nation until it was conquered by Muslim Arabs in A.D. 642.

   ANSWER: TRUE. Egypt still has a large minority of Coptic Christians.

2. Which of the following describes the political system of Egypt in the twentieth century?
   a. British protectorate
   b. Constitutional monarchy
   c. Republic
   d. All of the above

   ANSWER: d. The British protectorate over Egypt ended in 1922. It was followed by a constitutional monarchy, which was overthrown in 1952. Egypt today is a republic.

3. Match the following Egyptian Nobel Prize laureates with the correct category:
   a. Naguib Mahfouz   1. Nobel Peace Prize
   b. Anwar al-Sadat   2. Nobel Prize in chemistry
   c. Ahmed Zewail   3. Nobel Prize in literature

   ANSWERS: a. 3: Mahfouz won the 1988 prize in literature; b. 1: President Sadat shared the 1978 peace prize; c. 2: Zewail shared the 1999 prize in chemistry.

▶ TIPS ON DOING BUSINESS IN EGYPT

- Egypt is one of the most westernized nations of the Middle East. You will encounter some international executives who are very familiar with Western business customs. Other Egyptian executives may have traditional Arab manners. Be prepared for any extreme.
- As a general rule, keep both feet on the ground. Traditional Arabs do not cross their legs when sitting. Never show the bottom of your foot to an Egyptian; this is considered offensive. Even when a person removes his or her shoes (as when entering a Mosque), the soles of the shoes are placed together, preventing the sole from being pointed at anyone.
- Adjustments foreigners must make include the work week (Friday is the Islamic Sabbath, so the work week runs Saturday through Wednesday) and Ramadan (the month of fasting, when no one eats or drinks during the day).

Cultural Note

The terms "Upper Egypt" and "Lower Egypt" are oriented to the flow of the Nile—not our geographic concepts of North and South. Consequently, Lower Egypt is in the north of the country and ends at the Mediterranean. Upper Egypt ends in the south at the border with Sudan.

▶ COUNTRY BACKGROUND

History

Egypt's recorded history dates back 7,000 years. Protected by deserts on both sides, ancient Egypt achieved unprecedented levels of wealth, architecture, and culture. But its wealth made it an irresistible target of powerful outside states. The Persians occupied Egypt in 525 B.C. Later occupying forces included Alexander the Great, then the Roman Empire, various Islamic rulers (including the Ottoman Empire), and finally Great Britain, which established a protectorate over Egypt. For more than 2,000 years, the rulers of Egypt were not Egyptians.

Under Ottoman control, the French were allowed to build a canal connecting the Mediterranean and the Red Sea. This Suez Canal was completed in 1869. Claiming that the Suez Canal was endangered, the British sent troops to occupy Egypt in 1882. They would remain in control until 1956.

The First World War broke the final bonds between Egypt and the Ottoman Empire. Under British control, Egyptian troops were sent to fight Ottoman control of the Arabian peninsula. Nationalist disturbances broke out in 1919, and the British granted Egypt independence in 1922. But the British remained influential and manipulated the constitution to keep nationalists from gaining control.

During the Second World War, Egyptian territory was invaded by Italian and German troops. The Axis threat to Egypt was ended with the Allied victory at El Alamein in 1942.

The Kingdom of Egypt came to an end with the 1952 revolution, which marks the beginning of the Republic of Egypt. Both the British and the profligate King Farouk were eventually thrown out of the country. Gamal al-Nasir (known as Nasser in the West) emerged as Egypt's leader. Nasser played the great powers off against each other in the Cold War. He nationalized the Suez Canal (which almost provoked an invasion by the United Kingdom, France, and Israel) and accepted aid from the USSR to build the massive Aswan High Dam project.

From 1958 to 1961, Egypt and Syria were joined into the United Arab Republic. The experiment failed, and Syria withdrew from the union, although Egypt continued to be known as the United Arab Republic until 1971.

In 1967, Egypt closed the Suez Canal to Israeli shipping. Israel retaliated with an air strike that effectively destroyed the Egyptian Air Force. In the subsequent Six-Day War, Israel also routed the combined forces of Egypt, Jordan, and Syria. Israel occupied a large amount of formerly Arab territory, including Egypt's Sinai.

General Nasser died in 1970 and was succeeded by Vice President Anwar al-Sadat. In 1973, Egypt and Syria launched a surprise attack on Israel. Although Israel again came out on top, Egyptians felt that the improved performance of Egyptian troops restored their country's honor.

Sadat stunned the Arab world by visiting Israel in 1977, where he negotiated directly with Israeli Prime Minister Menachem Begin. The following year, at negotiations in the United States, Egypt and Israel hammered out a peace treaty. Over the next few years, the Suez Canal was reopened to Israeli shipping and Israel withdrew from the Sinai.

President Sadat's overtures to Israel were bitterly opposed by various groups within and without Egypt. Muslim extremists and other opponents within Egypt were silenced by mass arrests. In retaliation, Anwar al-Sadat was assassinated by religious extremists in 1981. He was succeeded by Vice President Hosni Mubarak in a smooth transition of government.

Type of Government

The Arab Republic of Egypt is a democratic republic. The president is the chief of state. The prime minister is the head of the government. The main legislative body is the People's Assembly, which has elected and appointed members. There is also a consultative council called the Shura; its function is mostly advisory. Under the current government, the judiciary has increased its independence. The legal system is derived from European models, primarily the French Napoleonic Code, but it is also influenced by Islamic law.

For current government data, check with the Embassy of Egypt at *www.egyptembassy.us*. Another interesting site is *www.arab.net/egypt/index.html*.

Cultural Note

Terrorist violence occasionally breaks out in Egypt, but it does not usually affect non-Israeli foreigners. The speaker of the Egyptian Assembly was assassinated in October of 1990 by Islamic Jihad, the same group responsible for the death of President Anwar al-Sadat in 1981. A number of tourists (mostly German) were killed in 1997.

In general, Egyptians are friendly and hospitable. However, Egypt faces serious economic and population problems, and sometimes, when Arab populations see no hope in political or economic solutions, Islamic Fundamentalism gains strength.

Language

The official language of Egypt is Standard Arabic. Linguists have identified eleven languages in Egypt, five of which are different versions of Arabic. One of these eleven languages, Coptic, is now extinct except for its use by the clergy of the Coptic Church.

Most businesspeople who work with foreigners speak English, French, or both.

The Egyptian View

About 90 percent of Egyptians are Sunni Muslims, and most of the remaining 10 percent are Coptic Christians. (The Copts are the direct descendants of the ancient Egyptians.) Before 1952 there were some 80,000 Jews in Egypt, but as a result of Arab-Israeli tensions, only a few hundred remain.

After centuries under foreign rule, the Egyptian people are intensely proud that their leaders are now native Egyptians. However, there is widespread discontent with the current regime. The current government is supported by the West because (it is believed) open elections would bring Muslim fundamentalists to power. The ruling class that dominated the country's politics and economy before 1952 is now much reduced in influence but will still be encountered in business affairs.

Living in Egypt requires patience. Few things seem to happen on time. Traffic is often gridlocked; the bureaucracy takes forever. The three words heard most often in Egypt are *bokra* (tomorrow), *insha'allah* (God willing), and *malesh* (never mind).

With a huge population and chronic unemployment, Egypt used manpower for services that are automated elsewhere. For example, instead of mailing utility bills, they have been delivered by hand.

Islam puts great value on charity. Consequently, there is little shame in begging in Egypt, and you will find beggars everywhere. They compete with taxi drivers, porters, trinket sellers, and others for cash from foreigners. Some Egyptians rely on irregular sources such as these for their entire living.

☑ Know Before You Go

Egyptians are manic drivers. Traffic lights tend to be ignored unless there is a police officer physically present to enforce it. Amazingly, they also tend to drive at night without turning their headlights on. (Some Egyptians believe headlights deplete their car battery; others turn them on and off to warn other drivers.) Foreigners should not attempt to drive; hire a driver.

Consequently, the greatest hazard to visitors comes from Egyptian traffic—not only when you are in a vehicle, but when you are on foot. Pedestrians must be on guard against unpredictable Egyptian drivers. Where sidewalks exist, cars may drive up on them.

If you travel outside populated areas, be aware that mines are still present from former conflicts. Minefields are not necessarily marked, although they are usually enclosed by barbed wire.

As in other Middle Eastern nations, Egypt has armed soldiers patrolling the streets and other public areas.

Egypt's crowded cities are heavily polluted, with poor air quality. Egyptians are also inveterate smokers. (Environmental protection—whether regarding air pollution or the damage to marine life caused by the Aswan High Dam—is still in a nascent stage in Egypt.)

▶ CULTURAL ORIENTATION

Cognitive Styles: How Egyptians Organize and Process Information

Egyptians are open to information that does not conflict with Islamic values. They tend to be more open to Western ideas than people in other Arabic cultures. Most Egyptians are trained to think associatively, so information is processed from a subjective, experiential perspective. Islamic law is adhered to in all situations, which leads to a universalistic outlook. However, this same law says that one trusts brothers and cousins before outsiders because you must take care of your own, and this is a particularistic (not universalistic) trait.

Negotiation Strategies: What Egyptians Accept as Evidence

Faith in the Islamic ideology is the primary source of truth. This truth is modified by the personal feelings one has about the problem or situation. The highly educated may use facts and reason objectively.

Value Systems: The Basis for Behavior

The Islamic religion is a critical component in Egyptian life, playing an important role in all aspects of social structure. Solutions to all problems are in the correct interpretation and application of Islamic law. The following three sections identify the Value Systems in the predominant culture—their methods of dividing right from wrong, good from evil, and so forth.

Locus of Decision-Making

The male leader is the locus of decision-making, but he makes decisions through the consensus of the group or collective. The individual Egyptian is always subordinate to the family, tribe, or collective. Leadership and identity come from a person's lineage and his or her ability to protect the honor of the extended family. This is a kinship culture with little social identity outside the network of kin relationships.

Sources of Anxiety Reduction

The family is the cornerstone of the individual's social identity. Security is found in family loyalty and absolute submission to Islamic law. The most deeply held values—honor, dignity, and security—are available to an individual only as part of a larger kin group.

In accordance with the precepts of Islam, one's destiny is in the hands of God. Furthermore, Egypt has historically had a stable, static society, in which an individual's job and destiny has been determined by his or her birth. Therefore, the status quo tended to be accepted.

Issues of Equality/Inequality

Within Islam all believers are equal and united in the *ulema*. There is some ethnic bias against the Bedouin nomads and the Nubians. Egypt is under the social, political, and cultural dominance of a small elite, and there is great disparity between rich and poor. Education is the best way for Egyptians to achieve upward mobility, but there are no guarantees—the unemployment rate is high, and many Egyptians with good educations work in menial jobs.

Men and women are not treated as equals. Women make up a relatively small percentage of the work force. While there are women in prestigious jobs like physicians and professors, few women achieve top executive positions in business.

▶ BUSINESS PRACTICES

Punctuality, Appointments, and Local Time

- Punctuality is not a traditional virtue in Egypt. Your client may be late for an appointment or not show up at all. However, as a foreigner, you should endeavor to be prompt.
- It is standard Arab practice to keep supplicants (including foreign businesspeople) waiting. Until you get to know your clients, it is unwise to schedule more than one appointment per day.
- Don't forget that Cairo has some of the worst traffic jams in the world. Delays are frequently caused by traffic.
- An appointment is rarely private among traditional Arab businesspeople. Expect your visit to be interrupted by phone calls and visits from your client's friends and family. Westerners frequently find these distractions infuriating; try to maintain your equanimity.
- Friday is the Muslim holy day; no business is conducted. Most people do not work on Thursdays, either. The work week runs from Saturday through Wednesday.
- Working hours for businesses, banks, and government offices are truncated during the month of Ramadan.
- Government hours are generally 8:00 A.M. to 2:00 P.M. Government offices are usually closed on either Thursday and Friday or Friday and Saturday (the variation is designed to reduce traffic on congested Cairo streets).
- Business hours vary widely. In the winter, many businesses close for much of the afternoon and reopen for a few hours in late afternoon. A typical business schedule would be 8:00 A.M. to 2:00 P.M. in the summer; 9:00 A.M. to 1:00 P.M. and 5:00 P.M. to 7:00 P.M. in the winter.

- Remember that the Islamic calendar uses lunar months of 28 days, so an Islamic year of 12 months is only 354 days long. Holidays will thus be on different dates (by the Western calendar) every year. Any listed Muslim holiday dates are approximations because they depend upon actual lunar observations.
- Paperwork should carry two dates, the Gregorian (Western) date and the Hijrah (Arabic) date. Be aware that Christian Egyptians (Copts) have yet another calendar, different from both of the above.
- Egypt is two hours ahead of Greenwich Mean Time (G.M.T. +2), or seven hours ahead of U.S. Eastern Standard Time (E.S.T. +7).

Cultural Note
Egyptians often consider their country to be a bridge between the European West and the Arab East. Thus, business practices may resemble European or Arab practices or anything in between.

Negotiating
- The pace of business is much slower in Egypt than it is in the West. Be patient.
- Business meetings always start gradually, with long inquiries into one's health and journey.
- Egyptians operate at their own pace. Trying to force them into making a decision will probably be futile, if not counterproductive.
- An Egyptian will not even consider doing business with you until he knows and likes you. Thus, the social aspects of a deal are just as vital as the business ones.
- Egyptians love language. Expect long discussions, using poetic language, emotional viewpoints, and hyperbole.
- You are required to have an Egyptian agent to do business in Egypt. If you are working in both Cairo and Alexandria, it is recommended that you have a separate agent for each city.
- Business cards should be printed in your language on one side and in Arabic on the other. (Remember, Arabic is read right-to-left. Adjust your graphics and text accordingly.)
- Your Web site designer should consider how Arabic is read as well. Colors, symbols, graphics and text should be reviewed by local Egyptian contacts before final launch.
- Egyptians speak at a much closer distance than do North Americans or northern Europeans. Do not back up or shy away. There is also more physical contact, and conversations usually involve touching (but not between the sexes).
- Coffee is often served toward the end of a business meeting. This is a signal that the meeting will soon conclude. Incense may be lit at this time as well.
- Arab men often walk hand-in-hand, although westernized Egyptians rarely do this. If an Egyptian holds your hand, take it as a sign of friendship.
- Arabic is a language of hyperbole. When an Egyptian says "yes," it usually means "possibly." Be encouraged by this, but do not assume that the negotiating is over.

- Preserving one's dignity is vital to Egyptians. You may have to compromise on issues to avoid embarrassing your contact.
- Do not bring up the subject of women unless your Egyptian counterpart does so first. Do not even inquire as to the health of an Egyptian's wife or daughter.
- The topic of Israel should similarly be avoided.
- Egyptian achievements, both ancient and modern, are good topics of conversation.
- Positive discussions of sports are appropriate. Soccer (football), basketball, and boxing (in which Egypt has won several Olympic medals) are the most popular sports. Horseracing, tennis, and all water-related sports (especially sailing and swimming) are also popular.
- While foreigners should make a point of visiting the pyramids and the antiquities museum, do not be surprised if some Egyptians are ambivalent about these tourist sites. Some Muslims dislike them because they were built by pagans; others dislike the fact that they represent a huge waste of resources to glorify the Pharaohs.
- Egyptians are fond of jokes and often make fun of themselves (Egyptian bureaucracy is a favorite target). However, no matter how self-deprecating their humor gets, you should never make light of Egypt or the Egyptians.

Business Entertaining
- Hosting visitors is considered a virtue among Egyptians, so they will take care of much of the entertaining within their country.
- Be prepared to remove your shoes before entering a building. Follow the lead of your host.
- In Egypt, the male guest of honor is traditionally seated to the right of the host (rather than at the opposite end of the table).
- Remember that alcohol and pork are prohibited to strict Muslims. If you invite an Egyptian to a social event, make sure that there are nonalcoholic drinks available.
- Some Egyptians will use Western eating utensils and have Western furniture in the home. Others eat Arab style, using only their right hand and sitting on a carpet.
- Traditionally, if you are invited to dine in an Egyptian home, it is considered insulting if you add additional salt to your food. Doing so implies that you find their hospitality lacking.
- In all but the most formal restaurants, the proprietor may visit your table and converse for a while. Egyptians consider this being hospitable, not being intrusive.
- Do not eat everything on your plate. Leaving a little food is a sign that you have had enough.

PROTOCOL

Greetings
- Since there are several styles of greetings in Egypt, it is safest to wait for your Egyptian counterpart to initiate the greeting, especially at a first meeting.

- Westernized Egyptian men shake hands with other men.
- Some Egyptian men will shake hands with Western women. Western businesswomen should wait for an Egyptian man to offer his hand.
- Most women are employed in the service and professional sectors. There are many female secretaries and physicians, but relatively few female executives. When you encounter a woman decision-maker in business, she will probably be very Western-oriented in her behavior. You can count on her to initiate a handshake, with either men or women.
- A traditional Arab male will not necessarily introduce his wife. Follow his lead; if he acts as if she isn't there, you should do the same.
- A more traditional Arab greeting between men involves each grasping the other's right hand, placing the left hand on the other's right shoulder, and exchanging kisses on each cheek. However, kisses are always between members of the same sex. Men may kiss men, women may kiss women, but men and women may not kiss in public.
- The verbal component of an Egyptian greeting is effusive. Tradition demands that an Egyptian welcome you several times at your first meeting.

Titles/Forms of Address

- Westerners frequently find Arabic names confusing. The best solution is to request the names—written in your native language—of any Egyptians you will meet, speak to, or correspond with. Find out both their full names (for correspondence) and how they are to be addressed in person.
- Egyptian names are written in Arabic. In part because short vowels are not written in Arabic, translating from Arabic to other alphabets is not an exact science. Thus, Arabic names may be spelled several different ways in English; for example, the revered name of the Prophet has been rendered various ways, including: Mohammed, Muhammad, Mohammad, or Mohamed.
- In general, Egyptian names are written in the same order as English names: title (if any), given name, sometimes a middle name (often a patronymic), and surname (family name). Thus, the former leader of Egypt was President Anwar al-Sadat; his title was president, his given name was Anwar, and al-Sadat was his family name.
- The term al (also written as el) literally means "from" in Arabic. A name like al-Barudi could mean "son of Barudi" or "from the town of Barudi." Do not mistake the term al for the Western nickname Al (short for Alex or Albert).
- Most Egyptians should be addressed by title and surname (e.g., Doctor al-Nahhas), just as you would address a westerner. Some Egyptians prefer title plus first name. In writing, use the full name. If an Egyptian does not have a title, just use "Mr.," "Mrs.," or "Miss."
- Egyptians may address one another in different ways, depending upon the setting. An Egyptian you were on a first-name basis with at a party might address you by your title in a business meeting.

Gestures

- The left hand is considered unclean in the Arab world. Always use the right hand in preference to the left (unless you are handling something that is considered unclean). Never eat with the left hand, and avoid gesturing with the left hand.
- While Egyptians constantly gesture with their hands while speaking, they do not point at another person. This would be considered impolite.
- As a general rule, keep both feet on the ground. (See "Tips on Doing Business in Egypt").
- The "thumbs-up" gesture is rude throughout the Arab world.
- A gesture meaning "calm down" or "wait a minute" is accomplished in this way: with your palm facing you, touch all your fingers to your thumb, and bob your hand up and down (as if you were weighing something).

Cultural Note

Not only do Egyptians speak to each other at a closer distance than North Americans, they naturally gravitate toward others in public. In a nearly empty theater, an Egyptian may choose the seat next to you. On public transportation, when you are sitting alone on a long seat, an Egyptian might sit right next to you instead of at the other end. This does not necessarily mean that he or she wants to talk to you.

Gifts

- If you are invited to an Egyptian home, bring a gift of baked goods or chocolates. Flowers are acceptable for very westernized Egyptians, but they were traditionally used at funerals and weddings.
- Sometimes a beautifully made compass can be a good gift. A compass enables a devout Muslim to always know where Mecca is, even when traveling.
- Small electronic gadgets make popular gifts.
- Make sure you give or receive gifts with the right hand, not with the left (although using both hands is acceptable).

Cultural Note

Egyptians are a hospitable people. Many are eager to establish friendships with foreigners. However, in Egypt, friends are expected to do favors for each other. These favors can range from small gifts to help in getting paperwork to work abroad. And your obligations are not limited to just one friend—they extend to your friend's entire extended family, which may include dozens of cousins.

Of course, favors are reciprocal. Your Egyptian friend (and his or her relatives) will be happy to accompany you on errands, to tourist sites, and to suggest places you never would have seen without a native guide. Your friend may help you deal with Egyptian utilities and bureaucracy. And you will be invited to visit your friend's many relatives.

Dress

- While foreigners are not exempt from Egyptian standards of modesty, do not immediately adopt traditional native clothing. Egyptians may find it offensive to see foreigners dressed in their traditional clothes.
- Despite the Egyptian heat, most of the body must remain covered.
- Men should wear long trousers and a shirt, preferably long-sleeved. A jacket and tie are usually required for business meetings. Keep shirts buttoned up to the collarbone. Men should avoid wearing visible jewelry, especially around the neck. (Gold jewelry is prohibited to observant Muslim men.)
- While few urban Egyptian women wear traditional clothing, all women—including foreigners—are expected to wear modest clothing in public. The neckline should be high, and the sleeves should come to at least the elbows. Hemlines should be well below the knee, if not ankle-length. The overall effect should be one of baggy concealment; a full-length outfit that is tight and revealing is not acceptable. Pants or pantsuits are not recommended. While a hat or scarf is not always required, it is wise to keep a scarf at hand. The suitability of your attire will be apparent as soon as you venture out; if Egyptian men stare lewdly at you, your dress is not sufficiently modest.

Cultural Note

Although we think of Egypt as a hot, desert destination, it can get uncomfortably cold in the winter. Many Egyptian homes are not heated. If you are staying in an Egyptian home in the winter, dress accordingly.

Finland

Republic of Finland
Local short form: Suomi
Local long form: Suomen Tasavalta

Cultural Note

The Finns are incorruptible—at least they were in 2003. The annual Corruption Perception Index (by Transparency International) rated Finland number 1 out of 102 countries ranked worldwide. Transparency International compiles reports on corruption and bribery around the world. For more information on this nongovernmental organization, headquartered in Germany, see *www.transparency.org*.

WHAT'S YOUR CULTURAL IQ?

1. Which of the following languages is mutually intelligible with Finnish?
   a. Estonian
   b. Hungarian (Magyar)
   c. Swedish

   ANSWER: a. Finnish, Estonian, and Hungarian are all members of the Finno-Ugric linguistic family, but only Finnish and Estonian are mutually intelligible. Hungarian has diverged too much for Finns and Hungarians to understand each other. Swedish, Danish, and Norwegian (or English, for that matter) are all Indo-European languages.

2. Finland did not become an independent nation until the twentieth century. TRUE or FALSE? The Russians ruled Finland for almost 600 years.

   ANSWER: FALSE. Although Russia occupied Finland off and on throughout recorded history, it only subjugated Finland for one extended period, from 1809 to 1917. The Swedes ruled Finland for some 600 years.

3. TRUE or FALSE? Although ice hockey and football (soccer) are extremely popular, the Finnish national sport is a variation of baseball.

   ANSWER: TRUE. Since its introduction in 1922, Finnish baseball, known as *pesäpallo* (a.k.a., *pesis*), is played by Finnish schoolchildren.

TIPS ON DOING BUSINESS IN FINLAND

- At the present time, Finland boasts the highest Internet and mobile phone penetration rates in the world. However, Finnish business is not all silicon-based. The country is still a leader in the paper and shipbuilding industries. Every fourth cruise ship is constructed in Finland.

- Finland is the closest Nordic nation to the former USSR. This makes it ideally located to conduct business with Russia and the Baltic Sates of Lithuania, Latvia, and Estonia. Currently, more than 40 percent of the European Union's shipments via truck to Russia travel across Finnish roads. When Scandinavia is added to Northwestern Russia and the Baltic States, there are 80 million prospective customers surrounding Finland!
- Unlike the other major Scandinavian (and European) languages, Finnish is not an Indo-European language. Finnish is in the Finno-Ugric linguistic group. Recognize the differences, and be particularly careful to avoid blunders in translations.

▶ COUNTRY BACKGROUND

History

The Finnish people have maintained their separate cultural identity throughout recorded history, despite centuries of domination by either their fellow Scandinavians or the Russians. Swedish involvement in Finland began in 1172, when Pope Alexander III charged the Swedes to protect Catholic missionaries in Finland. The Swedes eventually established control over the Finns and converted them to Catholicism. This lasted until 1397, when Queen Margaret I of Denmark established the Kalmar Union. This temporarily united all of Scandinavia under the Danish crown. Eventually, control of Finland returned to Sweden.

Gustavus Vasa, king of Sweden, replaced Catholicism with Lutheranism in Sweden and Finland in 1527.

Twice during the eighteenth century the Russians occupied Finland, causing great destruction. The first occupation lasted for eight years, a period the Finns refer to as the Great Wrath. The Russians later returned for a two-year occupation (the Small Wrath), and again many Finns were slain.

Russia overran Finland in 1808 during the Napoleonic Wars. Sweden was forced to cede Finland to Russia. The Russians insisted that Finland's capital be moved to Helsinki from its traditional site of Turku.

During the tumult of the Russian Revolution, a newly elected Finnish Parliament assumed all powers formerly held by the Czar in 1917. Finland was soon declared an independent republic.

From January to May of 1918, Finland was torn by a civil war. The government was supported by the Whites, who largely represented the anti-Communist, middle-to-upper class, Swedish-speaking Finns. The Whites received aid from Germany and use German-trained Finns, who are called the Jägers. The Reds tended to be poor, rural, Finnish-speaking Communists; they were assisted by the Russian troops. The civil war ended in a White victory. At the start of the Second World War, Finland declared its neutrality. However, the USSR wanted to secure the approaches to Leningrad and demanded that Finland cede certain territory in return for parts of Soviet-controlled Karelia. When the Finns refused, Soviet armies invaded Finland on November 30, 1939, initiating the Winter War. Finnish troops fought bravely but were eventually overwhelmed. Russia annexed Finnish land, and some 400,000 Finns moved, rather than live under Soviet rule.

When Nazi Germany attacked the USSR in 1941 the Finns again proclaimed their neutrality. But German use of Finnish territory led the Russians to bomb Finnish cities. Finland then declared war against the USSR, emphasizing that the Finns were not allies of Germany but merely cobelligerents. This conflict is referred to by the Finns as the Continuation War.

After a prolonged standstill, Marshal Carl Mannerheim (Finland's greatest war hero) was installed as president of Finland in August of 1944, with a mandate to secure peace. An armistice with the USSR was signed on September 19.

Finland (along with Austria and Sweden) became a member of the European Union on January 1, 1995.

Cultural Note
Helsinki is the northernmost national capital on the European continent.

Type of Government

Finland is a multiparty republic. In the executive branch, the president is the head of state and shares power with the prime minister, who is chief of government. The president is elected and serves for six years. The prime minister and other members of the cabinet, or Council of State, are appointed by the president. They are not necessarily affiliated with a certain party. There is a legislative house. Many coalition governments have existed over the last century; rarely does a single party have a majority.

Women are totally accepted in high levels of government and business. In 1906, Finland was the first country to grant women the right to vote. Many women hold seats in Parliament, and have served as Cabinet ministers.

Finland's social welfare system is highly developed and includes health and child care allowances.

For current government data, check with the Embassy of Finland, at *www.finland.org*.

Language

Finland has two official languages: Finnish and Swedish.

English is the most popular third language, and business may be conducted in English.

During the last century, Finns who grew up speaking Finnish were required to study Swedish in school, while Swedish-speaking Finns had to study Finnish. This has changed, but many Finns are multilingual.

Finnish is written in the Roman alphabet. The Finnish language does not utilize the sounds we associate with the letters *b, c, f, w, x,* and *z.* Consequently, these letters are not used in traditional Finnish words. (Of course, they do appear in words borrowed from other languages.) There are many double letters; this indicates that the sound is twice as long when spoken. About half of the words in Finnish begin with the letters *k, t, p, r,* and *v.* Two vowels—*a* and *o*—may use umlauts. The *å* and the *ø,* which are found in other Scandinavian languages, do not appear in Finnish. For foreigners who want to learn Finnish, Finnish words are almost always pronounced exactly as spelled.

J. R. R. Tolkien, author of *The Hobbit* and *The Lord of the Rings,* was an amateur linguist. He reportedly based his fictional Elvish language on Finnish.

Ethnologue has listed eleven different languages spoken in Finland.

Finland

Cultural Note

Sisu is a Finnish word that is difficult to translate. One translation would be "never say die"—but that does not sufficiently convey the fatalism inherent in sisu. Perhaps a more accurate translation would be "I may not win, but I will gladly die trying."

Sisu is more than a motto; it reflects the indomitable spirit of the Finnish character. It is a belief of a people who were known as "the Bloody Shield of Sweden" during the centuries that Finland provided the armies that protected their Swedish rulers. It also sustains a nation that has fought forty-two wars with the Russians—and, although they lost every one, fought bravely.

The Finnish View

There is no official religion in Finland. Most Finns belong to the Evangelical Lutheran Church of Finland, which is part of the worldwide Church of Christ. There is a Finnish Orthodox Church, patterned after the Greek Orthodox Church, which accounts for a small percentage of Finns. Nonreligious Finns make up about 12 percent of the population; the remaining is split between many different denominations. The Evangelical Lutheran Church of Finland maintains a Web site in English at *www.evl.fi/english/page.html.*

Unlike the Kingdoms of Denmark, Norway, and Sweden, Finland is a republic. Furthermore, while Danes, Norwegians, and Swedes all speak similar, mutually intelligible languages, the Finnish tongue is different. Finnish is quite alien to them; a Dane can no more understand Finnish than he could understand Swahili or Chinese.

Finland's isolation and harsh environment has left its mark on the Finnish character. Many Finns attribute their stoic personality traits to their unforgiving environment.

While Finland is well provided with woods, its stone is particularly difficult to work. Whereas other Scandinavian countries built houses of stone, the Finns built their homes out of flammable wood. Time and again Finnish towns and cities have burned to the ground. As they rebuilt their homes over and over, the Finns developed a pessimistic outlook combined with an indomitable will.

Certainly, a willingness to fight the Russians after losing forty-two wars to them displays an astonishing degree of determination.

The proliferation of mobile phones in Finland seems to have made Finns more comfortable with small talk, at least among the young. Interestingly, there was a trend toward more (not less) social formality in the 1990s. This involved using the formal form of address, rather than the more egalitarian informal form.

And finally, their language serves to isolate the Finns. Their Finno-Ugric tongue, incomprehensible to all outsiders (except for the approximately 1 million Estonians), puts a distance between the Finns and the rest of the world.

☑ Know Before You Go

The primary hazard to visitors comes from the Finnish weather. Finland's winter is cold and snowy.

Aside from that, Finland is a very safe country. Most visitors to Finland come away from a visit with no more damage than a hangover from trying to keep pace with Finns.

 ## CULTURAL ORIENTATION

Cognitive Styles: How Finns Organize and Process Information

The Finns are generally cautious toward outside information. New products and new ways of doing things are viewed with circumspection. However, once a product is accepted, the Finns enthusiastically make it their own. Finnish higher education has become more conceptual, with information being processed from an analytical perspective rather than a subjective, associative one. Finns tend to follow universalistic laws and rules of behavior rather than considering each situation as a unique problem.

Finns are a very low-context people. The Finns expect people to say what they mean and mean what they say. The Finnish propensity for silence can make them seem opaque to outsiders.

Negotiation Strategies: What Finns Accept as Evidence

The Finns have faith in their own indomitable determination to survive despite a harsh environment. Objective facts are preferred over subjective feelings. The Finns have a very competitive business environment; expect them to be tough negotiators.

Value Systems: The Basis for Behavior

Traditionally, Finns know how to fight, but they also know how to get along. The term *Finlandisation* refers to the acquiescence of a small nation, Finland, to demands of a larger, more powerful, neighbor—the USSR. Finland is also a social welfare state with strong humanitarian and environmental concerns.

The following three sections identify the Value Systems in the predominant culture—their methods of dividing right from wrong, good from evil, and so forth.

Locus of Decision-Making

The individual is expected to make decisions within the boundaries of the social welfare system. There is an emphasis on individual initiative and achievement, with a person's ability being more important than his or her station in life. Although the dignity and worth of the individual is emphasized, there is a strong feeling of obligation to help those who are not able to help themselves. Finns cherish their right to a private life and personal opinions.

Sources of Anxiety Reduction

Finns use laws and morality to give structure to their worldview.

The strong social welfare system and a strong nuclear family give Finns stability and security. This reduces life's uncertainties and the anxiety that comes with them. Finns are highly nationalistic, with a liberal philosophy of tolerance for dissent and deviation.

Issues of Equality/Inequality

Finland has an egalitarian society with a largely homogeneous population. While class differences exist, they are minor compared to many European countries. There is also a belief that hard work should be rewarded.

Finland is basically a middle-class society where the government helps with family needs. The minimizing of social differences also minimizes the evidence of poverty and wealth.

Child care is considered a priority, with husbands and wives sharing the responsibilities. Finland also boasts one of the most gender-neutral societies in the world.

And, of course, the Finnish sauna is a very egalitarian tradition. It is difficult to behave in an elitist manner if one is nude.

▶ BUSINESS PRACTICES

Punctuality, Appointments, and Local Time

- The Finns are one of the most punctual people in the world. Lateness demonstrates an insulting lack of concern.
- The residents of Finland, like most Europeans, write the day first, then the month, then the year (e.g., December 3, 2010, is written 3.12.10 or 3/12/10).
- Finns may take four or five weeks of vacation per year.
- Avoid business travel to Finland in July, August, and early September, when many Finns will be away on vacation.
- Finland is two hours ahead of Greenwich Mean Time (G.M.T. +2) or seven hours ahead of U.S. Eastern Standard Time (E.S.T. +7).

Negotiating

- As previously noted, the Finns have a highly competitive business culture. Expect them to be tough negotiators.
- A mix of British English and American English may be spoken. Titles reflect the British style (for example, the CEO is the managing director, etc). While it is considered courteous to have all materials translated into Finnish, it is not strictly required.
- The Finns tend to be more comfortable talking than writing. They prefer to communicate over the telephone or in person, rather than via e-mail or formal correspondence.
- Avoid any attitude of superiority.
- The propensity of Finns to remain silent for extended periods of time confuses some foreign negotiators. The Finns are comfortable being quiet and somewhat unemotional in public—so you should not be put off by long silences.

Cultural Note

Finns do not have a tradition of group cooperation. Managers from the United States and the United Kingdom sometimes complain that the Finns are not good "team players." (Of course, this view is subjective—the Japanese often consider workers from the United States and the United Kingdom to be uncooperative and too individualistic.) The Finnish lack of "team spirit" is not due to an unfamiliarity with team sports; most Finns play several team sports in school.

Business Entertaining

- Finns love coffee—cafés are everywhere, and breakfasts can be quite substantial.
- Lunch is usually eaten sometime between 11:00 A.M. and 1 P.M. In the past, a business lunch included alcohol and could last for as long as three hours. Today, 90 minutes is about average, and alcohol is rarely served.
- Although drinking has diminished somewhat in recent years, Finns may still engage in prodigious bouts of alcohol consumption. Pace yourself—drunk-driving laws are very strict in Finland.
- It is perfectly acceptable to converse about business during a meal. This may be one reason that Finland's businesses are considered among the most competitive in the world.
- In Finland, the guest of honor at a meal has specific duties. He (or she) is seated to the right of the host. He may not eat until everyone has been served, and should not drink until the host proposes a toast. After the meal, the guest of honor may make a short speech, which includes thanking the host for the meal.
- The cold table (buffet) is known as *voileipapoyta*.
- Good topics of conversation include Finnish history, politics, cuisine, sports, technology, hobbies, travel, and the traditions of the sauna. Avoid personal questions.
- The Finns also have a tradition of social dancing, especially their own version of the tango. Comparing the Argentine and Finnish tango is also a topic of interest.

- Most affluent Finns have a summer cabin away from the cities; their activities there make a good topic of conversation. Favorite rural activities include hiking, fishing, and mushroom picking.
- Finns love reading about their country in foreign books and publications. Make note of favorable mention about Finns or Finland in your country's press.

▶ PROTOCOL

Greetings

- Finns of all ages and genders usually greet each other with a brief, firm handshake. It should be accompanied by eye contact and a nod of the head. Even children are encouraged to shake hands.
- Finns do not often touch in public and are not particularly comfortable with additions to handshakes that involve touching (such as a hand on the arm or shoulder).
- Embraces are reserved for close friends and relatives.

Titles/Forms of Address

- Names in Finland are written in the same order as those in most of Europe: first name followed by the surname.
- Finns usually introduce themselves with their full name, minus academic or professional titles.
- In a business or academic setting, Finns expect to be addressed by their title and surname. Finns without a title may be addressed with an honorific (Mr./Mrs./Miss) and surname.
- Younger Finns are more comfortable using first names.

Gestures

- It is not appropriate to fold your arms: this signifies arrogance or a close-minded position.
- A toss of the head is a motion for "come here."
- Finns are not comfortable with physical contact such as backslapping.
- It is not polite to talk with your hands in your pockets.
- Sitting with the ankle resting on the knee is too casual.
- Look people directly in the eye when conversing.

Gifts

- Gift giving is not normally a part of doing business in Finland. Indeed, the Finnish reputation for honesty makes the giving of gifts problematic; a gift must not be interpreted as a bribe. Never bring a business gift to the first meeting.

- Fiskars scissors (with the orange handles) are a commonly imitated Finnish product. Avoid giving any type of gift that may compete with them.
- Personal gifts at a friend's home can include a good bottle of wine, flowers, books on a topic of interest to your client/friend/host, or something particularly meaningful from your home country.

Dress

- The weather in Finland is the primary determinant of clothing. Visitors should dress to stay warm, but be aware of local styles.
- Weather conditions aside, Finns are not an ostentatious people and prefer conservative clothing. Businesspeople still generally wear suits.
- If you are asked to be a guest at a Finn's summer cabin, he or she probably has a selection of outdoor gear to lend you, such as boots and rain slickers.

Finland

Cultural Note

"The Finns design products

The Swedes build them

The Danes market them

And the Norwegians buy them."

This is an old Norwegian saying, referring to the relative skills of the Scandinavian peoples. The Finns have often produced striking designs, while the Swedes have Scandinavia's largest manufacturing capacity, and the Danes are known for their salesmanship abilities.

France

French Republic
Local long form: République Française

> ### Cultural Note
> French attitudes about time are different from most of those in Northern Europe, the United States, or the United Kingdom. Surprisingly, a French businessperson might give an excuse for being a few minutes late to a meeting, yet say nothing if he is a half-hour late. No insult is intended by tardiness. To the French, life is complex and many things occur that can cause a delay. People and relationships are always more important than a soulless schedule. (Of course, there are exceptions—some executives will be as punctual as their exquisite watches.)

 WHAT'S YOUR CULTURAL IQ?

1. The French consider conversation to be an art. Which of the following are characteristic of most French conversations?

   a. Attentive listening
   b. Waiting for the other person to finish
   c. Scrupulous accuracy
   d. None of the above

   ANSWER: d. French conversation tends to be nonlinear. People frequently interrupt each other—even if the speaker has not finished answering a question. Cleverness is considered more important than accuracy.

2. TRUE or FALSE: It is probably useless to complain to the management about unsatisfactory service in a small French shop.

   ANSWER: TRUE. A store manager feels such loyalty to an employee that he or she usually supports the employee against the customer—even if the employee is in the wrong. "The customer is always right" is not a French aphorism.

3. TRUE or FALSE: Joan of Arc inspired the French to defeat the English during the conflict which came to be known as the Thirty Years' War.

   ANSWER: FALSE. It was the Hundred Years' War—which actually lasted 116 years, from 1337 to 1453.

TIPS ON DOING BUSINESS IN FRANCE

- During negotiations, the French may want to express every possible objection. It is not necessary to respond to each and every single statement—French conversational habits encourage all opinions to be voiced, even if they are not critical to the outcome.

- Before you ask for directions, assistance, or just plain information, apologize for not speaking French! You are in France, and the French will appreciate your acknowledgment that you cannot speak French well—if at all.
- Learn proper dining etiquette (including the identification of all the utensils) before you attend a formal French dinner. Understand the seven courses in a Parisian restaurant, in what order they arrive (soup, fish, sorbet, meat or fowl, salad, dessert, coffee) and study a bit about the wines of France. And never cut the point off the brie! (The best part of the brie is at the center, because there is less rind and more cheese. It is rude to leave just the edge of the wheel of brie, which is typically heavier on the rind, for the next diner.)
- Cultural Quote: "How can you be expected to govern a country that has 246 kinds of cheese?"—Charles de Gaulle

Cultural Note

France has a civil law system, rather than a common law system. Commercial agreements are short because they refer to the legal code. Many businesspeople have studied law and can draw up their own contracts. Parties to an international contract may choose which country's laws will govern it.

▶ COUNTRY BACKGROUND

History

The cultural roots of the French go back to the Celtic Gauls, who were conquered by Julius Caesar in 51 B.C. Five hundred years later, Clovis extended Frankish rule over much of Europe. Charlemagne is often considered the true founder of France; during his rule (A.D. 768 to 814), he made France the center of the Holy Roman Empire. But under Charlemagne's successors, both France and the Holy Roman Empire fell into disarray.

Some regions of France came under the control of English kings. The Hundred Years' War (1337–1453) ended with the English expelled from France by Charles VII—aided by Joan of Arc.

The Reformation made inroads into Catholic France, primarily in the form of the Huguenots, causing a series of civil wars. Eventually, most Protestants left, and France remained a Catholic nation.

The Thirty Years' War (1562–1698) devastated Central Europe. The great French ministers Richelieu and Mazarin successfully maneuvered to make France the leading power in Europe; France also annexed Alsace.

The French Revolution of 1789 abolished feudalism and absolute monarchy but failed to establish democracy. France was held together by Napoleon I, who established the First Empire. France was at war for most of his reign, which ended in France's defeat by a European coalition in 1815.

Like most of Europe, France suffered badly in the First World War (1914–1918). Unlike some European countries, France emerged from the war with its democracy intact. The Great Depression brought a radical-socialist-communist Popular Front alliance to power, which introduced many social reforms.

France entered the Second World War in 1939 and was soon overrun by Nazi Germany.

The Germans allowed the extreme right to set up a puppet dictatorship under Marshall Petain in Vichy. Resistance to the occupation was maintained by the Free French under de Gaulle.

The Allies landed in France at Normandy in June 1944, and the German occupation force was pushed back. Officials from de Gaulle's organization in Algiers and local Resistance leaders took over the administration. The war ended the following year. Trials of those who collaborated with the Nazis occupied postwar France for years. In 1957, France joined with five other Western European powers to form the EEC (European Economic Community), a common market of 165 million people largely unencumbered by tariff barriers. This eventually evolved into the European Union.

In 1968, students at the University of Paris, protesting police brutality, went on strike and occupied university buildings. Their example set off strikes of students and workers throughout the country, and by the third week of May, the country was virtually paralyzed by a general strike.

President Charles de Gaulle announced a referendum on two constitutional reforms and declared that he would resign if the voters should reject his proposals. In the voting on April 27, 1969, 53 percent of the voters cast negative ballots, and de Gaulle resigned the next day. Georges Pompidou succeeded de Gaulle in the elections held after his resignation.

Georges Pompidou died in 1974 and the Independent Republican candidate, Valéry Giscard d'Estaing, was elected president.

François Mitterrand replaced Giscard as president in 1981, following a Socialist victory at the polls.

The former prime minister, Jacques Chirac, won the French presidency in 1995 with 52.6 percent of the vote.

France refused to participate in the 2002 war against Iraq and strongly opposed the U.S.–led invasion.

Cultural Note

The first woman to serve as prime minister of France (albeit for only ten months) was Edith Cresson. Labeled "incredibly maladroit" at politics, this controversial politician claimed that the Japanese were successful economically because of their "antlike qualities" and declared that one in every four British men were "homosexuals" (presumably those who did not flirt with her). Subsequently, she became a senior EU official and, in 2003, was charged with fraud and abuse of confidence by Belgian prosecutors.

Type of Government

France is a multiparty republic. The head of the government is the prime minister; the president is chief of state. The French people elect the president and the two houses of Parliament. The president, who appoints the prime minister, serves for five years. The president has a large share of the power, including the right to dissolve the lower house of Parliament, the Assemblée Nationale, and call for new elections. According to the constitution, it is the government and not the president that decides on national policy.

For current government data, check with the Embassy of France, at *www.info-france-usa .org*, which can also provide guides on doing business in France.

Language

The French people are very proud of their language, which was the international language of diplomacy for centuries. The ruling classes of countries as distant as Russia and Mexico spoke French in preference to their own indigenous tongues. The fact that English is now the international language of finance, science, and aviation is inconsequential; the French believe their language is still superior. If you do not speak French, it is advisable to apologize for this—because as far as they are concerned, you are in France, and you should know French.

Many French businesspeople speak English but will prefer to conduct their meetings in French.

Ethnologue, at *www.Ethnologue.com*, lists twenty-eight different languages spoken in modern France—there are rapidly declining regional dialects and languages (Provençal, Breton, Alsatian, Corsican, Catalan, Basque, Flemish, etc.). Literacy is at 99 percent.

France

> ### Cultural Note
> In 1966, the French government established a commission to combat Franglais, a mixture of French and English. The Haut-Comité pour la défence et l'expansion de la langue Française created French terms to replace words borrowed from English.

The French View

There is no official religion. France is principally a Catholic country (70 percent), although new immigrants are raising the percentage of Islam (5–10 percent). Many other religions, including Protestantism and Judaism, are present, and there are also many people unaffiliated with any religion.

Are the French unfriendly? No—but they can be difficult to get to know. The average French citizen develops personal relationships with many people—including local sales clerks. Customers go to the same store, year after year, and get to know everyone in the shop. So much is accomplished through personal contacts in France that they do not feel any obligation to be deferential to strangers. Historically, the French have considered foreigners who grin and chat with strangers as either condescending or idiotic.

The strong tendency to build long-term networks is reflected in the French mode of communication. Prior to any major meeting, the French will generally talk with their contacts about any delicate issues that may arise on the agenda. They are thoroughly informed by their networks before, during, and after most meetings.

This dedication to maintaining and expanding one's network is vital to sales processes in France. French interviewers actually inquire, "Who do you know?" far more often than "What have you done or sold?" Sales managers care more about your potential network of leads and contacts than your closing ratio. Sales executives will have a variety of major networks—through their parents, their schools, industry contacts, clubs, associations, etc. Employers value that access and may prefer a candidate with excellent potential networks rather than the one with the largest tax return.

(As an aside, French interviewers may also do handwriting analyses of job candidates! The French use graphology to determine predominant work characteristics.)

Managers often have strong relationships with their employees. They feel responsible for their staff, treat them like family, and will back them in a dispute.

☑ Know Before You Go

The weather can be hazardous—with everything from flooding to drought, windstorms in the winter months to avalanches in the spring. Near the Mediterranean, they are prone to forest fires.

The island of Corsica has been under French rule since they invaded in 1769. In the 1960s, terrorist groups that craved independence became active—primarily utilizing homemade bombs. The bombings became an almost daily feature of life in Corsica—and escalated to as many as 700 a year in the 1980s. Recently, the island's growing Arab community has been the new target of these attacks. Be cautious when planning your visit.

▶ CULTURAL ORIENTATION

Cognitive Styles: How the French Organize and Process Information

The French will readily accept information for the purpose of debate and may change their minds quickly, but strong ethnocentrism will not allow the acceptance of anything contrary to the cultural norm. Ideas are very important to them, and they approach knowledge from an analytical and critical perspective. They look at each situation as a unique problem and bring all their knowledge to bear on it.

Negotiation Strategies: What the French Accept as Evidence

Arguments tend to be made from an analytical, critical perspective with eloquent rhetorical wit and logic. There is a great love for debate, striving for effect rather than detail and image over facts. Feelings and faith in some ideology may become part of the rhetoric.

Value Systems: The Basis for Behavior

Pride in their heritage sometimes makes them appear egotistical in their behavior. The following three sections identify the Value Systems in the predominant culture—their methods of dividing right from wrong, good from evil, and so forth.

Locus of Decision-Making

The French are strongly individualistic and have a centralized authority structure that makes quick decisions possible. The relationship between the participants becomes a major variable in the decision-making process. An individual's self-identity is based on his or her accomplishments in the social realm. Education is the primary variable in social standing. Individual privacy is necessary in all walks of life.

Sources of Anxiety Reduction

The French seem to be preoccupied with status, rank, and formality. Contacts are of utmost importance, and they may have a low tolerance for ambiguity in one's station. They feel comfortable with rules and regulations. If the French are provided with adequate details and assessments, they are more comfortable with business risks. Their attachment to a public figure gives them a sense of security. Yet, individuality is preferable to conformity. People are allowed to show both positive and negative emotions in public.

Issues of Equality/Inequality

An informal stratified class system still exists, but most people are middle class. Superiors expect obedience from subordinates in all walks of life. Power is a basic fact of society, and leaders with the ability to unify the country or group are highly prized. Gender roles in society are fluid, and a person's status is more important than his or her sex.

▶ BUSINESS PRACTICES

Punctuality, Appointments, and Local Time

- Always make appointments for both business and social occasions. Be punctual, although the French are more relaxed about time in the South.
- Most French get four or five weeks of summer vacation and take it in July and August. Indeed, except for the tourist industry, France virtually shuts down in August. Try to conduct business during other months.
- A law in 2004 created a full working day without salary, which reduced the number of public holidays in France by one day. Called a "solidarity journey," this day can be applied to any official holiday the company's employees select. If they cannot decide on which day should be the working day/holiday, it automatically forfeits to Pentecost Monday.
- Always present your business card. When receiving the cards of others, treat them very carefully.

- It is best to have your business card printed in French upon arrival. One side can be in English, with the translation in French on the other side. On the French side, include any academic credentials and your school if it is a prestigious one.
- The best times to schedule meetings are around 11:00 A.M. or 3:30 P.M.
- France is one hour ahead of Greenwich Mean Time (G.M.T. +1). This makes it six hours ahead of U.S. Eastern Standard Time (E.S.T. +6).

Cultural Note

Most English-speaking French have studied British-style English, which can lead to communication breakdowns with speakers of American-style English. For example, in the United States, a presentation that "bombs" has failed, but in England, it has succeeded.

Words in French and English may have the same roots, but different meanings or connotations. If you don't speak French, don't be offended too easily. For example, a French person might "demand" something, because demander simply means "to ask." If you speak some French, don't assume that an English word will have the same connotation in French. For example, if you ask for the bathroom and use the translation salle de bains, it will not be understood that you are asking for la toilette.

Negotiating

- Eye contact among the French is frequent and intense—so much so that some Asians and North Americans may be intimidated.
- Because of the strong "old-boy network" and lack of merit-based promotions, employees stick to their job descriptions. Know who does what. If you are in charge of a service-oriented company, make it a policy to promote your French nationals based on good service, because your French management may not do so. Be sure to effectively communicate your company's standards for service.
- The French are known for their formal and reserved nature. A casual attitude during business transactions will alienate them.
- During negotiations, the French may make you seem to be the demandeur (petitioner), thus putting you in the weaker position.
- Hierarchies are strict. Junior executives will pass a problem on to a superior. Try to cultivate high-level personal contacts.
- Women should not mistake French gallantry for condescension.
- Don't start a conversation by asking personal questions.
- Don't mistake a high-pitched voice and excited gestures for anger; they usually just mean great interest in the subject.

Business Entertaining

- Business can be conducted during any meal, but lunch is best.
- Though the French are familiar with "le power breakfast," they are not enthusiastic about it.

- Business lunches usually last one to one and a half hours. Dinner is late (8:00 or 9:00 P.M.).
- At a business lunch or dinner, show enthusiasm about the food before beginning a business discussion.
- The business drink should not be held in a café; they are too noisy. Try a quieter venue.
- Whoever initiates the meal or drink is expected to pay.
- Reservations are necessary in most restaurants, except in brasseries and in hotels. In choosing a restaurant, stick to French rather than ethnic ones.
- The French have a great appreciation for good conversationalists.
- When eating, keep both hands on the table at all times. Food comes gradually, so don't fill up too soon. When finished, place your fork and knife parallel across your plate.
- Cheese is served toward the end of the meal.
- Don't drink hard liquor before meals or smoke between courses. The French believe this deadens the taste buds.
- Respect privacy. The French close doors behind them; you should do the same. Knock and wait before entering.

▶ PROTOCOL

Greetings
- Always shake hands when being introduced or when meeting someone, as well as when leaving. In general, the woman offers her hand first. French handshakes do not usually involve a strong grip.
- In social settings, with friends, expect to do *les bises*, or touching cheeks and kissing the air.

Titles/Forms of Address
- Find out the titles of older French people you meet and address them in that way, both during the introduction and in the course of conversation. Even simple titles like "Madame" should be used as you converse, whether in English or French.
- Use "Madame" for all women except young girls.
- Don't use first names until you are told to do so. Don't be put off by the use of last names; it doesn't mean that the French are unfriendly. If you speak French, use the vous form until you are told to use tú.
- The French sometimes say their last names first, so that Pierre Robert might introduce himself as "Robert, Pierre." Ask!

Gestures
- The "thumbs-up" sign means "okay"; the North American "okay" sign (forming a circle with thumb and forefinger) means "zero" in France.
- Slapping the open palm over a closed fist is vulgar.

- To call for the check, make a writing gesture.
- Don't chew gum in public!
- Men may still stand up or make a move to stand up when a visitor or a superior enters the room.

Gifts

- Don't give a business gift at your first encounter.
- Avoid gifts that are either too lavish or too skimpy, as well as gifts with your company logo. Good taste is everything.
- You can insert a business card with your gift, along with a small card that states: "with the compliments of Mr./Madame. . . ."
- Good gifts include books or music, as they show interest in the intellect. Bring American bestsellers, especially biographies. The thicker and more complex the book, the better; simplicity is not a virtue in France.
- Bring flowers (not roses or chrysanthemums), fine chocolates, or liqueur to the host. Present them before, not after, the party.
- For thank-yous, send (at least) a note the next day.

Dress

- Clothes are very important in France. This is not surprising; the very words used in English to describe fashion—"haute couture," "chic," etc., are from the French language. The term haute couture dates back to 1908.
- Not everyone in France owns an extensive wardrobe, but what they do own is expensive, well made, and fashionable. Affluent executives purchase the best suits and styles possible.
- The French also tend to have excellent posture, which makes their clothes look even better.
- In the north and in the winter, men should wear dark suits.
- North American men should be aware that French suits are cut differently.
- Never be the first to remove your jacket or tie. Let your colleagues make the first move toward a more relaxed look.

> **Cultural Note**
> Bringing a bottle of wine is a common gesture when visiting friends around the world—would it be an appropriate gift for dinner at a French client's home?
>
> Probably not. As a citizen of France, your host may be a serious oenophile and has likely taken great pains to carefully select the correct wines for each course. Unless your charming little vintage is of interest because it is from your home country, it implies that you know more about wine than your host does. Or, by bringing your own bottle, you may inadvertently communicate that you have doubts about the quality of his or her wine cellar.

France

Germany

Federal Republic of Germany
Local short form: Deutschland
Local long form: Bundesrepublik Deutschland
Former: German Empire, German Republic,
German Reich

Cultural Note

Most Germans feel a deep connection to the environment. The historical image of brave German tribesmen successfully resisting the Roman Empire, fighting amidst the vast, majestic forest, is as important to Germans as the conquest of the western frontier is to North Americans. Germany was one of the first countries where a political party with an environmental platform (the Greens) won seats in a national legislature.

 ## WHAT'S YOUR CULTURAL IQ?

1. Ever since Martin Luther, Germany has been divided between Protestants and Roman Catholics. TRUE OR FALSE: Whatever their religious beliefs, most Germans are fond of a Catholic saint named King Gambrinus.

   ANSWER: TRUE. King Gambrinus is the patron saint of beer drinkers and brewers. German legend even credits him with the invention of beer. Many German breweries and taverns display an inscription honoring Gambrinus.

2. German literature is known for profound, serious authors. Which one of the following is the bestselling German author of all time?
   a. Johann Wolfgang von Goethe (1749–1832)
   b. Heinrich Böll (1917–1985)
   c. Günter Grass (1927–)
   d. Herman Hesse (1877–1962)
   e. Thomas Mann (1875–1955)
   f. Karl May (1842–1912)

   ANSWER: f. An author of cowboy-and-Indian adventures, Karl May was (and is) very popular in Germany.

3. In 1948, Adi Dassler started a now-famous company. In 1954, Mr. Dassler's company garnered tremendous publicity when Germany's entire soccer team wore his product and won the World Cup for the first time. TRUE OR FALSE: His company made sneakers.

   ANSWER: TRUE. Adidas do not really stand for "All Day I Dream About Sports" (or Soccer). The brand is a combination of the first three letters of his names.

TIPS ON DOING BUSINESS IN GERMANY

- In business matters, Germans do not like the unexpected. Sudden changes—even if they may improve the outcome—are unwelcome.
- Whether you know German or use your own language, speak in complete sentences. Make it obvious when a sentence is complete; don't let your sentences trail off. In the German language, the most important word in a sentence is usually the final one. Germans are in the habit of listening for the end of a sentence and can be annoyed if it doesn't materialize.
- The trade fair (a.k.a., trade show) was largely invented in Germany. Germany hosts almost two-thirds of the international trade fairs, so participation in their conferences is key.

Cultural Note

Like many things in Germany, advertising is highly regulated. It is illegal in an advertisement to compare your product to that of a competitor's product. You can say that your product is "#1", but you will be required to prove that with objective data. If you cannot, your ad may be pulled from the airwaves by the German government.

▶ **COUNTRY BACKGROUND**

History

After the fall of the Roman Empire, Germany was unified under Charlemagne, who established a kingdom that encompassed much of western Europe in A.D. 800. Charlemagne divided his holdings among his sons, and the first all-Germanic kingdom dates back to this division.

The first strong German king was Otto I, who defeated invading Danes, Slavs, and Magyars (Hungarians). In A.D. 926, Pope John XII crowned Otto I as the emperor of the Holy Roman Empire, a loosely organized domain that stretched from Germany down into northern Italy. To modern Germans, this Holy Roman Empire was the "First Reich."

The Holy Roman Empire encompassed many semiautonomous principalities that often fought with each other. The internecine warfare increased after Martin Luther's successful Reformation in 1519. Some areas remained Roman Catholic while others adopted Protestant beliefs. This conflict cumulated in the Thirty Years' War (1618–1648).

In 1740, Frederick II ("the Great") became ruler of Prussia. He greatly expanded Prussia's territory by annexing small German principalities (not to mention about a third of Poland). Prussia soon became one of Europe's great powers and began competing with Austria for leadership among the German-speaking peoples.

Napoleon I conquered most of Germany in 1806. This led to the dissolution of the Holy Roman Empire.

By the eighteenth century, two German-speaking kingdoms had come to dominate Central Europe: Prussia and Austria. Austria felt it was in its interest to keep the German principalities separate; Prussia wanted to unite (and rule) them. Austria's Metternich succeeded in replacing the Holy Roman Empire with a loose union called "the German Confederation" (the Bund). But Prussia eventually won out when Prime Minister Otto von Bismarck led his country into war, first against Denmark, then against Austria and the Austrian-allied German kingdoms, then against France.

As a result of Bismarck's efforts, the Prussian King William I was crowned Kaiser (emperor) of all Germany in 1871. The German nation dates its existence from this event. This "Second Reich" was to last until Germany's defeat in the First World War.

After the First World War, Germany became a republic. Burdened with enormous war reparations and the Great Depression, Germany fell into the hands of the "National Socialists," as they are known to Germans—the term "Nazi" was rarely used within Germany. The atrocities of Adolf Hitler's "Third Reich" present a moral dilemma that each new generation of Germans must face.

At the end of World War II, Germany was occupied by England, France, the United States of America, and the USSR. This resulted in the division of Germany into the capitalist, NATO-allied Federal Republic of Germany (FRG) and the Communist, Warsaw Pact German Democratic Republic (or GDR). Berlin was also divided into West and East. Consequently, Bonn was selected as the capital of West Germany. Only the changed priorities of Mikhail Gorbachev's Soviet Union allowed the two halves of Germany to reunite on October 3, 1990.

As the largest and most populous nation in the European Union, the reunited Germany has developed into a leading power, and one of the strongest members of the EU.

Type of Government

The reunited Federal Republic of Germany is a democratic federal multiparty republic. Voting is done by proportional representation. There are two legislative houses: the Federal Council and the Federal Diet. The president is the chief of state, and the chancellor is the head of the government.

The government's preoccupations include issues pertaining to the former East Germany. One current hot-button issue is the war on terrorism and the invasion of Iraq. In the past a staunch U.S. ally, Germany vigorously opposed the Second Gulf War.

Abjuring from military intervention after the Second World War, Germany influenced the world via "checkbook diplomacy," contributing far more than its share to international organizations. Germany gave much more to the European Union than it gained in return. However, Germany can no longer afford to be so generous.

In 2005 Germany elected its first female chancellor, Angela Merkel. For current government data, check with the Embassy of Germany at *www.germany-info.org*.

Language

The official language of Germany is German, which is called *Deutsch*. Ethnologue.com has identified twenty-seven languages spoken in Germany, two of which are now extinct. The extant languages include variants of German as diverse as Bavarian and Yiddish.

German has many dialects. The accepted national dialect is High German (or *Hochdeutsch*). It gained prominence after Martin Luther translated the Bible into High German in 1534. Low German *(Plattdeutsch)* was spoken in many low-lying northern regions of Germany.

English and French are currently the preferred foreign languages that Germans study. This is especially true among executives. Germans who grew up in the former German Democratic Republic were forced to study Russian in school. This is no longer the case, but you will find fewer English speakers in eastern Germany.

Cultural Note

German is now printed in Roman fonts similar to the typeface used in this book. The German typefaces known in English as "Gothic" (Germans refer to the most common forms as "Fraktur" or "Schwabacher") were dropped in the 1930s when studies indicated they were harder to read than Roman typefaces.

The German View

The population is split almost evenly between Roman Catholics and Protestants (mostly of various Lutheran sects). Many Germans describe themselves as nonreligious. There are small populations of Jews and Muslims.

The majority of immigrants are Turkish Muslims. Although Germany's aging population needs their labor, their presence is of great concern. Many Germans feel that the Turkish immigrants make an insufficient effort to adopt German customs. Violence against Turks occasionally breaks out.

Germany's powerful economy has been in the doldrums since the 1990s. Restrictive labor laws and high taxes made Germany an unwelcome place for foreign investment. Unemployment has remained relatively high. Many observers believe that Germans are unwilling to allow their industry the flexibility to compete in the global market.

German manufacturing has a reputation for high quality, which German consumers demand. Any instances of quality control failure are cause for worry among German society, not just the individual company involved.

Almost all Germans profess a love of nature. Many Germans enjoy outdoor activities, such as hiking, bicycling, camping, and skiing. They also enjoy long vacations to take advantage of their country's scenic landmarks. Most Germans get at least six weeks of paid vacation per year, plus numerous paid holidays and sick days with partial pay.

Germany

☑ Know Before You Go

The greatest hazards to visitors tend to be vehicular accidents. There is also the danger from exposure to cold during Germany's bitter winters.

Periodic flooding is a serious danger and has caused much destruction in low-lying areas.

Avalanches and landslides are also hazards. Germany has an active Green Party, which maintains that Germans are in danger from the many toxic waste sites in the former East Germany, as well as from Russian-built nuclear power plants throughout eastern Europe.

▶ CULTURAL ORIENTATION

Cognitive Styles: How Germans Organize and Process Information

Germans have historically been closed to outside information, and they did not freely share data among units of the same organization. However, the younger generation is becoming more open. Germans are analytic and conceptual in their information processing. They are strongly committed to the universal beliefs of their culture. Friendships are not developed quickly, but they are deep and highly selective.

Negotiation Strategies: What Germans Accept as Evidence

Data, data, data: Germans depend upon objective facts. Emotional involvement is unacceptable in negotiations. Once a position is decided upon, Germans rarely budge, which gives them the reputation for being tough negotiators.

A strong faith in their social democratic ideology influences Germans' perceptions of the truth.

Value Systems: The Basis for Behavior

One may find some differences in the value systems between what was once East and West Germany. There are also generational differences: for example, the postwar generation is less burdened by guilt over Nazi atrocities. The following three sections identify the Value Systems in the predominant culture—their methods of dividing right from wrong, good from evil, and so forth.

Locus of Decision-Making

A desire to seek consensus and a widespread respect for order are German characteristics. This is reflected in the German phrase: *"Ordnung muss sein"* (There must be order!). Every German has a responsibility to follow the rules, both written and unwritten. Actions that disrupt this social order are seen as inherently wrong. Decisions must be made in reference to larger units: society, one's company, and one's family.

Curiously, the ability of Germans to compartmentalize allows for substantial individual freedom. As long as an individual's duties to society and employer are met, Germans have a wide latitude for private individual behavior.

Germany

Decision-making is slow and involved, as all peripheral concerns must be taken care of in the process. Once a decision is made, it is unchangeable. Individual privacy is necessary in all walks of life, and personal matters are not discussed in business negotiations.

Sources of Anxiety Reduction

Germans have a fairly high index of uncertainty avoidance. As a result, Germans use laws and morality to give structure to their worldview. Germans tend to be risk-averse and cautious about making decisions. They also buy every conceivable sort of insurance: life insurance, fire insurance, theft insurance, travel insurance, personal liability insurance, and so on.

As the German population ages, it can be expected that Germans will become even more risk-averse.

Universal rules and regulations combined with strong internal discipline give stability to life and reduce uncertainty. There is a high need for social and personal order, and a low tolerance for deviant behavior. There is very little show of emotion because of strong internal structures and control.

Germans are more oriented toward near-term issues. German skepticism about the future (economic, political, and social) can breed anxiety and pessimism. There is a sense of helplessness about humanity's ability to produce a desirable outcome in the long-term.

Issues of Equality/Inequality

Titles of nobility were gradually abolished after the First World War, but Germany still has a class system with very little flexibility. Business leaders tend to come from the upper class. Although equality is guaranteed by law, German businessmen sometimes denigrate women as "lacking self-confidence" and "unable to command male subordinates." This is changing, as evidenced by the 2005 election of Angela Merkel, the first female Chancellor of Germany. One thing is clear: Germans respect self-assurance. If you don't project it, whatever your gender, you will not be well-received in Germany.

▶ BUSINESS PRACTICES

Punctuality, Appointments, and Local Time

- Nowhere in the world is punctuality more important than in Germany. Be on time for every appointment, whether for business or social engagements.
- Arriving just four or five minutes late can be insulting to a German executive, especially if you are in a subordinate position.
- When writing the date, Germans write the day first, then the month, then the year (e.g., December 3, 2010, is written 3.12.10 or 3/12/10).
- Appointments should be made well in advance. Give at least one week's notice for an appointment made by telephone. If you don't have that much lead time, a short preliminary meeting may sometimes be arranged on a few days notice.

- E-mail has substantially changed the process for setting up appointments in Germany. Both the historical mode of communicating (sending a written letter to the firm in general rather than to an individual executive) and the lag time required for correspondence via the mail have been streamlined.
- Still, be aware that if your e-mail (or your posted letter) is addressed to an executive who is on vacation, the response may be a long time in coming. Most Germans take at least six weeks of (paid) vacation per year.
- If two Germans sign a business letter, or if more than one German is consistently copied on e-mail, this indicates that both of them must be in agreement before a decision is made.
- Do not schedule appointments on Friday afternoons; some offices close by 2:00 or 3:00 P.M. on Fridays. Many people take long vacations during July, August, and December, so check first to see if your counterpart will be available. Also be aware that little work gets done during regional festivals, such as the Oktoberfest or the three-day Carnival before Lent.
- In the former East Germany, businesses did not usually schedule appointments on Wednesdays. This has been changing since reunification.
- Germany is one hour ahead of Greenwich Mean Time (G.M.T. +1). This makes it six hours ahead of U.S. Eastern Standard Time (E.S.T. +6).
- Germans use a twenty-four-hour clock. In German, midnight is *null Uhr* (zero hour).
- When identifying a half-hour, the usage in German is unlike the usage in English. Where an Englishman might refer to 9:30 A.M. as "half-nine," a German may call the same time "half-ten." If you are in doubt, ask for clarification.

Cultural Note

German negotiators can be very tough customers. Many of them view being forced to compromise as a personal failure. As some observers have noted, "Germans come in expecting 110 percent. They might settle for just 100 percent."

Negotiating

- The pace of German corporate decision-making is methodical—much slower than in the United States or Great Britain.
- The decision-making process in German firms can be a mystery to outsiders. In addition to the official chain of command, German companies often have a parallel "hidden" series of advisers and decision-makers. The approval of this informal "kitchen cabinet" is mandatory.
- Directness is appreciated. Germans may bluntly criticize your product or your company; don't take it personally.
- Germans abhor hype and exaggeration. Be sure you can back up your claims with lots of data. Case studies and examples are highly regarded.
- Be prepared to supply reams of information at short notice. Some of the requests may seem trivial; be assured that they are important to the Germans.

- The German reputation for quality is based (in part) on slow, methodical planning. Every aspect of the deal you propose will be pored over by various executives. Do not anticipate being able to speed up this process. This slowness extends through all business affairs. Germans believe that it takes time to do a job properly.
- German punctuality does not extend to delivery dates. Products may be delivered late without either explanation or apology.
- Germans also take a lot of time to establish a close business relationship. Their apparent coldness at the beginning will vanish over time. Once they get to know you, Germans are quite gregarious.
- German bookkeeping practices historically allowed a high degree of secrecy. It was exceedingly difficult (if not impossible) to get a German company to reveal a true and accurate financial record. Due to new EU requirements, this is changing.
- Even if the German executives speak your language, all promotional materials and instruction manuals should be translated into German.
- Bring plenty of business cards; quite a few Germans may wish to exchange them with you.
- If your company has been around for many years, the date of its founding should be on your business card. If you have a large number of employees, that number should be included too.
- Since education is highly respected in Germany, consider including any title above the bachelor's level on your card.
- Germans may or may not socialize before getting down to work. It is quite possible that you will walk into an office and start talking business immediately after introducing yourself.
- If your German associates decide to chat at the beginning of a meeting, expect to be asked about your flight, your accommodations, where you are from, and so forth.
- Germans smile to indicate affection. They generally do not smile in the course of business, either at customers or at coworkers.
- Business is serious; Germans do not appreciate humor in a business context.
- Compliments tend to embarrass Germans; they expect to neither give nor receive them. They assume that everything is satisfactory unless they hear otherwise.
- When a problem arises, be prepared to explain it clearly, in detail, and unemotionally. You may have to do this in writing. Germans are not accustomed to informally "passing the word."
- Never follow the U.S. business habit of saying something positive before saying something negative. This compliment/complaint juxtaposition will sound contradictory to Germans, and they may reject your entire statement.
- Privacy is very important to Germans. Doors are kept closed, both at work and at home. Always knock on a closed door and wait to be admitted.

Germany

- Avoid asking personal questions of a German executive. If a businessperson wants you to know if he or she is married or has children, he or she will find a way to communicate this to you. Family life is kept separate from work in Germany.
- Obviously, embarrassing political questions should be avoided. Do not ask about the Second World War or anti-Semitism.
- Germans tend to be well informed about politics and to have firm political opinions. They are also honest and may tell you their opinions about your country (or its actions), even if these opinions are negative.
- Sports are a good topic for conversation. Many Germans are passionate soccer fans; skiing, hiking, cycling, and tennis are also popular. Less well-known sports enjoyed by Germans include ice-skating, curling, and gliding.

Cultural Note

Germany makes some of the finest beer in the world. A German beer drinker will be happy to explain about the local brews, especially the seasonal beers and the specialty brews like Berliner Weisse, a Berlin beer made from wheat.

Business Entertaining

- Breakfast meetings are still somewhat uncommon in Germany. However, business lunches are customary.
- At lunch, be aware that business may be discussed before and (sometimes) after a meal, but never during the meal itself. If you are invited out to a luncheon, you may offer to pay, but expect your host to decline your offer. Insist on paying only when you have made the invitation.
- Be on time to social events. Drinks are served before the meal, but usually with a few appetizers. The meal itself will start soon after.
- Germans do not often entertain business associates in their homes. If you are invited to a home, consider it an honor.
- When eating, always use utensils; very few items are eaten with the hands. Place your utensils vertically side by side on the plate when you are finished eating.
- If you smoke, always offer your cigarettes to everyone else before lighting up. Of course, ascertain if smoking is banned at your location.

Cultural Note

If you arrive late to a concert, production, or show, the doors will probably be closed, and you must wait until the intermission to gain access to the event.

▶ PROTOCOL

Greetings

- In business situations, most Germans shake hands at both the beginning and the end of a meeting.
- The German handshake may be accompanied by a nod of the head. Although this gesture is subtle, it is important.
- While Germans are open and generous with close friends, they tend to be formal and reserved in public. You will not see many smiles or displays of affection on German streets.
- The avoidance of public spectacle is reflected in the way Germans will get quite close to each other before offering a greeting. Only the young and the impolite wave or shout at each other from a distance.
- To get someone's attention, raise your hand, palm facing out, with only the index finger extended. Don't wave or beckon.
- When sitting, cross one knee over the other, rather than resting your ankle over one knee. Do not prop your feet on anything other than a footstool.
- The eldest or highest-ranking person generally enters a room first.
- Many traditional practices of etiquette have changed in the last few decades; however, if you are with senior executives, behave in the most formal, reserved manner possible.
- Never talk to someone while chewing gum.
- Expect to be hushed if you so much as cough while attending an opera, play, or concert. German audiences remain extraordinarily silent, rarely even shifting in their seats.
- Carry a good supply of business cards.
- Extended, direct eye contact is expected when conversing. Failure to meet a German's gaze will give the impression that you are untrustworthy.
- Never put your hands in your pockets for longer than it takes to retrieve an object. Germans find it insulting when people speak to them with their hands in their pockets.

Cultural Note

Germans keep a slightly larger personal space around them than do most British or North Americans, and a much larger personal space than most Latins. Stand about six inches beyond handshaking distance.

Germans are also protective about the positioning of their office furniture. When invited into a German office, do not move your chair closer; a German executive could find that very insulting.

This expanded personal space extends to their automobiles. Expect an outburst from a German driver if you so much as touch his or her car. Never put a package down on any car except your own.

Titles/Forms of Address

- The order of names in Germany is the same as in most of Europe: the first name followed by the surname.
- Traditionally, only family members and close friends addressed each other by their first names. You may never establish a close enough relationship with your older German colleague to get to a first-name basis; however, younger Germans will move more quickly to a first-name basis.
- When speaking to persons who do not have professional titles, use "Mr.," "Mrs.," or "Miss," plus the surname. In German, these titles are
  Mr. = *Herr*
  Mrs. (or Ms.) = *Frau*
  Miss = *Fräulein*
- Fräulein is now used only for young women (under age eighteen). Any businesswoman you meet should be addressed as "Frau," plus her surname, whether or not she is married.
- It is very important to use professional titles. Attorneys, engineers, pastors, and other professionals will expect you to address them as "Herr" or "Frau" plus their title. This goes for anyone with a Ph.D. as well (e.g., Herr (or Frau) Doctor/Professor). However, make sure you know the correct professional title.
- When entering or leaving a shop, it is considered polite to say "hello" and "goodbye" to the sales clerk.
- There are significant regional variations in behavior throughout Germany. For example, Bavarians have a reputation for being warm, hospitable, and casual: they tend to progress quickly from formal to informal speech and from surnames to first names. Do not expect northern Germans to behave this way.

Germany

Cultural Note

Many foreigners have described Germans as positively manic once they get behind the wheel of a car. Certainly pedestrians must keep an eye on the traffic, especially when crossing the street. However, even when driving, Germans tend to obey traffic regulations. Difficulties arise when foreigners do things that violate unwritten rules, such as jaywalking.

Gifts

- German businessmen do not give or expect to receive expensive gifts. A gift should be of good quality but not of exorbitant cost. Gifts that are small in size are preferred.
- German civil servants are prohibited from accepting any form of gift whatsoever.
- Appropriate gifts include good-quality pens, reasonably priced electronics (MP3 players loaded with music that your associate will like, etc.), or imported liquor. Gifts from your home region or country are good choices, such as an illustrated book of your home city.

- The only article of clothing considered an appropriate gift is a scarf. Other clothing, perfume, and soap are considered too personal.
- An invitation to dinner at a German home is considered an honor, and you should send a bouquet of flowers ahead of time for your host. The bouquet should not be ostentatiously large and should have an uneven number of flowers (but not thirteen). Do not choose red roses; they are reserved for courting. Also avoid such funeral flowers as white carnations, white chrysanthemums, and calla lilies. In Northern Germany, do not include heather in a bouquet. (Because of its hardy nature, heather is often planted on graves, and deemed bad luck to bring into a house.)
- While an imported liquor is appropriate, a gift of a locally available wine might be interpreted as saying that your host's wine cellar is inadequate. However, a good wine brought from your home country (one not sold in Germany) or a top-quality imported red wine will be appreciated.
- Germans make some of the finest beers in the world, so it is unlikely that you could bring a foreign beer that would truly impress them.
- Business gifts are usually given at Christmastime, although many German companies restrict themselves to sending Christmas cards and/or a calendar.
- For further guidelines on gift giving, visit *www.kissboworshakehands.com*.

Cultural Note

If your home region or country has any oddities, be prepared to discuss them. Germans are known for odd hobbies and enthusiasms. For example, Germany has many fans of odd facets of Americana; it is not unusual to run into a German aficionado of cowboy novels, jazz, or zydeco music. If one of your business associates is in this category, a gift from the United States in his or her area of interest (for example, a well-reviewed jazz CD or an Indian arrowhead) would be greatly appreciated.

Dress

- Business dress in Germany is very conservative. Virtually all businessmen wear dark suits, sedate ties, and white shirts. However, blue blazers and gray flannel pants are also considered formal. Khaki or seersucker suits are not acceptable! Women dress equally conservatively, in dark suits, pantsuits, and blouses of a neutral color.
- Follow the lead of your German colleague with regard to removing your jacket or tie in hot weather. Do not be surprised if he or she remains fully dressed in sweltering heat.
- Business wear is also appropriate for most formal social events: parties, dinners, and the theater. Remember that you are obliged to check your coat in German theaters; if you tend to be cold, bring a sweater. On the opening night of an opera, concert, or play, men are expected to wear their best dark suit or tuxedo, and women a long evening gown.
- Casualwear consists of comfortable shirts and jeans, although these clothes should be clean and in good repair. Most German men wear sandals during the summer.

Greece

Hellenic Republic
Local short form: Ellas or Ellada
Local long form: Elliniki Dhimokratia
Former: Kingdom of Greece

Cultural Note
Backgammon is the national pastime of Greece. Men can be found playing backgammon in every taverna. If you don't know how to play, learn before you go to Greece.

WHAT'S YOUR CULTURAL IQ?

1. Even people who have never studied ancient Greek literature and philosophy have heard of Homer (the blind poet credited with writing the *Iliad* and the *Odyssey*), and the great Greek philosophers Plato and Aristotle. TRUE or FALSE? All three of these men were contemporaries.

   ANSWER: FALSE. Plato and Aristotle were contemporaries; Plato was Aristotle's teacher. But Homer lived several centuries before them.

2. The Greek language is written in the Greek alphabet, which is over 2,000 years old. Which of the following alphabets did not evolve from the Greek alphabet?
   a. The Coptic alphabet
   b. The Cyrillic alphabet
   c. The Phoenician alphabet

   ANSWER: c. The Phoenician alphabet came before the Greek alphabet. In fact, it is believed that the Phoenician alphabet inspired the Greek alphabet. Other alphabets, including the Coptic (used by Christian Egyptians) and the Cyrillic alphabet (used by Russians, among others) evolved out of the Greek alphabet.

3. Although many Greeks have immigrated to the United States, there has been a substantial amount of anti-Americanism in postwar Greece. What is the source of this?
   a. During the Greek civil war of 1945–1949, the United States (and the United Kingdom) intervened against the Communists, who had considerable popular support.
   b. The United States supported the right-wing military junta of 1967–1974; the junta drove many Greeks into exile.
   c. During the Cypriot crisis of 1974, the Greeks felt that the United States sided with Turkey over Greece.
   d. All of the above.

   ANSWER: d. However, this animosity is not usually directed toward individual citizens of the United States.

TIPS ON DOING BUSINESS IN GREECE

- Greeks tend to be physically demonstrative. They kiss, hug, and walk arm-in-arm with both relatives and friends. Even Greek soldiers often walk arm-in-arm. This is not private behavior; it can be seen every day in the streets, to a degree that surprises visitors from northern Europe and North America.
- The Greek Orthodox Church forms an integral part of the Greek identity. Unlike Western branches of Christianity, Greek Orthodoxy stresses individual choice and does not emphasize guilt or shame. Some view this as important to the Greek character.
- Greek (also called "Hellenic") is written in the Greek alphabet, rather than the Roman alphabet used by most western European nations. (Even Turkey uses the Roman alphabet.) The Cyrillic alphabet used by the Russians and Bulgarians is derived from this Greek alphabet.

Cultural Note

Historic Macedonia stretches through several countries: Bulgaria, Greece, the former Yugoslavia, and Albania. For some 2,000 years, control of historic Macedonia switched from country to country. Greece now has a northern province called Macedonia, and the Greeks are adamant that no other country be allowed to use the name "Macedonia." Many Greeks feel that any non-Greek area that calls itself Macedonia is making a territorial claim to Greek Macedonia.

The existence of Macedonian separatists in Greek Macedonia makes this threat credible. Some Greek citizens in Greek Macedonia want to break away from Greece and form their own independent state. This is also a concern for neighboring countries. (For example, if Greek Macedonia became independent, the Macedonians in Bulgaria would strive to add their corner of Bulgaria to an independent Macedonia.)

▶ **COUNTRY BACKGROUND**

History

The ancient Greeks are credited with the invention of democracy. However, the democratic era of Athens was relatively short-lived and was followed by various forms of dictatorship. Occupation and domination by outsiders—Romans, Turks, and (in this century) Nazi Germany—has made the Greek people ferociously nationalistic.

During the Second World War, resistance to the German and Italian occupying armies was carried out by guerrilla bands, which fought each other almost as frequently as they fought the Nazis. With the end of World War II, Greece tried to form a democratic government, despite the presence of these competing guerrilla organizations.

The Communist guerrillas, seeing their brethren in neighboring Eastern European states come to power, decided to revolt. The Communist rebellion in Greece lasted from 1946 to 1949 and was ended only when neighboring Yugoslavia left the Soviet orbit. The Yugoslavs closed their borders to the Soviet-backed Greek Communists. The United States took over

Greece

the responsibility for Greek reconstruction from an impoverished Great Britain, and U.S. intelligence agencies worked frantically to deprive the Communists of any power in the new Greek government. In 1952 Greece joined NATO and allowed the United States to create military bases on Greek soil in 1953.

At the time, Greece was a constitutional monarchy. Distressed by the inability of the Parliament to maintain stability, in 1966 King Constantine II authorized the formation of an extraparliamentary government to rule until new elections could be held the following year. This resulted in a military coup d'etat in 1967, first ruling "in the king's name" and then, when the king tried to stage his own coup, without the king.

The junta, ruled by Colonel George Papadopoulos, gave Greece stability and a degree of economic prosperity at the cost of some human rights. By 1973, opposition to the authoritarian regime had grown strong enough that Papadopoulos decided to institute reforms. The monarchy was formally abolished, civil liberties were promised, and free elections were scheduled. But the head of the Greek military police, General Ioannides, staged a coup in late 1973 before the planned elections could be held.

Within a year this new coup had yielded to the demand for elections. The new Greek Republic was declared on December 9, 1974. A new constitution was adopted in 1975, and Greece has had peaceful transitions from one government to the next ever since.

Greece became a full member of the European Economic Community (now the EU) in 1981.

Despite fears that the facilities would not be completed in time, the 2004 Summer Olympic Games in Greece took place in a secure, efficient, and successful manner.

Type of Government

Today, Greece is a presidential parliamentary republic. Its constitution dates from 1975. There is a president elected by the Parliament and served by an advisory body, the Council of the Republic. The president is the chief of state. The real power is held by the prime minister, who is the official head of the government. The prime minister is the leader of the majority party of the unicameral Parliament. The Parliament is called the Greek Chamber of Deputies.

For current government data, check with the Embassy of Greece at *www.greekembassy.org*.

Cultural Note

There are two versions of the Greek language today. The popular form, known as Demotic, has been used in government documents and in the media only since 1976. Previously only Katharevousa, the "pure" language, was used for these purposes. Today Katharevousa is usually found in technical publications.

Language

Greek is the official language. It is written in the Greek alphabet, which was developed around 1000 B.C. The second most commonly spoken tongue is Romanian.

Today, the Greek people speak a form of the Greek language known as Demotic Greek. This is a modern form of the Ancient Greek spoken 2,000 years ago. Classical studies programs usually teach Ancient Greek, not modern Demotic Greek.

In addition to Greek, linguists have identified fifteen languages, two of which are now extinct. (One of the languages classified as extinct is Ancient Greek, which is still used as a liturgical language by the Greek Orthodox Church.)

The Greek View

The Greek Orthodox Church is the official religion, and 98 percent of Greeks are members. Greek Orthodox principles are learned in school, and the state supports the church. However, freedom of religion is guaranteed. There is a small minority of Muslims, Roman Catholics, Protestants, and Jews.

Much of Greece's rural population has lived in privation for generations. While the quality of life has improved since the end of the Greek civil war in 1949, the memory of poverty is strong. Some attribute the Greek tradition of hard bargaining to this adversity.

Rainfall is sparse in Greece, making fresh water a valuable commodity. Wildfires are common in the parched woods and fields. Greece is also subject to periodic seismic activity, such as the devastating earthquakes in 1999. This contributes to a sense that humans are not in control of their fate.

The environment is a serious issue in Greece. In addition to the severe air pollution in cities like Athens, Greece suffers from severe deforestation. Ancient Greece was a country of forests and wooded hills. Since classical times, the trees have been stripped for lumber, for charcoal, and for fuel. What man did not destroy, wildfires and goats did. Reforestation efforts are still in their infancy in Greece and are hampered by the country's sparse rainfall.

Some foreigners doubted the ability of the Greeks to host the 2004 Summer Olympic Games. The fact that the games were peaceful and successful was uplifting to the Greeks, although they now have to deal with the exorbitant cost of the event.

Many older Greeks opine that the younger generation is becoming too Europeanized and losing its respect for Greek tradition.

☑ Know Before You Go

The greatest hazard to vacationers in Greece is probably sunburn in the strong Mediterranean sunlight. For business travelers in Greece, the risk is split between vehicular accidents and petty street crime (such as pickpocketing).

Greeks are heavy smokers; it is estimated that 45 percent of adults smoke. Smoking in many public places was outlawed in September 2002, but people often ignore the rules. (Greece is also a large tobacco producer.)

▶ CULTURAL ORIENTATION

Cognitive Styles: How Greeks Organize and Process Information
Greeks are open to discussion of most topics but may find it difficult to change their position on issues. They process information more from a subjective, associative perspective than an objective, abstractive one. Interpersonal relationships are of major importance in the overall scheme of things. This leads them to consider the specifics of a situation rather than making decisions on the basis of universal rules or laws.

Negotiation Strategies: What Greeks Accept as Evidence
Subjective feelings are the basis for the truth, although faith in various ideologies (religion, ethnocentrism) may strongly influence the outcome. Objective facts will not be accepted if they contradict either of these.

Value Systems: The Basis for Behavior
Greece is the historical home of democracy. Although it has toyed with other forms of government, it has always returned to a democratic form of government. The following three sections identify the Value Systems in the predominant culture—their methods of dividing right from wrong, good from evil, and so forth.

Locus of Decision-Making
The individual is responsible for all decisions, but he or she takes into consideration those who depend on him or her (family, group, and so forth). A person's private life is influenced by family, friends, and organizations. Through this process an individual develops opinions. Friendships are deep and carry obligations. One must establish a relationship with his or her counterpart before negotiations can be successful. Education is the primary vehicle for moving up the social ladder.

Sources of Anxiety Reduction
Greeks have a high index of uncertainty avoidance. As a result, Greeks use laws and morality to give structure to their worldview.

It is one's role in the social structure, the extended family, and deep friendships that give structure and security to the individual. There is a strong work ethic, but a laid-back approach to life contributes to an image of much activity but slow progress. There is a strong need for consensus in groups. Failures are often attributed to external circumstances.

Issues of Equality/Inequality
There is a definite social hierarchy, with some bias against classes, ethnic groups, and religions. Greeks have an inherent trust in people because of the social interrelationships between extended families and friends. There are extreme contrasts between rich and poor,

but Greeks are people oriented, with quality of life and the environment being important considerations. Machismo is very strong.

▶ BUSINESS PRACTICES

Punctuality, Appointments, and Local Time
- Always be punctual, although you will note that punctuality is not generally stressed by your Greek counterparts.
- Scheduling an appointment is not always necessary, but it is courteous.
- It is not considered necessary to set a limited time for a business appointment.
- Greeks, like most Europeans, write the day first, then the month, then the year. For example, December 3, 2010, would be written 3.12.10 or 3/12/10.
- The work week may change. From May to October (Monday through Friday), it is generally 8:00 A.M. to 1:30 P.M. and from 4:00 P.M. to 7:30 P.M.). From October to May, hours are usually from 8:00 A.M. to 1:00 P.M. and from 4:30 to 7:30 P.M.
- Greeks observe Orthodox Easter, (which is different from the Gregorian Calendar), however, they celebrate Christmas on the 25th of December.
- Greece is two hours ahead of Greenwich Mean Time (G.M.T. +2), making it seven hours ahead of U.S. Eastern Standard Time (E.S.T. +7).

Negotiating
- The senior members of a group are always shown great respect. Authority usually rests with them.
- To do business in Greece, one must be patient, yet ready to use quick judgment. Greeks are excellent bargainers.
- It is advisable to have one side of your business card printed in English and the other in Greek. Present it with the Greek side up.
- Avoid making judgments about the Greek style of describing things. Many Greeks may use hyperbole in discussions; this is not unusual.

Business Entertaining
- Business is usually done over a cup of coffee—often in a coffeehouse or taverna.
- Lunch is the main meal of the day, between noon and 2:00 P.M.
- The elderly are always served first.
- Dinner is a small meal and is eaten at around 8:00 or 9:00 P.M.
- Often, many dishes are ordered and shared by all at the table.
- When dining in a Greek home, you will probably be offered seconds and thirds in an insistent way. Accepting more food is a compliment to your host.

- Bad topics to bring up include Greek conflicts with Turkey, Macedonia, or other nations. In general, just avoid political discussions.

PROTOCOL

Greetings
- Remember that Greek people tend to be physically demonstrative. Expect your Greek associates to stay in relatively close proximity to you.
- In first business encounters, a handshake is typical.
- The greeting can take many forms in Greece; a handshake, an embrace, or a kiss can all be encountered at first meetings or among friends and acquaintances.

Titles/Forms of Address
- Older people are greatly respected in Greece and therefore are always addressed formally (using titles, etc.).
- The order of Greek names is the same as in North America: given name first, followed by surname.

Gestures
- The Greeks are an active and energetic people, and their mannerisms reflect this. Gestures tend to be strong and used frequently.
- Greeks gesture, not only with their hands and heads, but with their eyes and lips as well.
- Greeks may exhibit nervous energy through foot tapping or fidgeting. This may be a reason why Greeks sometimes play with worry beads (called kombologion). This fidgeting does not necessarily indicate boredom or impatience.
- Traditionally, Greeks indicated "no" with an upward nod of the head. (This movement is also used to signify negation in Greek sign language.) This is not as common with the younger generation. Recently Greeks have begun to use North American gestures for "yes" and "no," which can be confusing.
- Anger is sometimes expressed by a smile.
- After giving or receiving a compliment, Greeks sometimes make a puff of breath through the lips to ward off the "evil eye."
- Sometimes Greeks express thanks by placing their right hands over their hearts. The gesture is usually accompanied by a verbal expression of thanks.

Gifts
- Greeks are very generous; if you compliment an object too enthusiastically, it may be given to you.
- For business associates, you do not need to give a gift during the first encounter.

- Avoid gifts that are too lavish or too skimpy, as well as gifts that are only a means of showing your company logo.
- If you are invited to a home, compliment the children of the household and give them a small gift; flowers or a dessert is also appropriate for the hostess.
- For further guidelines on gift giving, visit *www.kissboworshakehands.com*.

Dress

- Conservative business clothing is best.
- Women should wear dresses or suits in subtle colors.

Cultural Note

The Nazi occupation of Greece decimated the country's Jewish population. Between 1492 (when the Jews were expelled from Spain) and 1941, the majority of the population in Salonika, the second largest city, was Jewish. When the Nazis captured Salonika in April of 1941, the entire Jewish population was transferred to concentration camps. About 96 percent of these Jews were slain in the camps—a higher proportion than in any other city in the world. The Nazis also did their best to destroy all evidence of Jewish Salonika. (For example, they took gravestones from the Jewish cemetery and used them to line a swimming pool.) Today, there is virtually no sign of the lost Jewish community of Salonika.

Greece

Guatemala

Republic of Guatemala
Local long form: Republica de Guatemala

Cultural Note

The resplendently plumed quetzal bird is the national symbol of Guatemala. Its name is used for the country's currency as well as its second largest city. However, due to widespread environmental devastation, it is difficult to see a live quetzal in the wild. Aside from a few reserves, most of the mountain forests that were the quetzal's habitat have been decimated.

 WHAT'S YOUR CULTURAL IQ?

1. Which civilization achieved supremacy in what would become Guatemala and southern Mexico around 800 B.C.?
   a. The Olmecs
   b. The Mayans
   c. The Toltecs

   ANSWER: a. The Olmecs were the first identifiable civilization that ruled Guatemala prior to the Mayans. After the great Mayan cities were mysteriously vacated in approximately A.D. 900, the Toltecs were one of their successors.

2. TRUE or FALSE? Two Nobel Prizes have been awarded to Guatemalans.

   ANSWER: TRUE. The 1967 Nobel Prize for literature was awarded to Miguel Ángel Asturias, while the 1993 Nobel Peace Prize went to Rigoberta Menchú Tum.

3. TRUE or FALSE? The Guatemalan civil war was the longest-running insurgency in Central America in the twentieth century.

   ANSWER: TRUE. By the time a treaty was signed in 1996, the war had lasted thirty-six years.

 TIPS ON DOING BUSINESS IN GUATEMALA

- In Guatemala—as elsewhere in Latin America—successful business relationships hinge on friendly social relationships. Guatemalan decision-makers are free to base their decisions on gut instincts. If they dislike you—or even if you just made a poor first impression they may not do business with you.

- Unlike members of the Latin upper class elsewhere, Guatemalan executives tend to be open and blunt-spoken. Also, foreigners are frequently surprised at the accessibility of the decision-makers. Even high-ranking leaders in business and government tend to be willing to see foreign salespeople.

- Price is the single most important factor in a purchasing decision. After sales service is also a high priority. Guatemala is a small market, and a negative reputation (especially for such things as service) spreads quickly.

COUNTRY BACKGROUND

History

Guatemala was home to the Mayan people, who developed a highly advanced civilization. In 1519, Hernando (Hernán) Cortés led the first European expedition to subdue Mexico. A lieutenant of Cortés, Pedro de Alvarado, made the first Spanish inroads into Guatemala in 1524.

Independence from Spain was declared in 1821; in 1823, representatives of the five Central American states (Guatemala, Honduras, El Salvador, Nicaragua, and Costa Rica) founded the United Provinces of Central America, independent from Mexico.

Following years of internecine fighting, the United Provinces of Central America was dissolved in 1838. Guatemala became a solitary independent state, led by Rafael Carrera. A semiliterate mestizo farmer, Carrera seized power during an Amerindian uprising. He remained dictator until 1865 and undid all the reforms enacted by the leaders of the United Provinces.

Justo Rufino Barrios, hailed as the "Great Reformer," became president in 1873. He encouraged European immigration, coffee growing, and reduced the power of the Catholic Church. He died in 1885 while trying to forcibly reunite the United Provinces.

Manuel Estrada Cabrera came to power in 1898 in a rigged election for the presidency. He managed to hold on to power until 1920. It was Cabrera who gave huge concessions to the foreign plantation owners, especially the United Fruit Company. He was ousted in a bloody coup in 1920.

Juan José Arévalo was elected president in 1944. Calling himself a "Spiritual Socialist," he enacted reforms and granted political liberties. He also survived twenty-five coup attempts by Conservative forces during his six-year term in office!

Colonel Jacobo Arbenz Gúzman was elected president in 1951. He continued Arévalo's reforms, including the expropriation of land from foreign owners, such as the United Fruit Company. Angered, the United States supported a 1954 coup to overthrow him. The conservative oligarchy took power. There would not be free and fair elections in Guatemala until the 1990s.

After 1960, guerrilla movements began to grow in force, finally erupting into full-scale terrorist activities concentrated in Guatemala City. Many leading political figures, including the U.S. ambassador, were killed. By 1966, Guatemalan military and death squads began to make thousands of Guatemalan citizens "disappear."

Guatemala

General Efraín Ríos Montt seized power in 1982. His sixteen-month dictatorship was marked by a scorched-earth campaign against rebels. His ruthlessness restored a measure of order and was popular with the oligarchy. He seized power a second time in 1989.

Jorge Serrano was elected president in 1991. His inauguration marked the first time in fifty-one years that one freely elected civilian government followed another in Guatemala. In 1993, faced with public unrest and official corruption, Serrano dissolved the Congress and Supreme Court. His attempt to seize dictatorial powers failed, and he was forced to flee into exile.

In 1992 the Nobel Peace Prize was awarded to Rigoberta Menchú Tum for her work with Guatemala's Mayan Indians. In 1996, after five years of negotiations, President Alvaro Arzu signed a peace treaty with URNG guerrilla front leader Rolando Moran and Amerindian peace activist Rigoberta Menchú. This marked the official end to Guatemala's thirty-six-year civil war.

In December of 2003, President Óscar Berger Perdomo won a run-off election.

Type of Government

Guatemala has had a difficult political history since its independence from Spain in 1821. It has seen dictators, revolutions, and violent transfers of power. Since 1986, however, the country has been under civilian rule.

The Republic of Guatemala has a unicameral legislative house, called the Congress of the Republic. The president is both chief of state and head of the government.

Voting is compulsory for all literate persons over the age of eighteen.

For current government information, check with the Embassy of Guatemala at *www .guatemala-embassy.org.*

Language

Spanish is the official language. Many Amerindian languages and dialects are used in the interior of the country. Not all are mutually intelligible. Ethnologue, at *www.ethnologue.com*, has identified fifty-six separate languages in Guatemala, two of which are extinct.

The Guatemalan View

Guatemala has no official religion. Until the 1950s the vast majority of the people were Roman Catholic. Recently, Evangelical Protestantism has made the greatest number of converts amongst a traditionally Catholic population. Estimates show that approximately a quarter of Guatemalans are now Protestants. Evangelical Protestants have even been elected president of Guatemala. Televangelists have also become popular.

Much of the Guatemalan ruling elite has come to embrace the "prosperity theology" of some Neopentecostal sects. As elements of the Catholic Church became associated with the betterment of the poor, Catholicism lost popularity among the wealthy. (Indeed, those

Catholics whose "liberation theology" allied them with guerrillas came to be considered enemies of the state.). Some of Guatemala's Amerindians retain their traditional religious beliefs.

In its long civil war, Guatemalans have suffered enough to acquire a sense of fatalism and helplessness.

☑ Know Before You Go

Guatemala is subject to occasional violent earthquakes and volcanic eruptions. The country's Caribbean coast is extremely vulnerable to hurricanes and tropical storms.

Mudslides often follow heavy rains.

The history of Guatemala's various capitals shows the country's propensity for natural disasters. The first capital of Guatemala was Santiago de los Caballeros de Guatemala. Founded in 1527, it was destroyed by mudslides in 1543. (It was later rebuilt under the name Ciudad Vieja.) Next, nearby Antigua became the capital, until it was leveled by an earthquake in 1773.

The current capital, Guatemala City, was founded in 1776. While it has endured its share of disasters, it has survived.

Street crime remains a problem. As a result of years of civil war, Guatemala is awash with weapons. Not only does this mean that criminals are liable to be armed, but there have been a substantial number of land mines in the countryside. Although Guatemala tried to clear all land mines and unexploded ordnance by 2004, persons traveling in areas that were planted with mines should use extreme caution.

Guatemala is a major transit country for drug smuggling.

▶ CULTURAL ORIENTATION

Cognitive Styles: How Guatemalans Organize and Process Information

Guatemalans love to converse. In a discussion, foreigners can easily construe the acceptance of information by Guatemalans where no such acceptance exists. Guatemalans process information subjectively and associatively rather than objectively or abstractly. They will look at the particulars of each situation, rather than appeal to a rule or law to solve their problems.

Negotiation Strategies: What Guatemalans Accept as Evidence

Subjective feelings are much more important than objective facts in determining the truth. There is some faith in the ideology of the Church (Protestant and Catholic) in providing the truth, but Guatemalans are more apt to trust in the ideology of their ethnic heritage.

Value Systems: The Basis for Behavior

The value systems of the indigenous Indians are very different from those of the ruling class.

Locus of Decision-Making

The individual is responsible for his or her decisions, but these must be viewed in the context of the needs of the family, group, and organization. In Guatemala, "friends do things for friends"—thus it is necessary to develop friendships with business associates. In the workplace, your ability to get along with colleagues can be more important than your expertise.

Sociologists have proposed that Guatemala has one of the highest scores in terms of power/distance in Latin America. This translates into a large gap between authoritarian figures and their subordinates. Not surprisingly, economic power (in the form of business ownership) in Guatemala is concentrated in less than 1 percent of the population.

Sources of Anxiety Reduction

Wealth and family ties give the individual status and security. Trust and loyalty are centered on close kin. The Catholic Church has little influence in the government, but its precepts permeate the population and give structure to life. Often, it seems more important to make a pronouncement than to actually carry out the action. Progress in any endeavor takes a long time, which protects those who are threatened by change.

Guatemala has been ranked as having the lowest score in Latin America for individuality. This indicates a highly collectivist culture in which loyalty to one's group is paramount.

Issues of Equality/Inequality

Deep-seated social, economic, and political inequity exists, particularly between the mestizos and the Mayans. These ethnic relations have been changing and are dynamic, ranging from cordial and tolerant to open hostility and violence. Changes in the political system are often made by revolution or military coups. Women are still considered subordinate (they did not receive the right to vote until 1945, and under current law, only women may be charged with adultery).

 ## BUSINESS PRACTICES

Punctuality, Appointments, and Local Time

- Punctuality, although not strictly adhered to in daily living, is expected from foreigners and in business situations.
- There are many Asian-owned manufacturing companies in Guatemala. A company that runs along Asian management lines will consider punctuality extremely important.
- Guatemalans, like many Europeans and South Americans, write the day first, then the month, then the year (e.g., December 3, 2010, is written 3.12.10 or 3/12/10).
- Make appointments as far in advance as possible by telephone or e-mail.
- The best times to visit Guatemala are February through July and September through November. Common vacation times are the two weeks before and after Christmas and Easter, Independence Day (September 15), and the month of August.
- Local time is six hours behind Greenwich Mean Time (G.M.T. –6); Guatemala is in the same time zone as U.S. Central Standard Time (E.S.T. –1).

Negotiating

- Contracts are done among Guatemalans only after a relationship has been established. Spend time forming a friendship before jumping into business discussions.

  Business tends to take place at a much slower pace than in Europe or North America. Be calm and patient with delays. Several trips may be necessary to accomplish a transaction.

- There is a strong sense of personal honor on the part of the Guatemalan businessperson. Therefore, do not criticize a person in public or do anything that will cause him or her embarrassment.

- The majority of Guatemalan *maquiladoras* (manufacturing plants) are Asian-owned (primarily by South Koreans). Among Asians (as among Guatemalans), it is very important to avoid humiliating a person in public.

- Business is discussed in an office or over a meal in a restaurant. It is not discussed in a home or around family.

- Guatemalans find loud voices annoying. Speak in soft, well-modulated tones (especially in public).

- Contacts are very important in establishing business relationships. Your embassy may have a foreign commercial service officer who can provide you with contacts in your industry segment. Banks, accounting or legal firms, shipping and export corporations can also expand your network.

- Women executives are still the exception in Guatemala. Visiting businesswomen should act extremely professional and convey that they are representing their company, rather than speaking for themselves personally.

Business Entertaining

- Business breakfasts or lunches are preferred to dinners.

- An invitation to a Guatemalan home is offered for the purpose of getting to know you personally. This is not the time to discuss work. Spouses are usually invited to such gatherings.

- Good topics of conversation are Guatemalan tourist sites, your family, hobbies, travel, and so forth. Topics to avoid include political unrest and violence.

> **Cultural Note**
> Do not be surprised if some Guatemalans claim that the military is defending Guatemala's "territorial integrity" against incursion from neighboring Central American nations. It is true, however, that Guatemala has Latin America's longest-running guerrilla opposition. Neither of these topics are appropriate dinner conversation.

- If you speak to a married couple, the man will generally be the one who will converse or answer your questions.

- The main meal of the day is eaten at noon. This will probably include black beans, tortillas or meat, and fruit and vegetables.
- Meals are usually eaten "family style," with each person serving herself or himself. It is rude to take food and leave it on your plate uneaten.

PROTOCOL

Greetings

- Men always shake hands when greeting. Women sometimes shake hands with men; this is done at the woman's discretion.
- The handshake is usually accompanied by a verbal greeting, such as *¡Buenos días!* (good morning/day), *¡Buenas tardes!* (good afternoon), or *¡Buenas noches!* (good evening).
- Do not expect firm grips when shaking hands; if you can, modify your own handshake to mirror your Guatemalan associate's.
- Close male friends may hug or pat each other on the back in greeting. Women will often pat your right forearm or shoulder instead of shaking hands. If they are close friends, they may hug or kiss each other on the cheek.
- At parties or business gatherings, it is customary to greet and shake hands with everyone in the room.

Titles/Forms of Address

- Most people you meet should be addressed by their title alone, without their surname. Traditionally, only children, family members, and close friends address each other by their first names.
- Younger businesspeople will quickly move to a first name basis with their peers.

Gestures

- Guatemalans wave good-bye using a gesture that looks like someone fanning themselves: hand raised, palm toward the body, and a wave of the fingers back and forth, with the fingers together as if encased in a mitten.
- To beckon someone, extend your arm (palm down) and make a slight scooping motion toward your body (more with the fingers than the wrist).
- The "fig" gesture (thumb-tip protruding from between the fingers of a closed fist) is considered obscene in Guatemala. (However, in some parts of South America it is considered a "good luck" gesture.)
- The "okay" sign (thumb and forefinger forming a circle) is considered obscene.
- Make eye contact while speaking with Guatemalans.

Guatemala

Gifts

- If invited to a home, it is appropriate to bring flowers or candy, and something for the children.
- Always take a more personal gift with you after an initial visit.
- Do not bring white flowers; they are reserved for funerals.
- If you will be returning to Guatemala, you may ask your counterpart if there is something you can bring from your home country.

Cultural Note

Remember that Guatemala is in a tectonically active zone, with frequent earthquakes and occasional volcanoes. Easily breakable gifts may not be the best choice.

Dress

- For business, a lightweight suit is appropriate for men; women should wear a suit, dress, or skirt and blouse.
- When dressing casually, men should wear pants and a shirt in cities and a sweater in the cooler highlands; women should wear a skirt and blouse. Short pants and jeans are not appropriate for cities and more rural areas. Women in pants are becoming more common but still may offend some people.

Cultural Note

Military clothing is illegal; it can neither be worn nor brought into the country.

Honduras

Republic of Honduras
Local short form: Honduras
Local long form: Republica de Honduras

WHAT'S YOUR CULTURAL IQ?

1. Of the many Amerindian groups of Honduras, the Lenca were the only tribe to mount a serious offense against the Spanish. TRUE or FALSE: Modern Hondurans honored the Lenca chief Lempira by naming their national currency after him.

   ANSWER: TRUE. Chief Lempira led 30,000 Lenca warriors against the Spanish in 1537. Unable to defeat him in battle, the Spanish seized and executed Lempira while under a flag of truce. By 1539, the Spanish had suppressed the Lenca revolt.

2. U.S. citizen Sam (the Banana Man) Zemurray is considered the man responsible for turning Honduras into the archetype of a banana republic. Zemurray did far more than simply buy land to grow bananas—he deposed Honduran governments at will. TRUE or FALSE: Zemurray hired a U.S. mercenary with the unlikely name of General Lee Christmas to persuade recalcitrant Honduran politicians.

   ANSWER: TRUE. Lee Christmas even became commander in chief of the entire Honduran Army.

3. Competition for control of the banana market was fierce. Which company eventually won out to become the leading banana producer in Honduras?
   a. Sam Zemurray's Cuyamel Fruit Company
   b. The United Fruit Company (which eventually became United Brands)
   c. The Vaccaro Brothers (which became Standard Fruit)

   ANSWER: b. United Fruit became the leader after buying out Zemurray's company in 1929. This made United Fruit the primary target during the 1954 general strike that united

Hondurans against the foreign corporations that all but ran their country. Coffee has since replaced bananas as Honduras's chief agricultural export.

▶ TIPS ON DOING BUSINESS IN HONDURAS

- Hondurans are status conscious. At least one member of the negotiating team should be from senior management. Emphasize qualifications, titles, degrees, etc.—stay in good hotels, and eat at fine restaurants.
- While Honduran law does not require that a foreign firm utilize a local agent, hiring one is strongly recommended. However, be judicious because Honduran representatives of foreign companies often sell products made by competitors. Also, if things do not work out with your agent, it can be exceedingly difficult to terminate him or her.
- Price remains the primary motivator for purchases, but Honduran consumers also list customer service as important. The lack of reliable local service will impact your sales. This is hinged to the perception that once a product is purchased, it cannot be returned.

▶ COUNTRY BACKGROUND

History

The Mayan Indians achieved an advanced level of civilization in Honduras. But the Mayan empire had passed its peak before the arrival of Europeans. Christopher Columbus arrived in Honduras in 1502, but no Spanish outpost was immediately established.

The Spanish found their first permanent outpost in 1525 at Trujillo. It became the first capital of Honduras, but it was hot and malaria-ridden.

In 1537, the Spanish established a new capital at Comayagua in the cooler interior highlands. In the same year, 30,000 Lenca warriors nearly drove the Spanish out of Honduras. The Lenca are the only Amerindian tribe to mount an effective opposition to the Spanish.

Subsequently, control of Central America (including Honduras) was centralized in Guatemala by the Spanish Crown.

Both gold and silver were discovered near Tegucigalpa in the 1570s. Until the ore ran out, Honduras was the wealthiest nation in Central America. Amerindians were enslaved on a massive scale to work the mines and plantations.

The Mexican Revolution of 1821 eliminated Spanish authority in the region. Honduras (along with the rest of Central America) declared its independence from Spain. The new Mexican empire claimed sovereignty over all of Central America, but Mexican troops never reached as far south as Honduras.

In 1823, Honduras joined the new Central American Federation, which was led by a Honduran, General Francisco Morazán. But the federation was rent by factional disputes and soon dissolved. Honduras declared its independence on November 5, 1938. Honduras became one of the five independent successor states of the federation.

The United Kingdom ceded the island of Roatan (formerly Ruatan) to Honduras in 1860. U.S. mercenary leader William Walker, who had previously conquered Nicaragua, tried to capitalize on the situation by leading the English-speaking residents of Roatan against Honduras. When this scheme was thwarted by British warships, Walker decided to invade the Honduran mainland instead. He landed his small force of men at Trujillo and captured the local fort, but British marines forced Walker to surrender. The British turned Walker over to the Hondurans, who executed him.

Honduras became a major exporter of bananas in 1910, when Sam (the Banana Man) Zemurray, a naturalized U.S. citizen, bought 15,000 acres of Honduran land near the Caribbean coast. The very next year, Zemurray helped to overthrow an unfriendly Liberal Honduran government. He then hired mercenary Lee Christmas to enforce his will. Lee Christmas later became commander in chief of the entire Honduran Army.

A general strike was called against the largest banana producer, the United Fruit Company, in 1954. Some concessions were granted, but the strike's greater significance was in the unified opposition of Central Americans to the foreign corporations that had controlled their economies for decades.

Cultural Note

Honduras's capital and largest city is Tegucigalpa (colloquially known as Tegus, pronounced "TEY-goose"). Many Honduran corporations have their offices in Tegucigalpa. However, Honduras's boom town is its second largest city, San Pedro Sula. Before Hurricane Mitch in 1998, San Pedro Sula was the fastest-growing city in Central America.

Type of Government

The Republic of Honduras is run by a president (who is both chief of state and head of the government), a Council of Ministers, and a unicameral National Congress. Voting is compulsory over the age of eighteen.

Since independence from Spain in 1821, Honduras has experienced great political instability. There have been nearly 300 civil wars, rebellions, and changes of government—almost half of them during this century. However, in comparison to the turbulence of its Central American neighbors, the political situation has been relatively stable.

For current government data, check with the Embassy of Honduras at *www.honduras emb.org*.

Cultural Note

The name "Honduras" comes from the Spanish word *la hondura* (depth), a reference to the deep water off the country's Caribbean coast. The Hondurans refer to themselves as *hondureños*.

Language

Spanish is the official language, although several Amerindian dialects are also spoken in remote areas. Many Hondurans have a basic understanding of English, and it is widely understood in urban and tourist centers. A form of Creole English is the main language in many communities on the Caribbean coast, but this may be unintelligible to foreign English speakers.

Ethnologue.com has identified eleven distinct languages in Honduras, all of them still extant.

The Honduran View

The Roman Catholic Church has a strong cultural influence in Honduras, with 97 percent of the population following its teachings. Various Protestant sects account for the remainder.

Ever since the country's mines ran out 200 years ago, wealth has always come from outside Honduras. Although Hondurans love their beautiful country, many long to leave it. They often seek prosperity and security elsewhere.

A sign on the jail in Trujillo reads *"La Ley es Duro, pero es la Ley"* (The law is hard, but it is the law). This aphorism says much about the attitudes of average Hondurans toward their government. The law is seen as a harsh master from which there is neither appeal nor escape—rather than as an even-handed form of protection for every citizen. The upper classes may view the law differently.

☑ Know Before You Go

The greatest hazard for a visitor comes from erratic drivers and street crime. The prevalence of crime and corruption are a serious drawback to conducting business in Honduras.

Violent earthquakes, volcanoes, and mudslides occur periodically. The Caribbean coast of Honduras is particularly prone to hurricanes and tropical storms. In 1998, Hurricane Mitch devastated Honduras's second largest city, San Pedro Sula.

Unlike most of its neighbors, Honduras never planted antipersonnel mines on its territory. However, during the Nicaraguan civil war, combatants planted over 50,000 mines on both sides of the border. Since 1990, over 200 civilians have been injured by mines near the Honduras-Nicaragua border.

A 2001 survey reported no mines on the border between Honduras and El Salvador.

Along the Honduras–El Salvador border there are still some disputed areas, as well as in some small islands in the Caribbean.

Law enforcement agencies report that Honduras is a transshipment point for illegal drugs.

▶ CULTURAL ORIENTATION

Cognitive Styles: How Hondurans Organize and Process Information

Honduras is a relatively open society that readily accepts change. Negotiations may take a long time to complete. Education is by rote, so information processing is subjective and associative. Hondurans become personally involved with all problems, seldom using universal rules or laws to make decisions.

Negotiation Strategies: What Hondurans Accept as Evidence

Subjective feelings are the primary source of truth, ameliorated by faith in the Church or the cultural heritage. Objective facts are seldom seen as a useful basis for the truth.

Value Systems: The Basis for Behavior

The pluralistic atmosphere of Honduran social and political life stems from a more homogeneous mestizo society, which developed without extensive, institutionalized slavery.

Locus of Decision-Making

People gain their identity from family lineage and their role in society, so the individual's capacity to make decisions is compromised by his or her need to satisfy family and social groups. A person's ability to maintain a harmonious group is more important than his or her expertise. A small elite group, mostly foreigners, control the majority of economic resources. They are relatively weak politically, because they have not formed a cohesive group.

Sources of Anxiety Reduction

The Catholic Church gives social structure to life through its precepts and holidays, though it is not a strong political force. A person's role in the social structure and the presence of a strong extended family gives him or her a sense of security. Hondurans are always busy, but progress is not necessarily the primary goal. This laid-back behavior helps to reduce anxiety.

Issues of Equality/Inequality

Honduras is the poorest country in Latin America. The homogeneity of the mestizo society only makes for a large, poor middle class, with the few rich above and the poorer Miskito Indians in the east at the bottom of the social ladder. Yet Hondurans feel they are all equal because each individual is unique, and there is an inherent trust in people because of the social interrelationships of extended families and friends. Machismo is strong, and there are clear and classic role differences between the sexes.

▶ BUSINESS PRACTICES

Punctuality, Appointments, and Local Time

- Scheduled appointments may be delayed, and punctuality is not strictly adhered to in daily life. However, punctuality is expected of foreigners.
- Arrive about thirty minutes late for social events.
- In Honduras, as in many European and South American nations, it is customary to write the day first, then the month, then the year (e.g., December 3, 2010, is written 3.12.10 or 3/12/10).
- Personal relationships are extremely important. Be sure to make contacts through appropriate intermediaries.

- The best time to visit Honduras is between February and June. The rainy season lasts from May to November. December and August are popular vacation times.
- Meetings may take place at breakfast, lunch, or dinner. Let your counterpart suggest the time.
- Honduras is six hours behind Greenwich Mean Time (G.M.T. –6), which is the same as Central Standard Time in the USA (E.S.T. –1).

Negotiating

- Business tends to take place at a much slower pace than in Europe or North America. Be calm and patient with delays. Several trips may be necessary to conclude a transaction.
- Personal friendships are vital to business in Honduras. Hondurans are looking for a long-term relationship based on mutual trust and reliability. It is important to spend time building a relationship before jumping into discussions. Plan to make repeated visits and maintain contact after your trips.
- Try to keep the same person as the linchpin during all your negotiations. Much of the business relationship will be based on this personal friendship.
- Latin Americans respect the value of individual dignity and honor, regardless of social status or wealth. Never publicly criticize a Honduran, or do anything that would cause him or her humiliation.
- In their desire to please, Hondurans are likely to give you the answer they think you want to hear. Be careful how you phrase your questions. For example, a question such as "Does the market open at 8:00?" will probably be answered "yes," whether this is the truth or not, because this is the answer they think you want. Instead, phrase questions so that they require more detailed answers, such as "What time does this market open?"
- Remember to avoid saying "no" in public while in Honduras. "Maybe" or "we will see" generally means no.
- Because of Hondurans's desire to tell people what they want to hear, get all agreements in writing. A verbal agreement may have been given out of politeness and may not be considered binding.
- When negotiating, emphasize the trust and mutual compatibility of the two companies. Stress the benefits to the person and his or her family and pride. An argument based upon feelings and personal priorities will be more effective than the logical bottom line of a proposal. If there is a disagreement, do not expect a compromise, since this is seen as a show of weakness.
- Decisions are not made quickly. Indeed, snap decisions are suspect; take time before announcing a final decision, even if your mind is already made up.
- Include a margin for bargaining in your initial offer, but do not overinflate your prices. That will erode the level of trust people will have in you. Using powerful graphics will leave a strong impression after your presentation is over.

- Although the situation is rapidly changing, women in upper levels of management are still the exception rather than the rule. A woman may face some initial lack of respect in Honduras. Since titles and position are valued, a businesswoman should emphasize her qualifications with the firm, and that she has the authority to make decisions for her company.
- Hondurans are proud of their heritage and their individuality. Therefore, be careful of sensitivities in referring to citizens of the United States as "Americans." That term applies to all North and Latin Americans.
- Do not be offended if another person is served before you in a line. Preference is given to the elderly and those with higher positions and social status.
- Never overly admire another's belongings. The owner may feel obligated to give them to you.
- Have business cards and other material printed in Spanish as well as in your native language. Present your card to a Honduran with the Spanish side up.

Business Entertaining
- Good topics of conversation are Honduran tourist sites, your family and job at home, and sports (especially soccer, the national sport). Topics to avoid are local politics and unrest in Central America.
- The best times for business meetings are breakfast and lunch, the main meal of the day. If you are invited to a local home or invited to a meal where spouses are also included, do not expect to discuss business. Instead, socialize and get to know the family. Dinner is eaten between 8:30 and 9:00 P.M. Arrive about thirty minutes late.
- Foreign businesswomen should never invite their male counterparts to a business dinner unless spouses also attend. For business lunches, eat at your hotel and have the bill added to your tab; otherwise your male guest will not want to let you pay.

▶ PROTOCOL

Greetings
- Men shake hands in greeting. Women often pat each other on the right arm or shoulder instead of shaking hands. If they are close friends, they may hug or kiss each other on the cheek.
- Do not be surprised if handshakes are light, with a relatively weak grip; give the same in return.
- At parties it is customary to greet and shake hands with everyone in the room.

Gestures

- Several gestures are unique to this area. Placing a finger below the eye indicates caution. A hand below the elbow means that a person is stingy. "No" is indicated by waving the index finger. Joining one's hands together shows strong approval.
- Conversations take place at a much closer distance than may be considered comfortable in northern Europe or North America. Pulling away from your counterpart may be interpreted as rejection.
- Honduran men are warm and friendly and make a lot of physical contact. They often touch shoulders, or hold another's arm. To withdraw from such a contact is considered insulting.

Dress

- Business: Men should wear a conservative suit. Women should wear a suit, skirt and blouse, or a dress. Honduran businessmen commonly wear a guayabera, which is a decorative shirt, rather than a shirt and tie.
- Casual: A light shirt and pants for men and a skirt and blouse for women may be worn in urban areas. Revealing clothing for women and shorts for either sex are not appropriate. Pants for women are not as common as in North America and may offend some locals.

Honduras

Cultural Note

In the 1980s, revolutions in neighboring Nicaragua and El Salvador had wide-ranging effects on Honduras. To suppress leftist governments in these countries, the United States trained anti-Communist Salvadoran and Nicaraguan troops inside Honduras. This training of foreign troops brought in millions of U.S. dollars. Nevertheless, the Honduran people wanted the United States and foreign troops off their soil. This sentiment was so strong that Honduran president José Simeón Azcona del Hoyo was forced to ask the United States to leave.

Hungary

Republic of Hungary
Local short form: Magyarorszag
Local long form: Magyar Koztarsasag

> **Cultural Note**
> For a relatively small country, Hungary has produced an astonishing number of top scientists. Many of the scientists who worked on the U.S. Manhattan Project (which produced the first nuclear bombs) were Hungarian expatriates. Some were Hungarian Jews who were fleeing fascism, some were Hungarian Christians, and others were born in the United States but had Hungarian ancestry.

WHAT'S YOUR CULTURAL IQ?

1. No one can prove whether or not today's Hungarians are descended from the fifth-century warriors of Attila the Hun. TRUE or FALSE? Despite this uncertainty, "Attila" remains a fairly common name in Hungary.

   ANSWER: TRUE. It has been used both as a first name and a surname. Interestingly, whatever the legendary "Scourge of God" called himself, it wasn't Attila. The name "Attila" is a Gothic name derived from the Gothic word atta, meaning "father." Attila was probably a term given him by the Gothic peoples he conquered.

   The main alternative theory is that the ancestors of today's Hungarians arrived in Europe from Asia much later, sometime in the ninth century. This theory—that the Hungarians arrived after the empire of the Huns fell apart—was promoted by the Austrians and the Soviets. Both groups had a vested interest in blurring the Hungarian national identity. Neither wanted the Hungarians to think of themselves as descended from the most feared invaders Europe has ever known.

2. Hungary also has a number of well-known composers. Which of the following musicians is better known today for his efforts in music education?
   a. Béla Bartók
   b. Franz Lehár
   c. Zoltán Kodály

   ANSWER: c. There is a Zoltán Kodály Pedagogical Institute of Music in Hungary, as well as other institutes using his techniques all over the world. Lehár was a composer of operettas; he is best remembered for the operetta *The Merry Widow*.

3. Hungary's southern border marks a dividing line between Catholic/Protestant Europe and Orthodox Europe. TRUE or FALSE? Since 2004, this border delineates another new and important divide.

ANSWER: TRUE. Hungary was admitted to the European Union in 2004. The countries to the south—Romania, Bulgaria, and Turkey—applied but were not admitted (for now). Hungary's southern border is the border of the European Union, and the Hungarians are charged with keeping illegal immigrants out of the EU.

▶ TIPS ON DOING BUSINESS IN HUNGARY

- Remember that Hungary is a landlocked nation, although a limited amount of shipping is done via the Danube River, which passes through the capital, Budapest. Hungary's infrastructure of highways and railroads has been improved, however, many roads are still in need of upgrades.
- The Hungarian language is called Magyar and is difficult for outsiders to learn. Unlike most European languages, Magyar is not a member of the Indo-European linguistic family. It is a Finno-Ugric tongue, distantly related to Finnish and Estonian. Fortunately, Hungarians have a tradition of learning other languages. You can present written materials in English or German; many Hungarians read these languages.
- When holding important business discussions through an interpreter, stop and reiterate points on a regular basis. This avoids misunderstandings. Magyar has suffixes that convey degrees of ambiguity and subtleties, which can easily be lost in translation.

▶ COUNTRY BACKGROUND

History

King Stephen (later canonized) is credited with uniting the Hungarian people and adopting Roman Catholicism as the national religion. The dates of his rule are usually given as A.D. 1000 to 1038. The Árpád dynasty he established ruled Hungary for some 300 years.

After the fall of Constantinople in 1453, the Hungarians became Europe's front line of defense against the Ottoman Turks. The two groups fought off and on for some 300 years. Finally, the Turks managed to conquer the Hungarians.

At the Battle of Mohács in 1526, the Ottomans dealt the Magyars a crushing defeat and slew the Hungarian king. The Ottomans occupied the then-capital of Buda. All of southern Hungary became a vassal state of the Ottoman Empire. The Habsburg kings of Austria took control of the northernmost remnant of Hungary, and they slowly pushed back the Ottomans. By 1683, they had expelled the Turks from central Hungary, and they incorporated most of Hungary into their empire.

Hungary

Unhappy under Habsburg rule, the Hungarians revolted in 1848. The Austrians were unable to put down the revolt by themselves and accepted an offer of Russian aid. The Hungarian revolt was crushed in 1849.

Realizing that they could not permanently stifle Hungarian nationalism, the Habsburgs created the dual monarchy: Hungary became a separate state under the Habsburg Crown. The name of the empire was changed to the Austro-Hungarian Empire.

The Austro-Hungarian Empire entered the First World War in 1914. When the war ended in 1918, Hungary was dismembered along with the rest of the Austro-Hungarian Empire.

Hard hit by the Great Depression, Hungary developed its own fascist movement, the Arrow Cross. When the Second World War began, both Hungary and Romania allied themselves with Nazi Germany. Hungary suffered great destruction and emerged from the war both reduced in size and under the control of the USSR.

As in its neighboring countries, Hungary was forced to accept a Communist government. In 1956 the Hungarian government tried to withdraw from the Warsaw Pact. This resulted in a Soviet military crackdown, during which many Hungarians died, others fled to the West, and Prime Minister Imre Nagy was executed.

The liberalism that swept Eastern Europe in the late 1980s fostered changes in Hungary. Long-time Communist leader János Kádár was forced to resign in 1988. The Communists became just another political party and were roundly defeated in the elections of 1990.

Hungary joined NATO in 1991 and the European Union in 2004.

Cultural Note

An amazingly fertile country, Hungary was intentionally kept agricultural while it was part of the Austro-Hungarian Empire. After the Second World War, the Communists instituted massive industrialization projects. Industry now provides almost half of the Hungarian GNP. Besides the soil's fertility, Hungarian resources include coal, natural gas, and bauxite.

Type of Government

The Republic of Hungary is now a multiparty republic. There is a single legislative body, the National Assembly.

The prime minister is the head of the government. The state president of Hungary is commander in chief of the armed forces, in addition to being head of state; this gives the position more importance than in most European countries.

Formerly one of the most prosperous members of the Warsaw Pact, Hungary underwent a relatively smooth transition from a one-party Communist state to a democracy.

For current government data, check with the Embassy of Hungary at *www.huembwas.org*.

Language

The official language of Hungary is Hungarian, which the Hungarians call "Magyar."

Although Hungary has a significant minority population (primarily German, Slovak, Romanian, and Gypsy), over 95 percent of the people speak Magyar (Hungarian).

Ethnologue, at *www.ethnologue.com*, has identified twelve languages spoken in Hungary, all of which are extant.

The Hungarian View

The majority of Hungarians are Roman Catholic; approximately 28 percent belong to Protestant denominations. Other religions are also present. By and large, Hungary marks the end of Catholic and Protestant Europe. Romania and Bulgaria are Orthodox countries. Some believe that Hungary's economic success is due in part to the "Protestant Work Ethic"—something that is relatively absent in Romania and Bulgaria.

Hungarians have a reputation for melancholy. Rates of depression in Hungary are difficult to measure, but the suicide rate is relatively high.

On the bright side, Hungarians also rank among the top in number of Olympic medals per capita.

☑ Know Before You Go

As in many former members of the Warsaw Pact, street crime is present. There are also various scams, from bars that charge foreigners outrageous prices for drinks, to elaborately plotted scams using criminals disguised as police officers.

Under the Communist regime, Hungary suffered massive environmental pollution. This is slowly being ameliorated. Hungary has substantial deposits of coal, but new regulations require many coal-fired plants to be shut. They are usually replaced with power plants using natural gas, which Hungary must import. Hungary also uses aging, Soviet-built nuclear power plants, the safety of which is cause for concern.

Although most Hungarians were anxious to join NATO, they still want to balance military and environmental concerns. In 2004, protesters halted the construction of a NATO radar station near Pecs in southern Hungary.

Hungary's overriding international concern is the treatment of ethnic Hungarians living in Romania, Serbia, and the Slovak Republic. In addition to this, Hungary and the Slovak Republic have long-standing disagreements over a dam on the Danube River.

▶ CULTURAL ORIENTATION

Cognitive Styles: How Hungarians Organize and Process Information

Hungary engaged in a degree of free-market enterprises before the collapse of Communism. Consequently, there is now an entire generation of businesspeople with experience in capitalism.

Under Communism, the educational system taught most Hungarians to process information associatively. Today, between a more diverse educational system and training abroad, there are a substantial number of Hungarians who think more abstractly. Hungarians have a tendency to see laws as something written by those in power for the benefit of those in power, not as something to protect the powerless. Personal relationships tend to be valued more than stringent adherence to regulations.

Negotiation Strategies: What Hungarians Accept as Evidence

The cataclysmic demise of the Communist Party as the ideological focus for all arguments has opened the door to other forms of reasoning. The more exposed to outside influences the participants are, the more they may use objective facts in their reasoning rather than subjective feelings or faith in the ideology of party or group. Intentions, feelings, and opinions are now openly expressed. Because it is considered better to be direct than devious, spontaneity of action is favored.

Surrounded by peoples (especially Slavs) who speak languages radically different from their own, Hungarians tend to feel isolated. Their typical worldview is that Hungarians are a misunderstood, put-upon people, oppressed by their neighbors. Information is often filtered through this worldview.

Value Systems: The Basis for Behavior

With the fall of Communism, Hungary is now open to explore the values of other systems and is subject to all the internal turmoil this brings. The following three sections identify the Value Systems in the predominant culture—their methods of dividing right from wrong, good from evil, and so forth.

Locus of Decision-Making

As the movement toward freedom and privatization advances, it is putting the responsibility for decision-making on the shoulders of the individual. In many instances the individual may transfer this responsibility to the group as a whole or to a consensus of privileged individuals. It is not clear yet whether the model to be followed will be that of capitalist or socialist democracy.

Sources of Anxiety Reduction

Formerly, the party structure, power, and full employment were the primary stabilizing forces in the lives of the people. Now there is a great deal of day-to-day anxiety over job and family security. The family unit is still recognized as a stabilizing force in society. Hungarian churches, which have always been influential in family life, are taking a more active role.

Except for a minority of successful entrepreneurs, Hungarians tend to have low expectations out of life. For example, when Hungary joined the European Union, most Hungarians surveyed said that they thought EU membership might bring a degree of prosperity to future generations, but not to their own.

Issues of Equality/Inequality

The removal of Communist Party control has allowed perceived feelings of inequality to surface. Ethnic disputes have become visible, along with humanitarian needs for equality and the establishment of strong, hierarchically structured systems in government, business, and society.

While Hungarian women hold important positions in academia and various professions, business is still dominated by men. Although Hungarian tradition demands that men treat visiting women with great courtesy, this does not apply to the women they see on a daily basis. In mixed company, men tend to dominate the conversation.

> **Cultural Note**
> While private ownership of property is permitted in Hungary, the concept of joint responsibility for property has not completely sunk in. Property not owned by an individual is often allowed to deteriorate. For example, the common areas in Hungarian buildings are sometimes dirty and shabby, because tenants often don't see such upkeep as their responsibility.

▶ BUSINESS PRACTICES

Punctuality, Appointments, and Local Time

- Punctuality is expected in all matters related to business: appointments, deliveries, payments, and so forth.
- Establish a relationship with a Hungarian representative prior to your visit. This individual can initiate contacts for you and accompany you to your appointments. Select this contact person carefully, because your new Hungarian clients will expect you to keep that representative ad infinitum.
- Request your appointment via e-mail or by regular letter as far in advance as possible. Always reconfirm the day before the meeting.
- Business letters may be written in English. While all businesses can translate letters from English, not all of them have staff members who can speak it. Consider hiring an interpreter.
- Avoid making business trips to Hungary during July and August, and from mid-December to mid-January. These are holiday and vacation periods.
- Hungary is one hour ahead of Greenwich Mean Time (G.M.T. +1) and six hours ahead of U.S. Eastern Standard Time, (E.S.T. +6). There is a daylight-saving system in the summer; the clocks are turned one hour ahead from April to September.

Cultural Note

In addition to vacations, August is interrupted by two important feast days. The Feast of the Assumption of the Virgin Mary is on August 15: the Virgin Mary is very important to Catholic and Orthodox Hungarians. Before the Second World War, many Hungarians referred to the month of August as "the Month of the Virgin Mary." August 20 is the Feast of King St. Stephen (Hungary's patron saint). On his death in A.D. 1038, King Stephen entrusted the protection of Hungary itself to the Blessed Virgin.

Negotiating

- It is difficult to predict how long it will take to negotiate a deal. Under the Communists, any type of contract would take months. However, some of Hungary's entrepreneurs will be anxious to move quickly.
- Whether fast or slow, deals in Hungary cannot be finalized without a lot of eating, drinking, and entertainment.
- Except for businesspeople trained abroad, Hungarians do not tend to stick to a linear agenda. Foreigners may perceive a Hungarian business meeting as loud and disorganized. Despite this perception, Hungarians are effective at accomplishing their goals.
- Have someone in your party take notes during meetings.
- Bring plenty of business cards, and give them out to everyone you meet.
- If you speak English, it is not necessary to have your business card translated into Hungarian. Indeed, Hungarian has many foreign loanwords, so your title in English may be similar to what it would be in Hungarian.
- Hungary's relations with its neighbors (especially those it ruled during the days of the Austro-Hungarian Empire) have not always been cordial. Do not bring up your background if you are of Romanian, Slovak, Polish, or Gypsy descent.

Business Entertaining

- Hungarian hospitality is legendary. You will have to fight with your Hungarian counterparts to pay a bill.
- Meals are primarily social occasions. Very little can be accomplished during a lunch, and nothing related to business should be brought up at dinner.
- Expect dinners to last a long time; restaurants usually have musicians or entertainers in the evening.
- If your schedule will not permit a full night's entertainment, suggest a business lunch instead.
- Once you have signed or completed a contract, throw a cocktail party at a prestigious hotel.
- Hungarian food, wine, horses, and sightseeing are good topics to discuss. So are sports: football (soccer) is the most popular sport, and chess is a national preoccupation.

Hungarians consider themselves a "nation of horsemen." If you get outside the city, invitations to go horseback riding are not uncommon.

Cultural Note

Hungary produces a variety of fruit brandies, and an excellent selection of wines. The best-known Hungarian wine-producing region is Tokaj, which produces wines by that name (known as "Tokay" outside Hungary).

When offering a toast, Hungarians will toast to your success—not to their own. In response, you should toast to their success—even if you are all in business together. Hungarians believe that toasting one's own success is pompous and arrogant.

▶ PROTOCOL

Greetings

- A handshake is customary not only when being introduced, but also when departing. Men sometimes wait for women to extend their hands before shaking.
- Only close friends will greet each other with an embrace. For men, the sequence goes as follows: shake hands, embrace, and make cheek-to-cheek contact on the left cheek, then on the right cheek. Close female friends do the same but omit the handshake.
- Hungarians typically "talk with their hands," using a lot of gestures.
- Personal space is small in Hungary; people talk at a closer distance than is common in northern Europe or North America.
- Extended eye contact is expected. Failure to meet a Hungarian's gaze will convey that you are untrustworthy.

Titles/Forms of Address

- Relatives and close adult friends address each other on a first-name basis; they will also call children by their first names. Young people typically use each other's first names. However, it is prudent to address adults by their titles and surnames until you are invited to do otherwise.
- In Hungary, the surname is listed before the given (first) name. Thus, the Hungarian musicians Béla Bartók and Franz Liszt are known in their homeland as Bartók Béla and Liszt Franz (or, more precisely, Liszt Ferenc, since Ferenc is the Hungarian equivalent of Franz). Foreign names, however, are listed in the order that is customary in their country of origin.
- Always use professional titles (Doctor, Director, Minister, and so forth) when addressing someone. Either use a title and surname (Professor Szabo) or add "Mr.," "Mrs.," or "Miss" to the title (Mrs. Architect).

Gifts

- When visiting a company, it is not always necessary to bring gifts. However, if you do, bring many small gifts and give them out freely.
- Because of a housing shortage, you may not be invited into a Hungarian home. This is especially true in Budapest, where some 20 percent of the total Hungarian population resides. If you are asked to visit, Western liquor (not wine, as Hungarians are proud of the wines they produce) and wrapped flowers (but not red roses or chrysanthemums) are appropriate.

Dress

- Dress tends to be conservative, especially among businesspeople.
- Appropriate business dress for men is a dark suit, a white shirt, and a tie. Women should wear suits or dresses.
- Jeans are standard casualwear. Shorts are somewhat uncommon in the city and are best reserved for the beach or the countryside.
- Standard business wear is appropriate for formal social occasions, restaurants, and the theater.
- Hungarians enjoy dressing up for their many formal events. Dark suits, tuxedos, and formal gowns are popular.

Cultural Note

Chess is one of the most popular pastimes among Hungarians. Hungary has produced world-class chess players, including two grandmasters: Judit and Zsuzsa (Susan) Polgár, and their sister, Zsófia (Sofia), an International Master. Judit is regarded as the strongest female player of all time, and has defeated almost every top player in the world, including Garry Kasparov. Susan was the top-ranked female chess player in the world by the age of fifteen.

Inviting your Hungarian prospects to play a game of chess might be an excellent opening move.

India

Republic of India

> **Cultural Note**
>
> On March 12, 1930, Mahatma Gandhi began a 240-mile march, on foot, from Sabarmati to the coastal village of Dandi, in order to gather salt from the sea. The Salt March was in direct violation of British law, because the sale or production of salt by anyone but the British government was a criminal offense. However, up to one-fifth of a peasant's annual income could be consumed by the tax because salt was critical to the vegetarian diet of many Indians (particularly in India's intensely hot and humid climate). The twenty-three-day Salt March ultimately proved to be one of the major steps in India's fight for independence.

▶ WHAT'S YOUR CULTURAL IQ?

1. In 2004, a new prime minister of India was sworn in. TRUE or FALSE: He was the first Sikh to hold this position.

   ANSWER: TRUE. Prime Minister Manmohan Singh was a former International Monetary Fund official and finance minister. His priorities included better relations with Pakistan.

2. Many countries have decided to eradicate "colonial" or westernized versions of their cities' names. This movement began in western India in the 1990s and resulted in many changes all across India. Match the current city title with its former name.

   a. Mumbai   1. Calcutta
   b. Chennai   2. Bombay
   c. Kolkata   3. Madras

   ANSWER: a. 2; b. 3; c. 1

3. "Civilization is the encouragement of differences" is a quote by:

   a. Jawaharlal Nehru
   b. George W. Bush
   c. Mahatma Gandhi

   ANSWER: c. Mahatma Gandhi's dreams for a peaceful India have been buffeted by harsh realities in recent history, but his views are available online. One site is *www.mahatma .org.in*.

▶ TIPS ON DOING BUSINESS IN INDIA

- The workplace in India has changed drastically in the last few decades—from high-tech booms to Bollywood—the pace of decision-making has sped up in many industry segments. However, traditional elements of doing business essentially remain the same. Networking, face-to-face meetings, and building relationships are still the means to success in India.

- Highly educated Indians enjoy heated debates and feel strongly about defending their country's viewpoints. Keep an open mind, and never criticize India's poverty, belief systems, politics, caste system, or any business practices you may not understand or appreciate.
- Bargaining and negotiating is a continual lifestyle in India. Be prepared for multiple contract iterations.

COUNTRY BACKGROUND

History

The Indian subcontinent was home to advanced civilizations since before recorded history. It has also known its share of invaders. The Aryans (predecessors of the Hindus) conquered most of the subcontinent before 1500 B.C. The Muslim Moghuls ruled much of India until the advent of the European invaders. The Portuguese first arrived in 1489. French, Dutch, and English traders followed. The British East India Company became ascendant, essentially ruling India from 1760 to 1858, when India was formally transferred to the British Crown.

After long years of struggle, and nonviolent resistance to British colonialism under Mohandas Gandhi and Jawaharlal Nehru, India became an independent country on August 15, 1947.

When the British left in 1947, British India was partitioned into primarily Hindu India and mostly Muslim Pakistan. The centuries-old antagonism between Hindus and Muslims has repeatedly erupted into open warfare between India and Pakistan since independence.

Type of Government

The Republic of India is a multiparty federal republic. The head of government is the prime minister, while the president is the chief of state. There are two multiparty legislative houses: the Council of States and the House of the People.

In the 1920s, Mahatma Gandhi made the Indian National Congress into India's leading political force. Its successor, the Congress Party, has ruled India for most of the years since independence.

India's first prime minister was Mahatma Gandhi's compatriot Jawaharlal Nehru. Power remained with the Congress Party until 1977, when Prime Minister Indira Gandhi (Nehru's daughter) was voted out of office. Janata Party leader Morarji Desai became prime minister, but his Janata coalition broke up in 1979. An interim government called new elections, and Indira Gandhi returned to power in 1980. She was assassinated by her own Sikh bodyguards in 1984, and she was succeeded by her son, Rajiv Gandhi. He attempted to steer the country toward a more market-oriented economy but was defeated in the 1989 elections by another Janata coalition, and Vishwanath Pratap Singh became prime minister.

V. P. Singh's minority government's most serious crisis resulted from its determination to reserve some 49 percent of government jobs for lower castes (which make up 54 percent of India's 890 million people). Insurgencies in Punjab, Kashmi, and Assam further weakened the government. The Singh government fell in November 1990.

Rajiv Ghandi was assassinated during the elections of May 1991. In 1998 the Hindu nationalist BJP party formed a coalition under Prime Minister Atal Behari Vajpayee, and India performed their first nuclear tests. President Abdul Kalam, the former architect of India's missile program, was elected in 2002, and Manmohan Singh was sworn in as prime minister in a surprise victory for the Congress Party in 2004.

For current government data, visit the Embassy of India at *www.indianembassy.org*.

Cultural Note

India's government is determined to achieve self-sufficiency, and for decades has declined offers of outside help. In fact, after the tragic Boxing Day tsunami of 2004, not only did India decline outside aid, it provided assistance to its neighbors.

Indians tend to be very patriotic, and most support their government's efforts to increase their country's prestige. They believe that India should take its rightful place as one of the world's leading nations and as the leading military power in South Asia.

Language

Hindi is the national language, and English is an associate official language (widely used for business and political communications), but there are 14 other official languages and almost 400 others acknowledged by linguists. The 14 additional official languages are:

Assamese, Bengali, Gujarati, Kannada, Kashmiri, Malayalam, Marathi, Oriya, Panjabi, Sanskrit, Sindhi, Tamil, Telugu, and Urdu. Hindustani is a popular variant of Hindi/Urdu that is spoken widely throughout northern India but it is not an official language. The literacy rate is listed at approximately 60 percent.

The Indian View

Religion plays a major role in the daily lives of most Indians, and two of the world's great religions—Buddhism and Hinduism—were born here.

The majority of Indians are Hindu. Unlike many religions that are traced to a particular founder, Hinduism grew out of Indian mythology. Hinduism has many variants and lacks a single, authoritative text (like the Christian Bible or the Muslim Koran). It is a religion with multiple gods, and it teaches a belief in karma and reincarnation. To escape the cycles of reincarnation and achieve nirvana, one must stop committing both bad deeds and good deeds—a difficult process that requires virtual nonintervention with humanity. India's caste system is supported by most variants of Hinduism. Many Hindus venerate cows and neither eat beef nor wear leather. Many Hindus are vegetarians.

Interestingly, Hinduism is still an evolving, dynamic religion. In some Hindu variants, new gods continue to be added to the pantheon. Indian film stars sometimes find themselves added to the Hindu pantheon!

A minority of Indians are Muslim. Islam is a monotheistic religion with ties to both Judaism and Christianity. Shiite Muslims outnumber Sunni Muslims by about three to one in India. Surrender to the will of Allah is a central belief. Pork and alcohol are prohibited to observant Muslims. While the majority of Hindus and Muslims coexist peacefully in India, violence does sometimes break out. Hundreds of people in both religions have died in religious conflicts.

About 2 percent of Indians are Sikhs. Sikhism combines tenets of both Hinduism and Islam. Sikhs believe in reincarnation but do not recognize caste distinctions. Unlike Hindus, Sikhs reject nonintervention with the world as cowardly.

India also has Christians, Buddhists, Jains, and Zoroastrians. The Republic of India has no official religion.

The origins of the caste system are unclear, but it has existed in India for thousands of years. Even though the government has outlawed discrimination on the basis of caste, castes still play a significant role in the politics and business of the country. Although there are only four traditional castes, these are broken down into thousands of subcastes.

☑ Know Before You Go

India has suffered everything from cyclones (in 1999 at least 10,000 died in the eastern state of Orissa) to massive earthquakes (approximately 30,000 dead in Gujarat during 2001) to the devastation of the tsunami in southern India in 2004. Additional hazards include droughts, flash floods from monsoons, and extreme weather changes in the Himalayas.

Stay healthy on your trip. Listen to your doctor's advice prior to your visit (and take your vaccinations against hepatitis A, cholera, etc.). Many travelers fall ill because of overindulging in spicy foods, or eating raw fruits or vegetables that have been contaminated. Drink bottled water, wear sunscreen, and be certain to bring any required medications with you.

▶ CULTURAL ORIENTATION

Cognitive Styles: How Indians Organize and Process Information

In India information is accepted openly as long as it does not challenge religious and social structures. Because of rote learning and tradition, most thinking is associative. However, highly educated Indians are more abstractive and analytical. Although universal rules of behavior exist within the social structure, immediate situations and people are of major concern, but always within the constructs of the caste system.

Negotiation Strategies: What Indians Accept as Evidence

Personal feelings form the basis for the truth, but a strong faith in religious ideologies is always present. The use of objective facts is less persuasive than a combination of feelings and faith.

Value Systems: The Basis for Behavior

Although it is constantly being challenged by younger citizens, India still has an attachment to the caste system, with all of its social structure and liabilities. The following three sections identify the Value Systems in the predominant culture—their mode of dividing right from wrong, good from evil, and so forth.

Locus of Decision-Making

India is a moderately collectivistic culture in which an individual's decisions must be in harmony with the family, group, and social structure. Success and failure are often attributed to environmental factors. Friendships and kinships are more important than expertise, although diplomas and certificates are coveted. One must build a relationship with other participants in the negotiation process by discussing friends and family. Indians may often be too polite to say "no."

Sources of Anxiety Reduction

With such a strong social structure, there is little anxiety about life because individuals know and accept their place in the society or organization. Behaviors contrary to religious traditions are not easily tolerated. There is a strong sense of what westerners call "fatalism," so time is not a major source of anxiety, and passivity is a virtue. Emotions can be shown, and assertiveness is expected.

Issues of Equality/Inequality

There is a very rigid structure of inequality, even though there is equality under the law (seldom enforced). The belief that there are qualitative differences between the castes is ingrained. Traditional male chauvinism is strong, and women do not have equal privileges. The abundant sexual symbols in society do not translate into an acceptance of public intimacy.

> **Cultural Note**
> Tipping in India is more than just a reward for good service; it is often the way to ensure that things get done. The term baksheesh encompasses both these meanings. Judicious (and discreet) use of baksheesh will often open closed doors, such as getting a seat on a "sold-out" train.

▶ BUSINESS PRACTICES

Punctuality, Appointments, and Local Time

- Indians appreciate punctuality but do not always practice it themselves. Keep your schedule loose enough for last-minute rescheduling of meetings.
- Request appointments as far ahead as possible. Advances in communication systems have made it far easier to schedule meetings, but it is still appropriate to get on the schedule of executives as early as possible.
- Be aware that your Indian contacts may request impromptu meetings, at late hours.
- Make sure that you are fully equipped with the latest wireless and telecom devices before you arrive in India—your prospects will want multiple ways to contact you and will expect you to invest in technology.
- Although they usually do not make final decisions, middle managers do have input. A middle manager on your side can forward your proposal. Often they are more accessible, and they are willing to meet at any time of the day.
- Go to the top of the company for major decisions.
- Indian executives generally prefer late morning or early afternoon appointments, between 11:00 A.M. and 4:00 P.M.
- The best time of year to visit India is between October and March, bypassing the seasons of extreme heat and monsoons.
- Business is not conducted during religious holidays, which are numerous. Dates for these holidays change from year to year, so confirm your schedule with local contacts.
- India is five and a half hours ahead of Greenwich Mean Time (G.M.T. +5½), or ten and a half hours ahead of Eastern Standard Time (E.S.T. +10½ hours).
- India operates in one time zone, and although it does not observe daylight-saving time, many visitors have mentioned their use of IST (Indian Stretchable Time).

Negotiating

- Indians have a less hurried attitude toward time than North Americans. The concept "time is money" is alien to many Indians.
- While you should get sound legal and tax advice before negotiating any agreement, it is important to be flexible and not appear too legalistic during negotiations.
- Be prepared to offer competitive technology packages with close technical follow-up. The technical assistance you can provide and how effective your training support is will be critical factors in the decision.
- Expect delays; they are inevitable. The Indian government moves at its own pace, and communication within India may still be somewhat difficult. Be patient, and make a realistic assessment of the steps and time involved in finalizing any agreements.

- Always present your business card. It is not necessary to have it translated into an Indian language.
- Business in India is highly personal. A great amount of hospitality is associated with doing business. Tea and small talk are preludes to most discussions.
- When refreshments are offered, it is customary to refuse the first offer, but to accept the second or third. To completely refuse any refreshment is an insult. Drink slowly if you wish to limit your intake of the sugary, milky Indian tea.
- The word "no" has harsh implications in India. Evasive refusals are more common and are considered more polite. Never directly refuse an invitation—just be vague and avoid a time commitment. "I'll try" is an acceptable refusal.

Cultural Note

In a monetary transaction, your change is simply placed in your hand, without explanation of the amount. If you remain standing with your hand outstretched, you may receive more change.

Be sure to keep lots of small change on hand, because street merchants and taxi drivers often claim they do not have change.

▶ BUSINESS ENTERTAINING

- Business lunches are preferred to dinners.
- Remember that Hindus do not eat beef and Muslims do not eat pork.
- Businesswomen may host Indian businessmen at a meal without embarrassing the men, although the men may try to pay at the end of the meal. Female executives should arrange to pay the bill with the waiter before the meal.
- If you are invited to dinner, be a few minutes late unless it is an official function. If the dinner is in a home, you may arrive fifteen to thirty minutes late.
- Eat only with the right hand, because the left hand was traditionally used for hygienic purposes and is considered unclean.
- Touching a communal dish with your hands may cause fellow diners to avoid it.

    Never offer another person (even a spouse) food from your plate, as it is considered "polluted" as soon as it is placed on your plate.
- Washing your hands both before and after a meal is important. In Hindu homes, you are expected to rinse your mouth out as well.
- Do not thank your hosts at the end of a meal. Saying "thank you" for a meal is insulting because the thanks are considered a form of payment. Returning the meal by inviting your hosts to dinner shows that you value the relationship.
- India's two major religions abjure beef and pork, so it is not surprising that Indian cuisine uses mostly chicken, lamb, or vegetables.

PROTOCOL

Greetings

- In large cities, men and very westernized Indian women will offer to shake hands with foreign men and sometimes with foreign women. Western women should not initiate handshaking with Indian men.
- There are numerous ethnic, linguistic, and religious groups in India, each with its own traditions.
- The majority of Indians are Hindu. Most Hindus avoid public contact between men and women. Men may shake hands with men, and women with women, but only westernized Hindus will shake hands with the opposite sex.
- A minority of Indians are Muslim. Traditionally, there is no physical contact between Muslim men and women. Indeed, if an orthodox Muslim male is touched by a woman, he must ritually cleanse himself before he prays again. Because of this, women should not offer to shake hands with Muslim men (nor should men offer to shake hands with Muslim women). Of course, if a westernized Indian offers to shake hands, do so. Other Indian religious groups, such as Sikhs, also avoid public contact between the sexes.
- The traditional Indian greeting is the *namaste*. To perform the namaste, press the palms of your hands together (as if praying) below the chin, near the heart, and gently nod or bow slightly. There are many Web sites that describe the meaning of the namaste, and how this peaceful greeting can be appropriate for individuals or for large meetings.
- A namaste is useful for foreigners in any situation where a handshake might not be acceptable. It is also a good alternative to a handshake when a Western businesswoman greets an Indian man.
- Indians of all ethnic groups disapprove of public displays of affection between people of the opposite sex. Do not touch (except in handshaking), hug, or kiss in greeting.

India

Titles/Forms of Address

- It is important to note that India's naming conventions are changing. For example, the Southern region of India seems to be gradually moving toward the naming customs of the North, and professional females are starting to keep their maiden names.

- Titles are highly valued by Indians. Always use professional titles, such as "Professor" and "Doctor." Don't address someone by his or her first name unless you are asked to or you are close friends; use "Mr.," "Mrs.," or "Miss."

- Status is determined by age, university degrees, caste, and profession.

- Occupationally, government service is more prestigious than private business.

- Traditionally, Hindus did not have family surnames. A Hindu Indian male used the initial of his father's name first, followed by his own personal name. For example, V. Thiruselvan is "Thiruselvan, son of 'V.'" For legal purposes, both names would be written out with an "s/o" (for "son of") between the names: Thiruselvan s/o Vijay. In either case, he would be known as Mr. Thiruselvan. However, long Indian names are often shortened. He may prefer to be called either Mr. Thiru or Mr. Selvan.

  Hindu female names follow the same pattern: father's initial plus personal name. When fully written out, "d/o" (for "daughter of") is used instead of "s/o." When an Indian woman marries, she usually ceases to use her father's initial; instead, she follows her personal name with her husband's name. For instance, when S. Kamala (female) marries V. Thiru (male), she will go by Mrs. Kamala Thiru.

- Some Indians will use Western-style surnames. Christian Indians may have biblical surnames like Abraham or Jacob. Indians from the former Portuguese colony of Goa may have surnames of Portuguese origin, such as Rozario or DeSilva. Such a person could be addressed as Dr. Jacob or Mr. DeSilva.

- Muslim names are usually derived from Arabic. Generally, a Muslim is known by a given name plus *bin* (son of) plus their father's name. For example, Osman bin Ali is "Osman, son of Ali." He would properly be called Mr. Osman, not Mr. Ali—Mr. Ali would be Osman's father.

- A Muslim woman is known by her given name, plus *binti* (daughter of) and her father's name. For example, Khadijah binti Fauzi is "Khadijah, daughter of Fauzi." She would be known as Miss Khadijah or, if married, as Mrs. Khadijah. For business purposes, some Indian women attach their husband's name. Thus, if Khadijah was married to Osman, she might choose to be known as Mrs. Khadijah Osman. Note that in English, binti may also be spelled "binte.

- Some westernized Indians drop the bin or binti from their name.

- A Muslim male who has completed his pilgrimage to Mecca is addressed as Haji. A woman who has done so would be addressed as Hajjah. Note that these titles are not automatically conferred on spouses; they must be individually earned by making the pilgrimage. However, when in doubt, err on the side of generosity. It is better to give a superfluous title than to omit one.

- Indian Sikhs generally have a given name followed by either Singh (for men) or Kaur (for women). Always address them by a title and first name. While Singh literally means "lion," to refer to a Sikh male as Mr. Singh is as meaningless as saying Mr. Man in English.

Gestures

- Many Indians consider the head to be the seat of the soul. Never touch someone else's head, not even to pat the hair of a child.
- As in much of the world, to beckon someone, you hold your hand out, palm downward, and make a scooping motion with the fingers. Beckoning someone with the palm up and wagging one finger can be construed as an insult.
- Standing tall with your hands on your hips—the "arms akimbo" position (also the gesture for "Offsides!" in soccer)—will be interpreted as an angry, aggressive posture.
- The comfortable standing distance between two people in India varies with the culture. In general, Hindu Indians tend to stand about three or three and a half feet apart.
- Pointing with a finger is rude; Indians point with the chin.
- Whistling under any circumstances is considered impolite.
- Winking may be misinterpreted as either an insult or a sexual proposition.
- Grasping your ears designates sincerity or repentance. Ears are considered sacred appendages; to pull or box someone's ears is a great insult.
- Never point your feet at a person. Feet are considered unclean. If your shoes or feet touch another person, apologize.

Gifts

- Gifts are not opened in the presence of the giver. If you receive a wrapped gift, set it aside until the giver leaves.
- If you are invited to an Indian's home for dinner, bring a small gift of chocolates or flowers. Don't give frangipani blossoms, however—they are associated with funerals.
- Don't wrap gifts in black or white, which are considered unlucky colors; green, red, and yellow are lucky colors.
- If you know that your Indian counterpart drinks alcohol, bring imported whiskey. High taxes can be avoided by purchasing the liquor on the airline or at the duty-free shop before arriving.
- Muslims consider dogs unclean. Do not give toy dogs or gifts with pictures of dogs to Indian Muslims.
- Should you give money to an Indian, make sure it is an odd number. Usually this is done by adding a single dollar; for example, give $11 instead of $10.

Dress

- For business dress, men should wear a suit and tie, although the jacket may be removed in the summer. Businesswomen should wear conservative dresses or pantsuits.
- For casualwear, short-sleeved shirts and long trousers are preferred for men; shorts are acceptable only while jogging. Women must keep their upper arms, chest, back, and legs covered at all times. Women who jog should wear long pants.
- Note that wearing leather (including belts, handbags, or purses) may be considered offensive, especially in temples. Hindus revere cows and do not use leather products.

Cultural Note

In the 1800s, the British East India Company created an enormous barrier between their territories and the then-independent Indian kingdoms. Rather than building a wall, they grew a huge hedge, 2,504 miles in length! The Great Hedge (as it was known) was designed to keep out untaxed goods. At some 1,700 breaks in the hedge, the British erected customs houses, from which they would demand taxes on imported goods. The most profitable of these was the Salt Tax. The profits from the Salt Tax justified the cost of building the Great Hedge, as well as paying for 12,000 Indians to maintain and guard it.

The Great Hedge was at least eight feet in height and five feet in width. Over rocky ground where nothing would grow, stone walls took the place of the hedge. As the British annexed the lands on the other side of the Great Hedge, the barrier lost its main purpose. Maintenance on the Great Hedge was abandoned in 1879. Some parts were torn down, others burned in the dry season or simply died. Few stretches of the Great Hedge remain today, and its existence is all but forgotten.

India

Indonesia

Republic of Indonesia
Local long form: Republik Indonesia
Former: Netherlands East Indies;
Dutch East Indies

Cultural Note

While the word for "tomorrow" in Bahasa Indonesian is *besok*, this word does not literally mean "within the next 24 hours." It can mean the day after, or the day after that, or it might even mean next week. Besok is much more like the Spanish mañana in that it denotes an indeterminate time in the near future.

 WHAT'S YOUR CULTURAL IQ?

1. Indonesia is an equatorial archipelago, marking the boundaries of the Indian and Pacific Oceans. TRUE or FALSE? Indonesia comprises at least 13,000 islands.

   ANSWER: TRUE. The exact number varies, according to one's definition of what constitutes an island. Some sources put the figure as high as 17,000.

2. Indonesia contains an astonishing diversity of wildlife, from giant lizards to orangutans. TRUE or FALSE: Zoologists say that Indonesia straddles what is known as the "Wallace Line."

   ANSWER: TRUE. The Wallace Line is the dividing point between Asian and Australian flora and fauna. Parts of Indonesia are on either side of this line.

3. Which of the following leaders is considered Indonesia's first freely elected head of state?
   a. Sukarno   c. B. J. Habibie
   b. Suharto   d. Megawati Sukarnoputri

   ANSWER: d. Sukarno and Suharto seized power. B. J. Habibie was Suharto's vice president, and took over when protestors forced Suharto out in 1998. The country's first free election for president occurred in 1999, when the daughter of Sukarno, Megawati Sukarnoputri, was elected president.

Cultural Note

As Indonesia is a relatively new nation, it is not surprising that it has a relatively short literary history. Indonesia has proven to be a fairly difficult place for journalists as well. Journalists who write things that displease the government have often been arrested (or, if foreigners, ordered to leave the country). Journalists found guilty of "criminal defamation" have been imprisoned (the editor of *Tempo* magazine, Bambang Harymurti, was sentenced to twelve months imprisonment in 2004).

TIPS ON DOING BUSINESS IN INDONESIA

- Indonesians show great deference to a superior. Consequently, supervisors are often told what they want to hear. The truth is conveyed in private, "up the grapevine"—often by a friend of the superior. Indonesians honor their boss by shielding him from bad news in public. This Indonesian trait, called *asal bapak senan* (which translates as "keeping father happy") is instilled in Indonesians from childhood. A foreign executive must establish a network through which he or she can be told the truth in private.

- Because Indonesians believe it is impolite to openly disagree with someone, they rarely say "no." The listener is expected to be perceptive enough to discern a polite "yes (but I really mean no)" from an actual "yes." This is rarely a problem when speaking in Bahasa Indonesia, because the language has at least twelve ways to say "no" and many ways to say "I'm saying yes, but I mean no." This subtlety is lost when translated into many foreign languages, including English.

- Indonesians are comfortable with silence, in both business and social settings. A silent pause does not necessarily signal either acceptance or rejection. Westerners often find such pauses uncomfortable, but Indonesians do not 'jump' on the end of someone else's sentence. A respectful pause may last as long as ten to fifteen seconds. Westerners often assume they have agreement and resume talking before an Indonesian has the chance to respond.

▶ **COUNTRY BACKGROUND**

History

Thanks to its central location, Indonesia has been a trading outpost for many centuries. Chinese trading settlements in Indonesia were established as early as the third century B.C. However, it was Indian traders who eventually had the greatest influence upon early Indonesia. By the second century A.D., several small states had organized on Indian models and flourished on Sumatra, Java, and Borneo.

Many Indian influences are to be seen in modern Indonesia. Although Hinduism was superseded by Islam on most islands, it is still the main religion on Bali. The native language of Java is written in a variant of the Indian Devanagari alphabet.

Contact with Europe began in the sixteenth century. Beginning in 1511, the Portuguese dominated the region from their base in Malacca, in neighboring Malaysia. The Dutch arrived in 1596; they eventually reduced the Portuguese holdings in Indonesia to the eastern half of the island of Timor. Indonesia was ruled by the Dutch East India Company from 1602 to 1798, when the Dutch government took direct control. Nationalist sentiments grew during the early twentieth century, but Indonesia remained a Dutch colony until World War II. The Japanese occupied Indonesia from 1942 to 1945. During this occupation, native Indonesians were finally placed in positions of power and allowed by the Japanese to run the nation. One such leader, Sukarno, declared Indonesia an independent republic on August 17, 1945. The Dutch fought to regain control of Indonesia, but they finally relinquished all claims to their former colony in 1949.

When the Western powers refused to support him against the remaining Dutch presence in the area, Sukarno became hostile toward the West and received military assistance first from the USSR, then from the People's Republic of China. Most Indonesian political parties were restricted to allow the Communist Party of Indonesia (PKI) to become the dominant political force.

With Sukarno in ill health, the PKI decided to take power in a coup on September 30, 1965. The coup failed, and for the next six months Indonesia writhed in civil disorder. In 1966, President Sukarno was forced out of power and General Suharto became president.

Although Indonesia was officially a nonaligned nation, Suharto pursued friendlier relations with the West. Since Suharto's accession in 1966, Indonesia pursued a probusiness, proinvestment policy that brought increased prosperity and development.

In May of 1998, the long-simmering political discontent with the authoritarian rule of President Suharto erupted into violence. Under pressure, President Suharto resigned, and Vice President B. J. Habibie took power. An election—the first free election in Indonesian history—was held in May 1999. Despite the advantages of money, experience, and control of the media, the long-ruling party of Habibie and Suharto failed to win a majority in the election.

After the people of the Indonesian state of East Timor voted for independence in August of 1999, the government in Jakarta allowed legions of Indonesian soldiers and militias to run riot in East Timor. Thousands of Timorese were slain, tens of thousands fled the country, and many homes and businesses were burned. The world was outraged, and Jakarta reluctantly agreed to allow UN troops into East Timor. Peace was eventually restored, and East Timor became an independent country on May 20, 2002.

Type of Government

The Republic of Indonesia declared its independence in 1945. Fighting against the Dutch continued until 1949, which is the usual date given for Indonesian independence.

Indonesia is a unitary multiparty republic. The president is both head of state and head of the government. The Republic of Indonesia has two legislative houses. The House of People's Representatives and the People's Consultative Assembly.

As a diverse nation, separated by geography, language, ethnicity, and religion, Indonesia must constantly struggle against separatism and secession. Areas of Indonesia threatened by separatist movements are Aceh, Kalimantan, Sulawesi, the Molucca Islands, and Papua (formerly known as Irian Jaya). After a referendum and international pressure, East Timor was granted independence in 2002.

For current government data, visit the Embassy of Indonesia at *www.embassyofindo nesia.org.*

Cultural Note

The government has established an official doctrine called Pancasila, which affirms the existence of a single Supreme Being. This is in harmony with both Islam and Christianity, Indonesia's second largest religious grouping (9.6 percent of the population). It is, however, in opposition to Indonesia's minority Hindus (1.8 percent).

The five principles of Pancasila are:

- Belief in One Supreme God.
- Belief in a just and civilized humanity.
- Belief in the unity of Indonesia.
- Belief in Democracy.
- Belief that adherence to Pancasila will bring social justice to all the peoples of Indonesia.

All Indonesian government employees and all students are indoctrinated in Pancasila.

Language

The Republic of Indonesia has designated Bahasa Indonesia as the official language. Written in the Roman alphabet, Bahasa Indonesia evolved out of the "market Malay" trade language used throughout the region during the colonial era. The selection of Bahasa Indonesia as the official tongue was a conscious effort to unify all Indonesians; as a trade language, it did not have the literary history or prestige of other Indonesian tongues (notably Javanese). Bahasa Indonesia is written horizontally, left to right, using the Roman alphabet used in the West.

While as many as 140 million Indonesians use Bahasa Indonesia as a second language, no more than 30 million consider it their mother tongue. Almost half the population of Indonesia uses Javanese as its first language.

The Indonesian archipelago encompasses one of the most linguistically dense areas of the world. Ethnologue, at *www.ethnologue.com*, has identified 731 languages in Indonesia, 3 of which are extinct. All advertising, media, and official communications are required to be in Bahasa Indonesia, and it is taught in all elementary schools.

The Indonesian View

The early traders and settlers brought Hinduism and Buddhism to Indonesia (the Majapahit empire merged the two into a single state religion). Islam arrived in the sixteenth century and eventually became Indonesia's major religion. As with earlier religions, the Indonesians adapted Islam to suit their needs, especially on the island of Java. Indonesia is the world's most populous Islamic nation; its population of 185 million is more than double Pakistan's 90 million. However, Islam in Indonesia is fragmented into numerous sects, many of which are antagonistic toward one another.

The majority of Indonesians are Muslim. While Islam is not the official religion, Indonesia has declared itself to be officially monotheistic. Of course, this position is in accordance with Islam and in opposition to Hinduism.

In addition to ethnic and religious factionalism, Indonesians must deal with economic problems, a developing democracy, and a history of corruption on the part of their leaders. Under Sukarno, Indonesia had a system of "crony capitalism," in which business licenses were dependent upon the favor of friends and family of Sukarno.

Indonesia's former colonial owner, the Netherlands, exerts relatively little influence over Indonesia today (although the Netherlands remains a highly desired destination for Indonesian emigrants). The United States is a major influence, although Indonesians have some justification for being angry at the United States in regard to East Timor (in 1976 the United States indicated that it did not object to Indonesia's annexation of East Timor, but by 1999 the United States started putting pressure on Indonesia to grant independence to East Timor). Since the terrorist attacks of September 11, 2001, Indonesian terrorists have become a large concern. However, when foreign troops are on Indonesian soil—as with the majority of the UN troops in East Timor—they are usually Australian. Until the recent bombings, Australians also made up the bulk of foreign tourists in Indonesia.

The new player in Indonesian affairs is the People's Republic of China, which is increasing its influence all over Asia. Because much of Indonesian business is in the hands of ethnic Chinese, the PRC has a built-in advantage. However, this advantage is tempered by the distrust that many ethnic Malays have for Indonesian Chinese. If there is another pogrom by Malays against Indonesian Chinese, the PRC may decide to act.

☑ Know Before You Go

Indonesia is well within the Pacific "Ring of Fire" and, like many other countries, suffered horribly from the tsunamis generated by the earthquake of 2004.

There is no aspect of Indonesia that was not touched by the tsunami. While it is well nigh impossible to predict such a terrible event, travelers should take precautions when visiting any of the countries that were hit by the tragedy. Be certain to register with your country's embassy or consulate when you visit, and leave details of your trip with multiple contacts at home. Make it as easy as possible for people to track you down in an emergency.

Indonesia is also subject to volcanoes. Flooding and typhoons are a danger as well.

While Western foreigners—especially from the United States and Australia—have been targeted by bombings, the majority of visitors experience no hostility in Indonesia. However, check with your country's government as to whether or not there are any current travel advisories for Indonesia. Mob violence is probably more of a danger than the occasional terrorist acts.

Air quality is a sometimes a problem in Indonesian cities. Smoking is common and there are relatively few non-smoking areas. During extended dry seasons, smoke from slash-and-burn agriculture has become so omnipresent that it sometimes darkens the sky and poses a threat to aviation.

▶ CULTURAL ORIENTATION

Cognitive Styles: How Indonesians Organize and Process Information

Indonesians have a history of assimilating new ways of doing things into their indigenous systems. They are open to information. Independent thinking is discouraged in their education, so they tend to process information associatively. Those educated abroad may be more abstractive. Their focus is on the immediate situation and the people involved rather than on rules or laws that might govern behavior in similar situations.

Negotiation Strategies: What Indonesians Accept as Evidence

Most people will rely on the truth of their subjective feelings. However, this truth may be modified by a faith in the ideology of their religion. The most powerful influence is the desire for harmony. Those with higher education may accept objective facts more readily.

Value Systems: The Basis for Behavior

One should be aware of the value system of the Chinese, who conduct much of the business in Indonesia. Indonesians have blended Hinduism, Buddhism, Islam, and Christianity into their theology. The following three sections identify the Value Systems in the predominant culture—their methods of dividing right from wrong, good from evil, and so forth.

Locus of Decision-Making

Decision-making traditionally goes through deliberation and consensus. All interested parties are welcome to participate. They strive for balance; conciliation without resentments or grudges is a trait of the Indonesian culture. Many government officials and entrepreneurs adhere to a mystical form of spirituality called Kebatinan, a metaphysical search for inner harmony and guidance in decision-making. They do not subjugate the will of the individual to the will of the group.

Sources of Anxiety Reduction

There is a strong belief in the supernatural for protection and security. This faith goes beyond any one religion, although most Indonesians are at least nominally Muslims. The nuclear and extended families are basic to security and economic support, with marriage being used to reinforce economic and social alliances. The *adat* (common law) has become one of the major stabilizing factors maintaining the traditional rural societies. The military is the main arbiter of power in the government.

Issues of Equality/Inequality

In most organizations there is a strong authoritarian hierarchical system that demands obedience of subordinates. Although there are strong ethnic identities, there is also a strong national identity that is taught to all children in the primary school years. The husband is considered the head of the household, but the wife is not inferior in status, and both are expected to cooperate in maintaining their household and family. Equal rights for women have always been upheld in the community.

Nevertheless, Indonesia has a multiethnic society with many historic antagonisms. In particular, ethnic Chinese and Christian Indonesians are sometimes the targets of antagonism.

 ## BUSINESS PRACTICES

Punctuality, Appointments, and Local Time

- As a foreign businessperson, you are expected to be on time for all business appointments. This is especially true when you are meeting someone with a higher social standing than yourself.
- In general, the higher the status of an Indonesian, the more he or she is likely to appreciate punctuality. Sometimes Indonesian laborers consider themselves punctual if they arrive within a few hours of an appointment. Executives and government officials will understand promptness—but they still have the prerogative to make a subordinate wait.
- A majority of Indonesian businesspeople are Chinese. Their culture is very work oriented, and they are likely to be prompt. Other businesspeople and the majority of government officials are ethnic Malays. Their culture is very different from that of the Chinese, and they have a looser concept of time. Promptness has never been a virtue in the Malay culture of Indonesia.
- Social events in Indonesia involve different rules. In general, Indonesians arrive a half-hour late.
- The casual Indonesian attitude toward time may allow you to schedule appointments on short notice.
- Indonesian executives tend to be more accessible than executives in many countries. Even an Indonesian CEO is likely to meet with foreign businesspeople.
- English is used in many business transactions and correspondence. However, attempts to use Bahasa Indonesia are appreciated.
- Bahasa Indonesia is the official language of Indonesia. Although many government officials will speak some English, they may prefer to hold meetings in their native tongue. Fortunately, an English-speaking translator is usually close at hand.
- All official correspondence with government officials must be in Bahasa Indonesia. Use of the language is also mandated for many advertisements and publications.
- The holidays in Indonesia attempt to accommodate the celebrations of Islam, Hinduism, and Christianity.
- Observant Muslims fast from dawn to sundown during the month of Ramadan. Be sure not to eat or drink in front of fasting Indonesians. It can be difficult to conduct business during

Indonesia

Ramadan, when many Indonesians leave to visit relatives in rural areas—or even on another island. The price of food, clothing, and transportation tends to rise during Ramadan.

- As in most countries, Indonesians write the day first, then the month, and then the year (e.g., December 3, 2010, is written 3/12/10 or 3.12.10).

- Indonesia spans three time zones. Java and Bali are on West Indonesia Standard Time, which is seven hours ahead of Greenwich Mean Time (G.M.T. +7). Central Indonesia Standard Time is eight hours ahead of Greenwich Mean Time (G.M.T. +8); Lombok and Nusatenggara are on Central Time. The East Indonesia Standard Time Zone, which includes Maluku and Papua (Irian Jaya), is nine hours ahead of Greenwich Mean Time (G.M.T. +9).

Cultural Note

Expect to encounter tough negotiations. Indonesians negotiate virtually every aspect of their daily lives, from taxi rides to groceries. You should anticipate considerable haggling over even the smallest point. In addition, Indonesians are good at wearing down the opposition, because the concept "time is money" is not a cultural norm.

Negotiating

- Indonesians do business with people they know and like. Establishing this personal relationship will take time, but it is vital for success.

- The pace of business negotiations in Indonesia is far slower than in the West. Be patient and do not rush.

- It would be unusual to complete a complicated business deal in only one trip. Expect to take several trips over a period of months. Indeed, little will happen at the first meeting except getting acquainted.

- Politeness is one of the most important attributes for successful relationships in Indonesia. This politeness in no way hinders the determination of Indonesian businesspeople to get their own way.

- Everyone has a defined status in Indonesia. In Bahasa Indonesia, you generally converse with a person after you know whether he or she is your superior, inferior, or equal. Even when the conversation is in English, Indonesians will not feel comfortable until they know your position. This is one reason why Indonesians will ask you very personal questions about your job, your education, and your salary.

- Indonesians rarely say "no." This subtlety is lost in English. Westerners sometimes interpret this as deceit, but Indonesians are simply being polite by their own cultural standards.
  - This "no" is clear even in English: anytime an Indonesian says "yes, but . . . ," it means "no."
  - When there are any qualifications attached (such as, "It might be difficult"), it means "no."

- A clear way to indicate "no" is to suck in air through the teeth. This sound always indicates a problem.
- Evasion is indicative of a "no," even if the person has said neither "yes" nor "no." He or she may even pretend the question was never asked.

- A deal is never complete until all the paperwork is signed. Indonesians (especially the Chinese) often consult astrologers, so the signing may be delayed until an "auspicious" day arrives.
- People in Indonesia may smile or laugh in situations that westerners consider inappropriate. Smiles may hide embarrassment, shyness, bitterness, or discord. If an Indonesian nurse giggles while tending to a seriously ill male patient, this could be from embarrassment at having to touch a man, not callousness. Learning to interpret smiles and laughter may take a foreigner years.
- In Indonesia, an individual who expresses anger in public is considered unable to control himself or herself. Such a person will not be trusted or respected.
- Being embarrassed publicly (also called "losing face") is known as *malu*. One result of "malu mentality" is that Indonesians may allow a person to continue to err rather than risk embarrassment by correcting him or her in public. In effect, an Indonesian may "honor" someone's authority by allowing him or her to make a disastrous error.
- In Indonesia, individuals are rarely singled out in public, either for praise or for condemnation. People are expected to be part of a group, and it is the group that is addressed. If you must reprimand an individual employee, do it calmly and in private.
- Always be aware of social hierarchy. If you are part of a delegation, line up so that the most important persons will be introduced first. If you are introducing two people, state the name of the most important person first (e.g., "President Suhardjono, this is Engineer Wong").
- Speak in quiet, gentle tones. Always remain calm. Leave plenty of time for someone to respond to a statement you make(as long as ten to fifteen seconds) before speaking again. Westerners often assume that they have agreement and resume talking before a Indonesian has the chance to respond.
- Topics to avoid in conversation include any criticism of Indonesian ways, religion, bureaucracy, human rights record, or politics. Also, avoid any discussion of sex or the roles of the sexes. (However, do not be surprised to hear graphic discussions of birth control methods. The Indonesian government supports major population control programs.)

Business Entertaining

- Some Indonesians have negative images of foreigners. Indonesia was exploited by foreigners for some 300 years. Social encounters are the best way for you to dispel that preconceived image.
- Understand that there may be little conversation while eating. Do not be concerned by a silent meal.

- Take advantage of any invitations to social events. Establishing a successful business relationship hinges on establishing a social relationship as well.
- Invitations to social events may not come immediately. Be patient and let your Indonesian associates make the first invitation. You generally do not host a social event until you have already been a guest.
- Respond to written invitations in writing. Among the Chinese, white and blue are colors associated with sadness; do not print invitations with those colors. Red or pink is a good choice.
- Generally, spouses may be invited to dinner but not to lunch. However, no business will be discussed at an event where spouses are present.

Cultural Note

Hosting a party for Indonesians can be complex. Send out written invitations (addressed to husband and wife) a week in advance, but do not expect many responses in writing, even if your invitations say RSVP. Indonesians are somewhat averse to committing themselves to a social event. Find excuses to follow up (either by phone or in person) to remind your guests of the affair. Be prepared to explain (1) what event the party is celebrating, (2) the guest list, and (3) who the guest of honor is. Hold the party early; the guests will probably leave by 9:30 P.M. Indonesians find buffets more comfortable than sit-down dinners with assigned places. Be sure the food is sophisticated; if you depend on Indonesian servants to plan the meal, they are likely to select working-class fare (tasty but not prestigious). Remember that observant Muslims do not drink alcohol. Finally, show great respect toward your guest of honor. He (or she) is the last to arrive and the first to be served.

▶ PROTOCOL

Greetings

- Indonesia has more than 300 ethnic groups, each with its own traditions. These range from isolated Stone Age tribes in the jungles of Irian Jaya to the cosmopolitan denizens of Jakarta.
- Expect to shake hands only upon initial introductions and before and after a long separation. Most Indonesian handshakes are more like handclasps; they are rather gentle and last for some ten or twelve seconds. (By contrast, most North American handshakes last for only three or four seconds.) For special emphasis, the handshake can be intensified by placing your hand over your heart.
- Most ethnic Indonesians are Muslim; the majority of the others are Hindu. Traditionally, there is no physical contact between men and women in these cultures. (Indeed, if a religious Muslim male is touched by a woman, he must ritually cleanse himself before he prays again.) Because of this, women should not offer to shake hands with Indonesian men (nor should men offer to shake hands with Indonesian women). Of course, if a westernized Indonesian offers to shake hands, do so.

- Upon greeting, the traditional Muslim Indonesian salutation is the word *selamat*, which means "peace."

- Among Indonesian Chinese, the traditional greeting was a bow. However, most now shake hands or combine a bow with a handshake. Chinese men are more likely than other Indonesian ethnic groups to be comfortable shaking hands with a woman.

- The traditional Hindu greeting involves a slight bow with the palms of the hands together (as if praying). This greeting, called the namaste, will generally be used only by older, traditional Hindus. However, it is also an acceptable alternative to a handshake when a Western businesswoman greets a Hindu Indonesian man.

- Above all else, greetings in Indonesia are stately and formal. Do not rush. Take your time; hurried introductions show a lack of respect. This applies to all Indonesians, from executives to laborers.

- Among all ethnic groups, kissing in public (even a quick peck on a cheek) is considered unacceptable. Only the most fashionable and cosmopolitan of Indonesians will give even a quick kiss in greeting.

Cultural Note

Just as the British greeting "How do you do?" is rhetorical, Indonesians have many rhetorical greetings. Chinese greetings often involve food. "Have you eaten?" and "Have you taken food?" are rhetorical greetings; answer "Yes," even if you are hungry. Similarly, a typical Indonesian greeting when meeting on the street is "Where are you going?" This is also rhetorical; "For a walk" or "Nowhere of importance" is a perfectly acceptable answer ("I'm eating the wind!" is a local idiomatic response). You are not expected to reveal your itinerary.

- Business cards should be printed (preferably embossed) in English. Since ethnic Chinese constitute the majority of Indonesian businesspeople, you may wish to have the reverse side of some of your cards printed in Chinese (gold ink is the most prestigious for Chinese characters).

- Your business card should contain as much information as possible, including your business title and your qualifications. Indonesians include all of this data on their card, as well as any titles of nobility.

- Westerners should use their usual academic titles, rather than translate them into the Indonesian equivalent (which are sometimes derived from Dutch academic titles).

- The exchange of business cards can be quite stately. After introductions are made, the visiting businessperson should offer his or her card to each person present. Present your card with both hands. (The most deferential method is to present your card in your right hand, with your left hand lightly supporting your right wrist.) Give your card to the recipient with the print facing him or her (so he or she can read it). The recipient will receive the card with both hands, then study the card for a few moments before carefully putting it away in a pocket. You should do the same when a card is presented to you.

- Never put a business card in your back pocket, where many men carry their wallets. While it is useful to write information such as the pronunciation of a name on someone's business card, do not let the person see you writing on his or her card. Either of these actions may be interpreted as "defiling" a business card.

Titles/Forms of Address

- Every variation of personal naming patterns can be found among Indonesia's myriad ethnic groups. People may have one name or two, short names or long, given name followed by a family name or vice versa, or one name and one initial.
- Names are considered sacred by most Indonesians. Indeed, among some Javanese, a person who has a string of misfortunes will change his or her name to one considered luckier.
- Most businesspeople you meet should be addressed with at least a title and their name. If a person does not have a professional title (such as Engineer, Doctor, or Teacher), a Westerner may use "Mr." or "Madam," "Mrs.," or "Miss," plus their name. However, be aware that you may be omitting other titles, important both to the person and your understanding of that person.
- As you inquire of an Indonesian how you should address him or her, be forward in explaining what he or she should call you. Indonesians may be equally unsure as to which of your names is your surname. Follow their lead as to the degree of formality. Do not tell an Indonesian "just call me Tony" when you are calling him Dr. Armizal.

Gestures

- Aside from handshakes, there is no public contact between the sexes in Indonesia. Do not kiss or hug a person of the opposite sex in public—even if you are husband and wife. On the other hand, contact between people of the same sex is permitted. Men may hold hands with men or even walk with their arms around each other; this is interpreted as nothing except friendship.
- Among both Muslims and Hindus, the left hand is considered unclean. Eat with your right hand only. Where possible, do not touch anything or anyone with your left hand if you can use your right hand instead. Accept gifts and hold cash in the right hand. (Obviously, when both hands are needed, use them both.)
- The foot is also considered unclean. Do not move anything with your feet, do not point with your feet, and do not touch anything with your feet. Feet should not be rested on tables or desks.
- Do not show the soles of your feet or shoes. This restriction determines how one sits: you can cross your legs at the knee but not with one ankle on your knee.

- Pounding one fist into the palm of your other hand is an obscene gesture among some Indonesians.
- The head is considered the seat of the soul by many Indonesians. Never touch someone's head, not even to pat the hair of a child.
- As in much of the world, to beckon someone, you hold your hand out, palm downward, and make a scooping motion with the fingers. Beckoning someone with the palm up and wagging one finger can be construed as an insult.
- It is impolite to point with your forefinger. Point with your right thumb and a closed fist (like a hitchhiker). This gesture is also used to mean "you go first."
- Standing tall with your hands on your hips—the "arms akimbo" position—is always interpreted as an angry, aggressive posture. Indeed, this position is used as a ritualized symbol of anger in the Indonesian *wayang* (shadow puppet) theater.

Gifts

- Gift giving is a traditional part of Indonesian culture. Although gifts may be small, they are often exchanged.
- Gifts can celebrate virtually any occasion: when you return from a trip, when you are invited to an Indonesian home, when a visitor comes to tour your office or workplace, and in return for services rendered.
- It is not customary to unwrap a gift in the presence of the giver. To do so would suggest that the recipient is greedy and impatient. Worse, if the gift is somehow inappropriate or disappointing, it would embarrass both parties. Expect the recipient to thank you briefly, then put the still-wrapped gift aside until you have left.
- Food makes a good gift for most occasions. When a person visits an area of Indonesia where a delicacy is available, he or she is expected to bring some back for friends.
- Pork and alcohol are prohibited to observing Muslims, so do not give them as gifts to Indonesians. Other foods may be appropriate, although meat products must be *halal* (the Muslim equivalent of kosher). The prohibition against pork and alcohol also precludes pigskin products and perfumes containing alcohol.
- Muslim Indonesians consider dogs unclean. Do not give toy dogs or gifts with pictures of dogs.
- Pets that are prized by Indonesians include cats and birds, especially songbirds. Recordings of the songs of champion songbirds are distributed and may make a good gift for an Indonesian bird fancier.
- Remember that personal gifts from a man to a woman can be misinterpreted as romantic offerings. When a foreign businessman gives a gift to an Indonesian woman, he must let everyone know that he is simply delivering a gift from his company, or his wife.
- For information on gift giving to ethnically Chinese contacts, see the chapter on China.

Indonesia

- Observant Hindus do not eat beef or use cattle products. This eliminates most leather products as appropriate gifts.

Dress

- Indonesia straddles the Equator and thus is hot and humid all year long. Most of the lowlands have a daytime temperature range of 75 to 95°F, and humidity around 75 percent.
- Lower temperatures occur only in the mountainous areas.
- The rainy season runs from September through February, but sudden showers occur all year long. Some people carry an umbrella every day.
- Because of the heat and humidity, business dress in Indonesia is often casual. Standard formal office wear for men is dark trousers and a light-colored long-sleeved shirt and tie, without a jacket. Many businessmen wear a short-sleeved shirt with no tie.

  Businesswomen wear long-sleeved blouses, skirts, business suits, and more recently, pantsuits. The colors should be dark and muted; bright, vivid colors are not appropriate for a businesswoman.
- As a foreigner, you should dress more conservatively until you are sure what degree of formality is expected. Men should expect to wear a suit jacket and tie, and remove them if it seems appropriate. Whatever you wear, try to stay clean and well groomed—which is a feat in the tropics.
- Many Indonesian men wear an open-necked batik shirt to work. This is also popular for casual attire. Jeans are good for casualwear, but shorts should be avoided.

  In deference to Muslim and Hindu sensibilities, women should always wear blouses that cover at least their upper arms. Skirts should be knee-length or longer.

Cultural Note

Three calendars are in common use in Indonesia. The Western (or Gregorian) calendar is the official calendar. Islamic holidays are dated by the Arabic calendar, which loses approximately eleven days each year against the Western calendar. In addition, there is a Hindu-influenced Javanese calendar.

When certain days from different calendars coincide, it is considered lucky. For example, when the fifth day of the Western week falls on the fifth day of the Javanese week (which is only five days long), the occasion is considered auspicious.

Ireland

The Republic of Ireland
Local short form: Éire

> **Cultural Note**
> The Republic of Ireland joined the European Community in 1973, and trade with the European Union moved Ireland out from under the United Kingdom's shadow. Originally one of the poorest members of the EU, Ireland became eligible for EU loans and assistance, and many multinational corporations placed their headquarters there. EU influence also helped women to achieve more equality in Ireland. Historically a male-dominated society, Ireland now has many women in politics—including its recent presidents.

 ## WHAT'S YOUR CULTURAL IQ?

1. What service did the Irish render after the fall of the Roman Empire?
   a. They protected England from invasion by fierce Icelandic Vikings.
   b. They preserved Roman and Greek literature and disseminated it throughout Europe after the continent had been overrun by illiterate Germanic tribes.
   c. They became the primary provider of alcoholic beverages to the world.

   ANSWER: b. Greco-Roman heritage was lost to much of Europe after the fall of Rome. Irish priests and monks kept literary treasures safe within their monasteries while the western Roman Empire collapsed. Then, Irish missionaries spread out over Europe to convert the barbarians. In the process, they introduced them to Greek and Roman literature.

2. TRUE or FALSE? English is the sole official language of the Republic of Ireland.

   ANSWER: FALSE. They have two official languages: Irish (a.k.a., Irish Gaelic, or Erse) and English.

3. Which of the following Irish-born authors did not win the Nobel Prize for literature?
   a. Samuel Beckett   d. George Bernard Shaw
   b. Seamus Heaney   e. William Butler Yeats
   c. James Joyce

   ANSWER: c. Joyce might be the most famous novelist of the twentieth century, but he never won the Nobel.

> **Cultural Note**
> The Irish propensity for talk is exaggerated; not all Irish are gregarious, nor do all speak with great cleverness. But enough do to give foreigners this impression. Many Irish will talk to any foreigner they meet. A stranger's name, marital status, occupation, and reason for visiting are quickly ascertained, and this information is passed around from person to person. The contrast with cultures that ignore strangers is striking.

TIPS ON DOING BUSINESS IN IRELAND

- The Irish have an ambivalent attitude toward wealth. The founding father of the Irish Republic, Eamon De Valera, envisioned Ireland as a pastoral land of simple virtues. Moneymaking was not included as a virtue. People who have achieved financial success are not automatically respected. Ostentation is frowned upon, except in giving to charity.
- Irish hospitality and friendliness are well known. Most Irish look forward to chatting with friends and strangers alike over a cup of tea or a pint of Guinness (naturally, in a country with such a changeable climate, the weather is a constant topic.) It would be considered impolite not to talk to anyone in whose company you found yourself, whether in a waiting room or a pub.
- In the 1990s, Ireland experienced unprecedented economic growth. Ireland's rates of employment and growth outstripped that of most other European Union nations. After decades of seeking work in other countries, Irish emigrants began returning home. This has brought the Irish a degree of satisfaction, but not the exuberance one might expect. The Irish continue to have a deep strain of pessimism. Many feel that success today is no guarantee of success tomorrow.

▶ COUNTRY BACKGROUND

History

Although Ireland's economy and image have changed incredibly since 1990, its history reaches back to around 350 B.C., when Ireland was occupied by Celtic tribes from Europe. They overwhelmed the original inhabitants and became Ireland's dominant culture. Written Irish history began circa A.D. 400, and in A.D. 432 Saint Patrick brought Christianity to Ireland.

Anglo-Norman troops conquered most of Ireland in 1170, and the overlords loosely ruled a portion of Ireland known as the Pale for the next 400 years. In 1541, the Irish Parliament granted Henry VIII the title of King of Ireland, and the king's establishment of the Church of England eventually resulted in the persecution of Irish Catholics. The harp (which became Ireland's national symbol) was first used on Irish coinage under Henry VIII.

In 1801, the Act of Union made Ireland part of the United Kingdom and dissolved the Irish Parliament. Then in 1916, a rebellion in Dublin called the Easter Rising became a rallying point for Irish nationalism. The Anglo-Irish War, between the Irish Republican Army and the Royal Irish Constabulary, followed from 1919 to 1921. Years of negotiations resulted in independence from the United Kingdom for twenty-six southern Irish counties in 1921. The other six counties in the North (known as Ulster) remained part of the United Kingdom.

The Republic of Ireland formally withdrew from the British Commonwealth and became fully independent in 1948. In 1973, it joined the EC (now the EU).

"The Troubles" began in 1970, when the Irish Republican Army began fighting the Protestant government in Northern Ireland. Relatively little violence occurred in the Republic of Ireland. A peace settlement for Northern Ireland, called the Good Friday Agreement, was approved in 1998 but has not been implemented.

> ### Cultural Note
> In 1957, corporate taxes on foreign multinationals that invested in Ireland were almost eradicated. Low corporate taxes, free trade with the United Kingdom, relatively low wages, and English as an official language made Ireland extremely attractive to many corporations. After the setbacks of the 1970s, the Republic of Ireland experienced tremendous growth in the 1990s and was nicknamed the Celtic Tiger.

Type of Government

Ireland is a parliamentary democracy. Its president, or chief of state, is a somewhat ceremonial figure elected by popular vote to a seven-year term. According to the Irish Constitution, the president needs advance cabinet approval of speeches and travel.

The prime minister is the head of government and is nominated by the House of Representatives and appointed by the president.

The Bicameral Parliament, or Oireachtas, is comprised of the Seanad or Senate and the Dail Eireann or House of Representatives. The Dail representatives are elected by universal suffrage for a maximum of a five-year term. Members of the Senate also hold office for a five-year term; however, eleven Senate members are nominated by the prime minister and the remaining are elected by local universities and from panels of candidates in the following five areas: cultural and educational, agricultural, labor, industrial and commercial, and administrative. The Dail is the more powerful body. The electoral system features proportional representation in multicandidate constituencies. Current government data can be found at the Embassy of Ireland at *www.irelandemb.org*.

> ### Cultural Note
> The use of Gaelic in the Academy Award–winning movie *Million Dollar Baby* thrilled many Irish and Irish-American viewers. However, the heartfelt phrase *Mo chuisle*, which was printed on the character Maggie Fitzgerald's green silk boxing robe, generated some controversy. Some Gaelic speakers claimed it was spelled incorrectly, and some said it was mistranslated. The phrase from which Mo chuisle was evidently culled is "A chuisle mo chroÃ" (pulse of my heart).

Language

Ireland has two official languages, English and Irish (also called Irish Gaelic, Erse, or Gaeilge).

Irish is from the Gaelic (a.k.a., Goidelic) group of Celtic languages, which includes Scottish Gaelic and the now-extinct Manx; Welsh is a more distant relation. It was suppressed by the English overlords of Ireland and was close to dying out by the end of the nineteenth century. It survived in the most rural areas of Ireland (such regions were known as *Gaeltacht*). Organizations such as the Gaelic League helped revive its use. When Ireland achieved independence, the new government encouraged the use of Irish. Politicians gave speeches in Irish (often to audiences with little knowledge of the language). Today, some programs are broadcast in Gaelic, and Irish is a mandatory subject in schools. Proficiency in Irish is a qualification for a successful career in academia and the civil service. For those who master it, Irish is a second language. English is the everyday language of Ireland.

Ireland is not unique in the European Union for having two official languages. However, Ireland is alone among EU members in that one of those tongues is a revived language—Irish was near extinction until the Gaelic League revived it in the early twentieth century.

The Embassy of Ireland has a deeper explanation of Gaeilge at *www.irelandemb.org/gaeilge.html*.

Ethnologue, at *www.ethnologue.com*, lists five various languages for Ireland (Éire), all of which are living languages. They are English, Irish Gaelic, Scottish, Shelta (also called the Cant, Cant, Irish Traveler Cant, Sheldru, and Gammon) and Irish Sign Language for the Deaf.

Cultural Note

The Irish character can seem complex and contradictory at times. (Sigmund Freud is alleged to have said that the Irish are the only people who cannot be helped by psychoanalysis.) Ireland is still a Catholic country, yet the Irish people are inevitably described as rebellious by nature and sarcastic about authority. Ireland has the lowest rate of marriage per capita in the European Union, yet the highest fertility rate (2.1 children per woman). And even when Ireland was a poor country with high unemployment, the Irish often gave more per capita to charities than far wealthier nations.

The Irish View

It is not possible to define the Irish identity without reference to two seminal influences: the British Empire and the Catholic Church.

Ireland was invaded by the British many times. Subjugation began in earnest after Henry VIII changed England's official religion from Catholicism to Protestantism, which had the side effect of making wealthy Catholic monasteries into legitimate military targets. The Irish were dispossessed and the Protestant gentry set up farms known as "plantations." In the North of Ireland, even the plantations' tenant farmers were Protestant Englishmen. Southern Ireland was brutally subjugated by Cromwell the Protector in the 1650s. Catholic Irish lands were confiscated. By the eighteenth century, Catholics owned less than 15 percent of Irish lands.

The height of British misrule of Ireland occurred during the Potato Famine of the 1840s. The potato crop failed in 1842 and then failed again in 1846. While 1 million Irish starved and another million fled Ireland, British-owned plantations in Ireland continued to export grain. By the time the famine eased, the population of Ireland had dropped from over 8 million to some 6 million. Emigration had become a way of life and continued until the economic turnaround of the 1990s. As in other occupied countries, the Church became a guardian of the national identity during the hard years.

While Ireland has no official religion, about 92 percent of the citizens of Éire claim to be Catholic. The Church's influence has waned in recent history, and there is a more liberal view on sexuality. A referendum was narrowly passed in 1995 to allow divorce, and contraceptives are now widely available. (Condoms were illegal until 1980; after that, they could only be sold to married couples—by prescription.) Abortion is still illegal, but there are no sanctions against women traveling to England for abortions.

The Irish are exceedingly proud of their history and of their tremendous successes in the last few decades.

☑ Know Before You Go

Ireland does not have any natural hazards, unless one includes winter weather. But business travelers may even enjoy the look of the Isle in the misty rain and cold—it certainly makes pubs look warm and inviting.

There is some water pollution from agricultural runoff, and Ireland has been listed as a transshipment point for illicit drug trade.

▶ CULTURAL ORIENTATION

Cognitive Styles: How the Irish Organize and Process Information

Historically, Ireland has been seen as a traditional, conservative country—however they have always been interested in outside information and different opinions. Over many decades, the Irish have shown they are comfortable with risk. Their strong cultural identity has allowed them to accept the rapid changes that foreign investment and economic success have brought.

Negotiation Strategies: What the Irish Accept as Evidence

Historically, the Irish primarily used a combination of feelings and facts to discern the truth in a situation. With the recent changes in Ireland, younger Irish are more prone to consider the validity of facts as the primary basis for evidence. However, one's feelings for an individual still weigh heavily on business decisions. Again, they are comfortable with a short-term risk and may perceive a work decision almost like a bet.

Value Systems: The Basis for Behavior

The Irish are generally ambivalent about authority and, despite recent economic growth, do not feel as though immense success and wealth is an attractive goal. There is a belief that the poor should receive the same respect as the powerful. Besides the structure of the family and the Catholic Church, the Irish do not require additional rules to make them feel secure.

Locus of Decision-Making

Decisions are often made individually, usually by a senior executive, after some discussion with associates. The Irish will be polite but are more straightforward with good or bad news about business situations than in the past. An individual's right to make his or her own decisions is vital.

Sources of Anxiety Reduction

The immediate and extended family are the primary units of social organization, and they give the Irish a strong sense of identity and stability. This is followed by the precepts of Catholicism. The Irish are relatively open with their emotions but may have an aversion to saying a definitive "yes" or "no." Pressurized deadlines generate large amounts of stress.

Despite the economic gains that Ireland has made, there is often a sense of melancholy and cynicism that is expressed in songs and literature.

Issues of Equality/Inequality

There is a high level of masculinity in the culture, and sex roles were historically differentiated in a clear manner. The Irish are becoming more open to equality for women, as evidenced by recent elections and more women in executive positions. The Irish are very competitive and will grasp at opportunities as they arise.

⊙ BUSINESS PRACTICES

Punctuality, Appointments, and Local Time

- As in most countries, the Irish write the day first, then the month, and then the year (e.g., December 3, 2010, is written 3.12.10 or 3/12/10).
- Punctuality is expected for business appointments. The rules for social engagements, especially between friends, are more flexible.
- Perhaps because of the Irish tendency to do things differently from the British whenever possible, the Irish have traditionally taken a more relaxed view toward time.
- Because promptness has not historically been valued in Ireland, some Irish companies instituted unusual measure to encourage people to pay their bills on time. For example, the Irish telephone and electric utilities automatically enter paid-on-time bills into a raffle!
- Irish attitudes toward time may extend to deadlines and delivery dates. Do not automatically expect something to be executed at the time or date promised, unless you have been careful to explain why that deadline must be met.
- Avoid scheduling many appointments around July and August, because many Irish executives will be on vacation. Most businesses also close from December 24 through January 2 during the Christmas period.
- Ireland's national holiday is Saint Patrick's Day, on March 17.
- Ireland, like England, is on Greenwich Mean Time. This is five hours ahead of U.S. Eastern Standard Time (EST +5).

Negotiating

- Historically, the Irish did business with people they knew and liked. They still feel far more comfortable working with people they know but have extended their personal contacts into the global market.
- Money was minimally discussed and seemed to be an almost embarrassing topic.
- A handshake and a verbal promise were good enough for many Irish, as was the fact that a delivery date was an approximation.
- It can still be considered poor manners to directly tell someone "No, we haven't any of those products" or "No, we cannot do that work for you." A softer answer (which may stretch the truth a bit) is more civilized.
- With the economic changes over the last two decades, negotiations have taken on a more assertive tone. Do not expect the Irish to accept initial offers—they will expect to bargain for the best possible margin that they can.
- A fast cash profit is generally viewed as better than a long-term market share.
- However, the Irish will still want to do business on a personal level, and even brief meetings for coffee can be the key to building a valuable relationship.
- Never cancel an appointment without a serious reason—it is insulting to not only that potential contact but all his or her close contacts as well.
- Many Irish businesses are family owned, and nepotism is considered as a good thing. This is one reason it can be difficult to enter a network without an appropriate contact or introduction. The Irish like to work with their own, and they do not offer referrals or introductions without trusting you first.
- Never praise England or use any British symbolism during your negotiations with the Irish.
- Never make inflated claims about your product or yourself. The Irish do not like hype.
- Since sports are generally a good topic, you might want to use a sports analogy in your presentation—that is, if you are up-to-date with popular Irish teams.
- Leave the pressure for quick decisions on the airplane. Deadlines can be problematic.

> **Cultural Note**
> St. Patrick was born a Romanized Celt called Patricius. His mission to Catholicize Ireland occurred between A.D. 431 and 461. He died on March 17, and his Confessio (which he wrote) tells much of his life story.

Business Entertaining

- Offer to take your Irish associates to a popular restaurant or pub. Make sure you confirm that you are picking up the tab, and do not try to initiate a serious work discussion until after the meal is over.
- Do not expect table service at a pub. Go to the bar to order your pint of Guinness.

- After-hours Guinnesses or ciders are primarily for establishing social relationships; you may never get to the topic of business in a pub.
- Going to the pub is traditionally a daily routine for many Irish. Be aware of your limitations.
- Avoid bringing up topics of discussion like abortion, religion, and politics with older Irish citizens—they will generally have conservative views. If these topics do arise, refrain from commenting unless you fundamentally agree with your Irish hosts.
- Younger Irish citizens are far more liberal and open to change; however, do not expect them to appreciate your views. Many foreign executives feel too comfortable too soon chatting with the Irish, and air their opinions far too readily.

▶ PROTOCOL

Greetings
- A handshake is the most common form of greeting. The grip is generally firm. Both men and women shake hands.
- Foreigners should not initiate a hug.
- Give your Irish associates enough room to stand a few feet apart from you after the handshake is over.
- Generally, the further you are from an urban setting, the further the acceptable personal distance.
- Whether it is a formal introduction in a business setting, or a chance meeting with a stranger in rural Ireland, you will find yourself spending time chatting about yourself, where you come from, your trip, etc. Always allocate enough time to visit a bit; the Irish will want to know something about you. Do not rush them.
- Whether you are leaving a serious meeting at headquarters or a little shop on a corner street, always say "goodbye."

Titles/Forms of Address
- During introductions, the Irish may use "Mr." or "Ms." and a last name with each other for the first meeting. However, many people go to first names right away (particularly younger members of the work force).
- Most Irish have two Christian, or given, names that are conferred upon them at baptism. Usually, people use just one of their first names, along with their family name (another name is bestowed upon Catholics during the Sacrament of Confirmation). This means that many Irish Catholics have rather long names (e.g., Patrick Joseph Sían Conaway).
- Many women do not take their husbands' last names. Alternatively, they may combine their own names with their husbands'.

- You may hear some of your Irish associates called by either Gaelic or English versions of their names. For example, Liam is William, and Máirín is Maureen. Some Gaelic names have no English equivalent.
- The prefixes "Mac" and "O" originally meant "son of." For example, Brendan MacCarthy meant Brendan, "son of" Carthy ("Mac" was changed to "Mc" by the English).
- Some names originally indicated an occupation; for example, Ms. Rose MacGowan would have been the daughter of a blacksmith—in Gaelic, she would be Ms. MacGabhann. (Gabha is Gaelic for "blacksmith.")

Gestures

- The Irish are comfortable with prolonged eye contact. Do not shift your gaze around when speaking with someone.
- Men do not usually touch or hug each other, unless they are participating at a sporting event.
- Winking is usually inappropriate.
- At work, the Irish are rather restrained in their gestures. Do not gesticulate emphatically during a presentation.

Gifts

- Gift giving is not common at work; however, a small, thoughtful present will be appreciated.
- Extravagant gifts can make the Irish uncomfortable. Dinners, visits to a pub, tickets to sporting events, etc., are more advisable.
- Bring wine, chocolates, and gifts for the children when you visit someone's home.

Dress

- Although business dress is usually casual among the Irish, they will expect you to wear more formal attire because you are a foreign executive.
- Fashions are changing in Ireland, so be adaptable.
- Visiting female executives will not want to wear any low-cut attire at work.
- While it may sound conservative, your garments will be scrutinized, so you should be more formal to maintain your credibility.

Cultural Note

Remember that Éire, Southern Ireland, the Free State, the Republic, and the South all mean the Republic of Ireland. If you confuse it with Northern Ireland, the North, or Ulster, you have definitely started out on the wrong foot with your Irish Republican associates. Northern Ireland is part of the United Kingdom. The Republic of Ireland is not.

Israel

State of Israel
Local short form: Yisra'el
Local long form: Medinat Yisra'el

Cultural Note

Until the founding of the state of Israel, the Hebrew language was primarily used for religious purposes, as Latin was used among Roman Catholics. Hebrew was not the daily tongue of any Jewish population. It has now been revived and serves as a unifying force among Jews.

The Hebrew alphabet has two characteristics that distinguish it from most European alphabets. First, it traditionally only denotes consonants, not vowels. (In modern usage, vowels may be represented by diacritical marks.) Second, the letters are not connected; there is no traditional cursive form. This contrasts with Arabic, which is a Semitic tongue closely related to Hebrew. Arabic also represents only consonants, but most of the Arabic alphabet consists entirely of connected letters. Even when Arabic is typeset, it is (in essence) written only in cursive. Both Hebrew and Arabic are written right to left.

▶ WHAT'S YOUR CULTURAL IQ?

1. Which of the following are official language(s) of the State of Israel?

   a. Arabic   c. Hebrew

   b. English   d. Yiddish

ANSWER: Both a. and c. Israel is a multicultural society, with a large Arab population.

2. Visitors to Israel are often stunned at encountering things they know only from holy books such as the Bible or the Koran. TRUE or FALSE? The Samaritans still exist in Israel.

ANSWER: TRUE. Known from the biblical "Parable of the Good Samaritan," this offshoot of Judaism has dwindled to about 600 members but still exists in Israel.

3. All of the following Israelis have won a Nobel Prize. Which of the following laureates is not an Israeli politician awarded the Nobel Peace Prize?

   a. Menachem Begin

   b. Avram Hershko

   c. Shimon Peres

   d. Yitzhak Rabin

ANSWER: b. Avram Hershko and Aaron Ciechanover, his colleague at the Technion-Israeli Institute of Technology, shared the 2004 Nobel for chemistry. The others were all (at different times) Israeli prime ministers: Begin won in 1978, while Peres and Rabin shared the prize in 1994.

> **Cultural Note**
> For a young nation, Israel has a strong literary tradition. Some, like Shmuel Yosef Agnon (winner of the 1966 Nobel Prize for literature), concentrate on writing about life in his eastern European birthplace. Others, such as S. Yizhar, have written about the Israeli War of Independence. Contemporary Israeli authors such as Amos Oz and David Grossman tend to focus on personal lives of Jews.
>   Arab-speaking Israelis also boast many authors, notably Anton Shammas, Michel Haddad, and Emile Habibi.

▶ TIPS ON DOING BUSINESS IN ISRAEL

- The typical Israeli that does business internationally is secular, not religious. He or she will probably deal with you much as any North American businessperson would. The most obvious differences will be that Israelis tend to be less formal, speak louder, and stand closer to you than most North Americans.
- Expect Israelis to ask you very personal questions. Nothing is considered off-limits, from your age to your marital status to how much you earn. You can answer such questions or not, as you please.
- To foreigners, it often seems that Israeli businesses operate at only two speeds: glacially slow, or right now. Even if your deal seems to be indefinitely delayed, be prepared to deliver quickly if the situation changes.

▶ COUNTRY BACKGROUND

History

Israel (including the West Bank) was the historical homeland of the Jews in biblical times. In A.D. 66 the Jews staged their Great Revolt against the Roman Empire, temporarily throwing off the Roman yoke. But the Roman armies returned, capturing Jerusalem and destroying the Temple in A.D. 70.

The Diaspora (dispersion) of the Jews began; the Jewish people were scattered all over the ancient world. Some Jews remained in Israel, but they constituted a small minority.

In the late nineteenth century, some European Jewish thinkers concluded that the Jewish people would never be safe until they had a country of their own. Led by a Viennese journalist named Theodor Herzl, the Zionist movement was born. Jews began moving back into Palestine (as the area was known), which was then part of the Ottoman Empire.

The United Kingdom promised to support the Zionists in return for Jewish support in World War I. However, in part because of the opposition of the local Arab peoples, Israel did not become a reality until after World War II. The modern state of Israel was created in 1948; the neighboring Arab states immediately declared war. Israel won that war, as it did the subsequent wars in 1967 and 1973.

In the Six-Day War of 1967, Israel routed the combined forces of Egypt, Jordan, and Syria. Israel occupied a large amount of formerly Arab territory: the Egyptian Sinai, the Syrian Golan Heights, and a sizeable part of Jordanian land.

During Yom Kippur in 1973, Egypt and Syria launched a surprise attack on Israel. Although Israel again came out on top, their opponents achieved a better result than the first time. By not being routed as they were in 1967, the Egyptians and Syrians felt that they had restored their lost honor.

With U.S. assistance, Israel and Egypt stunned the Arab world by signing a peace treaty in 1978. Over the next few years, Israel withdrew from the Sinai and Egypt reopened the Suez Canal to Israeli shipping.

In the 1990s, the Palestinian intifada, or uprising, eventually prompted the Israelis to negotiate territorial settlements with the Palestinians. Several peace accords were negotiated but never fulfilled their promise. Usually, both sides accused the other of violating the peace accords.

At the present time, the Palestinian Authority runs portions of the Occupied Territories. Palestinians hope that this limited self-rule will one day evolve into an independent Palestinian state. The death of the long-time Palestinian leader Yasir Arafat in 2004, and the return of the Gaza Strip may lead to changes in the long stalemate between the Israelis and the Palestinians.

Syria still hopes for the return of the Golan Heights, occupied by Israel since 1967. The return of the entire Golan seems unlikely; Israel unilaterally annexed the Golan in 1981. Not only are the Golan Heights strategically important in any battle between Israel and Syria, they provide one-third of Israel's water supply.

Type of Government

Israel is a parliamentary multiparty democracy. There is one legislative house, called the Knesset. The chief of state is the president, who is allowed to serve for no more than two five-year terms. The head of government is the prime minister, who is also the head of the Cabinet.

Most of the Palestinians in the Occupied Territories are not Israeli citizens. They have had no vote and were not tried in the Israeli criminal courts but in special military courts. The planned limited self-rule will offer them a chance to elect leaders and police themselves.

Current government data can be found on the Web at the Embassy of Israel at *www .israelemb.org.*

Language

The official languages of Israel are Arabic and Hebrew. Other languages frequently heard in Israel are English, French, Yiddish, and Russian. Ethnologue, at *www.ethnologue.com*, has catalogued thirty-three languages spoken in Israel, three of which are now extinct.

The Israeli View

Although Israel was established as the Jewish homeland, the state of Israel has no official religion. Except for the failed Soviet experiment of the "Jewish Autonomous Oblast" near the Russian-Chinese border, Israel is the only Jewish homeland in existence.

A large segment of Israeli Jews are secularists, who rarely observe the forms of the Jewish faith.

Ethnic Jews now make up slightly more than 82 percent of the population. The rest are primarily Arabs, mostly Palestinian. The majority of Palestinians are Sunni Muslims, but there are Christian Palestinians as well. There are even Muslims in Israel who are not Arabs, such as the ancient Circassian community in the north of Israel. There are also small numbers of a bewildering array of ethnic and religious groups. The largest of these are the Druze (1.6 percent), an obscure Arab people who keep their religious beliefs a secret. The Druze community has closed itself to outsiders since approximately A.D. 1050. This self-segregation is typical of many Israeli groups; Israel views itself as a multicultural mosaic, not a melting pot.

As for the candor encountered by many visitors to Israel, some believe that, because Israel is a new, multicultural nation, there has not been enough time for universal standards of politeness to evolve. Others blame Israel's universal military service: not only have most Israelis endured the shouts of drill instructors, many have damaged hearing from weapons fire.

Israel

☑ **Know Before You Go**

At various times, terrorist activity has occurred on a daily basis in Israel. While usually directed at Jewish Israelis, such attacks can victimize visitors as well. Attacks are often delivered by suicide bombers, which have sometimes been women and even teenagers. The most frequent targets are buses, bus stops, shopping areas, and malls; visitors should avoid these. Check with your government for current travel warnings for Israel.

Rocket or mortar attacks are launched without warning from across the Israeli border, most often from southern Lebanon.

Even during high levels of terrorist activity, the average visitor in Israel does not even witness violence, let alone be harmed by it.

The most common victimization experienced by a visitor to Israel is being cheated by cab drivers, who often avoid turning on their meters.

In addition to barbed wire and other barriers, Israel has deployed a large number of land mines. Always check for warning signs before you go off well-traveled routes.

▶ CULTURAL ORIENTATION

Cognitive Styles: How Israelis Organize and Process Information

Israelis are open to information that advances the state. Information is processed analytically and abstractly. The personal aspects of a situation are more important than obeying universal rules or laws, but these aspects may involve the principles of Judaism and the needs of the state.

Negotiation Strategies: What Israelis Accept as Evidence

Subjective feelings tend to be the basis for the truth. However, faith in the ideologies of Judaism, including the fact that the state must succeed, problems have to be solved, and security has to be maintained, may modify the truth as one sees it. Objective facts are used to supplement feelings and faith.

Value Systems: The Basis for Behavior

Israel's need to survive as a state permeates all value systems. The following three sections identify the Value Systems in the predominant culture—their methods of dividing right from wrong, good from evil, and so forth.

Locus of Decision-Making

Although there are still some collectives, there is an emphasis on individual initiative and achievement and a strong belief in individual decisions within the social and business context. Decisions are made with an effort to blend idealism with reality, emotion with pragmatism, physical labor with respect for the intellectual and spiritual realms, and a strong military posture with a sincere desire for peace. The dignity and worth of the individual is always emphasized, along with the right to a private life and opinions.

Israel

Sources of Anxiety Reduction

A strong nuclear family is the basis for socialization and gives its members a sense of social identity. It also serves as a focal point for emotional and physical security. The revival of Hebrew and its successful adaptation as a modern language ties the society together with a linguistic identity. A deep consciousness of Jewish history and tradition produces a bond that gives structure and stability to everyday life and also sensitizes people to the anti-Jewish sentiment in the surrounding Arab countries.

Issues of Equality/Inequality

Israel is a democratic and egalitarian culture built on competition. The leveling and educational influences of general military service help to develop a sense of equality. Although there are inequalities in roles, equal rights are guaranteed to all. Strong negative biases exist against the Palestinians and other Arabs, as do some biases against Jews from different countries. The emphasis on the equality of women and men can be seen in all spheres of national life; for example, both are subject to compulsory army training. Expect to see many women engaged in business.

▶ BUSINESS PRACTICES

Punctuality, Appointments, and Local Time

- Punctuality is not a traditional virtue in most Middle Eastern cultures. If your clients are Sephardim or Palestinians, they may be late for an appointment or not show up at all. However, they may have adopted a more Western attitude toward punctuality. Unless you know the individuals, it is difficult to know this in advance.
- Most—but not all—Ashkenazim tend to be more prompt to appointments.
- It is standard Middle Eastern practice to keep supplicants (including foreign businesspeople) waiting. Until you get to know your clients, it is unwise to schedule more than two appointments per day.
- The population of Israel comes from all over the world (only 60 percent of Israeli Jews are native-born), so many different cultural traditions are represented. As a result, business practices may be North American, Russian, European, or anything in between.
- An appointment is rarely private among traditional Arab businesspeople. Expect your visit to be interrupted by phone calls and visits from your client's friends and family. Westerners frequently find these distractions infuriating; try to maintain your equanimity.
- The Jewish holy day, the Sabbath, begins at sunset on Friday and ends at sunset on Saturday. In deference to the religious Jewish community, no business is conducted on the Sabbath. The work week runs from Sunday through Thursday.
- Business hours vary widely. Even the days businesses are open depends upon the religion of the owner. Most Jewish businesses close on Fridays (especially in the afternoon) and

Saturdays. Islamic-owned establishments will be closed all day on Fridays; Christian-owned ones will be closed Sundays. (Remember that Palestinians may be either Muslim or Christian.)

- A typical schedule for a Jewish-owned business would be 8:00 A.M. to 4:00 P.M. Sunday through Thursday, and 8:00 A.M. to 1:00 P.M. on Fridays.
- Both Judaism and Islam use lunar calendars that are different from the Gregorian (Western) calendar. However, for official business purposes and when dealing with foreigners, Israelis will use the Gregorian calendar.
- The Jewish and Islamic lunar calendars use lunar months of 28 days, so a lunar year of twelve months is only 354 days long. Holidays will thus be on different dates (by the Western calendar) every year.
- Note that when a schedule is agreed upon in terms of months (e.g., delivery in two months), an Israeli may be thinking in terms of twenty eight-day months while a westerner may be assuming thirty or thirty-one-day months.
- Israel is two hours ahead of Greenwich Mean Time (G.M.T +2), or seven hours ahead of Eastern Standard Time (E.S.T. +7).

Cultural Note

Perhaps as a result of being surrounded by hostile Arab countries that have frequently sought to destroy Israel, the Israeli people exhibit a strong strain of fatalism. When one assumes that one may be dead in a year, long-term plans are not given a high priority. Successful business deals in Israel must promise an immediate return. Long-term guarantees and warranties are rarely selling points.

Similarly, an Israeli's vigorous opposition to a plan may suddenly vanish without warning. There is an attitude of "Life is too short to keep arguing; let's make a deal and be done with it."

Negotiating

- It often takes a long time for decisions to be made.
- Most Israelis have a very confrontational negotiating style, which may become very emotional. Expect shouting.
- Unlike most Israeli Jews, an Israeli Arab will not even consider doing business with you until he knows and likes you. Thus, the social aspects of a deal are just as vital as the business ones.
- In general, the pace of business is slower in Israel than it is in the West. Be patient.
- Middle Eastern business meetings traditionally start slowly, with long inquiries into one's health and journey.
- Business cards are important. Although most Israeli businesspeople speak English, many foreigners have cards printed in English on one side and in Hebrew on the other. English is read from left to right; Hebrew is read from right to left.

- The front cover of an Israeli magazine is where English speakers would expect the back cover to be. While most Israeli businesspeople read English, they may instinctively look first at the back cover of English promotional literature. Keep that in mind when you design the back cover of your literature or marketing materials.
- Most Israelis speak at a much closer distance than North Americans.
- Do not back up or shy away. There is also more physical contact, and conversations often involve touching. However, foreign businesswomen should avoid initiating physical contact.
- Coffee is often served toward the end of a traditional Middle Eastern business meeting. This is a signal that the meeting will soon conclude. Arabs may light incense at this time as well.
- Arab men often walk hand in hand, although westernized Israeli Arabs rarely do this. If an Israeli holds your hand, take it as a sign of friendship.
- Arabic is a language of hyperbole. When an Israeli Arab says "yes," it usually means "possibly." Be encouraged by this, but do not assume that the negotiating is over.

     English-speaking Jews are often surprised to find themselves referred to as "Anglo-Saxons" by Israeli Jews. It is not meant as an insult.
- Israelis love to argue and are rarely at a loss for an opinion. You need not agree with all of their positions.
- Sports are always a good topic of conversation. Swimming, soccer, and basketball are among the most popular Israeli sports.
- Religion is usually a bad topic of conversation, as is U.S. aid to Israel.

Cultural Note

Because strictly observant Orthodox Jewish men are supposed to avoid the touch of any woman (in case she is "unclean"), women should not hand anything directly to Orthodox men. Instead, the woman places the object on a table within easy reach of the man, who then picks it up. This technique should be used by foreign businesswomen, even when they are presenting their business cards.

Business Entertaining

- Hosting visitors is considered a virtue in the Middle East, so most Israelis will take care of the entertaining within their country.
- Be prepared to remove your shoes before entering an Arab building. Follow the lead of your host.
- Remember that religious Israelis have strict dietary laws. Pork is prohibited to observing Jews; strict Muslims do not consume either alcohol or pork. If you decide to host a gathering, know the dietary restrictions of your guests.
- The left hand is considered unclean in the Arab world. Among Arabs, always eat with the right hand only. Even if you are left-handed, eat with your right hand.

- Do not eat everything on your plate. Leaving a little food is a sign that you have had enough.
- Realize that tipping (baksheesh) is expected for many types of services and courtesies.

▶ PROTOCOL

Greetings

- While different cultural groups in Israel may have different styles of greetings, most Israelis who do business in foreign environments shake hands upon introduction. The usual greeting is either *Shalom* (peace) or the English word "Hello."
- A traditional Arab or Orthodox Jewish male will not necessarily introduce his wife. Follow his lead; if he acts as if she isn't there, you should do the same.
- A traditional Arab greeting between men involves each grasping the other's right hand, placing the left hand on the other's right shoulder, and exchanging kisses on each cheek. However, Arabs used to dealing with foreigners will probably confine themselves to shaking hands on a first meeting.

> **Cultural Note**
>
> Because of the Orthodox prohibition against touching women, a foreign businesswoman should not offer to shake hands with an Orthodox Israeli man. Wait to see if they offer to shake hands, then follow their lead. Over 50 percent of Israeli Jews are considered "secular"—they do not observe the traditional Jewish rituals. The majority of businesspeople dealing on an international basis belong to this group, and they will shake hands. Orthodox Jewish men traditionally wear a skullcap (yarmulke) or hat and black clothing.

Titles/Forms of Address

- Israeli Jews come from all over the world, and their names usually reflect the tradition of their previous country. For example, Russian Jews will have a given name, followed by a patronymic ("son of . . ."), and a surname.
- In general, an Israeli Jew's given name will come first and the surname will come last. Address them by their title, or "Mr.," "Mrs.," or "Miss," and their surname, unless they indicate otherwise.
- Israeli Arabs have traditional Arabic names, which westerners frequently find confusing. The best solution is to request the names—written in English—of any Arabs you will have to meet, speak to, or correspond with. Find out both their full names (for correspondence) and how they are to be addressed in person.
- Israeli Arabs write their names in Arabic. In part because short vowels are not written in Arabic, translating from Arabic to other alphabets is not an exact science. Thus, Arabic names may be spelled several different ways in English.

- In general, Arabic names are written in the same order as English names: title (if any), given name, sometimes a middle name (often a patronymic), and surname (family name). Thus, the previous leader of Egypt was President Anwar al-Sadat; his title was President, his given name was Anwar, and al-Sadat was his family name.
- The term al literally means "from" in Arabic. A name like al-Barudi could mean "son of Barudi" or "from the town of Barudi."
- The term *abu* means "father of" in Arabic. Israeli Arabs frequently refer to revered elders as Abu.
- Most Arabs should be addressed by title and surname (e.g., Doctor al-Nahhas), just as you would address a westerner. In writing, use their full name. If they do not have a title, just use "Mr.," "Mrs.," or "Miss."

Gestures

- The left hand is considered unclean in the Arab world. In the Middle East, always use the right hand in preference to the left (unless you are handling something that is considered unclean). Never eat with the left hand; eat only with your right hand. Avoid gesturing with the left hand.
- While Israelis constantly gesture with their hands when speaking, they avoid pointing at another person. This would be considered impolite, especially among Arabs.
- As a general rule, keep both feet on the ground. Traditional Arabs do not cross their legs when sitting. Never show the bottom of your foot to an Arab; this is considered offensive. When a person removes his or her shoes (as when entering a mosque), the soles of the shoes are placed together, preventing the sole from being pointed at anyone.
- Any gesture that displays an extended thumb—including the "thumbs-up" gesture or a hitchhiker's gesture—is offensive throughout the Middle East.

Gifts

- Avoid giving a gift until you know something about the person you are giving it to. Especially with Orthodox Jews and Arabs, a gift must not violate one of the restrictions of their belief systems.
- Because of past problems with bribery, some Israeli companies forbid their employees from accepting any gifts.
- Small office-related gifts are almost always acceptable. These include anything that would be displayed on a desktop. It is acceptable for such items to include your company logo.
- If you are invited to an Israeli home, bring a gift of flowers or candy. Be sure a gift of food is kosher if it is going to an Orthodox person.
- Make sure you give or receive gifts with the right hand, not with the left (although using both hands is acceptable).

Israel

Cultural Note

The roads within ultra-Orthodox Jewish communities are typically closed on Friday nights and Saturday days in observance of the Sabbath. Women visiting such areas should take care to avoid wearing revealing clothing, which is liable to incite insults from the ultra-Orthodox.

Dress

- While foreigners are not exempt from Israeli standards of modesty, do not adopt traditional native clothing. Non-Jews should not wear yarmulkes (except when inside a synagogue), and non-Arabs should not wear turbans or other Arab headgear.

   Because Israeli law is mostly secular, there are few laws regarding clothing. But "immodest" dress will result in vocal disapproval from both Orthodox Jews and traditional Muslims.

- Despite Israel's heat, conservative tradition dictates that most of the body remain covered.

- Men should wear long trousers and a shirt, preferably long-sleeved. A jacket and tie are often required for business meetings. However, many Israeli businessmen rarely wear a tie. Keep shirts buttoned up to the collarbone.

   Israeli social events almost never require tuxedos; the only regular black-tie affairs are those hosted by foreign embassies.

- Remember that Israeli summers tend to be hot and humid, while the winters are often chilly enough to require overcoats. Indoor heating is often poor, so sweaters or shawls are useful. Away from the coast, winters can be cold enough to require hats and gloves, especially at higher elevations.

Cultural Note

All women—including foreigners—are expected to wear modest clothing in public, especially in areas of religious significance. These include temples, mosques, churches, and the communities in which various religious groups live.

   The neckline should be high and the sleeves should come at least to the elbows. Hemlines should be well below the knee, if not ankle-length. The overall effect should be one of baggy concealment; a full-length outfit which is tight and revealing is not acceptable. Therefore, pants or pantsuits are not recommended. While a hat or scarf is not always required, it is wise to keep a scarf at hand.

   On the other hand, there are places—nightclubs, certain resorts, etc.—frequented only by secular Jews. In such locations, women's fashions can be as tight and revealing as in any similar place in Europe.

Italy

Italian Republic
Local short form: Italia
Local long form: Repubblica Italiana
Former: Kingdom of Italy

Cultural Note

The Italians—and their ancestors, the Romans—invented many of the business practices we use today. Their innovations included banking, insurance, and even double-entry bookkeeping. Do not let Italian friendliness and chatter lull you into forgetting that they are very astute businesspeople.

WHAT'S YOUR CULTURAL IQ?

1. Leonardo is the name of an Italian police database that tracks what?
   a. Illegal drugs
   b. Stolen art
   c. Suspected terrorists

   ANSWER: b. According to the United Nations, more than half of the world's cultural treasures are in Italy. At least for now. Thousands of precious and historic artifacts are being smuggled out every year, and the Italian police have the formidable job of investigating and prosecuting the Italian art crime wave—with the help of "Leonardo."

2. The Italian language has many dialects, some of which are not mutually intelligible. From which region did modern Italian evolve?
   a. Rome
   b. Sardinia
   c. Tuscany

   ANSWER: c. Since the 1500s, Tuscan has been the preferred dialect, in large part because it was favored by some of Italy's greatest writers of the Middle Ages (such as Dante, Petrarch, and Boccaccio).

3. The former Italian prime minister, Silvio Berlusconi, drew a lot of attention in January of 2004 because:
   a. After four years of legal battles, he was cleared of charges of corruption.
   b. He revealed his new, cosmetically enhanced face.
   c. His right-wing party, Forza Italia, eradicated the budget deficit.

ANSWER: **b.** The sixty-seven-year-old thanked his wife, Veronica, for convincing him to undergo plastic surgery.

 TIPS ON DOING BUSINESS IN ITALY

- Italians generally behave in a formal, refined manner—or with a *bella figura*—what Western executives might call a "consultative image." It can mean anything from an attractive-looking appearance, to appropriate behaviors, to a good performance. Dignified, smooth mannerisms are important from the first meeting—through each dining experience—to your final departure.
- While you may be extremely well prepared with factual details for your meetings, you should also invest a great deal of effort in developing a strong, trusting relationship with your Italian associates. Initially they will care more about you, and whether you are worth knowing personally, than the specifics of your product.
- The Italian bureaucracy and legal system is notoriously slow. One reason for this is because Italy is burdened with over 2,000 years of laws. While new laws are added, old ones are rarely removed from the books—even laws dating back to the Roman Empire still exist!

Cultural Note:

July and August are poor months for scheduling appointments, since many firms close for vacation. The observance of many regional holidays may also close businesses, and if a holiday falls on a Tuesday or Thursday, Italians tend to extend their weekend to the holiday—giving themselves a four-day weekend. And of course, many businesses celebrate Christmas and New Year for at least a week. Check with your local representatives to confirm whether offices may be closed during your visit.

COUNTRY BACKGROUND

History

Italy has been the name of this region for over 3,000 years. Evidence of early Latin/Italic tribes dates from 2000 B.C. The Etruscans arrived around 1200 B.C., bringing their own culture and laws, and conquered vast central areas of the peninsula.

Greek civilization dominated southern Italy around 600 B.C., and much of Greek culture was subsequently adopted by the Romans. The Roman Empire had tremendous impact on Italian social, legal, political, artistic, and military culture.

With 3,000 miles of coastline, Italy proved a logical prey for invaders. After the fall of the Roman Empire, there were repeated invasions from many countries, including France, Austria, Spain, and Germany. Italy became a country of sharply diverse city-states.

By 1870 Italy had become a politically unified monarchy. The final monarch abdicated in 1946.

The most notorious political figure from Italy's recent past is Mussolini, the fascist dictator known as Il Duce. Mussolini controlled Italy's government from 1922 to 1943. He supported Hitler during World War II, until the Allies' Italian supporters assassinated him and overthrew the Fascists.

Italy did not become a politically unified constitutional republic until the 1946 national elections. Corruption scandals in the early 1990s tainted most major political parties, resulting in the 1994 election of reform candidates led by Prime Minister Silvio Berlusconi.

Type of Government

The Italian Republic is a multiparty parliamentary republic. There are two legislative bodies, a Senate and a Chamber of Deputies. The president is the chief of state, while the prime minister is the head of the government.

For current government data, check with the Embassy of Italy at *www.italyemb.org*.

Language

Italian is the official language. There are many diverse dialects. Modern Italian originally evolved from spoken Latin. Although modern Italian is spoken in most of Italy, many Italians also speak one of the regional dialects as their first language. English is spoken by many businesspeople.

> **Cultural Note**
> Europe's oldest university was founded in Bologna in the twelfth century.

The Italian View

The vast majority of Italians are raised Roman Catholic, although the Republic of Italy has no official religion. While the Catholic Church remains very influential in Italy, it was unable to prevent the legalization of divorce and abortion in the 1970s.

Historically, Italy's geographic structure produced distinct regions, each with its own dialect, politics, and culture. These regions frequently warred with one another, which was one of the reasons why family life became a central focus. The motto "Family First" reflected Italians' need to preserve and protect not only their relatives but their regional cultures. However, while there is great respect in Italy for the family, for age, and for the power of the patriarch and matriarch—the institution of the family has changed.

Recently, both a falling birthrate and economics have changed the family. Currently, Italy's birthrate is not even sufficient to offset its death rate. Households now need two incomes, so more women work, and many Italians have moved away from their traditional homes in search of employment. Today the extended family, with several generations living under one roof (and most of the adults working in the family business) is the exception, not the rule.

Italians do appreciate the more refined aspects of life. They have a cultivated awareness of art, science, history, literature, music, fine wines, beautiful clothes, excellent meals, the list goes on. . . . They will respect a well-educated, civilized businessperson with accomplishments beyond just the workplace.

✓ Know Before You Go

Although it is not a consistent issue, traveling by train in Italy can be problematic.

In January of 2005 railway workers went on strike to protest unsafe practices. The strike followed a head-on collision between two trains, which resulted in the death of seventeen people (five of whom were railway workers). Developments for increasing the safety standards, as well as the efficiency of the trains are ongoing.

Italy's natural hazards vary by region. Mudflows, landslides, volcanic eruptions, and avalanches can occur, but there are more gradual issues that are of great concern as well—like Venice's land subsidence.

Crimes like money laundering and smuggling are well publicized, but business travelers who are cautious will probably not even encounter a pickpocket. (Unless they ride the subway in Rome.)

▶ CULTURAL ORIENTATION

Cognitive Styles: How Italians Organize and Process Information

In Italy information is readily accepted and great discussions occur, but little movement is seen in the opinions of the participants. Information tends to be processed subjectively and associatively. Italians will look at the particulars of each situation rather than appeal to a law or rule to solve a problem.

Negotiation Strategies: What Italians Accept as Evidence

Subjective feelings are more important than faith in an ideology or objective facts when deciding what is true. However, the ideologies of the Church do permeate many transactions. Italians who have a higher education tend to use facts to back their arguments.

Value Systems: The Basis for Behavior

The ideologies of the Roman Catholic Church exert the most influence. The following three sections identify the Value Systems in the predominant culture—their methods of dividing right from wrong, good from evil, and so forth.

Locus of Decision-Making

The individual is responsible for his or her decisions but is often expected to defer to the interests of the family or organizational unit. There is an admiration for urban life and an enduring loyalty to region and family.

Sources of Anxiety Reduction

The extended family is getting smaller but is still the major source of security, order, and stability. Anxiety, as well as security, is produced by seeking success in the eyes of the extended family and society. There are strong Catholic and Communist segments that can work in opposition, but they are not completely incompatible. The Church gives a sense of structure to the majority. Italians are remarkably diverse, but they also have a strong capacity for social and cultural resilience and continuity.

Issues of Equality/Inequality

There are extreme contrasts between rich and poor. The population is stratified by income. Patron-client relationships provide a strong social and political base. Even though there is a large German-speaking group in the north, and many mutually unintelligible dialects, there is one standard language that binds the country together. Women have made progress toward equality.

> **Cultural Note**
> Everyone tends to speak at once at Italian gatherings. This goes for business meetings as well as social events. Of course, it is possible for Italians to conduct a meeting in a more orderly fashion, if those parameters are established at the beginning—but do not take offense at being interrupted.

▶ BUSINESS PRACTICES

Punctuality, Appointments, and Local Time

- Be on time, especially in the industrial north, where business is often conducted with pressure and efficiency.
- The more important the person, the later he or she may arrive to a business meeting. *Le persone importante si fanno aspettare* (important people arrive late). However, at many events, Italians will be more punctual—to church, a doctor's office, and particularly to the theater or the opera.
- Italian businesspeople prefer to deal with people they know, even if that acquaintance has been a perfunctory handshake at a trade fair. Before you invest in travel to Italy, be sure to engage a strong representative who can make appropriate introductions and appointments for you.
- Write first for an appointment, in Italian if you want an immediate reply.
- Follow up your letter by phone and by e-mail.
- Be very aware of summer vacation periods. Most firms are closed in August. If you write for an appointment in mid-July, you may not get a satisfactory reply until September.
- Italians like to get acquainted and engage in small talk before getting down to business. They are hospitably attentive. Expect to answer questions about your family.

- Plan appointments between 10:00 and 11:00 A.M., and after 3:00 P.M.
- There may be fewer public holidays in Italy than in many Latin countries, but business-people must be aware that practically every Italian city celebrates the feast of its patron saint as a legal holiday and much of the city literally shuts down.
- Italy is one hour ahead of Greenwich Mean Time (G.M.T. +1), or six hours ahead of U.S. Eastern Standard Time (E.S.T. +6).

Cultural Note

Corporations often have a horizontal chain of authority. Italians call it a *cordata* (which actually means a team of mountain climbers on the same rope). This parallel channel is based on levels of personal, reciprocal concern—and should never be taken lightly.

Negotiating

- It is important to understand corporate hierarchy. Titles may not coincide with a foreign-er's conception of responsibility. Authority often goes with the individual, not necessarily the title. Status is exceedingly important, and respect for authority pervades work and social environments.
- The cordata concept is very difficult to explain fully to outsiders. But it exists and, to facilitate business, one should have a reliable contact who has full knowledge of a compa-ny's internal structure.
- The pace of negotiations is usually relatively slow. The more important the contract, the more study is going on behind the scenes. Any obvious sense of urgency is thought to weaken one's bargaining position.
- A dramatic change in demands at the last minute is often a technique to unsettle the other side. Be patient and calm; just when it appears impossible, the contract may come together.
- One does not exchange business cards at social occasions, but it is normal at business functions—especially because an Italian would feel it impolite to ask a foreigner to spell out her or his name.
- Italian cards are often plain white with black print. Usually, the more important the per-son, the less information is on the card.
- Conversational subjects that are highly appreciated are Italian culture, art, food, wine, sports such as bicycling and especially soccer, family, Italian scenery, and films.
- Your host may be negative about something in his or her country or its politics, but don't agree too strongly and never offer criticisms of your own.
- Avoid talking about religion, politics, and World War II.
- Italians do not usually tell off-color jokes and are uncomfortable when acquaintances do.
- Never ask someone you have just met at a social gathering about his or her profession. To do so is considered gauche, even insulting.

Italy

> **Cultural Note**
> When dining, Italians keep both hands above the table, not one resting on the lap. There may be three plates to start: a small one for antipasto, a deep dish for pasta or soup, and a large plate on the bottom—which may be for the main course, or may be removed with the soup, and replaced with a fresh plate.

Business Entertaining

- Italian hospitality plays an important role in business life, and most often means dining in a restaurant. No matter how you feel, refusing an invitation will be offensive.
- Use your utensils (not your fingers) to pick up cheese, and don't eat any fruit except grapes or cherries with your hand.
- Italians consider wine as a food to be sipped, not as a means of relaxation. Therefore, to drink too much is considered rude.
- Business dinners involve only a small, important group. If you are the host, consult with your Italian contact before extending invitations. You cannot be aware of all the "inside" personalities and ranks, so ask for help.
- Ask your Italian client's secretary to suggest a favorite restaurant.
- Dining is a serious business, and real prestige can be gained or lost at the table. At a propitious moment one may bring up business.
- Paying may equate to prestige, and Italians may even slip the waiter a generous tip before dinner to make sure you do not get the bill.
- The check will not be brought until you ask for it. And female executives may find it extremely difficult to pay.
- Keep the receipt for the restaurant bill. Sometimes "tax police" check restaurant bills outside for adherence to tax laws.
- In a restaurant you will have to ask for ice, because Italians usually do not serve drinks cold (they think ice-cold things are unhealthy—except for "gelato").

> **Cultural Note**
> Breakfast (*la prima colazione*) is usually around 8:00 A.M. and consists of rolls, bread, butter, perhaps some jam, and strong coffee or chocolate.
> Lunch (*la colazione*) is the full-course, main meal of the day, and serving starts at 1:00 P.M.
> Dinner (*la cena*) is again a light meal. Service starts around 7:00 P.M. and may be served until after 10:00 P.M.

 PROTOCOL

Greetings

- As a guest, you will probably be introduced first. The most senior or eldest person present should also always be given special deference.

- Shake hands with everyone present when arriving and leaving. At a large gathering, if no one is giving formal introductions, it is proper to shake hands and introduce yourself.
- Handshakes may include grasping the arm with the other hand.
- Women may "kiss" good friends on either cheek (it is rather more like pressing the sides of each face together).
- Close friends and male relatives often embrace and slap each other on the back.

Titles/Forms of Address

- Do not use first names unless you are invited to—formality is still appreciated.
- Traditionally, executives and subordinates in offices would not address one another by their first names; however, this is changing.
- Professors and doctors are highly esteemed; use the title Dottore for a man and Dottoressa for a woman. It is better to use a title (even if you are unsure); always err on the side of caution. It will be accepted as an understanding of "status earned" even if not academically achieved.
- Personal titles are used in all forms of address, spoken and written. Like "Dottore," they can be used with or without the surname. Attorney Green is "Avvocato Verdi," Signorina Avvocata is "Miss Attorney," and so forth. Find out these details before the meeting if possible.

Gestures

- Latins "talk with their hands," and most gestures are usually both expressive and innocuous.
- You may see a disgruntled man quickly stroke his fingertips under his chin and thrust them forward. This is a sign of defiance and/or derision, somewhat like thumbing your nose in the United States.
- Another gesture has two versions: Holding your hand palm down with the index and little fingers straight out, and the others curved inward, symbolizes the devil's horns, and the message is to ward off evil. If the same gesture is done with the fingers pointing upward, it is an obscene message.
- Further information on gestures is accessible at *www.kissboworshakehands.com*.

Gifts

- Business gifts are sometimes given at a senior managerial level. They should be well designed and made by craftsmen of prestige.
- Consumables like liquors or delicacies, or crafts from the visitor's country, may be appropriate.
- Do not give gifts that are obviously a vehicle for your company's logo.
- Note that some Italian firms have privately published glossy, top-quality illustrated books suitable for display on a bookshelf or coffee table.

- A small gift may be given to any staff member who has been particularly helpful. Travel alarm clocks, pens, electronic gadgets, silver key chains, or local handicrafts from your home are good gifts. If it is not a handicraft, be certain that you purchase prestigious name brands.
- If you require a more substantial gift, consider loading an iPod with a gracious message from your CEO to the recipient, or music from a prestigious orchestra in your country.
- Flowers or chocolates are acceptable for a secretary.
- If you are invited to someone's home, bring gift-wrapped chocolates, pastries, or flowers. Never give an even number of flowers. Do not give chrysanthemums; they are used for funerals. Do not give a brooch, handkerchiefs, or knives, all of which connote sadness.
- If you give wine, be certain it is of excellent vintage—many Italians are oenophiles.
- For further guidelines on gift giving, visit *www.kissboworshakehands.com*.

Dress

- In the business world, good clothes are a badge of success. Women dress in quiet, expensive elegance; men's ties and suits should also be fashionable and well cut.
- Keep in mind Italy is a major center of European fashion. Even casual clothes are smart and chic.
- Women wear pants in cities, but shorts are a rarity. You may be stopped if you try to go into a church while wearing shorts, a shorter than knee-length skirt, or a sleeveless top.
- Italians appreciate refined clothes, and they will take note of your garments. But again, your clothes are just part of your image. Italians value a bella figura and will consider all aspects of the individual simultaneously—from their attire and the scent they wear, to their technical knowledge and reputation in the field. Investing some time in your personal appearance, as well as your technical research, before you arrive in Italy, will help you to be successful.

Cultural Note:

Italy is renowned for its opera and boasts a variety of magnificent venues for staging major works. The world's most famous opera house is La Scala, in Milan. It recently reopened in December of 2004, after undergoing a major restoration.

The Arena of Verona, a Roman amphitheatre built in the first century A.D., has seen gladiators, jousts, and tournaments over thousands of years—and is now the host of one of Italy's spectacular summer opera festivals.

Another extremely important locale is Florence, where the first opera was said to have been created. Many popular locations exist for Florentine music—including the Teatro Comunale, Teatro Verdi and, in the summer, the Boboli Gardens of the Palazzo Pitti.

Japan

Japan

▶ WHAT'S YOUR CULTURAL IQ?

1. TRUE or FALSE? Within a generation or two, Japan may have its first female emperor.

   ANSWER: FALSE. Although Japan has historically had male emperors, there had not been a male born into the Japanese royal family for some forty years . . . until September of 2006!

   The current heir to the throne, Crown Prince Naruhito, has a daughter as his heir, which might have forced the change in tradition. However, his brother Prince Akishino and his wife, Princess Kiko, had a baby boy who can theoretically become the next Emperor of Japan. The baby was named Hisahito, and he may be heir to the world's oldest hereditary monarchy.

2. More than fifty-five years after the end of the Second World War, one of the following Japanese islands remains occupied by a foreign power. Which one is it?
   a. Hokkaido   b. Kurile Islands   c. Okinawa

   ANSWER: b. As of this writing, Russia remains in control of the Kurile Islands, which the Japanese refer to as the Northern Territories. Russia's refusal to return the islands is the reason Japan has never signed a formal peace treaty ending the Second World War with Russia (or with its predecessor, the USSR). Although the United States maintains a controversial military base on Okinawa, it returned the island itself to Japanese control.

3. The Japanese have at least ten distinct breeds of dogs. TRUE or FALSE? The Japanese Tosa makes a fine lap dog for the many Japanese who live in small apartments.

   ANSWER: FALSE. The Tosa is a large dog, originally bred for dog fighting and nicknamed the "Japanese Mastiff." The lap dog bred for upper-class Japanese ladies is the Chin.

TIPS ON DOING BUSINESS IN JAPAN

- A "poker face" is of great use in Japan. The Japanese dislike strong public displays of emotion. If you show shock or anger during business negotiations, they will believe that you lack self-control and are questionable as a business partner.
- The younger members of your team should generally remain quiet and defer to their seniors during the meetings. Their real job will be to go out drinking with the Japanese team's young executives at night. The Japanese like to convey important information (e.g., "Our boss was very angry at your offer today") via junior executives.
- The Japanese may ask international visitors many questions—including information about your job, your title, your age, your responsibilities, the number of employees that report to you, etc. Japanese is a very complex language with many forms of address and honorifics. They will need a lot of information to decide which form to use when speaking to you. (Most of this subtlety will be lost when translated into English, but it is important to the Japanese.)

COUNTRY BACKGROUND

History

The Japanese Islands have been occupied for thousands of years. The dynasty of the current emperor is said to have been founded in 660 B.C.

Japan

Historically, Japan has resisted outside influences and frequently closed itself to foreigners. The United States forcibly opened Japan to foreign markets in 1853 when Commodore Perry sailed his war fleet into Tokyo Bay.

What westerners consider World War II was only part of a long-running Asiatic war in which Japan invaded neighboring nations. Korea was annexed in 1910, Manchuria was annexed in 1931, and China proper was invaded in 1937.

Japan surrendered to the Allies in 1945, and was occupied until 1952. The United States, wishing to demilitarize and democratize Japan imposed many reforms after World War II. These efforts included a decrease in the power of the emperor and decentralization of the government. Subsequently, the Japanese recentralized much of their government. Japan's bureaucracy of civil servants became just as powerful (if not more) than its elected officials.

Devastated by the war, the Japanese rebuilt their factories and infrastructure. Japan's economy boomed in the 1970s and 1980s. During this time, cash-rich Japanese bought property and businesses all over the world. This boom ended in the 1990s.

Since then, the Japanese economy has largely been in a state of stagnation. Unable to continue providing traditional lifetime employment, many Japanese workers were laid off. This breaking of the postwar social contract has caused a major change of attitude among many Japanese.

Recently, the government led by Prime Minister Junichiro Koizumi has made some painful changes to the economy. While this resulted in economic improvement in 2003, it remains to be seen if this recovery will be sustained.

Cultural Note

The term "Japan Inc." has often been used to describe the totality of Japanese business: the tight government control; the huge, interlocking corporate alliances; the hard-working salary men who began each day by singing the company song and getting lifetime employment in return for their loyalty; the postwar Japanese economic miracle. But "Japan Inc." was always an exaggeration, and a decade of poor economic performance has just about ended the myth.

However, business is still conducted differently in Japan than in North America or the EU. The Japanese still prefer to do business in a network of old friends, facilitated by favors and obligations.

Type of Government

Japan is a parliamentary democracy under a constitutional monarch. The chief of state is the emperor; Emperor Akihito was crowned in 1990 after the death of his father, Emperor Hirohito. The head of the government is the prime minister.

Power within the government resides mainly in the prime minister, who is the leader of the majority party of the Diet, or Parliament. The prime minister dissolves the House of Representatives every two or three years. The prime minister also appoints the Supreme Court and leads the Cabinet.

The Diet is made up of two houses, the House of Representatives and the House of Councilors. Both are elected, with the House of Representatives having more authority. Finally, the Cabinet is responsible to the Diet. In the Cabinet, it is the Ministry of Finance (MOF) and the Ministry of International Trade and Industry (MITI) that are the most important.

MITI, through involvement in business and industry following the Second World War, helped Japan gain its strength. Today MITI does not have the same authority it once did, both because it is not needed as much as before and because of pressure from other governments (such as the United States). The government does not control industry; government ministries instead serve as intermediaries and as think tanks.

For current data, visit the Embassy of Japan at *www.us.emb-japan.go.jp*.

Cultural Note

Japanese uses not one but three different forms of writing: *kanji, katakana,* and *hiragana*. As a rule, kanji represents blocks of meaning. Katakana is used for foreign names and words. Hiragana expresses the grammatical relationships between words.

As a foreigner, your name and your company's name will probably be written in katakana characters.

Language

Japanese is the official language of Japan. It is a complex and subtle language, spoken nowhere else in the world as a primary tongue. Most sentences in Japanese can be expressed in at least four different levels of politeness. Japanese women almost always use one of the more deferential forms. Communication in Japan is often marked by great subtlety; information is left unspoken yet is perfectly understood.

Ethnologue.com has identified fifteen languages currently spoken in Japan. These range from Korean (with some 670,000 speakers) to Ainu (with just 15 active speakers).

Cultural Note

Literacy is close to 100 percent in Japan, and 95 percent of the population has a high school education. The Japanese educational system includes difficult qualifying exams that students must pass, which puts enormous pressure to study and to get good grades. Once a student has passed the entrance exam for college, however, exams are over. Students accepted to the top colleges are almost guaranteed top jobs.

All Japanese students begin classes in English around age twelve. However, the goal for students of English is to pass their exams rather than to learn to verbally communicate in English. Although many Japanese learn to read English, less are able to speak with English-speaking foreigners.

Reflecting the increased influence of China, some Japanese are now studying Mandarin Chinese as their second foreign language.

The Japanese View

The Japanese have a unique culture and language. Despite increasing scientific evidence, many Japanese believe that they are genetically unique as well. (One good way to make yourself unpopular in Japan is to quote studies that indicate the Japanese are descended from immigrants from mainland Asia.) Foreign pharmaceuticals are often prohibited in Japan on the basis that they have not been proven to be safe and effective for the Japanese people.

Wherever the Japanese originated, they are extremely protective of their culture and their society. They discourage large numbers of foreigners from coming to work and live in Japan. Even Korean workers who have lived in Japan for several generations are not accorded full citizenship. Foreigners in Japan are often considered to be the source of crime and public disorder.

The prejudice against foreigners can even be directed at native-born Japanese. Often, Japanese who spend too much time studying abroad are stigmatized for "not being Japanese enough."

One important aspect of Japanese behavior is apology. Not only do individuals apologize for missteps, but companies do as well (in the person of their highest-ranking officers).

Japan has its own unique belief system, called *Shinto*. Shinto means "the way of the gods," yet it is not always categorized by westerners as a religion, in part because Shinto lacks an official religious text or a system of ethics to live by.

The Japanese are surprisingly tolerant of religious differences and may even practice both Buddhism and Shinto concurrently. Many people are married in a Shinto ceremony but select a Buddhist funeral.

Christianity (less than 5 percent) and other religions (under 20 percent) are also present in Japan. There is no official religion. The Japanese tend to adapt their religion to modern life; for example, they will have new businesses blessed.

☑ Know Before You Go

The greatest difficulty for foreigners involves finding one's way about. Most signs are only in Japanese (some tourist attractions and large avenues have multilingual signs). Not all buildings have street numbers. The layout of most cities is chaotic and confusing. Efforts to use public transportation are often made difficult by impatient crowds. Unless they have a guide, first-time visitors to Japan are often overwhelmed.

Japan is one of the most tectonically active nations in the world. The country has suffered many devastating earthquakes. It also has several active volcanoes: Mt. Usu on Hokkaido erupted in April 2000. Visitors to Japan should know that they may be viewed with suspicion in the aftermath of a natural disaster; foreigners have often been blamed for "causing disruption" (i.e., looting) after earthquakes.

Japan is also occasionally the victim of destructive typhoons or tsunamis.

North Americans should know that they are, on average, larger (both taller and wider) than the average Japanese. Consequently, they may find Japanese accommodations (everything from shower stalls to train seats) difficult to use. You may also find it difficult to purchase clothes in your size.

Japan has occasionally experienced terrorist attacks. The Red Brigade carried out attacks in the 1970s. More recently, in 1995, a religious sect released the deadly nerve gas sarin on the Tokyo subway, causing a dozen deaths and injuring thousands.

Open prejudice against foreigners is occasionally encountered in Japan. You may be told that certain services are "for Japanese only," especially when you travel outside areas frequented by tourists.

Japanese taxi drivers are notoriously erratic and can be a danger to both pedestrians and other drivers.

If you are staying in Japan and are considering buying a car, realize that the purchase price is only part of your costs. In addition to insurance, you must first rent a registered parking space for your car. Old cars are sold very cheaply because they require expensive repairs to pass inspection (this is one reason all the cars in Japan look so well maintained).

▶ CULTURAL ORIENTATION

Cognitive Styles: How Japanese Organize and Process Information

The Japanese generally close all doors to outside influences, although they are open to ideas from within their group. They are subjective and experiential in their thinking, holding fast to traditional values. Strong loyalty to their groups makes the Japanese look to the particular and specific rather than the universal and abstract. While the Japanese pride themselves on anticipating others' needs, they can also be very compartmentalized.

Negotiation Strategies: What Japanese Accept as Evidence

The Japanese may rely more on their feelings than on facts, because they tend to be more subjective than objective. Since they strive for consensus within their groups, individuals are prepared to change their position for the sake of group harmony.

Foreigners sometimes interpret the Japanese dismissal of facts and decision-by-consensus process as evidence that the Japanese believe that they are superior to others. The opaqueness of their decision-making and their tightly controlled communicative behavior exacerbates this situation with unknowing foreigners.

Value Systems: The Basis for Behavior

Traditional Japanese value systems have recently eroded due to the failure of the postwar social compact (especially the loss of lifetime employment). These views are especially prevalent among the younger generation.

The following three sections identify the Value Systems in the predominant culture—their methods of dividing right from wrong, good from evil, and so forth.

Locus of Decision-Making

Decisions are made within the group with little or no personal recognition. A person's actions reflect on the group, particularly his or her family. Outsiders must be accepted into the group before they can participate in decision-making. The Japanese are only moderately collective.

Sources of Anxiety Reduction

The Japanese have very high anxiety about life because of the need to avoid embarrassment. There are constant pressures to conform. A very strong work ethic and strong group relationships give structure and stability to life. Emotional restraints are developed in childhood, and all behaviors are situation-bound. This makes it extremely difficult for a foreigner to understand the culture.

Issues of Equality/Inequality

Age is revered. There is a great deal of competitiveness among equals, but also an inherent trust in people. Ethnocentrism is very strong.

Male dominance is still strong in public situations. Gender roles in society are clearly differentiated, but a desire for Western-style equality is growing among Japanese youth.

Cultural Note

Japanese politics, like most areas of power, has been almost exclusively male for decades. Recently this has begun to change.

In February 2000, Fusae Ota became the first Japanese woman to win a gubernatorial election when she became governor of Osaka. She was a former officer in the powerful Ministry of International Trade and Industry (known as MITI).

▶ BUSINESS PRACTICES

Punctuality, Appointments, and Local Time

- Be punctual at all times. Tardiness is considered rude.
- The work week is generally forty-eight hours without overtime pay, spread over five and a half working days. Some large firms have instituted a five-day week. While the Japanese work long hours, few executives take their work home with them.
- During holidays, banks and offices close, although some stores remain open.
- During three weeks of the year (New Year's holidays, December 28 to January 3; Golden Week, April 29 to May 5; and Obon, in mid-August), many people visit the graves of their ancestors. Conducting business and traveling are difficult during these periods.
- When writing the date in English, the Japanese may write the year first, then the month, then the day (e.g., December 3, 2010, would be 10.12.3 or 10/12/3) or they may write the day first, then the month, then the year (e.g., December 3, 2010, would be written 3.12.10).
- Japan is nine hours ahead of Greenwich Mean Time (G.M.T. +9), or fourteen hours ahead of Eastern Standard Time (E.S.T. +14).

> **Cultural Note**
> The Japanese also have a non-Western method of designating the year: they use the year of the current emperor's reign. This year is now considered to begin on the first of January in the Gregorian (Western) calendar.
>
> The New Year is the most important holiday in Japan. Businesses close for three to five days. Many people send greeting cards to celebrate. *Bonekai* parties ("year forget parties") are held to put all of the old year's worries to rest. People visit shrines, eat specific foods, and even play obscure games, such as *hanetsuki*, a Japanese form of badminton.

Negotiating

- A Japanese response "I'll consider it" may actually mean "no."
- Negatively phrased questions typically get a "yes" if the Japanese speaker agrees. For example, a question such as "Doesn't Company A want us?" will be answered "yes" if the Japanese thinks that Company A indeed does not want you. In English, the answer would be "No, they do not want you."
- Incorporate the words "I'm sorry" into your vocabulary when you go to Japan. However, don't be ingratiating out of fear of offending; just be polite.
- Hard-sell techniques will fail in Japan. Instead, find the points on which you and your Japanese counterparts agree, then build upon those. A positive, persuasive presentation works better with the Japanese than does a high-pressure, confrontational approach.
- Negotiations are begun at the executive level and continued at the middle level (working level).
- Connections are very helpful in Japan. However, choose your intermediaries carefully, because the Japanese will feel obliged to be loyal to them. Do not choose someone of lower rank than the person with whom he or she will be negotiating. Intermediaries should not be part of either company involved in the deal.
- If you don't have a connection, a personal call is better than a letter or e-mail.
- Use an intermediary to convey bad news.
- Using a Japanese lawyer rather than a Western one indicates a cooperative spirit.
- The Japanese usually use the initial meetings to get to know you, while at the same time asking to hear about your proposal. Agreements of confidentiality are vague.
- Contracts are not perceived as final agreements. You or they may renegotiate.
- Because age equals rank, show the greatest respect to the oldest members of the Japanese group with who you are in contact.
- You will not be complimented on good work, because the group and not the individual is rewarded. It is a bad idea to single out Japanese workers.
- The Japanese will not explain exactly what is expected of you.
- Most Japanese go through job rotation, in which they change jobs within the same company every few years. In this way, the employees get to know the company and its work force well.

- Suggestion boxes, so often ignored in the United States, are useful in Japan, because Japanese employees stuff them full of suggestions.
- Do not make accusations or refuse anything directly; be indirect.
- At work the Japanese are very serious and do not try to "lighten things up" with humor.
- When working with Japanese who know English, or when using an interpreter, be patient. Speak slowly, pause often, and avoid colloquialisms. Your interpreter may seem to be taking more time with the translation than you did with your statement; this is because she or he is using lengthy forms of respect.
- Do not be surprised if your interpreter translates Japanese into English almost simultaneously but waits until English speakers are finished before translating into Japanese. Unlike English, Japanese is a very predictable language. By the time a Japanese businessperson is halfway through a sentence, the translator probably knows how the sentence will end. Indeed, it would be very impolite of a Japanese to end a sentence with an unexpected choice of words.
- At times, you may need to pretend you are sure that your Japanese colleague or friend has understood you, even if you know this is not the case. This is important for maintaining a good relationship.

Cultural Note

Asian psychology requires that people observe the proper order of things. When three Japanese hostages were released from Iraq in 2004, they had to pay for their own flights home. Instead of being welcomed back to Japan, they returned to widespread animosity because they had entered Iraq against their government's recommendation. This was a violation of protocol, and they were perceived to have put the government and the Japanese people in a bad position.

Business Entertaining

- Business entertaining usually occurs after business hours, and very rarely in the home. You will be entertained often, sometimes on short notice. While the first evenings will probably be spent going from bar to restaurant to "hostess bar" (not a good idea for businesswomen), you may suggest alternatives later. These may include sumo wrestling or karaoke ("empty orchestra") bars, where you sing along with prerecorded music.
- When you are taken out, your host will treat.
- Allow your host to order for you (this will be easier, too, since the menus are in Japanese). Be enthusiastic while eating, and express your thanks afterward.
- While business entertaining is primarily for building friendships rather than for doing deals, you may discuss business during the evening.
- If you are invited to a Japanese home, keep in mind that this is a great honor: show your appreciation.
- For social occasions, it is appropriate to be fashionably late.

- When entering a Japanese home, take off your shoes at the door. You will wear one pair of slippers from the door to the living room, where you will remove them. You will put them on again to make your way to the bathroom, where you will exchange them for "toilet slippers." Do not forget to change back again.
- In a home, you will sit cross-legged, or with your legs to the side, around a low table with the family. You may be offered a backrest.
- Meals are long, but the evening usually ends at about 11:00 P.M.
- Never point your chopsticks at another person. When you are not using them, you should line them up on the chopstick rest.
- Use both hands to hold a bowl or a cup that you wish to be refilled.
- Eventually, you will wish to invite your hosts out. Be insistent, even if they claim that a foreigner should not pay for anything.

PROTOCOL

Greetings
- The Japanese are very aware of Western habits and will often greet you with a handshake. Their handshakes will often be gentle; this gives no indication of their assertiveness of character.
- The handshake may last longer than customary in northern Europe or North America.
- The bow is their traditional greeting.
- If someone bows to greet you, observe carefully. If you are greeting an equal, bow to the same depth as you have been bowed to, because the depth of the bow indicates the status of the relationship between you.
- As you bow, quickly lower your eyes. Keep your palms flat against your thighs.

> **Cultural Note**
>
> Business cards are extremely important for establishing credentials. Have them prepared in advance and checked by a Japanese business representative. It is best to have one side printed in your native language, with extra information such as membership in professional associations included; the reverse side should be in Japanese. If your status changes, have new cards printed immediately.
>
> Cards are presented after the bow or handshake. Present your card with the Japanese side facing your colleague, in such a manner that it can be read immediately.
>
> Read the card presented to you, memorizing all the information. Ask for help in pronunciation and in comprehension of the title; if you understand without help, make a relevant comment.
>
> Handle cards very carefully. Do not put them in your pocket or in your wallet if you plan to put it in your back pocket. Never write on a person's business card (especially not in his or her presence).

Japan

Titles/Forms of Address

- In person, use last names plus San, meaning "Mr." or "Ms." Do not immediately assume that the Japanese will call you by your first name.
- In correspondence, it is more respectful to add –dono or –sama to the last name.

Gestures

- Japan is a high-context culture; even the smallest gesture carries great meaning. Therefore, avoid expansive arm and hand movements, unusual facial expressions, or dramatic gestures of any kind.
- The American "okay" sign (thumb and forefinger curled in an O) means "money" to the Japanese.
- Some Western gestures convey nothing to the Japanese. These include a shrug of the shoulders or a wink between friends.
- Pointing is considered impolite. Instead, wave your hand, palm up, toward the object being indicated, as the Japanese do.
- Beckoning "come here" is done with the palm down.
- Moving the open hand, with the palm facing left, in a fanning motion in front of the face indicates a negative response.
- Sniffing, snorting, and spitting in public are acceptable, but nose blowing is not. When you must blow your nose, use a disposable tissue and then throw it out.
- To get through a crowd, the Japanese may push others. There is also a gesture meaning, "excuse me," which involves repeating a bow and a karate chop in the air.
- The Japanese do not approve of male-female touching in public.
- Men do not engage in backslapping or other forms of touching.
- In conversation, the Japanese remain farther apart than do North Americans.
- Prolonged direct eye contact is not the norm.
- A smile can mean pleasure, but it can also be a means of self-control, as when it is used to hide disapproval or anger.
- Keep a smile, even when you are upset.
- Laughter can mean embarrassment, confusion, or shock, rather than mirth.
- Silence is considered useful.

Cultural Note

Should you have occasion to visit a Japanese person who is ill, never bring him or her white flowers. The color white is associated with death. Also, avoid giving a potted plant, which suggests that the sick person will soon be planted in the ground.

Gifts

- Gift giving is very common in Japan. Business gifts absolutely must be given at midyear (July 15) and at year-end (January 1). They are often given at first business meetings.
- Make sure your gift was not made in China.
- For the Japanese, the ceremony of gift giving is more important than the objects exchanged. Do not be surprised by either modest or extravagant gifts.
- Take your cue from the Japanese with whom you are working. Allow them to present gifts first, and make your gift of the same quality as theirs.
- The Japanese do not usually open gifts directly upon receipt. If they do, they will be restrained in their appreciation. This does not mean that they do not like your present. Again, follow their lead.
- Good gifts are imported Scotch, cognac, or frozen steaks; electronic gadgets and toys for children of associates; or items made by well-known manufacturers. Elite, foreign name-brands are always best.
- Always wrap your gifts in Japan or have them wrapped by hotel or store services. It is best to buy the paper there, so as not to choose a paper that is considered tasteful in your home country but unattractive in Japan (for example, black and white paper is unacceptable). Rice paper is ideal.
- If you are invited to a Japanese home, bring flowers, cakes, or candy.
- Avoid giving gifts with even numbers of components, such as an even number of flowers in a bouquet. Four is an especially inauspicious number; never give four of anything.

Dress

- Men should wear conservative suits. Avoid casual dress in any business meeting.
- Because shoes are removed frequently, many people wear shoes that slip on.
- Women should dress conservatively, keeping jewelry, perfume, and makeup to a minimum. Pants are becoming more common. High heels are to be avoided if you risk towering over your Japanese counterparts.
- Summer is usually very hot in Japan, so bring lightweight cotton clothing. Be sure to have plenty of changes of attire, because the Japanese are very concerned with neatness.
- If you wear a kimono, wrap it left over right! Only corpses wear them wrapped right over left.

Kuwait

State of Kuwait
Local short form: *Al Kuwayt*
Local long form: Dawlat al Kuwayt

▶ WHAT'S YOUR CULTURAL IQ?

1. Before the discovery of oil, which of the following was the most important resource in Kuwait?
   a. Figs
   b. Religious sites visited by Muslim pilgrims
   c. Pearls

   ANSWER: c. Pearl divers provided much of Kuwait's foreign income until the Japanese began marketing cultured pearls in the 1930s.

2. Oil revenues brought great wealth to Kuwait. TRUE or FALSE? Oil revenues are shared by every resident of Kuwait.

   ANSWER: FALSE. Only a small proportion of Kuwaiti residents get a share of the oil wealth. Many residents are long-term noncitizens, even though they are the second or third generation born in Kuwait. There are also thousands of foreigners residing in Kuwait, working at everything from highly technical oilfield jobs to domestic help positions.

3. Kuwait is a desert country, with very little land suitable for agriculture. TRUE or FALSE? Kuwait is entirely dependent upon food imports to survive.

   ANSWER: FALSE. While most of Kuwait's food is imported, it has an active fishing industry. Kuwaiti cuisine includes many seafood dishes. There are also some farms subsidized by the government.

▶ TIPS ON DOING BUSINESS IN KUWAIT

- Kuwaiti men who deal with foreigners usually offer to shake hands with other men. Although Kuwaiti women do not have as much freedom as men, they make up a substantial portion of the work force. Kuwaiti women do not traditionally shake hands with other women. As in other Islamic countries, there is no physical contact between the sexes in public. However, if a Kuwaiti woman offers to shake hands, do so.
- Kuwait is the only Gulf nation with universal military conscription. The term of service is two years, or one year for persons with a university deferment. However, in practice, a large number of wealthy Kuwaitis manage to get total deferments.
- To the surprise of many Europeans, truffles also grow in certain desert environments—including Kuwait. In the past, many Kuwaitis made family outings to search for truffles. This has declined since the Iraqi invasion of 1990, because thousands of antipersonnel mines were planted in the desert.

▶ COUNTRY BACKGROUND

History

In medieval times, Kuwait was under the nominal rule of the Ottoman Empire. In practice, the Kuwaitis have always maintained autonomy by playing one ruler against another. During that era, they usually pitted the Ottomans against the Persians (modern Iran).

In the sixteenth century, the Portuguese established forts to protect their shipping trade routes. Two centuries later, the British supplanted the Portuguese as the dominant European power in the Gulf. Again the Kuwaitis sought alliances, and they decided that they would have the most freedom under the British flag. The first treaties between Britain and Kuwait were signed in 1899.

Despite its ancient history, Kuwait has been recognized as a fully independent nation only since 1961, when British rule ended.

Kuwait's massive oil reserves were not discovered until the 1930s, and development of the oilfields was delayed by World War II. Only in the 1950s did oil wealth remake Kuwait. The wealth transformed Kuwait's economy without making any basic changes in the political structure.

Following Kuwait's independence in 1961, Iraq made territorial claims on the country. Threatened intervention by Britain kept the Iraqis from invading in the 1960s. By 1990, Britain was no longer the dominant military power in the Gulf, and Saddam Hussein convinced himself that the United States would not intervene militarily. Iraq invaded and then annexed Kuwait in 1990. The emir and his cabinet fled to Saudi Arabia.

After Iraq refused to obey a UN resolution to withdraw, a coalition of many nations, led by the United States, invaded in January of 1991. The shooting war was over within a

Kuwait

month, as Iraqi forces quickly retreat from Kuwait. However, before leaving, the Iraqis set many Kuwaiti oil wells on fire. The emir returned in March of 1991; under international and domestic pressure, he allowed the National Assembly to be restored.

Kuwait and Iraq finally moved toward normalizing relations in 2002. But the following year, the Second Gulf War broke out. Coalition forces—this time primarily belonging to the United States and the United Kingdom—invaded and occupied Iraq. Saddam Hussein was captured, ending the military threat to Kuwait.

Type of Government

The emir now rules Kuwait as a constitutional monarchy. Traditionally, the emir of Kuwait—always a member of the al-Sabah family—exercised total authority. However, the emir was always careful to allow the powerful Kuwaiti merchant families to prosper. In effect, the merchants yielded their political power in return for economic power.

By and large, the al-Sabah emirs ruled adroitly. They managed to maintain Kuwait's identity despite being surrounded by powerful neighbors. Oil wealth brought changes. Health and educational services were transformed, and the populace (now educated and familiar with Western political ideas) agitated for a voice in government. By 1962 a constitution had been written for Kuwait, establishing a National Assembly patterned after an assembly that had evolved back in the 1930s. Despite being an essentially conservative body, this modern assembly did not support the emir on all issues. Friction between the assembly and the emir increased until, in 1976, the assembly was dissolved and the constitution was suspended. The assembly remained suspended at the time of Iraq's 1990 invasion, although an advisory body, the National Council, was in existence. While in exile, the emir promised that the assembly would be reconvened. After the war, a new National Assembly was elected, and in 2006 a new emir took office: Sabah al-Sabah.

A proposal by the former emir to allow women to vote and hold public office was passed in the National Assembly in 2005. (See the Cultural Note at the end of the chapter for information on Kuwait's first female Cabinet Minister.) The emir is both head of state and head of government. There is an appointed prime minister and an independent judiciary.

Current government data can be found at the Embassy of Kuwait's Web site at *www .kuwait-info.org*.

Cultural Note

The official language of Kuwait is Arabic. Classical Arabic (the language of the Koran) is revered by the Arab people. However, in daily life, people speak modern dialects of Arabic. Kuwaitis speak the dialect known as Gulf Arabic, which is shared by most of the people of the Arab peninsula. Gulf Arabic is mutually intelligible with that spoken by Egyptians and Palestinians. However, speakers of Gulf Arabic may have a difficult time communicating with speakers of the Arabic dialects used in Iraq or North Africa.

Kuwait

Language

Arabic is the national language, but English is widely spoken among the business classes.

For data on the languages of Kuwait, visit Ethnologue at *www.ethnologue.com.*

The Kuwaiti View

Kuwait is an Islamic country. The majority—including the Kuwaitis in positions of power—are Sunni Muslims. Friction sometimes exists between the Sunnis and the Shiite minority (about 20 percent), which escalated into terrorist violence in the 1980s. Kuwait's version of Sunni Islam is quite conservative and is influenced by the fundamentalist Wahabism of Saudi Arabia.

Women are gaining more rights since the passage of the law in 2005 that allows them to vote and run for public office. Additionally, they are not forced to wear traditional clothing. Indeed, despite their status, women make up more than 10 percent of the Kuwaiti work force (particularly since the Persian Gulf War).

Only a small portion of Kuwait's population are fully enfranchised citizens. There are over 100,000 Bidun (disenfranchised) Kuwaitis, who are classified as "long-term noncitizens." They do not get the stipends or educational and health benefits given to citizens.

Kuwait is still dealing with the trauma of the 1990–1991 Iraqi occupation. In addition to the destruction, oppression, and torture inflicted on the Kuwaitis by the Iraqis, there are other ramifications. Kuwaitis accused of collaborating with the Iraqis have been dealt with. Since PLO leader Yasir Arafat publicly supported Saddam Hussein, the thousands of Palestinians who worked in Kuwait were deported after the country was liberated. They were replaced by workers from different parts of the world, mostly from Bangladesh. (Among other duties, Bengali workers were given the unenviable task of removing the thousands of land mines left by the Iraqis.) Kuwaiti women also filled some of the vacancies left by the Palestinians.

There are also thousands of refugees from Iraq in Kuwait.

The presence of thousands of soldiers from many countries on Kuwaiti soil has been troublesome; their existence was considered a regretful necessity to the security of Kuwait.

☑ Know Before You Go

The greatest hazard to visitors to Kuwait involves vehicular accidents.

As a strict Islamic country, Kuwait prohibits the importation of alcohol, pork products, or pornography. Persons found in possession of these may be dealt with harshly.

The effects of the huge oil well fires set by the retreating Iraqi occupiers in 1991 are debated, but they certainly caused severe air pollution.

Iraqis also planted millions of antipersonnel mines throughout the country. At this point, contractors have removed some 1.5 million land mines. However, many more remain, and travelers should be cautious when venturing off heavily trafficked areas.

▶ CULTURAL ORIENTATION

Cognitive Styles: How Kuwaitis Organize and Process Information

Kuwaitis' minds are generally closed to most information that does not reflect Islamic values. Most university education is in North America or Europe, which brings with it a degree of abstractive thinking. However, Kuwaitis are taught from youth to think associatively. They generally approach problems subjectively according to the tenets of Islamic law.

Negotiation Strategies: What Kuwaitis Accept as Evidence

Truth is found in Islamic law, so faith in its ideologies permeates all discussions. Subjective feelings are the predominant way of discerning the truth in any situation.

Value Systems: The Basis for Behavior

Islam is the state religion and the main source of legislation. All behavior is judged by Islamic principles. The following three sections identify the Value Systems in the predominant culture—their methods of dividing right from wrong, good from evil, and so forth.

Locus of Decision-Making

The male leader is the locus of decision-making, but he respects the consensus of the group or collective. The individual is always subordinate to the family, tribe, or collective. Solutions to problems primarily lie in the correct interpretation and application of divine law. Leadership and identity come from a person's lineage and his or her ability to protect the honor of the extended family.

Sources of Anxiety Reduction

Security is found in family loyalty and absolute submission to Islamic law. Tribal loyalty will influence hiring and employment even among foreign companies. Loyalty to the ruling clan, not nationality, brings a feeling of national security. Tribal membership remains the cornerstone of the individual's social identity.

Issues of Equality/Inequality

Within Islam, all believers are equal and united in the ulema. However, some tribes feel superior to others. Traditional respect for literacy and aversion to manual labor has created a need for large numbers of foreign workers, with varying degrees of acceptance. Men and women are often considered to be qualitatively different in emotion and intellect.

Historically, public life had been the exclusive domain of men. However, in 2005, women were given far more freedom through the passage of a law that granted them the right to vote and to hold elective office.

▶ BUSINESS PRACTICES

Punctuality, Appointments, and Local Time

- Punctuality was not traditionally considered a virtue in Kuwait. Your client may be late for an appointment or not show up at all. You, however, should endeavor to be prompt, particularly if your Kuwaiti contact was educated in the West. They will expect you to be on time.

- It is standard practice to keep supplicants (including foreign businesspeople) waiting. Do not expect to be able to keep more than one appointment per day.

  An appointment is rarely private. Expect your visit to be interrupted by phone calls and visits from your client's friends and family. Westerners frequently find these distractions infuriating; try to maintain your equanimity.

- Kuwaiti officials traditionally worked no more than six hours per day. Some may do more, but mornings are usually best for appointments.

- Understand that government employment of Kuwaitis is often an aspect of the welfare system rather than a method of running an industrialized state. Kuwaiti officials may show up to work or not, as they please. The day-to-day work is done by foreigners, mainly non-Kuwaiti Arabs.

- Of the several people present at Kuwaiti business meetings, the person who asks you the most questions is likely to be the least important (this is often a non-Kuwaiti professional). The real decision-maker is probably a silent, elderly Kuwaiti who watches everything but never speaks to you directly.

- Because people wander in and out of meetings, you may be asked to repeat the entire presentation several times. Do so gracefully. Do not become angry, even if you are asked to repeat the presentation for an obviously unqualified, uncomprehending family member.

- Kuwaitis try to maintain their calm in any and all circumstances, and you are expected to do the same.

- Bring plenty of copies of promotional materials.

- Friday is the Muslim holy day, and no business is conducted. Most people do not work on Thursdays, either. The work week runs from Saturday through Wednesday.

- Paperwork should carry two dates, the Gregorian (Western) date and the Hijrah (Arabic) date.

- Kuwait is three hours ahead of Greenwich Mean Time (G.M.T. +3), or eight hours ahead of U.S. Eastern Standard Time (E.S.T. +8).

Kuwait

Cultural Note
Some foreign businessmen recommend holding business meetings in the lobby of an international hotel, rather than in a Kuwaiti's office. This has several advantages. There will be fewer people wandering in and out of the meeting. Their willingness to come to you demonstrates that the Kuwaitis are truly interested. Finally, you will have access to refreshments that may be more to your taste. (The local tea and coffee served by Kuwaitis is quite strong; in a hotel, you can get a variety of drinks.)

Negotiating

- The pace of business is much, much slower in Kuwait than it is in the West. Be patient.
- Since they are in no hurry, Kuwaitis have no fear of silence. Do not feel obligated to speak during every period of silence.
- Business meetings always start slowly, with long inquiries into one's health and journey. You may have two or three preliminary meetings (consisting entirely of small talk) before you ever get to make your presentation. The Kuwaitis will let you know when they are ready to talk about business.
- Business cards should be printed in English on one side and in Arabic on the other. Hand your card to a Kuwaiti with your right hand, with the Arabic side facing him.

    Kuwaitis speak at a much closer distance than North Americans are used to. Do not back up or shy away. There is also more physical contact.

- Coffee is often served toward the end of a business meeting. This is a signal that it the meeting will soon conclude. Incense may be lit at this time as well.

    Kuwaiti men often walk hand in hand. If a Kuwaiti holds your hand, take it as a sign of friendship.

- Arabic is a language of hyperbole. When a Kuwaiti says "yes," it usually means "possibly." Be encouraged by this, but do not assume that the negotiating is over.

    It is possible that you will never meet the true decision-maker. It is also possible that the decision-maker was silently observing you while you made your presentation.

- A sage Kuwaiti adviser will sound out the opinions of various decision-makers before you meet with them. He will then put you in contact only with the ones most likely to favor your proposal. Do not rush your contact into introducing you. To do so is to risk having your proposal turned down because you met with the wrong persons.
- When business partners in Kuwait cannot come to an agreement, the case may be taken to court. Unlike Western courts, which hand down a decision, Kuwaiti courts are intended to be arbitrators, recommending an out-of-court settlement. A westerner is usually prudent to accept such a compromise, even in a case where the westerner feels he should win a judgment. Never allow a dispute between you and your Kuwaiti sponsor to be settled by a judge, unless you plan on terminating your Kuwaiti operations. If the judge rules against your sponsor, you will have caused your sponsor to be publicly humiliated, and he will probably obstruct all future dealings you have in the country.

- Avoiding shame is extremely important to Kuwaitis. Always be aware of this. You may have to compromise on some issue not for any practical reason but to protect someone's ego.
- When a contract is finally drawn up, keep it as brief as possible. Arab contracts are traditionally only a few pages long.
- The legal, binding contract must be in Arabic, even if there is an English-language one as well.

Business Entertaining

- Hosting visitors is considered a virtue among Kuwaitis, so they will take care of all of the entertaining within their country.
- Be prepared to remove your shoes before entering a building. Follow the lead of your host.
- Remember that alcohol and pork are proscribed for orthodox Muslims, and that eating is done with the right hand only. Even if you are left-handed, eat with your right hand.
- Expect to encounter eating utensils only in the most westernized of Kuwaiti homes.
- Do not bring up the subject of women unless your Kuwaiti counterpart does so first. Do not even inquire about the health of a Kuwaiti's wife or daughter.
- The topic of Israel should similarly be avoided.
- Sports are a good topic of conversation. Soccer (football), horse and camel racing (with betting prohibited), hunting, and falconry are the most popular Kuwaiti sports.
- Truffles are also a good topic of conversation. The truffles that grow in the Kuwaiti desert are often larger and milder than those that grow in Europe.

Cultural Note
Kuwaitis have a reputation for being generous, affable hosts. Once you have established a relationship with them, they will feel free to stop by your office without an appointment. You are expected to do the same to them, even though this concept is very alien to Western executives. Even if the time you stop by is very inconvenient, they will put on a smile and greet you in an unhurried fashion.

 Kuwait

▶ PROTOCOL

Greetings

- As several styles of greetings are currently in use in Kuwait, it is safest to wait for your Kuwaiti counterpart to initiate the greeting, especially at a first meeting.
- Westernized Kuwaiti men shake hands with other men.
     Some Kuwaiti men will shake hands with Western women. Western businesswomen should wait for a Kuwaiti man to offer his hand.
- Before the war, Kuwaiti women made up little more than 10 percent of the work force, and few were in positions where they met with foreigners. Since the war, the Kuwaiti

government has been deporting "unreliable" foreigners, and many of these jobs have been taken over by Kuwaiti women. Wait for a Kuwaiti businesswoman to offer her hand.

- When a veiled Kuwaiti woman is with a Kuwaiti man, it is not traditional to introduce her.
- A more traditional Kuwaiti greeting between men involves grasping each other's right hand, placing the left hand on the other's right shoulder, and exchanging kisses on each cheek.

Cultural Note

In addition to offices, Kuwaitis have a traditional meeting place known as a *diwaniyah*. Decades ago these were tents set up to entertain male guests away from one's home. Today, they are simply shaded areas adjacent to homes—rather like a large porch in a Western home. Benches with colorful cushions are set up, often in the shape of a square. This allows many men to sit and converse together. Men will come and go, smoking, eating nuts, drinking tea, and socializing.

Diwaniyahs are used in the early evening, after the heat of the day. Sometimes, a television is brought out for people to watch. Although these seem to be entirely social gatherings, a great deal of business is conducted in diwaniyahs.

Titles/Forms of Address

- Westerners frequently find Arabic names confusing. The best solution is to request the names—written in English—of any Kuwaitis you will have to meet, speak to, or correspond with. Find out both their full names (for correspondence) and how they are to be addressed in person.
- Kuwaiti names are written in Arabic. In part because short vowels are not written in Arabic, translating from Arabic to other alphabets is not an exact science. Arabic names may be spelled several different ways in English.
- In general, Kuwaiti names are written in the same order as English names: title, given name, middle name (often a patronymic), and surname (family name). Thus, the former ruler (emir) of Kuwait was Sheikh Jaber al-Ahmed al-Sabah; his title was Sheikh, his given name was Jaber (also spelled Jabir), al-Ahmed (or al-Ahmad) is a patronymic meaning "son of Ahmed," and al-Sabah was his family name.
- The terms al and bin (sometimes spelled ibn) both literally mean "from" in Arabic, so it is not immediately apparent whether a name like "bin Mubarak" indicates "son of Mubarak" or "from the town of Mubarak." Most Kuwaitis prefer al and use it in patronymics. However, both al and bin may be used in the same name.

   If an Arab's grandfather is (or was) a famous person, he sometimes adds his grandfather's name. Thus, Dr. Mahmoud bin Sultan bin Hamad al-Muqrin is "Dr. Mahmoud, son of Sultan, grandson of Hamad, of the house (family) of Muqrin."
- Westerners frequently mistake bin for the name Ben, short for Benjamin. Obviously, bin has no meaning by itself, and one cannot address a Kuwaiti as "bin." Kuwaitis do not use the name Benjamin.

- The female version of bin is bint. Thus, Princess Fatima bint Ibrahim al-Saud is "Princess Fatima, daughter of Ibrahim, of the house of Saud."
- Most Kuwaitis should be addressed by title and given name (e.g., Sheikh Khalil), just as you would address a member of the British aristocracy (e.g., Sir John). They can also be addressed as "Your Excellency." In writing, use the full name.
- In Kuwait, the title Sheikh (pronounced "shake") designates membership in the Kuwaiti royal family.

Gestures

- The left hand is considered unclean in the Arab world. Always use the right hand in preference to the left (unless you are handling something considered unclean). Never eat with the left hand; eat only with your right hand. Avoid gesturing with the left hand.
- While Arabs constantly gesture with their hands while speaking, they do not point at another person. This would be considered impolite.
- As a general rule, keep both feet on the ground. Arabs do not cross their legs when sitting. Never show the bottom of your foot to an Arab; this is considered offensive.
- The "thumbs-up" gesture is offensive throughout the Arab world.

Gifts

- Kuwaiti hospitality is legendary. You are not required to bring a gift when invited to a Kuwaiti home; however, one will be appreciated.
- Appropriate gifts include crafts or picture books from your home. Avoid images or pictures of people or dogs; Islam proscribes images of the human body, and dogs are considered unclean.
- Good gifts for businesspeople include gold pens, pencils, finely made compasses (so that they will always know where Mecca is), business card cases, and cigarette lighters. Have the items engraved, when possible.
- Traditionally, every Kuwaiti who must broker or approve a business deal takes a percentage. Be careful that you do not run afoul of the U.S. Foreign Corrupt Practices Act.
- Avoid admiring an item too effusively; a Kuwaiti will feel obligated to give it to you.
- When offered a gift by a Kuwaiti, it is impolite to refuse.

Cultural Note

The exchange of gifts is one way to acquire *wasta*, an Arabic word for "influence." Wasta is the way things get done in Kuwait. The best way to cut through Kuwaiti bureaucracy is to have someone with wasta intervene for you.

Dress

- While foreigners are not exempt from the Kuwaiti standards of modesty, do not adopt native clothing: for men, a *ghotra* (headdress) and *thobe* (flowing white robe); for women, a veil and an *abaya* (black head-to-foot robe). Kuwaitis may find it offensive to see foreigners dressed in their traditional clothes.
- Foreigners should wear Western clothes that approach the modesty of Kuwaiti dress. Despite the heat of the desert, most of the body must remain covered.
- Men should wear long trousers and a shirt, preferably long-sleeved. A jacket and tie are usually required for business meetings. Keep shirts buttoned up to the collarbone.
- Men should avoid wearing visible jewelry, especially around the neck.
- While not all Kuwaiti women wear traditional clothing, all women—including foreigners—must wear modest clothing in public. The neckline should be high, and the sleeves should come to at least the elbows. Hemlines should be well below the knee, if not ankle-length. The overall effect should be one of baggy concealment; a full-length outfit that is tight and revealing is not acceptable. Therefore, pants or pantsuits are not recommended. While a hat or scarf is not always required, it is wise to keep a scarf at hand. The suitability of your attire will be apparent as soon as you venture out; if Kuwaiti men stare lewdly at you, your dress is not sufficiently modest.

Cultural Note

Massouma al-Mubarak is Kuwait's first female Cabinet Minister. Her appointment to the post was met with insults from Islamic fundamentalists—and enthusiastic cheers from her supporters. The passage of the law in Parliament that allowed women to vote and hold office occurred in 2005.

Kuwait

Malaysia

Former name: Federation of Malaysia

> **Cultural Note**
>
> Malaysian authorities exert strong control over many aspects of society. They have stringent censorship laws in the media. TV or film scenes that include kissing or foul language are often censored.
>
> There is also no room for drug addiction in Malaysia. Any Malaysian citizen can be ordered to take a drug test, and failure to pass means a mandatory sentence in a rehabilitation facility.

WHAT'S YOUR CULTURAL IQ?

1. Malaysia was a colony until after the Second World War. TRUE or FALSE: Before the Japanese occupation, Malaysia was owned by the Netherlands.

   ANSWER: FALSE. Malaysia was a colony of the United Kingdom. Neighboring Indonesia was owned by the Dutch.

2. Malaysia shares which large island with two other nations?
   a. Borneo
   b. Java
   c. Sumatra

   ANSWER: a. The island of Borneo is shared by Malaysia, Indonesia, and the Sultanate of Brunei.

3. Malaysia is rich in natural resources and has developed a formidable manufacturing capacity. Which of the following does Malaysia produce?
   a. Computer disk drives
   b. Timber
   c. Protons
   d. Rubber
   e. All of the above

   ANSWER: e. "Proton" is the name of a car—c does not refer to subatomic particles.

TIPS ON DOING BUSINESS IN MALAYSIA

- Keep in mind that Malaysia is the only country in Southeast Asia that is divided between the Asian mainland and an archipelago. It shares the Malay Peninsula with Thailand. Business and politics are affected by events in adjacent countries. For example, Malaysia was very concerned about the treatment of ethnic Malays in southern Thailand in 2004.

Malaysia

- In Malaysia, a smile is not the ubiquitous gesture that westerners may expect. People in Malaysia may smile or laugh to hide embarrassment, shyness, bitterness, or discord. Malaysian businessmen may laugh during the most serious part of a business meeting; this may be an expression of anxiety, not frivolity.
- In multicultural Malaysia, it is good business to know something about each of the three main ethnic groups—Malay, Indian, and Chinese. Ethnic Malays, called *Bumiputera*, comprise the majority of Malaysia's government. The educated Indian population will generally be in a variety of professions, such as lawyers and journalists. The largest percentage of Malaysian businesspeople are Chinese.

▶ COUNTRY BACKGROUND

History

The proto-Malay people reached Malaysia several thousand years ago. Some of their modern-day descendants still live in the jungles of Borneo, where their traditional cultures have scarcely changed. There are also some 100,000 non-Malay aboriginal people; the Semang and Pangan.

Malaysia has long been a center of international trade. The country lies directly on the sea routes between China and India. For centuries, small kingdoms and sultanates in what is now Malaysia profited from this trade, either by assisting it or by preying upon it. In the sixteenth century, Europeans began trading in Asia. Trade bases were established, and the Malay "pirate kingdoms" were gradually conquered. Malaysia became a British colony.

The British were temporarily driven out by the Japanese during World War II. In 1946, faced with the nationalist aspirations of the Malay peoples, the British consolidated the patchwork of sultanates and states on the Malay Peninsula into a crown colony called the Malayan Union. The sultans were deprived of power, and all citizens were given equal rights.

Many ethnic Malays were dissatisfied with the Malayan Union. Some wished to restore the powers of their Islamic sultans. Furthermore, the Chinese minority had always been the most wealthy and educated ethnic group on the Malay Peninsula. The ethnic Malays, despite their numerical majority, feared that the aggressive Chinese would take over the new crown colony. (The Chinese-dominated Malayan Communist Party did conduct a guerrilla war against British and Malay forces from 1948 until 1960.)

As a result, the Malayan Union was replaced in 1948 with the Malayan Federation. The sultans were restored to power, and the ethnic Malays were guaranteed favorable treatment. In effect, a balance was established between the Malays and the Chinese: The Malays would run the government, and the Chinese would run the businesses. This division is essentially still in effect today. (The Indian population at that time consisted mostly of poor agricultural laborers. They were not considered in the settlement.)

The Federation of Malaya became independent from the United Kingdom in 1957. A new, expanded nation was proposed, uniting the Malay Peninsula, the island crown colony of Singapore, and the three British-controlled territories on the island of Borneo: Sarawak, Brunei, and North Borneo (later renamed Sabah). The sultan of Brunei, wealthy with oil revenues, declined to join. (Brunei remained a British protectorate until becoming an independent country in 1984.) The other Borneo territories, Sarawak and Sabah, joined the new federation, as did Singapore.

The new Federation of Malaysia came into being in 1963. Since 1963, the only change in the makeup of the Federation of Malaysia has been the secession of Singapore in 1965.

Cultural Note

The word "Malay" has several meanings. It can refer to the Malay linguistic group; Malaysia's official language, Bahasa Malaysia, is a standardized form of Malay (similar but not identical to Bahasa Indonesia). Malay can also refer to the dominant ethnic group of Malaysia. Finally, Malay has a geographic meaning; the peninsula shared by Thailand and West Malaysia is called the Malay Peninsula.

Geopolitically, several variants were used by the British during the colonial and postcolonial era: first Malaya, then the Malayan Union, and later the Federation of Malaya. The current nation was formed on September 16, 1963, with the name the Federation of Malaysia. The citizens of Malaysia are Malaysians, while the Malays are the dominant ethnic group in Malaysia.

Type of Government

Malaysia is a constitutional monarchy. The monarchy is rather unique: the nine hereditary sultans elect from among themselves a "paramount ruler" for a five-year term. The paramount ruler—essentially a king with a five-year reign—is the chief of state of Malaysia. "Paramount ruler" is the English term; the actual Malay title is *Yang di-Pertuan Agong*.

The head of government of Malaysia is the prime minister. The United Malays National Organization (UMNO) is the most powerful political party. There are two legislative houses: the Senate and the House of Representatives.

Current government data can be found at Malaysia's Web site of their Embassies worldwide at *www.my.embassyinformation.com*.

Cultural Note

Malaysia experienced tremendous economic growth under the leadership of Prime Minister Mahathir Mohamad. His New Economic Policy brought millions of Malaysian out of subsistence agriculture and into the working class. He and his UMNO Party proposed a New Development Policy designed to put at least 30 percent of Malaysia's wealth into the hands of ethnic Malays—a direct challenge to Chinese economic domination. And his "Vision 2020" plan called for Malaysia to be a fully developed nation by the year 2020.

But Mahathir was also a polarizing figure during his twenty-two-year reign. He instituted draconian laws covering many areas of life and allowed those laws to be used against his political opponents. (The world was stunned when Mahathir's expected successor, Deputy Prime Minister Anwar Ibrahim, fell out of favor and faced trial. He was sentenced to six years for corruption and nine years for sodomy!) Mahathir blamed international currency speculators for the Asian financial crisis that ended Malaysia's economic boom in 1997. And he clearly favored ethnic Malays over the other ethnic groups in his country.

Language

The official language of Malaysia is Bahasa Malaysia, which evolved out of the trade language called Bazaar Malay. It is now written in the Latin alphabet; spelling and orthography were standardized in 1972.

Ethnologue.com has identified 140 languages spoken in Malaysia, one of which is now extinct. As a result of British colonialism, the English language is widely understood in Malaysia, and there are many English loan words in Bahasa Malaysia. (This is one of the factors that separates Bahasa Malaysia from Bahasa Indonesia—Indonesia was a colony of the Netherlands, so Bahasa Indonesia's loan words come from Dutch.) Although English has had a unifying effect on the diverse Malaysian population, the Malaysian authorities have made Bahasa Malaysia the official language of government and education. At home, a Malay family might speak one of several Malay dialects, just as a Chinese family might speak Mandarin or Hakka or Cantonese, or an Indian family speak Tamil or Hindi or Gujarati.

Cultural Note

Islam has long been the predominant religion in Malaysia. Consequently, the use of Arabic script was widespread before the adoption of the Latin alphabet. The Latin alphabet has not entirely replaced Arabic; there are still Malaysian newspapers published in Arabic script. To write Bahasa Malaysia in Arabic script, five additional letters must be added to the traditional twenty-eight Arabic letters.

The Malaysian View

Most religions are represented in Malaysia: Islam, Buddhism, Daoism, Hinduism, Christianity, Sikhism, and Shamanism in Eastern Malaysia. Ethnic Malays and some Indians are Muslims. Most Chinese, when forced to choose, will describe themselves as "Buddhist," but they may follow several religious traditions concurrently.

Although Malaysia is officially an Islamic state, nearly half the population identifies itself as non-Muslim.

The former Malaysian Prime Minister Mahathir Mohamad defended Asian traditions in a book he coauthored called *The Voice of Asia*. He proclaimed:

> Westerners generally cannot rid themselves of (their) sense of superiority. They still consider
> their values and political and economic systems better than any others. It would not be so bad

if it stopped at that; it seems, however, that they will not be satisfied until they have forced other countries to adopt their ways as well. Everyone must be democratic, but only according to the Western concept of democracy; no one can violate human rights, again, according to their self-righteous interpretation of human rights. Westerners cannot seem to understand diversity.

Malaysians obviously feel comfortable with their own cultural traditions and will defend them.

☑ Know Before You Go

Malaysia is close to the epicenter of the tsunami of 2004, but it was shielded from full impact by the island of Sumatra in Indonesia. Besides the tragedy of the earthquakes and tsunamis, the greatest hazards faced by the average foreign traveler are those found in most countries near the equator: sunburn, heat stroke, and/or digestive upsets. Frightening incidents reported in the global news that also occur, but are relatively rare, include: mob violence, typhoons, and floods.

Malaysia maintains some of the strictest censorship laws in the world. It is official policy to insulate the Malaysian population from the "corrupting" foreign media. Foreign journalists are routinely asked to leave the country after writing something uncomplimentary about Malaysia.

Although Malaysia has virtually no Jewish population, anti-Semitism is common, especially among Muslims. Even former Prime Minister Mahathir Mohamad publicly blamed Jews for his country's financial problems.

Bribery and corruption are not unknown in Malaysia. Historically, Malaysia has been considered less corrupt than Indonesia but more corrupt than Singapore (which enforces strict antibribery laws).

▶ CULTURAL ORIENTATION

Cognitive Styles: How Ethnic Malays Organize and Process Information

Although the ethnic Malays have assimilated many indigenous religious rituals into their Islamic religion, they adhere to the closed thinking of Islam when it comes to accepting outside information into their everyday lives. Information is processed subjectively and associatively, and this leads to personal involvement in problems rather than abstract analysis.

Negotiation Strategies: What Ethnic Malays Accept as Evidence

The subjective feelings of the moment form the basis for truth, with faith in the ideologies of Islam having a very strong influence. Only the most westernized and secular of ethnic Malays will use objective facts as the sole source of the truth.

Value Systems: The Basis for Behavior

Much of the business in Malaysia is conducted by the Chinese and Indians, who have a very different system of values from the ethnic Malays. The following three sections identify the Value Systems in the predominant culture—their methods of dividing right from wrong, good from evil, and so forth.

Malaysia

Locus of Decision-Making

The individual ethnic Malay makes decisions based upon the immediate situation and the relationships among those involved. The highly religious may refer to Islamic guidebooks that detail the proper way to handle every decision in life.

Ethnic Malays are quick to organize and have the support of the group behind their decisions. They are not good at confrontations and try to communicate in such a way as to alleviate conflict. They seldom use a categorical "no." It is important for foreign business executives to develop a personal relationship with their Malaysian counterparts.

Sources of Anxiety Reduction

Solid religious beliefs among ethnic Malays give structure and stability to life. The norm is a nuclear household with strong ties to both the husband's and wife's extended families. The extended family is expected to help in time of need. There is little friction between common law and Islamic law, as they are often combined into a single pronouncement. Respect for authority, unbreakable family ties, and the performance of proper social behavior provide strength in times of stress.

Issues of Equality/Inequality

Most states have sultans, and the division between royalty and commoners is rarely bridged. Royalty is treated with great deference, which includes elaborate ritual and special terms of address. The ethnic Malays hold the political power, but they and the economically dominant Chinese continually joust with each other. Ethnocentrism and stereotypes abound, but virulent racism is stifled. Malaysians practice the strong masculine hierarchy of a secular Muslim state.

BUSINESS PRACTICES

Punctuality, Appointments, and Local Time

- It is important to be on time for all business appointments. Never make a Malaysian executive wait.
- The majority of Malaysian businesspeople are Chinese; they are likely to be prompt. The majority of government officials are ethnic Malays. Their culture is very different from that of the Chinese, and they have a more flexible concept of time. Although foreigners are expected to be on time, an ethnic Malay may or may not be prompt.
- The Indian minority conception of time is closer to the Malay than to the Chinese. However, the Indians a foreign businessperson is likely to come in contact with are professionals: lawyers, reporters, physicians, and so forth. They will expect punctuality.
- Social events in Malaysia involving different cultural groups have different rules. In general, when invited to a social event, most Malaysians arrive on time or slightly late. Never be more than a half-hour late.

- A social event hosted by observant Muslims will be without alcohol. There will be no predinner "cocktail hour" and (probably) no appetizers, so the meal may be served close to the time given on the invitation.
- Once a close friendship has been established, guests may arrive a few minutes early to a social occasion. If you are the host and your guests are close friends, it is important to be ready early.
- Try to schedule appointments as early as possible. Malaysian executives are extremely busy. Many travel frequently, especially to conferences in their area of specialization.
- English is the language of many business transactions and correspondence. However, the English spoken often has native inflections, syntax, and grammar, which can easily lead to misunderstandings.
- Bahasa Malaysia is the official language of Malaysia. Although most government officials will speak some English, they may prefer to hold meetings in their native tongue. Fortunately, an English-speaking translator is usually close at hand.
- All official correspondence with government officials must be in Bahasa Malaysia. You may accompany this correspondence with an English translation, if you wish.
- Unlike in nearby Singapore (which has mandated Mandarin Chinese as the official Chinese dialect), Malaysian Chinese often speak mutually unintelligible dialects of Chinese. As a result, the only spoken language a Cantonese-speaking Chinese may have in common with a Hakka-speaking Chinese is English. Similarly, the different linguistic groups within the Indian community often speak English between themselves. English is seen as a unifying force in Malaysia.
- Although lunch has generally been reduced to a single hour (from two hours), Muslims may take a two-hour break on Fridays to attend a mosque.
- Executives often work far longer days than their subordinates do. The Chinese, especially, have reputations as workaholics.
- Holidays in Malaysia vary from state to state. The heavily Muslim states do not celebrate any non-Islamic holidays (including Easter, Christmas, and Western New Year's Day).
- Malaysians usually write the day first, then the month, then the year (e.g., December 3, 2010, is written 3.12.10 or 3/12/10).
- Malaysia is eight hours ahead of Greenwich Mean Time (G.M.T. +8), making it thirteen hours ahead of U.S. Eastern Standard Time (E.S.T. +13).

Cultural Note

Although most Malays are Muslim, not all of Malaysia follows the traditional Islamic work week pattern (Friday is the Islamic holy day, so the traditional Muslim "weekend" is Thursday and Friday). The Malaysian capital city, Kuala Lumpur, is in the state of Selangor, where the work week is Monday through Friday.

Negotiating

- Malaysians prefer to do business with persons they know and like. Establishing this personal relationship will take time, but it is vital for success.
- The pace of business negotiations in Malaysia is slower than in the West. Be patient; it would be unusual to complete a complicated business deal in only one visit. Expect to take several trips over a period of months. Indeed, little will happen at the first meeting except getting acquainted.
- Courtesy is the single most important attribute for successful relationships in Malaysia. This civility in no way hinders the determination of Malaysian businesspeople to get their own way.
- Standards of polite behavior vary widely between cultures. Many Malaysians will ask you highly personal questions (such as "Why aren't you married?" or "How much do you earn?") without realizing that westerners find such questions intrusive. Simply smile and change the topic—and be aware that you, too, will unknowingly violate local standards of polite behavior.
- Because courtesy requires that a Malaysian not disagree openly, the word "no" is rarely heard. A polite but insincere "yes" is simply a technique to avoid giving offense. In Malaysia, "yes" can mean anything from "I agree" to "maybe" to "I hope you can tell from my lack of enthusiasm that I really mean 'no.'"
- "Yes" really means "no" when there are any qualifications attached. "Yes, but . . ." probably means "no." "It might be difficult" is a distinct "no."
- A clear way to indicate "no" is to suck in air through the teeth. This sound always indicates a problem.
- When it comes to making a decision, a "yes" often comes more quickly than a "no." This is because a way must be found to deliver the "no" politely. The "no" may even be delivered through a third party.
- Because Malaysians (especially the Chinese) often consult astrologers, signing a contract may be delayed until an "auspicious" day arrives.
- In Malaysia, as in Indonesia and much of Asia, people who lose their temper are considered unable to control themselves. Such individuals are not trusted or respected.
- Be cautious in asking Malaysian Chinese a question. English speakers would give a negative answer to the question "Isn't my order ready yet?" by responding "no" (meaning, "No, it's not ready"). The Chinese pattern is the opposite: "yes" (meaning, "Yes, it is not ready").
- Malaysians of all ethnic groups are comfortable with silence. A silent pause allows time for thought; it does not necessarily signal either acceptance or rejection. Westerners often find such pauses uncomfortable.
- Age and seniority are highly respected. If you are part of a delegation, line up so that the most important persons will be introduced first. If you are introducing two people, state the name of the most important person first (e.g., "President Smith, this is Engineer Wong").

- Business cards should be printed (preferably embossed) in English. The majority of Malaysian businesspeople are ethnic Chinese, so you may wish to have the reverse side of some of your cards translated into Chinese (gold ink is the most prestigious color for Chinese characters). Your business card should contain as much information as possible.
- The exchange of business cards is a formal ceremony in Malaysia. After introductions are made, the visiting businessperson should offer his or her card. Make sure you give a card to each person present. Present your card either with both hands or with your right hand (with the left hand lightly supporting your right). Give your card to the recipient with the print facing him or her (so the recipient can read it). He or she will receive the card with both hands, then study the card for a few moments before carefully putting it away in a pocket. You should do the same when a card is presented to you. Never put a card in your back pocket (where many men carry their wallets). Do not write on someone's business card.
- Topics to avoid in conversation include any criticism of Malaysian ways, religion, bureaucracy, or politics. Also, avoid any discussion of sex or the roles of the sexes.
- Good topics for discussion include tourism, travel, plans for the future, organizational success (talking about personal success is considered bombastic), and food (while remaining complimentary to the local cuisine).

Cultural Note

Speak in quiet, gentle tones. Always remain calm. Leave plenty of time for someone to respond to a statement you make; people in Malaysia do not jump on the end of one another's sentences. They often leave a respectful pause (as long as ten seconds) before responding. Westerners often assume that they have agreement and resume talking before a Malaysian has the chance to respond.

Business Entertaining

- Take advantage of any invitations to social events. Establishing successful business relationships hinges on establishing strong social relationships.
- Food is vitally important in Malaysian culture. Indeed, the standard Chinese greeting literally means "Have you eaten?"
- Invitations to social events may not come immediately. Be patient and let the Malaysians make the first invitation. You cannot successfully host a social event until you have been a guest at a Malaysian event.
- Respond to written invitations in writing.
- Generally, spouses may be invited to dinners but not to lunch. However, no business will be discussed at an event where spouses are present.

Cultural Note
Among all ethnic groups, kissing in public (even a quick peck on a cheek) is considered unacceptable. Only the most fashionable and cosmopolitan of Malaysians will give even a quick kiss in greeting.

▶ PROTOCOL

Greetings

- Malaysia has three major ethnic groups, each with its own traditions: Malay, Chinese, and Indian.

- With younger or foreign-educated Malaysians, a handshake is the most common form of greeting. The standard Malaysian handshake is more of a handclasp; it is rather gentle and lasts for some ten or twelve seconds. (By contrast, most North American handshakes last for only three or four seconds.) Often, both hands will be used.

- In Malaysia, westernized women may shake hands with both men and women. Malaysian businessmen usually wait for a woman to offer her hand. It is perfectly acceptable for a woman to simply nod upon an introduction rather than offering her hand. A woman should offer her hand only upon greetings; too-frequent handshaking is easily misinterpreted as an amorous advance. (Among themselves, men tend to shake hands both on greeting and on departure.)

- Ethnic Malays are generally Muslim. Traditionally, there is no physical contact between Muslim men and women. (Indeed, if a religious Muslim male is touched by a woman, he must ritually cleanse himself before he prays again.) Because of this, women should not offer to shake hands with Malay men, nor should men offer to shake hands with Malay women. Of course, if a westernized Malay offers to shake hands, do so.

- The traditional Malay greeting is the salaam, which is akin to a handshake without the grip. Both parties stretch out one or both hands, touch each other's hand(s) lightly, then bring their hand(s) back to rest over their heart. This greeting is done only between people of the same sex: from man to man or from woman to woman. However, if cloth (such as a scarf or shawl) prevents actual skin-to-skin contact, then a Malay man and woman may engage in the salaam.

- Among Malaysian Chinese, the traditional greeting is a bow. However, most now shake hands or combine a bow with a handshake. Chinese men are likely to be comfortable shaking hands with a woman—more so than men from other ethnic groups of Malaysia.

- Many Malay Indians are Hindu. Most Hindus avoid public contact between men and women, although not as assiduously as observant Muslims. Men may shake hands with men and women with women, but only westernized Hindus will shake hands with the opposite sex. Malaysian Indians may also be Sikhs or Christians or Muslims; all avoid public contact between the sexes.

Malaysia

- The traditional Indian greeting involves a slight bow with the palms of the hands together (as if praying). This greeting, called the namaste, will generally be used only by older, traditional Hindus. However, it is also an acceptable alternative to a handshake when a Western businesswoman greets an Indian man.
- Just as the British greeting "How do you do?" is rhetorical, Malaysians have many rhetorical greetings. Chinese greetings often involve food. "Have you eaten?" or "Have you taken food?" are rhetorical greetings; answer "yes," even if you are hungry. Similarly, a typical Malaysian greeting when meeting on the street is "Where are you going?" This is also rhetorical; "For a walk" or "Nowhere of importance" are perfectly acceptable answers—indeed, the latter is the English equivalent of the traditional Malay response. You are not expected to reveal your itinerary.

Titles/Forms of Address
- Addressing Malaysians properly is a complex affair, especially for westerners unfamiliar with the naming patterns of Malaysian ethnic groups. Take your time over an introduction, which will probably involve business cards. Repeat the title and name of the person and ask if you are pronouncing them correctly. This often invites an explanation of the history or origin of titles or names, providing you with personal information that may be useful.
- Malaysia is a constitutional monarchy with nine royal houses. With so many royals, international business visitors are likely to encounter one sooner or later. Titles and means of address vary; ask a native how a particular royal should be addressed.
- Never be overly-familiar with a business contact. Most executives you meet should be addressed with a title and their name. If a person does not have a professional title (such as Engineer, Doctor, or Teacher), a westerner may use "Mr." or "Madam/Mrs./Miss" plus the name. However, be aware that you may be omitting other titles that are important both to the person and to your understanding of that person.

    The traditional Malay forms of Mr., Mrs., or Miss are:
    Mr. = *Encik* (which may be abbreviated as "En")
    Mrs. or Madame = *Puan*
    Miss (an unmarried woman) = *Cik*

    These are used in front of an individual's name (e.g., Mr. Ahmadi would be properly addressed as Encik Ahmadi.) Although there is no Malay equivalent for "Ms.," the current trend is to use Puan for any adult female.
- There are additional titles that may be used once you become closer to your Malaysian associates. One title which is important in business circles is Tuan, which is conferred when a man is in a respected position of authority.
- When you ask Malaysian associates about their titles and names, explain about yours as well. They may be equally unsure as to which of your names is your surname. Follow

their lead as to the degree of formality. Don't tell a Malaysian "just call me Tony" when you are calling him Dr. Gupta.

- Each of the three major ethnic groups in Malaysia has different naming patterns. For further information on the proper titles and forms of address for Muslims, Indians, and Chinese, please consult Appendix A.

Gestures

- Aside from handshakes, there is no public contact between the sexes in Malaysia. Do not kiss or hug a person of the opposite sex in public—even if you are husband and wife. On the other hand, contact between people of the same sex is permitted. Men may hold hands with men or even walk with their arms around each other; this is interpreted as nothing except friendship.
- Among both Muslims and Hindus, the left hand is considered unclean. Eat with your right hand only. Where possible, do not touch anything or anyone with your left hand if you can use your right hand instead. Accept gifts and hold cash in the right hand. (Obviously, when both hands are needed, use them both.)
- The foot is also considered unclean. Do not move anything with your feet, and do not touch anything with your feet.
- Do not show the soles of your feet (or shoes). This restriction determines how one sits: You can cross your legs at the knee, but do not place one ankle on your knee. However, any form of leg crossing is ostentatiously casual in Malaysia; never cross your legs in the presence of Malaysian royalty.
- Do not prop your feet up on anything not intended for feet, such as a desk.
- It is impolite to point at anyone with the forefinger. Malays use a forefinger only to point at animals. Even pointing with two fingers is impolite among many Indians. When you must indicate something or someone, use the entire right hand (palm out). You can also point with your right thumb, as long as all four fingers are curled down. (Make sure all your fingers are curled—older Malays would interpret a fist with the thumb and little finger extended as an insult.)
- Pounding one fist into the palm of the other hand is considered obscene.
- The head is considered the seat of the soul by many Indians and Malays. Never touch someone's head, not even to pat the hair of a child.
- As in much of the world, to beckon someone, you hold your hand out, palm downward, and make a scooping motion with the fingers. Beckoning someone with the palm up and wagging one finger, as in the United States, can be construed as an insult.
- Standing tall with your hands on your hips—the "arms akimbo" position—is always interpreted as an angry, aggressive posture.
- The comfortable standing distance between two people in Malaysia varies with each culture. In general, stand as far apart as you would if you were about to shake hands (about two to three feet). Indians tend to stand a bit further apart (three or three and a half feet).

Gifts

- The Malaysian Anti-Corruption Agency has strict laws against bribery. Avoid giving gifts that could be interpreted as bribes.
- Gifts are exchanged between friends. Do not give a gift to anyone before you have established a personal relationship with her or him. Otherwise, the gift may have the appearance of a bribe.
- It is not the custom to unwrap a gift in the presence of the giver. To do so would suggest that the recipient is greedy and impatient. Worse, if the gift is somehow inappropriate or disappointing, both parties would be embarrassed. Expect the recipient to thank you briefly, then put the still-wrapped gift aside until you have left.
- Because pork and alcohol are prohibited to observing Muslims, do not give them as gifts to Malays. Other foods make good gifts, although meat products must be halal (the Muslim equivalent of kosher). The prohibition against pork and alcohol also precludes pigskin products and perfumes containing alcohol.
- Muslim Malays consider dogs unclean. Do not give toy dogs or gifts with pictures of dogs.
- Remember that personal gifts from a man to a woman can be misinterpreted as romantic offerings.
- Don't wrap gifts to ethnic Malays in white paper; white is associated with funerals.
- The Chinese traditionally decline a gift three times before accepting; this prevents them from appearing greedy. Continue to insist; once they accept the gift, say that you are pleased that they have done so.
- Gifts of food are always appreciated by Chinese, but avoid bringing food gifts with you to a dinner or party (unless it has been agreed upon beforehand). To bring food may imply that your host cannot provide enough. Instead, send food as a thank-you gift afterward. Candy or fruit baskets are good choices.
- For further information on Chinese gift-giving practices, see the chapter on China.
- Among Indians, the frangipani flower (used by Hawaiians to make leis) is used only for funeral wreaths.
- If you give money to an Indian, make sure it is an odd number (just the opposite of Chinese tradition). Usually this is done by adding a single dollar; for example, give $11 instead of $10.
- Observant Hindus do not eat beef or use products made from cattle. This eliminates most leather products as gifts.

Dress

- Just north of the Equator, Malaysia is hot and humid all year long. Most of the lowlands have a daytime temperature range of 75 to 95°F and humidity between 60 and 70 percent.

- Lower temperatures occur only in the mountainous areas, where businesspeople rarely venture (except for tourism). Mountain temperatures can actually dip below freezing at night.
- The monsoon season runs from September through December, but sudden showers occur all year long. Many people carry an umbrella every day.
- As a foreigner, you should dress conservatively until you are sure what degree of formality is expected. Men should wear a suit jacket and tie.
- Because of the heat and humidity, business dress in Malaysia is sometimes casual. Standard formal office wear for men is dark pants and a light-colored long-sleeved shirt and tie, without a jacket. Businessmen may also wear a short-sleeved shirt with no tie.
- Businesswomen wear light-colored long-sleeved blouses and skirts, or business suits.
- Many Malaysian men wear an open-necked batik shirt to work. This is also popular for casual wear. Jeans are acceptable for casual wear, but shorts should be avoided.
- In deference to Muslim and Hindu sensibilities, women should always wear garments that cover at least their upper arms. Skirts should be knee-length or longer.

Cultural Note

The use of electronic gadgets has become ubiquitous in Asia. Cell phones alone have changed cultural norms. One unfortunate example is that of a Malaysian football player who terminated his engagement via a text message the morning of the wedding! The bride then had to face 1,000 guests alone at their traditional Malaysian wedding feast. The incident appalled the player's Kedah State Football Association—and all his teammates, who had been invited to the wedding. Because he tarnished the game's image, the player's contract was terminated.

Malaysia

Mexico

United Mexican States
Local long form: Estados Unidos Mexicanos

Cultural Note

Mexico remains a very Catholic county; every town and village has a patron saint.

Many Mexicans consider themselves *Guadalupeños*, a nickname for those who believe in the miracle of the Virgin of Guadalupe (the Virgin Mary). She appeared three times to a poor Aztec, Juan Diego, in 1513, and told him to build a church in Tepeyac, where the Aztec goddess Tonantín was worshipped. Today the basilica is visited by more than 1 million pilgrims annually, and images of the Virgin of Guadalupe are everywhere, a symbol of unity between the Aztec and Spanish cultures and of Mexican nationality.

▶ WHAT IS YOUR CULTURAL IQ?

1. Dictator and military leader Antonio López de Santa Anna was famous for:
   a. Losing the Texas War of Independence
   b. Losing the U.S.-Mexican War
   c. Selling a strip of Mexican territory so the United States could build a railroad
   d. Seizing the presidency of Mexico no less than eleven times!
   e. All of the above

   ANSWER: e. During Santa Anna's tenure, Mexico lost half its territory to the United States. His career was ended by Mexican outrage after he sold southern Arizona and New Mexico to the United States in the Gadsden Purchase.

2. The Mexican Revolution lasted from 1910 to 1920 and cost over 1 million Mexican lives. TRUE OR FALSE: The United States of America supported the rebel Mexican leaders Pancho Villa, Pascual Orozco, and Emiliano Zapata.

   ANSWER: FALSE. The USA opposed the radical leaders. Although Villa and Zapata managed to occupy Mexico City, the U.S.-backed Constitutionalists eventually won.

3. Which of the following Mexican authors won a Nobel Prize for literature?
   a. Carlos Fuentes
   b. Jorge Ibargüengoitia
   c. Octavio Paz
   d. None of the above

   ANSWER: c. Octavio Paz won the 1990 Nobel Prize for literature. His acceptance speech is available at *www.nobel.se/literature/laureates/1990/paz-speech.html*.

Mexico

TIPS ON DOING BUSINESS IN MEXICO

- Elaborate, effusive courtesy is a characteristic of Mexican communications. This formal courtesy can conceal true feelings. It is quite possible for Mexicans to politely say one thing and do the opposite.
- Although the United States and Mexico are neighbors, their citizens have different attitudes toward eye contact. In the United States, someone who does not directly meet your gaze is often suspected of being untrustworthy. Mexicans find continued, intense eye contact to be aggressive and threatening. Mexican business executives expect intermittent eye contact.
- The family is the single most important institution in Mexico. Because of this, nepotism is an accepted practice. Mexican executives generally put a higher importance on the best interest of their families than on their place of employment.

> **Cultural Note**
>
> The official name of Mexico—Estados Unidos Mexicanos—translates to "The United States of Mexico." Consequently, referring to the United States of America as simply "The United States" can cause confusion. Curiously, the polite Mexican term for a citizen of the United States of America is norteamericano, although Mexico itself is technically part of North America. Canadians are called canadienses to differentiate them from norteamericanos. The term americanos—Americans—is insufficient to designate citizens of the United States of America, as it can apply to anyone in North, Central, or South America.

 COUNTRY BACKGROUND

History

The origins of Mexican culture date back to the Mayan and Aztec Indians. Their empires were destroyed by the Spanish conquistadors (assisted by European diseases, superior military technology, and infighting amongst the Amerindian tribes), and Mexico came under colonial rule in 1521.

By the 1700s, Mexico had become the heart of the viceroyalty of New Spain, which encompassed all of Central America down to Panama. One advocate of independence was a parish priest from the Mexican town of Dolores. This priest, Father Miguel Hildalgo, issued a call for independence, known as "the Grito de Dolores" (the Cry from Dolores). Delivered on September 16, 1810, the Grito de Dolores became one of the most famous speeches in Mexican history. Father Hildago led a rebellion against the viceregal forces, but he was captured and executed in 1811. After eleven years of rebellion, Mexican independence was finally achieved in 1821. But the new nation became a monarchy, rather than a republic, angering many of the rebels. A defector from the Spanish viceregency, Colonel Agustín de Iturbide had himself inaugurated as the first emperor of Mexico in 1822. After just nine months in office, Iturbide was forced to abdicate by military leader Antonio López de Santa Anna.

The first Mexican Constitution was approved in 1824, establishing the Republic of Mexico. Guadalupe Victoria became Mexico's first president.

Santa Anna seized the presidency of Mexico in 1833. During the next twenty-two years, Santa Anna occupied the presidency no less than eleven separate times.

In 1836, Texas successfully achieved independence from Mexico, following the defeat of Santa Anna's forces at the Battle of San Jacinto.

When Mexico protested the admission of Texas into the United States, the U.S. Congress declared war. By 1848, Mexico's forces were defeated, and the United States annexed the Mexican territory west of Texas. This annexed territory now forms all or part of the states of California, Nevada, Utah, Colorado, Arizona, and New Mexico.

In 1862, Napoleon III of France decided to conquer all of Mexico. Napoleon restored the Mexican monarchy and placed Archduke Maximilian of Austria on the throne. Following the end of the U.S. Civil War, the United States was in position to demand the removal of French forces from Mexico under the Monroe Doctrine. The French troops left, but Maximilian refused to abdicate.

Mexican forces under Benito Juárez defeated the remaining imperial forces in May 1867, and Maximilian was executed by firing squad the next month.

In 1876, Porfirio Díaz first came to power in Mexico. For the next thirty-four years, he ruled Mexico either directly as president or indirectly through his proxies. This period was known as the "Porfiriato."

Opposition to the dictatorship of the Porfiriato erupted into strikes in 1910. Rebel leaders Pancho Villa, Pascual Orozco, and Emiliano Zapata all led factions that fought the government. Eventually, Mexico was divided into two camps: the Constitutionalists and the Radicals. Slowly, the Constitutionalists gained the upper hand. By the time the rebellion ceased in 1920, the decade-long revolution had cost the lives of almost one out of every eight Mexicans.

As Mexico's economy continued to grow after World War II, so did the country's population. The population doubled, and the poor left their small farms and moved to the cities. During the presidency from 1988 to 1994 of a Harvard-educated technocrat, Carlos Salinas de Gortari, the Mexican economy improved. Salinas signed the North American Free Trade Agreement (NAFTA), which is known in Mexico as *Tratado de Libre Comercio (TLC)*.

Vicente Fox Quesada was elected president in 2000, ending seventy-one years of national dominance by the PRI (Institutional Revolutionary Party).

Type of Government

The United States of Mexico—as Mexico is officially known—is a federal republic. The head of the government is the president, who is elected to a six-year term and cannot be re-elected. During the seventy-one-year rule of the Partido Revolucionario Institucional

(PRI) Party, presidents were generally able to handpick their successors. Whether this will continue remains to be seen.

There is a bicameral legislature with a Senate and a Chamber of Deputies, plus a judicial Supreme Court.

For current government data, check with the Embassy of Mexico at *www.embassyof mexico.org*.

Language

Spanish is the official language of Mexico, although ethnologue.com also lists over 200 Amerindian languages.

In the past, French was the foreign language of choice of the upper class. English is now the most popular second language, and an English speaker is usually near at hand in most multinational firms.

The Mexican View

There is no official religion in Mexico, but almost 90 percent of Mexicans are Roman Catholic. Protestants account for around 5 percent, and their percentage is growing—notably among the Evangelical sects.

NAFTA and privatization have changed everyday life in Mexico, at least for consumers and nonagricultural workers. For example, after decades of protectionism, foreign consumer goods are readily available in Mexico.

Young Mexican executives are generally familiar with foreign business practices and online communications. Most Mexicans are highly skeptical of authority figures. Politicians and police alike are often seen as corrupt and self-serving. Outlaws who are honest about their criminality are sometimes glamorized, especially narcotics traffickers.

Mexico is one of the United States' most important trade partners. It is the third largest exporter to the United States, and its international trade products include oil exports, tourism, and the products of its many assembly plants (called *maquiladoras*).

☑ Know Before You Go

Currently, the greatest concern of foreign visitors in Mexico is street crime, up to and including kidnapping. Kidnappers range from highly organized groups who target specific individuals, to kidnappers-of-opportunity who grab random, affluent-looking targets.

Mexico City, with nearly 20 million inhabitants, is the second largest urban area in the world. Despite efforts to limit air pollution, the problems with air quality in Mexico City remain.

Mexico has numerous high-altitude sites. Altitude sickness can strike anyone, even if you have never experienced it before. There is no sure prevention except gradual acclimation to high elevation: once you get to 6,000 feet above sea level, spend at least two nights there. Repeat this acclimation period at each increase of 3,000 feet. Alcohol consumption tends to make the symptoms worse. Sunburn is also a danger at high altitudes because there is less atmosphere to protect you from the sun.

▶ CULTURAL ORIENTATION

Cognitive Styles: How Mexicans Organize and Process Information

In Mexico, information is readily accepted for purposes of discussion, but little movement in attitude is seen. Mexicans tend to become personally involved in each situation and look at the particulars rather than initially using a rule or law to solve problems.

Negotiation Strategies: What Mexicans Accept as Evidence

Subjective feelings generally form the basis for truth, and this can lead to the truth altering depending on perceptions and desires. Faith in the ideologies of the Catholic Church, though pervasive, does not greatly affect their perception of the truth. Those with a higher education more often use objective facts.

Value Systems: The Basis for Behavior

Mexico's long and unhappy history with the United States makes Mexicans suspicious of U.S. businesspeople—and, to a lesser extent, of foreigners from any industrialized country. The following three sections identify the Value System in the predominant culture—their methods of dividing right from wrong, good from evil, and so forth.

Locus of Decision-Making

The individual is responsible for his or her decisions, but the best interest of the family or group is a dominating factor. One must know a person before doing business with him or her, and the only way to know a person in Mexico is to know the family. Expertise is less important than how one fits into the group, so it is extremely important to cultivate personal relations with the right people in the right places.

Sources of Anxiety Reduction

It is one's role in the social structure and the presence of the extended family that give a sense of stability to life. However, families exert pressure on the behavior of their members. Group members are bound by intense friendship and personal relations and commit themselves to assisting one another in case of need. This network of relatives, friends, and memberships is crucial to class affiliation and social mobility. All of these expect mutual support—a lifelong commitment.

Mexicans have been charted as risk-averse and resistant to change. Their societal norms have not varied significantly in the last decade.

Issues of Equality/Inequality

There are extreme contrasts between rich and poor, but Mexico has the largest upper middle class of all Latin American countries—all interrelated in one way or another. Machismo is very strong, and there is a general belief that if there is an opportunity for sex to occur, it will. Mexicans are also known for their endless variety of sexual double-entendres. Many innocuous Spanish terms have slang sexual meanings.

For women, femininity is stressed in dress, makeup, and behavior. Despite widespread machismo, most Mexicans believe that mothers are the central figure in every family.

▶ BUSINESS PRACTICES

Punctuality, Appointments, and Local Time
- Punctuality, although admired, is not strictly adhered to in daily life. However, it is expected from foreigners and in business circles, so be on time for appointments—but bring some work in case your counterpart is late.
- Punctuality is not expected for parties, dinner invitations, and so forth. Be at least thirty minutes late when invited to a party at a Mexican home. In Mexico City, be at least one hour late; some guests will be two or even three hours late.
- Make appointments approximately two weeks prior to your arrival in Mexico by e-mail or phone, then reconfirm it a week before. Establish your contacts as high up in the organization as possible. Use a local *persona bien colocada* (well-connected person) to make introductions and contacts for you.
- Meetings may take place at breakfast, lunch, or dinner. Let your counterpart select which time.
- Mexico is six hours behind Greenwich Mean Time (G.M.T. –6), or one hour behind U.S. Eastern Standard Time (E.S.T. –1).

Negotiating
- The business atmosphere is friendly, gracious, and unhurried.
- The pace will tend to be slower than that of Canada, the United States or northern Europe. Decisions are made at top levels, with consultation at lower levels. This may take time. Be calm and patient with delays and build them into your expectations.
- Personal friendships are vital to business in Mexico. Mexicans look for long-term relationships based on mutual trust and reliability, or *personalismo*. It is important to spend time building these relationships, as your friendship will mean more to your prospects than the multinational firm you represent. Plan to make repeated visits and maintain contact after your trips.
- Be warm and personal, yet retain your dignity, courtesy, and diplomacy. Your Mexican counterparts may initially seem vague, suspicious, and indirect. Overcome this with trust and goodwill.

Mexico

- Mexicans highly value the individual dignity of a person, regardless of social standing or material wealth. It is important not to pull rank, publicly criticize anyone, or do anything that will cause an individual to be humiliated.
- Mexicans avoid saying "no." "Maybe" or "we will see" may actually mean "no." Get all agreements in writing, as the "yes" may have been said out of politeness and the agreement later reversed.
- When negotiating, emphasize the trust and mutual compatibility of the two companies. Stress the benefits to the person and his or her family and pride. This emotional approach may be more effective than the logical bottom line of a proposal.
- If there is a disagreement, do not overcompromise, because this would show weakness.
- Leave yourself a reasonable margin for negotiating in your prices.
- Use high-end, sharp visuals in your presentations.
- Although the situation is rapidly changing, there are still fewer women in upper levels of management than men. A woman should display her competence in a dignified manner, or she may face some initial lack of respect in Mexico.
- Mexicans are status conscious. At least one member of the negotiating team should be from higher-level management. Stay in prestigious hotels, eat at good restaurants, and mention major achievements (for example, advanced degrees from a prestigious university—if the topic arises).
- One major barrier in negotiations is the issue of financing the cost of foreign goods and services. Be prepared with some creative financing solutions.

Business Entertaining

- The best times for business meetings are breakfast or lunch, the main meal of the day. Business breakfasts are usually held at a guest's hotel and start at 8:00 or 8:30 A.M. and may last for up to two hours.
- If you are invited to a Mexican home, do not expect to discuss business. Instead, use this time for socializing and meeting the family. Dinner is never eaten before 8:30 P.M. Arrive about thirty minutes late.
- Good topics of conversation include Mexican sights and your family and job at home. Sports are also good topics: football (soccer), baseball, basketball, and bullfighting. Topics to stay away from include historically sensitive issues such as Mexico's territorial losses or the large numbers of Mexicans who work illegally in other countries, especially in the United States.
- It is customary for one person to pay the check for a group meal. This is often the oldest person in the group. It is good manners to haggle over paying the bill. Reciprocate by inviting the person out for another meal, insisting ahead of time that this will be your treat.
- You may be invited to a girl's fifteenth birthday party. This is called a *quinceañera* and is an important occasion.

- It is not wise for foreign businesswomen to invite their counterparts to a business dinner unless other associates or spouses also attend. For business lunches, eat at your hotel and have the bill added to your tab. Otherwise men will resist having you pay.

▶ PROTOCOL

Greetings
- Men will shake hands in greeting. Women will often pat each other on the right forearm or shoulder instead of shaking hands. If they are close, they may hug or kiss each other on the cheek. Men may wait for women to initiate a handshake.
- Be prepared for a hug on the second or third meeting.
- At a party, give a slight nod to everyone as you enter the room. It is customary to greet and shake hands with each individual. Usually your host will introduce you. You are also expected to shake hands with each person when you leave.

Titles/Forms of Address
- Titles are very important in Mexico. Address a person directly by using his or her title only, such as Profesor. First names are used only by people on familiar terms. Wait for your counterpart to initiate this switch to first names.
- For further information on the proper titles and forms of address in Mexico, please consult Appendix A.

Gestures
- Conversations take place at a much closer physical distance than what may be considered comfortable in the United States or northern Europe. Pulling away from your counterpart may be regarded as unfriendly—and your Mexican associate may simply step forward and close up the distance again.
- Mexican men are warm and friendly and make a lot of physical contact. They often touch shoulders or hold another's arm. To withdraw from such a gesture is considered insulting.
- Mexicans may catch another's attention in public with a psst-psst sound. This is not considered rude.
- Men should avoid putting their hands in their pockets. Hands on your hips indicate that you are making a challenge.
- When indicating height, always use the index finger. Only the height of an animal is shown by using the whole hand.
- In a store, pay for purchases by placing the money in the cashier's hand, rather than on the counter.

Gifts

- Giving gifts to executives in a business context is not required at an initial meeting. However, small gifts, such as items with a company logo (for an early visit) or a bottle of wine or Scotch (on subsequent trips) are appreciated. If a gift of greater value is called for, desk clocks, finely made pens, or gold cigarette lighters are good choices (smoking is still common in Mexico).
- Small electronics, like MP3 players loaded with your associate's favorite artist, or selections from prominent musicians in your country, make for a thoughtful gift. Make sure the electronic device was made in your country.
- Mexican secretaries expect gifts from foreign businesspeople. A government secretary who performs any service for you is generally given a token gift. For secretaries in the private sector, a more valuable gift should be given on a return visit.
- Gifts are not required from a dinner guest. An extension of thanks and a reciprocal invitation are considered sufficient. However, a gift will be happily accepted if offered. Good choices are candy, flowers (if sent ahead, impress upon the florist that the delivery must arrive early or on time), or local crafts from home.
- Regional viewpoints on the significance of specific flowers vary—check with your hosts or the local embassy to determine appropriate floral arrangements.
- Avoid giving gifts made of silver; it can be associated with trinkets sold to tourists in Mexico.
- Gifts of knives should be avoided in Latin America; they can symbolize the severing of a friendship.

> **Cultural Note**
>
> Mexicans feel compelled to help someone who asks for assistance. If you become lost in Mexico City, asking for directions can easily become a group event. There are many stories of travelers who ask one person for help, and that individual consults with another *Mejicano*, who asks a cab driver, etc. The process is only resolved when everyone is satisfied that the lost innocent is safely on his or her way—often with a personal guide.

Dress

- For business, men should wear a conservative dark suit and tie; women should wear a suit, pantsuit, or dress.
- Pants and a light shirt are casual wear for men; women may wear a skirt or nice pants. Jeans are not considered appropriate unless they are tailored and well pressed.
- Revealing clothing for women and shorts for either sex are still sometimes viewed as inappropriate except at a resort. Men may wish to wear the traditional guayabera, a light shirt worn untucked.

The Netherlands

Kingdom of the Netherlands
Local short form: Nederland
Local long form: Koninkrijk der Nederlanden

> **Cultural Note**
> The Kingdom of the Netherlands is often incorrectly called Holland. Holland refers only to a specific area in the Netherlands, encompassing the major cities of Amsterdam, Rotterdam, and the Hague. It is no more correct to call all of the Netherlands "Holland" than it would be to call all of Germany "Bavaria" or all of Spain "Andalusia."

▶ WHAT'S YOUR CULTURAL IQ?

1. Match the following notable Dutchmen with their fields of achievement:
   a. Christiaan Huygens
   b. Rembrandt van Rijn
   c. Baruch (Benedict) de Spinoza
   d. Anton van Leeuwenhoek

   1. Biology and the Microscope
   2. Philosophy
   3. Painting
   4. Mathematics and Physics

   ANSWERS: a. 4; b. 3; c. 2; d. 1

2. TRUE or FALSE: It is acceptable to discuss prostitution, soft drugs, and euthanasia with your open-minded Dutch coworkers.

   ANSWER: FALSE. Although all are legal in the Netherlands, none are an appropriate topic of conversation in a work environment.

3. TRUE or FALSE? During the 1600s, the Netherlands became a world power, with a globe-spanning fleet and a far-flung network of colonies.

   ANSWER: TRUE. The Dutch fleet even outclassed the British fleet in the early 1600s. Dutch supremacy started to unravel when both Britain and France attacked the Netherlands in 1672.

▶ TIPS ON DOING BUSINESS IN THE NETHERLANDS

- The Netherlands continues to rank among the top dozen trading nations in the world. Expect Dutch businesspeople to be experienced and sophisticated.
- The Dutch are a low-context, straight-speaking people. They can be blunt spoken and critical without meaning to offend.
- Do not make any promises you cannot keep. The Dutch expect honesty; any backpedaling on what they perceive as a promise will cause you to lose credibility. Even an offhand promise—such as "We'll take care of it"—is likely to be taken at face value.

▶ COUNTRY BACKGROUND

History

Julius Caesar's troops fought Germanic tribes in what is now the Netherlands. The strongest of these tribes were not subdued until 13 B.C. The Romans were neither the first nor the last to invade the Netherlands.

Following the collapse of the Roman Empire, Charlemagne incorporated the Netherlands into his Kingdom of the Franks.

The Low Countries, as the Netherlands and Belgium were then known, were subsequently claimed by one ruler after another, from the French duke of Burgundy to the Austrian House of Hapsburg. All of these rulers were absentee landlords; they controlled blocks of land in scattered locations throughout Europe. Lacking any political power, the Dutch put their energies into trade and industry.

When Charles I of Spain came of age in A.D. 1516, he inherited title to the Netherlands. But a nation as distant as Spain was bound to have difficulty ruling the increasingly self-sufficient Dutch. The Protestant Reformation increased Dutch opposition; many Dutch became Calvinists and resisted Catholic Spain on religious grounds.

The Dutch revolution spanned eighty years, from 1568 to 1648. Although Spain was then the most powerful nation in Europe, it was unable to subdue the Dutch rebels.

The northern districts of the Low Countries formally united in 1579 under the Union of Utrecht; this is often used as the date of origin of the Netherlands. An equally valid date is 1781, when those northern districts formally declared their independence from Spain. The Spanish agreed to a twelve-year truce with the Dutch in 1609 but did not recognize the Dutch Republic as an independent nation until the Peace of Munster in 1648. The southern Low Countries (Belgium) remained under Spanish control.

The Netherlands survived and prospered. They experimented with several forms of government, with and without kings. The current Kingdom of the Netherlands dates to the ascension of Prince William I as king in 1813.

Beginning in the seventeenth century, the Netherlands enjoyed a "golden era" of economic supremacy as its trade spanned the world. Dutch colonies were founded in Asia and the Caribbean. However, the tiny size and small population of the Netherlands made it inevitable that Dutch economic supremacy would be eclipsed by Britain, France, and Germany.

The Netherlands remained neutral in World War I. However, in World War II, they were invaded and occupied by the Nazis. The Netherlands' last major colony, Indonesia, was occupied by the Japanese during WWII as well. The Dutch never truly regained control of Indonesia after the war, and Indonesia became independent in 1949. The Dutch still rule the Netherlands Antilles and Aruba in the Caribbean.

In 1995, Dutch confidence in their military was shaken when their peacekeeping troops stationed in Bosnia failed to prevent the Srebrenica massacre. Subsequently, the Dutch were shocked again when the controversial Dutch politician Pym Fortuyn was assassinated in May of 2002.

Type of Government

The Kingdom of the Netherlands is a constitutional monarchy. There is a bicameral Parliament, with a First Chamber and a Second Chamber. The monarch is the chief of state; the prime minister is the head of the government.

The Netherlands is a member of both NATO and the European Community.

Although the Dutch are known for frugality in their personal lives, they have a very generous social welfare system. The government is seeking ways to reduce this system, which is seen as a burden on the economy.

For current government data, check with the Embassy of the Netherlands at *www .netherlands-embassy.org.*

Language

The official language of the Netherlands is Dutch. A minor percentage of the population speaks Frisian, Turkish, and Arabic.

The Dutch are among the most accomplished linguists in Europe. A majority of Dutch people speak at least one additional language. English is widely understood.

Ethnologue.com lists sixteen languages spoken in the Netherlands. All are currently in use.

Cultural Note

Frisian is the language of the inhabitants of Friesland province in the northeast Netherlands. The province's name is also spelled Vriesland. The people have a distinct culture and many native works of literature. There are perhaps 750,000 Frisians, of which some 300,000 live outside Friesland. At various times, the Frisians have demanded independence from the Netherlands. Frisian is considered the language most similar to English. English speakers can sometimes read portions of Frisian text.

The Dutch View

There is no official religion in the Netherlands. Although the Netherlands is thought of as a Protestant nation, Roman Catholics have a slight majority. The Dutch Reformed Church and Calvinists are the significant Protestant denominations. The largest group consists of persons professing no religion at all: nearly 40 percent.

The Dutch live with the knowledge that their tiny country was once, in the seventeenth century, the world's pre-eminent mercantile power. This is a source of great pride and gives business a great importance even today.

For better or worse, the Dutch also have to live with their legacy as a former colonial power, which involves them in the affairs of places such as Indonesia.

The Netherlands

Much of their land is below sea level. Only their elaborate system of dikes protects them from the North Sea.

Equality and tolerance are important aspects of Dutch society. A wide range of behavior is tolerated, as long as it is kept private.

 Know Before You Go

The Netherlands is a very safe country, although there is the ever-present worry about the system of dikes that hold back the North Sea. Failure in the dike system would devastate the country and take thousands of lives. This occurred in 1953, when nearly 2,000 people died when storm waters breached the dikes. Then in 1995, serious flooding occurred again, and 250,000 people were evacuated.

Street crime and vehicular accidents are probably the greatest hazards to visitors. The term "vehicular accidents" includes bicycle accidents; the Dutch are avid cyclists. By some reckonings, one-fourth of daily trips made by the Dutch are via bicycle. Bike theft is a problem.

 CULTURAL ORIENTATION

Cognitive Styles: How the Dutch Organize and Process Information

The Dutch are generally circumspect toward outside information. They are abstractive and process information objectively and analytically. There is an obligation to the universal rules of behavior, rather than to the individual. Friendships develop slowly and are very selective.

Negotiation Strategies: What the Dutch Accept as Evidence

Truth lies in the accumulation of objective facts, influenced by a strong faith in a social democratic ideology. Minimal credence is given to subjective feelings. The Dutch tend to offer as little information as possible, and moderation is the rule. Subjective, emotional arguments are not accepted.

Value Systems: The Basis for Behavior

Planning is a way of life in the Netherlands. Planning, regulating, and organizing are of major importance to the Dutch. The following three sections identify the Value Systems in the predominant culture—their methods of dividing right from wrong, good from evil, and so forth.

Locus of Decision-Making

The Dutch are strongly individualistic, but cultural history must be considered in the decision-making process. Individual privacy is considered a necessity in all walks of life.

Decision-making is slow and involved, as all peripheral concerns must be taken care of in the process. Once the decision is made it is unchangeable.

Even though universal values are adhered to, it is important to develop the respect and friendship of the participants.

Sources of Anxiety Reduction

Universal rules and regulations combined with strong internal discipline give stability to life and reduce uncertainty.

There is a high need for social and personal order and a low tolerance for deviant behavior. Everything is organized, including leisure time. The Dutch rarely show emotions, because of strong internal structure and control. But the Dutch have great faith in the ability of scientific method to solve human problems.

Some sociologists believe that the Dutch have a high index of uncertainty avoidance. As a result, they generally use laws and morality to give structure to their worldview.

Issues of Equality/Inequality

The Netherlands is a distinctly hierarchical society, with classes established to fill organizational roles and give structure and order. Protest in the Netherlands is a crucial part of the democratic process, because the densely populated and overly structured country breeds dissent.

Equal rights for all are guaranteed by law but may not be practiced in the marketplace. There is some racism (although its presence is often denied).

Although there is still a strong paternal nuclear family orientation (including well-defined roles for males and females), this structure is beginning to erode as more females enter the work force.

Cultural Note

The Dutch do not usually give compliments to individuals. Everything is considered a team effort, and accolades are awarded to the group, not to individuals. Conversely, individuals are not usually singled out for blame. When something goes wrong, it is considered the fault of a system that failed to exercise proper oversight. The Dutch find self-aggrandizement to be abhorrent.

▶ BUSINESS PRACTICES

Punctuality, Appointments, and Local Time

- The residents of the Netherlands, like most Europeans, write the day first, then the month, then the year (e.g., December 3, 2010, is written 3.12.10 or 3/12/10).
- Punctuality is very important in the Netherlands. Be certain to be on time for both business and social engagements.
- The Dutch place great importance on planning and efficient use of time. Arriving even a few minutes late to a business meeting may cause the Dutch to doubt your ability to utilize time well. In the Netherlands, a person who is late is suspected of being either incompetent or untrustworthy—or both!

- Another important aspect of punctuality in the Netherlands involves response time. Any company that cannot promptly deliver price quotes upon request will fail to win Dutch customers. It is also important to deliver products and services quickly.
- A very high percentage of Dutch businesspeople are fluent in English. In almost every situation, someone who can translate from English to Dutch will be close at hand.
- Appointments will be carefully scheduled; do not assume that they can be changed on short notice. Spontaneity is not considered a virtue in the Netherlands.
- Give as much notice as possible for an appointment made by telephone or e-mail.
- Always acknowledge the receipt of important communications immediately (contracts, price quotes, letters of intent, and so forth).
- Business letters may be written in English. Keep your letters formal, businesslike, and grammatically correct. When addressing individuals in writing, be sure to use their full and correct title, even if you are on a first-name basis.
- Many Dutch executives take long vacations during June, July, August, and late December, so confirm that your counterpart will be available.
- The Netherlands is one hour ahead of Greenwich Mean Time (G.M.T. +1), or six hours ahead of U.S. Eastern Standard Time (E.S.T. +6).

> **Cultural Note**
> Avoid conveying information that you want kept confidential. The Dutch prefer to keep their operations open to suggestions from all employees in a company, so all personnel are given access to information. Furthermore, the Dutch are generally uncomfortable with secrets.

Negotiating

- Do not be surprised if meetings begin with little or no preliminary socializing. The Dutch value the effective use of time and do not like to waste it on small talk.
- Dutch executives are often straightforward and efficient. However, the pace of corporate decision-making may be slower in the Netherlands than in North America.
- Decisions in Dutch firms are based upon consensus. Every employee who may be affected will be consulted. All opinions will be listened to, regardless of the status or seniority of the person. The process can take a good deal of time.
- Dutch society values diversity of opinion. Everyone has his or her say, and they do not have to agree. An effort will be made to accommodate all divergent positions. This will include an attempt to make dissenters change their minds.
- Once a positive decision has been reached, Dutch firms will move swiftly. Everyone will be committed to the project and will be prepared to act quickly.
- A negative decision may be slower in coming. The one area in which many Dutch are not blunt is in saying "no." They may prevaricate or predict insurmountable complications instead of giving a direct "no."

- The Dutch admire modesty and abhor exaggeration or ostentation. Be sure you can back up your claims with lots of data. Keep your presentation clear and straightforward.
- Keep every promise you make, no matter how minor. A person who cannot be trusted to be punctual or to deliver a proposal on time will not be considered responsible enough to fulfill a contract.
- Most executives in the Netherlands understand English, so it is not necessary to have your business cards translated. However, all promotional materials and instruction manuals should be translated into Dutch.
- History is very important in the Netherlands. If your company has been around for many years, the date of its founding should be on your business card.
- Education is well respected in the Netherlands; include any degree above the bachelor's level on your card.
- It is quite possible that you will walk into an office and start talking business immediately after introducing yourself. In a country with centuries of experience in commerce, Dutch executives believe that they can judge whether they wish to work with someone quickly.
- In addition, it is also possible that a Dutch executive will have had background research done on prospective clients. This gives the executives hard data to back up their impressions, while maintaining a reputation for being "canny judges of human character."
- When the Dutch decide to chat before getting down to business, expect to be asked about your flight, your accommodations, where you are from, and so forth. Contacts are vital to doing business in the Netherlands, so know the name of every possible person who could give you or your company a good reference. Be aware of recent political events, both in your own country and in the Netherlands; the Dutch frequently discuss politics.
- The Dutch respect honesty and forthrightness. It is better to be blunt than to appear devious or evasive.
- When an individual must be either complimented or chastised, the Dutch always do so in private.
- Always avoid giving an impression of superiority. Egalitarianism is a central tenet of Dutch society. Everyone in a Dutch company, from the boss to every laborer, is considered valuable and worthy of respect.
- Privacy is very important in the Netherlands. Doors are kept closed, both at work and at home. Always knock on a closed door and wait to be admitted.
- Keep personal questions superficial; if your counterpart wants you to know any detail about his or her family, he or she will tell you. Avoid talking about sex, including the fact that prostitution is legal in the Netherlands.
- The Dutch tend to stand somewhat further apart than North Americans when talking. The positioning of furniture reflects this, and you may find yourself giving a sales pitch from a chair that seems uncomfortably far away. Do not move your chair closer; it is not your place to rearrange the furniture.

- Dutch family life is kept separate from business dealings. However, executives do take work home with them and may be phoned at home about business matters.

Cultural Note

Although business is considered a serious matter, the Dutch occasionally enjoy humor in formal business presentations and official speeches. The Dutch sense of humor tends to be good-natured and earthy; wit, sarcasm, and verbal legerdemain are not prized.

Business Entertaining

- Although the Netherlands is not known for its cuisine, food constitutes an important part of Dutch entertainment.
- In addition to three meals a day, the Dutch often break for a snack at 10:00 A.M. and 4:00 P.M. Coffee is available at the morning break; the afternoon drink is usually tea.
- The Dutch enjoy hosting foreign businesspeople at lunches and dinners. These are usually held in restaurants rather than in Dutch homes.
- All social events will be carefully scheduled and planned. The Dutch do not appreciate spontaneity, and they do not "do lunch" on a moment's notice.
- Remember to be on time to social events.
- Fine coffee is prized in the Netherlands; expect to drink a lot of it.
- When eating, always use utensils; very few items are eaten with the hands. Many Dutch even eat bread with a knife and fork!
- At the dinner table, do not rest your hands in your lap. Keep both hands above the table, with your wrists resting on the tabletop.

Cultural Note

As an alternative to a formal dinner, the Dutch often invite guests to come to their home after dinner. The guests are offered numerous hors d'oeuvres, plus alcohol and coffee. The amount of food and drink at these events can rival a full meal, but the setting is more relaxed and informal.

 PROTOCOL

Greetings

- Virtually everyone shakes hands in the Netherlands, both upon greeting and upon departure. Men shake hands, firmly but briefly, with other men, with most women, and even when being introduced to a child.
- Upon introduction, repeat your last name while you are shaking hands. It is not traditional to utter any greeting phrase (such as "How do you do?"), although many Dutch businesspeople will do so to make a foreigner feel at ease.

When you have not been formally introduced to everyone at a business or social gathering, it is your job to introduce yourself. Failure to do so may leave a bad first impression.

- Avoid standing with your hands in your pockets, and never leave your left hand in your pocket while shaking hands with your right.
- Aside from handshakes, there is very little public contact in the Netherlands. Close friends or relatives may hug briefly.

Titles/Forms of Address

- The order of names among the Dutch is first name followed by surname.
- As a foreigner, it may take you a long time to establish a close enough relationship with a Dutch colleague to get to a first-name basis. However, Dutch associates will usually use their first names amongst themselves at work.
- On the other hand, many Dutch executives are experts at dealing with foreign business-people. Your Dutch counterpart may quickly suggest going to a first-name basis. Understand that he or she is trying to make you feel comfortable.
- Dutch surnames can be confusing to foreigners, especially when they are preceded by a prefix. Common Dutch prefixes include: de, der, den, and het (which all mean "the"); op means "on," and van, van't, van den, and van der all mean "from."
- There is usually a space between prefixes and the surname in the north of the Netherlands. In the south, the prefixes may be combined and attached to the surname. For example, the form "van der Heyde" is common in the north, while "vanderHeyde"—all one word—is common in the south.
- Professional titles are not always used when speaking. Usually, an attorney, engineer, or doctor who wishes you to use a title will introduce himself or herself to you that way.
- Written communication in the Netherlands is very formal. Know the recipient's correct professional title and be sure to use it in the letter or e-mail.
- When entering a shop, it is considered polite to say "good day" to everyone present, customers and employees alike. However, do not interrupt—Dutch clerks will wait on only one person at a time.

Gifts

- Any gift to a Dutch executive should be of good quality but not of exorbitant cost.
- Appropriate gifts to businesspeople include imported liquor, good-quality pens, pocket calculators, or any new gadget. Wine collecting is common, so do not give a gift of wine unless you can make an appropriate selection for that person.
- If you are invited to dinner at a Dutch home, bring a bouquet of unwrapped flowers for your host; or, you may send a bouquet or a plant the following day.
- Avoid bringing wine as a gift to dinner; you don't want to imply that your host's wine cellar is inadequate.

The Netherlands

- Chocolate or candy is also a good gift when you are invited to a Dutch home, especially if there are children in the house.

> ### Cultural Note
> The Netherlands is not the place to "dress for success." The wealthier and more successful a Dutch executive has become, the harder he or she must work at appearing ordinary. Wealthy Dutch citizens often may not wear fancy clothes, drive exotic cars, or live in expensive mansions. In a crowd, a Dutch CEO might not be distinguishable from a low-ranking executive.

Dress

- Business dress in the Netherlands is fairly conservative, but it varies with the industry. In the financial industries, most businessmen wear dark suits, sedate ties, and white shirts; women dress in dark suits and white blouses. Expect to wear the same clothes when invited to dinner.
- However, some industries allow very informal dress. Quite a few executives save their ties and jackets for outside the office.
- Surprisingly, the higher a person's rank, the more informally he or she can dress (in some industries). You may find the sales clerks in suits and the boss in jeans and a sweater.
- As in many countries, Dutch men remove their jackets when working. Follow their lead.
- When the occasion calls for it, the Dutch enjoy dressing up. A tuxedo for men and an evening gown for women may be required for formal social events. These include formal parties, dinners, and opening night at the theater.
- Casualwear is essentially the same as in North America. However, shorts are worn only when jogging or hiking.

> ### Cultural Note
> In March of 2004, the Netherlands' Queen Mother Juliana passed away. She was an extraordinary example of a royal personage with a streak of populism. She cast aside many of the formal protocols of sovereignty—and was comfortable riding a bike, buying bread in local markets, pouring her own tea, and helping those in need. The Queen Mother was particularly loved for the selfless work she did when the dykes burst in 1953. Donning Wellingtons, she slogged through her flooded country, taking food and supplies to the displaced. Her rule spanned thirty-two years.

The Netherlands

New Zealand

Abbreviation: NZ

> **Cultural Note**
> Three islands make up the bulk of New Zealand's land area. The North Island has fertile agricultural land with forests, a dairy region, and a volcanic plateau. About 75 percent of New Zealand's population lives there. The South Island contains a mountainous strip with glaciers, surrounded by plains, fjords, a heavily forested strip, and beaches. South Island has many opportunities for sports, including skiing. Stewart Island is a small island to the south with fewer than 600 inhabitants. The other islands are smaller and include the Antipodes, Auckland, Bounty, Chatham, and Kermadec Islands, and Campbell Island.

▶ WHAT'S YOUR CULTURAL IQ?

1. Which of the following is not correct about New Zealand?
   a. In 1893, New Zealand became the first country to give women the vote.
   b. Ancestors of the Aborigines were the first people to live in New Zealand.
   c. Gisborne, NZ, was the first city to see the rising sun of the millennium.
   d. New Zealand native Sir Edmund Hillary was the first man to scale Mount Everest.
   e. New Zealand's first female prime minister was elected in 1997.

   ANSWER: b. Ancestors of the Maori tribes people were the earliest known inhabitants of New Zealand, arriving somewhere around A.D. 800.

2. TRUE or FALSE: The French Secret Service blew up a ship in Auckland Harbour in 1985.

   ANSWER: TRUE. It was the "Rainbow Warrior," a ship owned by the environmentalist group Greenpeace. One person died.

3. The word "Kiwi" refers to:
   a. An appellation adopted by New Zealand's servicemen during WWI.
   b. A brand of shoe polish.
   c. A flightless bird with whiskers like a cat that lays a huge egg.
   d. All of the above.

   ANSWER: d. New Zealanders not only refer to themselves as "Kiwis" (in contrast to Australia's "Aussies"), they have made the Kiwi into a national emblem, which some would like to put on their national flag—to differentiate it from the very similar Australian flag.

> **Cultural Note**
> The English word "taboo" sounds very similar to the Maori word *tapu*, which means behaviors or items that were prohibited in their complex social system. Breaking sacred laws of tapu resulted in many violent incidents during early encounters between Maori and *Pakehas* (non-Maoris). One tragic event in the 1800s started with the flogging of a Maori chief by the captain of a trading ship from Sydney, the *Boyd*. This atrocious violation of tapu particularly infuriated the tribesmen because the chief's back and head were sacred. The Maoris killed almost all the people onboard the Boyd and set the ship on fire. In reprisal, whalers burned two Maori villages.

▶ TIPS ON DOING BUSINESS IN NEW ZEALAND

- Stick to the facts in your presentations. An emotional, hyped-up pitch will not impress the Kiwis.
- Relationships are not as inviolate as in other cultures—you can interchange employees without completely disrupting the sales process.
- New Zealanders will not find it difficult to say "no," and they are not afraid of taking a controversial position on a topic.
- Kiwis are a bit more formal than Aussies. Do not assume an instantly congenial demeanor in meetings. Build up a bit of credibility first.
- New Zealanders are comfortable setting precedents, politically, socially, and technically. Never assume that they are bound by traditions.

> **Cultural Note**
> As of this writing, New Zealand's prime minister is Helen Clark, who protested against the Vietnam War and opposed the invasion of Iraq in 2003. Her Labour Party propelled the free-market economics of the 1980s and oversaw various groundbreaking, progressive policies. She was New Zealand's first female deputy prime minister, and she became their second female prime minister.

▶ COUNTRY BACKGROUND

History

The earliest known inhabitants of New Zealand were the Maori tribespeople, who came across the sea from Polynesia around A.D. 900. The first European explorers were the Dutch, who arrived in 1642 and continued to visit while on whaling and trading expeditions. British exploration began in 1769 with Captain James Cook, who visited New Zealand on all three of his Pacific voyages. Cook thought highly of the islands and the natives; his journal, published in 1777, encouraged Europeans to trade with and colonize New Zealand.

Unlike nearby Australia, New Zealand never became a major penal colony for the United Kingdom. Most arrivals in New Zealand wanted to be there, although some were Australian

New Zealand

convicts or sailors seeking refuge. Increased colonization and missionary activity prompted the British to annex New Zealand in 1838.

The Maoris accepted English sovereignty in 1840 in return for legal protection and land ownership, although much of this land was taken away after the Anglo-Maori wars of the 1860s.

England granted the colony internal self-government in 1852, and New Zealand became an independent dominion within the British Commonwealth in 1907.

Along with Australia, New Zealand fought with the Allies in both the First and Second World Wars. During World War II, the early defeat of Britain's Pacific forces by the Japanese was a shock to New Zealanders. With Britain unable to defend it, New Zealand accepted military help from the United States.

Type of Government

New Zealand is a constitutional monarchy. Although independent from Great Britain, it acknowledges the British monarch as its chief of state. The monarch is represented in New Zealand by a governor-general.

The present government is a parliamentary system without a written constitution. There is a unicameral House of Representatives and an independent court system. The executive branch is headed by the prime minister and the Cabinet. The prime minister is the head of the government.

New Zealand is active in the United Nations. Relations with the industrial democratic nations of Asia are considered a priority. New Zealand also assists the underdeveloped countries of the Pacific region through economic and technical programs.

Because Great Britain was unable to defend them in World War II, New Zealand and Australia accepted military aid from the United States. In 1951, Australia, New Zealand, and the United States signed the ANZUS mutual defense treaty. This treaty has been suspended, however, because of disagreements arising from nuclear arms control.

The New Zealand government proclaimed its territory to be a "nuclear-free zone" in 1985, prohibiting ships that carried nuclear arms or were nuclear powered from using its ports. As a result, relations between New Zealand and the United States became strained. The U.S. government would not disclose which of its ships carried nuclear weapons and which did not, so all U.S. military ships were banned. Both the Labour and the National Parties pledged to keep this ban in effect; however, during the 1990s, the situation with the United States improved.

In the last decade, New Zealand's government moved into a globally competitive position technically, economically, and socially.

Current government data can be found at the Embassy of New Zealand at *www.nzemb.org*.

Language

English and Maori are the official languages. Efforts are being made to preserve the Maori language, but most Maoris speak English. A very distinct accent and slang has developed in New Zealand.

Ethnologue.com lists four languages in New Zealand, and the literacy rate is 99 percent.

Cultural Note

Remember that New Zealanders refer to themselves as "Kiwis." If someone calls you "mate" or a "hard case," consider it a compliment, for they mean you are a "friend" or a "funny person." Some Maori words are commonly used, including *kai* (food) and *pakeha* (non-Maori).

The New Zealander View

Most New Zealanders are Christian. Anglicans are the most numerous, with Roman Catholics, Presbyterians, and Methodists present as well. Almost 20 percent of New Zealanders describe themselves as nonreligious.

Rules and laws generally supercede emotional arguments, and self-sufficiency and pragmatism are admirable traits.

New Zealanders feel that their individual rights are extremely important, and they support an egalitarian viewpoint. The welfare of their citizens is a top priority.

☑ Know Before You Go

New Zealand is subject to earthquakes and volcanoes. In 1995 and 1996, Mount Ruapehu erupted, and the spreading ash clouds disrupted air travel.

Many indigenous fauna and flora were eradicated by the introduction of other species, indiscriminate forestry, and hunting. New Zealand has since established stringent regulations to protect its natural resources and has allocated large tracts of land as protected parklands.

New Zealand ranked second out of 146 countries on the corruption perception index in 2004. They were led only by Finland. For more information on Transparency International, visit their Web site at *www.transparency.org*.

▶ CULTURAL ORIENTATION

Cognitive Styles: How New Zealanders Organize and Process Information

The prevailing culture of New Zealand is somewhat closed to outside information. The culture has high regard for practical experience but processes information abstractly and conceptually. The New Zealanders' humanitarianism keeps the welfare of the person as a top priority, but New Zealanders tend to solve problems by looking to universal rules or impersonal laws.

New Zealand

Negotiation Strategies: What New Zealanders Accept as Evidence
The accumulation of objective facts forms the basis for truth. Faith in the ideologies of nationalism may have some influence on this truth, but subjective feelings are given very little credence.

Value Systems: The Basis for Behavior
The culture of New Zealand has a deep humanitarian orientation where humanistic progress is as important as materialistic progress. The following three sections identify the Value Systems in the predominant culture—their methods of dividing right from wrong, good from evil, and so forth.

Locus of Decision-Making
There is very high individualism in decision-making, but employees generally follow company policy; so one executive can be exchanged for another without disrupting business negotiations. New Zealanders have a high self-orientation, which emphasizes individual initiative and achievement. They do not expect others to assist them, but they do expect everyone to be subject to the same value system. Friendships are few and specific to needs.

Sources of Anxiety Reduction
There are enough external organizations and structures to insulate New Zealanders from everyday pressures and to provide a feeling of security.

Anxiety occurs over deadlines and performance, but emotions are not shown in public. An individual's greatest reward is to be recognized for his or her accomplishments. There are established rules for almost everything, but these rules can be changed if need be. Experts are relied upon at all levels.

Issues of Equality/Inequality
All ethnic groups have been integrated into a truly multiracial society, although some bias against the Maoris continues. There are structured social inequalities that give people an opportunity to work their way up the social ladder. While inequalities do exist, New Zealanders believe that equal rights should be guaranteed to all. Traditional sex roles are changing, as evidenced by the female leadership in the political and business sectors.

Cultural Note
New Zealand is known for its advanced social legislation. It was the first member of the British Commonwealth to create old-age pensions (in 1898!). Other early innovations include voting rights for women in 1893, labor arbitration in 1894, and widow's pensions in 1911.

▶ BUSINESS PRACTICES

Punctuality, Appointments, and Local Time

- Always be on time or a little early for appointments. Tardiness is viewed seriously.
- Social events tend to start on time.
- The best times to visit New Zealand for business are February through May, and October and November. December and January are summer months, and many people are on vacation.
- If possible, arrange meetings by telephone or e-mail several weeks prior to your arrival.
- New Zealanders write the day first, then the month, and then the year (e.g., December 3, 2010, is written 3.12.10 or 3/12/10).
- New Zealand is twelve hours ahead of Greenwich Mean Time (G.M.T. +12), or seventeen hours ahead of U.S. Eastern Standard Time (E.S.T. +17).

Negotiating

- New Zealanders value their egalitarian society and are very emphatic about equality among people. They respect people for who they are, and have little regard for wealth and social status. Therefore, emphasize honesty and forthrightness in negotiations. Avoid hype and ostentation.
- The business atmosphere may be faster than the pace in Australia.
- Initial meetings often take place in an office setting. After that, you may suggest meeting over lunch at a restaurant or hotel.
- Lunch appointments are for conducting business. If you receive an invitation for dinner, this will be a more relaxed social evening with spouses. This is not the time to discuss business.

> **Cultural Note**
> The Maori have not been as marginalized as indigenous peoples in other countries have. They have influenced New Zealand's culture, and their traditions place great value on humility and truth. Maori society is very communal.

Business Entertaining

- New Zealanders love to entertain in their homes; do not be surprised by an invitation to a meal. Note that there is a difference between "tea" and "afternoon tea." Afternoon tea is usually served between 3:00 and 4:00 P.M., and tea is the evening meal served between 6:00 and 8:00 P.M. "Supper" is a late–night snack.
- Don't expect much conversation during the meal. Most socializing takes place after you have eaten.

New Zealand

- Good conversation topics are sports and politics. New Zealanders love the outdoors and are very active in hobbies such as hiking, fishing, or sailing, as well as organized sports.
- Avoid discussing the treatment of the Maori people.
- New Zealanders strive to establish a separate and distinct identity from Australia. There is a strong rivalry between the two countries. Avoid praising Australia or Australians to New Zealanders, and never confuse the two nations.
- New Zealanders are also very opinionated about politics. Hold up your end of the conversation and debate, without becoming insulting or personal. A person who has no apparent beliefs or convictions is not respected in New Zealand. Have some knowledge of New Zealand's nuclear-free policy and how it leads to tension with other nations.

▶ PROTOCOL

Greetings

- New Zealanders are very friendly and polite but tend to be formal in a work environment. They may wait to be approached but are warm after an initial meeting.
- Men shake hands upon introductions and when preparing to leave. The handshake should be firm and accompanied by direct eye contact.
- Men in New Zealand may wait for a woman to extend her hand. Women generally shake hands with other women.
- The formal "How do you do?" is used until a more friendly level is achieved. After that, "Hello" or the New Zealand "G'day" is appropriate for informal settings.

Cultural Note

The beautiful traditional greeting among Maori is the *Hongi*—literally the "sharing of breath." They do this by gently pressing their noses together. While you may encounter Maori or part-Maori businesspeople, do not expect them to "share your breath"—they will probably expect to shake your hand.

Titles/Forms of Address

- The order of names for European-descended New Zealanders is the same as in the United States: first name followed by surname.
- At first meetings, expect to address New Zealanders by their title or "Mr.," "Mrs.," or "Miss" plus their surname.
- Once a relationship is established, New Zealanders progress to a first-name basis as quickly as possible. But continue to use titles and surnames until you sense that a more informal tone has been set or until you are asked to address someone by his or her first name.

Gestures

- Chewing gum or using a toothpick in public is considered rude.
- The "V for victory" sign is rude° and is considered obscene when done with the palm facing inward.
- New Zealanders usually keep their speech soft and find loud voices annoying. They do not open their mouths wide when they speak; indeed, they often seem to be speaking through clenched teeth.
- Expansive behavior of any sort, even when drinking, is looked down upon. New Zealanders maintain more of the traditional British reserve than do Australians.

Gifts

- When visiting a New Zealand home, you may bring a modest gift. Chocolates, flowers, or a good bottle of whiskey may be appreciated.
- Gifts should be simple and utilitarian. Ostentation is frowned upon.

Dress

- Business attire is conservative. Men may wear a dark suit and tie. Businesswomen should wear a suit, pantsuit, dress, or a skirt and blouse with a jacket.
- General dress is casual.
- New Zealand is in the Southern Hemisphere, so the seasons are reversed from those of North America. The climate is temperate, not tropical; bring some warm clothes and rain gear.

New Zealand

Norway

Kingdom of Norway
Local short form: Norge
Local long form: Kongeriket Norge

Cultural Note

Norway has been ranked as the best place to live in the world by the United Nations—for four consecutive years! The criteria include average income (U.S.$36,600 in 2004), life expectancy (seventy-nine years), and education levels (enrollment levels of 98 percent). Norway's vast oil and gas reserves help generate a high level of wealth, and their relatively small population uses that wealth to develop and sustain an economically and politically equal society with a high quality of life.

▶ WHAT'S YOUR CULTURAL IQ?

1. Norwegian names like Olsen, Hansen, and Nilsen originated as patronymics—that is, they originally meant "son of Ole," "son of Hans," and "son of Nils." TRUE or FALSE: All Norwegians use their patronymic as their surname.

   ANSWER: FALSE. In 1923, all Norwegians were ordered by law to adopt a hereditary last name. Many simply took their patronymic and used that. However, other surnames were adopted as well. Many took the name of the farm they worked on as a surname.

2. Which of the following cultural figures is not Norwegian?
   a. Composer Edvard Grieg
   b. Playwright Henrik Ibsen
   c. Painter Edvard Munch
   d. Composer Jean Sibelius

   ANSWER: d. Sibelius is from Finland, and his work comes from a different cultural tradition.

3. Norway was occupied by Nazi Germany during the Second World War. TRUE or FALSE? Norwegians wore a paper clip on their clothing as a sign of opposition to the Nazi occupation.

   ANSWER: TRUE. The invention of the modern paper clip is credited to Norwegian Johan Vaaler. (Although Norway had no patent law when he created the device in 1899.) During the occupation, wearing this Norwegian invention on one's clothing became a sign of Norwegian patriotism. It irritated the Germans so much that wearing a paper clip made one subject to arrest.

▶ TIPS ON DOING BUSINESS IN NORWAY

- Norwegians tend to be more informal than other Scandinavians (especially the Swedes, whom they generally consider stuffy.)
- Many observers consider the Norwegians to be the least punctual people in northern Europe. A fifteen-minute delay is not uncommon. However, as a foreigner, you are expected to be prompt.
- Norwegian businesspeople are sometimes uncomfortable communicating in writing, especially in a foreign language. Many prefer to do business by telephone rather than by letter. When writing is necessary, it will often be as short as possible: a brief e-mail message or fax suffices.

▶ COUNTRY BACKGROUND

History

The Vikings (also called "Norsemen") were feared for their raids throughout northern Europe from the eighth to eleventh centuries. These Vikings eventually became the Norwegians, the Swedes, and the Danes.

Political power became concentrated in Denmark, which came to rule much of Scandinavia, including Norway. Eventually, Sweden became a rival power. Denmark sided with Napoleon during the Napoleonic Wars. To punish Denmark, the postwar Congress of Vienna took Norway from Denmark and gave it to Sweden in 1815.

The fishermen, sailors, and merchants of Norway had little in common with the aristocrats of Sweden. Friction developed. Fortunately for the Norwegians, their rugged, rocky nation could not be divided up into the vast farming estates preferred by the Swedes. After a century of Swedish occupation, Norway peacefully gained its independence in 1905.

The Norwegian parliament invited a Danish prince to become their constitutional monarch, so King Haakon VII became the first king of Norway.

Norway remained neutral in World War I. However, despite its neutrality, Norway was occupied by Nazi Germany during World War II. For this reason, the Norwegians shifted from a belief in neutrality to one in collective security.

Norway

Norway signed the North Atlantic Treaty of 1949 and participated in the foundation of the United Nations.

Oil was discovered off Norway's coast in the late 1960s, and production of North Sea oil began in the 1970s. Today, Norway is the world's third largest producer of crude oil, behind Saudi Arabia and Russia. Norway also provides over 10 percent of the natural gas used in Europe. Oil revenues have made Norway one of the wealthiest nations in the world.

Norway declined to join the European Union in 1994. In 2001, Norway agreed to fight terrorism by sending troops to Afghanistan. However, Norway opposed the invasion of Iraq because it was not supported by the United Nations.

Type of Government

Norway is a multiparty (hereditary) constitutional monarchy. There are three branches of government. The executive branch is made up of the king, who is chief of state, the prime minister, who is the head of government, and a cabinet, also termed the Council of Ministers.

Executive power actually resides in the Council of Ministers in the name of the king, or King's Council. The prime minister sits on this council. The prime minister is chosen by the leading political parties. The legislative branch is a modified unicameral parliament, known as the Storting. Members of the Storting are elected according to a system of proportional representation. They serve for four years. Women comprise a strong percentage of the representatives in the Storting.

Norway became a major oil and gas producer in the 1970s. The income from this sector allowed it to further advance its social welfare system. Currently, it hopes to make the non-oil sector of its economy more efficient and less dependent on subsidies.

For current government data, check with the Embassy of Norway at *www.norway.org.*

Cultural Note

In accordance with the wishes of Swedish industrialist Alfred Nobel, five of the six Nobel Prizes are awarded by Sweden. The sixth prize—the Peace Prize—is awarded by Norway. No one knows for sure why Nobel wanted the Norwegians to award the Peace Prize, but it may have been because Norway lacked Sweden's militaristic history.

Language

The official language of Norway is Norwegian, which is a Germanic language related to Icelandic, Danish, and Swedish. It has two forms, a "book language," known as *Bokmål*, used in schools and broadcasting, and a commonly spoken language, known as *Nynorsk*. According to law, Nynorsk must sometimes be used in instruction and in the media.

Ethnologue.com has identified eleven languages spoken in Norway, all of which are extant. One notable minority language is Saami, spoken by the Laplanders.

Most Norwegians have studied English; it is widely spoken in business meetings and in major cities.

The Norwegian View

Norway has complete religious freedom, but it does have an official state church, the Evangelical Lutheran Church, or Church of Norway. About 94 percent of the people belong to this church.

The traditional occupations of Norwegians—farming the rocky soil or fishing—were very hard lifestyles. Norwegians attribute many of their national characteristics to this: toughness, stubbornness, and self-sufficiency.

Older Norwegians complain that, due to the country's growing wealth, young Norwegians are losing some of their self-sufficiency. Some affluent young Norwegians hire people to do gardening and home repairs—to the horror of their elders. Egalitarian Norwegians like to boast that there are no private housemaids in Norway, but that may not be true for long.

Protection of the environment is a major concern for Norwegians. In March of 2000, a dispute over whether or not to build power plants fired by natural gas (which cause air pollution) resulted in a change of government.

☑ Know Before You Go

Norway is an extremely safe country. The primary hazard to visitors comes from Norway's weather, particularly in winter.

Oddly, there have been recent terrorist threats against Norway by groups presumably related to Al Qaida.

Norway has two territorial disputes. The most serious one concerns fishing rights in the Barents Sea, which are also claimed by Russia.

The second dispute is about Antarctica. Norwegian explorers were among the first to explore the continent, and their territorial claims overlap those of other nations.

▶ CULTURAL ORIENTATION

Cognitive Styles: How Norwegians Organize and Process Information

Norwegians are generally cautious toward outside information. New products and new ways of doing things are viewed with circumspection.

Their education system has become more abstractive, and people are beginning to process information conceptually and analytically. Although they are deeply concerned with social welfare, their individualism dictates that everyone be subject to the same rules and regulations.

Negotiation Strategies: What Norwegians Accept as Evidence

Proud of the country they have built, Norwegians put their faith in the ideologies of their culture and their social welfare state. Truth tends to be viewed through this filter. Within that context, objective facts are preferred to subjective feelings.

Norway

Norwegians tend to be blunt and direct; subtlety is not a typical trait. This makes them more likely to accept evidence at face value. However, their acceptance of facts as evidence does not result in quick decisions.

Value Systems: The Basis for Behavior

Norway has a highly nationalistic culture with a liberal philosophy of tolerance for dissent and deviation. Independence is highly valued.

Debts of all sorts are avoided, since such obligations are seen to impinge upon an individual's freedom.

The following three sections identify the Value Systems in the predominant culture—their methods of dividing right from wrong, good from evil, and so forth.

Locus of Decision-Making

There is a strong belief in individual decisions within the social welfare system. Self-sufficiency is prized. There is an emphasis on individual initiative and achievement, with a person's ability being more important than his or her station in life.

Although the dignity and worth of the individual is emphasized, there is a strong feeling of obligation to help those who are not able to help themselves.

Sources of Anxiety Reduction

Life's uncertainties are accepted and anxiety is reduced through a strong social welfare system. Life is given stability and structure by a strong nuclear family. Young people are encouraged to mature early and take risks to develop a strong self-image.

Issues of Equality/Inequality

Nationalism transcends social differences, and ethnic differences are minimized within a largely homogeneous population. Norway has a fiercely democratic and egalitarian society.

Norwegians have been charted as having a very low masculinity index. This is indicative of a society free of gender roles, in which women have no limitations on their behavior. Child care duties are shared by Norwegian husbands and wives.

High taxes have helped to produce a middle-class society that strives to minimize social differences. There are no privileges granted to wealthy or high-status Norwegians—not even to government officials or the royal family.

▶ BUSINESS PRACTICES

Punctuality, Appointments, and Local Time

- Norwegians are not quite as insistent on punctuality as many Scandinavians. However, as a foreigner, you should always be punctual, both for business and social events.
- Norwegians generally get to work exactly at the start of the business day. They also like to leave exactly at the end of the day. They have even been known to hang up in the middle of a phone call at the end of the workday!
- Norwegians, like most Europeans, write the day first, then the month, then the year (e.g., December 3, 2010, is written 3.12.10 or 3/12/10).
- The work week is generally Monday through Friday, 8:00 A.M. to 4:00 P.M. Businesspeople leave their offices promptly and go home for dinner, which is typically held at about 5:00 P.M.
- It is best to avoid business trips to Norway around Easter and in July and early August— when most people take vacations.
- Norway's Constitution Day is May 17.
- Norway is one hour ahead of Greenwich Mean Time (G.M.T. +1), or six hours ahead of Eastern Standard Time (E.S.T. +6).

Cultural Note

Norwegians are not known for their ability to compromise: they tend to adopt a position and stick to it. There have been frequent conflicts between Norwegian offshore oil workers and major oil companies, most of which are based in the United States. The typical pattern is: Norwegian oil workers strike—a few weeks pass—the Norwegian government forces a mediation.

Negotiating

- Norwegians are relatively informal (far more so than the neighboring Swedes).
- It is wise to set a time limit on the meeting. However, Norwegians will abide by the schedule, so be ready to end the meeting at the designated time, whether or not there are matters left to discuss.
- Norwegians may adopt a "take it or leave it" attitude and will not appear dismayed if you reject their proposal and the deal falls through.
- Norwegians are wary of the American concern with legal matters. Written confirmation of business deals is sufficient; if you must mention bringing in a lawyer, be discreet.

Cultural Note

Both coffee and milk are mainstays of the Norwegian diet. However, the two are never mixed: Norwegians drink their coffee strong, black, and unsweetened. The closest they get to mixing coffee is at the end of a meal, when coffee is often accompanied by a glass of cognac or aquavit (potato whiskey flavored with caraway and other herbs).

Norway

Business Entertaining

- If you have a late morning meeting, invite your Norwegian colleague to lunch.
- In most Norwegian restaurants, alcohol is served only after 3:00 P.M. and only from Monday through Saturday.
- You may discuss business at any time during the meal.
- Good topics of conversation include family, Norwegian history, sports, and nature. Many affluent Norwegians have a second home in the country, where they can hike and ski.
- Norwegians will appreciate your knowledge about the differences among the Scandinavian countries.
- Avoid personal topics (employment of your host or family members, health issues, etc).
- Avoid criticism of other peoples or political systems. The Norwegians stress tolerance. Chastising Norwegians for permitting the hunting of whales will not win you any friends.
- Don't complain about the cost of living in Norway. Norwegians know how expensive their country is.
- Norwegians usually eat dinner early, starting at 5:00 or 6:00 P.M.
- When you go to a Norwegian home, wait to be asked in; wait again until you are asked to sit down. At the table, wait until the host invites everyone to begin eating.
- Some Norwegians have a cocktail before dinner; others do not. It is possible that you will be directed to the dinner table as soon as you arrive. Arrive on time.
- The fork is held in the left hand; the knife remains in the right hand.
- Hands should not be kept in the lap at the table.
- A dinner in a Norwegian home may have numerous courses and last several hours. Pace yourself.
- At the end of the meal, people thank the hostess by saying *takk for maten*, or "thank you for the food"; you will please your hosts by saying this in Norwegian.
- You should initiate your own departure, as your hosts will not. Expect the evening to end around 10:00 P.M. in the winter. However, in the summer, the sun does not set until around midnight. Your hosts may suggest a walk after dinner, followed by a final drink. In the summer, expect to leave around 11 P.M.

▶ PROTOCOL

Greetings

- The handshake is the standard greeting for men and women.
- People greet each other by saying "*morn*" (which means "morning") at any time of day.
- Norwegians are quiet people; avoid speaking loudly.

> **Cultural Note**
> Norwegians enjoy discussing sports. Cross-country skiing was invented in Norway. Most Norwegian children participate in outdoor sports, starting at a very young age. Many members of the Norwegian royal family are avid sportsmen; the late King Olav won an Olympic medal for sailing in 1928.

Titles/Forms of Address

- The order of names is the same as in most of Europe: first name followed by surname.
- Follow the lead of your hosts as to whether or not to go to a first-name basis. Many Norwegians prefer to be addressed solely by their surnames, without even a "Mr." in front.
- Among older people, titles are used; among younger people, usage varies. In general, professional titles (Doctor, Engineer, Professor, and so forth) are used, followed by a surname; business titles (Director, President, and so forth) are not typically used. With government officials, it is appropriate to use titles. Oddly, lawyers and clergymen do not use titles.

Gestures

- A toss of the head means, "come here."
- Norwegians do not always rise when another person enters the room. Don't be offended by this.
- However, do rise when you are being introduced to someone.
- Talking with your hands in your pockets is considered too casual.
- The North American "okay" gesture (thumb and forefinger forming a circle) is considered insulting.

Gifts

- Gift giving is not part of doing business in Norway. Antibribery legislation makes giving any gift in a business setting problematical.
- Flowers, liqueurs, wine, liquor, or chocolates are appropriate gifts for your hostess when invited to a Norwegian home.
- When giving flowers, avoid the following, since they are all used only for funerals: lilies, carnations, and all white flowers, as well as wreaths.
- Alcohol taxes are high, so fine alcohol is an appropriate gift.
- If you do decide to give a business gift, be sure it is wrapped in good-quality paper. Make the gift neither too extravagant nor too skimpy.

Norway

Dress

- In general, Norwegians dress more informally than North American businesspeople; however, visitors should dress as they would in a business context at home.
- Men should always wear a tie for business appointments, but a sports jacket rather than a suit is usually acceptable.
- Women may wear suits, dresses, or pants.
- Clean blue jeans and T-shirts are standard casualwear, but torn clothes are unacceptable. Shorts are worn for hiking; they are not common in urban areas.

Norway

Pakistan

Islamic Republic of Pakistan
Former: West Pakistan

Cultural Note

South Waziristan is a remote region of Pakistan that did not generally get noted on the news before the tragedies of September 11, 2001. But the attention of the world turned there after reports that Osama bin Laden may have been sheltered there by sympathetic Pashtun tribesmen.

To root out terrorists, the Pakistani army launched major assaults on hundreds of foreign militants in the South Waziristan region. Those actions were strongly influenced by the United States, which ended its sanctions against Pakistan in return for Pakistan's support to apprehend members of Al Qaeda.

 ## WHAT'S YOUR CULTURAL IQ?

1. Pakistan has incredible mountain ranges, which makes it an alluring destination for mountaineers (most of whom are Japanese). Which of the following peaks are not in Pakistan?
   a. Nanga Parbat (Naked Mountain)
   b. Mount Everest
   c. K2

   ANSWER: b. Mount Everest is in Nepal. But K2 is nearly as high and has a reputation as a harder climb. Nanga Parbat is so steep that even snow falls off it.

2. Pakistan has fought multiple wars with India. In the early 1970s, one of these wars resulted in East Pakistan becoming a separate, independent nation. What was the new country called?
   a. Bhutan
   b. Tajikistan
   c. Bangladesh

   ANSWER: c. Bangladesh, which lies to the east of India, seceded in 1971.

3. What are Punjabi, Sindhi, Siraiki, Pashtu, Urdu, Balochi, Hindko, Brahui, and Burushaski?
   a. Languages in Pakistan
   b. Cities in Pakistan
   c. Pakistani holidays

   ANSWER: a. They, along with English, are some of the sixty-nine languages extant in Pakistan.

Pakistan

Cultural Note

The famous Khyber Pass lies along Pakistan's border with Afghanistan. The twenty-eight-mile pass cuts through the Safed Koh mountain range, and it has been an invasion route for many armies, including Alexander the Great's in 326 B.C. At one point it reaches 3,500 feet above sea level, and it is guarded by an elite unit of Pakistan's army—the Khyber Rifles.

 TIPS ON DOING BUSINESS IN PAKISTAN

- Pakistan is a multiparty federal Islamic republic, and traditional beliefs prevail. Politically, the military is the most powerful force in government, but the clergy (the ulema) is also influential.
- There are varieties of taboo conversational topics. Those associated with Islam would include questions about a client's wife or daughter, as well as the equality of women. Discussing any aspect of the "war on terror," nuclear testing, the sale of nuclear secrets, etc., are all unwise.
- Be comfortable with prolonged visits, delayed appointments, or rapid changes of schedule. While a Pakistani will probably expect a Western foreigner to equate time with money, he or she will not be driven by the same perspective.

 COUNTRY BACKGROUND

History

The name "Pakistan" was first used in 1933, and the Pakistani nation was established as a separate Muslim state in 1947 during the British partition of India. However, the land that makes up the country has a history and cultural heritage more than 4,000 years old.

The Aryan tribes who invaded the Indian subcontinent over several centuries built up a sophisticated civilization long before the flourishing of the Greek and Roman Empires. Kingdoms rose and fell, frequently toppled by outsiders. In A.D. 712, the Pakistani province of Sind was the first to be occupied by Muslim invaders. More Muslim invaders came, and the entire subcontinent fell to the Mogul Empire in 1526. In what would become India, the Hindu citizenry often failed to adopt the Islamic faith of their Mogul rulers. However, in Pakistan, the majority of the people accepted Islam.

The Mogul supremacy fell before the technology of the European invaders who began arriving in 1498. Pakistan eventually became part of British-ruled India.

When the British promised independence to India after World War II, Muslim leaders became fearful that the more-numerous, better-educated Hindus would subordinate the Muslim population. Consequently, they insisted on a separate, independent Muslim state. Despite opposition from many Hindu leaders, including Mahatma Gandhi, the predominantly Muslim provinces of Punjab and Bengal became Pakistan (a Dominion within the

British Commonwealth) on August 15, 1947. Pakistan proclaimed itself a fully independent republic on March 23, 1956.

At independence, Pakistan consisted of two separate regions; East Pakistan and West Pakistan were separated by over 1,000 miles of Indian territory. Smaller East Pakistan sought more autonomy from Islamabad. These efforts resulted in war between the two regions in 1970. East Pakistan was no match for the military might of West Pakistan. Some 1 million East Pakistanis were slain, and 10 million fled into India. This prompted India to declare war in December 1971. Indian troops invaded East Pakistan and routed the West Pakistani occupation army. East Pakistan became the independent nation of Bangladesh.

In 1998, Pakistan conducted nuclear weapons tests in reaction to India's detonations.

And then in the aftermath of September 11, 2001, the leader of Pakistan's government, President Pervez Musharraf, allied Pakistan with the United States in its efforts to capture terrorists.

Cultural Note
At thirty-five years of age, Benazir Bhutto was the first and youngest female prime minister to lead Pakistan, a Muslim nation. Her publications include *Daughter of the East* and *Foreign Policy in Perspective*.

Type of Government
The Islamic Republic of Pakistan is a parliamentary democracy in a federal setting. Pakistan has frequently been ruled by its military, which has been tolerated because Pakistanis feel an urgent need for the military's protection. In Pakistan's short existence as a nation, its military has been involved in battles with China, Bangladesh, and India. Conflict with India continues over the status of the disputed territories of Jammu and Kashmir, which are claimed by both countries.

The government consists of a bicameral legislature made up of a National Assembly, which is elected directly by the people, and a Senate, which is elected by four provincial assemblies. The executive branch consists of the president, who is head of state, and the prime minister, who is head of government. The prime minister is elected by the National Assembly from among its members.

Current government data can be found at the Embassy of Pakistan at *www.embassyof pakistan.org*.

Cultural Note
In May 1991, the National Assembly declared that the Koran—the holy book of Islam—was the supreme law of Pakistan. All aspects of Pakistani life are now subject to Islamic law. This move met with the approval of the masses of impoverished peasantry, who form the majority of Pakistan's 159 million people. Some of the urban elite opposed the adoption of Islamic law, but it was implemented, and the changes were made to the legal code.

Language

Urdu, Sindhi, and English are the official languages of Pakistan; Urdu is being encouraged as a replacement for English, but English is used by the government and the educated elite. The provinces are free to use their own regional languages and dialects (such as Punjabi, Sindhi, Pashtu, and Balochi). Ethnologue.com recognizes sixty-nine languages in Pakistan.

The Pakistani View

Pakistan was created as a Muslim state, and as a result, religion is an important part of all aspects of life there. About 97 percent of the population are Muslims and belong to either the Sunni or the Shiite branches. Hindus make up a small percentage of the population, with even fewer Christians and adherents of other religions. Muslims are called to prayer five times a day, and you will find men bowed in prayer in shops and airports, as well as in the fields. The direction of Mecca is marked in every hotel room.

The various tribes of Pakistanis are loyal to their own families, and members of their tribes, but not necessarily to the government. The tribes include the Punjabi, Sindhi, Pashtun (Pathan), Baloch, and Muhajir (who were originally immigrants from India at the time of partition).

☑ Know Before You Go

Business travel to Pakistan will probably not take you into any regions that are security challenges. However, never be cavalier about your safety. Take general precautions (for example, notify your country's embassy upon arrival, make sure your firm arranges for private drivers that you can identify at the airport, etc.) and keep your headquarters apprised of your agenda.

Visitors who are there on holiday should be knowledgeable about the latest information on security and medical precautions. Military operations are constant along the Kashmir Line of Control, as well as in many of the Federally Administered Tribal Areas and Agencies (FATA).

If you are going mountaineering, be certain to be part of a reputable expedition. It should include guides who understand security measures and weaponry.

Pakistan suffers from earthquakes, pollution, and diseases like malaria and dengue fever. Purchase emergency medical evacuation insurance before your visit.

Drink bottled water.

▶ CULTURAL ORIENTATION

Cognitive Styles: How Pakistanis Organize and Process Information

In Pakistan, although some ethnic groups are more closed than others, in general there is an acceptance of information from the West among urban dwellers. Because education is still primarily available to the elite, most people process information subjectively and associatively. Islamic law offers solutions to personal problems.

Negotiation Strategies: What Pakistanis Accept as Evidence

Truth lies in one's faith in the ideologies of Islamic law. This may be modified by an individual's immediate feelings about the situation but objective facts are not generally considered irrefutable evidence.

Value Systems: The Basis for Behavior

Pakistan is the home of Islam, and all behavior is perceived through the lens of Islamic law. The following three sections identify the Value Systems in the predominant culture—their methods of dividing right from wrong, good from evil, and so forth.

Locus of Decision-Making

The male leader is the center of decision-making, but he is expected to consider the family group upon whom the decision is binding. Opinions are determined by the family, the ethnic group, and Islamic law, in that order. Membership in social organizations is the source of identity and pride, and private life is sacrificed to these memberships.

Sources of Anxiety Reduction

Pakistanis believe that their destiny is in the hands of Allah; westerners often view this as fatalism. Security is found in strong loyalties to family and ethnic groups, but not in national unity. Rules are only guidelines, and maintaining a relationship is crucial to inner peace. A strong military presence ensures internal stability and security from outside attack.

Issues of Equality/Inequality

Inequality follows ethnic lines. The Punjabis dominate the government and the military. A great gulf exists between the rich and the poor; most people live in absolute poverty. There seems to be a tolerance for some deviation in Islamic sects, as common practice differs from formal Islamic law. Prestigious positions are reserved for males, although Pakistan is the only Islamic state to elect a female prime minister. There are strict sex roles based on the Islamic code.

> **Cultural Note**
> The Urdu language uses the same word (*kal*) to describe both yesterday and tomorrow. Not surprisingly, Pakistanis do not share Western concepts of time and punctuality.

▶ **BUSINESS PRACTICES**

Punctuality, Appointments, and Local Time

- Punctuality: Pakistanis are not time conscious, but they expect foreign visitors to be prompt.

Pakistan

- Guests traditionally arrive anywhere from fifteen to sixty minutes late to a social event. However, it is the host's responsibility to be prepared for any eventuality. If a guest arrives three hours late with several uninvited family members in tow, the host must graciously accommodate them.
- Avoid scheduling trips during major Muslim holidays, such as Ramadan (which is observed for a month), Eid al Fitr (at the end of Ramadan), Eid Al Adha (the Feast of the Sacrifice), and Eid al-Mawlid (the Birthday of the Prophet Mohammed). Business patterns are often interrupted during these times, and Muslims fast from dawn to dusk during Ramadan.
- Dates for these holidays vary from year to year, so check with your Pakistani associates, the tourist office, consulate, or embassy before scheduling your visit.
- Schedule appointments as far in advance as possible via phone, e-mail, or fax. Once you are in Pakistan, confirm your meetings a week in advance, and never break an appointment.
- Make sure you give your Pakistani associates multiple ways to contact you—by e-mail, cell phone, etc.
- The best times for appointments with government officials and commercial establishments are morning and early afternoon.
- Offices, banks, and shops are closed on Friday, the Muslim Sabbath. Many offices close on Saturday as well.
- Pakistan is five hours ahead of Greenwich Mean Time (G.M.T. +5), or ten hours ahead of U.S. Eastern Standard Time. (E.S.T. +10).

Negotiating

- Pakistani businessmen are formal, reserved, and deliberate in negotiations.
- Business is conducted at a more leisurely pace than in the West, but you may encounter a "get right down to business" attitude as well.
- If you are negotiating with the government, expect to make several trips to Pakistan.
- The Pakistani government is the largest potential customer in the country and has many public and semipublic corporations, each with its own bureaucracy.
- Always present your business cards.
- Avoid discussing local politics, religion, Israel and Jews, and Pakistan's relationship with its neighbors (especially India).
- Never make jokes or bring up any topics that can be considered lewd.
- Pakistanis are a serious, unsmiling people. Jokes and levity have no place in Pakistani business affairs.
- Never call Muslims "Mohammedans"; they believe it makes them sound like followers of a cult figure.
- Women must be aggressive in banks and post offices or men will be waited on first.
- Be sure to accept the tea you will be offered during an office visit; to refuse is considered rude.

- Different units of measurement to know when discussing financial or demographic statistics are the *lakh*, which equals 100,000, and the *crore*, which is 100 lakhs (1,000,000). (These measurements are also used in India.)

Business Entertaining
- Foreign businesswomen should be aware that it may be difficult for them to pick up the check when entertaining Pakistani businessmen. If possible, arrange to pay for the check before you arrive at the restaurant. If you are entertaining in your hotel restaurant, you can make prior arrangements to have the meal charged to your room.
- If you wish to invite the wife of a business counterpart to dinner, find out discreetly if she is in purdah (the seclusion of women from public observation—a practice among Muslims and some Hindus).
- If you are invited to a Pakistani's home for a meal, expect to be served very late—perhaps as late as 11:00 P.M. Guests are expected to leave immediately upon completion of the meal.
- Many Pakistanis normally eat with their hands, but when they entertain guests, they usually provide forks and spoons. Use the fork with your left hand and the spoon in your right, pushing the food with the fork onto the spoon.
- If you do eat with your hands, use only the right hand, as the left is considered unclean.
- Muslims do not eat pork.

PROTOCOL

Greetings
- Men usually shake hands with other men. Although strict Muslim men avoid the touch of women, most Pakistani businessmen will shake hands with a woman.
- Pakistani women do not normally shake hands with other women.
- Men may embrace male friends, and women hug and kiss upon meeting. But people of the opposite sex do not show affection in public.
- Introductions at social gatherings will be done by your host.

Titles/Forms of Address
- Pakistani naming patterns can sometimes be so complex and unfamiliar that a foreigner might be wise to ask how a Pakistani associate would like to be addressed.
- Most Pakistanis will introduce themselves with all their names but without any titles. There will usually be three names. The clan name or surname may come first or last; it will not generally be in the middle. Pakistanis should be addressed as "Mr.," "Mrs.," or "Miss" plus surname. An academic or job title may substitute for the Mr. or Mrs.
- The Pakistani equivalent of "Mr." is Sahib. The female equivalent is (roughly) Begum. These titles follow the surname: Mr. Zia would be called "Zia Sahib" and Mrs. Hussein

would be addressed as "Hussein Begum." These titles can also follow academic or job titles (Doctor Sahib or Director Sahib).

- Another complexity is that some Pakistani names make sense only in context, relating a first name to a second name. If the name is broken down into each part, it conveys a different meaning. For example, the name Ghulam Hussein means "slave of (the Islamic martyr) Hussein." To call him simply Ghulam is to address him as slave.
- Do not use a Pakistani's first name until you have been invited to do so.

Gestures

- Gesturing with a closed fist is considered obscene.
- Beckoning is done with the palm down rather than up, waving all the fingers toward the body.
- Using individual fingers to make gestures is considered impolite.
- Never point the bottom of your foot or shoe toward another person.
- Women should never wink.

Gifts

- You are not obliged to bring a gift when you are invited to a meal at a Pakistani's home. If you choose to do so, however, chocolates or flowers are good choices.
- Alcohol is prohibited to Muslims. Do not give alcohol as a gift unless you know that a Pakistani drinks alcohol.
- Pens, Swiss knives, watches, and electronic gadgets make good business gifts.
- If you are invited to stay at a Pakistani home, hand each servant a small tip before you leave. (Most Pakistanis have servants.)

Dress

- When you meet with governmental officials, it is better to dress more formally. Suits and ties may be appropriate for private industry as well, but may not be as common.
- For women, a pantsuit is preferable to a knee-length dress. Women should keep their arms covered.
- Men wear a dark suit (no tuxedos) at formal events; women wear a long dress or skirt.
      In casual circumstances, men wear trousers and a shirt; something modest is the key for women.
- Pants and a shirt or a traditional Pakistani garment, a *salwar kameez* (or *shalwar qamiz*), is appropriate for tourists. Both men and women wear the long, loose salwar kameez.
- Shorts are never appropriate for women. Men should wear them only when jogging. Jeans are acceptable for either sex.

Pakistan

Panama

Republic of Panama
Local short form: Panama
Local long form: Republica de Panama

Cultural Note

Panamanians are sensitive about the influence of the United States on their country. Be careful not to remark how "Americanized" the people are, nor should you refer to U.S. citizens as "Americans," since everyone from North, Central, and South America is an American.

WHAT IS YOUR CULTURAL IQ?

1. Panamanians enjoy many sports. In which one have they produced fourteen world champions?

   a. Soccer
   b. Baseball
   c. Cockfighting
   d. Boxing

   ANSWER: d. Many Panamanians are avidly interested in boxing. Their fourteen world boxing champions include Roberto Duran.

2. TRUE or FALSE? In 1501, Spanish navigator Rodrigo de Bastidas led the first European expedition to reach Panama.

   ANSWER: TRUE. Rodrigo de Bastidas beat Christopher Columbus to Panama; Columbus arrived later, on his fourth and final voyage to the New World.

3. TRUE or FALSE: Alone among Spain's former colonies, Panama remained prosperous after Spain gave up its claims to Latin America.

   ANSWER: FALSE. Panama's importance declined when Spain lost her colonies in South and Central America. Revenues sagged. It took the 1848 discovery of gold in California to revive Panama's fortunes. As a result, thousands of U.S. citizens from the East Coast traveled to California via Panama (rather than making the long, dangerous land journey across the United States).

Cultural Note

Although its distribution of wealth is very unequal, Panama remains the wealthiest Central American nation, in large part due to the Panama Canal and investment from the United States. (Mexico is wealthier, but it is considered part of North America, not Central America.)

▶ TIPS ON DOING BUSINESS IN PANAMA

- Panamanians prefer to maintain an image of harmony in public. People are criticized in private, out of hearing of others. Do not criticize or disagree with other members of your negotiating team in public.
- White, urban Panamanians hold most of the country's wealth and power. They have *the* inelegant nickname *los rabiblancos* (whitetails). Many of them speak English as well as Spanish. They are a separate group from the rural landowners, who never achieved the political influence that is characteristic of agricultural barons elsewhere in Central America.
- Many Panamanians have nicknames. Even powerful politicians are often referred to by their nicknames. Dictator Manuel Antonio Noriega was known as *la Piña* (the Pineapple) due to his pockmarked complexion. His successor as president, the pleasant and rotund Guillermo Endara, was called *Pan de Dulce* (Honey Bun)!

▶ COUNTRY BACKGROUND

History

Columbus reached Panama in 1502 on his fourth and final voyage to the New World. In 1513 Vasco Núñez de Balboa crossed the width of the isthmus and proved it could provide a path for transport of goods between the Pacific and Atlantic. Subsequently, Panama became a transshipment point; Spain brought its silver and gold up to Panama via ship, then portaged overland via the *Camino Real* (Royal Road) and loaded it back onto ships bound for Spain. An alternate name for the cross-country trail was the *Camino de Cruces* (Road of the Crosses)—based on all the graves.

The Spanish included Panama as part of the viceroyalty of New Grenada. Most of Central America declared its independence from Spain in 1821. Rather than going it alone, Panama joined the already-independent nation of Colombia. This union (known as "Gran Colombia") was not entirely successful, and many Panamanians sought independence from Colombia.

The first major U.S. investment in Panama was in 1855, when a railroad was built to ferry people and goods between the coasts. This was prompted by the California gold rush of 1849. Thousands of miners traveled from the Atlantic coast of the United States by sea to Panama, traversed Panama, then took a ship from Panama's Pacific coast to California.

Gran Colombia was reorganized in 1886 as the Republic of Colombia. The autonomy that Panamanians enjoyed was lost in the reorganization. The Panamanian independence movement dates its origin to this time.

The French tried and failed to build a canal across Panama in the 1880s.

In the wake of the 1898 Spanish-American War, the United States of America became determined to build a canal. The Panama isthmus was the favored site, but Colombia refused to grant the required concessions.

The USA supported Panamanian independence, in return for concessions (primarily the establishment of the U.S.-controlled Panama Canal Zone). The canal was finally completed in 1914, and changed the nature of world trade. It returned to Panamanian control on December 31, 1999. In the same year, Panamanians elected their first female president, Mireya Elisa Moscoso Rodríguez. For better or worse, the Panamanian agency charged with running the canal, the Panama Canal Authority, is largely autonomous—beyond the control of elected Panamanian politicians.

Since its independence from Colombia in 1903, Panama has been a republic. The military often dominated the government until 1989, when dictator General Manuel Noriega was overthrown by U.S. forces and civil rule was instituted.

Type of Government

Panama is a multiparty republic, with a president, two vice presidents, a Cabinet, a unicameral Legislative Assembly serving five-year terms, and a Supreme Court. The president is the head of state and the head of the government.

Frequently dominated by its military, the Republic of Panama has had a peaceful transfer of power between civilian governments since General Manuel Noriega was removed in 1989. (However, even during the Noriega era, the appearance of elective government was maintained.)

For current government data, check with the Embassy of Panama in your country.

Language

Spanish is the official language of Panama. Many Panamanians are bilingual in English as well. There are several Amerindian languages. Ethnologue.com has identified fourteen distinct languages in current use in Panama. (Two of these are languages of Chinese immigrants.)

The Panamanian View

Traditionally a Roman Catholic country, Protestantism has made significant gains in the recent past. Around 80 percent of Panamanians identify themselves as Roman Catholics. Protestants now make up about 15 percent, more than half of them belonging to Pentecostal groups. There are also small numbers of Muslims, Hindus, and others.

Panama has no official religion.

The family remains the single most powerful social unit. Nepotism is considered proper at all levels of society.

Attitudes toward the United States—known as *El Gigante del Norte* (the Giant to the North)—are complex. Some Panamanians blame the United State's long domination of Panama for all their country's problems. Nevertheless, many Panamanians view the United

Panama

States as their best opportunity for education and advancement; thousands of Panamanians live in the United States.

 Know Before You Go

Aside from street crime, the greatest hazard to visitors comes from the heat and humidity.

Panamanian drivers also represent a danger. Many drivers ignore traffic signs in Panama.

If you go swimming in either the Atlantic or Pacific Ocean, there are dangerous riptides off many Panamanian beaches.

Despite the current government's best efforts, Panama is still listed as a major cocaine transshipment point and primary money-laundering center for narcotics revenue; money-laundering activity is especially heavy in the Colon Free Zone; official corruption remains a major problem.

▶ CULTURAL ORIENTATION

Cognitive Styles: How Panamanians Organize and Process Information

Perhaps because Panama has long been a transit port for goods and people from many nations, Panamanians are open to information of many kinds. Panamanians are also very politicized, which shades how they view this information. For example, members of anti-American or antiglobalization parties may resist any data from the United States. Panamanians typically process information subjectively and associatively. Their personal involvement in a problem may make it unlikely that they will apply rules or laws to solve it.

Negotiation Strategies: What Panamanians Accept as Evidence

Truth is found in the immediate feelings of the person involved. However, this truth may be influenced by a strong faith in the ideologies of nationalism. Unless they have been educated abroad, older Panamanians will seldom let objective facts stand in the way of their desires. Younger Panamanians may view matters less subjectively.

Value Systems: The Basis for Behavior

The following three sections identify the Value Systems in the predominant culture—their methods of dividing right from wrong, good from evil, and so forth.

Locus of Decision-Making

The individual makes the decisions, but always in light of their effect on the family or group to which he or she belongs. It is difficult for Panamanians to make a negative decision. Personal relationships are everything, and Panamanians strive to maintain them at all costs. A small, elite oligarchy is now in power, and they have historically made decisions favorable to the interests of the United States.

Panama

Sources of Anxiety Reduction

The extended family is the surest defense against a hostile and uncertain world. There is a strong work ethic, but levels of production are not highly evident. This is a laid-back society that does not let time dictate its behavior. Panamanians are followers of strong leaders. The rituals and precepts of the Catholic Church give structure to societal behavior.

Panamanians have been charted as having a relatively low individualism index. This indicates a collectivist society in which groups look out for the welfare of each individual member.

Issues of Equality/Inequality

There is a large gap between rich and poor, a fairly large middle class, and a large lower class. Panama has been listed as being tied with Guatemala for the highest power distance in Latin America. This indicates a great difference between the wealthy and the poor, as well as widespread acceptance of this situation. However, younger Panamanians no longer believe that the powerful elite are entitled to unlimited privileges. There is an inherent trust in people, so one needs to cultivate friendships. Machismo is strong. Most Panamanian men believe that the ideal focus for a woman is a home, family, and children.

▶ BUSINESS PRACTICES

Punctuality, Appointments, and Local Time

- Punctuality, although not strictly adhered to in daily living, is expected in business circles—particularly with foreigners.
- If you are invited to a party, never be on time. For dinner parties, it is appropriate to arrive up to one hour late if there are several guests, and up to thirty minutes late if you are alone. At large parties, you may arrive up to two hours late.
- Remember that many Europeans and South Americans write the day first, then the month, then the year (e.g., December 3, 2010, is written 3.12.10 or 3/12/10). Although Panamanians are familiar with the day-month-year format of the USA, they will generally write it in the conventional form for South America.
- Make appointments as far in advance of your arrival in Panama as possible. Confirm your arrival via phone or e-mail at least one week ahead of time.
- Local time is five hours behind Greenwich Mean Time (G.M.T. –5).

Negotiating

- Contract negotiations proceed at a much slower pace than in northern Europe or North America. Be patient with delays, and be prepared to travel to Panama more than once to finalize a transaction.
- Business is conducted among friends in Panama. Therefore, spend time establishing a relationship with your counterpart before jumping into business discussions. Emphasize

Panama

the personal compatibility of the two companies and develop a high level of trust, rather than focusing solely on the logical bottom line.

- Although more women are moving into higher managerial positions, they are still relatively rare. Women should emphasize the fact that they are part of a team from a company that is strongly committed to doing business in Panama.
- Have business cards and other material printed in Spanish as well as English.
- Adjust your starting price to allow a margin for bargaining.
- Latin Americans tend to be status conscious. At least one member of the negotiating team should be from a high level of management.
- Panamanians believe in the intrinsic worth of the individual and treat one another with respect and dignity, regardless of a person's social standing or material wealth. Therefore, it is very important not to publicly criticize a person.
- To avoid embarrassment, Panamanians rarely disagree with anyone in public. This can extend to a foreign businessperson trying to close a deal; a Panamanian may tell a foreigner "yes" simply to be polite. Lukewarm affirmatives, like "maybe" or "we will see," are polite ways of saying "no." A "yes" is not final until a contract is signed.
- A familiarity with Panamanian history, sites, culture, and art will impress your counterparts.
- Senior officials and the elderly are given preferential treatment. They should be greeted first and may be served before you in a line.

Business Entertaining

- Always stay at the best hotels and entertain your guests at premier restaurants. Ask your client's secretary about any preferences the client may have for restaurants or clubs.
- Good topics of conversation include sports, travel, and local cultural events. Avoid supporting claims that "the Canal was run better by the United States," even if they are made by a Panamanian.
- Foreign businesswomen should always include spouses in invitations to business dinners.
- To pay for either a lunch or dinner with male clients, women should arrange to take care of the bill privately with the waiter. If the check is brought to the table, the men will strongly resist letting a woman pay. Give the waiter your credit card beforehand or, if you are hosting a dinner at your hotel, arrange to have the charge added to your hotel bill.

Panama

Cultural Note

Citizens of the United States working in Panama have often remained separate from Panamanians in business and social networks. To encourage better cultural and business ties, businesses should plan and support fully integrated functions.

PROTOCOL

Greetings

- Men usually shake hands in greeting. Women will often pat each other on the right fore-arm or shoulder instead of shaking hands. If they are friends, they may hug or kiss each other on the cheek.
- At parties, it is customary to greet and shake hands with each person in the room.

Titles/Forms of Address

- Titles are very important in Panama and should be used whenever possible. When addressing someone directly, use the title alone and do not include a last name (Profesor, Doctor, and so forth). The title *Licenciado* is used for anyone with a bachelor's degree.
- Traditionally, first names were used only by persons on a familiar basis; however, younger executives may move to the use of first names with business associates from North America.
- For further information on the proper titles and forms of address for Spanish-speaking countries, please consult Appendix A.

Gestures

- Because of the long-standing presence of the United States in Panama, most North American gestures (and insults) are understood.

Gifts

- Gifts are not required in a business setting. However, after the first few meetings, you may want to bring a gift from your home state, such as a local craft or illustrated book. Other good gifts include the latest electronic gadgets or expensive liquor.
- Gifts are appropriate if you are invited to a Panamanian home or if you are visiting rural areas. Some good options are chocolates, wine, Scotch, or local crafts from home.
- Gifts are not expected, however, and it is enough to extend your thanks and to invite your hosts to a meal in return.

Dress

- In theory, men should wear a conservative business suit for work.
- In practice, jackets and ties are often dispensed with in Panama's hot, humid weather. Panamanian businessmen in higher positions wear suits; others wear *camisillas* (a light-weight, open-necked shirt that is not tucked inside the trousers).
- Women should wear a skirt and blouse or a dress.
- Pants, including jeans, and a shirt are appropriate casualwear in the city. Shorts are not often worn by either sex, and women should avoid any revealing clothing. A woman wearing pants in a rural area may draw some attention.

Panama

Paraguay

Republic of Paraguay
Local long form: Republica del Paraguay

 ## WHAT'S YOUR CULTURAL IQ?

1. TRUE or FALSE? Paraguay is the only landlocked country in South America.

   ANSWER: FALSE. Paraguay is landlocked, but so is neighboring Bolivia.

2. Which neighboring countries did Paraguay fight in the War of the Triple Alliance?
   a. Argentina
   b. Brazil
   c. Uruguay
   d. All of the above

   ANSWER: d. Paraguay unwisely fought all three of these countries simultaneously from 1864 to 1870. As a result, Paraguay lost half of its adult men and much of its territory—including its border with Uruguay.

3. Paraguay had the unsavory reputation as a refuge for exiled or fleeing criminals. If you hear German spoken in Paraguay, who is likely to be speaking it?
   a. Escaped Nazi war criminals
   b. Mennonite farmers
   c. German and Austrian tourists
   d. None of the above

   ANSWER: b. Today there are thousands of peaceful Mennonite farmers in Paraguay. Most of the few Nazi war criminals in Paraguay have died off.

TIPS ON DOING BUSINESS IN PARAGUAY

- Paraguay is the only South American nation with two official languages: Spanish and Guaraní. Guaraní, an indigenous language, is the most commonly spoken tongue spoken outside the capital, Asunción. Most executives speak Spanish, if not English.

- However, every politician and civil servant in Paraguay is required to be fluent in Guaraní. If you expect to deal with the government, you may find a Guaraní interpreter to be of use.
- Paraguay once had the reputation as a haven for Nazi war criminals hiding from justice. Today, most German speakers in Paraguay are peaceful Mennonite farmers. There are thousands of Mennonite *estancias* (ranches) in rural Paraguay.

▶ COUNTRY BACKGROUND

History

The city of Asunción, which today is the capital of Paraguay, was founded in 1537. For a time, Asunción was the capital city of the Spanish colonial provinces of Paraguay and Río de la Plata (encompassing most of the bottom third of South America). To the disappointment of the Spanish colonizers, Paraguay lacked the gold and silver they sought. Consequently, Paraguay remained undeveloped and attracted relatively few Spaniards. Most of the Spaniards who came married Indian women; the arable land was divided into huge plantations.

Jesuit missionaries, however, did venture into Paraguay. They instituted a major social experiment, establishing a series of self-sufficient missions among the Indians, the famous *reduccciónes* (reductions). This pitted the Jesuits against the Spanish-descended settlers, who wanted cheap Indian labor for their plantations. Unfortunately, the Jesuits were expelled from the continent in the 1700s; the reduccciónes failed, and the Indians fled into the jungle or were sold into slavery. (This saga was portrayed in the 1986 film *The Mission*.)

In 1811, Paraguay became the first nation in South America to gain its independence from Spain. This was accomplished without violence; Spain did not consider remote, agricultural Paraguay worth fighting for.

From 1814 to 1840, Paraguay's elected "supreme dictator," Dr. José Gaspar Rodríguez de Francia, cut the nation off from the outside world. Paraguay became totally self-sufficient, and intermarriage with the Indians was encouraged. As a result, Paraguay evolved into a highly nationalistic, ethnically homogeneous state.

At the time of its independence, Paraguay was about a third larger than it is today. Part of its land was lost when it became involved in territorial wars with all of its neighbors. Had Argentina and Brazil been able to agree upon a partition, Paraguay would have ceased to exist. As it was, the wars of 1865 to 1870 and 1932 to 1935 devastated the population. An astonishing 80 percent of the men in Paraguay were slain in the first war alone.

In 1954, General Alfredo Stroessner took control of Paraguay in a coup. His reign lasted until another coup, led by General Andrés Rodríguez Pedotti, ousted him in February 1989. Rodríguez was elected president of Paraguay in May 1989, and he restored some civil and political rights. Despite occasional irregularities—including coup attempts, resignations, and the assassination of a vice president in 1999—Paraguay has maintained an elective

Paraguay

government ever since. However, the threat of another coup will be present as long as economic instability continues.

Type of Government

Technically a constitutional republic, Paraguay has a powerful executive branch and has usually been under the thumb of one strongman after another. However, Paraguay has managed a relatively peaceful transition of power from one elected president to another since 1989. The president is both the chief of state and head of the government.

The government is divided between the executive branch (headed by a president who is elected for a five-year term), an independent judiciary, and a two-house legislature. Voting is mandatory for all citizens between the ages of eighteen and sixty.

For current government data, check with the Embassy of Paraguay at *www.paraguayem bassy.com.*

Language

Paraguay is unusual in that it has two official languages: Spanish and Guaraní (a language of most of the indigenous Amerindian population). While most writing is done in Spanish, there is some literature in the Guaraní language.

For data on the various languages of Paraguay, see Ethnologue at *www.ethnologue.com.*

The Paraguayan View

Roman Catholicism is the state religion of Paraguay and is adhered to by about 89 percent of the populace. The state pays all Church salaries and controls all Church appointments. However, religious freedom is guaranteed, and the remainder are primarily members of Mennonite and other Protestant denominations. Protestantism has been gaining in popularity. There is also a small community of Muslim immigrants.

☑ Know Before You Go

The police and intelligence services of many major nations take interest in persons who travel to and from Paraguay. The tri-border area—where the borders of Paraguay, Brazil, and Argentina meet—has been known for decades as a haven for counterfeiters and smugglers. Lately, the region's Muslim community has been named by the U.S. State Department as supporters and financiers of terrorism. Traveling to this area may get your passport flagged by the intelligence services of your home country.

Despite widely publicized political violence, the primary hazard for foreign visitors in Paraguay is automobile accidents. Roads vary in quality.

For visitors traveling outside the cities, the environment can be hazardous, especially the heat of the desertlike Chaco region. Poisonous snakes are common in the Chaco.

Earthquakes do occur on occasion. Hurricanes and tornadoes are uncommon. Malaria remains a hazard in many areas.

Paraguay suffered a hoof-and-mouth disease outbreak in 2001, which was of major concern in a beef-exporting nation. The country was declared free of the disease in 2003.

Paraguay

▶ CULTURAL ORIENTATION

Note: The people of Paraguay have not been studied as extensively as have the people of their neighboring countries. Further research is needed.

Cognitive Styles: How Paraguayans Organize and Process Information

Historically, strict government controls have insulated the people from most outside information. Paraguayans process information subjectively and associatively. This makes their solutions subjective and particular to each situation, rather than rule-based or law-based.

Negotiation Strategies: What Paraguayans Accept as Evidence

Paraguayans generally find truth in the subjective feelings of the moment. This truth may be influenced by faith in the ideologies of nationalism and religion. Objective facts are not commonly used to prove a point. (However, this is not true for young Paraguayans educated abroad.)

Value Systems: The Basis for Behavior

Paraguay has the most homogeneous population (95 percent mestizo) in Latin America. The following three sections identify the Value Systems in the predominant culture—their methods of dividing right from wrong, good from evil, and so forth.

Locus of Decision-Making

The male is the decision-maker, but he always keeps the interests of the family or group in mind. An individual's self-identity is based on his or her family genealogy and position in the social system. Decisions will always favor friends or family over expertise. There has always been a strong leader (usually a dictator) to make the decisions for the nation.

Sources of Anxiety Reduction

Family and kin, not the community, are the center of the social universe. They give stability and security to the individual. Godparents are a very important part of the web of kinship. Paraguayans like to follow strong leaders, and their nationalism gives them a sense of security. Catholicism is an essential component of social life, with its rituals, fiestas, and holidays all providing continuity and stability.

Issues of Equality/Inequality

There is a tradition of authoritarian rule and a concomitant lack of democratic institutions. There is an extreme contrast between the elite (educated, prosperous, and city-based) and the poor. The basic social dichotomy is between small farmers and a narrow stratum of elite families who control all the resources. Machismo is strong.

Paraguay

▶ BUSINESS PRACTICES

Punctuality, Appointments, and Local Time
- While punctuality is not a high priority for Paraguayans, foreigners are expected to be on time.
- Despite their formality, business meetings rarely start on time. It would be unrealistic to expect your Paraguayan counterparts to be prompt.
- Paraguayans, like many Europeans and South Americans, write the day first, then the month, and then the year (e.g., December 3, 2010, is written 3.12.10 or 3/12/10).
- Mornings are best for appointments.
- The best time of year to conduct business in Paraguay is from June through October. Little business is accomplished during the two weeks before and after Christmas and Easter, or during Carnival. December through February is vacation time in Paraguay, as is May around Paraguay's Independence Day.
- Paraguay is four hours behind Greenwich Mean Time (G.M.T. –4), making it one hour ahead of U.S. Eastern Standard Time (E.S.T. +1).

Negotiating
- The pace of business negotiations in Paraguay is usually much slower than in North America.
- Most Paraguayan men dislike confronting or offending women. Including a female representative on your team can be beneficial in negotiations.
- Personal relationships are far more important than corporate ones in Paraguay. Each time your company changes its representative in Paraguay, you will virtually be starting from scratch. A new relationship must be built up before business can proceed.
- Do not assume that each portion of a contract is settled as it is agreed upon. Until the entire contract is signed, each portion is subject to renegotiation.
- While many of the executives you meet will speak English, check beforehand as to whether or not you will need an interpreter.
- All printed material you hand out should be translated into Spanish. This goes for everything from business cards to reports to brochures. You are not expected to translate material into Guaraní.
- Paraguayans are great sports fans. Talking about sports is generally a good way to open a conversation. Football (called fútbol here, and soccer in the United States) is the most popular sport. U.S.-style football is fútbol americano. Basketball, volleyball, and horseracing are also popular.
- Most people in Paraguay are very proud of their country's massive engineering projects, especially their hydroelectric dams. The Itaipu Dam, a joint project of Paraguay and Brazil, is the world's largest. Inquiring about such projects is a good topic of conversation.

Business Entertaining
- Many people still go home for lunch. However, with enough notice, Paraguayan executives may consider a business lunch.

- Most business entertaining is done over dinner, which is held late, often at 9:00 or 10:00 P.M. Indeed, most restaurants will not serve dinner before 9:00 P.M.
- Dinner is considered a social occasion; do not try to talk business unless your counterpart brings it up.
- Paraguayans love to have long dinners under the stars. Many restaurants have shows that last until after midnight. There are also several casinos.
- Paraguay is a major cattle producer, so expect a lot of beef to be served in restaurants.

Cultural Note

At a gathering such as a party, it is important to shake hands with everyone, both as you arrive and when you leave.

▶ PROTOCOL

Greetings
- Except when greeting close friends, it is traditional to shake hands firmly with both men and women.
- Close male friends shake hands or embrace upon meeting; men kiss close female friends. Close female friends usually kiss each other.
- Close friends of either sex may walk arm in arm.

Titles/Forms of Address
- Remember that Paraguay has two official languages: Spanish and Guaraní. However, all the businesspeople you meet will be fluent in Spanish, so Spanish titles may be used.
- Most people you meet should be addressed initially with a title and their surname.
- For further information on the proper titles and forms of address for Spanish-speaking countries, please consult Appendix A.

Gestures
- As in much of Latin America, Paraguayans converse at a much closer distance than do most people in North America or northern Europe. Restrain yourself from trying to back away; a Paraguayan will probably step forward and close the distance.
- The traditional thumbs-up gesture means "okay."
- Displaying the thumb and index finger curled into a circle (which means "okay" in the United States) should be avoided. When done with the wrist bent and the other fingers pointed toward the ground, the gesture is obscene.
- Crossing the index and second fingers is also considered offensive.
- Winking in Paraguay has sexual connotations.
- Tapping one's chin with the top of the index finger means "I don't know."

- A backwards tilt of the head means "I forgot."
- Sit only on chairs, not on a ledge, box, or table. Manners dictate an erect sitting posture; don't slump.
- Do not rest your feet on anything other than a footstool or rail; it is very impolite to place them upon a table.

Gifts

- Gift giving is problematic in Paraguay, because corruption was widespread during the former regime.
- As in any country, any gift given should be of high quality. If the item is produced by your corporation, the corporate name or logo should appear discreetly, not emblazoned over the whole surface.
- Avoid giving knives; they symbolize the severing of a friendship.
- Gifts are not expected when invited to a Paraguayan home. However, a gift of flowers, chocolates, wine, or a single-malt whiskey may be appreciated.
- As in many other Latin American countries, gifts are exchanged not on Christmas but on January 6, (the Epiphany), commemorating the gifts given to the Christ Child by the Three Kings.

Cultural Note
Realize that Paraguay is a major trading center with plenty of affluent consumers. You may have to get creative to discover an item from your homeland that isn't for sale in Paraguay. In fact, many gifts can often be bought at a cheaper price in Paraguay if you are prepared to bargain with the merchants. Whatever you purchase, make sure it is made in your home country.

Dress

- Business dress in Paraguay is conservative: dark suits and ties for men; white blouses and dark suits or skirts for women. Men should follow their Paraguayan colleagues' lead as to wearing ties and removing jackets in the summer.
- Dress to handle the heat and humidity of Paraguayan summers. Most local people wear cotton. Don't forget that the seasons in South America are the reverse of those in North America.
- Sweaters are recommended during the winter. Although Paraguay never gets very cold, the heating in buildings is often poor.
- Whatever the season, be prepared for sudden changes in weather and temperature.
- Men may wear the same dark suit for formal occasions (such as the theater, a formal dinner party, and so forth), but women are expected to wear an evening gown. The invitation will specify that the affair is formal.
- Both men and women wear pants as casualwear. If you are meeting business associates, avoid jeans and wear a jacket or blazer. Women should not wear shorts.

Peru

Republic of Peru
Local long form: Republica del Peru

> **Cultural Note**
> Peru is rich in natural resources, some of which are intriguing to international oil, gas, and space industries. A major natural gas site exists in Camisea (an eastern jungle), and Peru has the world's highest plains near the equator. The high, clear characteristics of Peru's altiplano would make it an attractive location for potential space observations or launches.

WHAT'S YOUR CULTURAL IQ?

1. TRUE or FALSE: The magnificent ruins called "Machu Picchu" were built (and later abandoned) by the Aztecs before the Spanish reached Peru.

   ANSWER: FALSE. Yes, Machu Picchu (often called "The Lost City of the Incas") was abandoned, but it was built by the Incas, not the Aztecs.

2. The Spanish made Peru the seat of Spanish South America because:
   a. It was the location of South America's biggest silver mine
   b. It is free from earthquakes
   c. It was the seat of the Inca empire

   ANSWER: c. Peru was the center of Tahuantinsuyo, which was what the Incas called their empire (the name means "four corners"). Peru also used to rule Bolivia (where the great silver mine of Potosí is located). Peru is certainly not free of earthquakes; a 1971 quake measuring 7.7 on the Richter scale killed some 70,000 Peruvians.

3. TRUE or FALSE: After Peru's modest reserves of gold and silver were exhausted, and long before petroleum was discovered, Peru's most valuable mineral resource was *guano.*

   ANSWER: TRUE. The guano in Peru's southern provinces became so valuable as a fertilizer that Chile fought two wars with Peru to gain control of it. Chile won both times.

TIPS ON DOING BUSINESS IN PERU

- Peru has historically been a highly stratified society, with a wealthy oligarchy ruling over poor mestizos (persons of mixed European and Amerindian heritage) and even poorer Amerindians. There is also a small community of Japanese immigrants, from which the former president, Alberto Fujimori, descended.

- Peru has had difficult relations with some bordering countries. It lost valuable southern territory to Chile in the last century, and a dispute with Ecuador deteriorated into conflicts in the 1990s. In marketing, or even in conversation, be careful not to compare Peru to its neighbors.
- Peruvian consumers may tend to distrust the quality of items sold by mail. Traditionally, such products have had problems with after-sale service.

▶ COUNTRY BACKGROUND

History

Peru was a center of the powerful Inca empire until the Spanish conquistador Francisco Pizarro invaded in 1532. Peru then became the richest and most powerful of the Spanish colonies in South America.

Peru declared its independence from Spain in 1821. But the war of independence lasted several years, and a subsequent war with Spain lasted from 1864 to 1866. Independence did not bring a stable government. The first hundred years of Peru's existence is a record of one revolution after another.

Although Peru has had democratically elected governments since 1980, it is still seeking stability and freedom from the threat of revolution. Terrorist activities from two major insurgent organizations, the Sendero Luminoso (Shining Path) and the Túpac Amaru Revolutionary Movement (MRTA) have fortunately subsided.

Alberto Fujimori's election to the presidency was a major departure from conventional political elections in 1989. He made radical changes to the Peruvian economy, and in 1992 he dissolved Congress and suspended the constitution, after which he instituted multiple reforms.

On December 17, 1996, some twenty members of the Túpac Amaru Revolutionary Movement seized the Japanese Embassy in Lima. Over 400 guests were held hostage. The rebels demanded the release of imprisoned members of their group. Eventually, government forces entered the embassy and all the rebels were shot.

Following the ousting of President Fujimori in 2000 by the Congress, Alejandro Toledo was elected in 2001.

Peru

Cultural Note

The odd lines at Nazca (which have been called extraterrestrial maps) have been the center of controversy for years. Although these lines can in fact best be viewed by airplane, there is no proof that the lines are the work of extraterrestrials.

Type of Government

The Republic of Peru is a unitary multiparty republic with a single legislative house, the Congress. The president is the chief of state and head of the government.

For current government data, check with the Embassy of Peru at *www.peruvianembassy.us.*

Language

Peru has two official languages: Spanish and Quechua (an Amerindian language). Besides Quechua, another Indian language, Aymara, is spoken in the southern highlands. Although many businesspeople understand English, all written materials should be presented in either Spanish or Spanish and English.

The Peruvian View

The Spanish brought Roman Catholicism to Peru, and the majority of the population is considered Catholic. A minority belong to various Protestant faiths. Religion plays a significant part in Peruvian life and often reflects a mix of traditional Amerindian beliefs and Christianity.

Peru's social stratification permeates all facets of life. Unlike the Latin American nations to the south, Peru has a large Amerindian population—far too large to be ignored. This population segment has been marginalized economically and constitutes some of the poorest people in South America.

Mestizos make up the next level. Traditionally exploited by the ruling class, it was the mestizos who elected Alberto Fujimori as president in 1990.

Peru's most powerful economic class is still primarily "white." The majority of private business transactions will be with members of this class.

☑ Know Before You Go

Peru is subject to earthquakes and volcanoes, as well as severe weather due to fluctuations in the El Niño current.

Street crime remains a problem, in both the cities and rural areas.

Activity by the major rebel groups—the Sendero Luminoso (Shining Path) and the Túpac Amaru Revolutionary Movement (MRTA)—has been drastically reduced from its height in the 1980s and 1990s. Although these groups receive worldwide publicity, their actions do not generally affect the international business traveler. (The 1996 seizure of the Japanese Embassy in Lima by the Túpac Amaru Revolutionary Movement was an anomaly.) However, the remnants of such groups sometimes kidnap foreign travelers in rural areas and hold them for ransom.

The cocaine industry has more influence on international business, due to its high profitability, inherent violence, and government efforts to limit it. Peruvians grow more than half of the world's coca crop. The law enforcement agencies of many nations monitor the Peruvian drug traffic. Consequently, innocent business travelers to Peru may find police attention focused on them.

The greatest threat to foreign travelers in Peru is not cholera outbreaks, terrorism, or earthquakes: it's altitude sickness. Lima is near sea level, but other popular destinations (such as Cuzco and the area around Lake Titicaca) are high enough to cause this illness. Anyone can be struck by altitude sickness, and rest is the only sure cure. Be aware that Peruvian folk remedies for the sickness usually contain coca leaves. (Coca leaves, which are chewed by many Amerindians, are legal in Peru. Cocaine itself is highly illegal.)

Altitude sickness can strike anyone, even if you have never experienced it before. There is no sure prevention except gradual acclimation to high elevation. Once you get to 6,000 feet above sea level, spend at least two nights there. Repeat this acclimation period at each increase of 3,000 feet. Alcohol consumption tends to make the symptoms worse. Sunburn is also a danger at high altitudes, because there is less atmosphere to protect you from the sun.

Land mines are still present in Peru. There are estimates of over 100,000 antipersonnel mines on the Peru-Ecuador border. Mines are also present on the Peruvian-Chilean border. Furthermore, during the days of rebel attacks on electrical power stations, the Peruvian government planted mines around power stations and other critical infrastructures. The heavy rains from El Niño sometimes expose land mines or even wash them out of place. Since 1995, there have been 179 reported casualties due to land mines, and information indicates that the data is underreported. Further information is available at *www.icbl.org*.

▶ CULTURAL ORIENTATION

Cognitive Styles: How Peruvians Organize and Process Information

The culture of Peru is open to most information, but attitudes are not changed easily. Except for the highly educated, information is processed subjectively and associatively. Personal involvement in problems and solutions is more important than having a rule or law that dictates one's approach to life.

Negotiation Strategies: What Peruvians Accept as Evidence

An individual's personal feelings about a situation are the basis for truth. In Peru, the ideologies that may influence the truth are those of elitism and religion. Faith in either of these may have historically affected the truth. This may be changing in the younger work force, because objective facts are beginning to carry more weight.

Value Systems: The Basis for Behavior

The value systems of Peru were built around ideologies of an elitist system in which each level was controlled by the next step in the hierarchy. Some characteristics are changing, as evidenced in the election of an "outsider" in the late 1990s—Alberto Fujimori.

The following three sections identify the Value Systems in the predominant culture—their methods of dividing right from wrong, good from evil, etc.

Locus of Decision-Making

Individuals are responsible for their own decisions, but the best interests of the families or groups are dominating factors. A small upper class of the elite oligarchy still controls most of the resources of the country. Personal relationships are more important than one's expertise in business associations. A person's self-identity is based on the social system and the history of his or her extended family.

Peru

Peru has been charted as having a slightly higher than average index of uncertainty avoidance (for Latin America). This would indicate that Peruvians have a low level of tolerance for uncertainty and are generally averse to risk.

Sources of Anxiety Reduction

At every level of society, the family is the cornerstone of relationships. Kinships define the principal areas of trust and cooperation. At the highest levels of society, kinship and marriage reinforce and solidify political and economic alliances.

Issues of Equality/Inequality

All classes have ranks that are stratified along lines of deep-seated inequalities. Education is the gatekeeper to social advancement in the Peruvian elitist system. It appears that the economic ruling class tries to maintain the large gap between the rich and poor. Machismo is strong, but there are indicators that Peruvian women are gaining more liberties.

▶ BUSINESS PRACTICES

Punctuality, Appointments, and Local Time

- Punctuality is becoming more important in both private and public sectors. However, do not be insulted if your Peruvian contact is late.
- Remember that many Europeans and South Americans write the day first, then the month, and then the year (e.g., December 3, 2010, is written 3.12.10 or 3/12/10). This is the case in Peru.
- Make appointments about two weeks in advance. Upon arrival, do not make impromptu calls at business or government offices.
- Appointments should be scheduled in the morning and may involve a lunch invitation, so do not plan more than one meeting each morning.
- The work week is rather long in Peru, since businesses are often open six days a week. People may return home for lunch, so offices sometimes close between 1:00 and 3:00 P.M.
- Government offices and banks generally work different hours in the summer (January to March) and winter (April to December).

  Many Peruvians go on vacation between January and March, as well as two weeks before and after Christmas and Easter. Therefore, try not to schedule major appointments then or during national holidays.
- Peru is five hours behind Greenwich Mean Time (G.M.T. –5), or the same as U.S. Eastern Standard Time.

Negotiating

- During negotiations, be prepared to discuss all aspects of the contract concurrently, rather than discussing it in a sequential manner. Also accept that seemingly extraneous data may be reviewed and rereviewed. Try to be as flexible as possible; ask questions and avoid confrontations.

- Include a variety of materials in your presentations (Web-based communications, high-end graphics in printed format, interactive demonstrations, etc.).
- If you plan to invite your prospects to dinner or lunch during the negotiations, ask only the key participants. After the deal is completed, invite everyone who was involved in the project.
- You may be received with exceptional warmth, since Peruvians are open to foreign investment.
- Peruvians may be more comfortable discussing their Spanish heritage than their Indian background; therefore, it may be unwise to inquire about an individual's ancestry. Also, avoid making remarks about the Peruvian government, terrorists, relations with neighboring countries, or politics in general.
- Peruvians value personal relationships and relate more to an individual business associate than to a corporation. When approaching a prospect in Peru, it is always better to establish the connection through a highly regarded local contact. This representative will be able to navigate through the maze of networks that make up Peruvian business and government.
- Have your business cards and all company materials printed in both Spanish and English.

Cultural Note
Above all else, do not switch your company's players during negotiations. The Peruvian negotiation team might call a halt to the process as a result. Peruvians relate to the person they have come to know, not to the organization.

Business Entertaining
- Entertain at prestigious restaurants, and include spouses in the invitations if it will be a dinner.
- Discussing business over dinner is not common.
- Most dinner invitations will be for 9:00 P.M., which means dinner will probably be served around 10:30 P.M. Arrive around thirty minutes late, and stay about thirty minutes after dinner ends.
- Imported alcohol is very expensive.
- Stay at a first-class hotel, and feel free to use it to host a meeting or luncheon, particularly if you will be looking for wireless connections.
- An invitation to tea at a private residence is usually for 6:00 to 8:00 P.M.

Peru

▶ PROTOCOL

Greetings

- Men and women shake hands both in greeting and in parting.

    Once a friendship has been established, men may greet each other with a hug, and women may kiss one another on the cheek.

Titles/Forms of Address

- Titles are very important in Peru. Address a person directly by using his or her title, such as "Profesor" or "Doctor," and last name or surname. Wait for your counterpart to initiate this switch to first names
- For further information on the proper titles and forms of address in Peru, please consult Appendix A.

Gestures

- Peruvians communicate in close proximity. When they stand nearby, do not back away; you will offend them. Do not be surprised if your Peruvian associates take your arm as you walk—men sometimes walk arm in arm with other men, as do women with other women.
- To signal "come here," hold your hand vertically and wave it back and forth with the palm facing out, or put your palm face down, and wave the fingers back and forth.
- Crossing your legs by resting the ankle of one leg on the knee of the other is inappropriate; however, you may cross your legs at the knee.
- When eating out, be sure to rest both hands on the table, rather than leaving one in your lap.
- "I'm thinking" is represented by tapping your head.
- "Go away" is shown by holding your hand flat and flicking the fingers toward the irritation.
- "Pay me" is signified by an eyebrow raise, or by sweeping your hand toward your body.

> **Cultural Note**
>
> In Latin America, giving gifts is a normal part of business protocol. Peruvians sometimes consider it ironic that U.S. businesspeople feel hesitant about giving a well-thought-out gift to a Peruvian prospect or client, yet will insist on being overtly friendly by immediately calling the Peruvian by his or her first name.

Gifts

- Giving a gift is not required at the first meeting. Instead, buy lunch for your prospect to start the relationship. Subsequently consider the individual's tastes for future gift giving.
- Wait until after the formal meeting is over to present a gift. A relaxed social situation is the best time.

Peru

- A gift with a significant connection to your home region will be remembered (for example, local folk art, liquor produced in your region, or an illustrated book about your home city).
- Keep company logos small.
- Appropriate gifts are ones that "ground" or "locate" the firm. For example, a company might present gifts that incorporate stone quarried from the state where they are head-quartered (like paperweights, lighters, business card holders, etc.).
- Small electronic gadgets, such as calculators, MP3 players, a handheld GPS, cell phones, electronic organizers, or various wireless devices, are appropriate—particularly because import taxes would normally have to be paid on these items. Have items customized with your contact's initials when possible.
- Digital cameras and name brand pens are appreciated, as are ties, scarves, or other accessories in natural fabrics. (It is often too hot for man-made weaves.)
- When invited to a home, bring wine, whiskey or other liquors, or chocolates. Also bring gifts for the children, such as T-shirts or caps with the logos of popular sports teams or prestigious universities, CDs, electronic games, and so forth.
- Sending roses after a dinner is appropriate if they are not red (these have romantic connotations). Any other flower is regarded as cheap.
- Avoid sending thirteen of anything, any purple or black objects (which have connotations of religious ceremonies), knives (which can signify cutting off a relationship), or handkerchiefs (which represent grief).
- If you intensely admire one of a Peruvian's possessions, he or she may feel obligated to present it to you as a gift.
- There are some social idiosyncrasies in Peru related to the "caste" system. Various levels of family history, social standing, and education may influence the gifts exchanged. Be aware of these sociological issues.

Dress

- For business meetings, men should wear well-tailored suits.
- Female executives generally wear suits, but it may depend upon the environment.
- Foreigners should not wear native Indian clothing, even if they intend to honor the local culture.

Peru

Cultural Note

The noted author Mario Vargas Llosa is a cultural icon in Peru. His writings deal with corruption in politics and societal changes. This drew both praise and persecution. He ran for president of Peru in 1990 but lost to Alberto Fujimori, who had 60 percent of the vote.

Philippines

Republic of the Philippines
Local short form: Pilipinas
Local long form: Republika ng Pilipinas

> **Cultural Note**
> Culturally, Filipinos are unique. Although the majority are of Malay stock, most have Hispanic surnames, are Roman Catholic (this is the only Christian nation in Asia), and speak some English. This makes the Philippines the fourth-largest English-speaking country in the world, after the United States, the United Kingdom, and India.

 ## WHAT'S YOUR CULTURAL IQ?

1. The Philippine archipelago is comprised of 7,107 islands, over half of which are not inhabited. Which of these is not a large Philippine island?
   a. Java
   b. Luzon
   c. Mindanao

   ANSWER: a. Java is an island, but it is part of Indonesia.

2. TRUE or FALSE? Boogong and Balut are indigenous Philippine languages.

   ANSWER: FALSE. They are traditional delicacies. A rite of passage that will endear you to Filipinos consists of eating one of the few local dishes that foreigners are squeamish about. These include the foul-smelling shrimp paste called bogoong, or the boiled embryonic duck egg called balut.

3. Which of the following women have not served as president of the Philippines?
   a. Gloria Macapagal-Arroyo
   b. Imelda Marcos
   c. Corazon Aquino

   ANSWER: b. Imelda Marcos was the wife of former president Ferdinand E. Marcos.

 ## TIPS ON DOING BUSINESS IN THE PHILIPPINES

- Kinship is everything in the Philippines. You will be accepted more rapidly if you can explain your relationship to someone the Filipinos already know. Even if the relationship is distant (i.e., you are the friend of the brother of someone they know), it will help establish you as a related, connected person.

- Groups of Filipinos do not arrange themselves in neat lines. Instead, they form a pushing, shoving crowd, with each person out for him or herself. The only times that Filipinos have queued in neat lines was for armed soldiers (such as during the Japanese occupation army in World War II).
- There is a rather short-term orientation, so break down your projects into manageable sections. Deeply involved, long-term plans can be viewed as onerous and unrealistic.

▶ COUNTRY BACKGROUND

History

The Philippine Islands were inhabited before recorded human history. To this day, one can find human cultures living there at every level of technology. Many Filipinos live in modern, bustling Pacific Rim cities, while others live in isolated tropical jungles. This cultural diversity began in the tenth century A.D., when the Chinese began to trade with Filipinos. Eventually, some Chinese stayed in the Philippines. Although ethnic Chinese represent a small percent of the Philippine population, they control about half of the nation's commerce and banking. While many prominent Filipinos have Chinese ancestry, there is considerable hostility toward the Chinese dominance of business.

Arab traders introduced Islam to the Philippines in the fourteenth century. Concentrated in the southern islands, these Muslims fiercely resisted both Spanish and American authority. Their refusal to yield to colonial overlords is a source of pride to many Filipinos, Muslim and Christian alike.

The Portuguese navigator Magellan led a Spanish fleet to the Philippines in 1521 and named the islands after King Philip II of Spain. Spaniards subsequently ruled for 350 years and brought Catholicism to the islands, as well as the Latino attitudes and traditions that are now a major part of the Filipino makeup. After the Spanish-American War, the Philippines were ceded to the United States in 1898. Already fighting against their Spanish overlords, Filipinos had no desire to be ruled by another colonial power. The Philippine insurrection against the United States lasted over twelve years and cost the lives of hundreds of thousands of Filipinos. But after the war, the United States brought infrastructure development to the country. It was in the U.S.-built public schools that English became a predominant language. Under U.S. control, the nation became the Commonwealth of the Philippines in 1935.

In 1941, the Japanese conquest of the Philippines demonstrated to Filipinos that the United States was not unbeatable. The Philippines were liberated in 1945 by Allied troops, both U.S. and Filipino. Full independence for the Philippines came on July 4, 1946.

Philippines

Type of Government

The Republic of the Philippines has been an independent nation since 1946. Many Filipinos see their history as a struggle against foreign domination, first by Spain, then by the United States.

The Republic of the Philippines is a unitary republic patterned after the United States. The president of the Philippines is both head of state and head of the government. There are two legislative houses: the Senate and the House of Representatives.

The first Philippine Constitution dates back to 1935. After the Philippines became an independent republic, U.S. military bases were a source of contention, a constant reminder of colonial domination. Furthermore, the USA exerted tremendous influence, as when it helped to keep the corrupt dictatorship of Ferdinand Marcos in power for twenty-one years! The end of the Cold War reduced the importance of the two major U.S. bases in the Philippines, Clark Air Force Base and Subic Bay Naval Base. While the U.S. and Philippine governments were negotiating over the future of the bases, Mount Pinatubo erupted in June 1991. Buried under volcanic ash, Clark Air Force Base was rendered unusable. A new deal was negotiated to allow Subic Bay Naval Base to remain open. President Corazon Aquino agreed, but the Philippine Senate rejected it. The Philippine people themselves were split over the issue; had it been put to a referendum, the majority might have voted to allow U.S. forces to remain at Subic Bay Naval Base.

In 1992 Corazon Aquino's defense minister, Fidel Ramos, was elected president. He had a stable six-year term. Following President Ramos, a former movie star was elected in 1998—Joseph Estrada. His term in office was cut short because he was charged with taking bribes, and was impeached. After President Estrada capitulated, he was replaced by the vice president, Gloria Macapagal-Arroyo. President Arroyo won a second term in 2004.

The Philippines faces a future relatively free of foreign influences, but without the millions of dollars the U.S. military presence pumped into the economy. The country struggles with unemployment, a fluctuating economy, and a huge debt load, not to mention periodic natural disasters.

Current government data can be found at the Embassy of Philippines at *www .philippineembassy.org*.

Cultural Note

Filipinos grow up in extended families and are rarely alone. Indeed, solitude makes most Filipinos uncomfortable. A foreigner's desire for privacy is not usually understood. If you are sitting alone on a bus or in a cinema, a Filipino is likely to ignore all the empty seats and sit next to you. Such action is not about you; it is simply a cultural trait.

Philippines

Language

Tagalog (Pilipino, Filipino) and English are the official languages of the Republic of the Philippines. There are eight major dialects: Tagalog, Cebuano, Ilocan, Hiligaynon or Ilonggo, Bicol, Waray, Pampango, and Pangasinense. The literacy rate is approaching 90 percent.

Ethnologue.com acknowledges 172 languages in the Philippines, 3 of which are extinct.

The Philippine View

The Philippines has no official religion, but approximately 83 percent of Filipinos consider themselves Roman Catholic. While only 9 percent of Filipinos are Protestant, their Evangelical sects are growing rapidly. There is also a Philippine Independent Church, which claims some 6 percent of the population (they were Roman Catholics but broke with Rome). Followers of Islam are concentrated in the south.

Thanks in part to the Catholic Church's opposition to birth control, the Philippines has a very high birth rate. (Former President Estrada himself had at least ten children.)

Social scientists have found that most Filipinos have a fairly low uncertainty avoidance index. Societies that score high on this scale feel the need for creating rigid rules of behavior and extensive sets of laws to enforce them. At the opposite end of the scale, Philippine society and behavior exhibits flexibility and adaptability. The letter of the law is not strictly observed, and there are not regulations to cover every situation. This situation is probably ideal for a sprawling, geographically divided, multicultural society. But it has disadvantages for foreigners who assume that laws exist to be followed. For example, comprehensive building codes do not exist in all areas of the Philippines, and where they are present, they may not be strictly adhered to or enforced.

Curiously, this does not prevent companies from adopting extensive in-house regulations for their employees. This reflects the difficulty that a supervisor has in disciplining an employee who is probably related to several company employees (or even related to the boss). By detailing punishments for various infractions, the manager stays at a dignified distance from any necessary disciplinary action.

Great inequalities exist in the Philippines. The majority of the population is poor. But mobility (or the hope of mobility) exists. The most important influence on Filipinos is the family. Nepotism is common and is not considered to be detrimental.

☑ Know Before You Go

The Philippines is prone to disasters. Many are natural events, such as volcanoes, floods, mudslides, earthquakes, and typhoons. But some are within human control, like boat accidents. If you are considering taking a ferry, examine it closely—if it looks unsafe or overcrowded, seek alternative transportation. Whatever your travel plans, be sure to obtain medical evacuation insurance.

To avoid the monsoon season, try to schedule your visits between September and May. Avoid major Catholic holidays as well, as many Filipinos will observe Christmas and Easter celebrations.

There is a risk of getting malaria, typhus, or cholera outside of the major urban areas. Be sure to review the inocula-tions that your physician or the CDC (at *www.cdc.gov*) suggests.

Illegal logging has added to the high number of disasters in the Philippines. More than half of the Philippines' forests were ravaged over the last century. This deforestation, combined with fierce tropical storms, promoted flash flooding and landslides in the eastern and northern regions. These catastrophes took at least 5,000 lives in 1991, and thousands more in the northeast in late 2004.

▶ CULTURAL ORIENTATION

Cognitive Styles: How Filipinos Organize and Process Information

Filipinos love to converse. They are generally open to information but do not change their attitudes readily. Because most of their education is by rote, they tend to process informa-tion subjectively and associatively. They tend to become personally involved in problems rather than using rules and laws to solve them.

Negotiation Strategies: What Filipinos Accept as Evidence

Most truth comes from direct feelings. Although some absolute truths may rest on faith in ideologies (such as those of the Catholic Church), few are easily traced back to objective facts.

Value Systems: The Basis for Behavior

The culture of the Philippines is rich and diverse. China, Islam, Spain, and the United States all left their marks. The following three sections identify the Value Systems in the predomi-nant culture—their methods of dividing right from wrong, good from evil, and so forth.

Locus of Decision-Making

Individuals act in the context of a group (the family is the most important group). Thus, they must seek the consensus of the group, because the individual rarely feels that he or she has the final say on anything. Decisions are made from a relational perspective. Filipinos must get to know you, and this involves asking about your family and personal background. Rather than presenting their own ideas, they more often react to the input of others. It is difficult for them to be confrontational and give an outright "no."

Sources of Anxiety Reduction

The nuclear and extended family is the main source of support and stability. The whole family may be shamed by the action of one member. Much of the stability of life is found in the adherence to tradition, especially the observance of rituals that maintain relationships. Many of these are connected with religion. Interpersonal relationships bring with them a sense of obligation. Reciprocity in relationships is practiced on all levels, and paying one's obligations binds the persons involved more closely.

Issues of Equality/Inequality

Filipino politics is a system that serves its players, not the people. However, Filipinos are strongly in favor of democracy, individual freedom, education, and freedom of the press. Filipinos are very status conscious. This sometimes extends to issues of race—for example, the lighter the skin, the higher the status. There is a preoccupation with chastity and safety.

▶ BUSINESS PRACTICES

Punctuality, Appointments, and Local Time

- Time is malleable. Foreign executives are expected to be on time to business meetings. Filipinos tend to be reasonably punctual.
- Everyone, even a foreigner, is expected to be late for social events. But the exact measure of the delay depends upon the status of each person. (The highest-ranking person should arrive last.) Rather than try to decipher the ranking of each party guest, foreigners should just ask their host (in private) what time they should actually arrive.
- The exception to the socially correct delay is the Filipino wedding. Guests are expected to arrive on time. Only the bride may be late.
- Appointments can be scheduled far in advance of your arrival in the Philippines.
- English is the language of most business transactions and virtually all business or government correspondence.
- Without introductions, it is very difficult to meet decision-makers. You will end up scheduling many appointments with subordinates. Not only will you have to progress through levels of influence, but you must progress through levels of formality—from introductions at social events, to semiofficial luncheons, to scheduled business meetings.
- A skilled representative is often hired to cut through several levels of management to get to the decision-maker.
- Midmornings, midafternoons, or late afternoons are usually best for appointments.
- The official national Independence Day holiday is June 12th, which was the date of declaration of independence from Spain (in 1898). July 4, 1946, was their date of independence from the United States.
- The Philippines is eight hours ahead of Greenwich Mean Time (G.M.T. +8), or thirteen hours ahead of U.S. Eastern Standard Time (E.S.T. +13).

Philippines

Cultural Note

Filipinos are strong believers in forging relationships and maintaining *pakikisama* (smooth relations) at all costs. Confrontation is unthinkable and a sign of disrespect. Part of this process is the *utang na loob* (reciprocity) system whereby one business (or political) connection leads to other, more lucrative, deals. Acceptance of a favor or reference will call for a larger one in return. Beware the Filipino bearing gifts—a simple "thank you" will not suffice.

Negotiating

- The pace of business negotiations in the Philippines is slower than in northern Europe or North America. It would be unusual to complete a complex transaction in only one trip.

- Negotiating is generally done in a formal, precise manner. Pay attention to the hierarchy of the negotiators, and maintain a respectful, professional demeanor. The higher the negotiator's position, the more formal your interactions should be.

- Speak in quiet, gentle tones. Filipinos revere harmony. The only time you are likely to hear loud Filipinos is when they are boisterously happy.

- Filipinos want to please the people they are speaking to, so they are liable to say "yes" to various offers. This simply means that the Filipinos do not want to offend you with an outright "no." In the Philippines, "yes" can mean anything from "I agree" to "maybe" to "I hope you can tell from my lack of enthusiasm that I really mean 'no.'"

- To ensure that a Filipino really means yes, you must get it in writing. If possible, try to get written agreement at each stage in your negotiations. Filipinos feel honor-bound to fulfill a written commitment.

- Expect to see your Filipino business partners often at social situations. Never decline an invitation to a social event.

- When you interrupt Filipinos during a meal, they are obliged to ask you to join in. This is a formality; just thank them and decline, saying that you have already eaten.

- Remember that social contacts are more important in the Philippines than business ones. A Filipino must like you and be comfortable with you to do business. This relationship does not extend to your company. If your company replaces you with another executive, the new executive will have to forge this relationship anew (unless the new executive is a blood relative of yours).

- Business cards may be printed in English; it is not necessary to translate them into Pilipino. The exchange of business cards is more casual than in other parts of Asia; a Filipino businessperson to whom you have given a card may—or may not—give you one of his or hers. The visiting businessperson should be the first to offer a card.

- If a Filipino gives you a business card with their home phone handwritten upon it, take that as an invitation to call. Business in the Philippines evolves out of social interaction, most of which takes place outside the office.

- Once you are accepted, Filipinos are very sociable and love to talk. Expect to be asked very personal questions, such as "Why are you not married?" They will also ask how much you paid for something, out of concern that you may have been cheated.

Cultural Note

Filipinos smile constantly. However, as with the Japanese, a smile is not a ubiquitous sign of pleasure, affection, or amusement.

Filipinos may smile or laugh in situations that westerners consider inappropriate. Smiles hide embarrassment and discord. Filipino businessmen may laugh at the most serious part of a business meeting, and a Filipino physician may smile while telling a patient he is seriously ill.

While foreigners are not expected to smile as much as Filipinos, they are expected to restrain their temper. As in other parts of Asia, it is considered shameful to express anger in public; a person who loses his or her temper is not respected.

Furthermore, because the Philippines is a more violent country than Japan, Thailand, etc., expressing anger at someone can easily provoke a similar response. Foreigners can unintentionally push a Filipino into a public outburst, as the Filipino feels he must act to regain his honor—whatever the cost. If you must reprimand a Filipino employee, do it calmly and in private.

Business Entertaining

- Food is vitally important in Filipino culture. Social occasions always involve food. In reality, the standard Pilipino greeting "*Kumain ka na ba?*" translates as "Have you eaten?"
- Celebrate the conclusion of a business deal by inviting your Filipino partners to a restaurant. The person who issued the invitation always pays—unless it was a woman, in which case most Filipino businessmen will insist upon paying.
- Invite the wives of your business partners to dinner, but not to a luncheon.

  Expect to be invited to dinners and parties at the home of your Filipino partner (unless he or she is Chinese; Chinese rarely entertain at home). Such parties traditionally have numerous guests, including many relatives. Remember to show respect for elders. You may or may not be individually introduced to everyone.
- Most households have servants, including a cook. Compliment the hostess on the decor, but be aware that she probably did not prepare the food herself.
- Desserts are very popular in the Philippines at both lunch and dinner. If you are hosting a luncheon, be sure to provide a dessert.
- Social events often end with dancing and singing. Expect to be invited to sing.
- Despite boisterous partying and hard drinking (by men), Filipinos find public drunkenness shameful. Do not get out of control.

Cultural Note

Never appear too eager to begin eating at a party; allow the hostess to ask you several times to sit down. A person who jumps at food is considered uncouth and greedy.

This behavior holds true for social invitations also. Invitations must be extended multiple times, and Filipinos will probably respond with a polite "yes" without feeling committed to attend. Reconfirm the invitation at least once. Do not be surprised if someone declines via a third party. You can try sending out written invitations with an RSVP, but because Filipinos feel honor-bound by written commitments, few will respond.

PROTOCOL

Greetings
- Foreign businessmen should expect to shake hands firmly with Filipino men, both upon introduction and at subsequent meetings.
- Traditionally, there is no physical contact between men and women in public. Men should wait for a Filipino woman to offer her hand, which most Filipino businesswomen will do.
- Foreign businesswomen may initiate a handshake with Filipino men or women.
- Close female friends in the Philippines hug and kiss upon greeting. Similarly, close male friends may exhibit extended physical contact, such as holding hands or leaving an arm around a friend's shoulder.

Titles/Forms of Address
- Most people you meet should be addressed with a title and their surname. Many professionals have titles, because Filipino companies may reward employees with titles instead of additional pay or responsibilities.
- Persons who do not have professional titles should be addressed, in English, as "Mr.," "Mrs.," or "Miss," plus their surname.
- Wives of persons with important titles are sometimes addressed as "Mrs." plus the husband's title (e.g., Mrs. Senator or Mrs. Mayor).
- Upper-class Filipinos may follow the Hispanic tradition of having two surnames: one from their father, which is listed first, followed by one from their mother.
- Most Filipinos have nicknames, many of which sound incongruous to foreigners. Once a Filipino invites you to address him or her by a nickname, you are expected to do so. An example is the recent vice president of the Philippines, Manuel de Castro, who went by "Noli."
- After such an invitation, you should invite a Filipino to address you by your nickname. (If you don't have one, you might like to make one up).
- Flattery by means of "verbal promotion" is common in the Philippines. A police officer may be referred to as "Captain," a police captain may be called "Major," and so on.

Gestures
- A great deal of information can be communicated via eye contact and eyebrow movement. Filipinos may greet each other by making eye contact followed by raising and lowering the eyebrows.
- A traditional Filipino may demonstrate respect upon greeting an elder by placing the elder's hand or knuckles on his or her forehead.
- Because of the years of U.S. military presence in the Philippines, most North American gestures are recognized.

- The foremost obscene gesture in both the United States and the Philippines involves an extended middle finger. However, in the Philippines, that finger is pointed at the person or thing being insulted.
- Since pointing can easily be taken for an insulting gesture, Filipinos rarely indicate objects or directions by pointing with their fingers. Instead, they indicate with a glance or by pursing their lips.
- Indicating "two" with the fingers is done by holding up the ring and little finger, instead of the forefinger and middle finger. The thumb is not used to count numbers in the Philippines.
- Staring has various nuances in the Philippines, most of them negative. Foreigners should avoid staring at Filipinos, who can easily interpret a stare as belligerence. If you are stared at, look away.
- As in much of the world, to beckon someone you hold your hand out, palm downward, and make a scooping motion with the fingers. Beckoning someone with the palm up and wagging one finger, as in the United States, can be construed as an insult.
- To stand tall with your hands on your hips—the "arms akimbo" or "offsides" position in soccer—is always interpreted as an aggressive posture. Worse, it expresses an aggressive challenge—and in the Philippines, belligerence is often met with belligerence.
- Looking down is useful to avoid giving offense when making one's way through a crowd or between two people who are conversing. This may also be accompanied by an outstretched, flat hand (like a karate chop) or with both hands clasped together; the hand(s) are in front, preceding the direction of motion.
- A Filipino may try to attract your attention by brushing a finger against your elbow.

Gifts

- Gift giving is an important part of Filipino society. Flowers and food are the most common gifts, although there are situations in which a handful of small coins is traditional.
- When invited to a Filipino home, bring (or have sent before you arrive) flowers or a delicacy to your hostess. Avoid bringing alcohol or a substantial food, as this may imply that your host cannot serve enough to satisfy guests.
- However, exceptions are made for a specialty dish or food that only you can provide, such as a recipe from your home country. A thank-you note is appropriate afterward; some people also send a small gift.
- After a dinner party, Filipinos often give their guests extra food to take home, an ancient tradition called *pabaon*.
- At Christmas, you will be expected to give a token gift—such as a company calendar—to seemingly everyone you know or do business with. Your list should include everyone who works for you, all service personnel you deal with regularly (your postal clerks, your

security guards), and anyone who makes your life easier by cooperating with you, such as the secretary of an important client.

- Filipinos follow the Asian habit of not opening gifts in the presence of the giver. Traditionally, if the recipient is not happy with the gift, he or she avoids embarrassment by opening it away from the giver. Furthermore, Filipinos abhor appearing greedy; to open a gift immediately would give this impression. Do not be dismayed if your gift is casually set aside and ignored; you will be thanked for it at a later date.

> **Cultural Note**
> Foreigners are honored in the Philippines by being invited to family events: weddings, anniversaries, baptisms, and so on. It is an even greater honor to be asked to participate in such events as a sponsor in a wedding or a godparent in a baptism. Bring a gift, whether you are a guest or a participant. These events are part of establishing the personal relationships that are all-important in Filipino business practices.

Dress

- Because of the heat and humidity, business dress for Filipinos is often casual: dark trousers and white, short-sleeved shirts for men, without a tie; white long-sleeved blouses and skirts or pantsuits for women. Despite this simplicity, these clothes will be neat, clean, and fashionable. Filipinos are very style conscious.
- As a foreigner, you should dress more conservatively until you are sure what degree of formality is expected. Men should expect to wear a suit and tie; businesswomen wear white blouses and dark suits, pantsuits, or skirts.
- Men may wear a business suit for formal occasions, such as the theater, a formal dinner party, and so forth, but women are expected to wear a cocktail dress. Long evening gowns are required only on rare occasions, such as diplomatic functions.
- Neither men nor women should wear shorts or sandals in public, except at the beach.

    Because Filipinos are so competitively fashionable, some offices require their workers to wear uniforms.

> **Cultural Note**
> Filipinos consider everyone worthy of respect. The more important you are, the more you are expected to be humble and generous. Even the requests of a Filipino beggar are rejected with the phrase "*Patawarin po*" (Forgive me, sir). The Filipino is literally apologizing to the beggar for not giving him anything. Never brusquely dismiss anyone in the Philippines.

Philippines

Poland

Republic of Poland
Local short form: Polska
Local long form: Rzeczpospolita Polska

Cultural Note

Poles sometimes describe themselves as living between the bear and the wolf. To counter the (Russian) bear, Poles joined NATO. They hoped that they would need no protection from the now-peaceful (German) wolf. One of the earliest acts by unified Germany was the ratification of its borders, assuring Poland that it would not seek to regain German land lost to Poland after World War II.

However, without the support of the German government, some Germans are suing for the return of Polish property they lost in 1945. Some 10 million ethnic Germans were deported from the new Poland, under the supervision of the USSR. At least 30,000 of these Germans died in the exodus, from disease, starvation, or violence. (This is not an incident Poles like to talk about.)

Now that Poland has joined the European Union, it is subject to rulings from the European Court in Strasbourg. The German deportees may yet succeed in regaining land from Poland.

▶ WHAT'S YOUR CULTURAL IQ?

1. The name "Poland" describes the country's geography. What does "Poland" mean in Slavic?
   a. The hill country
   b. The flatlands
   c. The borderlands
   d. That unpronounceable place straddling the Vistula River

   ANSWER: b. Poland is mostly flat.

2. TRUE or FALSE? Although the Poles have been in their current location for some 2,000 years, the country of Poland has sometimes disappeared off the map of Europe.

   ANSWER: TRUE. Most notably, Poland was partitioned three times, with Polish land divided up by Germany, Russia, and Austria. Poland vanished entirely in 1795 and did not reappear as an independent entity until 1918.

3. Several Polish writers have won the Nobel Prize. Match the following Nobel Laureates with their works or genre:
   a. Czeslaw Milosz (1911–2004)
   b. Wladyslaw Stanislaw Reymont (1867–1925)
   c. Henryk Sienkiewicz (1846–1916)
   d. Isaac Bashevis Singer (1904–1991)

   1. *Quo Vadis?* and historical novels
   2. Poetry, essays, and translations
   3. Stories on Jewish life
   4. The Peasants and epic novels

ANSWERS: a. 2; b. 4; c. 1; d. 3. Singer, although he was born in Poland and worked in Warsaw as a journalist before moving to the United States in 1935, wrote in Yiddish, not Polish.

Cultural Note

In addition to these male Nobel laureates, two Polish women have won Nobel prizes. Poet Wislawa Szymborska won the Nobel for literature in 1996. And, with her husband Pierre Curie, Warsaw-born scientist Maria Skłodowska-Curie won twice: in 1903 for physics (the first Nobel awarded to a woman) and in 1922 for Chemistry.

▶ TIPS ON DOING BUSINESS IN POLAND

- Polish is one of the more difficult European languages for native speakers of English. It is complex, subtle, and formal. Certain sounds in Polish—notably the soft s, sh, cz, and szcz—are particularly hard for English speakers to master. However, learning even a few phrases in Polish will endear a foreigner to the Polish people. Polish businesspeople often speak German or English.
- In common with other Slavic groups, Poles give the appearance of being rather dour. Smiles are reserved for friends; they are rarely used in public. (When U.S. game shows were adapted for Polish television, the biggest problem was getting the serious Polish contestants to look happy and excited on camera!)
- Despite theoretical equality under the law, Poland is still a male-dominated society. International businesswomen report that Poland is one of the more difficult places in Europe to be taken seriously. Businesswomen must also consider how they want to socialize with Polish executives—a process that invariably includes large quantities of alcohol.

Cultural Note

The Communist regime was overthrown in 1989, so an entire generation of Poles has grown up in a free society. While they are not nostalgic for that era, there is an ironic appreciation among some young people for the "socialist-realist style." Propaganda posters from the Stalinist era have recently become collectables.

▶ COUNTRY BACKGROUND

History

The very existence of Poland is a testament to the tenacity of the Polish people, considering that it has disappeared from the face of Europe several times.

The Slavic tribes that would later become the Polish people settled in this northern corner of Eastern Europe more than 2,000 years ago. The nation took its name from one of these tribes, the Polane (the people of the plain). The Polish nation dates its existence to

Poland

the tenth century, with the ascension of King Mieszko I in A.D. 963. Mieszko adopted the Roman Catholic faith in 966, and the country remains staunchly Catholic to this day.

Poland flourished culturally and economically, but not politically. The country's flat, fertile plains and lack of defensible frontiers have made it a constant target for its aggressive neighbors. In 1386 the Polish state opted for unification with neighboring Lithuania, and for a time Polish fortunes were strengthened. But again political decline set in, and the country was partitioned three times between the German, Russian, and Austrian empires. By 1795, the time of the third partition, Poland had vanished.

The 1815 Congress of Vienna decreed that a Kingdom of Poland still existed, but only within the confines of the Russian Empire, where it was legally ruled by the Russian czar.

For the next hundred years the Poles continually worked for independence, with Catholicism serving as a rallying point against their Russian Orthodox overlords.

It was World War I that returned Poland to the map. When Russia sued the Central Powers for peace, the Treaty of Brest-Litovsk in 1918 dismembered the Russian Empire. Poland re-emerged as an independent state. But this independence proved to be short-lived. World War II began when Nazi Germany invaded Poland. Over 6 million Poles, including virtually the entire population of Polish Jews, died during the occupation. The Germans were pushed out by the Soviet Army in 1945, and the Polish borders were redrawn in their current configuration.

But Poland was not yet free. Instead, Poland became a Communist state under Soviet domination. Again, the Poles protested against their Russian overlords.

The first glimmering of success came in 1981 with the organization of the Solidarity labor union. Martial law was unable to stifle the will of the people, and (after the Polish regime ascertained that the Soviets would not intervene) Solidarity was legalized in 1989.

Political liberalization and a transition to a market economy were followed by the election of Solidarity leader Lech Walesa as the leader of the Polish Republic in late 1990.

Despite the opposition of Russia, Poland joined the North Atlantic Treaty Organization (NATO) in 1999. Poland joined the European Union in May of 2004.

Type of Government

The Republic of Poland is a multiparty democracy. The president is the chief of state; the prime minister is the head of government. There are two legislative houses: the upper house (the Senate) and the lower house (the Sejm). Within the legislative branch of the government, the Sejm has most of the power; the Senate may only suggest amendments to legislation passed by the Sejm or delay it. Both bodies are democratically elected.

Poland contributed troops to the U.S.-led Coalition in the occupation of Iraq in 2003.

For current government data, check with the Embassy of Poland at *www.polandembassy.org*.

> **Cultural Note**
>
> Polish has several aspects that make it different from other Slavic tongues. There are nasal vowels that are unique to Polish. Also, only in Polish does the stress typically fall on the penultimate syllable. In Czech and Slovak the stress is on the first syllable, while in Russian the stress shifts.

Language

Polish is the official language. Closely related to Czech, Polish is placed in the Slavic branch of the Indo-European linguistic family (English is also part of this family). Polish is written in a modified Latin alphabet, not the Cyrillic alphabet of Russian.

Ethnologue.com has identified twelve languages spoken in Poland; one of these, Prussian, became extinct around 1700.

> **Cultural Note**
>
> Pope John Paul II, the first Polish pope of the Roman Catholic Church, remains a hero to most Poles. They also believe that he had a major role in preventing the USSR from crushing the Solidarity Movement in the 1980s, which eventually led to Poland becoming free of Soviet domination.

The Polish View

Catholicism is essentially the only religion in Poland today. Only 1.5 percent of the population is identified as belonging to another religion (Orthodox), although almost 10 percent of Poles are nonreligious (an atheist legacy of Soviet-dominated Poland).

During centuries of foreign domination, the national aspirations of the Polish people were sublimated into the Catholic Church. The Church was the single most important influence in preventing Poland's cultural absorption by Lutheran Prussia and Orthodox Russia. The Polish people are in debt to their Church for preserving their cultural identity.

With Poland free and independent at last, it is not surprising that the Catholic Church should want to collect on that debt by having a say in how Poland is run. Poland is now challenging Ireland for the honor of being "the most Catholic country in the world." As in Ireland, the major friction arises over the Church's prohibition of contraception and abortion. But unlike Ireland, Poland had abortion on demand during the decades of Soviet domination. New restrictions on abortion have been passed, but they are opposed by many Polish citizens. Businesses (including medical insurers) whose products or services touch on birth control issues should be prepared for further changes in Poland.

While capitalism has been more successful in Poland than in any other former Warsaw Pact nation, it has also created a society of haves and have-nots. While most Poles are better off than they were under Communism, some (including farmers, miners, pensioners, and teachers) are not.

Poland

Despite the fact that virtually all of Poland's Jews were exterminated by the Nazis in World War II, anti-Semitism is still extant in Poland. Anti-Semitism can be found in many sectors of Polish society.

The overriding concern for Poles is national security. After centuries of domination by Russians and Germans, the Poles are determined to maintain their freedom. The Polish government does not believe that their fellow Europeans will guarantee their security, so they place their faith in the United States. Poland is the greatest ally the United States has in Europe; Poland even sent 2,600 troops to support the occupation of Iraq and led a multinational force (most from Eastern Europe) of 8,000.

Poland and Russia are locked into a complex historical relationship that colors all cross-border interactions. Many Poles see Russia as the architect of Poland's misfortunes. Some interactions that involve Poles and Russians will involve these beliefs.

In the short-term, Poles seem to be open to change and welcome the introduction of new business products or ideas.

☑ Know Before You Go

As with other Eastern European countries, the greatest hazard to travelers is property crime. Pickpocketing, theft from hotel rooms, and auto theft are common. Violent crime is rare but is an increasing problem.

The weather can be a hazard. Poland is subject to a highly variable climate. Winters can be very cold and snowy, or mild and wet. Summers are sometimes very hot and dry, especially in the eastern portion of the country. Poland is very flat, and flooding is common.

Much of Poland's infrastructure is in need of repair. Be cautious of road conditions when driving. Rural roads can be dangerous at night.

Poland has had some problems with bribery, and several Polish politicians have been removed for corruption.

Most business travelers come away from Poland with no more damage than a hangover (from trying to keep pace with Poles drinking vodka).

▶ CULTURAL ORIENTATION

Cognitive Styles: How Poles Organize and Process Information

The Polish culture has always been open to information from the West. With the demise of Communism, many aspects of education in Poland are in a state of flux. Poles tend to be abstractive, processing information conceptually and analytically. However Poles also value personal relationships as much as the law.

Cultural Note

Interpersonal relationships are all-important to Poles, even in business. This makes business use of the Internet problematic. Although Internet access is substantial, few small to medium-sized businesses currently make purchases online.

Poles are not technophobes, though. Cell phones and electronic gadgets are popular, and text messaging is widespread.

Negotiation Strategies: What Poles Accept as Evidence

In Poland, truth consists of objective facts combined with subjective feelings. Faith in ideologies has changed rapidly, shifting from the ideologies of the Communist party to those of
nationalism, democracy, and the Catholic Church. Truth may be viewed through the prism
of such ideologies.

Value Systems: The Basis for Behavior

Since the fall of Communism and the rise of democracy, the value systems of Poland are
being influenced more and more by those of the West. This includes both the United States
and Poland's fellow members in the European Union.

Poles are discovering a newfound respect for the law. In the past, Poles often felt that
rules were made to benefit the rulers (who were often not Polish). Today, Poles make their
own rules. How well Poles will adhere to the multitudinous regulations of the European
Union remains to be seen.

The following three sections identify the Value Systems in the predominant culture—
their methods of dividing right from wrong, good from evil, and so forth.

Locus of Decision-Making

In the new, democratic Poland, more decision-making responsibility has been placed on
individuals. Poles have a strong sense of individualism and democracy, plus a belief that all
citizens should influence the way the society is governed. In many instances, the individual
may transfer decision-making responsibility to the group as a whole or to a consensus of
privileged individuals. There is a tendency to expect decisions to be made at a higher level.

Sources of Anxiety Reduction

Studies have shown that Poles have a high index of uncertainty avoidance. As a result, Poles
use laws and morality to give structure to their worldview.

Post-Communist freedom is perceived as threatening most of the structures the Poles have
depended upon for stability and security. However, since most Poles are Catholics, the Church
is a significant factor in filling this need. Polish Catholicism has been described as emotional
and traditional, and the Poles are considered the most devout of all European Catholics. A
strong extended family also helps to give structure and security. Many Poles are unsure about
whether Poland's membership in the European Union will be a benefit or a detriment.

Issues of Equality/Inequality

Traditionally, Poles have lived in a hierarchical society. The structure of the organization is
dictated from above.

Although Poland has a largely homogeneous population, there are substantial inequalities between its citizens. There is some disjunction between private and public morality.

Poland is a male-dominated society. Only recently have a substantial number of women
advanced beyond clerical status in Polish businesses.

Poland

▶ BUSINESS PRACTICES

Punctuality, Appointments, and Local Time

- As a foreigner, you are expected to be on time for all appointments.
- Poles have become more punctual since the end of the Communist regime. Today, most Poles will be prompt for business appointments.
- The Polish workday starts early, generally at 8:00 A.M. Do not be surprised if someone offers you an 8:00 A.M. appointment.
- Many Polish workers do not take a lunch break but work straight through the end of the day. Factory workers tend to be finished by 3:00 P.M.; office workers by 4:00 P.M. Even executives are usually done by 5:00 P.M. Many people also work on Saturday.
- Business "lunches" are often held quite late, around 4:00 or 5:00 P.M., after the end of the business day. No one goes back to work after lunch, so only the time of day differentiates the business lunch from a business dinner. Dinner in Poland starts around 8:00 or 8:30 P.M.
- Requests for appointments should be made in writing (via e-mail) when possible. Translating the request into Polish will make a good impression.
- Poles count six distinct seasons. In addition to spring, summer, winter, and fall, they recognize early spring (*przedwiosnie*) and early winter (*przedzimie*).
- Sunday is the traditional day for visiting family and friends in Poland.
- Poland's Independence Day is celebrated on November 11.
- Poland is one hour ahead of Greenwich Mean Time (G.M.T. +1), and thus six hours ahead of U.S. Eastern Standard Time (E.S.T. +6).

Negotiating

- It is difficult to predict how long it will take to negotiate a deal. Poles used to be very cautious, and contracts could take months to complete. However, Poland's new entrepreneurs are more amenable—almost anxious to move quickly. This is more common with small enterprises.
- Poles can be very tough customers, insisting on their own terms. They sometimes take pride in being difficult—as the rest of the European Union found out once Poland became a member.
- The single most commonly heard objection in Poland is "the price is too high." Foreign companies must be flexible to penetrate the Polish market. For example, some foreign companies ship their products unassembled to reduce Polish import duties.
- Office doors are usually kept closed in Poland. Knock and wait before you enter. Either you will be told to enter or the occupant will open the door.
- A local Polish representative will be vital to successful operations. Polish business runs on relationships, and, as an outsider, you will need a Polish native for his connections. He

Poland

will also be able to get you things in short supply, from prestigious office space to scarce restaurant reservations.

- Bring plenty of business cards and give one to everyone you meet. Poles tend to bring more than one person to a meeting, so you should bring a good supply of cards.
- One side of the card should be in your native language, the other in Polish. However, because English is the most popular second language, opinions differ on whether or not it is necessary to translate an English business card into Polish.
- Proposals, reports, and promotional materials should be translated into Polish. If graphics are included in this material, make sure they are well done and neatly printed. Standards are high, because Poland has graphic artists that are the equal of any in Europe.
- While your presentation materials are important, Poles tend to operate on their gut feelings. If no bond has been established between you and your Polish counterparts, no presentation will be good enough.
- To counter objections from your Polish prospects (who may be somewhat more risk-averse), cite examples of similar deals that were successful.

Business Entertaining

- Business lunches and dinners are popular, but breakfast meetings are virtually unknown.
- Poland is still recovering from a housing shortage. Because apartments can be very cramped, do not be surprised if a Polish businessperson does not invite you home. Most entertaining is done in clubs and restaurants.
- The person who issues the invitation to a restaurant is usually the one who pays the bill. However, it is customary for a foreigner to offer to pay. Foreign businesswomen should intercept the waiter before dinner starts to arrange to pay. This will avoid any controversy over the tab, since Polish men may not want to let a woman pay.
- Despite having to go to work early, Poles love to stay up late, talking and drinking. Leaving early may insult them, so be prepared for a long night.
- Although there is an effort to promote beer as an acceptable drink (most Poles consider beer a chaser), vodka is still the drink of choice. (Poland makes an excellent potato vodka.) Don't get trapped in a vodka-drinking contest with Poles; you'll lose. Expect your glass to be refilled every time it is empty until the vodka runs out.
- Learn to give a Polish toast: "*Na zdrovya*" and the optional answer "*Dai bozhe*"—God grant it.
- Do not bring up your background if you are of German, Hungarian, or Russian descent. Poland's relations with those neighbors have not always been cordial.
- Anti-Semitism is also a subject to avoid. Remember that the Nazis located most of the death camps on Polish soil, not in Germany itself.

Poland

▶ **PROTOCOL**

Greetings

- Shake hands when you meet, and when you leave.
- You may want to wait for a Polish woman to extend her hand before offering to shake hands. If you feel an additional expression of respect is called for, simply make a short bow.
- Close Polish friends or relatives may greet each other effusively, with much hugging and kissing of cheeks. These are most common between women or between women and men, but Polish men occasionally kiss each other on the cheek. Three kisses, each one on an alternate cheek, are traditional.
- Food and sports are good topics to bring up, but expect conversations to be wide-ranging.
- Most of the businesspeople you meet will be male. Admonishing Poles for sexist attitudes, real or perceived, will not help your relationship.

Titles/Forms of Address

- As in some other Slavic cultures, the final letter in a woman's surname may be different from that of a man's. Where this is the case, a woman's surname will end in the letter a—thus, it is Mr. Solski and Mrs. Solska.
- The simplest way to address a Polish professional is by using "Mr.," "Mrs.," or "Miss" and their job title.
  - Mr. = *Pan* ("pahn")
  - Mrs. = *Pani* ("pah'-nee")
  - Miss = *Panna* ("pah'-nah")
  - Mr. Executive = *Pan Dyrektor*
  - Mr. Reporter = *Pan Redaktor*
- If a Pole lacks a title, be sure to address him as Mr., plus his surname. Only close adult friends will address each other by their first names.

Gestures

- In social situations, when a Pole flicks his finger against his neck, he is inviting you to join him for a drink (probably vodka).
- Do not chew gum while speaking to someone.
- Do not litter; Poles are shocked at the sight of anyone throwing trash anywhere but in a trash receptacle.
- Avoid loud behavior in public; Poles tend to be a quiet people. You will notice that Poles speak more softly than North Americans do.
- Polish men tend to have traditional views of acceptable female behavior. Women who speak forthrightly may encounter resistance from Polish men.

- When asking directions from strangers, a woman should approach either a police officer or another woman. Approaching a man will probably be interpreted as flirting.

Gifts

- A foreign gift is appropriate the first time you meet a Polish businessperson. Liquor (anything except vodka) is a good choice.
- Always bring a gift when visiting a Polish home, even for a brief visit. Flowers are the most common gift. Give the flowers, unwrapped, to your hostess. Always bring an odd number of flowers, and avoid red roses (used for courting) and chrysanthemums (used at funerals).

Dress

- Business dress is formal and conservative: suits and ties for men, dresses for women. Colors tend to be muted.
- For casualwear, jeans are ubiquitous for both men and women. Jeans with a dressy shirt or blouse will get one through most nonbusiness situations. Exceptions are:
  - Expensive restaurants, the theater, and the opera (these require suits and ties or dresses)
  - Dinner invitations in a Polish home (these require jackets and ties or dressy pants or skirts)
  - Formal invitations, as on New Year's Eve (these require tuxedos or gowns)

Cultural Note

Living in a hostile environment, often ruled by enemies, the Poles have developed two separate codes of behavior. In public, Poles can be demanding, distant, and abrupt. But in private, among friends or relatives, Poles tend to be warm, generous, and talkative. Long conversations lasting late into the night are a Polish tradition.

To see private behavior in a public setting, go to a train station or an airport. There, Poles engage in intimate farewells that last until the transport pulls away. There is a Polish saying that goes, "The English leave without saying good-bye. The Poles say good-bye but do not leave."

Portugal

Portuguese Republic

Local long form: Republica Portuguesa

Cultural Note

Although Portuguese is related to Spanish, and many Portuguese understand Spanish, foreigners should never presume that knowledge of Spanish is sufficient to do business in Portugal. The Portuguese consider it insulting when foreigners constantly try to communicate in Spanish.

▶ WHAT'S YOUR CULTURAL IQ?

1. Like Rome, Lisbon—the capital of Portugal—was built on seven hills near a river. Tradition holds that Rome was founded by Romulus. Which mythological character is credited with founding Lisbon?

   a. Aeneas   c. Bacchus

   b. Apollo   d. Ulysses

   ANSWER: d. According to local legend, Ulysses founded Lisbon (which the Romans called Olisipo) during his wanderings after the fall of Troy.

2. TRUE or FALSE? Geographically speaking, Portugal is not a Mediterranean country.

   ANSWER: TRUE. Portugal's only coastline is on the Atlantic Ocean. It is not on the Mediterranean Sea at all. However, its culture has much in common with other Mediterranean nations.

3. The *fado* is the most important indigenous style of music in Portugal. TRUE or FALSE? The fado is a happy, celebratory harvest song associated with the Portuguese countryside.

   ANSWER: FALSE. The fado is associated with urban life and is invariably melancholy and wistful.

Cultural Note

"God gave the Portuguese a small country as a cradle but all the world as their grave."
   —Jesuit priest Antonio Vieira (1608–1697), referring to the all-too-common fate of Portuguese explorers and colonizers.

Portugal

▶ TIPS ON DOING BUSINESS IN PORTUGAL

- Portugal was a highly stratified society for hundreds of years, and hierarchy remains important in the business climate. If an owner of a firm basically runs the company for his own benefit, that is accepted as natural. The owner can use it as an employment vehicle for members of his family or friends, or dispose of the firm as he wishes.
- This emphasis on social and business positions helps explain why it is vital to develop contacts and relationships with Portuguese executives. When the network is open, business is done.
- Women should be aware that machismo is a cultural norm in Portugal. Be certain to present a professional, capable image at all times, and do not be surprised if your Portuguese contacts consistently look to the men on your team for answers—even if you are the senior executive at meetings. Resolve this problem before the first meeting by briefing your male employees; to confirm your position, they should defer to you during discussions, and reinforce your opinions.

Cultural Note

Personal honor has historically been considered supremely important. Traditionally, one's honor could be lost not only through one's own actions, but through the actions of one's family as well. Challenges to a person's honor had to be addressed immediately. Even humor at someone's expense can still elicit an angry response. Naturally, these traditions evolved in small communities where everyone knew each other and extended families lived together. They are less applicable now in the anonymity of urban life.

▶ COUNTRY BACKGROUND

History

Over the course of history, Portugal's coastline has been populated by a succession of cultures. Ancient Phoenicians, Carthaginians, and Greeks preceded the Romans, who conquered the region in 27 B.C. Subsequently, the Visigoths and the Moors governed until the twelfth century. In 1140, Portugal became an independent nation under King Alfonso Henriques. During the fourteenth and fifteenth centuries, Portuguese explorers immensely expanded their empire. Both Spain and France temporarily ruled Portugal before the Republic of Portugal was established in 1910.

Type of Government

From 1974 to 1976, Portugal underwent a nearly bloodless transition from an authoritarian government to a constitutional democracy. Today, Portugal is a multiparty parliamentary democracy.

The parliament is known as the Assembly of the Republic. It is unicameral, and its members are elected by direct universal suffrage. Deputies serve for four years. The president is the chief of state, while the prime minister is the head of the government.

The 1976 constitution was revised in 1982 and 1989. It placed the military under civilian control and eliminated the Marxist rhetoric and socialist goals of the first document. This led to the privatization of many sectors of the economy, such as the financial and telecommunications industries. It also called for increasing decentralization of the administration. Portugal joined the European Community (now the European Union) in January of 1986. Membership stimulated liberalization of economic policy, which resulted in one of the best economic performances and one of the lowest unemployment rates in the 1990s. Performance diminished in recent years, partly based upon a poor educational system.

For current government data, check with the Embassy of Portugal at *www.portugal.org*.

Language

Portuguese, a Romance language, is spoken throughout Portugal. Outside Portugal, (i.e., in Brazil) the language has altered somewhat due to the influence of other language and speech patterns. Ethnologue.com has categorized six different languages spoken in Portugal.

Cultural Note

Many people who have written about Portuguese characteristics mention several terms: a sense of *saudade* (the sad knowledge that one is living in diminished times); *siso* (which is similar to a sense of prudence), and *loucura* (which would almost be the opposite of prudence—more like "excess"). While these terms are often quoted and may apply to many Portuguese, viewpoints are changing as the economy improves, and a younger generation looks to the future more than to the memories of the country's glory days.

The Portuguese View

As a colonial power, Portugal retained its colonies far longer than most other European powers. Italy, Germany, and Belgium held their colonies for less than a century; England, the Netherlands, and France held most of theirs for less than 200 years. Spain lost Latin America after about 250 years, and the Philippines after about 330. But Portugal's final African colonies were lost only after some 400 years of contact! This may help explain the Portuguese melancholy for past glories.

Portugal, like Spain, emerged from decades of repression under a dictator in the 1900s. This suddenly gave social and political freedom to a tightly controlled society. A rising standard of living (in large part due to Portugal's joining the EU) has generated more economic choices and opportunities, and the Portuguese finally have personal and political freedoms.

Portugal

This change has lightened the saudade attitude that has been referred to in literature about Portugal. Portuguese culture is slowly changing with developments in their economy and technology.

There is a Portuguese tradition of delegating hard or distasteful labor to others. They do not consider work to be the purpose of living and will not generally dwell long on conversations about their jobs.

☑ Know Before You Go

Portugal's Azores are subject to severe earthquakes. Water pollution is a serious problem in the coastal areas and has affected the fish populations.

Smoking is still common.

Portugal does have a drug problem since it is a gateway country for Latin American cocaine and Southwest Asian heroin entering the European market (especially from Brazil); it is reported to be a transshipment point for hashish from North Africa to Europe.

▶ CULTURAL ORIENTATION

Cognitive Styles: How the Portuguese Organize and Process Information

In Portugal, information is readily accepted for the purpose of discussion, but negotiations may be extensive with little movement from the initial perspective. Teaching is formal and innovation is discouraged, which fosters a subjective, associative mode of information processing. Because interpersonal relationships are of major importance, Portuguese are more inclined to maintain a relationship than to abide by rules and laws.

Negotiation Strategies: What the Portuguese Accept as Evidence

Truth is found in the personal feelings of those involved in a situation. While faith in the ideologies of humanitarianism and religion may influence their perspective, the Portuguese will not often let objective facts unduly sway their opinions.

Value Systems: The Basis for Behavior

The Portuguese's value systems are still in transition from the old authoritarian political and economic systems to the present democratic and capitalistic systems. The following three sections identify the Value Systems in the predominant culture—their methods of dividing right from wrong, good from evil, and so forth.

Locus of Decision-Making

Individuals are responsible for their decisions, but they are usually subject to the pressures of the family or the working group. The elite control all seats of power, intermarry for stability, and rely on extended kinship ties for control. One's self-identity comes from the history of one's extended family and one's position in society. A person's connections are much more important than his or her expertise when finding a job.

Sources of Anxiety Reduction

Most Portuguese are members of the Catholic Church, and its teachings and social structure provide stability and security to the individual. Friendship and patronage networks are the cement of Portuguese society and the primary means of communication within and between social classes. The family is the primary unit of social interaction, and it is an individual's role in the social structure and the presence of the extended family that give a sense of stability and security to life.

Issues of Equality/Inequality

There is ethnic and linguistic homogeneity in Portugal and this brings a sense of equality to the people. Although there are extreme contrasts between rich and poor, with a small upper class, a larger middle class, and a massive lower class, in general people feel that they are all equal because they are all unique. Failures are often attributed to external circumstances rather than personal inadequacies. It is a strongly macho society.

▶ BUSINESS PRACTICES

Punctuality, Appointments, and Local Time

- Punctuality is not a high priority in Portugal. Although foreigners are always expected to be on time, your Portuguese counterpart could easily be thirty minutes late.

    This indigenous casual attitude toward punctuality is affected by rank. A person of high social standing has the option to show up late to a meeting with a person of lower rank. Prior appointments are necessary.

- Remember that many Europeans and South Americans write the day first, then the month, then the year (e.g., December 3, 2010, is written 3.12.10 or 3/12/10). This is the case in Portugal.

- Lunch has traditionally been from noon to 2:00 P.M.; however, businesspeople may take shorter lunches. Try to avoid appointments between noon and 3:00 P.M.

- Portugal is the same as Greenwich Mean Time (G.M.T.), or five hours ahead of U.S. Eastern Standard Time (E.S.T. +5).

Negotiating

- Establishing a strong rapport through constant personal contact is essential.

- Emphasize your commitment to your clients; frequent visits are highly recommended. Do not expect negotiations to proceed at a rapid pace.

Persistence and patience are vital. Nothing is accomplished quickly in Portugal. The Portuguese do not consider themselves slaves to the clock. Appreciate their viewpoint, and you will have little difficulty conducting business there.

- After-sale service of your product is necessary. You must prove to your clients that this support will be provided.
- Good topics of discussion are the family, the excellent food, positive aspects of Portuguese culture, and personal interests.
- Avoid discussing politics and government.
- Avoid sounding too curious about your associates' personal matters.
- Many Portuguese study British English, so avoid idioms from the United States.
- Business cards are used. It is best to have yours translated, so that English is on one side and Portuguese on the other.
- Present your business card to your colleague with the Portuguese side facing him or her.

Business Entertaining

- Lunch is the main meal of the day and is eaten at approximately 1:00 P.M. Business lunches are common.
- Wine is generally the typical beverage consumed with meals.
- If you are invited out to lunch or dinner, be certain to reciprocate; however, do not mention that you "owe" the other person the favor.
- Women eating alone in a restaurant may be approached unless they obviously take work with them.
- The fork is held in the left hand and the knife remains in the right hand.
- Hands should not be kept in the lap at the table.
- It is impolite to eat while walking down the street.
- People often meet at tea houses (*casas de chá*).

PROTOCOL

Greetings

- A warm, firm handshake is the standard greeting.
- For social occasions, men greet each other with an embrace.
- Women kiss on both cheeks when greeting each other.
- The Portuguese tend to be less physically demonstrative in public than Spaniards.

Titles/Forms of Address

- The order of names is first name followed by the surname. This is the reverse of their neighbors in Spain.
- Use of first names has traditionally been reserved for friends, but this is changing.

- Some professionals are introduced as "Doctor" or "Doctora" even if they are not officially doctors.

Gestures
- "Come here" is indicated by waving the fingers or hand, with the palm facing down.
- It is considered very impolite to point.
- To call a waiter to your table in a restaurant, simply raise your hand.

Gifts
- It is not appropriate to give a business gift at the first meeting.
- When you give a business gift, do not include your business card; instead, include a handwritten card.
- Do not make your gift too extravagant or too cheap.
- The gift should not be a vehicle for your company logo.
- It is not necessary to bring a gift when you are invited to a home. Instead, you may invite your hosts out at a later date.
- If you do wish to give something to your Portuguese hosts, fine chocolates or other candy is the preferred gift.
- If you send flowers to your Portuguese hosts, have them sent ahead, and do not send thirteen of them, as that number is considered bad luck. Do not send chrysanthemums or roses. Do make sure that the bouquet is impressive; a gift of cheap flowers will have a negative effect.

Dress
- Conservative, formal dress is essential. Portuguese men may wear jackets and ties even when going to the movies!
- Despite the hot Portuguese weather, men should not remove their jackets unless their Portuguese colleagues do so first.
- Portuguese businesswomen usually wear subdued colors, so avoid the red power suit.

Portugal

Cultural Note
"This is the story of heroes who, leaving their native Portugal behind them, opened a way to Ceylon, and further; across seas no man had ever sailed before. They were men of no ordinary stature, equally at home in war and in dangers of every kind: they founded a new kingdom among distant peoples, and made it great. . . ."

—The opening lines of "The Lusiads," the classic epic poem of Portuguese exploration, written by Luis Vaz de Camões in 1572 (English translation by William C. Atkinson).

Romania

Romania

 ## WHAT'S YOUR CULTURAL IQ?

1. TRUE or FALSE? Modern Romania is situated in the province known in the Roman Empire as Dacia.

   ANSWER: TRUE. The Romans conquered the Dacians in the second century A.D. The territory of Dacia was approximately the same as present-day Romania.

2. Nazi Germany considered it vital that they controlled Romania during the Second World War. TRUE or FALSE: This was because of Romania's coastline on the Black Sea.

   ANSWER: FALSE. It was because the Nazi war machine needed oil, and Romania had the largest petroleum reserves then known in continental Europe.

3. Match the following
   - a. Constantin Brâncuşi
   - b. Eugène Ionesco
   - c. George Palade
   - d. Tristan Tzara

   1. Symbolist poet; founder of Dadaism
   2. Nobel prize winner for medicine
   3. Sculptor
   4. Absurdist playwright

   ANSWERS: a. 3; b. 4; c. 2; d. 1

Romania

TIPS ON DOING BUSINESS IN ROMANIA

- The Romanian elite has always traveled and studied abroad. Paris has been the favorite destination, and many French customs and habits are followed by upper-class Romanians.
- Romanians have reputations as hard bargainers. One useful technique is to delineate the limits of what your negotiators can and cannot do. This should be done at the beginning of a meeting.
- Romanians also have a reputation as risk takers. Unpredictability, spontaneity, and boldness are considered part of the Romanian character. So is their sense of humor, which includes a fine appreciation of the absurd.
- Filing paperwork at Romanian government offices can try the patience of a saint. It may involve waiting in line at a half-dozen offices.

▶ COUNTRY BACKGROUND

History

Modern Romania can be dated to 1861, when the principalities of Moldavia and Wallachia were freed from the control of the Ottoman Empire and united as the Romanian nation.

Despite having a Prussian king, Romania did not join the Central Powers at the outbreak of the First World War. When the Allies offered Transylvania to Romania, the Romanians joined their side. But without Allied armies on the ground, the Romanians were no match for German and Austrian armies. The Central Powers occupied Romania, while the Romanian government retreated to Moldavia, where the Russians protected them.

Russian protection ended with the Bolshevik Revolution of 1917. Romania surrendered to the Central Powers in May 1918. But the Central Powers soon collapsed. Romania retracted its surrender and occupied both Bessarabia and Transylvania. Romanian troops even briefly occupied the Hungarian capital of Budapest.

The Romania that emerged from the First World War was the largest it had ever been, but it had earned the enmity of all its neighbors. The victorious Allies allowed Romania to keep its winnings, provided that they sign a treaty with Hungary. The Trianon Treaty was signed in 1920.

As the Second World War swept over the Balkans, the Romanian army became involved. They assisted the Austrians and the Italians in the invasion of Yugoslavia. Then, once Hitler invaded the USSR, Romanian troops marched into Ukraine. The Romanians also exterminated the Jews in the Soviet land they occupied.

When the war turned and the Red Army marched into Romania in August of 1944, the Romanians switched sides. The Romanian army fought the Germans with the same fervor they displayed in Ukraine. The Red Army occupied Romania until a Communist government was established.

Gheorghe Gheorghiu-Dej took power in 1953. He deviated from Moscow's orders by encouraging anti-Hungarian and anti-Russian nationalism. These policies were continued by his successor, Nicolae Ceaușescu, who came to power in 1965. Ceaușescu ultimately held dictatorial power over Romania for twenty-four years.

As Moscow's control over the Warsaw Pact nations began to slip, desperate Romanians began to protest against their government. An underground movement, the National Salvation Front, rose up to oppose the regime. A populist uprising in late 1989 overthrew the government. Ceaușescu and his wife were captured, tried, and executed—which was videotaped and subsequently broadcast on television—on Christmas Day, 1989.

After the overthrow of the Ceaușescu regime, an interim government led by the National Salvation Front took control. The National Salvation Front leader, Ion Iliescu, was elected president in May of 1990, despite his Communist background and close ties to the Ceaușescu government. Because former Communist officials remained in charge, some refer to the events of 1989 as "the stolen revolution."

Romania joined NATO on March 29, 2004, and is scheduled to be admitted to the European Union in 2007.

Type of Government

Romania is now a multiparty republic with two legislative bodies: the Romanian Senate and the Assembly of Deputies. The president is the chief of state. The prime minister is the head of the government.

Previously one of the poorer countries in Europe, Romania's efforts toward improving their economy is generating positive results.

For current government data, check with the Embassy of Romania at *www.roembus.org.*

Language

The official language of Romania is Romanian. Ethnologue.com lists a total of fifteen languages currently in use in Romania. Romanian is mutually intelligible with Moldavian; many consider the two to be dialects of the same language.

Romanian is derived from Latin, and it is in the same linguistic family as Italian, French, Spanish, and Portuguese.

While French had been the most popular foreign language in Romania for decades, English has recently supplanted it. Many young Romanians study English and attend English-speaking universities.

Cultural Note
Although Romanian is quite similar to the Genoese dialect of Italian, some 12 percent of the Romanian vocabulary is derived from Slavic languages; do not expect to be able to conduct business by speaking Italian to your Romanian-speaking client.

The Romanian View

Some 87 percent of the population belongs to the Romanian Orthodox Church. The remainder of the population is Protestant, Roman Catholic, Greek Orthodox, Jewish, Islamic, or atheist.

Romanians consider themselves to be descended from the native Dacians and the Roman legions who conquered them in A.D. 101. Of course, this original population has been influenced by some 1,650 years of subsequent conquest and migration by many other peoples.

Foreigners have often commented on the fierce intensity of Romanians. They are fearless soldiers.

In Orthodox churches and at funerals, Romanians sometimes display a religious fervor that sedate—or repressed—foreigners find frightening. And in business, Romanians attack obstacles with a will—particularly when their path is clear.

Romania is subject to occasional serious earthquakes, which may contribute to the Romanian mindset that they are not in control of their destiny.

☑ Know Before You Go

The greatest hazard for visitors to Romania is probably nonviolent crime, such as pickpocketing. Visitors also complain about being gouged by taxi drivers, who often drive without meters or with nonoperational meters. Violent crime seems to be on the rise, ranging from simple muggings to sophisticated confidence schemes in which a criminal impersonates a law officer.

Romania is the second largest nation in Eastern Europe (after Poland). Consequently, it has a wide variety of terrain and climate. These include mountains and coastlines, each of which present different hazards. Romania is subject to occasional earthquakes, floods, and mudslides. Romania's prevailing weather patterns flow through Ukraine and Russia, yielding hot summers and cold winters.

While public transportation in Romania is in good repair, the roads are not—especially in rural areas. Travelers on rural roads at night should be especially careful of pedestrians, bicyclists, and horse-drawn carts—none of which will probably be carrying lights. Also, be aware that Romanian traffic laws are very strict. Romanian police may confiscate your driver's license for infractions, even if it was issued in your home country.

As in other former Warsaw Pact nations, little thought was given to the environment in the past fifty years. There is severe industrial and chemical pollution in parts of Romania. And Romania's first nuclear power plant was built on the country's most active earthquake zone.

There is a high degree of computer competence in Romania. Cybercrime is a growing problem, especially for foreign companies (which are the most frequent targets). Typical cybercrimes include: Internet fraud, credit card fraud, auction site fraud, and hacking or extortion schemes.

Despite anticorruption regulations, bribery is still common in Romania. The country has been described as "a nation of brown envelopes," referring to the typical enclosure for a bribe.

▶ CULTURAL ORIENTATION

Cognitive Styles: How Romanians Organize and Process Information

The people in Romania have always been independent (even under Communist rule) and open to outside information. Their basic education fosters associative thinking, but most of them are now processing information conceptually and analytically. They are also returning to personal involvement in situations rather than following the rules of a party line.

Negotiation Strategies: What Romanians Accept as Evidence

The more educated the participants are, the more they will use objective facts to define the truth. Subjective feelings are still strong, but faith in an ideology, other than freedom, does not cloud the issue of truth.

Value Systems: The Basis for Behavior

The following three sections identify the Value Systems in the predominant culture—their methods of dividing right from wrong, good from evil, and so forth.

Locus of Decision-Making

As the movement toward freedom and privatization advances, it puts the responsibility for decision-making on the shoulders of the individual. The individual may, in turn, transfer this power to the group as a whole or to selected experts within the group. It is not clear yet who will be the beneficiary of the individuals' decision-making skills: the decision-maker or the people as a whole. It seems that the Romanian tendency is to work for the betterment of the people.

Sources of Anxiety Reduction

Family cohesion is the basic social unit that gives identity and security to the individual. However, this has changed somewhat as more women work outside the home. Romanians are very nationalistic, which has been augmented by the departure of Communist rule. Religion fills some of the need for structure and security.

Issues of Equality/Inequality

A discernible hierarchy of classes has evolved, from the peasant to the bureaucratic elite. Although egalitarianism is favored, some resentment is found among the various ethnic and social groups. Hungarian and German minorities are very distinct, with their own languages, and present potential social and political problems. The ethnic Romanians do not hide their emotions; they tend to express their intentions, feelings, and opinions freely. In marriage both spouses have equal rights, and their roles are not clearly delineated.

Cultural Note

The most famous foreign author to write about Romania is Bram Stoker, who located the home of his vampire, Dracula, in Romania. He placed Castle Dracula at the convergence of three regions: Transylvania, Moldavia, and Bucovina.

▶ BUSINESS PRACTICES

Punctuality, Appointments, and Local Time

- Romanians tend to be very punctual; be on time.
- Appointments should be made well in advance.
- Appointments may be requested by e-mail or mail. Business letters can be sent in English. Not only do Romanians expect to translate foreign correspondence, but such a letter may be accorded more attention than one written in Romanian.
- An interpreter will be necessary for the meeting unless you are positive that you and your Romanian counterpart are fluent in a common language.
- Because more Romanian students now study at English universities than French, English is the most widely spoken foreign language. French is still widely studied as well, and many other languages are heard in various parts of Romania. For example, Hungarian is spoken in Transylvania, and Russian is common near the Romanian-Russian border. Older Romanian businesspeople tend to speak some German. Major hotels and resorts have English-speaking staff members.
- Official holidays include January 1 and 2, Easter Sunday and Monday, May 1 (Romanian Labor Day), December 1 (National Day), and December 25 and 26.
- Romania is two hours ahead of Greenwich Mean Time (G.M.T. +2), or seven hours ahead of Eastern Standard Time (E.S.T. +7).

Negotiating

- Patience is necessary for establishing business contacts in Romania; the process can seem glacially slow. However, once the connection is established, one can expect to continue the relationship for a very long time.
- Stay at one of the more prestigious international hotels. Staying elsewhere will diminish your importance in the eyes of Romanians.
- Like many Eastern Europeans who lived under totalitarian regimes, older Romanians learned to communicate obliquely. Even today, they are not accustomed to answering questions directly. Instead, they prefer to respond to questions with long stories that suggest an answer.
- Be prepared to hand out a large number of business cards. Your cards need not be translated into Romanian; a card in English or French is satisfactory. Your title and any advanced degrees should be listed on the card.

Business Entertaining

- Remember that Romania remains one of the poorer countries in Europe. As a foreigner, your hard currency gives you priority access to available goods. You should also bring some gift items with you from home.

Romania

- Your Romanian colleagues will do the majority of the entertaining. However, if you wish to reciprocate, begin with an invitation to lunch or dinner at your hotel.
- Romanian business lunches typical last at least two hours and involve the consumption of alcohol. Romania produces excellent wine and plum brandy; these are commonly served drinks.
- Romanians are avid fans of soccer (fútbol). Not only does soccer make an excellent topic of conversation, be aware that everything stops during the World Cup when a Romanian team is in contention.

▶ PROTOCOL

Greetings
- Romanians shake hands constantly: when they are introduced, when they leave someone, and every time they meet. No matter how many times they run into each other during the day, they will shake hands each time. Men should wait for a woman to extend her hand first.
- Men may still rise when being introduced to someone; women may remain seated.
- Good friends will greet each other expansively. Romanians may kiss each other on both cheeks. Men may kiss each other.
- At social gatherings, wait for your host to introduce you to everyone there.

Titles/Forms of Address
- The order of names in Romania is the same as in most of Europe: first name followed by surname.
- Historically, only close adult friends and relatives addressed each other by their first names. This may change when working with younger Romanians. Adults address the young by their first names.
- Surnames commonly end in escu or eanu. The escu ending means "son of"—Ionescu means "son of Ion" (Ion is the Romanian version of John). The eanu ending indicates a location—Constantinescu means "from Constantin."
- Always address Romanian professionals by their title (Doctor, Engineer, Professor, and so forth) and surname.

Gestures
- Romanian gestures tend to be expansive, reflecting both Italian and Slavic influences.
- The "fig" gesture—the thumb between the index and middle fingers of a clenched fist—is an insult.

Gifts

- Gift giving is very much a part of business in Romania. Sometimes it can be hard to decide where gift giving becomes bribery.
- While substantial gifts are expected on holidays (such as Christmas) and contract sign-ings, it is also useful to stock up on items such as pens, calculators, or lighters discreetly imprinted with your company name for incidental meetings.
- Items that are produced in your home state or region are of interest. Local artifacts (Native American handicrafts, etc.) or gourmet items may be appropriate. A more significant gift would be an iPod, or whatever advanced portable electronic tool is currently hot.
- If you are invited to dinner at a private home, bring wine, liquor, or have flowers sent ahead. Roses (but not red) are a good choice.
- Romanians have a tradition of hospitality. Indeed, some have called it aggressive hospi-tality. Romanians typically refuse to allow a guest to leave for hours and attempt to give all manner of items to the guest.
- If you are staying at a Romanian home, you can try to repay their hospitality by offering to help with some household chores, although your offer will probably be refused. You may be allowed to purchase groceries.

Dress

- Casual Western-style dress is common; jeans are everywhere. However, businesspeople are still expected to dress in conservative business apparel. Men wear dark suits except during the summer, when short-sleeved shirts with ties are acceptable; women wear suits and heels. Make sure your shoes are well polished.
- Business wear will generally suffice for formal occasions.
- Shorts are appropriate only for the country or the shore, not the cities.
- Unless specified otherwise, assume that invitations to a Romanian house or restaurant call for the same clothes you wear for business.
- Women should wear a skirt that covers their knees, and have their shoulders covered when entering an Orthodox church. Covering up one's hair is generally not required, but it is wise to carry a scarf just in case.

Cultural Note
With its varied scenery, Romania is popular as a low-cost venue for filmmakers. A number of Hollywood films, from the prestigious U.S. Civil War epic *Cold Mountain* to the camp horror sequel *Seed of Chucky*, have been filmed in Romania.

Romania

Russia

Russian Federation
Local short form: Rossiya
Local long form: Rossiyskaya Federatsiya
Former: Russian Empire, Russian Soviet
Federative Socialist Republic

Cultural Note

Russia is developing at an intense pace, absorbing new viewpoints and business styles. In some aspects they have changed their negotiating styles substantially (they rarely lose their tempers and walk out of meetings anymore). However, one crucial characteristic remains the same: they have tremendous patience. Russians prize endurance, which often puts impatient North Americans at a disadvantage.

 WHAT'S YOUR CULTURAL IQ?

1. The USSR launched the first artificial satellite in 1957. TRUE or FALSE: The Soviet space program shut down with the breakup of the USSR and has not launched since.

   ANSWER: FALSE. The program is still operational. The Russians run it out of the old USSR launch site in Kazakhstan. Currently, it is supporting the manned international space station Freedom.

2. Which of the following Russian authors have won the Nobel Prize for Literature?
   a. Ivan Bunin
   b. Boris Pasternak
   c. Mikhail Sholokhov
   d. Alexander Solzhenitsyn
   e. All of the above

   ANSWER: e. Pasternak, however, was persuaded by the Kremlin not to accept the prize.

3. The Russian Federation has many different ethnic, religious, and linguistic groups—some of whom, like the Chechens, want to be independent of Moscow. TRUE or FALSE? Ethnic Russians are actually a minority within the Russian Federation.

   ANSWER: FALSE. Although the Russian Federation is the largest single nation on Earth, its population contains approximately 87 percent ethnic Russians.

Russia

TIPS ON DOING BUSINESS IN RUSSIA

- When managing Russian employees, be clear and precise in your communications. Don't try to be subtle and make "suggestions," assuming that Russians will "take the hint." Give concise instructions. Russians accept authority figures; be one.
- If necessity is the mother of invention, Russians are very, very inventive. Historically faced with shortages of funds and equipment, they have learned how to improvise. Do not be surprised to find creative solutions to every type of problem everywhere you look.
- Very little is done in Russia without using *blat*—which is Russian for "connections" or "influence." Blat involves an exchange of favors; when you do something for someone, they now owe you a favor. Gifts—monetary or otherwise—are often part of this exchange.

Cultural Note

The breakup of the USSR added fifteen new independent nations to the map of the world. Historically, Russia often insulated itself from Europe by creating client "buffer states" between Russia and the outside world. Today, these former buffer states are now independent. Thus, Russia today shares no borders with any former Warsaw Pact nation except Poland. Neither does it share a border with Afghanistan, nor six of the former republics of the USSR!

▶ COUNTRY BACKGROUND

History

The former USSR, also known as the Soviet Union, lasted from 1917 through 1991. Before 1917, most of the territory in the USSR was part of the Russian Empire. The Russian Empire expanded outward from Moscow, the historic capital of the Russian Republic and of the Soviet Union itself. (Czar Peter the Great moved the capital in 1712 from Moscow to Saint Petersburg—Peter's "window on the West"—but the Communists moved the capital back to Moscow in 1918.)

The authoritarian, one-party rule of the Communists collapsed with surprising speed. Theories for this collapse abound. The precipitating event was the August 1991 coup attempt, when hard-line Communist leaders briefly imprisoned President Mikhail Gorbachev. Faced with resistance on all sides (from Gorbachev, who refused to acknowledge their authority; from President Boris Yeltsin, who became a popular hero for facing down tanks in the streets; and from thousands of Russians who took to the streets in protest), the coup failed in less than a week. The coup attempt ended the careers of the coup leaders (the "gang of eight") and of Gorbachev as well; Gorbachev had appointed the very men who had plotted against him.

In disarray, Moscow was unable to prevent the non-Russian republics from leaving the Soviet Union. The USSR ceased to exist on December 25, 1991. The Russian Soviet Socialist

Republic was renamed the Russian Federation and remains the largest and most powerful of the former republics.

As the hero of the popular uprising against the coup attempt, Boris Yeltsin became the first president of the independent Russian Federation. Initially a strong head of state that encouraged decentralization of power, Yeltsin became increasingly isolated as his health deteriorated. Corruption and favoritism had grown to alarming proportions by the time of his resignation at the end of 1999.

Various regions of the Russian Federation (especially those populated by non-Slavs) agitated for autonomy. The republic of Chechnya, whose population is predominantly Muslim, went further and declared independence. Russian troops invaded Chechnya late in 1994 and virtually destroyed the capital city of Grozny. A pro-Moscow government was eventually installed, but much of the country was never pacified. Chechen terrorists began attacks both inside Chechnya and in other areas of Russia—even in Moscow itself.

Russia's second president, Vladimir Putin, was elected in 2000. He initiated reforms in the economy and the legislature and cut back military expenditures. He also promised to combat corruption. His term was marred by more combat in the breakaway region of Chechnya.

In 2004, Muslim terrorists held hostage and slew hundreds of schoolchildren. Following his re-election to the presidency, Putin used this as a justification to consolidate power in his hands, to "protect Russia from terrorism."

Cultural Note

Despite their mistrust of Moscow, most of the former republics have united in an alliance called the Commonwealth of Independent States. (The exceptions are the three Baltic states of Lithuania, Latvia, and Estonia, which direct their attention toward Europe, not Moscow.) Thus, although Moscow no longer rules the USSR, it retains great influence (and responsibilities) in most of the former constituent republics.

The central Asian republics are particularly dependent upon Moscow for aid, both economic and military. Furthermore, the presence of ethnic Russians in every republic gives Moscow a reason for intervention, as it did to "protect" ethnic Russians in Moldova.

Type of Government

The Russian Republic is a federal multiparty republic with a bicameral legislature.

There is an upper house called the Federation Council, and a lower house, the State Duma.

The Russian president is the chief of state. The Russian prime minister is the head of the government.

Although there has been a considerable amount of legal reform (especially as it relates to business), Russian law remains in a state of flux. For years after the breakup of the USSR, multiple authorities tried to impose taxes—so many that taxes sometimes exceeded the gross income of businesses. As it was impossible to pay such a tax burden, most businesses in Russia declined to pay their taxes. In 2004, the administration of President Putin tried to enforce reformed tax legislation; it remains to be seen how successful this effort will be.

For current government data, visit the Embassy of Russia's Web site at *www.russianem bassy.org*.

Language
Russian is the official language. The literacy rate is approximately 99 percent. Ethnologue .com lists 103 languages for Russia, 3 of which are extinct.

The Russian View
The Russian Federation is so huge and contains so many ethnic, religious, and linguistic groups that it is impossible to generalize about its citizens. For example, the Russian Federation includes the autonomous republics of Chuvashia and Tatarstan, both of which are populated predominantly by Turkic peoples. However, the Chuvash adopted the Russian Orthodox faith centuries ago. The Tartars (or Tatars), like most Turkic peoples, remain Muslim.

That said, the following information should be considered to apply to the predominant culture of Russia, which is mostly ethnic Russian.

The USSR was officially an atheist nation; religion was suppressed, and some 50 percent of the population considered themselves nonreligious or atheist. Religious worship is now permitted. Many religions are represented in Russia, including Russian Orthodoxy, Protestantism, Islam, and Judaism. Religious participation is increasing.

Periodic hostility exists between officials of the Russian Orthodox Church and religions seen as not native to Russia. This hostility is often directed at the Roman Catholic Church but can be aimed at missionaries of any religion operating in Russia.

To older Russians who remember the constant shortages and endless lines of the USSR, the plethora of modern consumer goods available today is a source of amazement. But there is also a new generation of Russians who grew up amid this consumer culture; to them, it is normal.

There is substantial dissatisfaction among young Russians today. They face high levels of unemployment, poverty, and drug addiction. Emigration is more common, and the birth rate is low. Russia's population is shrinking.

☑ Know Before You Go
Russia is so large that almost any type of natural disaster can (and does) occur within its borders, including earthquakes, blizzards, floods, and forest fires.

As in other former republics of the USSR, street crime is present.

Russian roads are not in good condition.

While there has been some improvement in the Russian health care system, the U.S. State Department recommends that foreigners who experience medical emergencies in Russia seek medical evacuation for treatment elsewhere.

Although the 1986 Chernobyl nuclear accident occurred in Ukraine, the prevailing winds blew some of the fallout into Russia. However, there are many sources of radioactive and chemical pollution within Russia. Recently, dozens of radioactive hot spots were found around Moscow itself, from badly stored nuclear waste and decades-old experiments. The incidence of HIV and AIDS is growing rapidly in Russia.

▶ CULTURAL ORIENTATION

Cognitive Styles: How Russians Organize and Process Information

Historically, Russians have not been open to outside information. With the downfall of Communism, many Russians acknowledge that they must learn new ways. But it is a struggle, and they may once again close themselves off from outside information. Their tendency is to process information subjectively and associatively. Some Russians are able to transfer this predilection to the abstract rules of science and technology.

Negotiation Strategies: What Russians Accept as Evidence

Some executives—especially those trained in Western business traditions—will let objective facts dictate the truth. Others will still look to faith in some ideology or their own personal feelings to guide them to the truth.

Value Systems: The Basis for Behavior

Having rejected the values of Communism, Russian are still struggling to master those of a free-market economy and democracy. The following three sections identify the Value Systems in the predominant culture—their methods of dividing right from wrong, good from evil, and so forth.

Locus of Decision-Making

Although the Russians are by nature collectivistic, Communist Party rule put decision-making in the hands of the party. Soviet executives made their decisions in line with party policy; as long as the party rules were followed, the decision could not be wrong. Now these individuals have to make decisions on their own—and take responsibility for those decisions. In many instances, executives are delegating this authority to the group as a whole or to specialists within the group.

The presence of a strong, yet predictable, boss actually works to reduce anxiety in many Russians.

Sources of Anxiety Reduction

The demise of Communism has abolished many of the structures the people depended upon for stability. This stability is now being sought in religion, social groups, the family, or elsewhere. The transition to a free-market economy and democracy will not succeed unless the people can be shown that these changes provide increased security and stability.

Issues of Equality/Inequality

Today, the most obvious area of inequality is ethnicity. Terrorism is associated with Russians from the Caucasus area, so there is suspicion of anyone with darker skin. (People from the Caucasus resemble Mediterraneans more than pale-skinned Slavs.) In Moscow and other predominantly-Slavic areas, dark-complexioned people are frequently stopped on the street by security forces. They also find it difficult to get hired or to rent lodgings.

Despite the Communist premise of gender equality, there had always been a great deal of inequality between the sexes. Russian women are still struggling for equality with men, but more female business leaders are emerging. Despite new legal standards, sexual harassment is still extant in business and government.

Cultural Note

The avoidance of people in power has a long tradition in Russia. Even in modern businesses, employees tend to avoid talking to the boss. They do not even voice complaints to the boss (although they will to everyone else). Often, the first time a Russian boss knows that an employee is unhappy is when that employee resigns.

Western managers who have run businesses in Russia state that it is extraordinarily difficult and time consuming to get feedback from employees. Sometimes, the best solution is to ask the same question in several different ways at different times.

▶ BUSINESS PRACTICES

Punctuality, Appointments, and Local Time

- Always be punctual, but do not be surprised if the Russians are not on time. It is not unusual for Russians to be fifteen to thirty minutes late.
- Historically, patience, not punctuality, was considered a virtue in Russia.
- Allow plenty of time for each appointment. Not only may they start late, but they may run a bit longer than originally planned.
- Remember that the date is written differently in many countries. In Russia and the CIS, the day is normally listed first, then the month, then the year. (For example, 3.12.10 or 03.12.10 means December 3, 2010, not March 12, 2010).
- Obtaining an appointment can be laborious. Be patient and persistent. Once your appointment is scheduled, avoid a cancellation.
- Russia's Independence Day (from the Soviet Union) is August 24 (1991), and their National Holiday is Russia Day, June 12.
- Moscow and Saint Petersburg are both in the westernmost time zone, three hours ahead of Greenwich Mean Time (G.M.T +3), or eight hours ahead of U.S. Eastern Standard Time (E.S.T. +8).

Russia

- The huge Russian Federation spans eleven time zones. Daylight-saving time changes usually occur on a Saturday night at the end of March and October.

Negotiating

- It is said that Russians are great "sitters" during negotiations. Traditionally, Russians regard compromise as a sign of weakness. Some even see compromise as morally incorrect. Russians would rather out-sit the other negotiator—and gain more concessions from the other side.
- Be certain that all members of your negotiating team know and agree on exactly what you want out of the deal. Write this down (perhaps adding a few "nice to haves" that can be given away later) and bring it with you. Do not show the Russians anything other than unity among your team.
- Be factual and include all levels of technical detail.
- "Final offers" are never final during initial negotiations. Be prepared to wait; the offer may be made more attractive if you can hold out.
- Until you have a signed a formal agreement, do not get overconfident about the deal at hand. And never expect that you can renegotiate later for a better deal. This contract is as advantageous as you will ever get.
- The Russians may request that some funds be paid to them directly in cash, or to an account in a foreign bank. This may be because of their historic concern over the oppressive Russian tax system and the rarity of being paid in cash. Be prepared to propose various options.
- One Russian tactic is to allow (after long negotiations) the foreign partner to own 51 percent of a joint venture. However, contracts usually require unanimity among the partners for major decisions anyway, so 51 percent is not a controlling interest.
- Include a clause requiring the joint venture partners to submit to arbitration in a neutral country if they can't come to an agreement. Sweden is the most popular choice for third-country arbitration.
- Russian regulations represent the biggest liability to a successful joint venture. These regulations are in constant flux (reforms are being made all the time), so don't count on your Russian partner to have a full grasp of the legal issues involved. Get your own expert in Russian law. Don't be surprised when something you did yesterday is disallowed tomorrow; some laws are nebulous, and their interpretation is subject to change.
- Appearances can be deceiving. Russian firms may look prosperous and full of potential. Select a partner based upon full knowledge of the assets it owns or controls.
- Since it is not customary for Russians to disclose their home phone, or other personal telephone numbers, no official residential phone books are issued at all. However, various directories are produced, and many of them are accessible free on the Internet.

Russia

- In many countries—such as Japan—people tend to respond to a question by saying "yes." In the USSR the tendency used to be just the opposite; managers and bureaucrats said "no" at every opportunity. However, Russian executives now often say yes to proposals— even if they lack the authority to do so. They make promises to buy time, and expand the contacts they want with foreigners.
- Historically, there were many reasons why Russians said no to business proposals. One was that innovation was traditionally discouraged. Also, Russians were afraid that if they gave the go-ahead and a project failed, they would be held responsible. Another reason had to do with the position of an individual in a rigid, hierarchical bureaucracy. You rarely met a Russian bureaucrat who had the power to push a project forward without the agreement of others. But one individual could cancel a project, all by himself or herself. Often, the ability to say no was the only real power many bureaucrats possessed; not surprisingly, they used it frequently.
- Peace, international relations, the changes in Russia, and difficult economic situations are all common topics of conversation. People will ask what you think of Russia and what life is like in your home country.

Cultural Note
Traditionally, a restaurant table had two bottles on the table: one had water, the other vodka. If you opened a bottle of vodka, the idea was to drink it all at one sitting! Recently, Russians have started drinking more beer, but bars are usually well-stocked, and many preferences can be accommodated.

Business Entertaining
- Always have a good supply of soft drinks, tea, coffee (not in plastic cups!), Danish, cookies, snacks, and so forth, on the meeting table. Russians try hard to provide a variety of refreshments when conducting business and appreciate your reciprocating in kind.
- Russian hotels and restaurants may still have doormen who seem less than gracious. This is probably because doormen often double as security guards. Do not try to engage them in conversation.
- Russian restaurants have improved over the last decade. Menus generally reflect the available fare, and service is faster.
- Dinner generally begins around 7 P.M., because most offices close around 6 P.M.
- Quite often, Russians will state the time in a simple military format, so if you say "Meet me at 7 o'clock," they will assume that is 7:00 A.M. If you mean 7:00 P.M., specify nineteen o'clock, or nineteen hundred. Just try to avoid sounding artificially militaristic; Russians do not say "zero seven hundred" for 7:00 A.M.
- Russians are very confident of their ability to drink heavily and still remain "clear." They may prefer to conduct business when you are drunk.

- It is a great honor to be invited to a Russian home. It may also be a great burden for the host. Russian tradition demands that you be served a lunch or dinner that far exceeds everyone's appetite and, sometimes, the financial capabilities of the hosts. For example, caviar might be served with huge spoons.
- It is good to know a few toasts. The most common is *Na zdorovye* (pronounced "Nah-zda-ROE-vee-ah"), which means "To your health."
- In a restaurant or nightclub, Russians may invite you to dance or to come over to their table. Accept graciously.

Cultural Note

The Russian word *nyekulturny* (literally, "uncultured" or "bad mannered") signifies the wrong way to do something. Foreigners are often judged by the same standards Russians apply to themselves. Some nyekulturny behaviors include:

- Wearing your coat (and heavy boots) when you enter a public building—particularly the theater—is considered bad manners. You are expected to leave your coat in the *garderob* (cloakroom). One does not sit on one's coat at a concert, restaurant, and so forth. Many office buildings also have a garderob.
- Standing with your hands in your pockets, or generally lounging around, is viewed as uncultured behavior. This is especially true in public buildings.
- Wearing business clothes that are less than conservative—for example, pastel shirts with white collars—is nyekulturny. Colors have a substantial impact in many cultures, and foreign executives should notice that Vladimir Putin rarely wore a red tie. (See the article on "International Colors and Symbols" at *www.kissboworshakehands.com*.)
- Speaking or laughing loudly in public is considered uncultured behavior.
- Not only is whistling indoors considered nyekulturny, but there is a superstition that it may chase out good fortune.

▶ PROTOCOL

Greetings

- Russians only display affection in public during greetings. Relatives and good friends will engage in a noisy embrace and kiss each other on the cheeks.
- Except at formal or state occasions, Russians usually greet a stranger by shaking hands and stating their name, rather than uttering a polite phrase (such as "How do you do?"). Respond in the same way.

Titles/Forms of Address

- Russian names are listed in the same order as in the West, but the Russian middle name is a patronymic (a name derived from the first name of one's father). Thus, Fyodor Niko-laievich Medvedev's first name is Fyodor (a Russian version of Theodore), his last name is Medvedev, and his middle name means "son of Nikolai."
- Russian women add the letter a to the end of their surnames; Medvedev's wife would be Mrs. Medvedeva.

Russia

- Unless invited to do so, do not use first names. If a Russian has a professional title, use the title followed by the surname. If he or she has no title, use "Mr.," "Miss," "Mrs.," or "Ms.," plus the surname.
- Among themselves, Russians use a bewildering variety of diminutives and nicknames. They also address each other by first name and patronymic, which can be quite a mouthful. As you establish a relationship with them, you will be invited to call them by one of these. This is the time to invite them to call you by your first name.
- Despite the length of their names, there are relatively few variations of first names and surnames in Russia. Indeed, some names (e.g., Ivan Ivanovich Ivanov) are so common that you will need additional information to be able to identify the correct person. In official circles, Russians may use a person's birth date to differentiate between identically named individuals.

Gestures

- Russian is a language abundant in curses, and there are quite a number of obscene gestures as well. Both the American "okay" sign (thumb and forefinger touching in a circle) and any shaken-fist gesture will be interpreted as vulgar.
- Whistling is not taken as a sign of approval in a concert hall; it means you did not like the performance.
- The "thumbs-up" gesture indicates approval among Russians.
- You may encounter some superstitious behaviors if you are invited into a Russian's home. These include sitting for a minute before leaving a home, or knocking three times on wood to avoid bad luck.

Cultural Note

As a society historically subject to police surveillance, the Russians evolved gestures that would foil eavesdroppers. For example, to avoid saying the name of Brezhnev, Russians would touch a finger to an eyebrow (a reference to Brezhnev's hairy eyebrows). The free speech that has accompanied the breakup of the Soviet Union has reduced the need for such gestures, but they have not entirely disappeared. Nowadays, a gesture may be used to refer to a member of the Russian Mafia.

Gifts

- Muscovites now have access to much of the same products as Manhattanites, and as a result it is more difficult to select a good gift for your Russian counterparts.

  Presents that represent your hometown or country are appropriate. Russians still identify cigarettes and rare Zippo lighters with the United States, so they may be appreciated. Currently popular electronic gadgets like digital cameras, MP3, DVD or CD players, high-quality pens, illustrated books of your homeland, or well-reviewed, sophisticated books are other good gifts.

- Bring flowers, liquor, or a gourmet food item if invited to a Russian home.
- Feasting is also a part of religious holidays. Remember that the Russian Orthodox Church follows the Julian calendar, not the Gregorian calendar in official use throughout the Western world. Currently, the Julian calendar runs approximately thirteen days behind the Gregorian one.

Dress

- If you go to Russia during the winter, bring very warm clothes or buy Russian-style hats and gloves upon arrival. In addition, bring a pair of shoes or boots with skid-resistant soles.
- Russian buildings are usually well heated, so a layered approach is best.
- Business dress is conservative. Russians generally prefer European styles more than American. Business visitors should always appear in refined, well-cut clothes.
- While shorts are frowned upon for casualwear, you will note that Russians strip down to as little as possible on those rare days when it is sunny enough to sunbathe.

Cultural Note

Be cautious of using credit cards and ATM cards in Russia. Russia has many underemployed computer experts, some of which engage in such cybercrimes as capturing credit card numbers.

Saudi Arabia

Kingdom of Saudi Arabia
Local short form: Al Arabiyah as Suudiyah
Local long form: Al Mamlakah al
Arabiyah as Suudiyah

Cultural Note

Non-Muslims may not enter Saudi Arabia without an invitation, which usually involves being sponsored by a prominent Saudi. Once you enter the country, realize that you are beyond the protection of your government. You are subject to Saudi Islamic law, and something as innocuous (to westerners) as dressing immodestly in public can result in your being arrested or even whipped. Study the rules for acceptable behavior carefully. Also be aware that you may not leave Saudi Arabia without an exit permit, no matter what the emergency.

As for foreign businesswomen, the limitations on allowable behavior are stringent—and the activities they will be permitted to engage in (like driving) may seem restricted.

 WHAT'S YOUR CULTURAL IQ?

1. The Saudis use the Muslim calendar, which is different from the Gregorian calendar used in most Western countries. Which of the following abbreviations indicates that a date is written using the Muslim calendar?
   a. h
   b. A.D.
   c. C.E.

   ANSWER: a. The h (usually written in English without a period) stands for Hijrah (sometimes spelled Hijra or Hejira). A.D. (of course) is used for the Western calendar; it stands for "anno Domini," meaning "in the year of our Lord." C.E. is a more recent indicator of the Western calendar. It means "Common Era" and is a way of referring to the Gregorian calendar without referencing Christianity.

2. TRUE or FALSE? Saudi Arabia occupies the entire Arabian Peninsula.

   ANSWER: FALSE. Although Saudi Arabia takes up most of the Arabian Peninsula, it shares it with many other nations, including the United Arab Emirates, Oman, and Yemen.

3. Match the following Saudi cities with the appropriate reference:
   a. Jeddah   1. The capital of Saudi Arabia
   b. Makkah (Mecca)   2. A seaport and major commercial center of Saudi Arabia
   c. Riyadh   3. The birthplace of the prophet Mohammad

   ANSWERS: a. 2; b. 3; c. 1

> **Cultural Note**
>
> Observant Muslims pray five times a day in the direction of Makkah. The five prayer times are:
>
> - *Fajr* (dawn)
> - *Dhuhr* (midday)
> - *Asr* (afternoon)
> - *Maghrib* (sunset)
> - *Isha* (night)
>
> Not everyone arises at dawn to pray. Dawn prayers can be completed a little later, at *Shuruq* (sunrise).
>
> As a non-Muslim foreigner, you are not expected to pray. However, you are expected to avoid distracting those who are praying. If you are within earshot of a praying Muslim, you should be silent. And it is considered a great insult to walk in front of praying Muslims—in doing so, you are coming between them and Makkah.

▶ TIPS ON DOING BUSINESS IN SAUDI ARABIA

- Public activities in Saudi Arabia are strictly segregated by gender. Do not try to change traditions through any controversial behavior.
- Punctuality is not a traditional virtue in Saudi Arabia. Many Saudis do not even make appointments with specific start times. Instead, they set appointments for the time between particular prayer times. If you don't know when the prayer times are (they vary with the season of the year), check a daily newspaper.
- Don't expect Western-style checks and balances in Saudi Arabia. Government contracts do not need competitive bids, and transparency is almost nonexistent. The Saudis have their own way of doing business, and they feel that it works just fine.

> **Cultural Note**
>
> All countries consider their flag important, but the Saudi Arabian flag is important to all Muslims. This is because it contains the name of Allah, written in Arabic. Muslims all over the world object when the Saudi flag is not treated with respect, because it shows contempt for the name of Allah.
>
> For example, when the World Cup is held every four years, many manufacturers market soccer balls decorated with the flags of every qualifying nation. When the team from Saudi Arabia qualified, Muslims were outraged—the name of Allah was placed on something designed to be kicked!

▶ COUNTRY BACKGROUND

History

Although the Arabian Peninsula has been occupied for thousands of years, the Saudi Arabian nation was only founded in 1932. In that year, after thirty years of fighting, Abdul Aziz Bin Abdul Rahman Al-Saud united the tribes of the Peninsula.

Much of the day-to-day running of Saudi Arabia is left in the hands of foreign workers. Technical and managerial workers tend to come from North America, Europe, and Japan. Manual and unskilled laborers are primarily from Africa and Asia. The Saudis have been replacing the Middle Eastern workers that formerly constituted a large part of their foreign work force; these Palestinians and Lebanese are not considered politically reliable by the Saudi government. Guest workers may not become citizens, no matter how long they stay in Saudi Arabia.

While most of the citizens of Saudi Arabia are quite well off, some segments of the population have not benefited from the country's wealth. Some nomadic Bedouins still maintain their traditional lifestyle. But the Bedouins are given the opportunity to change, whereas the Shiite minority is not. (Concerned by the Shiite power in Iran, the Saudi government allows its Shiite citizenry to remain poor and powerless.)

Thus far, Saudi Arabia has had a relatively peaceful succession from one king to another. However, King Faisal Bin Abdul Aziz Al-Saud deposed his brother, King Saud, in 1964. In 1975, King Faisal himself was assassinated by his nephew. Faisal was succeeded by his brother, King Khalid, who died in 1981. Khalid was succeeded by his brother, King Fahd Bin Abdul Aziz Al-Saud.

The 1990 invasion of neighboring Kuwait by Iraq proved a traumatic experience for Saudi Arabia. Iraqi Scud missiles struck Saudi territory, and a Saudi border town was briefly occupied by Iraqi troops.

To support the allied liberation of Kuwait, Saudi Arabia found itself hosting troops from thirty-three nations. Both foreign troops and Saudis had to adjust. (In deference to Western sensibilities, public beheadings were delayed until after the effective conclusion of the war; upon resumption of the executions, sixteen men were beheaded in one day.)

After the war, opposition to the continued presence of foreign troops in Saudi Arabia (along with the many foreign workers in the oil industry) became a rallying point for opponents of the Saudi royal family.

In 1992, King Fahd initiated the first of a series of reforms, including the establishment of a new Consultative Council. The council was composed of a chairman and sixty members chosen by the king. The number of members was increased from sixty to ninety in 1997.

The September 11, 2001, terrorist attacks on the U.S. World Trade Center and the Pentagon caused great consternation to Saudi Arabia, especially when it was revealed that fifteen of the nineteen terrorists involved were Saudi nationals. Saudi officials have vehemently denied that they gave Al Qaeda terrorists any financial support.

Once considered one of the safest countries in the world, Saudis must now contend with terrorism. In the past few years, terrorists associated with Al Qaeda have targeted foreigners—especially U.S. citizens—working in Saudi Arabia.

Type of Government

Saudi Arabia is an Islamic monarchy. It was united, is ruled, and is run by the house of Saud (al-Saud). There is no written constitution, although it is traditional to say that the Koran is the constitution of Saudi Arabia. King Abdul Aziz Bin Abdul Rahman Al-Saud (known incorrectly in the West as ibn Saud) united the Arabian Peninsula in 1932. Saudi Arabia was named after him, and he became the new country's first king. All of the successive kings have been sons of Abdul Aziz; indeed, the majority of government officials are members of the al-Saud family. (King Abdul Aziz united his kingdom by marriage and by conquest. He married more than 300 times and had thousands of descendants.)

The king of Saudi Arabia is also prime minister, making him both the head of state and head of government. An appointed Council of Ministers advises the king. In 1993, a Consultative Council was established; its members are also appointed by the king. There is no elected government at this time, although eventual elections have been promised. The only codified restraint on the power of the king is Islamic law. In practice, however, the king is careful not to alienate either the religious fundamentalists or his people. He receives members of the general public at the Majlis, the weekly meeting where his subjects can discuss issues and raise grievances.

Current government data can be found on the Web at the Royal Embassy of Saudi Arabia at *www.saudiembassy.net.*

Language

Arabic is the official language. English is the most popular foreign language and is spoken by the majority of Saudis who conduct business internationally. Ethnologue.com has identified four variants of Arabic spoken in Saudi Arabia, plus a sign language for the deaf.

Cultural Note

The Arabic phrase *Abu al-Hol* (Father of Terror) has been applied to numerous people and things. In Egypt, for example, it is the local name given to the Great Sphinx in the outskirts of Cairo. But in Saudi Arabia, Abu al-Hol is the name given to a great cave formation.

Saudi Arabia has a vast network of caves, many of which have yet to be explored. Except when hunting for precious water, Saudis tended to avoid the sinkholes that lead to caves. Bedouin tradition held that sinkholes were the home of *djinn*—spirits who were best left alone. If you happen to be traveling in the interior and see a flock of rock doves apparently rise from nowhere, they probably live in a cave and just emerged from a nearby sinkhole.

The Saudi Arabian View

Saudi Arabia is an Islamic nation. Saudi citizens are Muslim and are not permitted to change religions. Westerners are frequently surprised to learn that Saudi Arabia is a more fundamentalist nation than the Islamic Republic of Iran.

The official religion of Saudi Arabia is the Wahabi branch of Sunni Islam. Wahabism is a rigid, puritanical sect that reflects Islam as it was practiced during the lifetime of Mohammed, over 1,300 years ago.

A massive education campaign has raised the literacy level. But many older, rural Saudis are still illiterate; around post offices you can find scribes who write letters for the illiterate. Educational levels for males have traditionally been far above those for females, as Wahabi tradition dismissed education for girls as counterproductive.

Many Western observers believe that Wahabism is insufficiently flexible for the wealthy, modern state that Saudi Arabia has become. However, it is firmly entrenched, and adherence to its precepts is enforced daily by the Matawain (religious police).

Since 1972, when Saudi Arabia began taking control of Aramco Oil, Saudi leaders have forged their own destiny, free of foreign control. However, Saudi Arabia's leaders can only push their people in a direction they wish to go. Unprecedented public protests in 2003 suggest that Saudi leaders are not changing quickly enough.

In recent years, suicide bombers have caused much soul-searching. The Saudis have referred to the 2003 attacks that killed thirty-five people in the capital of Riyadh as "our own 9-11."

Saudi Arabia is home to the two holiest cities of Islam: Makkah and Madinah. Hundreds of thousands of Muslims from all over the world make the pilgrimage to Makkah each year. Entry into Makkah and Madinah is prohibited to non-Muslims. Guardianship of these sites poses difficult security issues. Stampedes during the Makkah pilgrimages can result in hundreds of deaths.

☑ Know Before You Go

The importation of alcohol, pork products, and pornography is prohibited.

Terrorists (presumed to be associated with Al Qaeda) have attacked, kidnapped, and killed foreigners in Saudi Arabia.

Although terrorists have sometimes disguised themselves in police or military uniforms, foreigners are still required to stop at all police checkpoints. Failure to comply can lead to arrest and detention by Saudi authorities.

Malaria is endemic in the low-lying coastal plains of southwest Saudi Arabia, especially around the port of Jeddah.

Homosexual activity is considered a criminal offense, punishable by lashing, imprisonment, or even death.

Other prohibited activities include criticizing Islam, the Saudi royal family, and public practice of any religion except Islam. Foreigners are warned against wearing visible signs of non-Islamic religions, including wearing a crucifix.

▶ CULTURAL ORIENTATION

Cognitive Styles: How Saudi Arabians Organize and Process Information

Saudis find it difficult to accept any outside information that does not reflect Islamic values. Most Saudis are trained to think associatively. However, the majority of Saudi males complete their higher education in the United States, where they learn to process information conceptually and analytically. They do become personally involved in all situations rather than using rules or laws to solve problems.

Negotiation Strategies: What Saudi Arabians Accept as Evidence

Generally, a Saudi's faith in Islamic ideologies shapes the truth, but it is also affected by the immediate feelings of the participants. Reliance solely on objective facts seldom overrules a Saudi's feelings and faith in a decision.

Value Systems: The Basis for Behavior

Saudi Arabia is a very strong Islamic state and finds it difficult to integrate Western ideas into its value systems. The following three sections identify the Value Systems in the predominant culture—their methods of dividing right from wrong, good from evil, and so forth.

Locus of Decision-Making

The male leader is the decision-maker, but he always seeks out and considers the opinion of the group or collective. The individual is always subordinate to the family, tribe, or collective. Solutions to all problems are found in the correct interpretation and application of divine law. Leadership and identity come from one's lineage and one's ability to protect the honor of the extended family.

Sources of Anxiety Reduction

Tribal membership remains the cornerstone of the individual's social identity, and security is found in family loyalty and absolute submission to Islamic law. There is a strong sense of fatalism, with one's destiny in the hands of Allah. Individuals can do nothing about this, so they tend to accept the status quo. Loyalty to the house of Saud, not nationality, historically brought a feeling of national security—although this loyalty is increasingly being challenged.

Issues of Equality/Inequality

Within Islam all believers are equal and united in the ulema. There is cultural homogeneity among tribes. Most are Sunni Muslims adhering to Wahabi religious tenets. There are a great number of foreign workers who are accepted with varying degrees of bias. Men and women are seen as qualitatively different in emotion and intellect. Public life is primarily the domain of men. However, there are more highly educated Saudi women who pursue professional careers nowadays, like medicine or teaching. Within the confines of the home, the position of women has changed somewhat. Many of the traditional housekeeping duties of a mother are now often assigned to servants. Many husbands now share decisions concerning the home with their wives. And fewer Saudi men take multiple wives.

Cultural Note

Visitors to Saudi Arabia, whatever their nationality, are subject to the same rigorous Islamic law as Saudis. It is not uncommon for westerners to be imprisoned in Saudi Arabia for possessing an illegal substance. (Alcohol, pornography, pork, and narcotics are all highly illegal.) Saudi law is draconian; thieves still have their hands amputated, and capital crimes are punished by public beheadings. Not surprisingly, the populace is quite law-abiding.

▶ BUSINESS PRACTICES

Punctuality, Appointments, and Local Time

- Punctuality is not considered a virtue in Saudi Arabia. Your client may be late for an appointment or not show up at all. You, however, should endeavor to be prompt.
- It is standard practice to keep supplicants, including foreign businesspeople, waiting. Do not expect to be able to keep more than one appointment per day.
- You will need a Saudi sponsor before you may enter Saudi Arabia. This sponsor will act as intermediary and arrange appointments with the appropriate individuals.
- An appointment is rarely private. Expect your visit to be interrupted by phone calls and visits from your client's friends and family. Westerners frequently find these distractions infuriating; try to maintain your equanimity.
- Saudi officials were traditionally prohibited from working more than six hours per day. Mornings are usually best for appointments.
- Because of the summer heat, some Saudi businesspeople work after dark. They may request an evening appointment at any time up to midnight.
- Friday is the Muslim holy day; no business is conducted. Most people do not work on Thursdays, either. The work week runs from Saturday through Wednesday.
- Business hours vary widely, but most businesses close for much of the afternoon and reopen for a few hours in late afternoon.
- Holidays: Remember that the Islamic calendar uses lunar months of 28 days, so an Islamic year of 12 months is only 354 days long. Holidays will thus be on different dates by the Western calendar every year. Paperwork should carry two dates, the Gregorian (Western) date and the Hijrah (Arabic) date.
- Check with your Saudi sponsor as to which holidays the persons you intend to meet will observe. There is only one secular holiday, the Saudi National Day, which commemorates the unification of the kingdom. Many businesses remain open on Saudi National Day.
- Everyone observes the two most important holidays, and no business will be conducted during them. They are:
  - Eid al-Fitr—The festival of breaking fast. This is a three-day feast celebrating the end of the fasting of the month of Ramadan.
  - Eid al-Adha—The feast of the sacrifice. This is a three-day festival beginning on the tenth day of the month of Zul-Hijjah.
- Saudi Arabia is three hours ahead of Greenwich Mean Time (G.M.T. +3) or eight hours ahead of U.S. Eastern Standard Time (E.S.T. +8).

Negotiating

- The pace of business is much slower in Saudi Arabia than in the West. Be patient.
- Business meetings always start slowly, with long inquiries into one's health and journey.
- Decision-making can be a protracted process.
- An experienced Saudi contact will sound out the opinions of various decision-makers before you meet with them. Then, he will put you in contact only with the ones most likely to favor your proposal. Do not rush your contact into these important introductions. To do so is to risk having your proposal turned down because you met with the wrong persons.
- Your Saudi contact-sponsor is the single most important key to success in Saudi Arabia. You must find one who has the right temperament and influential friends or relatives. Once you choose a sponsor, you will not be permitted to switch.
- Business cards should be printed in English on one side and in Arabic on the other.
- Remember that Arabic is read right-to-left, so place your company logo accordingly.
- Many Saudis have unlisted telephone numbers. When a Saudi gives you his business card, be aware his numbers, e-mails, etc., may not be listed on it.
- Be prepared to leave multiple copies of all brochures and materials. The person you spoke to might not be the real decision-maker, and your proposal may have to be relayed to many others.
- Saudis speak at a much closer distance than North Americans. Do not back up or shy away. There is also more physical contact (but only between the same gender). Conversations usually involve touching.
- Coffee is often served toward the end of a business meeting. This is a signal that the meeting will soon conclude. Incense is often lit at this time as well.
- Saudi men often walk hand in hand. If a Saudi holds your hand, take it as a sign of friendship.
- Arabic is a language of hyperbole. When a Saudi says "yes," it usually means "possibly." Be encouraged by this, but do not assume that the negotiating is over.
- Protecting one's dignity is vital to Saudis. You may have to compromise on some issue just to ensure that your Saudi contact is not mortified by an inadvertent action or decision.
- Do not bring up the subject of women unless your Saudi counterpart does so first. Do not even inquire as to the health of a Saudi's wife or daughter.
- The topic of Israel should similarly be avoided.
- Sports are a good topic of conversation. Football (soccer), horse and camel racing (with betting prohibited), hunting, and falconry are the most popular Saudi sports.

Business Entertaining

- Hosting visitors is considered a virtue among Saudis, so they will take care of all of the entertaining within their country.

- Be prepared to remove your shoes before entering a building. Follow the lead of your host.
- Remember that alcohol and pork are illegal, and that eating is done with the right hand only. Even if you are left-handed, eat with your right hand.
- If you cannot keep up with Saudi appetites during a meal, try to nibble on something while they finish eating.
- Expect to encounter eating utensils only in westernized Saudi homes.
- Also expect constant inquiries of "How are you?" Your host will be concerned that you have everything you want to eat or drink, and this is a common way of asking.

▶ PROTOCOL

Greetings

- As there are several styles of greeting currently in use in Saudi Arabia, it is safest to wait for your Saudi counterpart to initiate the greeting, especially at a first meeting.
- Westernized Saudi men shake hands with other men.
- Some Saudi men will shake hands with Western women. Saudi women are generally not involved in business. When a veiled Saudi woman is with a Saudi man, it is not traditional to introduce her. Again, follow the Saudi's lead.
- A more traditional Saudi greeting between men involves each grasping the other's right hand, placing the left hand on the other's right shoulder, and exchanging kisses on each cheek.

Titles/Forms of Address

- Westerners frequently find Arabic names confusing. The best solution is to ask your Saudi sponsor to provide you with the names—written in English—of any Saudis you will have to meet, speak to, or correspond with. Find out their full names (for use in correspondence), and how they are to be addressed in person.
- Saudi names are written in Arabic. Translating from Arabic to other alphabets is not an exact science. Arabic names may be spelled several different ways in English. For example, the founder of the Kingdom of Saudi Arabia was King Abdul Aziz Bin Abdul Rahman Al-Saud. However, his name is also rendered in English as King Abd-al-Aziz Al Saud. History books tend to render his name as King Ibn Saud.
- For further information on the proper titles and forms of address for Arabic-speaking countries, please consult Appendix A.

Cultural Note

It can be difficult to achieve the correct balance between respect and familiarity with a Saudi. One way to do this is to address a parent by his *kunya*—that is, as "father of . . . ." If a Saudi's eldest son is named Fawaz, he may be addressed simply as "abu Fawaz" (father of Fawaz).

While it is less common, you can address a Saudi woman in a similar way. Use the word *umm* (mother of), as in "umm Fawaz" (mother of Fawaz).

Gestures

- The left hand is considered unclean in the Arab world. Always use the right hand in preference to the left (unless you are handling something considered unclean). Never eat with the left hand; eat only with your right hand. Avoid gesturing with the left hand.
- Although Arabs constantly gesture with their hands while speaking, they do not point at another person. This would be considered impolite.
- As a general rule, keep both feet on the ground. Arabs do not cross their legs when sitting. Never show the bottom of your foot to an Arab; it is offensive.
- The "thumbs-up" gesture is crude throughout the Arab world.

Gifts

- Saudi hospitality is legendary. However, you are not expected to bring any gift when invited into a Saudi home.
- Saudis have great appreciation for craftsmanship. To show respect for the gift, a Saudi is likely to open it immediately in the presence of the giver. Then he and everyone assembled will examine it minutely. Never present any gift that is of inferior craftsmanship.
- Some gifts for men are prohibited by tradition. Muslim men do not wear gold jewelry or wear silk clothing; these are reserved for women.
- Typical gifts for Saudi men include oriental carpets (which must be handmade), jewelry (silver or platinum, never gold), incense, and perfume. Be aware that prestigious incense and perfumes can be extraordinarily expensive. The traditional male scent is called *oud* and is made of an extract of aloes wood.
- Another woman must present gifts to a Saudi woman. It would be inappropriate for a foreign man to give a gift to a Saudi woman.
- Traditionally, every Saudi who must broker or approve a business deal takes a percentage. Be careful that you do not run afoul of your government's foreign corrupt practices law.

Cultural Note

Only close friends give gifts in Saudi Arabia. To give a gift to a Saudi before a close relationship has been established may mortify him, or at a minimum, make him uncomfortable.

When gifts are given, it is traditional to give the best gift one can afford. Saudi businessmen are often quite wealthy, so it is not unusual for such gifts to cost thousands of dollars.

Dress

- While foreigners are not exempt from Saudi standards of dress, do not adopt native clothing: for men, a *ghutra* (headdress) and *thobe* (flowing white robe); for women, a veil and an *abaya* (black head-to-foot robe). Saudis may find it offensive to see foreigners dressed in their traditional garments.
- Foreigners should wear Western clothes that approach the modesty of Saudi dress. Despite the heat of the desert, most of the body must remain covered.
- Men should wear long trousers and a shirt, preferably long-sleeved. A jacket and tie are usually required for business meetings. Keep shirts buttoned up to the collarbone. Saudi law prohibits the wearing of neck jewelry by men, and westerners have been arrested for violating such rules.
- Women must wear modest clothing. The neckline should be high, and the sleeves should come to at least the elbows. Hemlines should be well below the knee, if not ankle-length. The overall effect should be one of baggy concealment; a full-length outfit that is tight and revealing is not acceptable. Therefore, pants or pantsuits are not recommended. While a hat or scarf is not always required, it is wise to keep a scarf at hand. The suitability of your attire will be apparent as soon as you venture out; if Saudi men stare lewdly at you, your dress is not sufficiently modest. These same stares are used to determine when a Saudi girl is old enough to start wearing an abaya.

Cultural Note

The Matawain (often called "the religious police") enforce the modesty of dress in public. They have the authority to punish violators with their camel hair whips. While they do not possess the power to arrest, they are often accompanied by police officers that can make such arrests. Where the jurisdiction of the civil and religious police overlap, the civil authorities generally defer to the Matawain. While the ranks of the Matawain include a surprising number of foreign-educated Saudis, the ones enforcing Islamic law on street corners—and there are many—are often less-educated zealots brandishing camel whips. Western women who wear skirts that are too short may have their legs whipped. The Matawain can be neither reasoned with nor bribed, only endured.

Singapore

Republic of Singapore

Cultural Note

Singapore remains a booming center of capitalism in Southeast Asia. It is considered exceptionally safe (even antiseptic), however, visitors should remember that Singapore's myriad laws apply to natives and foreigners equally. Before arrival, travelers should become familiar with these laws: for example, no littering, no nonprescription chewing gum, no illegal drugs, no pornographic materials, no weapons, no jaywalking, no spitting, and no smoking in most public places. There is speculation that some of these stringent laws will ease in the future, but to date, they are unfailingly enforced.

 ## WHAT'S YOUR CULTURAL IQ?

1. Which of the following is true about driving in Singapore?
   a. Singapore enforces traffic regulations with cameras that monitor violations.
   b. Many Singaporean drivers are erratic and unpredictable on the road.
   c. A branch with green leaves adorning a stopped car indicates that the vehicle has broken down.
   d. Cars are driven on the left side of the road.
   e. All of the above are true.

   ANSWER: e. Traffic is a combination of high-tech (cameras), tradition (a branch stuck in the bumper of a broken-down car), and temperaments.

2. The government of Singapore applies its draconian legal code to citizens and visitors alike. TRUE or FALSE: Singapore is one of the few nations that still sentences criminals to be caned.

   ANSWER: TRUE. In fact, a teenager named Michael Fay (a U.S. citizen) was caned for vandalism in 1994, despite the intercession of then-U.S. president Bill Clinton.

3. After Sir Stamford Raffles established a trading post on Singapore Island in 1819, it was ruled by the United Kingdom for over a century. TRUE or FALSE: Singapore briefly joined with newly independent Indonesia in 1963.

   ANSWER: FALSE. Singapore joined the Federation of Malaysia in 1963. In 1965, Singapore left and became independent.

▶ TIPS ON DOING BUSINESS IN SINGAPORE

- All of the ethnic groups in Singapore prefer intermittent eye contact. This is especially true in situations between persons of unequal station: the person with lower status does not meet the gaze of his or her superior. Westerners sometimes interpret this failure to "look me in the eye" as evidence of untrustworthiness. On the contrary, in Singapore, sustained eye contact is considered hostile and threatening.

- One reason for the government's tight control over Singapore's populace is that it is a multicultural society. Singapore's ethnic Chinese dominate the business sector, just as they do in nearby Malaysia and Indonesia. Traditionally, this generated resentment on the part of the Indian population and the native ethnic Malays. The government has multiple programs to foster national unity.

- Offer your most advanced technical proposals in Singapore. It is a country where they are aggressive about innovative training in their schools and technology in their industries. Determined not to be left behind in the high-tech arena, Singapore is striving to become a center for stem-cell research.

▶ COUNTRY BACKGROUND

History

A crossroads of trade for centuries, Singapore was annexed by the British in 1819. British rule was to last some 120 years and gave the island British legal traditions and the English language. During World War II, the Japanese occupied Singapore from 1942 to 1945. After the war Singapore became a British crown colony, but the power of the British Empire was fading.

Singapore's first election was held in 1959. The People's Action Party (PAP) took the election and has remained in power ever since. The first prime minister was Cambridge-educated Lee Kuan Yew. Singapore experienced tremendous development under Lee and the PAP.

Singapore joined the Malayan Federation in 1963, but it seceded just two years later. Since 1965 it has been a separate, sovereign nation and a member of the British Commonwealth.

Many did not believe that Singapore could survive as an independent country. The tiny island had no natural resources aside from its harbor, and no way to defend itself against populous and often aggressive neighbors. Realizing that Singapore's people were its greatest national asset, Prime Minister Lee Kuan Yew's government embarked upon social engineering on a grand scale. The people would be educated, and capitalism would be encouraged. Old traditions were suppressed, and Singapore was turned into a true meritocracy.

No aspect of life was considered beyond the reach of the government. The "3-S Plan" of Social Responsibility, Social Attitude, and Skill became an official credo. Citizens were constantly reminded of the threat from Singapore's populous neighbors, and internal dissent was silenced. Tiny Singapore built up defense forces with the most up-to-date technology in the world. However, opponents of the government were sometimes jailed without trial; overly critical foreign journalists were deported, and any publication that employed such a journalist was liable to be banned from sale in Singapore.

Thankfully, Singapore was spared serious damage in the disastrous Boxing Day tsunami of 2004. Singapore has also made progress in its various long-term disputes with neighboring Malaysia.

Type of Government

The Republic of Singapore is a parliamentary democracy that has been ruled by one party since the nation achieved independence from Malaysia in 1965. The government exhorts its people to accept stringent limitations on freedom in return for peace and prosperity. These limitations often make Singapore more attractive from a business standpoint. (For example, Singapore's citizens have a high rate of savings, because participation in the Central Provident Fund—a pension program—is mandatory for all citizens.)

The leaders of Singapore are fond of saying that their island's only resources are the wit, industry, and inventiveness of the Singaporean people. They have successfully turned a developing nation into a center of capitalism.

Singapore has a unicameral parliament. The prime minister is the head of government. The chief of state is the president.

Current government data can be found at the Embassy of Singapore at *www.mfa.gov .sg/washington.*

Cultural Note
Although English is commonly spoken, it is a unique version. Singaporeans tend to imprint English with the patterns of their native tongue. There is even a term for this Singapore-English: Singlish.

Language

Singapore has four official languages: Malay, Tamil, Chinese, and English. To unify Singapore's three fractious ethnic groups—the Chinese, Malays, and Indians—English (native to none of these groups) became the language of instruction, business, and government. (This process has not ended; to unify the diverse Chinese populations, only Mandarin Chinese movies may be shown—despite the fact that most Singaporean Chinese speak Cantonese, not Mandarin.) Both Malay and English are printed using the Latin alphabet; Tamil and Chinese use their traditional forms of writing.

For data on the various languages of Singapore, see Ethnologue at *www.ethnologue.com.*

Cultural Note

Islam conquered much of the Middle East and Africa by the sword. In the islands of Southeast Asia, however, Muslim traders from the Indian subcontinent brought it peacefully. Some believe that this historical distinction yields a gentler, less rigorous type of Islam. Others disagree. And it may no longer matter, as fiery fundamentalist *mullahs* have come to Singapore, Malaysia, and Indonesia to agitate the Muslim populace. The authorities in Singapore try to keep out such individuals, but they can't totally halt the distribution of fundamentalist literature and recordings.

The Singaporean View

Most indigenous Malay are Muslim, but not all Muslims are Malay. Muslims account for over 15 percent of the population. Similarly, Christianity is adhered to by several different ethnic groups. Those Singaporeans who trace their roots to the Indian subcontinent come from many different ethnic groups; they may be Hindu, Muslim, Christian, Zoroastrian, Sikh, or adherents of yet another religion. The majority Chinese may profess to follow Buddhism, Confucianism, Taoism, none of these, or several of the above simultaneously. Wisely, Singapore has no official religion.

☑ Know Before You Go

Singapore is a very safe nation. Aside from running afoul of the country's regulations, visitors are most at risk from the hot and humid weather.

Although rarely seen outside garden areas, Singapore does have some dangerous wildlife, including poisonous snakes, spiders, and centipedes.

CULTURAL ORIENTATION

Cognitive Styles: How Singaporeans Organize and Process Information

Singapore's culture is closed to all but select information. Singaporeans' basic education teaches them to think associatively, but higher education brings in conceptual and analytical thinking. They have strong loyalties to their nation, companies, and groups, but particular relationships are more important than personal values.

Negotiation Strategies: What Singaporeans Accept as Evidence

Immediate feelings have a strong influence on the truth. This is usually biased by faith in the ideologies of nationalism, and supplemented by the accumulation of objective facts.

Value Systems: The Basis for Behavior

The strong Malay and Indian subcultures have different value systems from those of the Chinese. The following three sections identify the Value Systems in the predominant culture—their methods of dividing right from wrong, good from evil, and so forth.

Locus of Decision-Making

Individuals must work within the consensus of the group and forgo personal triumphs. The person with the highest ethos in the group (usually the oldest member) is the de facto leader. One must not lose face or cause another to be publicly embarrassed, so Singaporeans would rather use polite vagaries than utter an outright "no." There is a very strong authoritative structure that demands impartiality and obedience. One must build a relationship with the participants of a group before conducting business.

Sources of Anxiety Reduction

The family is the most important unit of social organization. Political power, wealth, and education are the criteria for social status. There is a very strong work ethic in which emotional restraint is prized and aggressive behavior is frowned upon. Although this is a multiracial society with a strong national identity, the social structure continues to change, and this leads to uncertainty. Multiracial housing has fostered feelings of insecurity, not community.

Issues of Equality/Inequality

Businesses are more competitive and ethnocentric than in the United States. Emphasis is on competence, merit, and team play. Performance, progress, excellence, and achievement are highly prized for the group. There is an inherent trust in people of the same ethnic group, with a strong feeling of interdependency among members of a group or business. There is some evidence of ethnic bias among the dominant Chinese against the Malays and the Indians. There are clearly differentiated sex roles in society, but gender equality is creeping in. Men still dominate in most public situations.

 BUSINESS PRACTICES

Punctuality, Appointments, and Local Time

- Always be on time for all business appointments. Making a Singaporean executive wait is insulting and impolite.
- Try to schedule appointments at least two weeks in advance. Executives travel frequently—especially to conferences in their area of specialization.
- English is the language of virtually all business or government correspondence, and most transactions in Singapore. However, the English spoken often has native inflections, syntax, and grammar, which can easily lead to misunderstandings.
- Remember that Singapore is a meritocracy. Few people get ahead, either in business or in government, without hard work and long hours. Executives will often work far longer days than their subordinates.
- Singaporeans write the day first, then the month, then the year (e.g., December 3, 2010, is written 3.12.10 or 3/12/10).

- Singapore is eight hours ahead of Greenwich Mean Time (G.M.T. +8), making it thirteen hours ahead of U.S. Eastern Standard Time (E.S.T. +13).

Negotiating

- The pace of business negotiations in Singapore may be slow compared to the West. Be patient.
- It would be unusual to complete a complicated business deal in only one trip. Expect to take several trips over a period of months.
- Because polite Singaporeans rarely disagree openly, evasion, or even pretending that a question was never asked, is indicative of a "no."
- Remember that a Singaporean must like and be comfortable with you personally to do business. This relationship does not extend to your company. If your company replaces you with another executive, the new person will have to forge this relationship anew (unless the new executive is a blood relative of yours).
- Unwavering civility is the single most important attribute for successful relationships in Singapore. However, diplomacy in no way hinders the determination of Singaporean businesspeople to get their own way.
- People in Singapore may smile or laugh in situations that westerners consider inappropriate. Smiles may hide embarrassment, shyness, bitterness, and/or discord. Singaporean businessmen may laugh at the most serious part of a business meeting; this may be an expression of anxiety, not frivolity.
- In Singapore, a person who loses his or her temper in public is considered unable to control himself or herself, and will not be trusted or respected.
- Be cautious in asking Singaporean Chinese a question. English speakers would give a negative answer to the question "Isn't my order ready yet?" by responding "no" (meaning, "No, it's not ready"). The Chinese pattern is the opposite: "yes" (meaning, "Yes, it is not ready").
- Age and seniority are highly respected. If you are part of a delegation, line up so that the most important persons will be introduced first. If you are introducing two people, state the name of the most important person first (e.g., "President Smith, this is Engineer Wong").
- Speak in quiet, gentle tones. Always remain calm. Leave plenty of time for someone to respond to a statement you make; people in Singapore do not jump on the end of someone else's sentences. Politeness demands that they leave a respectful pause (as long as ten to fifteen seconds) before responding. Westerners often assume that they have agreement and resume talking before a Singaporean has a chance to respond.
- Business cards should be printed (preferably embossed) in English. Because ethnic Chinese constitute the majority of Singaporeans (and an even higher percentage of businesspeople), it is a good idea to have the reverse side of your card translated into Chinese (gold ink is the most prestigious color for Chinese characters).

- The exchange of business cards is a formal ceremony. After introductions are made, the visiting businessperson should offer his or her card. Make sure you give a card to each person present. With both hands on your card, present it to the recipient with the print facing him or her, so that he or she can read it. The recipient may receive the card with both hands, then study it for a few moments before carefully putting it away in a pocket. You should do the same when a card is presented to you. Never put a card in your back pocket, where many men carry their wallets. Do not write on someone's business card.
- Topics to avoid in conversation include any criticism of Singaporean ways, religion, bureaucracy, or politics. Also avoid any discussion of sex.
- Good topics for discussion include tourism, travel, plans for the future, organizational success (talking about personal success is considered impolite boasting), and food (while remaining complimentary to the local cuisine).

Business Entertaining

- Take advantage of any invitations to social events; successful business relationships hinge on strong social relationships.
- Food is vitally important in Singapore culture. Indeed, the standard Chinese greeting literally means "Have you eaten?"
- Respond to written invitations in writing. Among the Chinese, white and blue are colors associated with sadness; do not print invitations on paper of these colors. Red or pink paper is a good choice for invitations.
- Generally, spouses may be invited to dinners but not to lunch. However, no business will be discussed at an event where spouses are present.
- Singapore's anticorruption laws are so strict that government officials may be prohibited from attending social events.

> ### Cultural Note
> Cleanliness and order is strictly enforced. Trash collection occurs seven days a week and there are heavy fines for littering. Even the harbor is refuse-free and generally devoid of oil slicks.

PROTOCOL

Greetings

- Singapore has three major ethnic groups, each with its own traditions: Chinese, Malay, and Indian.
- With younger or foreign-educated Singaporeans, a handshake is the most common form of greeting. The standard Asian handshake is more of a handclasp; it is rather gentle and

lasts for some ten or twelve seconds. (By contrast, most North American handshakes are very firm but last for only three or four seconds.) Often, both hands will be used.

- In Singapore, westernized women may shake hands with both men and women. Singaporean men usually wait for a woman to offer her hand. It is perfectly acceptable for a woman to simply nod upon an introduction rather than offer her hand. Women should offer their hands only upon greetings; too-frequent handshaking is easily misinterpreted as an amorous advance. (Among themselves, men tend to shake hands on both greeting and departure.)

- Among Singaporean Chinese, the traditional greeting was a bow. However, most now shake hands or combine a bow with a handshake. Chinese men are likely to be comfortable shaking hands with a woman—more so than other ethnic groups of Singapore.

- Singaporean Malay are generally Muslim. Traditionally, there is no physical contact between Muslim men and women. Indeed, if a religious Muslim male is touched by a woman, he must ritually cleanse himself before he prays again. Because of this, women should be careful about offering to shake hands with Malay men, and men should not offer to shake hands with Malay women. Of course, if a westernized Malay offers to shake hands, do so.

- The traditional Malay greeting is the salaam, which is akin to a handshake without the grip. Both parties stretch out one or both hands, touch each other's hand(s) lightly, then bring their hand(s) back to rest over their heart. This greeting is done only between people of the same sex. However, if cloth such as a scarf or shawl prevents actual skin-to-skin contact, then Malay men and women may engage in the salaam.

- Many Singaporean Indians are Hindu. They avoid public contact between men and women, although not as vehemently as most Muslims. Only westernized Hindus will shake hands with the opposite sex.

- The traditional Indian greeting involves a slight bow with the palms of the hands together (as if praying). This greeting, called the namaste, will generally be used only by older, traditional Hindus. However, it is also an acceptable alternative to a handshake when a Western businesswoman greets an Indian man.

Titles/Forms of Address

- Most people you meet should be addressed with a title and their name. If a person does not have a professional title (President, Engineer, Doctor), simply use "Mr." or "Madam," "Mrs.," or "Miss," plus their name.

- Each of the three major ethnic groups in Singapore has different naming patterns. For further information on the proper titles and forms of address in Chinese, Muslim, and Indian cultures, please consult Appendix A.

- With so many complexities, it is best to ask a Singaporean what you should call him or her. Repeat it to confirm your pronunciation is correct. Clearly explain your name and choose the same degree of formality. Don't tell a Singaporean "just call me Tony" when you are calling him Dr. Gupta.

Gestures

- Aside from handshakes, there is no public contact between the sexes in Singapore. Do not kiss or hug a person of the opposite sex in public—even if you are husband and wife. On the other hand, contact is permitted between people of the same sex. Men may hold hands with men or even walk with their arms around each other; this is interpreted as nothing except friendship.
- Among both Muslims and Hindus, the left hand is considered unclean. Eat with your right hand only. Do not touch anything or anyone with your left hand if you can use your right hand instead. Accept gifts and hold cash in the right hand. (Obviously, when both hands are needed, use them both.)
- The foot is also considered unclean. Do not move or touch anything with your feet.
- Do not show the soles of your feet or shoes. This restriction determines how one sits: You can cross your legs at the knee, but you probably do not want to sit with one ankle on the other knee. Also, do not prop your feet up on anything not intended for feet, such as a desk.
- It is impolite to point at anyone with the forefinger. Malays use a forefinger only to point at animals. Even pointing with two fingers is impolite among many Indians. When you must indicate something or someone, use the entire right hand (palm out). You can also point with your right thumb, as long as all four fingers are curled down. (Make sure all your fingers are curled—older Malays would interpret a fist with the thumb and little finger extended as an insult.)
- Avoid pounding one fist into the palm of your other hand. It is considered an obscene gesture.
- The head is considered the seat of the soul by many Indians and Malays. Never touch someone's head, not even to pat the hair of a child.
- Among Indians, a side-to-side toss of one's head indicates agreement, although westerners may interpret it as meaning "no." Watch carefully; the Indian head toss is not quite the same as the Western negative nod (which leads with the jaw).
- As in much of the world, to beckon someone, you hold your hand out, palm downward, and make a scooping motion with the fingers. Beckoning someone with the palm up and wagging one finger can be construed as an insult.
- Standing tall with your hands on your hips—the "arms akimbo" position (or "offsides" in soccer)—is always interpreted as an angry, aggressive posture.
- The comfortable standing distance between two people in Singapore varies with the culture. In general, stand as far apart as you would if you were about to shake hands (about 2 to 3 feet). Indians tend to stand a bit further apart (3 or 3½ feet).

Gifts

- Singapore prides itself on being the most corruption-free country in Asia. Consequently, it has strict laws against bribery. Government employees may not accept any gift at all.
- Gifts are given between friends. Do not give a gift to anyone before you have established a personal relationship with that person. Otherwise, the gift may have the appearance of a bribe.
- It is not the custom to unwrap a gift in the presence of the giver. To do so would suggest that the recipient is greedy and impatient. Worse, if the gift is somehow inappropriate or disappointing, both the recipient and the giver would be embarrassed. Expect the recipient to thank you briefly, then put the still-wrapped gift aside until you have left.
- The Chinese traditionally decline a gift three times before accepting; this prevents them from appearing greedy. Continue to insist; once they accept the gift, thank them profusely.
- Further guidelines on gift-giving to Chinese/Singaporean associates is in the chapter on China.
- As pork and alcohol are prohibited to observing Muslims, do not give them as gifts to Malays. Other foods make good gifts, although meat products must be halal (the Muslim equivalent of kosher). The prohibition against pork and alcohol also precludes pigskin products and perfumes containing alcohol.
- Malays consider dogs unclean. Do not give toy dogs or gifts that picture dogs.
- Among Indians, the frangipani flower (used by Hawaiians to make leis) is used only for funeral wreaths.
- Should you give money to an Indian, make sure it is an odd number (just the opposite of Chinese tradition). Usually this is done by adding a single dollar; for example, give $11 instead of $10.
- Observant Hindus do not eat beef or use cattle products. This eliminates most leather products as gifts.

Dress

- Singapore is only some eighty-five miles (136.8 km) north of the Equator. It is hot and humid all year long, with a temperature ranging between 75 and 88°F (24 to 31°C), and humidity above 90 percent.
- The rainy season is November through January, but sudden showers occur all year long. Some people carry an umbrella every day.
- As a foreigner, you should dress more conservatively until you know what degree of formality is expected. Men should be prepared to wear a suit jacket but can remove it if it seems appropriate.

- Because of the heat and humidity, business dress in Singapore is often casual. Standard formal office wear for men is dark trousers, light-colored long-sleeved shirts, and ties, without jackets. Some businessmen wear a short-sleeved shirt with no tie.
- Businesswomen may wear business suits and/or pantsuits. Fashions for businesswomen tend to be more frilly and decorative than those worn by Western businesswomen.
- Some Singaporean men may wear an open-necked batik shirt to work. These are also popular for casualwear. Jeans are good for casual situations, but shorts should be avoided.
- In deference to Muslim and Hindu sensibilities, women should always wear blouses that cover at least their upper arms. Skirts should be knee length or longer.

Cultural Note

Standards of polite behavior vary widely between cultures. Some Singaporeans will ask you highly personal questions (such as "Why aren't you married?" or "How much do you earn?") without realizing that westerners find such questions intrusive. Simply smile and gracefully change the subject—and be aware that you, too, will unknowingly violate local standards of polite behavior.

South Africa

English long form: Republic of South Africa
Afrikaans long form: Republiek van Suid-Afrika
Former name: Union of South Africa

Cultural Note
Trade unions remain a strong force in South Africa. During the country's most repressive years, when political freedoms were suppressed, trade unions were the only way most people could express their displeasure with the way things were.

 WHAT'S YOUR CULTURAL IQ?

1. TRUE or FALSE: The number 46664 has special significance to South Africans.

   ANSWER: TRUE. This was the identification number assigned to Nelson Mandela during his years of imprisonment. Today, Mandela uses it as the name of his social improvement organization, the 46664 Campaign. This organization has addressed many social problems; in 2005, it focused its efforts on preventing the spread of AIDS among women.

2. South Africa has three official capitals, each with its own branch of government. Match the city with the appropriate description:
   a. Bloemfontein   1. Legislative branch
   b. Cape Town   2. Executive branch
   c. Pretoria/Tshwane   3. Judicial branch

   ANSWER: a. 3; b. 1; c. 2. When a single city must be named as the capital of South Africa, Pretoria is usually given. This name may be changed to Tshwane in the future.

3. Match the following South African musicians with their primary form of music:
   a. Drakensberg Boys Choir   1. Jazz
   b. Hugh Masekela   2. Fusion of Western and African music
   c. Johnny Clegg and Savuka   3. Sacred and gospel

   ANSWERS: a. 3; b. 1; c. 2

 TIPS ON DOING BUSINESS IN SOUTH AFRICA

- White South Africans usually begin talking about business after a very brief exchange of small talk, whether in the office or at a restaurant. South Africans of other races may spend more time chatting. African tradition requires long inquiries about your health and your family.
- South Africa is in the Southern Hemisphere, so the seasons are reversed from those in the Northern Hemisphere. Summer vacation is centered around Christmas and New Year. Most businesspeople take a month-long vacation around that time; in fact, most of South Africa seems to shut down from mid-December to mid-January!

- South Africa is one of the most beautiful countries on Earth, and its inhabitants take full advantage of their environs. Outdoor activities are common, and work does not intrude. Few South Africans work weekends; they are reserved for leisure.
- While executives are respected in South Africa, they are not expected to be cutthroat. Businesspeople who gloat over crushing their competitors are not appreciated. The ideal business deal (to white South Africans) is a "win-win situation." Both parties should gain from the deal. On the other hand, Indian and Chinese populations came to South Africa as merchants; they have generations of trading experience and are considered shrewd businesspeople.

▶ COUNTRY BACKGROUND

History

There is evidence of human habitation in South Africa dating back some 100,000 years. The oldest remaining group in South Africa are the San (also called "Bushmen") and the Khoikhoi (also known as "Hottentot"). These two interrelated peoples have lived in southern Africa for 40,000 years.

The first Europeans to encounter South Africa were Portuguese sailors searching for a new route to Asia. Bartholomeu Dias rounded the Cape of Good Hope in 1487. The Dutch were the first to establish a permanent outpost, when a Dutch East India Company expedition arrived on April 6, 1652. This is the date celebrated in South Africa as "Founders' Day."

Chafing under the rule of the Dutch East India Company, some farmers migrated to areas beyond company rule. This is the origin of the Boers. They took self-sufficiency to an extreme, carving out homesteads in lands already occupied by Africans.

The racial group known in South Africa as "coloured" also originated at this time. Coloureds are a mixed-race group, the offspring of Boers, Khoikhoi, and Asians (primarily Malay) imported by the Dutch. Like the Boers, they speak Afrikaans.

The Napoleonic Wars had a great influence on South Africa. After the French captured the Netherlands, the British took control of the South African colony in 1795. South Africa was not formerly ceded to Great Britain until 1914.

South Africa might have remained an agricultural country were it not for the discovery of diamonds in 1869 and gold in 1886. The gold was in the Transvaal, which doomed the Boer's independence. Thousands of miners poured into the Witwatersrand gold fields from all over the world. Britain decided to annex the Transvaal. After decades of small incidents, full-fledged warfare broke out between the British and the Boer in 1899.

After the war, the British ruled South Africa, but accommodation had to be made with the Boers. The Union of South Africa was formally established on May 31, 1910. The Boers, defeated in battle, became politically powerful in the new Parliament. At Boer insistence, only whites were allowed to serve in Parliament. The process of disenfranchising the nonwhite population had begun. Blacks were prohibited from owning land (in 1913), intermarrying with other races (in 1949), and even from living in areas designated for whites (in 1950). The separation of the races, apartheid, had begun.

Internal opposition to apartheid built, yet the restrictions grew ever stronger. In 1960, after fifty years of nonviolent struggle, the African National Congress was outlawed. Only then did the ANC embrace violent revolution. The international community also began to impose sanctions on South Africa, to punish it for apartheid.

Finally, the combination of international condemnation, constant rioting in the black townships, and the collapse of international Communism convinced South Africa's leaders it was time to change. Faced with an ungovernable nation, President F. W. de Klerk finally made some real reforms in 1990. He freed ANC president Nelson Mandela, and began to dismantle apartheid.

South Africa's first one-person, one-vote election took place on April 27, 1994. The black majority was finally allowed to vote. The transitional government, with Nelson Mandela as president, took office on December 7, 1994.

Type of Government

The Republic of South Africa is a multiparty parliamentary democracy. The president is both chief of state and head of the government. There are two legislative houses, a National Assembly (whose members are elected by popular vote) and a National Council of Provinces. Each of South Africa's nine provincial legislatures elects members to the National Council. The National Council has special powers to protect cultural and linguistic traditions among ethnic minorities For current government data, check with the Embassy of the South Africa at *www.saembassy.org*.

Language

There are eleven languages designated as "national" or "official." They are Afrikaans, Ndebele, Northern Sotho, Southern Sotho, Swati, Tsonga, Tswana, Venda, Xhosa, Zulu, and English.

Ethnologue.com has identified thirty-one languages in South Africa, twenty-five of them in current use. Of the remainder, three are now extinct and three have no speakers who use it as a mother tongue.

Almost 25 percent of South Africans speak Zulu as a first language. Fortunately for foreign visitors, over 57 percent of South Africans speak some English. South African English follows the British spelling pattern.

Cultural Note

Afrikaans is the most widely spoken language of European origin in South Africa. It is the mother tongue of over 6 million people; another 4 million use it as a second language. Afrikaans is derived from the Dutch spoken by seventeenth-century colonists, with borrowings from Malay, Bantu languages, Khoisan languages, Portuguese, and others. In addition to the Afrikaaners themselves, it is also the mother tongue of 150,000 Cape Malays people, the descendants of laborers brought over from Java almost 300 years ago. However, Afrikaans is seen by many Africans as the language of the oppressor, while English is seen as an international language.

The South Africa View

There is no official religion in South Africa. The country's diverse population follows many religious beliefs. Historically, the most powerful church in South Africa was the Dutch Reformed Church. The Calvinist tradition has had a strong influence on South Africa's development. For example, blue laws long restricted shopping to weekdays and Saturday mornings. Consequently, workers had to do all their shopping between 8:00 A.M. and 1:00 P.M. on Saturdays. (Thankfully, shopping hours have since been extended.) Most other religions are represented in South Africa.

In 2004, South Africa held its third national election since the end of white rule. The ruling African National Congress (ANC) won 70 percent of the vote, insuring its continued dominance. South Africa seems on track to becoming a one-party state, and one-party states are inherently undemocratic. Outside observers attribute much of South Africa's governmental corruption and inefficiency to the lack of a viable challenger to the ANC.

Ever since the discovery of mineral wealth, most immigrants have considered South Africa as a place to become rich. Consequently, South Africa is a place where drive and ambition are considered positive traits. In this respect, white South Africans are unlike their relatives in Britain or the Netherlands. As in the United States, South Africans love a good rags-to-riches story.

By virtue of its leadership, its democratic government, and its military superiority, South Africa views itself as the leading state in sub-Saharan Africa. South Africa often leads peace negotiations in other African countries, especially in Central Africa. Despite its efforts, it has been unable to bring a lasting end to the civil warfare in the Democratic Republic of the Congo. (In some ways, this is the mirror image of apartheid-era South Africa, which used to send its armed forcers to pursue black Nationalist guerrillas into other African nations.)

The literacy rate varies widely. Because Afrikaans and English were the tongues of the privileged elite, white speakers of these languages have literacy rates approaching 99 percent. The literacy rate for South African Asians is 69 percent; for mixed-race "coloureds" it is 62 percent. The government gives an average literacy rate for all races of 86 percent.

☑ Know Before You Go

Hazards in South Africa depend on where you go. There are many townships (the usual term for poor black areas) and urban areas where violence is common. In wilderness areas, the hazards come from the wildlife. International business visitors who stay in well-patrolled areas face relatively few dangers. Sunburn is probably the greatest danger that most pale-skinned visitors will face.

In addition to rare but well-publicized violent crimes like home invasions and carjacking, there is also a substantial amount of petty crime, such as theft and pickpocketing.

In the bush, be sure to obey warnings about the wildlife. This includes not just large animals like elephants and hippos and feline predators, but smaller creatures. Baboons, for example, have lost their fear of humans and may approach you or sit on your parked car. They are far stronger than humans and can deliver a wicked bite. South Africa also has its share of poisonous snakes and insects (mosquitoes, ticks, and biting flies) that transmit disease.

▶ CULTURAL ORIENTATION

There have been four distinct educational systems for the four classes of people in South Africa: whites, "coloureds," Asians, and blacks. Those who have gone on to higher education in any of these groups will be abstractive in their thinking because all of the educational systems are patterned after the European system. The less educated will generally be associative. Unless otherwise noted, this following information pertains primarily to the dominant business culture, which (at this time) is overwhelmingly white.

Cognitive Styles: How South Africans Organize and Process Information

Historically, the South African ruling class was closed to outside information—of necessity, since apartheid drew the condemnation of the entire outside world. Today, successful South African businesspeople tend to be moderately open to information and are generally more analytic than associative. Nevertheless, they may place more value on relationships than obedience to abstract rules of behavior.

Negotiation Strategies: What South Africans Accept as Evidence

While most South Africans find truth through a mixture of subjective feelings and objective facts, businesspeople generally make decisions based on facts.

Value Systems: The Basis for Behavior

The following three sections identify the Value Systems in the predominant culture—their methods of dividing right from wrong, good from evil, and so forth.

Locus of Decision-Making

The responsibility for decision-making rests on the shoulders of the individual. Individualism has always been encouraged, and individual achievement is more important than family in determining status. Hospitality is considered a virtue in most of South Africa's cultures. Many South Africans entertain a wide circle of friends, but these tend to be from one's own ethnic group.

Sources of Anxiety Reduction

Most South Africans feel considerable anxiety for the future. Many white South Africans feel that their quality of life (especially in matters of security) has declined since the advent of majority rule. Many whites have considered the advisability of leaving the country. The Asian population is also unsure of their future, although "moving back to India" (or Malaysia, or wherever) is not an enviable solution, especially since many Asians have lived in South Africa for more than four or five generations. The "flight option" may be a choice of last resort, but this option serves to reduce anxiety.

Only the African and coloured populations usually lack the prospect of emigration to an ancestral country. Even if they can trace their roots to another part of Africa, there is no where else on the continent that offers South Africa's possibilities of quality of life. Although many are disappointed that majority rule has not yet brought them a better life, they still have hope for the future.

Religion and family also provide an important source of anxiety reduction for South Africans of every racial group. So do various organizations, from the African National Congress to the labor unions, which have long protected workers.

Issues of Equality/Inequality

South Africa is a hierarchical country. Under apartheid, the racial aspect of the social hierarchy was encoded into law. Today, things are less formal but the hierarchy still exists. Hierarchical structures are also found in government, business, and other organizations.

South Africa is also a paternalistic country. In most ethnic groups, the husband remains the titular head of the home; many husbands still refuse to do anything they perceive as "women's work." Although women have legal equality with men, the treatment of women varies widely between racial groups. In general, women have the most opportunity for business advancement among English-speaking whites. Many women's organizations seek improvement in women's lives.

Homosexuals are widely discriminated against in much of Africa but are relatively free in South Africa. The coastal city of Durban is considered a mecca for African homosexuals.

Cultural Note

Currently, South Africa has one of the highest percentages of HIV-infection in the world. Over 1 million people have died of AIDS, and at least 5 million more are infected with HIV. Obviously, this creates anxiety for South Africans.

▶ BUSINESS PRACTICES

Punctuality, Appointments, and Local Time

- Punctuality is important; be on time for all business engagements.
- Punctuality is not enforced for social events, but do not be more than a half-hour late.
- In South Africa, as in most other countries, the day is written first, then the month, then the year (e.g. December 3, 2010, is written 3.12.10 or 3/12/10).
- Prior appointments are necessary in business.
- As white South Africans frequently entertain at their homes, some will offer blanket invitations to stop by "anytime." However, it is wise to phone first.
- Due to the hot temperatures, the South African morning is often the most comfortable part of the day. As a result, most South Africans are early risers. It is not unusual for businesspeople to be in their offices by 8:00 A.M.
- A convenience store in South Africa is called a "café" and will stock almost anything except alcohol. They are open long hours, seven days a week.

- The national holiday is Freedom Day (since 1994), celebrated on April 27.
- South Africa is two hours ahead of Greenwich Mean Time (G.M.T. +2), or eight hours ahead of U.S. Eastern Standard Time (E.S.T. +8).
- South Africa does not use any sort of daylight-saving time.

Negotiating

- White South Africans usually begin talking about business after a very brief social exchange of data.
- South Africans of other races may spend more time on small talk. They will take more time getting to know you.
- White South Africans may be very concerned that foreigners might try to take advantage of them.
- High pressure and strong emotions have little place in dealings with white South Africans. Most would rather let a deal fall through than be rushed.
- In general, foreign businesspeople find South Africans of English heritage to be somewhat more open than Afrikaners.
- White South African's ancestors probably started as miners or farmers. On the other hand, many Indians and Chinese came as merchants. Some have generations of trading experience and are shrewd businesspeople. Their negotiations may be more aggressive and assured than those of white South Africans.

Business Entertaining

- Although South African executives usually arise early enough to attend a breakfast meeting, business breakfasts are relatively uncommon. However, they might discuss business at an early-morning tee time on the golf course.
- Business meetings can be held over lunch or dinner.
- Business may be discussed in a restaurant, but generally not over a meal at home.
- Invitations to white South African homes are not unusual. In good weather, these will often be barbecues, or braais, out by the pool.
- Feel free to ask your host what you can bring. Even if your host says you don't need to bring anything, at least bring a bottle of wine, or a dessert.
- Alcohol can be purchased only at very limited times.
- Large amounts of alcohol are often consumed at a braai. On a weekend, a lunchtime braai can last all afternoon and into the evening.
- Even though business is rarely discussed at braais, they are important for successful business relationships. A white South African must like and trust you to work with you.
- Invitations to the homes of the nonwhite business community are rare. Most business entertaining will be done in restaurants.

▶ PROTOCOL

Greetings

- Each of the many cultures of South Africa has its own traditions. However, the majority of businesspeople in South Africa will be from either the English or the Afrikaans ethnic groups.
- Among most black ethnic groups, men precede women when entering or exiting. Only a highly westernized black man will hold open a door for a woman and allow her to enter first.
- Although South Africa has a small Muslim population, the Muslim preference for the right hand is common among South Africans of many ethnic groups. When you give anything to a South African, hold it in your right hand, not your left.
- The years of foreign boycott made South Africans quite sensitive about foreigners interfering in their affairs. Avoid discussing South African politics. If pressed for your opinion, be sure you can offer a knowledgeable evaluation.
- Good topics of conversation are sports, outdoor recreation, travel, food, and music.
- Rugby is the most popular team sport among white South Africans. Be sure not to say anything derogatory about the sport. After rugby, the most popular sports are football (soccer), squash, tennis, and golf. Jogging and bicycling are also very popular; as is swimming. Afrikaners have an indigenous sport called *jukskei*, which is analogous to throwing horseshoes.
- At a dinner in a white South African home, do not compliment your host on the cooking unless you know she prepared the meal herself, because blacks still do most of the manual labor (including cooking) in white South African homes.
- The prevalence of black manual labor has numerous effects on South African society. For example, television commercials for beer never depict beer as refreshment after hard work. White South Africans may play hard, but they rarely do hard manual labor.
- Most (but not all) businesspeople have business cards. There is no formality involved in exchanging cards.
- Your card will not be refused, but you might not be given one in exchange. Don't be offended by this.

Titles/Forms of Address

- Among the English and Afrikaans-speaking South Africans, the order of names is the same as in most countries: first name followed by a surname.
- Traditionally, only family members and close friends address each other by their first names.
- It is important to use professional titles.

Cultural Note

South Africa remains a male-dominated society. While foreign businesswoman are usually accepted, they may be referred to as "girls" and individually addressed as "my dear girl." This can happen to any woman, regardless of age or job title.

Gestures

- South Africa is still a puritanical country. Although brief hugs or a kiss on the cheek is acceptable between friends, extended public contact between the sexes is frowned upon.
- Among both Muslims and Hindus, the left hand is considered unclean. Favor your right hand over your left. Where possible, do not touch anything or anyone with your left hand if you can use your right hand instead. It is permissible to accept gifts and hold cash with either the right hand or both hands—but never the left hand alone.
- The foot is also considered unclean by many South Africans. Do not move anything with your feet, and do not touch anything with your feet.
- Do not show the soles of your feet (or shoes). This restriction determines how one sits: you can cross your legs at the knee but not with one ankle on your knee. Also, do not prop your feet on anything not intended for feet, such as a desk.
- Bantu porters (at the airport and elsewhere) may approach you with their hands together, palms out, and fingers slightly curled. These are a traditional gesture of respect to you.
- The raised right fist known in North America as the "Black Power salute" has been adopted by the Bantu in South Africa. Even Nelson Mandela has been photographed in this position.
- As in much of the world, to beckon someone you hold your hand out, palm downward, and make a scooping motion with the fingers.

Gifts

- Gifts are given between friends. Do not give a gift to anyone before you have established a personal relationship with them. Otherwise, the gift may have the appearance of a bribe.
- Always bring something when invited to a house. Wine, candy, or flowers are the traditional choices. Small electronics are becoming more common.
- Some South African ethnic groups (such as the Chinese) traditionally decline a gift three times before accepting; this prevents them from appearing greedy. Continue to insist.
- For further guidelines on gift giving, visit *www.kissboworshakehands.com*.

Dress

- Dress in South Africa is fairly casual, although it varies from city to city. In general, Johannesburg is the most formal. Cape Town is only formal in the business district. Seaside resorts like Durban are the most casual.
- In general, businessmen in South Africa are expected to wear a coat and a tie. Follow the lead of your South African colleagues.
- Depending upon the formality of the office, businesswomen may wear anything from business suits to light-colored long-sleeved blouses and skirts.
- South Africans love the outdoors, and much entertaining is done outside. Jeans or shorts are accepted casualwear for both sexes. Women may wear short-sleeved shirts or even halter tops. Many people wear sandals all summer long.
- The sun in South Africa is very intense. Protect your skin, either with clothing or sunblock.

South Korea

Republic of Korea
Local long form: Taehan-min'guk
Note: the South Koreans generally use the term
Han'guk to refer to their country
Abbreviation: ROK

Cultural Note

While there are many religions in Korea, Confucianism exerts the strongest influence on society. It is not a religion centered around the worship of a supreme deity, but rather a rigid ethical and moral system that governs all relationships. It was established by Confucius, a Chinese scholar and statesman who lived during Chinese feudal times over 2,000 years ago.

 WHAT'S YOUR CULTURAL IQ?

1. Which of the following games are the most popular in Korea?
   a. Chess
   b. *Changgi* (also called "*Janggi*")
   c. Go (also called "*Baduk*")

   ANSWER: c. Go is so popular, there is at least one Korean television channel dedicated solely to its broadcast in South Korea. Koreans have won the $400,000 "Ing Cup" since its inception and clearly believe in the Chinese proverb—chess is a battle, but go is war. (Janggi is a variant of chess.)

2. TRUE or FALSE? There are less than 300 family names in Korea.

   ANSWER: TRUE. Some of the most common are *Kim* (meaning gold), *Lee* (meaning plum), and *Park* (which means gourd).

3. Confucianism is a belief system, which contains five constant superior/subordinate relationships that must be maintained. TRUE or FALSE? They are: ruler and subject, parent and child, elder and younger brother, husband and wife, elder friend and younger friend.

   ANSWER: TRUE. Confucianism also mandates *Jen* (a sense of duty to humanity), *Shu* (reciprocity—"Do unto others as you would have them do unto you," similar to the Gospel of Matthew 7:12), *Chih* (wisdom), *Wen* (representing all the arts), and respect for the *Chun tzu* (the civilized man who has developed all the virtues).

Cultural Note

After over fifty years of hostility, the leaders of South Korea (Kim Dae Jung) and North Korea (Kim Jong Il) shook hands at Pyongyang airport in 2000. Despite the significance of this event, there are still major concerns over North Korea's nuclear ambitions.

TIPS ON DOING BUSINESS IN SOUTH KOREA

- Koreans are more independent and individualistic than their Asian neighbors. They are the most straightforward of all Asians but can also be defensive, a trait stemming from a history of invasion by their neighbors.
- Foreigners should attempt to show proper respect to Korean supervisors. This includes not putting anything on the manager's desk (not even sales literature) during a presentation. Korean executives are very territorial about their desks.
- Koreans do not maintain as much eye contact as North Americans. As a general rule, Koreans of equal status will look at each other only half of the time during their conversation. When persons are of unequal status, the lower-ranking person will often avert his or her eyes during much of the conversation. Extended or intense eye contact can be associated with anger. North Americans who try to maintain continuous eye contact with a Korean may appear hostile or aggressive.

COUNTRY BACKGROUND

History

Korea's original name, *Choson*, meant "land of the morning calm." The country's history has been shaped by frequent invasions from its neighbors. Korean history is divided into three main periods: the Silla (668–935), Koryo (935–1392), and Yi (1392–1910) dynasties. The name "Korea" is derived from the middle dynasty of Koryo. Foreign influence—direct and indirect—occurred throughout these dynasties. All of Korea's foreign overlords—Mongolian, Chinese, and Japanese—instituted a closed-door policy to solidify their rule. This isolation earned Korea the name of the Hermit Kingdom.

In 1910, Japan annexed Korea and enforced ruthless control, outlawing Korean culture and language. Despite resistance, several generations grew up more familiar with Japanese than with Korean customs. At the Yalta Conference at the end of World War II, the United States and the Soviet Union jointly established temporary administrative trusteeship over Korea until democratic elections could be held. Japanese forces south of the thirty-eighth parallel surrendered to the United States and forces in the north surrendered to the USSR. The Soviets blocked attempts to hold nationwide elections, and the two sides became deadlocked. When authorities in the north ignored a United Nations resolution for supervised elections in 1948, a pro-Western government was established in the south (the Republic of

Korea). Later the Soviet Union established the Democratic People's Republic of Korea in the north. In June 1949, U.S. troops withdrew.

One year later, North Korean forces invaded South Korea. A United Nations–backed coalition of sixteen member nations sent assistance to South Korea. The resulting war lasted three years and ended in a stalemate. On July 27, 1953, an armistice agreement was signed and a Military Armistice Commission with five members for each side was set up to supervise the implementation of the armistice. Neither the United States nor South Korea ever signed the agreement (although they respect the terms as members of the United Nations), so a state of war is formally still in effect.

The United States still maintains a military presence in South Korea, although feelings that this should end are growing.

The year 1980 marked the beginning of Korea's focused development of a high-tech industry. It was also the year of the Kwangju massacre, when government troops killed hundreds of demonstrators who were part of a prodemocracy movement. In 1988 Seoul hosted the Olympic games (when restaurants removed dog from their menus in deference to delicate Western sensibilities), and Korea held their first free parliamentary elections. South (and North) Korea joined the United Nations in 1991, and in 2000, former president Kim Dae Jung received the Nobel Peace Prize. In 2004, a site was chosen for the new capital city in the Yeongi-Kwangju area.

Type of Government

South Korea is a unitary multiparty republic, governed by a president, prime minister, deputy prime minister, and State Council (cabinet). There is also a unicameral National Assembly and a Supreme Court.

The prime minister is the head of the government. The chief of state is the president, who is elected to a five-year term. Members of the National Assembly serve a four-year term.

Current government data can be found at the Embassy of South Korea at *www.korea embassyusa.org.*

Language

Korean is the official language of South Korea. English is widely taught in schools. Therefore, businesspeople are often familiar with English, especially in urban areas.

Korean is a Ural-Altaic language, but, unlike Japanese and Chinese, Korean does not use tones. Approximately 1,300 Chinese characters are used in modern Korean. The literacy rate is 92 percent, and newspaper readership is very high in South Korea.

Cultural Note
Which of the following is the correct method of transliterating the twenty-four-letter Korean alphabet into the twenty-six-letter Roman alphabet?

- The McCune-Reischauer method
- The Korean government's method
- Everyone else's method
- All of the above

The correct answer is "all of the above." Because of the variety of transliterations, Korean words can be spelled multiple ways in English.

The South Korean View

Dominant religions include Confucianism, Christianity (28 percent of the population), Buddhism, Shamanism (spirit worship), and Chondokyo (religion of the heavenly way). South Korea is a society run along Confucian precepts. In fact, Confucianism may have had a more profound effect on Korea than it had even in China, where Confucianism originated. (Remember that Confucianism is not a religion in the classic sense of the word. Rather, it is a philosophy and guide for living.)

Confucius taught that the basic unit of society is the family. To preserve harmony in the home, certain reciprocal responsibilities must be preserved in relationships. These relationships are between ruler and subjects, between husband and wife, between father and son, between elder brother and younger brother, and between friends. Because all but the last are hierarchical, rank and age are very important in all interactions. While all actions of the individual reflect upon the family, filial piety is of utmost importance. Virtues of kindness, righteousness, propriety, intelligence, and faithfulness are also revered.

The only relationships of equality in Korea are between members of the same class. One's closest friends are drawn from this group.

Korea has no official religion. Buddhism has traditionally been the major Korean religion, but Buddhism has gone through periods where it has been repressed by Korea's Confucian rulers. Buddhism is Korea's most popular religion, although only 27.6 percent of Koreans identify themselves as Buddhist. (Over half of Koreans follow no formal religion at all.)

Koreans are proud that Christianity did not reach Korea through missionaries. Instead, a Korean scholar studying in Beijing was baptized a Catholic in 1777. It was this scholar, on his return, who introduced Catholicism to Korea. Protestantism gained a foothold in 1884, via a Protestant physician who became the royal physician.

Whatever their formal religion, most Koreans also follow traditional Shamanistic beliefs. These include a belief in spirits, the veneration of ancestors, and the usefulness of fortune-telling. If there is one classic Korean characteristic, it would be resiliency. Koreans seem to be able to survive almost any hardship. Sacrifice has been demanded of one generation after another of Koreans. The results of this sacrifice in South Korea are evident to any visitor: a poor, war-torn agricultural country with few resources has transformed itself into the twelfth largest economy in the world.

☑ Know Before You Go

Korea suffers from occasional typhoons and low-level seismic activity. Air pollution is an issue in large cities, along with minor crimes like burglaries and pickpocketing.

Overall, Korea's crime rate is low; however, only use legitimate taxis or public transportation.

Avoid demonstrations; they can become confrontational and violent.

▶ CULTURAL ORIENTATION

Cognitive Styles: How South Koreans Organize and Process Information

In South Korea, one finds a culture that is closed to many foreign influences. Its basic education teaches one to think associatively and subjectively. In all situations, personal involvement is stronger than the rules and laws one might use to control behavior.

Negotiation Strategies: What South Koreans Accept as Evidence

One's personal feelings about an issue have traditionally been perceived as the truth.

The use of objective facts is becoming more common in negotiations. Faith in the ideologies of nationalism may have some influence on an individual's view.

Value Systems: The Basis for Behavior

Koreans are strong adherents of Confucianism. They strive to build a society in which individuals are aware of their relative position, fulfill their obligations to superiors with obedience and respect, and recognize their responsibility to treat inferiors with justice and benevolence. The following three sections identify the Value Systems in the predominant culture—their methods of dividing right from wrong, good from evil, and so forth.

Locus of Decision-Making

This is a collectivistic culture in which the individual may speak for the group, but decisions are made by a consensus of the group, with deference given to the one in the group who has the highest ethos—usually the oldest member. Loyalty to kin always supersedes loyalty to friends, neighbors, or the state. The self is downplayed, but Western-style individualism is felt. One must not cause another person to be embarrassed, so an outright "no" is rarely used.

Sources of Anxiety Reduction

The nuclear family is the basic unit of society, but the extended family gives stability and security to its members. There is a very strong work ethic, but intragroup harmony must also be maintained. Giving gifts to acquire favors is a common practice in the workplace, and reciprocity is expected. Friends expect to rely on each other for everything. They spend a lot of time together, and friendships last a lifetime.

Issues of Equality/Inequality

In business, the emphasis is on entry-level skills and team play. There is an inherent trust in people because of the homogeneity of the populace and social pressure. This produces a strong feeling of interdependency among members of a group or business. Age is revered. Respect and deference are directed from the younger to the older, and authority and responsibility from the older to the younger. There are clearly differentiated sex roles in society, but Western-style equality is creeping in and there is a strong feminist movement. Men still generally dominate in public situations.

▶ BUSINESS PRACTICES

Punctuality, Appointments, and Local Time

- Be punctual to meetings. This is expected from foreigners as a sign of good business practice. Do not get upset, however, if your counterpart is late.
- Punctuality is also expected at social events.
- Koreans often arrange one-on-one business meetings (as opposed to the Japanese, who prefer group meetings). Nevertheless, this one Korean businessperson will have to sell your proposal to his or her entire company. It is important that you establish a strong relationship with your contact person.
- Age and rank are very important in Korea. It is sometimes easier to establish a rapport with a businessperson your own age.
- When entering a group meeting, the senior member of your party should enter the conference room first, then the next-highest-ranking person, and so on. The Koreans will be lined up inside in order of importance.
- English is the most widely studied foreign language. Your business meetings can be conducted in English. Promotional materials and correspondence may be in English as well.
- The best times for business meetings are usually 10:00 to 11:00 A.M. and 2:00 to 3:00 P.M. Prior appointments are necessary. Business dinners are common.
- Korean businesspeople vacation from mid-July to mid-August; avoid trying to schedule appointments at this time of year. Other bad times include early October, a time of many holidays, and Christmastime.
- Many Europeans and Asians write the day first, then the month, then the year (e.g., December 3, 2010, is written 3.12.10 or 3/12/10).
- Local time is nine hours ahead of Greenwich Mean Time (G.M.T. +9), or fourteen hours ahead of U.S. Eastern Standard Time (E.S.T. +14).

Negotiating

- At each meeting, take time to talk to your counterpart. The first meeting should be solely for that purpose; never jump right into business discussions. Expect tea to be served at the beginning of the meeting; it is good manners to accept this sign of hospitality. Retain your formality as long as your counterpart does; do not become "chummy."

- Do not be fooled into thinking that Korea is completely westernized because of its façade of modernization. While the younger generation is open to globalization, traditional values run deep, especially with the older generation. You may find younger executives easier to negotiate with, as they will follow more westernized patterns.

- Business will tend to take place at a slower pace than in Europe or North America. Be patient with delays in decision-making. Often, this is a tactic to wear down the other side. Therefore, do not talk about your deadlines. Expect to make several trips to Korea before reaching an agreement.

- Do not be surprised if a Korean executive does not call you back immediately when you notify his or her office of a problem. Korean employees are very protective of their supervisors' harmony and traditionally will not upset their boss with a problem until the timing is just right. This is especially true at the start of the workday.

- Find out who will be included in the negotiating team for the other side and match the rank of the persons represented. Status is very important, and a mismatch may prove embarrassing to both sides. Generally, representatives should be older and hold senior positions in the company.

- Although this is changing, it is still not common to have women participate in business in Korea. This means that women will have the additional challenge of overcoming an initial hesitancy. It is best to consider this factor and mention to your Korean contact that a woman will be included in the team. This will allow them some time to adjust to the situation.

- Negotiations in Korea will be much more emotional than in Western countries that stress logic and the bottom-line cost. Mutual trust and compatibility will be the basis of a good business relationship. Also be prepared for the style to be aggressive at times. Koreans are much more direct and quicker to express anger or frustration. Remain calm yourself, and do not take everything said during these sessions seriously.

- Consider sending your proposals in advance of your visit for your host to preview. At a presentation, recap the major points at the beginning and the end. Break up the information into small segments with pauses and question-and-answer periods in between. Be patient with extensive questioning. Address the chief negotiator occasionally, even if he does not speak English. Do not use triangular shapes in your promotional material, because triangles have negative connotations.

- Look for cues that your counterpart did not understand you. Silence is one such sign.

- Do not ask or expect Koreans to tell you when this happens, as it will embarrass them. Instead, rephrase your statement or inquire if they would like more information.

- The use of a translator is recommended to avoid these miscommunications.

- Make a beginning bid that will leave you plenty of room to negotiate. Your counterparts will start off with an extreme position but will be prepared to meet you in the middle. This way both sides come away having gained a lot of ground.
- Brute honesty is not appreciated in Korea. While a direct "no" is more accepted in Korea than in other Asian countries, Koreans are not as direct as many westerners. To avoid saying "no," Koreans will often give the answer they think the other wants to hear. It is more important to leave you with good feelings than to be accurate and cause you dismay. Therefore, learn to listen to subtleties by asking questions that do not require a yes or no answer. A "yes" or nod of the head may mean "maybe" or "I understand." A "maybe" usually means "no." A negative response is sometimes indicated by a squint of the eyes or by tipping the head back while drawing air in through the teeth and waiting for you to speak again.
- Be sensitive to the overall length of the meeting. If the Koreans appear curious, take this lead and pursue it. If they return to social chitchat, take this as a sign that they are finished discussing business for the day.
- Bow at the beginning and end of a meeting. An exit bow that is longer than the greeting bow is an indication that the meeting went well.
- Treat the elderly with respect. Acknowledge them first in a group, and do not smoke or wear sunglasses when they are near. If you meet in a doorway, allow the older person to pass through first.
- Modesty is very important. Do not enter a home or office until you are invited, and do not seat yourself until you are asked to do so. Wait for the invitation to be extended several times before accepting. Be modest about your position and accomplishments in your company, and if you receive a compliment, politely refute it. Expect others to do the same. This should not stop you from complimenting another, however, as compliments are appreciated.
- Not losing "face"—the dignity of another person—is a very important and delicate matter. Therefore, never embarrass another person, especially in public. Never criticize your competition or admit that you do not know the answer to a question.
- Do not confuse Korean history and culture with those of any of its Asian neighbors. Korea has a distinctive language, history, and culture, and they are very proud of this. This pride and sense of history is quite strong and constitutes a large part of their self-image. Koreans are especially sensitive about Japan, so do not bring gifts from Japan or make reference to personal contacts there.
- Be careful not to overly admire an object belonging to another person; he or she may feel obliged to give it to you.
- Koreans tend to be suspicious of people they do not know, or people with whom they do not have a mutual contact. Try to obtain a personal introduction.

- Be prepared to give out a lot of business cards. Have your name, company, and title printed in English on one side and in Korean on the reverse. Cards are very important, since they indicate your rank and are a key to the respect you deserve in their culture.
- Offer your card with your right hand. Never place a Korean's card in your wallet if you intend to put your wallet in your back pocket. Never write on a business card.
- Do not sign a contract or write a person's name in red ink. To many Buddhists, this indicates that the person is deceased.
- Do not be surprised if you are asked personal questions, such as how much you paid for something or your salary. These questions are not considered in bad taste in Korea and often reflect an attempt to determine your rank and status.
- Attempts by foreigners to adhere to Korean modes of etiquette will not go unnoticed and may be instrumental in your eventual business success.

Cultural Note

Faux Pas: In 1998, the Swedish automobile firm Volvo bought 85 percent of Samsung's construction equipment business. Volvo's corporate culture is very different from that of the average Korean firm. In particular, Volvo tried to institute its culture of transparency, sharing all its plans with its employees in the hope that they will offer useful suggestions. It was expected that Volvo's Korean employees would keep the corporation's plans secret. They did not. Male Korean executives, like Japanese executives, spend most nights drinking and singing karaoke with their friends. In Korea, these friends will be a group of people who graduated from the same college in the same year. Some of them may work for competing companies. Information that should be proprietorial tends to leak during these drinking sessions. Volvo is not the only foreign firm to have had problems in this arena.

Business Entertaining

- The largest meal of the day is eaten in the evening, usually between 6:00 and 8:00 P.M.
- Entertaining is most often done in a restaurant or coffee shop; rarely is it done at home. If you are invited to a home, consider this an honor. Do not discuss business during a meal unless your host brings it up first. Do not expect to be shown around the house, and do not wander about the home or look in such rooms as the kitchen.
- Remove your shoes when entering a Korean home, restaurant, or temple building. Leave them with the toes pointing away from the building. When putting your shoes back on, do not sit with your back toward the temple.
- Call ahead before visiting a home. When taking your leave, express your thanks and bow slightly. Send a thank-you note to your host after a meal. It is polite to reciprocate by inviting your host to a meal of equal value at a later date.
- It is common to be invited out after business hours to a bar or dinner where there will be a lot of alcohol. This is an important part of establishing an informal relationship and judging the character of the other person. The alcohol is a stimulus to expression of more direct opinions; however, all comments and promises made during these times will be

taken seriously afterward. Do not refuse these invitations, and do not bring your spouse. Try to reciprocate before you leave.

- The person who invites the other(s) is expected to pay for the meal. It is polite for the younger to pay for the older. In all cases, a good-natured argument over who will pay is expected.
- Koreans eat a lot of garlic in their food. The smell is emitted from the skin. In getting used to this, remember that Koreans may find the odors emitted from red meat eaters, or heavy caffeine drinkers, offensive. Remember that the sense of olfaction is in a primitive part of the brain, and any strong reaction you may have to different scents should be guarded.
- When sitting on the floor for a meal, men should cross their legs while sitting on the cushion. Women (and men) may sit with their legs to the side, but never straightened out under the table.
- Koreans use chopsticks for eating and a porcelain spoon for soup. Your attempts at using chopsticks will be appreciated. When you are finished, set your chopsticks on the chopstick rest. Placing them parallel on top of your bowl is considered a sign of bad luck, and leaving them sticking out of rice is in bad taste, because this is how offerings are made to ancestors.
- Pass food with your right hand, supported by your left. Do not be shocked to see unusual foods. (There are many delicacies in Korea that might surprise a Western palate). It is polite to refill your neighbor's cup and soy sauce bowl when empty; expect the same. Drinking partners will often trade filled cups to drink. If you do not want a refill, do not finish your glass.
- Do not put food taken from a serving dish directly into your mouth. Transfer it to your plate or bowl first. Never pick up food with your fingers. Even fruit is eaten in slices with chopsticks.
- At a meal, do not finish everything on your plate. This indicates that you are still hungry and that the host did not provide enough for you. The host will offer more food several times. Even if you want more, refuse at least twice before accepting more. If you are hosting a party, offer food at least three times.
- At the end of a meal, there may be singing. It is impolite to refuse to sing if asked.
- Good topics of conversation include Korea's cultural heritage (which is extensive), kites, sports (especially the Olympics), and the health of the other's family (although family inquiries on topics other than health are considered an intrusion). Topics to avoid are local politics (discussions of which may be forbidden by the government for reasons of national security), socialism, Communism, Japan, and your host's wife.

> ### Cultural Note
>
> "Without question, the trait that sets Koreans apart from the Chinese, Japanese, and other Asians is their emotionalism. . . . They are quick to anger and just as quick to reconciliation. They are the only Asians among whom you will commonly see public tears or public displays of affection. . . ."
>
> "Korean men are very emotional even when making business decisions. If you strike the right emotional cord, the Korean decision-maker will often respond favorably simply on impulse. On the other hand, a Korean, unlike Japanese, will not be polite when you get on his wrong side. Korean tempers can get awfully hot. . . ."
> —From *The Asian Mind Game* by Chin-ning Chu.

 ## PROTOCOL

Greetings

- Korean men greet each other with a slight bow and sometimes an accompanying hand-shake while maintaining eye contact. Indicate added respect by supporting your right forearm with your left hand during the handshake.
- The junior person will initiate the greetings and be the first to bow. The senior person will be the first to offer his hand. A gentle handshake or nod of the head may be sufficient in business circles. Women rarely shake hands. Generally, men should not try to shake hands with Korean women; Western women will have to initiate a handshake with Korean men.
- Elderly people are very highly respected, so it is polite to greet them first—and spend a few minutes speaking with them.
- A compliment on an elder's good health is always appreciated.
- Wait to be introduced to another at gatherings and parties. Avoid introducing yourself, and employ a third person if there is someone you wish to meet.

Titles/Forms of Address

- Korean names are different from Western names. Traditionally, a person had a family name, a generational or clan name, and a given—or first—name (in that order). For example, Kim Hyong-Sim has the family name of Kim, the generational name of Hyong, and a first name of Sim. While this is confusing to westerners, our system is equally confusing to them, so they, too, may mix Western names around.
- Korean family names tend to be one-syllable, while generational names are more likely to be two-syllable.
- Note that family names can be transliterated into English in several ways; in English, the surname Lee might be Rhee, Yi, Li, or Lee.
- Address people by their title alone or by both their title and their family name. Kim Hyong-Sim would be referred to as Mr. Kim, Kim Sonsaengnim (meaning "Mr." or "teacher") or Kimssi, with the suffix -ssi added, which can mean "Mr.," "Mrs.," or "Miss." Given names are not used unless permission is granted to do so.

South Korea

- Married women will keep their maiden names. If you do not know a woman's maiden name, it is permissible to refer to her as "Madame" with her husband's family name.

Gestures

- Do not put your arm around another person's shoulders. People of the same sex may hold hands. Physical contact is inappropriate with older people, with people of the opposite sex, or with people who are not good friends or family.
- Feet are considered dirty and should not touch other people or objects. Men should keep their feet flat on the floor during formal situations. At other times men should take care that the soles of their shoes are pointing down. Women are permitted to cross their legs.
- Show respect to older people by touching your left hand, palm up, lightly to your right elbow when shaking hands or passing objects such as food or documents.
- Get someone's attention by extending your arm palm down and moving your fingers up and down. Beckoning a person by moving a single finger toward you is very rude.

    Cover your mouth when yawning or using a toothpick. It is not necessary to cover your mouth when laughing, as many Korean women do.
- Blowing your nose in public is considered gauche. If the highly spiced Korean food affects you, get up and move away from the table before blowing your nose.
- If embarrassed, a Korean may laugh excessively.
- Intermittent eye contact is important to convey sincerity and attentiveness to the speaker.

Gifts

- When visiting a family, it is appropriate to bring a gift of fruit, imported coffee, or quality tea such as ginseng, chocolates, or crafts from home. Liquor may be given to a man but never to a woman.
- Gift giving is often practiced within a business setting. Good gifts for a first trip include impersonal products with your company logo on them. (Be sure these gifts were not produced in Korea or Japan.)
- When giving or receiving a gift, use both hands. The gift is not opened in the presence of the giver. A gift of money should be put in an envelope. Expect initial resistance to receiving a gift. This is polite, so be persistent.

Dress

- Men should wear a conservative suit and tie and a white shirt for business.
- Fashions are changing for women; they may wear a conservative suit, pantsuit, skirt and blouse, or dress. Whatever you select, avoid tight skirts, because many people sit on the floor in homes and restaurants.
- Dress modestly for informal times. Revealing clothing for women will be a mark of poor character. Shorts are appropriate for young people. Avoid the colors yellow and pink.

Spain

Kingdom of Spain
Local short form: Espana

Cultural Note

Spain suffered through a horrendous civil war from 1936 to 1939. Over 350,000 Spaniards were killed.

WHAT'S YOUR CULTURAL IQ?

1. The year 1492 was highly significant for Spain. Which of the following events did not occur in that year?
   a. The Spanish recaptured all of the Iberian Peninsula from the North African Islamic invaders.
   b. Spanish Jews were required to convert to Catholicism or leave Spain.
   c. The Spanish and Portuguese thrones were effectively united.
   d. Columbus reached the Americas.

   ANSWER: c. This occurred earlier, in 1479. The countries remained technically separate but were ruled in concert until 1504.

2. The modern Spanish flag consists of two horizontal red stripes flanking a center yellow band. TRUE or FALSE: The design allegedly dates back to a French king wiping his blood-stained hands on a Spanish nobleman's yellow shield.

   ANSWER: TRUE. The story goes that the colors originated when the ninth-century King Charles I (also known as Charles the Bald) of France wiped his bloodstained hands on the plain yellow leather shield of the Count of Aragon.

3. TRUE or FALSE: The Prado, one of the most famous museums in the world, is located in Granada.

   ANSWER: FALSE. The Prado is in Madrid. Another famous site, the Alhambra, is in Granada.

TIPS ON DOING BUSINESS IN SPAIN

- Spaniards are independent and proud. They respect authority and a refined demeanor.
- Do not try to get too friendly too soon with your Spanish associates, and never underestimate a person based upon a job title.
- Spanish businesses tend to be very hierarchical. Departments may be compartmentalized to the extent that personnel are not very familiar with what other divisions are doing. Their part of the decision-making process is to pass their recommendations on to the supervisor.

Spain

- "Teamwork" generally means a team that follows and supports a clearly designated leader. It is not usually a give-and-take relationship among equals.

▶ COUNTRY BACKGROUND

History

Iberians, Celts, and Basques settled Spain. Then, conquering Carthaginians, Romans, Visigoths, and Moors subsequently influenced its development. The seizure of Granada in the fifteenth century by Christians was the culmination of their reconquest of the Iberian Peninsula over the Moors. This united Spain for the first time under a Christian king and marked the beginning of Spanish nationalism. Spain began its acquisition of a colonial empire in 1492.

Over the next few centuries, Spain gained a global network of possessions, then gradually lost them all. The first losses were those non-Iberian possessions inherited by the royal house of Spain: the Netherlands and parts of Italy and Germany. Then came the loss of much of North, Central, and South America. Finally, defeat in the Spanish-American War of 1898 resulted in the loss of Cuba, the Philippines, and Puerto Rico, ending Spain's global ambitions. Spain retained a few African colonies until recent times.

The Spanish civil war lasted from 1936 to 1939 and caused the deaths of more than 350,000 Spaniards. At the end of the war, Francisco Franco became dictator of Spain, and he retained control for nearly four decades.

Franco's long rule was marked by centralization and repression of regional ambitions. One of his most implacable opponents was the underground organization Euskadi Ta Askatasuna (which means "Basque Homeland and Freedom"). ETA is dedicated to achieving independence for the Basque region, by any means necessary. Formed in 1959, ETA first resorted to violence in 1961, when it attempted to derail a train. Their terrorist attacks—usually bombings—continue to this day, although they can no longer claim the support of a majority of Basques.

Franco remained in power until his death in 1975. To ensure political stability, Franco had already designated Prince Juan Carlos as the future king of Spain in 1969.

King Juan Carlos ascended to the throne of Spain in 1975 and soon had to put down an attempted military coup. He rapidly and independently mustered the support of many other parts of the military, allowing Spain to remain under civilian rule. In 1977, Spain held its first democratic elections in four decades. Spain has enjoyed democratic elections ever since, although there was an aborted attempt at a military coup in 1981.

Spain joined NATO in 1982 and the European Economic Community (now known as the European Union) in 1986.

In 1992—the five-hundredth anniversary of Columbus's first voyage—the Summer Olympic Games were held in Barcelona and Expo 92 was held in Seville. Both events were considered successes.

Just before the national elections in March 2004, radical Islamic terrorists bombed rush-hour trains in Madrid. Over 200 people were killed. The incident (and the government's clumsy reaction to it) was enough to upset the election. Aznar was voted out, and José Luis Rodriguez Zapatero of the Socialist Party became prime minister.

Zapatero soon fulfilled his campaign promise to withdraw all Spanish troops from Iraq. This was accomplished by May of 2004.

Type of Government

The Kingdom of Spain is a parliamentary monarchy. The current constitution was written in 1978 and made Spain a constitutional monarchy. The king is the chief of state. Legislative power resides in the Cortes (parliament), consisting of two chambers: the Congress of Deputies and the Senate. Deputies and senators are elected by universal suffrage and serve for four years. The executive branch consists of a prime minister (who is the head of the government), his deputy, and ministers, all of whom are responsible to the Cortes.

Spain is organized into multiple Autonomous Communities; each is granted considerable local control.

Spain continues to request the return of Gibraltar, which has been under British control since 1704.

In May of 2003, Spain lost sixty-two Spanish peacekeepers when their plane crashed in Turkey. They were returning from duty in Afghanistan.

For current government data, check with the Embassy of Spain at *www.spainemb.org.*

Language

Spanish, or Castilian, is the official language nationwide (it is also referred to as *español*, or *castellano*). There are other official regional languages: the Basques of the north, the Galicians of the northwest, and the Catalans of the extreme northeast all speak their own languages.

Dialects include Andalusian, Murcian, Aragonese, Navarrese, and a Canary Islands Spanish. Spanish is classified as a member of the Indo-European linguistic group: it is a Romance tongue. Ethnologue.com has identified fifteen languages in Spain, two of which are extinct. Worldwide, Spanish is one of the most commonly spoken languages, with an estimated 350 million speakers.

The Spanish View

Although Spain is an overwhelmingly Catholic country, Spain has no official religion. Approximately 94 percent of Spaniards practice Catholicism to some extent. Spaniards are known to have a deep religious sensibility—they appreciate the stability and structure of the Catholic Church and may have a profound mystical connection to their faith.

Every Spaniard, religious or not, is familiar with the basic precepts of Catholicism.

Spaniards observe many Catholic holidays and rituals. Besides the elaborate *Semana Santa* (Holy Week) processionals during the week that precedes Easter in many cities, there is a famous pilgrimage to Santiago de Compostela. *Santiago* is Spanish for "St. James," and the apostle's tomb is believed to be located under the church. During the Middle Ages, the relics made Santiago de Compostela the most important city of pilgrimage after Jerusalem and Rome. The saint's relics are still credited with miracles.

Many Spaniards are highly independent but rely heavily on the support of their families. Work will rarely be a Spaniard's first or second priority in life.

☑ Know Before You Go

The explosions on commuter trains in Madrid killed over 200 people in March of 2004. Responsibility for the terrorist bombings was initially placed upon the Basque separatist group *ETA*, but subsequently the investigation pointed to Al Qaeda. However, political tension continues in the northern Basque region, and *ETA* is suspected in other bomb blasts. Foreign executives are not at any particular risk.

Driving can be hazardous in Spain. Traffic is unpredictable, and drivers can be very aggressive.

There is a problem with air pollution, and smoking is still extremely common.

▶ CULTURAL ORIENTATION

Cognitive Styles: How Spaniards Organize and Process Information

The culture of Spain was released with the fashioning of a working democracy. Spaniards are open to information on all issues but do not change their attitudes easily. Most information is processed associatively and subjectively. Spaniards' personal involvement with issues makes it difficult for them to use more abstract rules and laws to solve their problems.

Negotiation Strategies: What Spaniards Accept as Evidence

One's subjective feelings on an issue are the ultimate source of truth. However, faith in the ideologies of the church or nationalism may help to formulate this truth. Objective facts may be used to prove a point, but they are rarely the sole source of evidence.

Value Systems: The Basis for Behavior

The philosophy that all people are equal because each person is unique is a fundamental Spanish principle. Therefore, one must get to know each person as an individual. The following three sections identify the Value Systems in the predominant culture—their methods of dividing right from wrong, good from evil, and so forth.

Locus of Decision-Making

Individuals shoulder responsibility for their own decisions, but the best interests of the family or group are always kept in mind. Self-identity is obtained from the family, and one's position in society. Relationships (both kinships and friendships) are generally as important as one's expertise in obtaining a job. The elite at the top of the social scale are a privileged minority with substantial control over economic resources.

Spain

Sources of Anxiety Reduction

Although the Catholic Church has lost most of its direct influence, the more educated a person is, the more likely he or she is to be a practicing Catholic. The Church's teachings are basic to most of the population and are a source of structure, stability, and security. The extended family is being replaced by the nuclear family as a source of security. There is a strong belief in nationalism.

Issues of Equality/Inequality

Society is differentiated along class, occupational, and professional lines, with an expanding middle class and a decreasing proportion of rural poor. Changes in the system were made by revolutions or military coups in the past, but now the democratic form of government seems to be well in place. Machismo is still very strong. However, women figure more prominently in education, politics, and the work force. Women have complete equality with men before the law.

BUSINESS PRACTICES

Punctuality, Appointments, and Local Time

- While you should be on time for all business appointments, Spaniards are not always punctual. Be prepared to wait, and never take offense at your Spanish associates' late arrival.
- Social events rarely begin at the scheduled time. Try to ask what time you are really expected to arrive; it is likely to be from fifteen to thirty minutes after the scheduled time.
- Spaniards, like many Europeans, write the day first, then the month, then the year (e.g., December 3, 2010, is written 3.12.10 or 3/12/10).
- Always make business appointments well in advance, and confirm them by phone and/or e-mail just before your arrival.
- The work week is generally forty hours in Spain, but hours of operation may vary.
- If a holiday falls on a Thursday or Tuesday, many people take a four-day weekend.
- Most Spaniards have thirty days paid vacation per year and usually take them in July or August. Also avoid scheduling appointments around Easter or Christmas.
- Some Spaniards like to go home for lunch, so do not be surprised if your invitation is politely declined.
- Conducting business over lunch can be problematic; wait for your Spanish counterpart to begin the discussion. It will probably be at the very end of the meal—over coffee.
- Do not schedule breakfast meetings before 8:30 A.M.
- Spain is one hour ahead of Greenwich Mean Time (G.M.T. +1), or six hours ahead of U.S. Eastern Standard Time (E.S.T. +6).

Negotiating

- Personal contacts are essential for business success in Spain. Select your Spanish representatives with great care, because once a representative is associated with you, it is very difficult to switch to another person.
- To the Spanish, information is considered a valuable commodity. For this reason, they may not be anxious to share useful facts with you, no matter how encouraging they may seem.
- Be warm and personal during your negotiations yet retain your dignity, courtesy, and diplomacy. Your Spanish counterparts may initially seem restrained and indirect, but this is normal until your relationship has been established.
- Do not expect to discuss business at the start of any meeting.
- Politics, sports, and travel are good topics of conversation. Avoid discussions of religion.
- Bullfighting is considered an art and should not be judged on any but Spanish terms; derogatory remarks about bullfighting are inappropriate.
- The Spanish give advice to one another and to foreigners freely; don't be offended by this.
- Have business cards printed with English on one side and Spanish on the other. Present your card with the Spanish side facing your Spanish colleague.
- Expect protracted negotiations, and be prepared to renegotiate topics that already seemed to have been resolved.

Cultural Note

Spaniards are known for their pride and personal sense of honor. However, international visitors are sometimes surprised that business acumen and expertise are not always highly regarded in Spain. (As with the upper class English, to call someone "clever" in Spain is a veiled insult.) Spaniards often take more pride in personal characteristics than in business skills.

Business Entertaining

- Always invite Spanish clients to excellent restaurants; many Spaniards are highly conversant about gourmet food and vintage wines.
- If a prospect or client accepts your invitation to lunch, remember to keep the discussion on a social level at least until coffee is served following the meal.
- At around 5:00 or 6:00 P.M., many Spaniards go out for hors d'oeuvres, called "tapas." These tapas are eaten at a series of bars or cafés (also called *tabernas* or *mesónes*) and can vary from salted almonds and olives to octopus and potato omelets. Spaniards will walk from bar to bar, eating tapas, drinking sherry, and visiting friends for an hour or two.
- Dinner is not served before 8:00 P.M., and often not until 10:00 P.M.

- You will probably not be invited to a Spanish home, as this type of socializing is reserved for intimate friends. You might, however, be invited out to dinner.
- If an invitation to a Spanish home is extended, you may decline at first, and accept it only when pressed; first invitations are often offered out of politeness. If the invitation is repeated, you may accept.
- In the continental style of eating, the fork is held in the left hand and the knife in the right, and they are never switched. Push food onto the fork with the knife. When you are finished, place knife and fork side by side on the plate; if they are crossed or on opposite sides of the plate, you will be offered more food. Hands should be kept above the table.
- Pay compliments to your host (and to the waiters in a restaurant).
- If you have been invited out, reciprocate at a later date, being careful not to mention "repaying" your hosts.
- Be aware that many restaurants close for a month of vacation.

 ## PROTOCOL

Greetings
- A handshake is a normal greeting.
- You will note that among close friends, Spanish men will add a pat on the back or a hug to the handshake.
- Women may lightly embrace and touch cheeks while kissing the air. A professional woman may also greet a Spanish man who is a close colleague in this way.
- Be ready to repeat the process when you depart.

> **Cultural Note**
> In Spain, the use of the familiar (tú) and formal (Usted) forms of address are different from their usage in Latin America. For example, Spaniards generally speak to domestic employees in the formal (Usted) manner; they feel this confers dignity and shows respect for the person.

Titles/Forms of Address
- First names are appropriate among friends and young people. Although things are changing in Spain, it is better to err on the side of formality at work. Wait for your Spanish counterpart to initiate the use of first names or the use of the familiar form of address (tú) as opposed to the formal form (Usted).
- Most people you meet should be addressed with a title and their surname.
- For further information on the proper titles and forms of address for Spanish-speaking countries, please consult Appendix A.

- As a general rule, use only one surname when speaking to a person, but use both surnames when writing.
- It is important to address individuals by any titles they may have, followed by their surnames. For example, teachers prefer the title Profesor, and engineers go by Ingeniero.

Gestures

- There are many gestures used in daily Spanish conversation. Their significance may vary from region to region, so observe local behaviors, and ask if you are unsure.
- To beckon another person, turn the palm down and wave the fingers or whole hand.
- Snapping the hand downward is used to emphasize a point.
- The "okay" gesture (making a circle of the first finger and thumb) is rude.
- Hands are a form of communication unto themselves in Spain. Motions are often made near the face, and they reflect the emotional aspects of a conversation.

Gifts

- Generally, if you are given a gift, you should open it immediately.
- If you are invited for a meal at a Spanish home, it is appropriate to bring chocolates, pastries, or flowers (but not dahlias or chrysanthemums, which are associated with death).
- Don't give thirteen flowers—it is considered bad luck.
- Business gifts are usually not given at a first meeting.
- If you give a business gift, choose it carefully; it should not be a vehicle for your company logo.
- Local crafts or illustrated books from your region are appropriate; university or sports team shirts and caps are good gifts for children.
- The latest electronic gadgets, fine writing implements, lighters, quality crystal, etc., can all be appropriate.
- Gifts should always be name-brand items of high quality, and they should be beautifully wrapped.
- For further suggestions on culturally correct gifts, visit *www.kissboworshakehands.com*.

Dress

- The Spanish are highly aware of dress. They like to project a refined image, and they will scrutinize clothing to ascertain a person's social position or business success.
- Always select well-made conservative attire. Name brands will be noticed. Dress in subdued colors.
- Men dress conservatively, while women are expected to be stylish.

Sweden

Kingdom of Sweden
Local short form: Sverige
Local long form: Konungariket Sverige

Cultural Note

Swedes were some of the first Europeans to own a cell phone, use the Internet, and invest in technical gadgets. This has led to a large number of technology firms coming to Sweden, despite the country's high taxes.

▶ WHAT'S YOUR CULTURAL IQ?

1. TRUE or FALSE: The Swedish firm Stora Kopparberg is the oldest known company in the world.

   ANSWER: TRUE. Stora Kopparberg began as a medieval copper mine, and its earliest records are more than 700 years old. The copper has long since run out, but its successor firm, Stora-Great, is still around as a forest products firm.

2. Swedish director Ingmar Bergman made some of the most important movies of all time. Which of the following was not directed by Bergman?
   a. *Cries and Whispers*
   b. *Fanny and Alexander*
   c. *My Life as a Dog*
   d. *The Seventh Seal*
   e. *Wild Strawberries*

   ANSWER: c. This film about a twelve-year-old boy in 1950s Sweden was directed by Lasse Hallström.

3. Which of the following is characteristic of Swedish business methods?
   a. Careful, meticulous planning
   b. Insisting on quality
   c. Considering a verbal agreement and a handshake binding
   d. Being punctual
   e. All of the above

   ANSWER: e. Violation of any of these norms by foreign executives may dissuade Swedish firms from doing business with them.

▶ TIPS ON DOING BUSINESS IN SWEDEN

- Swedes traditionally find outward displays of emotion to be distasteful. While this trait is common to all Scandinavians, it is especially pronounced in Sweden. Sales techniques that use hype or high enthusiasm are generally not as successful in Sweden.

- Swedish executives have a reputation as good negotiators, who can remain polite even while driving a hard bargain. They also consider quality to be one of the most important issues.
- Among themselves, Swedes prefer to make decisions via a consensus. However, they can be so subtle about it that foreigners never even know that the process is taking place. Instead of a formal vote, Swedes can establish a consensus through eye contact, slight nods, and murmurs.

Cultural Note

Berries are an important delicacy in Swedish cuisine. Besides the lingonberry jam that the retailer IKEA has made popular in households worldwide, Sweden also produces wild bilberries (with strong medicinal properties), caramel-flavored cloudberries (used in the ice cream at gala Nobel dinners), and the cherished *smultronställe* (wild strawberries). It is said that finding a pristine patch of wild strawberries can bring a tear to a Swede's eye.

Swedish berries are prepared in many different ways, including blueberry soup—a staple of Sweden's largest cross-country ski race, the Vasa (*Vasaloppet*). The Vasa runs from Sälen to Mora—fifty-five miles (89 km).

▶ COUNTRY BACKGROUND

History

The Vikings (also called "Norsemen") were feared for their raids throughout northern Europe from the eighth to eleventh century. These Vikings eventually became the Swedes, the Norwegians, and the Danes.

Christianity was introduced to Sweden by Saint Ansgar in A.D. 829.

Political power was concentrated first in Denmark, which came to rule much of Scandinavia. In 1389, the Union of Kalmar formally united Sweden with Denmark and Norway under Margaret I. Sweden left this union in 1448.

Denmark conquered Sweden in 1520. Many prominent Swedes were slain by the Danes in this "Stockholm Bloodbath." Denmark's rule did not last long; Sweden broke away from Denmark in 1523 and became a rival power under Gustav I. He later established Lutheranism as the state religion.

By 1660, expansionist Sweden had reached its greatest extent, gaining control of the Danish territories around Göteborg and Malmö, as well as parts of Norway.

Peter the Great of Russia defeated Swedish forces at the Battle of Poltava in 1709. Swedish power in Europe declined after this point.

In 1809, Sweden lost Finland to Russia during the Napoleonic Wars. Sweden and Denmark fought on opposite sides during this time. To punish Denmark for supporting Napoleon, the postwar Congress of Vienna took Norway from Denmark and gave it to Sweden in 1814.

Sweden had become an aristocratic nation of landed noblemen and had little in common with the fishermen, sailors, and merchants of Norway. Friction developed. Fortunately for the Norwegians, their rugged, rocky nation could not be divided up into the vast farming estates preferred by the Swedes. Norway finally broke away from Sweden in 1905 and was recognized as an independent nation.

Sweden remained neutral in both World Wars. In 1946, Sweden joined the United Nations but retained its policy of neutrality.

During the 1960s, Sweden enjoyed strong economic growth and became one of the world's most prosperous nations.

Prime Minister Olaf Palme was assassinated in Stockholm in 1986, shocking the nation.

Faced with soaring costs and high unemployment during the 1990s, Sweden implemented tax reforms and reductions to its comprehensive welfare system.

Sweden became a member of the European Union in 1995, but as of this writing, Swedish voters continued to turn down entry into the euro system.

Cultural Note
Alfred Nobel invented dynamite in 1867, helping speed the growth of the mining industry and Sweden's development as an industrial nation. Nevertheless, over the next twenty years, economic dislocations and food shortages caused half a million Swedes to immigrate to North America.

Type of Government

The Kingdom of Sweden is a parliamentary state under a constitutional monarchy. Sweden's current constitution was adopted in 1975. In the executive branch, the Cabinet (which consists of the prime minister and the advising ministers) is responsible to Parliament. The Parliament has one house, the Riksdag. Its members are elected by universal suffrage and serve for three years.

The king is the chief of state, while the prime minister is the head of the government.

Sweden has a free-enterprise economy, while maintaining an extensive social welfare system. State benefits include child care, health care, and extensive pension plans. Taxation is very high.

Sweden historically maintained neutrality and felt that membership in the European Union would not be consistent with this policy. However, the end of the Cold War put Sweden's entire foreign policy into question. Sweden did join the European Union in 1995 but declined to join NATO.

For current government data, check with the Embassy of Sweden at *www.swedenabroad.se*.

Language

The official language of Sweden is Swedish.

Ethnologue.com lists a total of fifteen different languages spoken in Sweden. Swedish is closely related to Danish and Norwegian.

> **Cultural Note**
>
> Silence is golden in Sweden. A good child is always described as quiet. Swedish children are also taught that it is impolite to interrupt. This puts Swedes at somewhat of a disadvantage when dealing with loquacious Europeans (such as the French and Italians) who expect several people to speak at the same time.

The Swedish View

Sweden once had an official church, the Church of Sweden (a form of Lutheranism). While Sweden has complete religious freedom, until 1996 all Swedish citizens were automatically registered from birth as members of the Church of Sweden. This automatic registration has been dropped, and today, baptism is required for church membership. Furthermore, the official status of the Church of Sweden was revoked in the year 2000. Since then, the Church has been fully independent (although it continues to receive some government subsidies). Many Swedes attend church on holidays.

Other Christian denominations are also represented in Sweden. There are small Jewish and Muslim populations.

One-eighth of the population is foreign-born, and absorbing these foreign influences is a major concern for Swedes. Certain incidents, such as the tragedy in which a Kurdish father killed his own daughter because she adopted Swedish customs, are becoming more common and generating alarm.

Sweden's egalitarianism is considered a cornerstone of Swedish society. Although authority is respected, positions of authority do not grant one special privileges. And Swedes believe that hierarchy can and should be bypassed when necessary.

Neutrality has been Sweden's foreign policy for over 190 years. This enabled Sweden to stay out of both World Wars. However, Sweden does send personnel out on international peacekeeping missions.

Despite their neutral status, Swedes often consider themselves the conscience of the world. They feel free to comment on real or perceived injustices occurring anywhere, worldwide.

In the past, Swedes looked upon lifetime employment as a right. This ended with economic dislocations in the 1990s. Younger Swedes do not have the same loyalty to their employers that their parents had, nor do they expect to be employed by the same company their entire lives.

☑ Know Before You Go

The primary hazard to visitors comes from the weather. Sweden's winter is cold, dark, and snowy.

Aside from that, Sweden is a very safe country. The closest thing to a hazard a foreigner is likely to encounter in Sweden is bafflement at the impenetrable Swedish sense of humor. (Swedes tell jokes with a straight face, which has led many foreigners to believe that Swedes have no sense of humor.)

▶ CULTURAL ORIENTATION

Cognitive Styles: How Swedes Organize and Process Information
The Swedes are a proud people. Their education teaches them to think conceptually and analytically. Swedes tend to look toward universal rules or laws to solve their problems.

Negotiation Strategies: What Swedes Accept as Evidence
Truth is supported by objective facts. Subjective feelings are considered suspect. Belief in the beneficence and desirability of the social welfare state is itself an ideology.

Like most Scandinavians, Swedes tend to accept data on face value. They extend trust to others until the source proves unreliable. However, the cosmopolitan Swedes are not naive.

Value Systems: The Basis for Behavior
The Swedes have a humanitarian culture. Top priority is given to the quality of life and to the environment.

The following three sections identify the Value Systems in the predominant culture—their methods of dividing right from wrong, good from evil, and so forth.

Locus of Decision-Making
Although decisions are made by group consensus, Swedes have a strong self-orientation and respect individual initiative and achievement. An individual's ability is considered more important than his or her station in life.

Swedes are very good at compartmentalization. They feel that they have a right to a private life totally apart from their careers. These lives are rarely discussed with business colleagues, but they can nevertheless affect business decisions.

Sources of Anxiety Reduction
Sweden has been rated as having a low level of uncertainty avoidance, which would indicate that Swedes are very tolerant of divergent opinions.

Sweden's comprehensive social welfare system is a great source of anxiety reduction. Swedes also tend to have strong nuclear families, which give stability and structure to their lives.

Issues of Equality/Inequality
Sweden has created a middle-class society that strives to minimize social differences, so there is very little evidence of poverty or wealth. The largely homogeneous population inhibits the development of largely divisive ethnic issues. Protected by their social welfare state, Swedes

Sweden

often feel a deep need to find a challenge in life, since most necessities are taken care of. Some ambitious Swedes seek their fortunes abroad, away from their country's high taxation rates.

Some sociologists believe that Sweden has the lowest masculinity index of any country in Europe. This reflects an extremely low degree of gender discrimination. Certainly, Swedes live in an androgynous society, with no limits to the roles women may fill. Men and women share the responsibilities of child care.

▶ BUSINESS PRACTICES

Punctuality, Appointments, and Local Time

- The Swedes respect punctuality. Be on time for all business and social appointments.
- Not only do Swedes expect meetings to start on time, they expect them to end at the appointed time as well. If your meeting runs overtime without good reason, they are likely to question your time management skills.
- Appointments should be made two weeks in advance.
- The residents of Sweden, like most of their European neighbors, write the day first, then the month, then the year (e.g. December 3, 2010, is written 3.12.10 or 3/12/10).
- Swedes set aside specific hours of the day for business meetings. They are usually from 9:00 to 10:00 A.M. and from 2:00 to 4:00 P.M. A well-planned day is considered very important in Sweden, and any last-minute attempt to change meeting times will not be appreciated.
- The minimum vacation in Sweden is five weeks per year (this has been legislated!) Most Swedes take off the entire month of July—so try to avoid scheduling any business trips during that time.
- During the Christmas holidays (from December 22 to January 6), many Swedish businesspeople are unavailable.
- Sweden is one hour ahead of Greenwich Mean Time (G.M.T. +1), or six hours ahead of U.S. Eastern Standard Time (E.S.T. +6).

Negotiating

- Although your first meeting with Swedes will be very low-key and seemingly informal, you are being evaluated. The Swedes will be well prepared and will expect you to be the same.
- Small talk is generally kept to a minimum at the start of business.
- Most Swedes consider humor inappropriate in a business setting. Swedes tend to be serious in general, and may appear downright stuffy during business hours.
- Swedes rarely express strong emotions in public, and certainly not in a business environment. They will react negatively to a foreigner who displays strong "feelings." Even "I'm

so happy to be here!" might put off the Swedes if it is stated too enthusiastically. The more remote the phrasing, the better; try "It is a pleasure to be here."

- Similarly, appearing reserved or even slightly shy can leave a positive impression with your Swedish hosts.
- Among themselves, Swedes prefer to make decisions via consensus. However, they can be so subtle about it that foreigners never even know such a process is taking place. Instead of a formal vote, Swedes can establish a consensus through nonverbal communication.
- Many Swedish businesspeople are fluent in English, particularly in large cities.
- While Swedes can be quite blunt, they also avoid confrontation. If a discussion begins to become heated, don't be offended if the Swedes cut it off abruptly.
- Avoid conducting private conversations in public areas.
- Do not ask personal questions or be offended if Swedes do not inquire about your family, your hobbies, and so forth.
- Swedes accept silence with ease. Do not rush to fill in pauses in the conversation.
- Swedes are very proud of each of their local regions. Be careful not to praise one locale over another.
- Scandinavians appreciate knowledge of the differences among the people of Finland, Norway, Sweden, and Denmark.
- The Swedes have an intense appreciation of nature.
- Relaxation is important to the Swedes. This includes breaks in their work schedule. Don't try to rush a Swede who is taking a long coffee break or an even longer lunch break, even if you are inconvenienced by it.

Business Entertaining

- Business lunches and dinners are quite popular. Make reservations in advance. Formal restaurants are recommended for business meals.
- Business breakfasts are becoming more common.
- Invite spouses to business dinners, but not to lunches.
- It is not uncommon for businesswomen to pick up the check in Sweden, especially if they are on an expense account.
- The Swedes generally do not socialize with coworkers after working hours, although they do consider their colleagues to be good friends.
- Swedes often remove their shoes when they enter their homes. There may be a place for your shoes to be stored in your host's hallway during your visit.
- Toasts, although uncommon among young people, are more formal in Sweden than elsewhere in northern Europe. Allow your host and your seniors to toast you before you propose a toast to them.
- *Skoal* is the Swedish word for "cheers." Wait until your host has said skoal before touching your drink.

- If you are seated left of the host as the guest of honor, you may be expected to make a speech.
- The *smörgåsbord* is a buffet (hot and cold) served year-round, and especially during Christmas and Easter. The cold foods are generally eaten first, then guests progress to the hot dishes.

PROTOCOL

Greetings

- The handshake is the standard greeting. Swedes also shake hands upon departure. Handshakes should be accompanied by direct eye contact.
- The handshake between men is short and firm. Handshakes between women—or between men and women—are less firm.
- Good friends (especially among the young) who see each other often may not bother to shake hands. Sometimes, they will exchange kisses on the cheek.
- Older, upper-class Swedes may be very formal. Be sure to shake their hands when greeting and when leaving. Older Swedes may avoid the pronoun "you," instead referring to people in the third person (e.g., when greeting Mr. Jarl, they will say "How is Mr. Jarl today?"). This is a rare but endearing custom.
- Swedes generally prefer to be introduced by a third person.

Titles/Forms of Address

- The order of names in Sweden is the same as in most of Europe: first name followed by surname.
- Young people are most likely to go to a first name basis quickly, and the egalitarian Swedes often use first names in the workplace.
- Older Swedes generally still expect to be addressed by their surnames.
- Persons with professional titles should be addressed by that title (Doctor, Engineer, Professor, and so forth) followed by a surname. In truth, Swedes are not as obsessed with titles as are many Europeans.
- It is important to say hello and goodbye to employees in stores and restaurants.

Gestures

- The Swedes are a restrained people and do not use many gestures. When dealing with them, you should avoid gesticulating or talking with your hands.
- Swedes are also a relatively quiet people. Keep your voice calm and well modulated.
- In general, Swedes do not like physical contact with anyone except close friends. Do not touch, backslap, embrace, or put your arm around a Swede.
- Direct eye contact is expected. Look a Swede in the eye when speaking with him or her.
- A toss of the head means "come here."

- While Swedes have a reputation for sexual openness, do not mistake a Swedish woman's forwardness for a sexual invitation. Swedish women often speak to strangers, especially foreigners, when they want to practice the foreigner's language.

Gifts
- In general, gift giving is not a part of doing business in Sweden. Sweden's anticorruption legislation makes gift giving problematical; a gift must not be interpreted as a bribe.
- For a foreigner, a practical rule of thumb is to have a gift ready for your Swedish business associates, but not to give the gift unless you get a gift from the Swedish contact.
- Despite recent tax abatements, liquor is still expensive in Sweden, so it is a highly appreciated gift. Fine liquor or wine from your home country makes a good business present.
- If you are invited into a Swedish home, you should bring a gift for your hostess. Appropriate gifts include flowers, liquor, wine, cake, or candy. If there are children in the home, you may also bring a small gift for them.
- Swedes often remove the paper, or wrapping, from bouquets before they present them to the hostess.

Dress
- Conservative dress is appropriate. For business appointments, men should wear suits and ties, while women should wear suits or dresses.
- During the snowy winter, many Swedes wear boots to work and change into regular shoes when they arrive.
- Swedes are usually fashionably well dressed in public. Even when jeans are worn, they should be neat and clean.
- Public ostentation is avoided in Sweden. Try not to dress in clothing that attracts too much attention.
- You can't always distinguish the boss by his or her clothes in Sweden. Swedish egalitarianism allows high-ranking executives to wear clothes similar to those of their employees.

Cultural Note

The government of Sweden tried to reduce the rate of alcoholism by imposing heavy taxes on alcohol. Many Swedes joke that the one tangible benefit of membership in the European Union is that the country was forced to reduce its alcohol taxes.

Switzerland

Swiss Confederation
French long form: Confederation Suisse
German long form: Schweizerische Eidgenossenschaft
Italian long form: Confédérazione Svizzera

Cultural Note

Switzerland has three official languages: French, Italian, and German, plus a fourth "protected" language called *Romansch*. In addition to one or more of these languages, businesspeople generally speak English as well.

WHAT'S YOUR CULTURAL IQ?

1. The flag of Switzerland is always easy to recognize, even among a host of flags. Why?
   a. It is the same as the flag of the Red Cross.
   b. By law, it must be larger than any other European flag.
   c. It is square.
   d. It is circular.

   ANSWER: c. Most flags are rectangular, but the Swiss flag is square. The Red Cross flag is a red cross on white, the reverse of the Swiss white cross on red.

2. Neutral Switzerland managed to avoid both World Wars. TRUE or FALSE? Switzerland has been peaceful for over 500 years.

   ANSWER: FALSE. Like most of Europe, Switzerland suffered from warfare. The last foreign incursion was from Napoleon in 1798. When Napoleon pulled his troops out in 1802, it prompted a short civil war.

3. Which of the following people were not born in Switzerland?
   a. Louis Chevrolet, founder of the U.S. Chevrolet Motor Company
   b. Albert Einstein, physicist and winner of the Nobel Prize for physics
   c. Alberto Giacometti, world-renowned sculptor
   d. Karl Jung, pioneering psychoanalyst

   ANSWER: b. Although Einstein was educated at the University of Zurich and taught at the University of Berne, he was born in Germany.

TIPS ON DOING BUSINESS IN SWITZERLAND

- Switzerland remains one of the world's most expensive nations (in terms of consumer goods). Cartels wield great influence over prices, and consumers pay the price. *The Economist*'s "Big Mac Index" often lists Switzerland as having the most expensive burger in the world. The upshot of this price fixing means that the Swiss do not allow competition to drive down prices.
- An influential contact is vital to success in Switzerland. All Swiss males serve in the military, where they also form friendships and networks. Businesses tend to be run by old-boy networks of men who were friends in the Swiss Army.
- Age and seniority are important in Switzerland. Young executives, sent alone to major appointments, may not be taken seriously. Expect to defer to the elderly. Also, if your company has a long lineage, the year it was established should appear on your business card and/or letterhead.

Cultural Note
The Swiss tend to judge a person by appearances. No matter how competent you are, if you are underdressed or ill groomed, the Swiss will not trust you.
The Swiss put great importance upon footwear. Wear good dress shoes and keep them shined.

 COUNTRY BACKGROUND

History
Archaeological evidence shows that Switzerland has been occupied for thousands of years. The Romans pacified and colonized an area they called *Helvetia* that more or less corresponds to modern Switzerland. In A.D. 260, the Alemanni invaded, destroying the local economy. The Romans kept nominal control of the region until they withdrew around A.D. 400.

In 1291, three Swiss cantons signed the Perpetual Covenant to defend against foreign domination. This Swiss Confederation achieved independence from the Holy Roman Empire in 1648.

During the Reformation, Switzerland did not escape religious violence. For example, Protestant reformer Huldreich Zwingli was slain in 1531. Switzerland eventually established Catholic cantons and Protestant cantons, and both religions coexist in Switzerland today.

Switzerland's borders were fixed in 1815 by the Congress of Vienna, which also guaranteed Switzerland's neutrality. Several Catholic cantons tried to secede from the Swiss Confederation in 1847, but a new Swiss Constitution in 1848 gave each canton enough control over its local affairs that the nation held together.

The International Red Cross was founded in Geneva in 1863.

Switzerland remained neutral in the First World War. Following the war, the League of Nations was established in Geneva in 1920. This league was powerless to prevent the outbreak of another world war.

With the rise of Nazi Germany, Switzerland accepted a substantial number of refugees fleeing Nazi persecution. Switzerland managed to remain neutral during the Second World War. At the time, their continued independence was attributed to the Swiss Army. Only later was it revealed how much Switzerland had to accommodate Nazi Germany to remain free.

During the postwar period, Switzerland joined the European Free Trade Association. In 1963, Switzerland joined the Council of Europe. They continued to resist joining international organizations that might violate their policy of neutrality—including the European Union.

During the late 1990s, revelations about Swiss compliance with Nazi Germany became public. Swiss banks refunded large sums of money to the heirs of depositors who were killed by the Nazis.

Cultural Note

Swiss women waited until 1971 for the right to vote in national elections—far longer than most other Europeans. Even then, Switzerland had to amend its constitution in 1981 to guarantee equal rights for women because some cantons still declined to grant them the right to vote. Then in 1991, the Federal Supreme Court had to force one recalcitrant canton to allow women onto the cantonal electoral roll.

Type of Government

The Swiss Confederation is a federal state of twenty-eight sovereign cantons. The president is head of both the state and the government. There are two legislative houses: the Council of States and the National Council.

Switzerland has a policy of permanent neutrality.

Switzerland did not enter into either world war; indeed, it has not been involved in a war since Napoleon invaded in 1798. Yet national defense is taken seriously, and all men must serve in the military.

For current government data, check with the Embassy of Switzerland at *www.swissemb .org.*

Language

Linguistically, Switzerland is complex. There are three official languages: French, German, and Italian. Around Lake Geneva (in the southwest), French is spoken. Italian is spoken by about 10 percent of the population of the country, concentrated in the Ticino region. German is spoken in many parts of Switzerland. A fourth language, Romansch, is a Romance language spoken by only 1 percent of the population. The Swiss take the preservation of traditional languages and cultures quite seriously.

In the cities, or in work environments, finding someone who speaks English does not pose a problem.

Most Swiss are multilingual, and the majority of businesspeople include English as one of their languages.

Ethnologue.com has identified a total of twelve languages spoken in Switzerland.

Cultural Note

Switzerland is a small, highly developed, multilingual market located at the crossroads of Europe. Its population of approximately 7½ million people (2004 estimates) is diversified, well educated, and affluent. It has a strong and stable economy, low inflation, relatively low unemployment, and a highly qualified work force—all factors that contribute to making the Swiss Confederation a desirable market environment. Per capita income is the highest in Europe and spending power for foreign goods and services is commensurately high.

The Swiss View

Switzerland's four cultures—German, French, Italian, and Romansch—encompass a variety of religious traditions. Roman Catholics, at 46 percent, constitute the majority, with various Protestant denominations making up 40 percent. Others include Muslims, Jews, Buddhists, and Mormons.

Switzerland was at the center of the Protestant Reformation. Reformer Ulrich Zwingli (1484–1531) lived in Zurich; Jean Calvin (1509–1564) was French but was exiled to Geneva. Years of warfare between Protestants and Catholics devastated Switzerland. As a result, the Swiss today consider religion to be a private concern. Religion is rarely discussed in public. The doomsday cult known as the Order of the Solar Temple came to international prominence when fifty-three members were found dead in October of 1994, the victims of murder and mass suicide. The Swiss were aghast at these events, which served to drive religion even further out of public discourse. Nevertheless, the Swiss consider themselves privately devoted to religious principals.

The Swiss believe that they have developed a fair and beneficent society and exert strong social pressures on their citizens to conform to Swiss patterns of behavior.

Divided by language and religion, the Swiss find unity in their devotion to their families, their work, and their country. The Swiss are patriotic and deeply involved in their country's politics. Their political system, which involves strong local government, allows each citizen's vote to have great effect on their everyday lives. Referendums are frequent.

Even the Swiss Constitution can be challenged by a system called the People's Initiatives.

The Swiss are intensely concerned about the environment. They recycle most consumer products, and are second only to Germany in environmental restrictions.

The Swiss have, to date, refused to join either the United Nations or the European Union. (However, Switzerland is a member of many UN agencies, such as the World Health Organization.)

Long a banking center, Switzerland's reputation was tarnished by its acceptance of assets from the Nazis in World War II, as well as its refusal to return funds to the heirs of persons executed by the Nazis. Under threat of a U.S. boycott initiated by the World Jewish Congress, Swiss banks agreed in 1998 to disburse $1.25 trillion in funds, most of it to the heirs of Jewish victims of Nazi atrocities.

As a prosperous, neutral nation, Switzerland remains a magnet for refugees. Thousands of would-be-refugees are turned back at the borders, but many manage to enter the country, legally or otherwise. During the Kosovo crisis of 1998 to 1999, Switzerland sheltered some 40,000 refugees.

☑ Know Before You Go

Violent crime is very rare in Switzerland.

The Swiss tend to divide foreigners into "those who bring" and "those who take." The former are visitors from wealthy countries, who have money to bring (and will leave some of it in Switzerland). The latter are refugees, who must take from the Swiss welfare system. While Switzerland has the highest rate per capita of political refugees in Europe, there is resentment against "those who take."

Because the Swiss are so law-abiding, the police in Switzerland are able to keep a low profile. However, they can be heavy-handed with foreigners. Be sure you can produce your passport at all times. If you and a traffic officer do not share a common language, you may have to accompany the officer to a police station.

The Swiss are very law-abiding, so graft and corruption are uncommon. However, some things that are illegal in other countries are legal under Swiss law. For example, price fixing may occur in Switzerland but is illegal in many other nations, like the United States.

▶ CULTURAL ORIENTATION

Cognitive Styles: How the Swiss Organize and Process Information

Swiss culture has historically been very ethnocentric and circumspect toward outside influence; however, the younger generation is becoming more open. The German and French segments of Switzerland process information conceptually and analytically; the rest tend to think associatively. The former will use universal rules to solve problems, while the latter tend to become personally involved in each situation.

Negotiation Strategies: What the Swiss Accept as Evidence

The German and French segments rely on objective facts to determine the truth, while those of Italian heritage generally use subjective feelings. In both cases, faith in the ideologies of nationalism and utopian ideals may influence the truth.

Value Systems: The Basis for Behavior

The culture of Switzerland is made up of four subcultures with differing value systems: German, French, Italian, and 1 percent of the indigenous population who speak Romansch. The following three sections identify the Value Systems in these predominant cultures—their methods of dividing right from wrong, good from evil, and so forth.

Locus of Decision-Making

The individual is the decision-maker. Although he or she may defer to the interest of the family, the company, or the state, he or she is still responsible. Decision-making is a slow and involved process in which a relationship must be developed between the negotiators. Ethnocentric values may shape the decision. In families there is joint decision-making between parents and older children.

Sources of Anxiety Reduction

The four languages and two religions are all very important to the Swiss, but they have come to terms with all cleavages and do not find them to be sufficient cause for civil unrest. They may acquire this ability to live together in the Swiss military, where all of the groups are brought together in a well-integrated force. The nuclear family is the basic social unit, and there is a very high feeling of ethnocentrism—a belief that languages and religions mix and work together as Swiss.

Issues of Equality/Inequality

Although there is a history of disagreement among the groups, the central government has been able to negotiate acceptable conditions for all. Equal rights for men are guaranteed by law, and those who feel discriminated against use the law to work out their problems. A Swiss motto is "Unity, yes; uniformity, no." The Swiss are competitive, responsible, tolerant, materialistic, proud, and private. There are still some classic role differences between the sexes, and discrimination against women still exists in some cantons.

▶ BUSINESS PRACTICES

Punctuality, Appointments, and Local Time

- The Swiss reputation for promptness is deserved. Always be punctual. This applies to both business and social events.
- The Swiss, like most Europeans, write the day first, then the month, then the year (e.g., December 3, 2010, is written 3.12.10 or 3/12/10).
- Introductions are necessary to conduct business in Switzerland. Cold-calling a potential customer will rarely be productive. Switzerland is a small country and everybody knows everybody else in each industry. If no one is willing to recommend you, the assumption is that you are not worth knowing.

- Most people take their vacations in July and August. It is not advisable to try to schedule important appointments during that time.
- Each canton celebrates its own holidays. The Swiss National Day is the first of August.
- Switzerland is one hour ahead of Greenwich Mean Time (G.M.T. +1), or six hours ahead of U.S. Eastern Standard Time (E.S.T. +6).

Negotiating

- Business is a serious and sober undertaking. Humor has little purpose in negotiations.
- Expect deliberations to proceed slowly. High-pressure tactics inevitably fail; there is no way to speed up decisions.
- Generally, the Swiss take a very long time to establish personal relationships. Be patient. A good relationship will help immensely down the road.
- German Swiss tend to get right down to business. The French and Italians will expect some small talk first.
- The Swiss are usually willing to negotiate anything except price. Once a price has established, the Swiss tend to stick to it—even if it costs them the deal.
- If you use an interpreter, speak slowly and clearly. Avoid idioms. Frequently confirm that what you have said has been understood.
- Ideally, you should translate one side of your business card into the language of your Swiss client. If you aren't sure what language to pick, choose German. However, many businesspeople speak English, so you can have English on your card as a default.
- If your firm is an old one, put the year it was established on your Web site, letterhead, and business cards. The Swiss respect longevity in business.
- Good topics of conversation are sports, positive aspects of Switzerland, travel, and food.
- The Swiss attribute their independence to their military preparedness, which includes universal military conscription. Opinions on this subject are passionately held. Bringing up the topic can result in an argument.
- It is not appropriate to talk about dieting, especially while eating. Avoid personal questions and talk about work.
- Keep your wrists on the table at meals. Never put your hands in your lap.
- The elderly are respected in Switzerland. On public transportation, younger people may relinquish their seat to the elderly.
- When entering a Swiss shop, say "Hello" to the clerk.
- It is not unusual for passersby to admonish strangers for "improper behavior" in the street. This is more common in German areas.

Cultural Note

The Swiss sense of humor tends toward understated wit. This form of humor requires both quickness and intelligence, and many Swiss excel at it. Typically, one Swiss makes a witty remark, and another responds in kind. These exchanges are more likely to elicit smiles than laughter—the Swiss rarely engage in loud guffaws.

If you are able to engage in this form of reparteé, feel free to do so. If you can't, you have the excuse that you are a foreigner, unaccustomed to such humor. However, don't ask a Swiss to explain his or her joke, unless there is a mistranslation involved. Explaining a witticism is tedious and sure to render the joke unfunny.

Business Entertaining

- Business lunches and dinners are popular, but business breakfasts are somewhat uncommon.
- Business lunches are often quite informal, sometimes taking place in the company cafeteria.
- Business dinners are the time to impress your client with a meal at a fine restaurant. The Swiss eat dinner as early as 6:30 P.M. You will have a hard time finding a good Swiss restaurant open after 11 P.M.
- The Swiss rarely invite business associates into their homes.
- If you are invited into a Swiss home, expect the evening to end early. Most Swiss are an early-to-bed, early-to-rise sort. Do not phone anyone after 9 P.M.
- Toasting is a formal process. After your host has proposed a toast, look directly at him or her and respond verbally ("To your health" covers most occasions, but try to say it in the local language), then clink glasses with everyone within reach—preferably the whole table; then you may drink.

Cultural Note

The Swiss frown upon ostentation and obvious displays of wealth. It is acceptable to spend a large amount on possessions—as long as the items do not look flashy or showy. Many Swiss buy pricey items that, to the uninitiated, look as if they might be modestly priced.

 PROTOCOL

Greetings

- The standard greeting is the handshake. Even children are encouraged to shake hands.
- Always rise to be introduced to someone. Wait to be introduced by a third person.
- In the German areas of Switzerland, women sometimes embrace, but men do not.
- In the French and Italian areas, both men and women may embrace. The French also kiss each other twice on the cheek.

Titles/Forms of Address

- The order of names is: first name followed by surname.

- Only children immediately address each other by their first names. Always address Swiss adults by their title or "Mr.," "Mrs.," or "Miss," plus their surname.

Gestures

- The German-speaking Swiss rarely display strong emotions in public. In fact, most Swiss never reveal what they are thinking—at least not initially.
- By and large, gestures are kept to a minimum. Avoid frequent or wild gesticulations.
- French-speaking and Italian-speaking Swiss tend to be more willing to be emotional in public.
- It is impolite to talk with your hands in your pockets.
- Gum chewing in public is inappropriate.
- Do not sit with one ankle resting on the other knee.
- Backslapping is not appreciated.

Gifts

- Gift giving is not normally part of business in Switzerland.
- If you are invited to a Swiss home, always bring a gift. Wine, flowers, or chocolates (boutique-quality Swiss chocolate, never Belgian!) are good gifts. A foodstuff from your home country would also be appreciated.
- A gift with a significant connection to your home region will be remembered (for example, local folk art, liquor produced in your region, or a book about your home city).
- Keep company logos small.
- If you give flowers, remember that red roses are reserved for lovers.
- Interpreters or guides appreciate personalized gifts rather than a tip.

Dress

- Conservative dress is expected of foreign businesspeople. Be sure to wear well-shined dress shoes.
- Swiss bankers are well-known for their formal attire. However, in some industries, the Swiss dress more casually.
- The Swiss appreciate discretion regarding wealth. Do not wear ostentatious jewelry—except for expensive Swiss watches.

Cultural Note

The Swiss attribute much of their success to their work ethic. They work hard (and play hard). Punctuality is required and planning is done in advance. Everything is kept clean (this also applies to the country as a whole). Perhaps the only negative is that the Swiss are not usually good at improvising.

Taiwan

Republic of China
Local short form: T'ai-wan
Local long form: Chung-hua min-k'uo
Former: Formosa

Cultural Note

The Taiwanese are justifiably sensitive about their relationship with mainland China (the People's Republic of China). Even though their economies are intricately interconnected, the PRC continues to issue threatening statements regarding the inadvisability of the "secession of Taiwan." Despite these declarations, the Taiwanese continue to hold onto their views on national identity.

 WHAT'S YOUR CULTURAL IQ?

1. Studies show that Asians sleep less hours each night than North Americans and Europeans. In Taipei, many businesses stay open twenty-four hours a day. Which of the following firms cater to Taipei's night owls?
   a. Florists
   b. Internet cafés
   c. Opticians
   d. Bookstores
   e. All of the above

   ANSWER: e. Residents of Taipei shop all night long.

2. In 1999, an earthquake measuring 7.6 on the Richter scale struck Taiwan. Over 2,000 people died, nearly 9,000 were injured, and approximately 10,000 were homeless. Which relief organization was most effective in immediately getting to the survivors?
   a. The Red Cross
   b. The Tzu-Chi Foundation
   c. The World Health Organization

   ANSWER: b. Tzu-Chi is led by a Buddhist nun, Dharma Master Cheng Yen. She mobilized hundreds of Tzu Chi volunteers immediately after the quake, long before other relief efforts arrived—because Tzu Chi volunteers were part of each neighborhood.

3. Taiwan's citizens are keenly competitive, and they look worldwide for new clients. The most common type of company in Taiwan is:
   a. A massive corporation with global reach
   b. A small family-run company
   c. A venture capital firm

Taiwan

ANSWER: b. While there are immense multinationals in Taiwan (which have done immense damage to the environment), the archetype company is the flexible, entrepreneurial enterprise.

▶ TIPS ON DOING BUSINESS IN TAIWAN

- The Taiwanese are a fairly small and slender people. The large size of average westerners can be intimidating. If you can find a way to compensate for this difference (such as sitting down, or standing on a lower level, so you and your Taiwanese counterpart are at comparable heights), do so. Also, large westerners should realize that everything from furniture to clothing is made to a smaller scale in Taiwan.
- Executives in the health care and medical supply industries must face the Taiwanese reluctance to discuss illness. People in Taiwan do not even like to give health warnings, nor do they comment on illness to a sick person. The insurance industry has gotten around this reluctance by speaking of insurance as if it were a bet (many Taiwanese love gambling). A life insurance salesperson will explain a policy by saying, "We will bet that you will live to age sixty, and if we lose, we will pay your beneficiaries."
- Although Taiwan does not have any official commercial relations with various countries, (including the United States), they may have specific offices that maintain unofficial diplomatic representation. In the United States, the Taipei Economic and Cultural Representative Office (*www.tecro.org*) has offices in Washington, DC, and other cities. Concomitantly, many countries maintain unofficial relations through their offices in Taiwan, like the American Institute in Taiwan (AIT) and the American Trade Center—both in Taipei. Further information is available at *www.roc-taiwan.org*.

▶ COUNTRY BACKGROUND

History

Migration to Taiwan from mainland China began in A.D. 500. Dutch traders claimed the island as a base for their trade in 1624 and administered it until 1661. In 1664, loyalists from the Ming dynasty fled to Taiwan to escape the Manchu invasion, and in 1683 it came under Manchurian control. When Taiwan became a Chinese province three years later, migration increased to the point where the Chinese dominated the aboriginal population. In 1895, following the first Sino-Japanese war, Taiwan was annexed to Japan. During the next fifty years, Taiwan underwent agricultural development and the construction of a modern transportation network. At the end of World War II, Taiwan again became governed by China.

A revolution founded the Republic of China (ROC) under Sun Yat-sen's Kuomintang (KMT) Party. However, a civil war was waged in China between the KMT forces (led by Chiang Kai-shek after the death of Sun in 1925) and the Communist forces of Mao Tse-tung. The

KMT was defeated, and the refugees fled to Taiwan. The provisional government they established claimed to be the only legitimate government over both the mainland and Taiwan.

Many countries supported Taiwan as the legitimate government until 1971, when the People's Republic of China was admitted to the United Nations in place of the Republic of China. The United States opened relations with the mainland government in 1979.

A peaceful solution to the Chinese situation is still being sought. Debate continues over Taiwan becoming a separate, independent country. More recently, hope has arisen that the PRC will democratize to the extent that reunification may occur.

After his death in 1975, Chiang Kai-shek was succeeded by his son Chiang Ching-kuo. Extensive modernization efforts created a growing and prosperous economy in Taiwan. Martial law was lifted in 1987, and political opposition was legalized in 1989, opening the way for multiparty democratic elections.

Relations with Japan, the United States, and other countries are good, and extensive trading continues.

Cultural Note

Modernization has come swiftly to Taiwan, making it one of the wealthiest countries in East Asia. Fast-food restaurants, the latest high-tech gadgets, and luxury items are evident. This is attributed in part to the long-term stability of the government and strong feelings of solidarity and nationalism. The Taiwanese are generally quiet and reserved, yet friendly and courteous to strangers.

Type of Government

The nation's official name is Republic of China. It is often known as Nationalist China.

After years as a one-party presidential regime, Taiwan is now a multiparty republic. Political opposition parties were legalized in 1989.

Taiwan's constitutional system divides the government into five branches, or Yuans. They are: the Executive Yuan, the Legislative, the Judicial, a Control Yuan that monitors public service and corruption, and the Examination Yuan that serves as a civil service commission. At the top of this structure is the chief of state, the president, who is chosen by the National Assembly. The head of government is the Premier, who is appointed by the president.

Taiwan held its first popular election for president in March of 1996. Since the People's Republic of China remains a one-party state, the Taiwanese election of 1996 was the first time in 4,000 years of recorded history that a Chinese nation held a free and fair election.

The KMT, which brought its political power and 2 million people over from Mainland China in 1949, was historically associated with the Mainlanders (i.e., people who fled to Taiwan with the KMT and their descendants).

For the first time, a member of the main opposition party, the Democratic Progressive Party (DPP), was elected in 2004. President Chen Shui-bian succeeded the KMT's Mr. Lee

Teng-hui. The DPP's most salient policy difference with the KMT has been the controversial issue of Taiwan's independence. The DPP modified its demand for immediate Taiwan independence and now calls for the people to decide Taiwan's future through a plebiscite.

The third-largest opposition party is the Chinese New Party, which consists mainly of second-generation "mainlanders" who have grown up in Taiwan. The New Party supports the eventual reintegration of Taiwan into the People's Republic of China.

The defining characteristic of Taiwan's international presence is its lack of diplomatic ties with most nations of the world. The ruling authorities in Taiwan call their administration the "Republic of China," and for many years claimed to be the legitimate government of all China. Foreign nations wishing to establish diplomatic relations with a government of China had two choices: to recognize the "Republic of China" or to recognize the People's Republic of China (PRC). Most chose to recognize the PRC. The PRC was admitted to—and Taiwan left—the United Nations and most related organizations in the early seventies. The United States switched diplomatic recognition to the PRC in 1979. Current government data can be found at the Embassy of Taiwan at *www.roc-taiwan.org*.

Cultural Note

Although Taiwan initially used only the old forms of written Chinese, they eventually adopted some (but not all) of the improved, simplified Chinese characters developed by the Communists. Visiting executives should make sure the Taiwanese variant is used for translations of their materials in Taiwan.

Westerners who wish to speak Chinese should be thankful that Mandarin was chosen as Taiwan's official language. Mandarin, with four different tones, is difficult enough to learn. The native Taiwanese language (imported from southern Fukien province) has six tones, which change depending upon the position of a word in the sentence!

Language

The official language of Taiwan is traditional Mandarin Chinese, although Taiwanese (called *Min*, a southern Fukien dialect), and Hakka dialects are spoken. English is a popular language to study in school, and many businesspeople can speak, understand, and correspond in English.

In general, Taiwan uses the Wade-Giles system for romanization, but the special municipality of Taipei adopted standard Pinyin romanization for street and place names. This means that the same Chinese word may be transcribed various ways into English.

For further data on the languages of Taiwan, see Ethnologue at *www.ethnologue.com*.

Cultural Note

The Chinese phrase that describes so much of Taiwanese life is *re nau*, which means "hot and raucous." This describes not just Taiwan's lively nightlife, but the aggressive nature of daytime Taiwan as well. The streets are jammed and the noise is overwhelming; everyone has something to do and is in a hurry to get there. It is this energy that developed Taiwan into a major industrial power in half a century.

The Taiwanese View

The religious distribution is over 90 percent Buddhist, Confucian, and Taoist; 4.5 percent Christian; and 2.5 percent other religions.

A Taiwanese citizen does not have to wonder about the meaning of life. The Mandarin term *shengyi* translates as "meaning of life." It also means "business." There could be no greater work ethic than this: the purpose of life in Taiwan is to work hard, be successful in business, and accumulate wealth for one's family.

Confucian ethics form the backbone of Taiwan society. Confucianism is not a religion in the Western sense, but it does provide guides for living. Unlike the People's Republic of China (where the Communists preached loyalty to one's work group), in Taiwan the family remains the central unit of society.

Taiwan has no official religion, reflecting the ability of the Taiwanese to simultaneously follow more than one religion. Aside from Confucianism and traditional folk beliefs, Taiwanese are likely to be Buddhist, Taoist, or Christian. (To make matters more complicated, many Taiwanese follow Taoist philosophy while ignoring the Taoist priesthood.)

☑ Know Before You Go

Taiwan sits in the Pacific's "Ring of Fire"—right above the juncture of the Philippine and Eurasian plates—in a seismically volatile region (as evidenced by the earthquake in September of 1999). Some geologists believe that Taiwan is ultimately doomed. Still, it is such an economic powerhouse that the risks are far outweighed by the monetary rewards of establishing facilities on the island. A similar situation exists in many parts of the U.S West Coast.

Earthquakes, typhoons, heavy air pollution, and contaminated drinking water are all hazards that Taiwanese face. Besides being continually cloudy most of the year, the monsoons generally hit Taiwan from June to August.

▶ CULTURAL ORIENTATION

Cognitive Styles: How the Taiwanese Organize and Process Information

Taiwan's culture is generally closed to outside information but willing to consider data that conforms to its vital interests. Taiwanese are trained to think associatively and to stress wholeness over fragmentation. They are more apt to let their personal involvement in a problem dictate its solution than to use rules or laws.

Negotiation Strategies: What the Taiwanese Accept as Evidence

One's immediate feelings are the primary source of truth. This may be biased by faith in the ideologies of nationalism. Recently, younger Taiwanese are moving toward the use of more and more facts to justify their decisions.

Value Systems: The Basis for Behavior

Confucianism has a great influence on Chinese society. It generates a rigid ethical and moral system that governs all relationships. The following three sections identify the Value Systems in the predominant culture—their methods of dividing right from wrong, good from evil, and so forth.

Locus of Decision-Making

Decisions are made by consensus of the group, which defers to those who have the most ethos—usually the oldest members. It is the individual's duty not to bring shame on any unit of which he or she is a member—family, group, or organization. Individuals must also be very careful not to cause someone else to lose face. Thus, Taiwanese may speak with vague politeness rather than saying "no." There is a strong authoritative structure that demands impartiality and obedience.

Sources of Anxiety Reduction

The family is the most important unit of social organization, and life is an organization of obligations to relationships. The Taiwanese are highly ethnocentric with a natural feeling of superiority and confidence in their political system. This gives them a feeling of national and personal security. One must work for harmony in the group, so emotional restraint is prized and aggressive behavior is frowned upon.

Issues of Equality/Inequality

There is a strong feeling of interdependence among members of the family, group, or organization. Businesses are very competitive and put heavy emphasis on entry-level skills and one's ability to get along in the group. Taiwan is still a male-dominated society with clearly differentiated sex roles. There is a strong women's movement.

▶ BUSINESS PRACTICES

Punctuality, Appointments, and Local Time

- Foreigners are expected to be punctual to meetings. Do not get upset, however, if your counterpart is late.
- Evening entertainment is an important part of doing business in Taiwan, so expect to be out late. It is wise to schedule morning appointments for late morning. This gives both you and your client a chance to rest.
- Plan a visit to Taiwan between April and September. Many businesspeople vacation from January through March.
- Traffic in Taipei is very congested. Unless your next appointment is so close that you can get there on foot, plan for long travel times between appointments.

- Taiwanese write the day first, then the month, and then the year (e.g., December 3, 2010, is written 3.12.10 or 3/12/10).
- Local time is eight hours ahead of Greenwich Mean Time (G.M.T. +8) or thirteen hours ahead of U.S. Eastern Standard Time (E.S.T. +13).

Cultural Note
Modesty is very important in Taiwan. Do not enter an office until you are invited, and do not seat yourself until you are asked to do so. If you receive a compliment, politely refute it and expect others to do the same. This should not stop you from complimenting another person, however, because compliments are always appreciated.

Negotiating

- The basis of a business relationship in Taiwan is respect and trust. Take time to establish a rapport with your counterpart. Initially, you will have to overcome the Taiwanese distrust of westerners. Meet face-to-face as often as possible, and keep in touch after your trip is over.
- Taiwan is relatively similar to other East Asian countries. The Chinese in Taiwan are capitalists with the same motivations for doing business as the Japanese. However, while Taiwan may seem very westernized, the heart of the culture is still very traditional.
- Business will tend to take place at a slower pace than in North America or Europe. Be patient with delays. Often, this is a tactic to wear down the other side. Therefore, do not talk about your deadlines. Expect to make several trips before reaching an agreement.
- Your negotiating team should include persons with seniority and a thorough knowledge of your company. Most importantly, include an older person. The Chinese revere age and status—sending a senior executive shows that a company is serious about starting a business relationship.
- Brute honesty is not appreciated in Taiwan. A direct "no" is considered rude. Learn to speak in and listen to subtleties. A "yes" or nod of the head may mean "maybe" or "I understand." A "maybe" usually means "no."
- When negotiating, be sincere and honest. Humility is a virtue, and a breach of trust, since trust is a vital factor in business relationships, will not be taken lightly. (Most proposals and potential business partners will be thoroughly investigated.)
- Emphasize the compatibility of your two firms, your personal amicability, and your desire to work with your counterpart. Profits are very important, but harmonious human interaction precedes them in importance. Avoid high-pressure tactics.
- Saving "face" or individual dignity is a very important and delicate matter. Therefore, never embarrass another person, especially in public.
- Never criticize your competition or avoid admitting that you do not know the answer to a question.

- Consider sending your proposals in advance of your visit for your host to preview. At a presentation, recap the major points at the beginning and at the end. Look for cues that your counterpart did not understand you. Do not expect him or her to tell you when this happens, because this will be embarrassing. Break up the information into small segments with pauses for question-and-answer periods. Be patient with extensive questioning. Address the chief negotiator occasionally, even if he does not speak English.
- Avoid using your hands when speaking. Chinese rarely use their hands while speaking and become distracted by a speaker who does.
- Business is competitive in Taiwan. Be prepared to discuss all parts of your proposal in detail. Bargaining is also a way of life, so be prepared to make concessions.
- Be sure to have products patented or registered in Taiwan to protect yourself against imitation.
- Have written materials translated by a Taiwanese expert. It is not acceptable to use the simplified Chinese script used in the People's Republic of China.
- Treat the elderly with respect. Acknowledge them first in a group, and do not smoke or wear sunglasses when they are near. When going through a doorway, allow older people to pass first. If they refuse, gently insist upon this point of etiquette.
- Try to obtain a personal introduction, possibly through your bank or government's Department of International Trade, since local contacts are extremely important.
- Be prepared to give out a lot of business cards. Your name, company, and title should be printed in English on one side and in Mandarin Chinese on the reverse side. (Gold ink is the most prestigious color for the Chinese side.) Cards are very important, because they indicate your rank and are a key to the respect you deserve in their culture. Never place a person's card in your wallet and then put it in your back pocket.
- For meetings, you will probably be taken to an informal sitting area and served coffee and tea. At the table, the member of your team with the highest seniority should sit in the middle of one long side. The second-ranked person will sit at his right, the third-ranked person to his left, and so forth. The Chinese delegation will do the same, so you will be able to identify key players on their team. If you are sitting on a sofa and chairs, follow the same pattern.
- Important issues to be aware of include observing hierarchy, respecting the elderly, modesty, and reciprocating gestures of goodwill.

Business Entertaining
- Hospitality is very, very important. Expect to be invited out every night after hours. This will entail visiting local nightspots and clubs, often until late at night.
- Be careful not to overly admire an object belonging to another person. He or she may feel obliged to give it to you.
- Remove your shoes when entering a home or a temple building.

- Do not be surprised if you are asked personal questions. You may be asked how much you paid for something, or what your salary is. These questions are not considered in bad taste in Taiwan.
- The largest meal of the day is in the evening, around 6:00 P.M. Entertaining is most often done in a restaurant and rarely in a home. If you are invited to a home, consider this an honor. Do not discuss business during a meal unless your host brings it up first.
- Never visit a home unannounced. Before leaving, express your thanks and bow slightly. Send a thank-you note to your host after a meal. It is polite to reciprocate by inviting your host to a meal of equal value at a later date.
- If you are the guest of honor at a round table, you will be seated facing the door. This is a custom carried over from feudal times that signified trust and goodwill on the part of the host, as the guest would be the first to see an attack and the host would be the last.
- At a meal, eat lightly in the beginning, because there could be up to twenty courses served. Expect your host to keep filling your bowl with food whenever you empty it. Finishing all of your food is an insult to your host, because it means that he did not provide enough and that you are still hungry. Leaving a full bowl is also rude. The trick is to leave an amount somewhere in the middle.
- Chinese use chopsticks for eating and a porcelain spoon for soup. Your attempts at using chopsticks will be appreciated. When you are finished, set your chopsticks on the table or on the rest. Placing them parallel on top of your bowl is considered a sign of bad luck.
- Sticking your chopsticks straight up in your rice bowl is rude, as they will resemble the joss sticks used in religious ceremonies. Hold your rice bowl near your mouth to eat.
- Do not put food taken from a serving dish directly into your mouth. Transfer it to your plate or bowl first. Bones and shells are placed on the table or a spare plate; they are never placed in your rice bowl or on your plate.
- Leave promptly after the meal is finished.
- Good topics of conversation include Chinese sights, art, calligraphy, family, and inquiries about the health of the other's family. Topics to avoid are the situation with mainland China and local politics. Generally, conversation during a meal focuses on the meal itself and is full of compliments to the preparer.

▶ PROTOCOL

Greetings
- With younger or foreign-educated Taiwanese, a handshake is the most common form of greeting. The standard Asian handshake is more of a handclasp; it is rather gentle and lasts for some ten or twelve seconds. (By contrast, most North American handshakes last for only three or four seconds.) Sometimes both hands will be used.

- When meeting someone for the first time, a nod of the head may be sufficient. When meeting friends or acquaintances, a handshake is appropriate and will be expected from westerners. Show respect by bowing slightly with your hands at your sides and your feet together.
- Chinese women shake hands more often these days. Western women may have to initiate a handshake with Chinese men.
- Elderly people are very highly respected, so it is polite to speak with them first. A compliment on their good health is always appreciated.
- Don't be surprised if you are asked if you have eaten. This is a common greeting, originating during the famines of feudal times. This phrase is comparable with "How are you?" in the West. A polite response is "yes," even if you have not eaten.
- Wait to be introduced to another at gatherings and parties. Avoid introducing yourself. Instead, employ a third person if there is someone you wish to meet.

Titles/Forms of Address

- A notable aspect of Taiwan is that, when they work with foreigners, they will list their names in the same order as westerners. The given name (or two hyphenated names) comes first, and their family (or surname) is last.
- Foreign executives may also notice that Taiwanese businesspeople will usually have an English first name, which they use constantly with English speakers. These English names (Sue, Tony, etc.) are often selected or assigned in school—and many Taiwanese just keep them for work purposes.
- If you require a Taiwanese businessperson to sign a document, he or she will probably use the Chinese version of his or her name. (When they sign, their names may be listed in traditional Chinese order—last name followed by two hyphenated given names.)
- For further information on Chinese naming conventions, please consult Appendix A.

Gestures

- Do not wink at a person, even in friendship.
- Do not put your arm around another's shoulders. While young children of the same sex will often hold hands, it is inappropriate for others to do so or to make physical contact with people who are not good friends or family.
- Do not touch the head of another person's child. Children are considered precious, and it is believed that they may be damaged by careless touching.
- Feet are considered dirty and should not touch things or people. Men should keep their feet flat on the floor, while women are permitted to cross their legs.
- Chinese point with their open hands, because pointing with a finger is considered rude. They beckon by extending their arms palm down and waving their fingers.

- While westerners point to their chests to indicate the first person, "I," Chinese will point to their noses to indicate the same thing.

Gifts

- Gift giving is often practiced within a business setting. Good gifts for a first trip include items with small company logos on them. Be sure the products were manufactured in your home country.
- Other popular gifts to business people include imported liquor, gold pens, and magazine subscriptions focused on your Chinese associate's hobbies or interests.
- When giving or receiving a gift, use both hands. The gift is not opened in the presence of the giver.
- The Chinese traditionally decline a gift three times before accepting; this prevents them from appearing greedy. Continue to insist; once they accept the gift, say that you are pleased that they have done so.
- Gifts of food are always appreciated, but avoid bringing food gifts with you to a dinner or party (unless it has been agreed upon beforehand). To bring food may imply that your host cannot provide enough. Instead, send food as a thank-you gift afterward. Candy or fruit baskets are good choices.
- The list of inappropriate and appropriate gifts in the chapter on the People's Republic of China can be applied to Taiwan as well.

Dress

- For business, men should wear a conservative suit and tie. A jacket may be removed during meetings if your Chinese counterpart does so first. Women should wear a conservative skirt and blouse or suit.
- Dress modestly for casual activities.
- Revealing clothing for women is considered a mark of poor character.
- Shorts are appropriate for young people.
- Neatness and cleanliness are important.

> ### Cultural Note
> Avoid being loud and boisterous around the Taiwanese. They sometimes interpret strong emotions, either positive or negative, as a loss of self-control. Westerners can be stereotyped in Taiwan as being raucous and emotional. Eschew lurid or gaudy attire as well.

Thailand

Kingdom of Thailand
Former: Siam

Cultural Note

Thailand is the only country in Southeast Asia never to have been a European colony. The country consistently remained free of European rule (a point of great national pride to the Thais). Thailand signed trade treaties with both France and Britain under the rule of King Mongkut and his son, King Chulalongkorn. By playing France and England off against each other, the Thai kings kept their country free. The name *Thai* means "free."

▶ WHAT'S YOUR CULTURAL IQ?

1. A *wai* is:
   a. A spicy dish made with peppers and rice
   b. An inquiry
   c. A form of greeting

ANSWER: c. A wai is the beautiful Thai greeting that is a combination of hands pressed together and a slight bow. Foreigners are not generally expected to know how to perform it correctly—but an attempt is appreciated.

2. Many of Thailand's cities celebrate *Songkran*, which is a Sanskrit word that refers to the orbit of the sun moving into Aries. It marks the beginning of a new solar year—the Thai New Year. TRUE or FALSE: The celebrations usually involve throwing water on people.

ANSWER: TRUE. From sprinkling water on statues of Buddha, to (politely!) dousing friends with buckets of water, Thais enthusiastically celebrate Songkran over several days in April. It is a cleansing, purifying holiday that Thais use to mark a new beginning, start fresh, and to give thanks.

3. Thailand's currency is the:
   a. baht   b. dong   c. rupee

ANSWER: a. The baht's currency code is THB. (Vietnam uses the dong, and Nepal and India use the rupee.)

▶ TIPS ON DOING BUSINESS IN THAILAND

• Thailand advertises itself as "The Land of Smiles," and the Thai people are genuinely friendly and polite. But their extreme politeness vanishes as soon as they get behind the

506

wheel of a car. Driving is aggressive, and pedestrians seem to be fair game. Be very cautious every time you cross a street; use an overhead walkway if possible.

- Because of travel difficulties in large Thai cities, many foreign executives plan on making only two meetings per day. The gridlock in Bangkok is so bad that many Thai businesspeople conduct business from their cars, with cell phones, laptops, and fax machines. (Remember that Bangkok and other Thai cities have passenger service on canals. When the street traffic is stalled, consider commuting by boat.)

- Entertaining is part of developing business relationships. Thais place great value on enjoyment (*kwam sanuk*). Laughter comes easily to Thais, and a foreigner can minimize his or her inevitable errors by laughing at them. Laughter can also be used to cover embarrassment.

▶ COUNTRY BACKGROUND

History

Like other countries of Southeast Asia, Thailand was peopled in prehistoric times through successive migrations from central Asia. Evidence of Bronze Age civilizations in northeast Thailand illustrate a high level of technology achieved by prehistoric people in Southeast Asia.

During the eleventh century, the Thai people began migrating from southern China. (Some research indicates that they were forced out by the Han Chinese.)

From the thirteenth century to the early twentieth century, the country was called Siam. The name was changed to Thailand in 1939.

Thailand was ruled by an absolute monarchy until a group of foreign-educated Thais directed a military and civilian coup d'état in June of 1932 and replaced the absolute monarchy with a constitutional monarchy. The current nation can be dated to that period.

In 1941 Japan occupied Thailand. After World War II, Thailand followed a pro-Western foreign policy.

Since the Second World War, a balance of power has been established between the military and the civilian leaders, with the king occasionally mediating. Whenever the military has felt threatened, it seized power. While many believed that the days of military coups were over, a constitutional crisis in September 2006 prompted another coup, overthrowing the government of Prime Minister Thaksin Shinawatra and his Thai Rak Party. The King has endorsed the coup, which appointed Surayud Chulanont as prime minister.

Whether Thailand is led by the military or elected officials, it must face an insurgency in its southern provinces from its minority Muslim population. Since the insurgency began in 2004, more than 2,100 people have been slain. The military government has promised to deal with the insurgents, but the outcome of its efforts is still in doubt.

Type of Government

The Kingdom of Thailand is a constitutional monarchy.

Thailand has a prime minister and a parliament with two legislative houses, but their power has been limited by the military. Membership in the lower house is by election, but in the upper house it is by appointment, and the military is well represented. Generally, the upper house has supported the military, while the lower house has been more likely to oppose it.

Current government data can be found at the Embassy of Thailand at *www.thaiembdc.org*.

Language

Thai, which is linguistically related to Chinese, is the official language. Other languages are spoken, including Chinese, Lao, Khmer, and Malay. The literacy rate is 89 percent.

The Thai alphabet is completely different from the Roman alphabet, and there are multiple ways to transliterate words, therefore, Thai words may be spelled different ways in English.

Ethnologue.com lists the number of languages in Thailand as seventy-five.

Cultural Note

Thai is a complex language with five different tones. While this makes it difficult for westerners to speak, Thais will appreciate a foreigner who takes the time to learn even a few phrases in Thai. There are only eight possible consonants that a word in Thai may end with: *p, t, k, m, n, ng, w,* and *y*. Consequently, when Thais speak English, they have trouble with words that end in other sounds. English words ending in *l* tend to be shifted to the *n* sound; for example, the word "Oriental Hotel" is pronounced "Orienten Hoten." And, because the *s* sound is not used in endings, Thais tend to leave the *s* off pluralized words. The Thai alphabet is similar to the alphabets used in Burmese and Laotian scripts. Thai is written from left to right. Adding to the difficulty for westerners, there are no spaces between individual words.

The Thai View

About 95 percent of Thais follow the Theravada form of Buddhism (an early form of Buddhism). About 4 percent of the population is Muslims, with the remaining split between other religions (including Christianity).

Adherents to the Theravada school consider themselves followers of the form closest to Buddhism as it was originally practiced. The spiritual liberation of the individual is a main focus of the Theravada school. Each individual is considered responsible for his or her own actions and destiny.

Each person in Thai society has a specific place. It is every person's job to fulfill his or her role with a minimum of fuss. Failure to do so involves a loss of personal dignity (called a loss of face). The Thai phrase *mai pen rai* (meaning "never mind" or "no worries") is frequently invoked as a reminder not to risk opposing the unopposable.

☑ **Know Before You Go**

If you are trying to keep correspondence private, it is probably not advisable to mark it "Confidential." Thai culture would consider that almost a teaser, which would bring it more attention than you wish.

The water table has been depleted in Bangkok, and the area now must deal with subsidence. Thais also face droughts, air, and water pollution, and the catastrophic effects of the 2004 tsunami.

▶ **CULTURAL ORIENTATION**

Cognitive Styles: How Thais Organize and Process Information

Thais cultivate alternatives and are usually open to information on most issues. They live in a concrete, associative, pragmatic world where the present is more important than the future and the person takes precedence over the rule or law.

Negotiation Strategies: What Thais Accept as Evidence

The truth develops from subjective, fatalistic feelings on the issue modified by faith in the ideologies of Theravada Buddhism. Thais with higher education from foreign universities may accept objective facts as a sole basis for evidence.

Value Systems: The Basis for Behavior

Religion plays a very important part in a Thai's life, but it does not dictate his or her every move. There are no absolute demands because their form of Buddhism permits selective conformity. They are free to choose which precepts of Buddhism, if any, they will follow.

Locus of Decision-Making

The individual is responsible for his or her decisions. Thais are nonassertive, as well as being very conscious of the feelings of others and their position in the social hierarchy. Decision-making revolves around the hierarchical, centralized nature of authority and the dependence of the subordinate upon the superior. Thus, the typical supervisor is authoritarian. He or she makes decisions autonomously, and the inferior unquestioningly obeys. A benevolent superior and a respectful subordinate is the Thai ideal.

Sources of Anxiety Reduction

The extended family is the basic social unit, with structure provided by the family, the village, and the *wat* (temple). The king is the primary provider of social cohesiveness. Thais refrain from developing specific expectations whenever possible because fate and luck play a major role in any event. You cannot plan because you cannot predict, so Thais live with a great deal of uncertainty. There is a high sense of self-reliance—what a person is depends on his or her own initiative.

Issues of Equality/Inequality

Status is of primary importance, as hierarchical relations are at the heart of Thai society. However, people gain their social position as a result of karma, not personal achievement. The royal family and the nobility are the only real class-conscious segment, although a class-conscious society is emerging. Regional and ethnic differences are socially and politically significant. This is a male-dominated society.

 BUSINESS PRACTICES

Punctuality, Appointments, and Local Time

- Punctuality is a sign of courtesy. Foreigners are expected to be on time.
- Traffic is extremely heavy in Bangkok, and floods make travel even worse. Allow plenty of time between appointments, especially during the rainy season.
- The best time to schedule a visit to Thailand is between November and March. Most businesspeople vacation during April and May. Avoid the weeks before and after Christmas, and the month of April. Thailand's Water Festival (Songkran) is held in April, and businesses close for an entire week.
- Arrange for a letter of introduction, and try to have an intermediary.
- Thais write the day first, then the month, and then the year (e.g., December 3, 2010, is written 3.12.10 or 3/12/10).
- Thailand is seven hours ahead of Greenwich Mean Time (G.M.T. +7), or twelve hours ahead of U.S. Eastern Standard Time (E.S.T. +12).

Negotiating

- Your initial meeting with Thai businesspeople may be over lunch or drinks, so they can get to know you. However, do not expect to discuss business during lunch.
- Because of the Thai deference to rank and authority, requests and correspondence usually pass through many layers before reaching top management.
- Be flexible and patient in your business dealings. Recognize that Thais do not follow the same relentless work schedule that other cultures do. Allow sufficient time to reach your goal.
- Never lose control of your emotions, and do not be overly assertive; that is considered poor manners.
- Thais avoid confrontation at all costs. They will never say "no" but will instead make implausible excuses or pretend that they don't understand English. They may even tell you that they must check with someone at a higher level, when such a person doesn't exist. Likewise, they find it difficult to accept a direct negative answer.
- Always present your business card, preferably with a translation printed in Thai on the opposite side. (You can have these printed in Bangkok.)

- Thai businesspeople will be impressed if you learn even a few words of Thai.
- If someone begins laughing for no apparent reason in a business meeting, change the subject. He or she is probably embarrassed.

Cultural Note

Direct confrontation is considered very impolite. Do not ask questions that require a value judgment (for example, "Which of these competing products is the best?"). Such questions are much too blunt. Use more subtle questions, and slowly work your way toward the answer ("Which of these competing products do you use?"). But don't make assumptions about the answer (for example, "So you use this one because it is best?" will probably elicit a "yes," even if the true reason for the preference is because a relative sells that brand).

Business Entertaining

- To entertain a small group, take them to an excellent restaurant in a prestigious hotel. For a large group, arrange a buffet supper. Always include Thai wives in business dinners.
- Expect to eat with Western-style forks and spoons. Keep the fork in the left hand and the spoon in the right (reverse this if you are left-handed). Cut with the side of the spoon, not the fork. Use the fork to push food onto the spoon.
- Never finish the last bit of food in a serving dish. Wait until it is offered to you and then refuse politely the first time. When it is offered again, accept; it is considered an honor to have the last bit of food.
- Drink tea or beer with meals. Drink water only if you have seen it being poured from a bottle.
- Many Thais smoke after dinner, but do not be the first to light up. Always pass cigarettes around to the men at the table. Although traditional Thai women do not smoke or drink in public, it is acceptable for Western women to do so.

Cultural Note

Monks are not permitted to touch the opposite sex. If you are female, do not expect them to shake your hand. If you need to give something to a monk, place it in front of him, or give it to a man to pass along. Monks are not expected to thank you for a contribution either—however, you always thank them for providing you with a means to better your life today, and in the future.

 ## PROTOCOL

Greetings

- The graceful, traditional Thai greeting is called a wai. Press your hands together as though in prayer, keeping arms and elbows close to your body, and bow your head to touch your fingers. The height of your hands is related to the level of deference or respect you are giving to the person you greet. The higher your hands, the more respect you show.

- A wai is used for both meeting and departing. You do not have to wai children.
- Thais will shake hands with westerners, but they will be pleased if you greet them with their traditional greeting.
- When introduced to a monk, never touch him; simply give a verbal greeting without shaking hands. Monks do not have to greet you with the wai.

Titles/Forms of Address

- Titles are very important.
- Many Thai businesspeople are Chinese.
- Chinese names generally consist of a family name, followed by two (sometimes one) personal names. In the name Chang Wu Jiang, "Chang" is the surname (or clan name). He would be addressed with his title plus Chang (Mr. Chang, Dr. Chang). For further information on the proper titles and forms of address for Chinese names, please consult Appendix A.
- Ethnic Thais predominate in government positions, but they will also be found in the business world.
- Since the adoption of surnames in the 1920s, ethnic Thais generally have two names. Their given name will come first, then their surname.
- Given names in Thailand are often unique and have a specific meaning. Only the most discerning travelers learn which ones apply to women and which to men.
- Address people by their title (or Mr./Mrs.) and their given (first) name. The short Thai term for "Mr.," "Mrs.," or "Miss" is *Khun* (although there are longer forms as well). Thus, former prime minister Chatichai Choonhavan could theoretically have been addressed as Khun Chatichai.
- Nicknames are popular in Thailand. Do not be surprised if the Thais give you a nickname, particularly if your name is hard for them to pronounce.

Gestures

- Public displays of affection between members of the opposite sex are not condoned. However, members of the same sex may touch or hold hands with one another.
- Never, ever point your foot at anyone; it is considered extremely rude. Don't cross your legs with one leg resting on the other knee, and never cross your legs in front of an older person.
- In contrast to the foot being foul, the head is sacred in Thailand. Never touch anyone on the head, not even a child.
- Do not pat people on the back or shoulders.
- Always give up your seat on a bus or train to a monk who is standing.
- Never walk in front of Thais praying in a temple.
- Beckoning is done with the palm down and the fingers waved toward the body.

Gifts

- Gifts are not opened in the presence of the giver.
- If you are invited for a meal, bring flowers, cakes, or fruit. Don't bring marigolds or carnations, however, because they are associated with funerals.
- High-tech gadgets (MP3 players, etc.), local handicrafts from your home, finely made pens and stationery, imported perfumes, select liquors, cigarettes, and illustrated books from your area are all suitable gifts.

Cultural Note

Much has been written about Thailand's sex industry. Since the proliferation of HIV (over 600,000 Thais live with HIV or AIDS as of this writing), it is an even more perilous occupation—endangering providers and patrons alike. It is projected that 40,000 to 60,000 Thais will die from AIDS-related causes each year; the majority being between twenty and twenty-four years of age.

Dress

- For business, men should wear a lightweight suit or slacks and a jacket, white shirt and tie; women should wear plain, conservative dresses or suits. Women should not wear black dresses, a color the Thais reserve for funerals or mourning.
- Dress for success. Thais are impressed with a neat appearance and refined clothing.
- In casual settings, men should wear slacks and shirts, with or without ties; women should wear light dresses or skirts and blouses. Short-sleeved blouses are acceptable, but sleeveless ones are not. Both sexes may wear jeans (but may find them too hot). Shorts are acceptable on the streets, but not in the temples.
- Men should wear traditional summer formal attire for formal occasions—white jacket, black pants, and black tie; women should wear long dresses. Black is acceptable to wear at a formal event if it is accented with color.
- Be certain to wear modest clothing when you visit temples—no shorts. It is also advisable to wear old or inexpensive shoes when visiting temples. You must remove them before entering, and once in a while they may be stolen.
- Never wear rubber thongs on the street; they are considered very low class.

Cultural Note

Never make fun of the royal family; they are regarded as a strong unifying influence. Faced with a fractious Parliament and a strong military, the Thai people turn to their constitutional monarch for leadership. Visiting executives should only use the most respectful terms when referring to the king. There is no room for criticism or humor in reference to royals—unless you want serious repercussions. Some Thai citizens who have made negative comments about the royal family have been charged with lèse majesté, and jailed.

Turkey

Republic of Turkey
Local short form: Turkiye
Local long form: Turkiye Cumhuriyeti

Cultural Note

Turkey's national hero, Kemal Atatürk, was president of the modern Republic of Turkey from its inception on October 29, 1923, until his death fifteen years later. He initiated an astonishing number of reforms. Turkey became a secular state—which was a major accomplishment in a Muslim land. Old titles were abolished, and all Turks were ordered to adopt surnames. Illiteracy was reduced by replacing Arabic script with the easier-to-master Roman alphabet. These and other reforms were not accomplished without considerable opposition. For most of his tenure, Kemal Atatürk found it necessary to rule Turkey as a one-party state. The surname Atatürk (father of the Turks) was awarded to Kemal by Parliament, and the government he founded was strong enough to endure even after his death.

▶ WHAT'S YOUR CULTURAL IQ?

1. Many of the places and events noted in Greek mythology did not occur in Greece. Which of the following were located in Turkey?
   a. The Temple of Artemis (one of the Seven Wonders of the Ancient World)
   b. King Midas (whose touch turned everything into gold)
   c. The Trojan Horse
   d. All of the above

   ANSWER: d. The Temple of Artemis was in Ephesus, Midas was king of Lydia, and the ancient city of Troy are all in modern Turkey.

2. Many persons and places associated with early Christianity were also in Turkey. TRUE or FALSE? Saint Nicholas (the inspiration for Santa Claus) lived in Turkey.

   ANSWER: TRUE. Nicholas was a fourth-century bishop of Myra, which is now the Turkish city of Demre. He was also born in the Turkish port of Patara.

3. Asia Minor—which more or less corresponds to modern Turkey—has been home to many civilizations. Place the following in the correct order, from oldest to youngest:
   a. The Republic of Turkey
   b. The Byzantine Empire
   c. The Ottoman Empire
   d. The Seljuk Empire

   ANSWER: b, d, c, a. "Ottoman" is a Western corruption of the Turkish name of Osman I (1281–1324), who was the most aggressive of the Seljuk Turkish leaders.

▶ TIPS ON DOING BUSINESS IN TURKEY

- Age is highly respected in Turkey. Elders are introduced first, served first, and are allowed to go through a doorway first. In a family-owned business, the decision-maker is probably an elder, even if some other member of the family does most of the negotiating.
- All meetings will begin with extensive small talk. Expect to be asked about your journey, your lodgings, and how you like Turkey. (Be sure to have good things to say about Turkey. Turks can say negative things about Turkey, but foreigners may not.)
- Although the majority of Turks are Muslim, the government and the military are determined to keep Turkey a secular state. While Muslim theocracies like Iran and Saudi Arabia insist that women cover their hair in public, the Turkish government has actually prohibited women from wearing head coverings in some situations, such as universities. Most women in Turkey do not live under harsh religious restrictions. In fact, Turkish women are well represented in business.

Cultural Note

Turkey occupies one of the most strategic locations in the world. Turkey controls access to the Black Sea. Russia's only warm-water ports lie on the Black Sea; Bulgaria, Romania, Ukraine, and Georgia also depend upon their Black Sea ports. Access out of the Black Sea into the Mediterranean is via the straits of the Bosporus and the Dardanelles, both of which lie entirely in Turkish territory. Furthermore, as the only member of NATO in direct proximity to Russia, Iran, and Iraq, Turkey's strategic importance cannot be underestimated.

▶ COUNTRY BACKGROUND

History

The Republic of Turkey is the successor to a series of empires that have existed on the Anatolian peninsula since the dawn of recorded history.

The Byzantine Empire ruled out of what is now Istanbul for over 1,100 years, until the Turks conquered it in 1453. In some ways, the Ottoman Empire represented a continuation of the Byzantines. (True, the Ottoman religion was Islamic rather than Christian, but the Byzantine Empire survived a change in religion: it began as the pagan Eastern Roman Empire.)

The current state emerged from the dissolution of the Ottoman Empire after its defeat in the First World War. The history of modern Turkey is inseparable from the biography of one man: Kemal Atatürk. A war hero, Mustafa Kemal (later known as Kemal Atatürk), held the ethnically Turkish areas of the empire together. Despite invading armies, fundamentalist opposition, and the total absence of a democratic tradition, he turned the core of a crumbling Islamic empire into a secular republic. The current Republic of Turkey dates to 1923.

Turkey managed to remain neutral in World War II. Choosing to ally itself with the West in the Cold War, Turkey sent an infantry contingent to fight in Korea in 1950 and joined NATO in 1952. Political turmoil following the introduction of multiparty elections sometimes resulted in the Turkish military involving itself in government. But throughout it all, Turkey has maintained a more stable, pro-Western government than most countries with Islamic majorities.

The 1990 invasion of Kuwait by Iraq put enormous strains upon Turkey. Turkey was a major trading partner of neighboring Iraq, but it supported both the embargo against Iraq and the multinational coalition that liberated Kuwait in 1991. Although Turkish troops did not serve in the liberation, the use of Turkish air bases was considered vital. Turkey experienced economic problems from both the embargo and high inflation during the Gulf crisis, although these were partially offset by $4 billion in grants and credits from Turkey's grateful allies.

In June 1992, Turkey initiated the Black Sea Economic Cooperation Treaty. Signed by Turkey, Greece, Bulgaria, Romania, and several ex-Soviet republics, the treaty was designed to enhance trade within the region.

Turkey suffered massive earthquakes in 1999. Turkey's traditional enemy, Greece, sent aid, which helped to relieve tensions between the two nations.

Like fellow NATO states France and Germany, Turkey declined to participate in the 2003 invasion and occupation of Iraq.

Cultural Note

The Turkish military is always in the background, ready to take over the reins of government if the politicians misstep. However, the military is not hated for this, at least not by most middle-class Turks. On the contrary, opinion polls repeatedly show that the military is the most trusted institution in Turkey. Many Turks view the military as well-meaning and paternalistic—rather like the rulers of the Ottoman Empire who preceded them.

Type of Government

The Republic of Turkey is a multiparty democracy. The president is the chief of state. The presidency was traditionally a largely ceremonial office, but the late President Turgut Ozal (who was also a former prime minister) turned it into a forum for directing Turkey's international affairs. The prime minister is the head of the government.

There is one legislative house, the Grand National Assembly.

The occupation of Iraq by the United States and allied forces put Turkey in a difficult position. Turkey supported the first Gulf War but has declined involvement in the second one.

Turkey is also concerned about conflict in various regions of the former USSR, especially between Armenia and Azerbaijan (centered on the autonomous region of Nagorno-

Karabakh). The Muslim Azeris are considered friends of Turkey, while there is historic animosity between the Turks and the Christian Armenians. The border between Turkey and Armenia is currently closed.

For current government data, check with the Embassy of Turkey at *www.turkishembassy.org.*

Language

Turkish is the official language. It is a member of the Ural-Altaic linguistic group—totally unlike any Indo-European language (such as English, German, or the Romance tongues). Turkish used to be written in Arabic script, but in 1928 the Latin alphabet was officially adopted. This made education much simpler, and today the literacy rate has increased to over 70 percent.

Ethnologue.com has identified thirty-six languages spoken in Turkey, two of which are extinct.

Many businesspeople speak a foreign language, usually English, German, or French. Executives often receive degrees from colleges outside of Turkey.

Cultural Note

With the breakup of the Soviet Union, Turkey and Iran are in a battle for influence over its former Islamic republics. This battle is waged on numerous fronts—even over which alphabet to use. All of the Muslim ex-Soviet republics wish to drop the Russian Cyrillic alphabet, which was forced upon them by Moscow. Whether they adopt the Arabic alphabet used by Iran or the Roman alphabet used by Turkey is a matter of great debate. Turkey and Iran try to influence the decision in multiple ways—for example, by sending books with their respective alphabets to the Muslim republics.

The Turkish View

Turkey has no official religion, although 90 percent of the Turkish population is Sunni Muslim, mostly of a nonorthodox sect called Alevi. The remaining 10 percent are primarily other Muslim sects, along with some Christians and Jews.

Since its founding in 1923, the Turkish Republic has been a secular state with no official religion. While there is considerable pressure to change this, other forces—including Turkey's powerful military—are determined to keep Turkey officially secular.

Every Turkish citizen, religious or not, is familiar with the basic precepts of Islam. The word *Islam* literally means "submission" (to the will of Allah). Consequently, success and misfortune are attributed to the will of Allah. Destiny is not under the control of man.

Most Turkish children are trained to be self-reliant, to care for others, and to be satisfied with their lot in life.

☑ Know Before You Go

The greatest hazard to visitors in Turkey comes from the chaotic vehicular traffic. Pedestrians, drivers, and passengers alike are at risk. Traffic is also made unpredictable by the variety of vehicles, from taxis to buses to minibuses (called a *dolmus*). Only bicycles are missing: Turks view bicycles as fit only for children.

Although terrorist incidents—usually car bombings—do occasionally occur in Turkey, foreign businesspeople are not usually affected.

In addition to heavy air pollution in the cities, tobacco is everywhere in Turkey. No-smoking zones are virtually nonexistent. If you are allergic to tobacco smoke, you will have a difficult time.

▶ CULTURAL ORIENTATION

Cognitive Styles: How Turks Organize and Process Information

Historically, Turks are generally closed to outside information. This is ameliorated somewhat by Turkey's position as a bridge between East and West. Turks are trained to process information subjectively and associatively. Turkey is a secularized Islamic nation, and one's personal involvement is more important than rules or laws.

Negotiation Strategies: What Turks Accept as Evidence

On any question, the answer comes from a combination of immediate feelings and faith in the ideologies of Islam. Among Turks, truth seldom comes solely from the accumulation of objective facts.

Value Systems: The Basis for Behavior

Turkey's territory lies in both Europe and Asia, and its value systems are an amalgam of East and West. The following three sections identify the Value Systems in the predominant culture—their methods of dividing right from wrong, good from evil, and so forth.

Locus of Decision-Making

The male leader is usually the decision-maker, but he always considers the family group upon which the decision is binding. Private life is overwhelmed by family, friends, and organizations, and these guide one's opinions. A relationship between participants must be established before any formal negotiations can take place. Identity is based on the social system, and education is the primary vehicle for moving up the social ladder.

Sources of Anxiety Reduction

Turks have been charted to have a fairly high index of uncertainty avoidance. They generally use laws and morality to give structure to their worldview.

In addition to the family, a Turk's identity derives from his or her role in the social structure. There is a deeply ingrained work ethic, but time is not a major source of anxiety. Pride in one's country, society, and family bolsters one's self-image and self-esteem. Emotions are shown, assertiveness is expected, and risks are taken to develop self-reliance.

Issues of Equality/Inequality

There is a definite social hierarchy, with some bias against classes, ethnic groups (especially the Kurds), and religions. The privileged elite control the country. There is not a lot of trust in people outside of the family and intimate friends. (Curiously, most ethnic Turks see the military as the nation's most trusted institution, despite the military's intervention in the political process.) The old dominate the young, and men often try to dominate women even though they have equal rights by law.

Historically, men and women had separate social subsocieties and did not mix in public. Today this is rapidly changing. Compared to most of its Arab neighbors, Turkey has more gender equality. However, although no jobs are barred to women, they still make up a minority of the full-time work force.

▶ BUSINESS PRACTICES

Punctuality, Appointments, and Local Time

- You are expected to be punctual for all business appointments.
- Traffic jams are frequent in both Istanbul and Ankara, so allow yourself plenty of travel time.
- Arrange appointments well in advance. A personal introduction (or at least a letter of introduction) will facilitate your acceptance.
- Turks have an unusual way of writing the date. They usually write the day first, then the month, then the day of the week, and finally the year. That is, December 3, 2010, is written as 3.12.Thursday.10 (periods are used rather than commas). Sometimes the day of the week is eliminated.
- Turkish businesspeople who work internationally are usually able to communicate in one or more foreign languages. English is commonly understood, as are German and French. Given advance notice, your Turkish colleagues should be able to conduct business in English; they probably have an English-speaking person on their staff. Business letters may also be in English. However, Turks will appreciate the effort if you learn at least a few phrases in Turkish.
- Do not expect to get right down to business at your appointment. The small talk that precedes business is important to Turkish executives—they want to get to know you.
- Although Friday is the Muslim holy day, offices are usually still open. Sunday is the government-mandated "day of rest."
- Business appointments can rarely be made during the months of June, July, and August; most Turkish businesspeople take extended vacations during that time.
- Obviously, you cannot expect to conduct business on a Turkish holiday. Be aware that many people will begin the holiday around noon the day before.
- November 10 is a secular holiday remembering the death of the founder of modern Turkey, Kemal Atatürk, in 1938. It is an insult not to observe the moment of silence at 9:05 A.M., the time of Atatürk's death.

- Visit kissboworshakehands.com for information on the Muslim holidays in Turkey, like: Ramadan (or Ramazan), Sheker Bayram, and Kurban Bayram. (Each year, these holidays will fall on different days.)
- Turkey is on Eastern European Time, which is two hours ahead of Greenwich Mean Time (G.M.T. +2). It is seven hours ahead of U.S. Eastern Standard Time (E.S.T. +7).

Negotiating

- The pace of negotiation is much slower in Turkey than it is in the West. Patience is exceedingly important; negotiations may take place over innumerable cups of tea or coffee. Meetings start slowly, with many inquiries as to your background, your education, and so on. Some of this may seem irrelevant to the purpose of your visit, but it is a serious breach of etiquette to cut this information-gathering process short.
- Negotiations are predicated upon the trust you have built with your new associates. Most business is conducted based upon personal relationships.
- In a family-owned business, the decision-maker may be quite elderly. Remember that elders are always respected in Turkey.

Business Entertaining

- By and large, most business entertaining will take place in restaurants. This is not a drawback, as Turkish cuisine is one of the finest in the world. However, you may not get the chance to act as host; Turkish hospitality is legendary, and your colleagues may insist upon doing (and paying for) all of the entertaining. When your colleagues invite you to a restaurant, you will not be allowed to pay for even part of the meal.
- Only when you issue an invitation to a meal will you be allowed to pick up the tab—and even then, you may have to fight off your colleagues' efforts to grab the check.
- In general, restaurants in the international hotels are bland and uninteresting compared to the average Turkish restaurant. However, Western-style alcoholic drinks are more readily available in such hotels.
- Turks use the same eating utensils used in Europe and the Americas. The fork is held in the left hand and the knife in the right; the knife is used for cutting and to push food onto the fork.
- Service in Turkish restaurants is very quick. Except in the international hotel restaurants, Turks do not usually order the entire meal at once. Instead they order the courses one at a time, deciding what to eat next only after finishing the last course.
- Turks usually smoke between courses.
- Good topics of conversations include Turkey's long history (avoiding the conflicts), sightseeing, cultural achievements, and sports. The most popular spectator sport is football (soccer).

- Wrestling is a traditional Turkish sport that remains very popular. Oddly, although Turks love horses, they have no tradition of organized horseracing.
- Always ask a Turkish father about his family; few subjects give a Turk more pride.
- Bad topics of conversation usually have to do with ethnic conflicts—with the Greeks, the Kurds, and especially with the Armenians.

Cultural Note

Tea, rather than coffee, is the national drink. Concentrated tea is poured into small, tulip-shaped glasses (hold the glass by the rim to avoid burning your fingers), and water is added to dilute the tea to your taste. Sugar may be added to tea, but never milk. As the glasses are small, you will probably go through many of them during a meeting. Outdoor tea gardens are common, and quite pleasant.

Turkish coffee is strong and is best appreciated as an after-dinner drink. Each cup is brewed individually, and the sugar is added at the time of the brewing, so you must indicate whether you want it plain or with little, medium, or lots of sugar. (U.S. palates usually require medium sugar.) Don't drain the cup; there will be coffee grounds at the bottom. Milk is not usually added to Turkish coffee but is generally available.

▶ PROTOCOL

Greetings

- Shake hands firmly when greeting or being introduced to a Turkish man. It is not customary to shake hands again upon departure.
- Male visitors should wait to see if a Turkish woman extends her hand before offering to shake. (Observant Muslims avoid physical contact with members of the opposite sex.)
- Turks may greet a close friend of either sex with a two-handed handshake and/or a kiss on both cheeks.
- Elders are respected in Turkey; if you are seated, rise to greet them when they enter a room. When being introduced to a group of men, shake hands with each one, starting with the eldest.

Cultural Note

The traditional Turkish greetings are *Merhaba*. (MEHR-hah-bah; Hello) and *Nasilsiniz*? (NAHS-sulh-suh-nuhz; How are you?). The response to the latter is *Iyiyim, teshekur ederim* (ee-YEE-yihm, tesh-ek-KEWR eh-dehr-eem; I'm fine, thank you!). Turks will appreciate any effort you make to speak their language.

Titles/Forms of Address

- The easiest and most respectful way to address a Turkish professional is by his occupational title alone. Simply say "Doctor" (Doktor) or "Attorney" (Avukat). If the professional is a woman, add the word Bayan after the title (e.g., Mrs./Miss Attorney is Avukat Bayan).

- When your Turkish colleague does not have a title, the situation becomes more complicated. Realize that most Turks did not have surnames until they were made mandatory by the 1934 Law of Surnames. The order of names is: first name followed by the surname.
- The traditional mode of address was to use a Turk's first name, followed by *bey* (for men) or *hanim* (for women). Use this form with older people unless instructed otherwise.
- Most of the Turks you will do business with use the modern form of address. The modern way is to use the surname, preceded by *Bay* (for men) or *Bayam* (for women). For example, Cengiz Dagci, a male novelist, would traditionally be addressed as Cengiz bey. The modern form of address is Bay Dagci (note the difference in spelling: Bey vs. Bay). Nezihe Meric, a female author, would traditionally be addressed as Nezihe hanim. The modern form of address is Bayam Meric.

Gestures

- It is safest to keep both feet flat on the ground when sitting. Displaying the soles of your shoes (or feet) to someone is insulting. Keep this in mind when changing from outdoor shoes into indoor slippers in a Turkish home.
- It is considered discourteous for women to cross their legs while facing another person.
- It is rude to cross your arms while facing someone.
- Keep your hands out of your pockets while speaking.
- Avoid blowing your nose in public, especially in a restaurant. If you must, turn away from others and blow as quietly as possible.
- Do not kiss, hug, or even hold hands with someone of the opposite sex in public.
- While Turks indicate "yes" by nodding their heads up and down (the same way as in North America), the gestures for "no" are different. Two ways to indicate "no" are as follows:
  1. Raising the eyebrows is a subtle way to indicate "no." This may be accompanied by the sound tsk.
  2. A broader way to indicate "no" is to accompany the eyebrow-arching with a backward tilting of the head and lowering of the eyelids (rather like someone trying to peer through the lower half of a pair of bifocals).
- The North American gesture for "no" (shaking the head from side to side) is a Turkish gesture for "I don't understand." If you inadvertently make this gesture in response to a question, a Turk may assume that you did not comprehend.
- Describing a desired length by holding the palms apart in midair (in the manner of a fisherman describing "the one that got away") will not be understood in Turkey. The Turks approximate length by extending one arm and placing the palm of the other hand on the arm; the length indicated is measured from the fingertips of the extended arm up to the side of the hand.
- To attract attention, Turks wave (palm out) with an up-and-down motion, rather than from side to side.

Turkey

- The Turkish "follow me" gesture is done with the entire curled hand moved in a downward "scooping" motion, not by curling an upraised index finger. It is considered rude to point your finger directly at someone.

Gifts

- If you know that your colleague drinks, a fine whiskey or liqueur is appropriate.
- If you are invited to a Turkish home—and an invitation may come more quickly from someone you meet socially than from a business colleague—a gift will be expected. Unless the gift needs immediate attention (such as foods that need to be refrigerated, or flowers that need to be placed in water) your gift will probably not be opened in your presence.
- Turks generally give presents in two ways: by leaving them or by presenting them apologetically. Often, a visitor simply leaves a wrapped gift near the door. The host will notice it but no verbal acknowledgement needs to be made by either party. Alternately, the gift may be presented while uttering a phrase such as "this gift is not worthy of you." Even then, the host might not open it immediately.
- Again, wine or liquor is appropriate if you are sure your hosts drink alcohol. Other suitable gifts are candy, pastries, or other treats. Fine glassware is also appropriate.
- Flowers are a good gift for a host, but tradition demands that the bouquet contain an odd number of flowers.
- If your invitation is for an extended stay (rather than a meal), further gifts are advisable. Items such as CDs, iPods, or other electronic gadgets are good. Be sure to bring gifts for the children, such as candy (especially chocolate) or small toys.
- Orthodox Islam prohibits alcohol and depictions of the human body (including photographs and drawings). Ascertain whether your hosts adhere to these strictures before giving such gifts.

Cultural Note

When entering a Turkish home, it is customary to remove your shoes and change into a pair of slippers. The homeowner provides the slippers. Sometimes, a Turkish host may tell you that you do not need to remove your shoes when you enter. This does not mean you should not do so; the host may simply be trying to save you from embarrassment in case your socks are dirty or worn.

Turkish hospitality demands that a guest be given the finest the household has to offer. You will be asked to sit in the best chair; you will be given the choicest cut at a meal. And if you use the bathroom, someone may offer you the finest guest towel in the house, stored away just for that occasion.

Dress

- Business dress is conservative: dark suits for men; suits and heels for women. However, Turkey is very hot in the summer, yet jackets and ties are rarely removed, even on the hottest days.

- Women's clothing may be comfortable but should remain modest; even in severe heat, necklines may not be low and skirts may not be short.
- Formal dress is required to attend the balls held at New Year's and on the Turkish national holiday (October 29). Men may need tuxedos; women may wear long gowns.
- Casual dress should also be modest. Shorts are appropriate only at seaside resorts. Jeans are acceptable for both men and women, but they should not be torn or frayed.
- Always wear clean socks in good repair. You will need to remove your shoes if you enter a mosque or if you are invited into a Turkish home.

Cultural Note

Should you enter a mosque, your clothing should be modest. Expect to leave your shoes at the door—one does not walk on mosque carpets in shoes. If you wish, you may rent slippers from an attendant at the mosque for a small fee. Pants are usually acceptable for women, but they are expected to cover their heads, shoulders, and arms. If your clothing is judged unacceptable, an attendant may offer you the loan of a long robe. A small donation to the mosque is always appreciated. Avoid visiting during prayer times or on Fridays (the Muslim holy day).

Ukraine

Local short form: Ukrayina

Former: Ukrainian National Republic, Ukrainian State, Ukrainian Soviet Socialist Republic

Cultural Note

The breakup of the USSR left Ukraine with a large military infrastructure, and an even larger stockpile of weapons and ammunition. This is as much a hazard as an asset; Ukraine has huge ammunition depots that are badly in need of decommissioning. One blew up in 2004, causing major damage.

 WHAT'S YOUR CULTURAL IQ?

1. TRUE or FALSE: The Cossacks are a legendary ancestral archetype to Christian Ukrainians, just as the Vikings are to the Scandinavians or cowboys are in the United States.

   ANSWER: TRUE. But they are not fondly remembered by Poles or Jewish Ukrainians, who were the victims of innumerable Cossack raids.

2. Which of the following cities was the capital of the first great civilization of Eastern Slavs?
   a. Kiev
   b. Moscow
   c. St. Petersburg

   ANSWER: a. Between the tenth and thirteenth centuries, Kievan Rus was the first great Eastern Slav city. A Russian proverb calls Moscow the heart of Russia, St. Petersburg its head, and Kiev its mother.

3. Match the following Ukrainian names with their identities:

   a. Taras Bulba   1. National poet; revived Ukrainian language
   b. Bogdan Chmielnicki   2. Mythic Cossack leader; Nikolai Gogol short story
   c. T. D. Lysenko   3. Cossack leader who incited revolt and pogroms
   d. Taras Shevchenko   4. Soviet agronomist; he persecuted scientists

   ANSWERS: a. 2; b. 3; c. 4; d. 1

 TIPS ON DOING BUSINESS IN UKRAINE

- Ukraine has proven to be a difficult country in which to conduct business, due to corruption and constantly changing laws. In one case, a European firm tried to buy a building and turn it into a restaurant. After giving gifts to numerous officials, they had all the required permits; then the land commission of the local State Property Fund ruled that the original permits were invalid. These commissioners wanted to be bribed as well.

- Of course, the November 2004 "Orange Revolution" and the poisoning of the then-presidential candidate Viktor Yushchenko illustrated Ukraine's hazardous, dynamic political environment.

- Overall, Ukraine's economy has grown in recent years. In 2004, Ukraine's rating was upgraded to "positive" by different investment-rating services. Then in 2005, economic growth decelerated somewhat. Although economic forecasts were for stronger growth in 2006, the standoff between Russia and Ukraine over natural gas prices showed how volatile Ukraine's fortunes can be. As of this writing, the dispute was settled.

Cultural Note

The name Ukraine means "borderland," and Ukraine has often constituted the border of several empires. This also resulted in the use of the definite article before Ukraine. English speakers said "the Ukraine" just as they said "the Bronx" or "the Netherlands." Current usage omits the article; the country is now just "Ukraine" or "Republic of Ukraine."

▶ COUNTRY BACKGROUND

History

Slavic peoples populated Ukraine at least 2,000 years before Christ. Kiev, the capital, dates to about the eighth century A.D.—some 400 years before Moscow. One of the oldest and most important of Slavic cities, Kiev is often considered the "mother" city of Ukraine, of the Russian Empire, and of the Slavic Orthodox churches.

Christianity came to Ukraine (and from there spread to Russia) when Prince Vladimir of Kiev was converted to Orthodoxy by Byzantine missionaries from Constantinople in A.D. 988.

Ukraine's flat, fertile expanses historically made it difficult to defend. The Mongols sacked Kiev in 1240, and from this point on, Moscow became the dominant Slav city. (Orthodox Russians see a progression of "holy cities of Orthodoxy," from Constantinople to Kiev to Moscow.)

Ukraine has been a prize coveted by many warring peoples. The Mongols were eventually driven back eastward, but other rulers took their place. The Lithuanians conquered Ukraine around 1392. When Lithuania and Poland merged in 1569, Polish influence became dominant. Under Polish rule, Ukrainian farmers were forced into serfdom.

Those who resisted began to band together and became known as Cossacks. They lived a harsh existence in frontier areas and gave only nominal allegiance to the Polish king.

In the 1600s, Polish Jesuits began to impose Catholicism on the Ukrainians by force. This rallied the Orthodox Cossacks, and in 1648 the Cossacks drove the Poles out of part of Ukraine.

Fearing that their independent state was too weak to stand alone, the Cossacks requested that Moscow rule them in 1654. Moscow tightened its grip on the Ukrainians decade after decade, reducing the Cossacks' power and completing the process of enserfment.

In 1871, the first of the modern-day pogroms against Jews occurred in Odessa. After the assassination of Czar Alexander II in 1881, pogroms became more frequent and were unofficially sanctioned by the Czarist government.

In the First World War, the subsequent Russo-Polish War, and the Russian Civil War, armies under several flags decimated Ukraine. In 1918, Ukraine experienced its first, brief period of independence, but it was soon absorbed into the new Soviet Union.

Between the World Wars, Stalin decided to enforce collectivization upon Ukraine. Thousands of peasants who resisted were slain. The result was widespread famine. Millions of Ukrainians starved to death in what was called the "bread basket of Europe."

Ukraine suffered again in the Second World War. Axis armies from Nazi Germany and Romania advanced far into Ukraine. Although some Ukrainians saw the Germans as liberating them from the USSR, Nazi atrocities soon turned most Ukrainians against the Axis. Many Ukrainians were slain. Over 2 million Ukrainian Jews were killed: some shot in their homes, some gassed in concentration camps.

From the start of the First World War to the end of the Second World War, over 5 million Ukrainians lost their lives—one in every six Ukrainians. This is a greater proportion than any other nation involved in the World Wars.

The breakup of the USSR in 1991 granted Ukraine its independence once more. Since independence, Ukraine has struggled to establish a democratic and capitalist society. The "Orange Revolution" of 2004 was a significant, peaceful event that resulted in a rerun of the election, and consequently, the swearing in of Viktor Yushchenko as president in January of 2005. (President Yushchenko had been poisoned with dioxins prior to the election and accused the former governmental authorities of the act.) The current government is seeking membership in the European Union and NATO.

Type of Government

Ukraine is a multiparty republic with a single legislative house, called the Supreme Council. The head of government is the prime minister. The president is the chief of state.

For current government data, check with the Embassy of Ukraine at *http://ukraineinfo.us*.

Cultural Note

Although it has long been in use by the Ukrainian people, Ukrainian is relatively new as a literary language. It was first used for comic effect in a 1798 novel written by a Russian-speaking bureaucrat. The man credited with first using Ukrainian as a serious literary tongue is Taras Shevchenko (1814–1859), a former serf who became a painter and poet.

Language

The official language of Ukraine is Ukrainian. There are several dialects. Until recently, Ukrainians were taught Russian in school, so people may switch from Ukrainian to Russian in the same sentence. Many technical terms in Ukrainian have been borrowed from Russian.

Ukrainian is similar, but not identical, to Russian. Modern Ukrainian has Polish linguistic influences that are absent in Russian. Today, Ukrainian and Russian are about as close as Dutch and German. Although the languages are different, native speakers can manage some communication. (However, foreigners who learn Russian usually report that they cannot understand Ukrainian without study.)

Ethnologue.com has identified eleven languages in Ukraine, one of which is extinct.

The Ukrainian View

There is no official religion in Ukraine, but over 27 percent of the population identify themselves as Ukrainian Orthodox, with a Moscow patriarchate; and over 20 percent say they are Ukrainian Orthodox with a Kiev patriarchate.

About 13 percent of the population belong to the Greek Catholic or Uniat Church, a church that follows Byzantine Orthodox rituals but accepts the authority of the Roman Catholic pope.

Immediately after the breakup of the USSR, Ukraine wanted to join both the European Union and NATO, but both moves were strongly opposed by Russia. However, President Leonid Kuchma revised Ukraine's military doctrine in June of 2004, and the new doctrine states that Ukraine does not view any nation as its military adversary.

Historically, Ukraine was usually ruled by either Poland or Russia. Poland's control, or suzerainty, ended before the Second World War, long enough ago that most Ukrainians have no animosity toward Poland. On the other hand, ethnic Ukrainians may have strong feelings about Russia. For many, it is a love-hate relationship: Ukraine was under Moscow's brutal rule, but Ukraine was also the most favored of Russia's possessions. For some former Communist Ukrainians, life was better under the USSR.

Under communism, a coal miner in the Ukraine was paid more than a chemical researcher. Today, salaries echo Western patterns: unskilled labor is paid less than jobs that require college degrees. Ukrainian youth now want to postpone marriage and children in favor of education and careers, so it expected that the birth rate in Ukraine will continue to decline.

☑ Know Before You Go

As of 1997, Ukraine requires all visitors to obtain mandatory health insurance from the state. The cost varies depending upon the anticipated length of stay but is generally modest. This insurance only covers medical care inside Ukraine. It does not cover the cost of medical evacuation.

Most travelers to Ukraine encounter no problems, despite a higher rate of street crime than in most Western European countries. Ukraine does have organized crime and computer hackers, but the majority of travelers are not affected by them.

The U.S. State Department has periodically recommended that visitors to Ukraine refrain from using bank or credit cards because of identity theft.

If you travel to Ukraine with young children, bring extra proof of your parenthood. Ukrainians are sensitive about foreigners (especially North Americans) coming to Ukraine to adopt Ukrainian children. They have initiated procedures at entry and exit points designed to prevent illegal adoptions.

There is still residual radiation from the Chernobyl nuclear accident in Ukraine. However, this is a problem throughout the region. Some studies assert that most of the Chernobyl radiation was blown into Belarus. And, recently, dozens of radioactive hot spots were found around Moscow itself, from badly stored nuclear waste and decades-old experiments.

▶ CULTURAL ORIENTATION

Cognitive Styles: How Ukrainians Organize and Process Information

Ukrainians have traditionally maintained freedom of discussion and have been open to out-side information. At the same time, they hold to their beliefs strongly and are quick to con-front. Ukrainians have excelled in the sciences, and higher education teaches abstractive and conceptual thought. However, their emotions bind them to the associative and the particular.

Negotiation Strategies: What Ukrainians Accept as Evidence

Ukrainians usually rely on the accumulation of objective facts. However, their ability to rea-son analytically and objectively is often influenced by subjective feelings.

Value Systems: The Basis for Behavior

The Ukrainian culture is one of contrasting value systems—Ukrainians are deeply idealistic, but just as deeply attached to the personal and subjective. The following three sections iden-tify the Value Systems in the predominant culture—their methods of dividing right from wrong, good from evil, and so forth.

Locus of Decision-Making

To Ukrainians, the individual is the primary unit for decision-making. He or she may be so independent that it is difficult to reach a consensus. Ukrainians tend to repudiate all forms of communal life that call for strict obedience. Decisions are not fixed on objective reality, but on idealistic viewpoints containing many elements. Ukrainians tend to confront reality with emo-tion, make decisions on the spur of the moment, and intermix theoretical and practical issues.

Sources of Anxiety Reduction

With the Communist Party no longer in control, religion is regaining its importance as the focal point for external structure and stability. Ukrainians are deeply religious but not fundamentalist; they look for ways to comprehend the essence of a creed rather than being fixated on dogma. Strong family ties help to ease the feelings of uncertainty. However, since feelings generally take precedence over reason, a person may go from deep love to great hatred or from great enthusi-asm to deep despair in a short time. Thus, the system may not seem to be in a stable condition.

Issues of Equality/Inequality

Ukrainians possess strong moral courage. They have a desire for harmony and an inclination to compromise and tolerate differences. Poetic by nature, they associate love not with eroticism but with a more philosophical, maternal love. There is a genuine softness of character that is expressed in politeness and high regard for the female sex. Women are considered the moral leaders of the nation.

▶ BUSINESS PRACTICES

Punctuality, Appointments, and Local Time

- Always be punctual, but do not be surprised if Ukrainians are not. It is not unusual for Ukrainians to be an hour late to an appointment.
- Punctuality was not considered essential under the Soviet system, since employment was guaranteed and no one could be fired for tardiness. Although this has changed, punctuality is still the exception rather than the rule.
- Even today, patience, not punctuality, is considered a virtue in Ukraine.
- Allow plenty of time for each appointment. Not only may they start late, but they may run two to three times longer than originally planned.
- The residents of Ukraine, like most Europeans, write the day first, then the month, then the year. (For example, December 3, 2010, is written 3.12.10 or 3/12/10).
- Obtaining an appointment can be a laborious process. Be patient and persistent. Once you have booked the appointment, make every effort to keep it.
- Ukraine is two hours ahead of Greenwich Mean Time (G.M.T. +2). This is seven hours ahead of U.S. Eastern Standard Time (E.S.T. +7). Daylight savings time is generally observed from spring through fall.

Negotiating

- Be factual and include technical details.
- Until you have a signed agreement, do not get overconfident about the deal at hand. Never expect that you can renegotiate later, either; the existing contract may be as advantageous as you will ever get.
- Never accept the first "no" as an answer. "No" is a quick and automatic response. Remain pleasant, try to establish a personal rapport, and ask again in a different way.
- "Final offers" are never final during initial negotiations. Be prepared to wait; the offer may be made more attractive if you can just hold out.
- Ukrainians may make dire proclamations that the deal is off during negotiations. Be prepared to play hardball.
- Haste always puts you at a disadvantage. If you give the impression that you cannot wait out your counterpart, you will inevitably lose.

- North Americans view negotiation as an exercise in compromise. However, the traditional Ukrainian view is that compromise equals weakness. If they can avoid compromising, they will. To yield on even an insignificant matter is something to be avoided.
- Ukrainian negotiators tend to speak with one voice. Foreign negotiators need to be in agreement among themselves and present a unified front.
- Ukrainians are fairly status conscious. They will probably have several people at any negotiation. They prefer you to have an executive whose rank is equivalent to that of their top negotiator at the discussions. A lone foreign executive in a room with a team of Ukrainians will have a difficult time.
- Include a clause requiring the joint venture partners to submit to arbitration in a neutral country if they can't come to an agreement. Sweden is the most popular choice for third-country arbitration.
- Ukrainian regulations represent the biggest liability to a successful joint venture. Since these regulations are in constant flux (reforms are being made all the time), don't count on your partner to have a full grasp of the legal issues involved. Get your own expert on Ukrainian law. Don't be surprised if the way you did something yesterday isn't permitted tomorrow; many laws are nebulous, and their interpretation is subject to change.
- Traits that many Ukrainians and North Americans have in common include a respect for nature and the outdoors, a fascination with technology and gadgets, and a tendency toward building things "big." All of these make good topics for conversation.
- Receiving a positive response from Ukrainians usually requires groundwork. Before making a decision, the bureaucrat should know who you are, what you want, what your project is, and which other bureaucrats have agreed to it so far. This information is best communicated through a third person, but e-mail or a letter will sometimes serve.

Cultural Note
While Ukrainians will criticize many aspects of life in Ukraine, they feel that only they have the right to do so. They quickly become defensive in the face of any criticism by a foreigner.

Business Entertaining
- In relation to other countries, dinner tends to be eaten early, around 6:00 P.M.
- Business success in Ukraine hinges upon establishing a personal rapport with your Ukrainian partners. Much of this will develop out of social events.
- Ukrainian restaurants historically had poor service and menus that did not reflect the dishes that were actually available. Today, Ukraine has restaurants that meet any international standards.

- Traditional Ukrainian restaurants had large tables set for many people. In such an establishment, if your party consisted of just two or three, you may have had to share a table with other people. Now, you will be able to reserve a table, or room, for your party.
- Two bottles will be on the table: one has water, the other has vodka. The vodka will not have a resealable lid—once it is opened, Ukrainians expect your party to drink it all.
- Ukrainians do most of their entertaining of foreigners in restaurants. Consider it an honor to be invited into a Ukrainian home.
- Ukrainians do not feel obligated to phone before dropping by a friend's house. Once you have established true friendship, a Ukrainian may stop by at any time—even late at night if a light is visible in your window.
- Guests are always offered food and drink (usually alcohol).
- Expect to do a lot of drinking—mostly vodka, champagne, and cognac.
- In a restaurant or nightclub, Ukrainians may invite you to dance or to come over to their table.
- Good topics of conversation include sports and music.

▶ PROTOCOL

Greetings

- Ukraine is home to several ethnic groups, notably Ukrainians, ethnic Russians, Belarussians, Moldavians, and Poles. While each group has its own cultural traditions, their similarities are greater than their differences.
- Throughout Ukraine, men shake hands with other men upon meeting and leaving.
- Allow women to take the initiative on handshaking.
- Although ethnic Ukrainians are generally less inhibited than Russians, both cultures can be rather dour and sedate in public. Smiles are reserved for close friends.
- Only during greetings do Ukrainians and Russians display affection in public. Relatives and good friends will engage in a noisy embrace and kiss each other on the cheeks.
- Ukrainians and Russians often greet a stranger by shaking hands and stating their name, rather than uttering a polite phrase (such as "How do you do?"). Respond in the same way.

Titles/Forms of Address

- Ukrainian and Russian names are listed in the same order as in the West, but the middle name is a patronymic (a name derived from the first name of one's father). Thus, Fyodor Nikolaievich Medvedev's first name is Fyodor (a Slavic version of Theodore), his last name is Medvedev, and his middle name means "son of Nikolai."
- Ukrainian and Russian women traditionally add the letter a on the end of their surnames; Medvedev's wife would be Mrs. Medvedeva.
- The variety of Russian names (both first and last) is quite limited. Ethnic Ukrainian names have somewhat more variety; surnames ending in -enko are characteristically

Ukrainian. Even so, it can be difficult to track down a person in Ukraine by a name alone. Additional data, such as birth date and place of birth, is often necessary.

- Unless invited to do so, do not use first names. Call Ukrainians and Russians by their surname preceded by "Mr.," "Miss," "Mrs.," or "Ms." If they have a professional title (e.g., Doctor), use their title followed by their surname.
- It is considered quite respectable to address friends, even elders, by their first names and patronymics, although many foreigners find this to be quite a mouthful. Do not be surprised to be asked about your father's first name, and to have that name scrambled into an unrecognizable patronymic.
- Among themselves, Ukrainians and Russians use a bewildering variety of diminutives and nicknames. As you establish a relationship with them, you may be invited to call them by a nickname or just their first name. Be sure to return the favor.

Gestures
- Ukrainians and Russians stand about one arm's length away from each other when conversing.
- The "thumbs-up" gesture indicates approval.
- The "fig" gesture—a clenched fist with the thumb protruding between the knuckles of the index and middle fingers—means "nothing" or "you will get nothing" in Ukraine. It is definitely not considered obscene, as it is in the Mediterranean. Indeed, a Ukrainian parent may use this gesture to his or her own child to indicate that the child cannot have something.
- When going to your seat in a Ukrainian theater, it is very impolite to squeeze in front of seated patrons with your back to them. Always face seated people as you move past them.

Gifts
- Good gift ideas include cigarette lighters, watches, currently popular electronics (like iPods) and thermos-type products (Ukrainians like to take food and drink with them on trips).
- If you are invited to a Ukrainian home, try to bring flowers, liquor, or a gourmet food item.
- Hard liquors that are easily available in Ukraine are vodka, champagne, cognac, and a Ukrainian honey-based cordial.

Dress
- While parts of Ukraine are quite cold in the winter, the country is generally warmer than Russia. In fact, the Ukrainian Crimea, which can be comfortable even in winter, was the major vacation area for all of the USSR.
- If you go to Ukraine during the winter, bring warm clothes or buy Russian-style hats and gloves upon arrival. In addition, bring a pair of shoes or boots with skid-resistant soles.
- Ukrainian buildings are usually well heated, so a layered approach is best in clothing, allowing you to take off clothes to be comfortable while inside.
- Business dress is conservative. Ukrainian clothing styles are not generally driven by the latest fashions in the West.

United Kingdom

United Kingdom of Great Britain and Northern Ireland
Abbreviation: UK

Cultural Note

England is only one part of the entity known as "the United Kingdom of Great Britain and Northern Ireland." Most of the United Kingdom's international business is conducted through England. Nevertheless, it is useful to know the following nomenclature:

- Britain refers to the island on which England, Wales, and Scotland are located. Although the English are in the habit of referring to all natives of Britain as "Brits," this term is not appreciated by many Welsh, Irish, and Scots.
- Northern Ireland shares the island of Eire with the Republic of Ireland. It is both incorrect and insulting to call someone from Eire a "Brit."
- Each of the four constituent parts of the United Kingdom (England, Wales, Scotland, and Northern Ireland) has a distinct history, culture, and ancestral language. There are also separatist pressures pulling each of these regions apart, and you must be sensitive to the individual ethnic heritage of your associates.

▶ WHAT'S YOUR CULTURAL IQ?

1. The Magna Carta is remembered as the first document delineating the rights of the English. TRUE or FALSE: King John I only signed the Magna Carta under duress.

   ANSWER: TRUE. In fact, John repudiated the agreement just months later. But he was then dethroned by the nobles, who forced successive monarchs to respect the document.

2. After King Charles I was executed in 1649, Oliver Cromwell led England for nearly a decade. Which of the following did not occur under Cromwell's busy rule?
   a. Scotland was brutally suppressed.
   b. Ireland was brutally suppressed.
   c. The Spanish Armada was defeated as it was about to invade England.
   d. England went to war against the Netherlands.

   ANSWER: c. The famous defeat of the Spanish Armada occurred in 1558, long before Cromwell became Lord Protector. However, the English fleet did battle a Spanish fleet during Cromwell's reign.

3. Sir Winston Churchill (1874–1965) inspired the allies with his oratory during WWII. In which of the following wars was he not actively involved?
   a. The Crimean War

b. The Boer War

c. WWI

d. WWII

e. The Korean War

ANSWER: a. Young Sir Winston was a war correspondent during the Boer War and was in the government—either in Parliament or as prime minister, during all or part of World War I and II, and the Korean War. He wasn't born until after the Crimean War of 1854–1856.

TIPS ON DOING BUSINESS IN THE UNITED KINGDOM

- The United Kingdom does not consider itself part of Europe—although it appreciates the economics of the European Union. Its first overture to join the European Economic Community in 1961 was vetoed by President Charles de Gaulle of France. The United Kingdom subsequently joined in 1973, but it still debates whether or not to adopt the euro.

- George Bernard Shaw has an oft-quoted line about the different meaning of words between England and the United States. He said, "America and Britain are two nations divided by a common language." Some terms that are innocuous in the USA have gotten companies in trouble in England. For example:

  - The 1993 Warner Brothers' film *Free Willy* left many Londoners helpless with laughter. This is because in England, the word willy is slang for "penis."

  - A Caucasian in England means a person from the Caucus republics: Armenia, Azerbaijan, and Georgia. In the United States, it means a white person.

Other English terms and their U.S. equivalents:			
English Term	**U.S. Term**	**English Term**	**U.S. Term**
Trainers	Sneakers	Single	One-way ticket
Suspenders	Garters	Return	Round-trip ticket
Braces	Suspenders	Ground floor	First floor
Dummy	Pacifier	First floor	Second floor
Bonnet	Car hood	Draughts	Checkers
Spanner	Wrench	Homely	Pleasant
Skip	Dumpster	Table a discussion	Begin a discussion

- Rapid change is not embraced wholeheartedly by most English. Traditional ways are valued, and the class system still has an impact on lifestyles.

Cultural Note

The English are tremendous sports fans. Football (soccer) is a national obsession, and millions of pounds are waged on important games. Other popular sports include horseracing, rugby, cricket, and golf.

▶ COUNTRY BACKGROUND

History

Britain was first brought into contact with the world when it was invaded by Rome in the first century B.C. Rome ruled much of the region until the fifth century A.D. Various tribes from Europe and Scandinavia—the Angles, Saxons, and Jutes—invaded after the Romans departed.

In 1066, the Normans invaded from France. This event, the Battle of Hastings, was the last successful invasion of Britain. The Normans transformed the region, making it a feudal kingdom.

Britain was frequently at war with continental powers over the next several centuries. Because it is an island, Britain had a tremendous defensive advantage. They realized they needed a strong navy to protect themselves, and this navy made the British Empire possible.

Great Britain was the strongest of the European powers in the nineteenth century, with many territories abroad. The Industrial Revolution first arose on British soil.

In 1926, the United Kingdom granted autonomy to New Zealand, Australia, and Canada; later in this century, it granted independence to India, Egypt, and its African colonies.

The First and Second World Wars caused great hardship for the United Kingdom; the First World War marked the end of the Victorian way of life. The Second World War ushered in the dismantling of the British Empire. After the war, many sectors of the British economy were nationalized. Britain did not fully recover from the destruction of WWII until the 1960s.

During the 1980s, Conservative prime minister Margaret Thatcher privatized many services, undoing some of the postwar nationalization policies.

In 1997, Tony Blair was elected prime minister, and the Labour Party assumed power in government once again. He was re-elected in 2001, and strongly supported the U.S. campaign against terrorism. Controversy surrounded him as he joined the United States in launching attacks against Iraq without UN approval.

Great Britain's devolution of powers has continued over the last decade. The Scottish Parliament in Edinburgh opened in 1999, as did the National Assembly for Wales in Cardiff.

Type of Government

England is a constitutional monarchy. Its constitution is unwritten and consists partly of statutes and partly of common law and practice. In its equivalent to the U.S. government's executive branch, the monarch is the chief of state, while the prime minister is the head of government. In practice, it is the Cabinet (selected from Parliament by the prime minister) that has power, rather than the monarch. The prime minister is the leader of the majority party in the House of Commons. The Parliament consists of the House of Commons and the House of Lords, with the Commons having more real power. The Commons is elected by universal suffrage every five years, although the prime minister may ask the monarch to dissolve Parliament and call for new elections at any time. Unlike the U.S. Supreme Court, the English judiciary cannot review the constitutionality of legislation.

For current government data, check with the Embassy at *www.britainusa.com*.

Language

In all its varieties, dialects, and accents, "the Queen's English" has had an immense influence on the languages of the world. Ethnologue.com estimates that worldwide, there are 341,000,000 English first-language speakers (1999 est.)—and obviously millions more if you consider those who learn English as a second language. English is spoken in 104 countries besides the United Kingdom. Some of these are: American Samoa, Andorra, Anguilla, Antigua and Barbuda, Aruba, Australia, the Bahamas, Barbados, Belize, Bermuda, Botswana, British Indian Ocean Territory, the British Virgin Islands, Brunei, Cameroon, Canada, the Cayman Islands, and the Cook Islands.

While there is a "Standard Oxbridge" or "BBC English accent" that most foreigners recognize, there are a multitude of dialects as well. Just ten minutes outside of London, pronunciations begin to change. In the United Kingdom alone, the dialects include Cockney, Scouse, Geordie, West Country, East Anglia, Birmingham (Brummy, Brummie), South Wales, Edinburgh, Belfast, Cornwall, Cumberland, Central Cumberland, Devonshire, East Devonshire, Dorset, Durham, Bolton Lancashire, North Lancashire, Radcliffe Lancashire, Northumberland, Norfolk, Newcastle Northumberland, Tyneside Northumberland, Lowland Scottish, Somerset, Sussex, Westmorland, North Wiltshire, Craven Yorkshire, North Yorkshire, Sheffield Yorkshire, and West Yorkshire.

In the United Kingdom overall, Welsh is spoken by about 26 percent of the population of Wales, and a Scottish form of Gaelic is used by approximately 60,000 people in Scotland.

The British View

England has an official religion—the Anglican Church, or Church of England. Most English belong to this church, which was founded when King Henry VIII decided to split from the Roman Catholic Church during his reign. The Church no longer has political power. Other religions represented in England are Roman Catholicism, Islam, Methodism, Hinduism, Sikhism, and Judaism. Religion is considered to be a very private subject. Scotland also has an official religion, the Church of Scotland. However, Wales and Northern Ireland do not have official religions.

Britain boasts some of the finest educational institutions in the world. A large portion of tax revenue is spent on the educational system. Schooling is free and compulsory from age five to age sixteen. Literacy is 99 percent, and school attendance is almost 100 percent. There are over forty universities in the United Kingdom, and many professional schools.

The stoic English "stiff upper lip" has changed in the last few decades. In some circles, the concept of personal responsibility for one's actions has morphed into a predilection for blaming someone else for life's problems, and seeking damages. The tabloids are calling it a "compensation culture"—and lawsuits for everything from personal injury to tenuous negligence claims are becoming more common. On the other hand, some believe that the change from the long-suffering English consumer to a more assertive comparison shopper is a positive development. This is not to ignore the fact that traditions still run deep in English society.

☑ Know Before You Go

The weather in England is generally less than balmy. Over half of the days are overcast, and it is subject to winter windstorms and floods. When a true warm spell occurs, the English suffer, because air-conditioning units are not ubiquitous. (However, more and more businesses now have air conditioning.)

Be aware there may be difficulties in rail transportation.

England has some territorial disputes—one with Spain over Gibraltar, another with Argentina over the Falkland Islands (Islas Malvinas), and several more.

▶ CULTURAL ORIENTATION

Cognitive Styles: How the English Organize and Process Information

(*Note:* we have included the predominant ethnic population for the United Kingdom in this section. Please be aware there is variation within other cultures of the United Kingdom.)

The English are somewhat closed to outside information on many issues. They will participate in debate but are not easily moved from their perspective. They are quite analytical and process information in an abstractive manner. They will appeal to laws or rules rather than looking at problems in a subjective manner. There is a conceptual sense of fairness—unwritten, as is the constitution—but no less vital. Company policy is followed regardless of who is doing the negotiating.

Negotiation Strategies: What the English Accept as Evidence

Objective facts are the only valid source of truth. Little credence is given to the feelings one has about an issue. Faith in few if any ideologies will influence decisions. They are the masters of understatement.

Value Systems: The Basis for Behavior

The usefulness of a monarchy is being questioned more seriously because of the expense of financing it. The following three sections identify the Value Systems in the predominant culture—their methods of dividing right from wrong, good from evil, and so forth.

Locus of Decision-Making

The English are highly individualistic, taking responsibility for their decisions, but always within the framework of the family, group, or organization. Individual initiative and achievement are emphasized, resulting in strong individual leadership. They do not find it difficult to say "no"; however, the English "no" is often communicated in a polite and somewhat subtle manner. The individual has a right to his or her private life, and this should not be discussed in business negotiations. Friendships are few and specific to their needs.

Sources of Anxiety Reduction

There are established rules for everything, and this gives a sense of stability to life. Well-entrenched external structures (law, government, organizations) help to insulate them from life. The English are very time oriented, and they are anxious about deadlines and results. However, many do not display their anxiety; traditionally emotions are not shown in public.

Habits are changing, though. The stalwart, emotionless "stiff upper lip" is seen less among the younger generation. And these habits are relative. By the standards of the optimistic entrepreneurs of the United States, the English are slow to take risks. But by the standards of the severe, conservative Slavs, the English are foolhardy risk-takers. In fact, the English take risks at about the same rate as many Europeans.

Issues of Equality/Inequality

There is an inherent trust in the roles people play (but not necessarily in the people) within the social or business system, and a strong feeling of the interdependency of these roles. There are necessarily inequalities in these roles, but the people are supposed to be guaranteed equality under the law. There is some bias against ethnic groups. There is a high need for success, and decisions are made slowly and deliberately. Women have a great deal of equality in both pay and power.

Cultural Note
Greenwich, England, is the home of the Prime Meridian—Longitude 0 degrees—which is an imaginary line that runs from the North Pole to South Pole. The line divides the Earth into the Eastern and Western Hemispheres and is the point from which all other lines of longitude are measured. In 1884, the "Transit Circle" telescope in the Royal Observatory's Meridian Building was chosen as the Prime Meridian. Delegates from twenty-five nations met in Washington, DC, to determine where the exact location was to be, and twenty-two voted for Greenwich. One (San Domingo) voted against, and France and Brazil abstained.

The principles established at the conference included:
- All countries would adopt a universal day.
- The universal day would be a Mean Solar Day, beginning at Mean Midnight at Greenwich and counted on a twenty-four-hour clock.
- Nautical and astronomical days everywhere would also start at mean midnight.

▶ BUSINESS PRACTICES

Punctuality, Appointments, and Local Time

- Always be punctual. In London, traffic can make this difficult, so allow plenty of time to get to your appointments.
- Schedule your visits at least a few days ahead of time, and then confirm your appointment upon your arrival in the United Kingdom.
- There is no designated national holiday in England; however, there are several weeks of official holidays in the United Kingdom—(including several bank holidays).
- The English are on Greenwich Mean Time, (obviously, since the Prime Meridian runs right through Greenwich), which is five hours ahead of U.S. Eastern Standard Time (E.S.T. +5).

Negotiating

- The best way to make contact with senior executives is through a third party.
- It is not appropriate to have this same third party intervene later if problems arise.
- The hierarchy in business is as follows: the managing director (CEO in the United States), the director (corporate vice president to U.S. executives), the divisional officers, the deputy directors, and, finally, the managers.
- Sometimes a secretary will introduce you to the executive; otherwise, introduce yourself.
- Businesspeople are normally more interested in short-term results than in the long-term future.
- Change is not necessarily a good thing to the British.
- The British do not often reveal excitement or other emotions; try to keep yours restrained as well. They also traditionally underplay dangerous situations.
- Similarly, they refrain from extravagant claims about products or plans.
- Some British executives stereotype U.S. businesspeople as condescending; to be safe, make every effort to avoid this impression.
- Avoid the hard sell.
- Do not rush the British toward a decision.
- Allow the British executive to suggest that the meeting has finished, then do not prolong your exit.
- Exchanging business cards is common, because of the necessity of e-mail addresses, cell phone numbers, etc.
- While U.S. executives are known for being direct, the British are even more so. Don't be offended if there's no hedging about whether your suggestion is good or not.
- It is wise to send your senior executives to the United Kingdom, as they may be received with more respect and are usually more restrained in conduct.

United Kingdom

- Some typical U.S. questions can sound inane, like "What part of England (or the United Kingdom) are you from?" because regional English accents are extremely distinct. For example, a Birmingham resident is immediately identifiable by his or her "Brummie lilt." An Englishman may simply respond "London," in order to graciously side-step a long explanation about accents and geography.
- In general, try to avoid interrogating your British contacts. They feel that excessive questions are intrusive.
- Avoid controversial topics such as politics or religion, and do not discuss comparative work ethics.
- Speak in complete sentences. Many U.S. executives have a habit of starting a sentence and then allowing it to trail off without ever completing the thought. This is a good way to provoke . . . (annoying, isn't it?).
- While the British are often self-critical, visitors should avoid joining in any criticisms—simply listen. Similarly, if they share their complaints with you, do not participate.
- The British apologize often, for even small inconveniences. They also have a habit of adding a question to the end of a sentence; for example: "It's a lovely day, don't you think?"

Business Entertaining

- Business breakfasts in hotels are becoming more common and are changing to a more Continental style—from the very large traditional breakfasts of eggs, bacon, sausage, kippers, etc.
- Lunch is generally between noon and 2:00 P.M.
- A business lunch will often be conducted in a pub and will be a light meal.
- Legislation to ban smoking in English pubs and private clubs was passed in 2006! A similar vote passed in Scotland, Northern Ireland, and the Republic of Ireland. That the traditional thick layer of smoke in pubs is now just one more English tradition left by the wayside.
- With senior executives, lunch will be eaten in the best restaurants or in the executive dining room.
- Dinner is generally from 7:00 to 11:00 P.M. in most restaurants.
- When you go out after hours, do not bring up the subject of work unless your British associates do—otherwise, you will be considered a bore.
- Most business entertaining is done in restaurants and pubs rather than at home.
- If you do smoke, always offer the cigarettes around to others before taking one for yourself.
- It is not polite to toast those who are older or more senior than you.
- If you are the guest, you must initiate your departure, as your hosts will not indicate that they wish the evening to come to an end.
- Do not invite a business associate out until you know him or her fairly well.
- When inviting the English out, it is best to include people of the same background and professional level in the invitation.

- When you are the host, be sure to offer the seat of honor to the most senior person. He or she may decline, offering it to you as host; accept it graciously.
- The English hold their forks in their left hands and their knives in the right.
- When passing items around the table, always pass them to the left.
- Always keep your hands above the table (but no elbows on the table!).
- The knife above your plate is used for butter.
- When dining out, it is not considered polite to inquire about the food you see around you.
- Likewise, you should not ask to sample the dishes of others.
- In general, maintain very proper manners.
- Animals are usually a good topic of conversation.
- Do not make jokes about the royal family.
- It is not good form to discuss one's genealogy.
- The English are only beginning to be concerned about diet and health; don't press your views on this matter. However, vegetarianism is popular, especially among women.

▶ PROTOCOL

Greetings
- A handshake is standard for business occasions and when visiting a home.
- Women do not always shake hands.
- When introduced, say "How do you do?" instead of "Nice to meet you." The question is rhetorical.

Titles/Forms of Address
- Business titles are not used in conversation.
- Find out the honorary titles of anyone you will be in contact with, and use them no matter how familiar you are with the person.
- Doctors, clergy, and so forth are addressed by title plus last name; however, surgeons are addressed as "Mr.," "Mrs.," or "Miss."
- Rather than "sir," you should use the title of the person you are addressing (i.e., "Yes, Minister," and not "Yes, sir").
- The use of first names is becoming more common. However, you should follow the initiative of your host.
- Avoid repeating the other person's name often during the conversation. This is generally viewed as an inane sales technique.

Gestures
- It is considered impolite to talk with your hands in your pockets.
- The British often do not look at the other person while they talk.

- In business, a light handshake is standard.
- When visiting a home, a handshake is proper; however, a handshake is not always correct at social occasions. Observe what others do.
- Don't point with your fingers, but instead indicate something with your head.
- Sitting with your ankle resting on your knee may be seen as impolite.
- If you give the "victory" sign (a V with two fingers), do so with the palm facing outward. If you reverse the sign, the deal is over.
- Tapping your nose means confidentiality, or a secret.
- It is inappropriate to touch others in public; even backslapping or putting an arm around the shoulders of another can make the English uncomfortable.
- In addition, the English maintain a wide physical space between conversation partners.
- Avoid excessive hand gestures when speaking.
- Men may give their seats to women on crowded public transportation.

Gifts

- Gifts are not part of doing business in England.
- Rather than giving gifts, it is preferable to invite your hosts out for a meal or a show.
- In a pub, never miss your turn to "shout for a round" (buy everyone a drink) in your party.
- When you are invited to an English home, you may bring flowers (not white lilies, which signify death), liquor or champagne, and chocolates. Send a brief, handwritten thank-you note promptly afterward, preferably by mail or e-mail—not by messenger.
- When bringing flowers, consult with the florist about the appropriate type and number.
- Be cautious in making purchases, as there is usually no refund or exchange policy.

Dress

- Conservative dress is very important.
- Men in executive positions still generally wear laced shoes, not loafers.
- Men's shirts should not have pockets; if they do, the pockets should be empty.
- Men should not wear striped ties; the British "regimentals" are striped, and yours may look like an imitation.
- Men's clothes should be of excellent quality, but they do not necessarily have to look new. Well-broken-in clothes are acceptable.
- Avoid plaid trousers, or any loud attire.
- Women should also dress conservatively.
- Avoid draping your camera around your neck, and ask permission if you intend on taking a picture. If it is digital (even a cell phone), show them the picture immediately afterward, and delete it if they so desire.

United States

United States of America
Abbreviation: U.S. or USA

> **Cultural Note**
>
> Things are big in the United States—trophy houses, super-sized stores, Hummers, and of course, large people. It is well-known that world obesity levels are highest in the United States, lending to the validity of the stereotype "overfed American." In foreign countries, one can often guess which tourists are Americans just from their girth. When international visitors arrive in the United States, the size of things and people in America can be disorienting.

▶ WHAT'S YOUR CULTURAL IQ?

1. When calling upon a prospect for the first time, what don't U.S. salespeople usually bring?
   a. A contract
   b. A product demonstration
   c. A gift

   ANSWER: c. U.S. executives do not generally exchange gifts—particularly between men. However, demos are expected, and contracts can follow rapidly.

2. TRUE or FALSE: By the year 2020, it is expected that white males will be the minority in the work force in the United States.

   ANSWER: TRUE. Attracting and training ethnically diverse employees in preparation for the changes in the work force is a common practice within many Fortune 500s.

3. The United States attracts many great minds. They come for the well-funded research positions, high-paying jobs, excellent universities, freedom of expression, etc. One of the results of this intellectual prowess is that the United States has won the most Nobel Prizes in all categories except for one. Which is it?
   a. Peace   d. Physics
   b. Economics   e. Chemistry
   c. Literature   f. Physiology or Medicine

   ANSWER: c. As of this writing, French authors have been awarded the most Nobel Prizes for literature.

> **Cultural Note**
>
> Executives from the United States are well-known for telling acquaintances to use their first names almost immediately. This should not be interpreted as a request for intimacy, but rather as a cultural norm. Even people in positions of great authority cultivate down-to-earth, accessible images by promoting the use of their first names, or nicknames.

TIPS ON DOING BUSINESS IN THE UNITED STATES

- No one needs to know you, trust you, or even see you to do business with you in the United States. Purchases for everything from books to cars to large-scale software systems are commonly made remotely.
- Never underestimate the speed at which business can be done in the United States. When clients do actually visit with you in person, purchasing decisions are often accomplished in one visit.
- The United States is a youth-oriented culture. Plastic surgery has burgeoned, hair-recovery systems proliferate, liposuction is common for men as well as women, and grotesque programs about these topics constantly draw high ratings on television. Be prepared.

COUNTRY BACKGROUND

History

Virtually all the land that is now the United States was previously occupied for thousands of years by the indigenous people known as Native Americans (or Indians).

The first permanent European settlement (by Spaniards) was in St. Augustine, Florida, in 1565. English settlers subsequently established Jamestown colony, in Virginia, in 1607.

The United States was assembled out of colonies owned primarily by the British, French, Russian, and Spanish empires. The Native Americans suffered greatly from this influx of Europeans. During the seventeenth and eighteenth centuries, the slave trade thrived in the colonies, with hundreds of thousands of Africans brought over to work on cotton and tobacco plantations.

The United States was formed following its Declaration of Independence from England in 1776. The constitution dates to 1787. The country has been a representative democracy since its founding.

General George Washington was elected the first president. He established many precedents, including a tradition of U.S. isolationism that continued until the middle of the twentieth century.

Slavery was abolished in 1865, after a horrific civil war resulted in the defeat of the Southern Confederacy.

The stock market crash of 1929 started the Great Depression, which continued until President Franklin D. Roosevelt launched the "New Deal" in 1933. This federal program generated jobs and provided social services.

The U.S. became involved in the First World War during 1917 and the Second World War in 1941. In 1945, following the surrender of Nazi Germany, the United States dropped atomic bombs on Hiroshima and Nagasaki. This prompted the surrender of the Japanese and marked the end of the Second World War.

United States

The 1960s was a period of social unrest. President John F. Kennedy, his brother Senator Robert F. Kennedy, and African-American leaders Dr. Martin Luther King and Malcolm X were all assassinated. Racial desegregation was implemented. The United States became involved in the war in Vietnam, which would eventually cost the lives of untold Vietnamese and nearly 60,000 U.S. soldiers. U.S. involvement in Vietnam ended with a cease-fire in 1973. The next year, President Nixon resigned over the Watergate scandal.

The subsequent presidents were Gerald Ford, Jimmy Carter, Ronald Reagan, George Bush, Bill Clinton, and George W. Bush. Investigations into scandals continued—from Irangate in the 1980s and a presidential sex scandal in the late 1990s, to the abuse of Iraqi prisoners in 2004, but the economy generally remained stable.

In 2000, there was great controversy over the election results for the presidency. It was exceedingly close, and the Supreme Court became involved. George W. Bush was enabled to take the presidency, although he had a smaller share of the national vote than Al Gore.

The attacks of September 11, 2001, by terrorists decimated the self-confidence and sense of security in the United States. Over 3,000 people were killed. There was a military retaliation by the U.S. government, which, as of this writing, did not result in the capture of Osama bin Laden, who evidently directed the attack. A Department of Homeland Security was established, and Iraqi leader Saddam Hussein was toppled.

Type of Government

The government is a federal republic system; individual states have sovereignty over their own territory. The president is both chief of state and head of the government and is elected for a term of four years. An electoral college of delegates from each state elects the president—an unwieldy system that gives disproportionate power to the most populous states. The legislative branch is elected by universal direct suffrage. It is made up of a bicameral Congress, consisting of the House of Representatives and the Senate.

Women were given the right to vote under the twenty-ninth amendment in 1920. Females have received more positions of power under recent administrations, such as positions as secretaries of state under President Clinton and Bush. However, the percentage of women in national politics is still relatively low. For current government data, check with *www.cia.gov./cia/publications/chiefs*.

Language

English is the official language. Spanish is the most widely used second language.

The number of languages listed by *www.ethnologue.com* for the United States is 231. Of those, 176 are living languages, 3 are second languages without mother tongue speakers, and 52 are extinct. Education is compulsory in most states from age five to age sixteen. It is free up through the secondary school level, although a large number of private schools exist.

The View from the United States

Church and state have always been separate in the United States; however, many citizens belong to a religious group. Most are Christian. Judaism, and Islam each account for about 2 percent of the population.

Certain parts of the United States will be more oriented toward religious activities than others. Some states are part of what has been termed the "Bible Belt." This region generally extends from South Carolina down and west toward Louisiana and Texas (these states are also more comfortable with delays). People in the Northeast are generally more formal, high-speed, driven by work, and reluctant to admit mistakes. The West Coast may be the most liberal area of the country—home to the most high-tech firms, and very diverse populations. There is little stigma associated with failure in the West (some attribute this to the "California Gold Rush" mentality—where the concept was to get out there and try to strike it rich). Statistically, the Midwest generates the most successful international executives. They are generally stable, hard-working employees who can adapt to many situations, yet feel secure in their own identities. Hawaii and Alaska have entirely different cultures than the rest of the United States.

Be aware that because the United States is the most litigious society on earth, corporations are extremely familiar with employment, health and safety, copyright, and every other type of law.

☑ Know Before You Go

Different parts of the United States present different hazards. The Northern states can have bitterly cold winters—and flooding in the springtime. The Midwest and southeastern states suffer from tornadoes. Some Atlantic and Gulf states are prone to hurricanes—and parts of the West Coast are cursed with mudslides, forest fires, and tectonic instability.

In 2005, the Gulf Coast region was hit by a hurricane that devastated New Orleans, Louisiana, as well as areas in several southern states.

Tsunamis, volcanoes, and earthquake activity occur around the Pacific Basin.

The weather is a common topic of conversation.

Security in airports has increased tenfold since the events of September 11. Security lines add hours to travel—and any traveler may be subject to protracted searches.

Private gun ownership is permitted, and the United States has more firearm deaths than any other industrialized nation.

▶ CULTURAL ORIENTATION

Cognitive Styles: How U.S. Citizens Organize and Process Information

The United States is generally ethnocentric and closed to most outside information. However, when a deficiency is recognized, outside information and techniques are eagerly accepted—such as Japanese just-in-time supply chain techniques. U.S. citizens are very analytical, and concepts are abstracted quickly. Innovation usually takes precedence over tradition. Universal rules are preferred, and company policy is normally followed regardless of who is doing the negotiating. There is minimal long-term orientation.

Negotiation Strategies: What U.S. Citizens Accept as Evidence

In negotiations, points are made by the accumulation of objective facts. These are sometimes biased by faith in the ideologies of democracy, capitalism, and consumerism, but seldom by the subjective feelings of the participants.

Value Systems: The Basis for Behavior

It is often said that Judeo-Christian values are the basis for behavior in the United States. However, these are heavily influenced by ego- and ethnocentrism. The following three sections identify the Value Systems in the predominant culture—their methods of dividing right from wrong, and good from evil.

Locus of Decision-Making

Although the United States has tested out as the most individualistic of all cultures (followed by Australia and the United Kingdom), people are considered replaceable in their organizations. There is a high self orientation emphasizing individual initiative and achievement. The individual has a life of his or her own that is generally private and normally not discussed in business negotiations. Friendships are few and specific to needs, but each person generally has loose ties with multitudes of acquaintances. In general, people from the United States do not find it difficult to say "no."

Sources of Anxiety Reduction

There is low anxiety about life, as external structures, religion, and science provide answers to important questions. Anxiety is developed over deadlines and results because recognition of one's work is a great reward. The work ethic is very strong, so that it appears that one lives to work. There are established rules for everything, and experts are relied upon at all levels. U.S. citizens are generally comfortable with risk.

Issues of Equality/Inequality

There is structured inequality in the roles people take, but personal equality is guaranteed by law. There is considerable ethnic and social bias against some minorities. Competition is the rule of life, but there is a strong feeling of the interdependency of roles. Excellence and decisiveness are prized characteristics. Material progress is more important than humanistic progress. The society is still male dominated, but traditional sex roles are changing rapidly. Women have become more assertive and fight for equality in pay and power.

Cultural Note:
Technological advances have resulted in massive changes over the last decade. The Internet, cell phones, and their associated capabilities have broken down hierarchical barriers, eliminated paper, and facilitated communications among all levels of people in private and public institutions. Remote learning is becoming ubiquitous, and quality online content is constantly sought.

▶ BUSINESS PRACTICES

Punctuality, Appointments, and Local Time

- Punctuality is highly emphasized. In some cities, such as Houston, Los Angeles, or New York, extreme traffic can cause delays. Be sure to allow enough driving time to your destination. If you are delayed, call to let your contact know.
- If you are invited for a meal, you should arrive promptly.
- If you are invited to a cocktail party, you can arrive a few minutes to a half-hour late without calling.
- People in the United States write the month first, then the day, then the year; e.g., December 3, 2010, is written 12/3/10. This is very different from many Europeans and South Americans, who write the day first, then the month, then the year (e.g., December 3, 2010, is written 3.12.10 or 3/12/10).
- Prior appointments are necessary.
- U.S. companies do not offer as generous a vacation benefit as businesses in Europe. The standard vacation policy is two weeks per year, in addition to some official holidays.
- The designated National Holiday is July 4.
- Many "convenience" stores (stores that carry frequently purchased products like gasoline, milk, and snacks, and so forth) are open twenty-four hours.
- The contiguous forty-eight states of the United States have four time zones. New York is five hours behind Greenwich Mean Time (G.M.T. - 5). The state of Hawaii is ten hours behind G.M.T.; most of the state of Alaska is nine hours behind G.M.T. In most states, daylight-saving time is in effect from midspring to midautumn.

Negotiating

- Business is done at lightning speed in comparison to many cultures. U.S. salespeople may bring final contracts to their first meeting with prospective clients. In large firms, contracts under $10,000 can often be approved by one middle manager in one meeting.
- Send all relevant information electronically to prospects prior to your visit, and be prepared to process invoices through their paperless online systems.
- Appointments are made by e-mail, conferences are broadcast live over the Web, information and presentations are archived on corporate intranets so employees can access them worldwide at their leisure. Speakers and presenters should remember that their recorded words may ring over speakers, through the Web, for years to come.
- Executives should keep up to date with new electronic gadgets and means of communications in the United States. Hot zones (wireless access) are proliferating; you can access e-mail and surf the net from a multitude of locations—including your airplane seat. The gadgets will only get faster and smaller, so stay current.

- The use of handhelds, cell phones, and associated devices are common in business meetings. Taking calls while others are in the room can be highly irritating to international visitors—but be aware that it is common practice.

- In response to an increase in the vehicular accident rate, some states (for example, New York and New Jersey) have made it illegal to talk on a hand-held cell phone while driving.

- While knowing the right people and having many contacts in an industry is valuable, it is not seen as being as important for a salesperson as a good history of sales. Sales staff are evaluated and compensated on their "track records" rather than the potential for exploiting their contacts.

- The "bottom line" (financial issues), new technology, and short-term rewards are the normal focus in negotiations.

- U.S. executives begin talking about business after a very brief exchange of small talk, whether in the office, at a restaurant, or even at home.

- Whether a colleague is a man or a woman should be ignored, except when it comes to personal questions. Women should not be asked if they are married. If a woman mentions that she is married, you should simply ask a few polite questions about her husband or children.

- Remember that the United States is the most litigious society in the world. There are lawyers who specialize in every industry and segment of society, from corporate tax attorneys to "ambulance chasers" (personal injury lawyers).

- The standard U.S. conversation starter is "What do you do?"—meaning "What kind of work do you do, and for whom?" This is not considered at all rude or boring. Actually, to many U.S. citizens, you are what you do.

- Compliments are exchanged very often. They are often used as conversation starters. If you wish to chat with someone, you can compliment something that person has (e.g., clothing) or has done (a work or sports-related achievement).

- Until you know a person well, avoid discussing religion, money, politics, or other controversial subjects (e.g., abortion, race, or sex discrimination).

- Some common topics of conversation are a person's job, travel, foods (and dieting), exercise, sports, music, movies, and books.

- Before smoking, ask if anyone minds, or wait to see if others smoke. Smoking is generally prohibited in public places: in airplanes, office buildings, in stadiums, and even in bars. Large restaurants in some states usually have a section where smoking is permitted. Many hotels designate rooms as smoking and nonsmoking.

- While businesspeople always have business cards, they are not exchanged unless you want to contact the person later. Be sure to include your e-mail address, Web site, etc., on your card.

- Your card will probably be put into a purse, wallet, or back pocket. People may write on your card as well. This is not meant to show disrespect.

Business Entertaining

- Business breakfasts are common and can start as early as 7:00 A.M.
- Business meetings are very often held over lunch. This usually begins around 12:00 noon and ends by 1:30 or 2:00 P.M. Lunch is usually relatively light, as work continues directly afterward. An alcoholic drink (usually wine or beer) may be ordered.
- Dinner is the main meal; it starts between 5:30 and 8:00 P.M., unless preceded by a cocktail party.
- On weekends, many people enjoy "brunch," a combination of lunch and breakfast beginning anywhere from 11:00 A.M. to 2:00 P.M. Business meetings can be held over brunch.
- When eating out, the cost can be shared with friends. This is called "splitting the bill," "getting separate checks," or "going Dutch."
- If you are invited out for business, your host will usually pay.
- If you are invited out socially, but your host does not offer to pay, you should be prepared to pay for your own meal.
- If you invite a U.S. counterpart out socially, you must make it clear whether you wish to pay.
- Before going to visit a friend, you should call ahead. However, in different regions of the country (e.g., the South) good friends and neighbors do "drop in" on each other.
- Most parties are informal, unless the hosts tell you otherwise.
- If you are offered food or drink, you are not obliged to accept. Also, your host will probably not urge you to eat, so help yourself whenever you want.
- U.S. coworkers or friends will probably enjoy learning a toast from your country.
- The fork is usually held in the right hand (by right-handed people, in any case), and it is used for eating (or sometimes cutting) relatively soft food. If something substantial needs to be cut, the fork switches from the right to the left hand, and a knife is used in the right hand to cut a bite-sized portion. Then the knife is put down, and the fork switches back to the right hand to continue dining.
- Many foods are eaten with the hands; take your lead from others, or if you are uncomfortable using your fingers to eat, do as you like.
- It is not considered rude to eat while walking; many people also eat in their cars (even while driving). However, it is usually illegal to eat on public transportation systems. There are many fast-food and drive-in restaurants.
- At a fast-food restaurant, you are expected to clear your own table.

 PROTOCOL

Greetings

- The standard greeting is a smile, often accompanied by a nod, wave, and/or verbal greeting.

- In business situations, (and some social situations) a handshake is used. It is very firm and generally lasts for a few seconds. Gentle grips are taken as a sign of weakness. Too long of a hand clasp may make businesspeople uncomfortable.
- Good friends and family members usually embrace, finishing the embrace with a pat or two on the back. Depending upon their ethnicity and upbringing, they may exchange kisses too, although that is much more common between women than men.
- In casual situations, a smile and a verbal greeting are adequate.
- If you see an acquaintance at a distance, a wave is appropriate.
- The greeting "How are you?" is not an inquiry about your health. The best response is a short one, such as "Fine, thanks."

Titles/Forms of Address

- The order of most names is first name, middle name, last name.
- To show respect, use a title such as "Dr.," "Ms.," "Miss," "Mrs.," or "Mr." with the last name. If you are not sure of a woman's marital status, use "Ms." (pronounced "Miz").
- When you meet someone for the first time, use a title and their last name until you are told to do otherwise (this may happen immediately). Sometimes you will not be told the last name; in this case just use the first name or the nickname.
- Nicknames may be formal names that have been shortened in surprising ways (e.g., Alex for Alexandra, or Nica for Monica).
- Be sure your U.S. acquaintances know what you wish to be called.
- The letters "Jr." stand for Junior and are sometimes found after a man's first name or surname.
- The Roman numerals III or IV indicates a third- or fourth-generation scion, with the same name as his predecessors (e.g., Patrick E. Ferrari III).
- Terms of endearment like "honey" or "baby" are commonly heard in the South, but elsewhere can be considered inappropriate and demeaning, particularly when directed toward businesswomen.

Cultural Note

Taboos at Work: Certain behaviors are prohibited in work situations, like making sexual innuendos, touching other employees, offering special benefits in exchange for a personal relationship (quid pro quo, harassment), etc. Guidelines on U.S. sexual harassment law are available at *www.abanet.org/publiced/practical/sexualharassment_liability.html*.

Gestures

- The standard space between you and your conversation partner should be about two feet. Most U.S. executives will be uncomfortable standing closer than that.

United States

- In general, friends of the same sex do not hold hands. If men hold hands, it will probably be interpreted as a sign of sexual preference.
- To point, you can use the index finger, although it is not polite to point at a person.
- To beckon someone, wave either all the fingers or just the index finger in a scooping motion with the palm facing up.
- To show approval, there are two typical gestures. One is the "okay" sign, done by making a circle of the thumb and index finger. The other is the "thumbs-up" sign, done by making a fist and pointing the thumb upward.
- The "V-for-victory" sign is done by extending the forefinger and index finger upward and apart. The palm may face in or out.
- A backslap is a sign of friendship.
- To wave goodbye, move your entire hand, palm facing outward.
- Crossing the middle and index fingers on the same hand has two meanings: either to bring good luck, or (when hidden) to indicate that the statement the person is making is untrue. Both gestures are used more often by children than by adults.
- There are many ways to call a waiter/waitress over: make eye contact and raise your eyebrows, or briefly wave to get his or her attention. To call for the check, make a writing gesture or mouth the words "check please."
- Direct eye contact shows that you are sincere, although it should not be too intense. Some minorities look away to show respect.
- When sitting, U.S. citizens often look very relaxed. They may sit with the ankle of one leg on their knee or prop their feet up on chairs or desks.
- In business situations, maintain good posture and a less casual pose.
- When giving an item to another person, one may toss it or hand it over with only one hand.

> ### Cultural Note
> In the United States, gift giving at work is less commonplace than in other countries. U.S. gift giving often symbolizes an emotional attachment. It is generally done only at Christmas or at retirement parties. It is not usually a normal part of business.

Gifts
- Business gifts are discouraged by the law, which allows only a modest tax deduction on gifts.
- When you visit a home, it is not necessary to take a gift; however, it is always appreciated. You may take flowers, a plant, a bottle of wine, chocolates, etc.
- If you wish to give flowers, have them sent ahead so as not to burden your hostess with taking care of them when you arrive.

- If you stay in a U.S. home for a few days, a gift is appropriate. You may also write a letter of thanks.
- At Christmas time gifts are exchanged. For your business associates, you can give business-related gifts that are useful at the office, or liquor or wine. Most stores gift-wrap at Christmas.
- Holiday greeting cards (which can apply to Christmas, Chanukah, or Kwanzaa) are often mailed to clients and prospects in late December.
- A good time to give a gift is when you arrive or when you leave. The best gifts are those that come from your country.
- Personal gifts such as perfume or clothing are generally inappropriate for women in a work situation. There are exceptions (e.g., a company shirt, jacket, or hat).
- Gifts for children are a good idea, but take into account the belief system of the parents. Pacifists (such as most Quakers) would probably object to your giving a toy gun to their child. As U.S. citizens tend to be poor at geography, gifts that demonstrate the location of your country are good choices. Electronic gadgets are generally appreciated.
- Business gifts are given after you close a deal. Unless the giver specifies a time at which the gift is to be opened (as may happen at Christmastime), gifts are usually unwrapped immediately and shown to all assembled.
- You may not receive a gift in return right away; your U.S. friend might wait awhile to reciprocate.
- Taking someone out for a meal or other entertainment is a common gift.

> **Cultural Note**
> If you stay in a U.S. home, you will probably be expected to help around the house by making your bed, helping to clear the dishes after a meal, and so forth. Relatively few U.S. households have domestic servants.

Dress

- In certain firms, conservative business attire may still be expected; however, many companies have adopted a "business casual" policy. Firms generally have guidelines about specific garments that are not appropriate (i.e., ripped or see-through clothing). However, many items that were not condoned a decade ago are now commonly worn everywhere from networking to manufacturing firms (i.e., khaki shorts, sportswear, etc.).
- In rural areas and small towns, clothing is less formal and more relaxed.
- When not working, dress casually. You may see people wearing torn clothing or in short pants and shirts without sleeves.
- If you wish to wear traditional clothing from your country, feel free to do so.

Uruguay

Oriental Republic of Uruguay
Local short form: Uruguay
Local long form: Republica Oriental del Uruguay
Former: Banda Oriental, Cisplatine Province

Cultural Note

Uruguay is a small country with few natural resources. However, Uruguay hopes to become to South America what Belgium is to the European Union: a regional capital where diplomats from many countries come to conduct business. Uruguay promotes itself as "The Gateway to Mercosur" (a customs union consisting of Argentina, Brazil, Paraguay, and Uruguay, with Chile and Bolivia as associate members). Montevideo, Uruguay's capital, is also the administrative capital of Mercosur.

▶ WHAT'S YOUR CULTURAL IQ?

1. TRUE or FALSE: The Uruguayan resort of Punta del Este is a favored tourist destination for thousands of Argentines.

   ANSWER: TRUE. It is also a favorite setting for international conferences, such as the Uruguay Round of the General Agreement on Tariffs and Trade (GATT), which led to the establishment of the World Trade Organization (WTO).

2. Which of the following statements are true about the military junta that ruled Uruguay from 1973 to 1980?
   a. The government classified every adult citizen in Uruguay as either A (reliable), B (questionable), or C (subversive).
   b. Thousands of citizens were imprisoned.
   c. Over one-tenth of the population fled into exile.
   d. All of the above.

   ANSWER: d. Life under the junta was brutal, but relatively few citizens disappeared—unlike in neighboring Argentina.

3. Which of the following countries did not claim Uruguay for their own?
   a. Spain
   b. Portugal
   c. Brazil
   d The United Kingdom

   ANSWER: d. In fact, the United Kingdom helped negotiate Uruguayan independence when both Brazil and Argentina claimed possession of it.

TIPS ON DOING BUSINESS IN URUGUAY

- Uruguay is considered the most literate nation in South America. Visitors should familiarize themselves with Uruguayan authors such as novelist Juan Carlos Onetti, essayist Eduardo Galeano, and José Enrique Rodó, who is considered the country's most famous author.
- In 2003, Uruguay had the highest percentage of citizens who used the Internet in Latin America.
- Like the Argentines, the Uruguayans are big fans of the tango. Tango refers to a style of music, not just a dance, and many tango compositions are intended for listening, not dance. Uruguay also has an indigenous form of Afro-Uruguayan music and dance called the candombe.
- A common drink in Uruguay is mate—pronounced "mah-tay." It is a drink prepared from the yerba mate leaf (Ilex paraguayensis) and is also known as Paraguayan tea. Uruguayans of every social and economic class drink it. It is not alcoholic, but, like other types of coffee and tea, it contains caffeine. (See the note under Paraguay for instructions on drinking mate.)

COUNTRY BACKGROUND

History

The first Europeans to settle in Uruguay were the Portuguese, who founded the town of Colonia in 1680. The Spanish established a fort at Montevideo in 1726, and the two groups fought for control of the area. Portugal ceded its claim to Uruguay in 1777. When Napoleon conquered Spain in 1808, Buenos Aires (in Argentina) declared itself in command of the viceroyalty of Río de la Plata, which included Uruguay. However, the Uruguayans had no desire to submit to Argentine domination.

José Gervasio Artigas, a captain of Spanish forces in the interior of Uruguay, gathered an army and fought Buenos Aires for control of the area. His efforts, lasting from 1810 to 1814, came to be known as Uruguay's war of independence. Neither Spain nor Argentina was ever to regain control of Uruguay, and Artigas is now revered as the father of his country.

However, Uruguay still had to defend its independence. The country was occupied by Brazilian troops in 1820; Artigas and many others were forced to flee. But in 1825, some thirty-three exiles—immortalized as the "33 Orientals" or "33 patriots"—returned and led Uruguay in a successful revolt. Uruguay had established itself as an independent country.

The first Uruguayan Constitution was signed on July 18, 1830; the main downtown avenue in Montevideo is named for this date.

Uruguay developed into one of the most stable and wealthiest nations on the continent. Its political stability earned it the nickname "the Switzerland of South America."

However, in the 1950s, Uruguay began to slip into an economic crisis. High tariffs, low productivity, inflation, debt, corruption, and other problems made life difficult for many Uruguayans. Social unrest increased. A Communist guerrilla group, the Tupamaros, became active in the late 1960s.

When the Tupamaros started killing government officials, police, and a U.S. advisor, the situation became serious. The military (some of whom trained in the United States) took over antiterrorist activities from the civil police. Political activities were banned in 1970. The military assumed control of more and more government functions until, by 1973, it was essentially running the country. In 1976 the military ousted the last elected president and openly ruled Uruguay.

The years of military rule were bloody and brutal. Since the Tupamaros had enjoyed widespread popularity before they turned violent, the junta seemed to regard the entire populace of Uruguay as enemies. Of a total population of fewer than 3 million Uruguayans, some 5,000 were imprisoned, and between 300,000 and 400,000 fled the country.

Initially, the junta's foreign economic advisers brought a measure of prosperity to Uruguay, and some speculators made millions. But soon the economic experiment turned sour, and the economy was in worse shape than before. The military decided to turn the government back to the civilians. General elections were finally held in 1984, and the military stepped down the following year.

Type of Government

The Oriental Republic of Uruguay has now celebrated over twenty continuous years of free and fair elections. Uruguay has two legislative houses: a Senate and a Chamber of Representatives. The president is both the chief of state and the head of the government.

The military continues to hover in the background, exerting influence but taking little direct action. However, human rights have been restored, and Uruguay is once again a democracy.

For current government data, check with the Embassy of Uruguay at *www.uruwashi.org*.

Language

Spanish is the official language, but many Italian words are commonly used in Uruguay.

Near the border between Uruguay and Brazil, some Uruguayans speak a Portuguese-influenced dialect called "Fronterizo." The Montevideo accent is considered the most prestigious among Uruguay's regional dialects.

For data on the various languages of Uruguay, see Ethnologue at *www.ethnologue.com*.

The Uruguayan View

Uruguay is one of the most secularized states in Latin America. Church and state are strictly separated, and only 70 percent of the population is classified as members of a religion.

Most Uruguayans are Roman Catholic; Protestants and Jews each number 2 percent of the population.

Few Uruguayans expect to become wealthy, especially if they stay within their country. Instead, Uruguayans typically search for security rather than take risks to achieve wealth.

Gambling is viewed as a valid means of achieving wealth.

The Uruguayan economy has been sluggish more often than not for several generations. This has helped inspire a widespread pessimism toward business success among many Uruguayans. The pro-business stance of the widely hated military junta of the 1970s also made business suspect.

☑ Know Before You Go

Uruguayans obey the rules of the road better than some Latin Americans do, but automobile accidents are still a major hazard, both to drivers and pedestrians.

Aside from that, Uruguay is a relatively safe nation, free from most natural disasters. Earthquakes, hurricanes, and tornadoes are uncommon. The country is currently free of malaria.

Uruguay suffered a hoof-and-mouth disease outbreak in 2001, which is of major concern in a beef-exporting nation. The country was declared free of the disease in 2003.

▶ CULTURAL ORIENTATION

Cognitive Styles: How Uruguayans Organize and Process Information

The prevailing culture of Uruguay values moderation and compromise. Uruguayans are generally open to outside information in discussion of most issues. They are trained to think subjectively and associatively. However, the state-supported Uruguayan educational system (which offers free tuition throughout the university level) does not encourage abstraction. Uruguayans are intensely loyal to the groups they associate with (primarily the family), and they are likely to chose personal loyalty rather than obey a rule or law.

Negotiation Strategies: What Uruguayans Accept as Evidence

Uruguayans find the truth in the immediate subjective feelings one has on an issue. This is sometimes biased by a faith in humanitarian ideologies. Uruguayans seldom resort solely to objective facts to prove a point.

Value Systems: The Basis for Behavior

The Uruguayans extol humanistic, spiritual, and aesthetic values but take a pragmatic, utilitarian, and materialistic approach to life. Each individual is considered unique yet equal. Traditionally, there has been an inherent trust in people and a strong belief in social justice, but this belief was undermined during the military junta of 1973 to1984. Uruguayan society as a whole is risk-averse and stable, making it highly resistant to change.

The following three sections identify the Value Systems in the predominant culture—their methods of dividing right from wrong, good from evil, and so forth.

Locus of Decision-Making

The individual is responsible for his or her decisions. Uruguayans respect individualism while regarding the family as the most important group. There is a tendency to adopt fatalistic attitudes. A person's self-identity is based on his or her role in the social system and the history of his or her extended family. Because expertise is less important than one's ability to fit into the group, kinships and friendships play a major role in business transactions.

Sources of Anxiety Reduction

The primary source of anxiety reduction in Uruguay is the family and an individual's role in it. (Interestingly, the Uruguayan nuclear family is smaller and has fewer kinship relationships than those in any other Latin American country.) There is a high need for personal relationships, as friendship networks are important to security, jobs, and socializing. The Roman Catholic Church is an important part of the national culture, offering another source of structure and security.

Research indicates that Uruguayans (along with Guatemalans) have the highest levels of uncertainty avoidance in Latin America. In theory, this means Uruguayans give higher importance to strict rules and regulations than most Latin Americans do. It also implies a dislike of ambiguity and an aversion to risk.

Issues of Equality/Inequality

There is less inequality of wealth in Uruguay than in many Latin American nations. The small upper class, which is extensively intermarried, controls much of the wealth and commerce. However, the large middle class is very influential. Men hold the dominant positions in society, but women are often involved in national life. They are considered equal in most respects. Women enjoy substantial freedom; they are independent and emancipated. Manual labor, which is disdained by many Uruguayans, helps define the class system.

Cultural Note

The military junta that ruled Uruguay from 1973 to 1984 held some 5,000 political prisoners. Considering the traditional Uruguayan dislike for uncertainty, it is not surprising that the political prisons utilized psychological pressure. Prison rules were changed constantly. One day a prisoner would be punished for leaving the window-shade to his cell open, the next day for leaving it closed, and so on.

▶ BUSINESS PRACTICES

Punctuality, Appointments, and Local Time

- Unlike in the past, punctuality is now considered important in business affairs in Uruguay. Promptness is not expected in social events.
- Business meetings may or may not start on time, but, as a foreigner, you are expected to be prompt.
- As in most South Americans countries, dates in Uruguay are written in this order: first the day, then the month, then the year (e.g., December 3, 2010, is written 3-12-10). Dates are usually separated with dashes.
- The best time of year to conduct business in Uruguay is from May through November. Little business is accomplished for two weeks before and after Christmas and Easter, as well as during Carnival. January through April is summer in Uruguay, and one or another of the decision-makers is liable to be off on vacation during this period.
- Uruguay is three hours behind Greenwich Mean Time (G.M.T. –3), making it two hours ahead of U.S. Eastern Standard Time (E.S.T. +2).

Negotiating

- The pace of business negotiations in Latin America is moderate to slow—much slower than that in the United States. However, many executives are accustomed to the business techniques of their major trading partners. Some younger Uruguayans will adapt to the negotiating style of their foreign counterparts, speeding up or slowing down in accordance with the foreigner's traditions.
- Most Uruguayan executives will be experienced and sophisticated; they may well have studied overseas.
- Most successful Uruguayan executives put in a very long workday.
- Uruguay is a nation of immigrants. While many of the businesspeople you encounter will be of Spanish descent, others will be German, Italian, or Jewish.
- Although many executives speak English, check beforehand as to whether or not you will need an interpreter.
- All printed material you hand out should be translated into Spanish. This goes for everything from business cards to brochures.
- Uruguayans are great sports fans. Talking about sports is always a good way to open a conversation. Football (which is called fútbol here, and soccer in the United States) is the most popular sport. (U.S.-style football is fútbol Americano.) Basketball is increasingly popular; the Uruguayan basketball team almost beat the U.S. team at the 2003 Pan-American Games.
- Foreign affairs are of great interest to Uruguayans, especially now that Uruguayan troops have been deployed overseas as part of UN peacekeeping missions. Currently, the largest Uruguayan deployment is in the Congo.
- Uruguay is a popular South American tourist spot, so ask about sights to see.

Business Entertaining

- Uruguayans are comfortable conducting business over lunch. Dinner, however, is a social occasion; don't try to talk business during an evening meal unless your counterpart brings it up.
- Business breakfast meetings, while not unheard of, are relatively rare.
- While you are in Uruguay, your counterpart will probably offer to take you out to—and pay for—lunch and dinner.
- Should you wish to reciprocate, the best choice will be an upscale French, Chinese, or Uruguayan restaurant.
- A good choice of location for a business dinner is the restaurant at an international hotel.
- Uruguay is a major cattle producer, and its restaurants serve some of the best beef in the world.
- Despite the traditional Uruguayan aversion to risk, the country has a number of casinos. Your counterpart may invite you out to one or more.

▶ PROTOCOL

Greetings

- Except when greeting close friends, it is traditional to shake hands firmly with both men and women.
- Close male friends shake hands upon meeting, but men kiss close female friends. Close female friends usually kiss each other.

Titles/Forms of Address

- For further information on the proper titles and forms of address for Spanish-speaking countries, please consult Appendix A.

Gestures

- While most Latin Americans converse at a much closer distance than North American citizens are used to, Uruguayans are generally aware that close proximity makes some people nervous. Consequently, most Uruguayan businesspeople will give such foreigners more "breathing room" than they would generally allow fellow Uruguayans.
- The "thumbs-up" gesture means "okay" in Uruguay.
- Curling the fingers around so that they touch the thumb indicates doubt. This gesture is usually done with the right hand.
- Sit only on chairs, not on a ledge, box, or table.
- Don't rest your feet on anything other than a footstool or rail; it is very impolite to place them on a table.
- Avoid yawning in public. Yawning is a signal that it is time to adjourn.

> **Cultural Note**
>
> Do not ask probing questions about an Uruguayan's family unless prompted to by your host. Remember that the country went through over fourteen years of brutal military dictatorship, during which more than 10 percent of the population fled into exile and one out of every fifty of the remainder were detained for interrogation (or worse).

Gifts

- Gift giving is not a major aspect of doing business.
- When you are given advance notice of an invitation to a Uruguayan home, bring (or have sent before you arrive) flowers or chocolates to your hostess. Roses are the most appreciated type of flower.
- Don't worry about a gift if an invitation is proffered on short (or no) notice. After business dinners in Uruguay, it is common practice to adjourn to someone's home for coffee. Guests are not expected to stay long if the following day is a workday.

Dress

- Business dress in Uruguay is conservative: dark suits and ties for men; white blouses and dark suits or skirts for women. Men should follow their Uruguayan colleagues' lead with regard to wearing ties and removing jackets in the summer.
- Uruguayans do not favor the bright colors popular elsewhere in Latin America. Choose subtle colors for your wardrobe.
- Men may wear the same dark suit for formal occasions (such as the theater, a formal dinner party, and so forth), but women are expected to wear an evening gown.
- Both men and women wear pants in casual situations. If you are meeting business associates, avoid jeans and wear a jacket or blazer. Women should not wear shorts.
- Don't wear anything outside that can be damaged by water during Carnival because drenching pedestrians is a favorite Carnival trick of the young.
- Summertime can be humid as well as warm, and winters are rainy and chilly. Bring appropriate clothing—and don't forget that the seasons in the Southern Hemisphere are the reverse of those in the Northern Hemisphere.

> **Cultural Note**
>
> If you graduated from the University of Chicago, leave your class ring at home. Under Uruguay's military junta, the generals took their economic policy from the "Chicago boys"—free-market economic advisers largely trained by Milton Friedman at the University of Chicago. The Chicago boys are not popular; some Uruguayans feel that they treated Uruguay as an economics experiment, enforced by the guns of the military. Opponents of the regime had a saying that "In Uruguay, people were in prison so that prices could be free."

Venezuela

Bolivarian Republic of Venezuela
Local short form: Venezuela
Local long form: Republica Bolivariana de Venezuela

> **Cultural Note**
> Venezuelans consider native son Simón Bolívar a national treasure, because he was not only the catalyst for Venezuela's independence from Spain but a liberator for much of South America. There is a Plaza Bolívar in the center of most Venezuela cities, and it is important to behave respectfully in that plaza. Venezuela's currency is named the bolívar. And President Hugo Chávez called his 1998 populist restructuring of Venezuelan government and society his "Bolivarian Revolution."

WHAT'S YOUR CULTURAL IQ?

1. Christopher Columbus was the first European explorer to reach Venezuela in 1498. (He named it Tierra de Gracia). After fighting the fierce native Caribs, the Spanish managed to establish their first mainland outpost at Cumaná in 1523. They hoped that Venezuela was the home of El Dorado (the lost city of gold). All they found were pearls, and those reserves were exhausted within a few decades. Instead, the Spanish colonists turned to farming and ranching. Obviously, they failed to discover Venezuela's oil, but what other mineral resources did they miss?

   a. Iron
   b. Coal
   c. Gold
   d. Diamonds
   e. All of the above

   ANSWER: e. Venezuela has significant deposits of all of these resources.

2. Independence for Venezuela itself was not enough for Simón Bolívar. He attempted to combine which of the following countries into his Confederation of Gran Colombia?

   a. Colombia and Panama
   b. Ecuador and Venezuela
   c. Peru and Bolivia
   d. All of the above

   ANSWER: d. He failed to keep this superstate together. Except for Panama (which remained part of Colombia), all of the above became independent nations within a few years of the death of El Libertador in 1830.

3. TRUE or FALSE: Today, baseball is the most popular sport in Venezuela.

   ANSWER: TRUE. Unlike most Latin American nations where football (soccer) reigns supreme, baseball is considered the national sport of Venezuela. Professional baseball teams play a four-month season and compete in the Caribbean Series. Many Venezuelans have played professional baseball in the United States. In the past few years, basketball has gained great popularity and is now Venezuela's number-two sport.

▶ TIPS ON DOING BUSINESS IN VENEZUELA

- In politics, as in business, Venezuelans tend to follow strong leaders. Leadership styles are often authoritarian, rather than inclusive.
- Venezuela is a highly status conscious country. Power flows from the top down, and bosses expect compliance. Employees do not contradict their bosses, so foreign teams in Venezuela should be careful not to argue with each other in public, because Venezuelans will interpret this as demonstrating poor leadership.
- Avoid dominating the conversation or putting pressure on your Venezuelan colleagues. Venezuelans like to be in control.

Cultural Note

Venezuela is a highly polarized country and has become even more so under the administration of President Hugo Chávez. The businesspeople you will deal with will almost all come from the middle or upper classes. If you deal with government officials, they may be from any background.

Venezuelan businesspeople can be divided into two types, with distinct differences in their styles of conducting business. Among the older generation, people will want to get to know you personally and will respond to you as an individual, rather than to your company or your proposals. The younger generations are often educated abroad and adopt foreign business practices. These executives may relate more to your firm, the proposal you are presenting, and so forth, than to you personally.

Many younger Venezuelans have been educated in the United States, and may own homes there. In fact, so many Venezuelans own property in Florida that the region around Miami has been nicknamed "Venezuela's twenty-first state."

▶ COUNTRY BACKGROUND

History

The original inhabitants of Venezuela were several Amerindian tribes, including the Caracas, Arawaks, and Cumanagotos. After Columbus discovered the area in 1498, the Spanish began conquering the coastal regions and offshore islands. Explorer Alonso de Ojeda named the land Venezuela, meaning "little Venice," because many Indian homes around Lake Maracaibo and the coast were built on stilts—which reminded him of Venice. Spain controlled Venezuela for more than two centuries, save for a period from 1529 to 1546, when the Spanish crown paid a debt to a German banking house by offering Venezuela for exploitation. The Spanish empire in the Americas was shaken when Napoleon conquered Spain in 1810. Independence movements grew among Venezuelans, and fighting broke out between rebels and royalists. Independence was finally secured when Simón Bolívar's forces (a Venezuelan) defeated the royalists at the Battle of Carabobo in 1821.

The Republic of Greater Colombia originally contained Venezuela, Ecuador, and Colombia. In 1830 Venezuela seceded and became an independent nation.

Type of Government

For its first century of existence, Venezuela was ruled by dictators. Since 1958, Venezuela has had continuous freely held democratic elections (peppered by several unsuccessful coup attempts). It is a federal multiparty republic, with a president who is both the head of government and the chief of state. There is a cabinet, or Council of Ministers, and a bicameral congress, composed of the Chamber of Deputies and the Senate. The judiciary is represented by the Supreme Court. Elections are held every five years. The administration of Hugo Chávez, who was elected president in 1999, rewrote the constitution and changed the way Venezuela is ruled. Whether or not the changes of Chávez's "Bolivarian revolution" will survive his administration remains to be seen.

For current government data, check with the Embassy of Venezuela at *www.embavenez-us.org*.

Language

Spanish is the country's official language. Venezuelans call their language *castellano*, not *español*. English and a variety of Amerindian dialects are spoken as well. There is also a native Venezuelan form of sign language, which has been taught in schools for the deaf since 1937.

Among older Venezuelans, there is a great loyalty to one's regional dialect. Younger Venezuelans tend to accept the Caracas dialect as the most prestigious, whether they speak it or not. For data on the various languages of Venezuela, see Ethnologue at *www.ethnologue.com*.

The Venezuelan View

Venezuela has no official religion, but the vast majority of people are Roman Catholic (over 92 percent). Upper-class Venezuelans tend to be strongly Roman Catholic, and the Church is historically seen to have ties to the ruling class. However, the Church does not have great influence on the daily lives of most businesspeople. Evangelical Protestant groups have become more popular in the past few decades, especially among the poor.

The single most important institution in Venezuela is the family. Extended families are the norm, and relatives often go into business with each other. When deciding between competing offers, a Venezuelan is likely to select an offer coming from a relative—even a distant relative—instead of going with an unknown provider.

Younger Venezuelans still consider their families as a top priority, although their global awareness tends to be wider. It is more likely that the younger generation of Venezuelan businesspeople has been educated abroad. Post-1990 graduates came of age during hard times in Venezuela and may lack the sense of entitlement and economic security that was present among their elders who prospered during the oil boom of the 1970s.

Venezuela is a male-dominated society. Sociologists who rank cultures along a masculinity index categorize Venezuela as one of the "most Masculine" in Latin America.

Another sociological finding puts Venezuela at the far end of the individuality index. This places the individual as the least-important person in a decision-making scenario. The best interests of one's family are considered first. (The United States ranks at the other end of this scale, with the individual decision-maker considering his or her self-interest above all.) A Venezuelan may make a decision by asking himself "Will this benefit or dishonor my family?"

In politics, business, and religion, Venezuelans tend to follow strong leaders. Leadership styles tend to be authoritarian rather than inclusive.

☑ Know Before You Go

Venezuelans tend to have casual attitudes toward the rules of the road. It is often stated that they regard traffic lights as "suggestions." Traffic accidents are a serious hazard to drivers and pedestrians alike.

Because of the regularity of these accidents, companies with fleets of vehicles in Venezuela must factor in the cost of frequent damage to their vehicles.

Earthquakes are a constant hazard. Historically, the first Venezuelan Republic fell in part because a massive earthquake in March of 1812 damaged the seats of the Pro-Independence movement.

▶ CULTURAL ORIENTATION

Cognitive Styles: How Venezuelans Organize and Process Information

In Venezuela, outside information is accepted on most issues for purposes of discussion. However, Venezuelans do not change their attitudes easily. Their educational system has historically trained them to process information subjectively and associatively. Their personal involvement in a situation is more important than the rules or laws that might be used to solve the problem.

Negotiation Strategies: What Venezuelans Accept as Evidence

The truth is usually found in the immediate subjective feelings of the participants. This may be influenced by their faith in the ideologies of humanitarianism, but not solely by the accumulation of objective facts.

Value Systems: The Basis for Behavior

Venezuela lost some of its humanitarian values when the oil market dropped and it had to increase taxes to maintain its economy. The following three sections identify the Value Systems in the predominant culture—their methods of dividing right from wrong, good from evil, and so forth.

Locus of Decision-Making

Individuals are responsible for their own decisions and any impact they may have upon their families or groups. The family, extended family, and friends are very important, and one must do nothing to shame them. Expertise is important in one's occupation, but less important than one's ability to get along with the group, so one usually has to make friends with the participants before meaningful negotiations can take place. The upper class dominates the economic structures of commerce and industry, but the middle class dominates politics.

Sources of Anxiety Reduction

Religion is not a strong force in their daily life, but Venezuelans are emotionally attached to the Church, and this gives them a sense of stability. The presence of the extended family also helps the individual to have a sense of security. Venezuelans seem to gain security by following charismatic leaders as well. Although they are always working on one or more projects, finishing them by a tight deadline does not seem to be a large priority. Time does not create anxiety.

Issues of Equality/Inequality

There are extreme contrasts between rich and poor, and Venezuelans feel that power holders are entitled to the privileges that come with the office. There is a small white elite, a large mestizo population, and a small black population. One notices some class and ethnic bias. Machismo is very strong. Women have some restrictions on their social and work behavior.

BUSINESS PRACTICES

Punctuality, Appointments, and Local Time

- Unlike the inhabitants of many countries in Latin America, Venezuelans tend to be prompt. Foreigners are expected to be on time to all business appointments. Social engagements also tend to start on time.
- Since promptness is expected, it is better to be a few minutes early than a few minutes late in Venezuela. Allow yourself plenty of time to compensate for traffic, which is a serious problem in Caracas.
- As in most countries, Venezuelans write the date in this order: day, month, year (e.g., December 3, 2010, is written 3.12.10).
- Avoid scheduling appointments two or three days before or after a holiday. Venezuelans often take extended vacations.
- Venezuela is four hours behind Greenwich Mean Time (G.M.T.–4).

Venezuela

Negotiating

- In a business meeting, begin by getting to know everyone. Don't rush into a discussion of the deal. At the same time, do not try to be instant friends with your prospects.
- Under the leftist administration of President Hugo Chávez, issues revolving around privatization could impact your deal.
- Never change your team during negotiations.
- Letters, brochures, and other documents should be translated into Spanish and followed up with a phone call.
- If you receive a reply from a Venezuelan in your native language, you may begin using your language in correspondence. English is spoken by many Venezuelan businesspeople.
- It is best to send an individual rather than a team for the first contact with a Venezuelan prospect. Later, you should send other members of your team.
- Even among Venezuelans educated in North America, expect negotiations to proceed more slowly than in the United States.
- Do not mention bringing in an attorney until negotiations are complete.
- After the first business contact in Venezuela, it is appropriate for the senior executive of the foreign firm to write a letter of thanks to the senior executive of the Venezuelan company.
- The focus of the business deal should be long-term, not solely geared to immediate returns. Venezuelans have had bad experiences with foreign firms that make a quick profit, then leave the country. You do not want to be categorized as another short-term player.
- Topics to avoid discussing are the government, personal relationships, and a comparison of your country's policies to Venezuela's.
- It is rude to ask direct questions about a person's family. However, such information is useful, especially because nepotism is common, and several family members may work for the same company. Try to find this information out through a third party.
- Venezuelans appreciate visitors who have some knowledge of their country's history and cultural achievements.
- Present your business card immediately following an introduction. Treat business cards with respect. Have your card printed in Spanish on one side and your native language on

the other. Be sure your job title is clearly identified; Venezuelans are very status conscious and will want to understand your position in your company.

- Venezuelans are generally comfortable with technological advances and are open to conference calls, e-mails, Internet-based training, Web conferences, etc.

Business Entertaining

- It is good practice to follow up morning appointments with an invitation to lunch, where you can continue your business discussions.
- In a restaurant, it is common for Venezuelans to compete with you for the check, even if you issued the invitation. To avoid this, arrange beforehand with the waiters to have the bill given directly to you (or pay it away from the table). This is particularly important for women, as they may encounter some resistance from their male Venezuelan counterparts in settling the bill.
- Unlike lunch, dinner is for socializing, not business.
- Dinner generally begins at 8:30 P.M. and can last until midnight.
- Spouses are usually invited to dinner.
- Businesswomen should be aware that going out alone with Venezuelan businessmen may be misconstrued. It is better for businesswomen to come to Venezuela as part of a team.
- At the table, the senior executive from each firm should sit facing each other.
- The senior visiting businessperson may give a toast offering good wishes for the negotiations, adding a comment about the pleasure of socializing with Venezuelans. This toast should be in Spanish. If the visitor does not understand Spanish, he or she should memorize it phonetically or be accompanied by an interpreter.
- If you are invited for a meal at a Venezuelan home, be aware that this is a sign of close friendship and is not to be taken lightly.

▶ PROTOCOL

Greetings

- A firm handshake is the standard business greeting.
- While shaking hands, announce your full name; the Venezuelan will do the same.

Titles/Forms of Address

- For further information on the proper titles and forms of address for Spanish-speaking countries, please consult Appendix A.

Gestures

- Venezuelans greet friends with a brief embrace called an abrazo, a squeeze of the arm, and sometimes a kiss on the cheek.

- Venezuelans converse in very close proximity to one another. Try not to waver or move away, as this will be interpreted as rejection.
- During a conversation, Venezuelans often touch each other's arms or jacket.

Gifts

- It is best to postpone giving business gifts until you have established a friendly relationship.
- The best time to present a business gift is during a long lunch. Try not to present a gift during business hours.
- For business, bring high-quality gifts that are somewhat useful—for example, a lighter with your company name, small electronics, carefully selected books, or an imported liquor like a twelve-year-old Scotch.
- Perfume and flowers (particularly orchids, the national flower) are good gifts for women and are not generally considered too personal. If, as a man, you feel the gift might be misconstrued, say it is a gift from your company.
- You may give gifts to the children of your colleagues; this will be greatly appreciated.
- In preparation for subsequent visits, ask colleagues if there is something from your home country that your Venezuelan counterparts would like you to bring back.
- Baseball is the national sport of Venezuela. If you are from Canada or the United States of America, sports attire from the professional baseball teams that have Venezuelans on their roster make good gifts.
- Foreign women should be wary about giving personal gifts to Venezuelan businessmen. This is best delegated to a male member of your team.
- When going to a Venezuelan home, never arrive empty-handed.

Dress

- Venezuelan women are very fashionable. Women should pack their best business clothes and something more formal for evening wear.
- Expect Venezuelans to notice both your dress and your accessories. Details such as high-quality watches or jewelry increase your status among most Venezuelans. Poorly dressed businesspeople do not command as much respect as executives with well-made clothes.
- Men should dress conservatively, in dark business suits of tropical-weight wool.

Cultural Note

In addition to its position as Venezuela's capital and largest city, Caracas has become the city of gardens. To alleviate hunger among Venezuela's 24 million impoverished citizens, the government ordered citizens to grow food crops on every available plot of land in the city—and on rooftops and in containers as well. Many foreign observers call the effort well intentioned, but point out that such projects have failed to provide enough food when tried in Communist countries.

Vietnam

Socialist Republic of Vietnam
Local long form: Cong Hoa Xa Hoi Chu Nghia Viet Nam
Local short form: Viet Nam

Cultural Note
The process of transforming from a Communist command economy to a market-oriented economy is never easy. The government's lack of transparency and low pay to government officials is a recipe for corruption. Another problem is competition among government agencies for jurisdiction over foreign investments. At present, multiple bureaucracies may claim control over foreign-controlled business—and each of them want to impose licenses and taxes.

▶ WHAT'S YOUR CULTURAL IQ?

1. Vietnam was divided into two antagonistic countries between 1956 and 1975. TRUE or FALSE: During this time, the south was known as "The Democratic Republic of Vietnam," while the north chose the shorter "Republic of Vietnam."

   ANSWER: FALSE. Reverse the names.. South Vietnam used the name Republic of Vietnam. In common with other Communist-bloc countries, North Vietnam added "Democratic" to its name (although it was nothing of the sort).

2. The traditional Vietnamese coat of arms is decorated with four animals. TRUE or FALSE: Three of these animals are mythological.

   ANSWER: TRUE. The coat of arms boasts a dragon, a unicorn, a phoenix, and a turtle.

3. Match the following Vietnamese terms with the comestibles they represent:
   a. Bia Hoi   1. Noodle soup
   b. Nuoc Mam   2. Fresh beer (freshly brewed and served)
   c. Pho   3. Rice wine
   d. Ruou   4. Fish sauce

   ANSWERS: a. 2; b. 4; c. 1; d. 3

▶ TIPS ON DOING BUSINESS IN VIETNAM

- The official governmental policy toward business in Vietnam is *doi moi* (renovation). While the execution may sometimes be rocky, there is official admission that changes must be made.

- The Communist government remains a major influence, corruption is common, and the infrastructure is still limited. However, labor costs are extremely low and the Vietnamese are anxious for outside investments.
- Vietnam has a million eager, aggressive businesspeople. In addition to this motivated work force, Vietnam has a variety of natural resources. Besides exporting rice and other agricultural products, Vietnam has started exporting oil. Their recently developed oil reserves are producing tens of millions of barrels.
- In common with other Confucian cultures, age is highly respected in Vietnam. Foreign business delegations should always include a senior member to whom the other members must defer in public. Similarly, foreigners must show great respect to the senior members of any Vietnamese organization. Older executives are viewed as more experienced, wiser, and should be held in esteem.

▶ COUNTRY BACKGROUND

History

Southeast Asia has been home to civilizations for thousands of years. China occupied the region for over 1,000 years, starting in 111 B.C. The region achieved independence from China in A.D. 939, and adopted a native dynasty of rulers. The ethnic Vietnamese were northerners who gradually moved south and eventually reached the Mekong delta.

The nation of Vietnam (as a country distinct from the rest of Southeast Asia) dates back only as far as the French colonization. The French began their conquest in 1858, and by 1885 they were in effective control of the entire country. The French allowed the Vietnamese emperors to remain on the throne, but they were subject to French orders.

By the start of the twentieth century, some French-educated Vietnamese began to agitate for independence. Ho Chi Minh, whom Vietnamese consider the father of Vietnamese independence, was one of these. Ho Chi Minh organized various groups into a nationalist front, although most anti-Communist groups refused to join.

Japan occupied Vietnam in the Second World War, demonstrating that the French could be defeated. At the end of the war, before the French could reassert power, Ho Chi Minh declared the birth of the independent Democratic Republic of Vietnam on September 2, 1945.

French forces returned and refused to acknowledge Vietnamese independence. An eight-year guerrilla war ensued. This ended with the defeat of the French and their anti-Communist Vietnamese allies at Dien Bien Phu in 1954. A peace conference convened in Geneva, Switzerland, resulting in the temporary division of Vietnam at approximately the seventeenth parallel. The Communists were given control of the north; the anti-Communists the south. The two halves of the country were intended to be reunited after a national election by July 1956.

However, the anti-Communists refused to participate in the election. Consequently, the division of the country into North Vietnam and South Vietnam lasted for almost two decades.

North Vietnam, with the support of the USSR and the People's Republic of China, began another guerrilla war. With the French unwilling to commit troops, the United States decided to support South Vietnam. U.S. military forces were initially sent into combat in 1965 by President Johnson. The level of U.S. forces in Vietnam peaked at 534,000 in 1969. Widespread opposition to the war led politicians in Washington, DC, to attempt to replace U.S. troops with South Vietnamese forces. But the Army of South Vietnam was unable to stop the Communist forces, and Saigon, the South Vietnamese capital, fell on April 30, 1975. By the end of the year, both halves of the country were united under a Communist government as the Socialist Republic of Vietnam.

After consolidating its power after reunification, the government of Vietnam felt threatened by the Khmer Rouge in neighboring Cambodia. Vietnam invaded Cambodia in December 1978. While most Western governments did not approve of the Vietnamese government, they considered the genocidal Khmer Rouge the greater evil.

In 1989, Vietnam withdrew its troops from Cambodia, and by 1991, it had forged diplomatic relations with many countries, including China and the United States. Vietnam and the United States signed a trade accord in 1991, finally allowing Vietnamese goods into the United States.

Vietnam's national holiday is Vietnamese National Day, celebrated on the second of September. However, the most important holiday is always the three-day celebration for the lunar New Year, or Tet.

Type of Government

The Socialist Republic of Vietnam is a constitutional republic dominated by the Communist Party. The National Assembly is the supreme organ of the state. The president and prime minister of Vietnam are elected by the National Assembly. The president is the head of state. The prime minister can be described as head of the government, because he is charged with the day-to-day handling of government organizations.

The Vietnamese Communist Party holds a national congress every five years to formalize policies and to outline the country's overall direction. The Party Congress also elects a Central Committee, which usually meets at least twice a year.

For current government data, check with the Embassy of Vietnam at *www.vietnamem bassy-usa.org.*

Language

The official language is Vietnamese. English has now replaced French as the preferred second language.

Ethnologue.com has listed a total of 103 languages in Vietnam. Only 1 of these languages is extinct: a pidgin combining French and Vietnamese known as Tay Boi.

> ## Cultural Note
> Vietnam has two large religious groups (sometimes described as cults) that are unfamiliar to outsiders. Hoa Hao is derived from Buddhism but advocates direct, simple worship without intermediaries. It was founded in 1939 by a man from the Mekong delta named Huynh Phu So. The French derided him as a "mad monk," and the political activities of his followers caused Hoa Hao to be banned periodically.
>
> Cao Dai is even more unusual: it is a syncretic faith that combines aspects of all the religions of Vietnam. Created in the 1920s, its leader, Ngo Minh Chieu, mixed such diverse beliefs as ancestor worship, Buddhism, Christianity, and Islam. Cao Dai has a pantheon of unusual saints, including Joan of Arc, Victor Hugo, Louis Pasteur, and Napoleon Bonaparte!

The Vietnamese View

The constitution of the Socialist Republic of Vietnam guarantees freedom of religion. The country's diverse population follows many religious beliefs. Confucianism (which is a philosophy more than a religion) has had a great effect on Vietnamese thought and tradition. Historically, the largest and most important religion in Vietnam was Buddhism. Although the Communist government describes Buddhism as currently "in decline," it acknowledges that 70 percent of Vietnamese are "strongly influenced" by Buddhist tradition.

Many other religions are represented in Vietnam. Also, as is common in Asia, religious beliefs often overlap. Vietnamese Catholics also may go to Buddhist temples; Vietnamese Muslims also may engage in ancestor worship. The current breakdown of religion in Vietnam is:

> **Buddhist**—about 70 percent
> **Roman Catholic**—about 10 percent (Catholicism entered Vietnam in the seventeenth century and was supported by the French colonials.)
> **Cao Dai**—approximately 2 million
> **Hoa Hao**—over 1 million
> **Protestant**—less than a half-million
> **Islam**—approximately 50,000 (Islam is concentrated among the Cham ethnic minority near the coastline in Central Vietnam.)

As you would expect, views on Vietnam vary between groups. Anti-Communists and supporters of the defeated South Vietnamese government view today's Vietnam rather critically. Many of these Vietnamese left around the time Saigon was overrun in 1975. The so-called "Boat People" who fled after the Communist absorption of all South Vietnam in 1976 may have cynical views of both Communist governments and the West, because many Boat People were left to languish in refugee camps for years by Western governments. (For example, some spent years in camps in British-ruled Hong Kong.)

Finally, some of the many ethnic minorities of Vietnam may also dislike the Communist government. These include the Hmong, who were persecuted as allies of the United States, and Vietnam's ethnic Chinese—a traditional merchant class who were devastated when the Communists made private trade illegal in 1978. Almost a half-million ethnic Chinese left Vietnam during that period, primarily by boat. Many were encouraged to leave by the Vietnamese government. (This mistreatment of Vietnam's ethnic Chinese contributed to the attack on the Vietnamese border by the People's Republic of China in 1979.)

☑ Know Before You Go

To the average business traveler in Vietnam, the greatest hazard is vehicular traffic. Traffic in Vietnam's fast-growing cities is chaotic, with trucks, cars, motorcycles, and bicycles all competing for space. Pedestrians can be in as much danger as drivers and their passengers. Exercise caution and hire a driver rather than drive yourself.

After dark, foreigners should avoid using the less-regulated forms of transport, such as motorcycle taxis and cyclos (also known as pedicabs). Also, at any time of day, you should negotiate the fee before entering a motorcycle taxi or cyclo: they have no meters. In a taxi, insist your driver use his meter.

Violence against foreigners is very rare, in part because the penalties for harming a foreigner are draconian. A Vietnamese who killed a foreigner in 1996 was quickly found, tried, and executed.

▶ CULTURAL ORIENTATION

Vietnam's recent history has been highly dynamic, and to date, there has not been much detailed study of Vietnamese cultural orientations. Pending further research, the following observations can be made:

Cognitive Styles: How Vietnamese Organize and Process Information

Historically, by accepting the foreign concept of Marxism, the leaders of Vietnam became closed to outside information. Because the Communist victory took the better part of a century, unswerving dedication to Marxist ideals became a necessity. However, the Communist reunification of divided Vietnam took place during the decline of global Communism. The dissolution of Vietnam's primary benefactor, the USSR, required the Vietnamese leadership to become more open to other, non-Communist ideals.

As a market-oriented society, Vietnam's decision-makers and businesspeople have—of necessity—become more open to outside concepts and more analytic than associative. Nevertheless, they may place more value on relationships than obedience to abstract rules of behavior.

Negotiation Strategies: What Vietnamese Accept as Evidence

Vietnamese relate each instance to their own experience, making search for truth highly subjective. Even experienced Vietnamese businesspeople may not make decisions entirely based on objective facts.

Value Systems: The Basis for Behavior

The following three sections identify the Value Systems in the predominant culture—their methods of dividing right from wrong, good from evil, and so forth.

Locus of Decision-Making

While responsibility for decision-making rests on the shoulders of the individual, decisions are always made with the family in mind. A Vietnamese will often consider "What is best for my family?" when making a choice.

Sources of Anxiety Reduction

Vietnam's current transition to a market-oriented economy offers exciting opportunities for its citizens, but it also causes great anxieties. There are clear winners and losers. Vietnamese laborers in inefficient, state-owned industries know that they will be among the losers.

The extended family forms the basic unit of Vietnamese society and also provides the main source of security. Ancestor worship reinforces the importance of the family as well.

Issues of Equality/Inequality

Vietnam remains a hierarchical country. Under Confucian tradition, each person has a place and knows to whom to defer. Hierarchical structures are also found in government, business, and other organizations.

The ethnic Vietnamese have traditionally looked down upon the country's ethnic minorities. The rural minorities, such as the Montagnards (mountain people), have often reinforced Vietnamese stereotypes by trying to remain separate from mainstream Vietnamese society.

The Communist ideal includes gender equality, and women have equal rights under the law. However, Vietnam is still a male-dominated country, both in business and government. In most ethnic groups, the husband remains the titular head of the home. The aged are considered more knowledgeable than the young, and their opinions are highly respected.

▶ BUSINESS PRACTICES

Punctuality, Appointments, and Local Time

- Punctuality is key; be on time for all business engagements.
- Being prompt is not as vital for social events, but do not be more than a half-hour late.
- In Vietnam, as in most other countries, the day is written first, then the month, then the year (e.g., December 3, 2010, is written 3.12.10).
- Prior appointments are necessary; do not try to make an impromptu office visit.
- Vietnam is seven hours ahead of Greenwich Mean Time (G.M.T. +7), or thirteen hours ahead of U.S. Eastern Standard Time (E.S.T. +13).

Negotiating

- The Vietnamese are great fans of bargaining. They dicker over the price of everything, from taxi rides to real estate. When you finally get around to talking about the price, expect them to negotiate aggressively.

Vietnam

- Connections are all-important in Vietnam. You cannot do anything unless you are know the right (that is, powerful) people. Personal introductions are preferred, but a letter of introduction is better than nothing.
- The Vietnamese need to personally trust you before they will do business with you. Expect to spend a substantial amount of time exchanging small talk, drinking tea, and developing a rapport. Do not consider this time wasted.
- In common with other Asian cultures, the Vietnamese will often say what they believe foreigners want to hear. It is your job to learn to tell the difference between honest agreement and a polite-but-insincere "yes."
- High pressure and emotion have little place in business in Vietnam. Most would rather let a deal fall through than be rushed.

Business Entertaining

- Your Vietnamese host will give at least one meal in your honor. You should return the favor by hosting a meal at an international hotel or fine restaurant.
- Business meetings are often held over lunch. Dinners are usually considered social occasions, but work can be discussed—if your Vietnamese counterpart initiates the topic.
- Expect beer or spirits to be served at a Vietnamese banquet. The senior member of your party will be expected to make a short speech—or, at least, a toast.
- Karaoke has become very popular in Vietnam. It is worthwhile to prepare a song if you are asked to sing.
- If you happen to visit a Vietnamese kitchen, you will probably find it decorated with the images of three Vietnamese kitchen gods.
- Vietnam is becoming a destination for culinary travelers. The Vietnamese have learned to make food out of virtually every nonpoisonous fish, beast, and plant native to their country. However, for those who are gastronomically timid, there are other cuisines available in Vietnam. In addition to Chinese and Thai food, Vietnamese cities have restaurants serving French and American cuisine. One can spend a considerable amount of time in Vietnam eating nothing but hamburgers and pizza.
- If you are a beer aficionado, you might want to visit one of the enormous beer halls that serve *Bia Hoi* (fresh beer)—brewed and served the same day.

Cultural Note
As a developing country, Vietnam boasts a relatively small number of entertainment venues. After the workday, the legal forms of entertainment consist of karaoke, traditional arts performances, such as music, dance, water puppets—or drinking. While the Vietnamese are usually happy to welcome foreigners into their bars and beer gardens, keep in mind that they have a number of drinking games. You're in trouble when a Vietnamese shouts *"tram van tram,"* which means "100 percent!" You are now in a race with the challenger to drain your drink! Of course, as soon as you drain that one, several more Vietnamese will undoubtedly challenge you again.

▶ PROTOCOL

Greetings
- The traditional greeting is a slight bow with the hands clasped together above the waist. There is no physical contact. However, the vast majority of businesspeople in Vietnam will greet you with either a slight bow or a handshake.
- It is not traditional for Vietnamese to introduce themselves, and their subordinates will often not introduce their boss, either. This is one reason that a personal introduction is extremely useful in Vietnam—from a person considered more-or-less an equal.
- Good topics of conversation are sports, travel, food, and music.
- If a Vietnamese superstition is discussed, take it seriously. There are many Vietnamese who will give it credence, and your host may be one.
- Most (but not all) businesspeople have business cards. There is little formality involved in exchanging cards.
- Your card will not be refused, but you might not be given one in exchange. Don't be offended by this.

Titles/Forms of Address
- Vietnamese names are written in this order: surname (a.k.a., family name) followed by two given names. Except in the most formal of situations, everyone will address the person by the second family name (that is, the final one in the series of three names), although this name may be preceded by an honorific.
- It is very important to use professional and governmental titles.

Gestures
- In common with other Communist states, Vietnam is a relatively puritanical country. Although brief hugs or a kiss on the cheek are acceptable between friends, extended public contact between the sexes is frowned upon.
- In general, do not touch your Vietnamese associates at work. Allow for more physical distance between you than is normal in the West.
- The foot is considered unclean by many Vietnamese. Do not move anything with your feet, and do not touch anything (except the ground) with your feet.
- Do not show the soles of your feet (or shoes). This restriction determines how one sits: you can cross your legs at the knee but not with one ankle on your knee. Also, do not prop your feet on anything not intended for feet, such as a desk.
- Among Vietnamese Muslims, the left hand is considered unclean. Favor your right hand over your left when you are among them.

- As in much of the world, to beckon someone you hold your hand out, palm downward, and make a scooping motion with the fingers. Beckoning someone with the palm up and wagging one finger—as in North America—can be construed as an insult.

Gifts

- Gifts are part of doing business in Vietnam. Come prepared with a gift for each participant on your first meeting. These gifts need not be expensive: pens, small electronics, and illustrated books of your home country are all acceptable gifts.
- A more expensive gift is expected to commemorate the successful conclusion of a business deal or your return to your home country.
- Gifts should be carefully wrapped. Currently, the old tradition of not opening a wrapped gift in the presence of the giver is fading away. Some Vietnamese will put a wrapped gift aside to open later; some will open it immediately. You should follow their suggestion as to when you open a gift.
- Avoid using wrapping paper that is primarily white or black. Both of these colors are associated with death and mourning.
- Always bring something when invited to a house. Wine, candy, or flowers are the traditional choices.

Dress

- Dress in Vietnam is fairly casual, although clothing should cover most of the body (despite the tropical heat).
- While Communist governments are often quite puritanical, the current government of Vietnam restored national beauty contests in 1992. The classic Vietnamese four-flap dress worn by everyone from schoolgirls to beauty pageant contestants is known as the *ao dai*. Traditionally, the ao dai was only worn once a year, during the Tet Festival.

Cultural Note

Modesty is a characteristic of Vietnamese culture. Consequently, bragging and hype are alien to them, and they are apt to respond badly to pompous behavior.

APPENDIX A
Titles and Forms of Address

There are many naming conventions within *Kiss, Bow, or Shake Hands*: single names, compound names, patronymics, names read right to left or left to right, honorifics, etc. For efficiency's sake, if multiple countries utilize the same naming customs, we have tried to consolidate them here. Some of this data may be repeated in certain chapters.

Titles and Forms of Address for most Spanish-Speaking Countries (excluding Argentina)

- Historically, many parents followed a Christian tradition and gave their children compound names at their baptism. For example: Juan Antonio, or Maria Rosa. The first names would usually include a saint's name, or a name of a relative or godparent—or both.
- At a confirmation ceremony, a middle name was often added, which might be derived from the person's "Saint's Day" (e.g., October 18 is the Feast of St. Luke, so a child born on that day might receive the name Luke, or Lucia). Confirmation names are not often included in business or social interactions.
- First (and possibly, middle names) would then be followed by compound family names (or surnames): one from the father, which would be listed first, followed by one from the mother. The father's surname was commonly used when addressing someone—e.g., Señor José Antonio Martínez de García would be addressed as Señor Martínez, and Señorita Pilar María Nuñez de Cela would be addressed as Señorita Nuñez.

  If the two people in the above example married, the woman would traditionally add her husband's surname and be known by that: Señora Pilar María Nuñez Cela de Martínez. Most people would refer to her as Señora de Martínez or, less formally, Señora Martínez.
- As women become increasingly independent, they may retain their maiden names, or use any combination thereof.
- As a general rule, use only one surname when speaking to a person, but use both surnames when writing.
- Additionally, it is important to address individuals by any titles they may have, followed by their surnames. For example, teachers may prefer the title Profesor, and engineers may go by Ingeniero.
- Don and Doña are additional titles of respect
- In Spain, the use of the familiar (tú) and formal (Usted) forms of address are different from their usage in Latin America. For example, Spaniards may speak to domestic employees in the formal (Usted) manner; they feel this confers dignity and shows respect for the person.

Chinese Naming Conventions

- Chinese names are listed in a different order from Western names. Traditionally, each person received three characters from the Chinese language. The first was the family name (from the father), then a middle name (which used to be called a generational name—one for all the brothers and another for all the sisters in a family), and finally a given name—in that order. Historically, generational names could have been planned out by a family's ancestors and served a great purpose across the generations.
- After the Cultural Revolution, generational names became less common and were supplanted by individual middle names. For example, in 2005, the President of the People's Republic of China and General Secretary of the Communist Party of China, President Hu Jintao had the family name of Hu, a middle name of Jin, and a given name of Tao. (His name could also be rendered Hu Chin-t'ao.)
- Chinese wives do not generally take their husband's surnames but instead maintain their maiden names. Although westerners commonly address a married woman as "Mrs." plus her husband's family name, it is more appropriate to call her "Madam" plus her maiden family name. For example, Liu Yongqing (female) is married to Hu Jintao (male). While westerners would probably call her Mrs. Hu, she is properly addressed as Madam Liu.
- For the sake of Western conventions, Chinese women sometimes use their husbands' last names.
- Similarly, many Chinese adopt English first names so that English speakers can have familiar-sounding names to identify them. Thus, Chang Wu Jiang may call himself Mr. Tony Chang. Others use their initials (Mr. T. J. Chang), which indicates that Chang is his surname.
- Another way that Chinese businesspeople may clarify their surnames is by underlining or capitalizing them in written correspondence.
- Chinese names can be rendered different ways in English, so do not be surprised by variations. Chinese may have two names but more often have three names, and the most common variant is whether or not to hyphenate the final two names. For example, the first chief executive of Hong Kong was Tung Chee Hwa. His name could also be rendered Tung Chee-hwa, or even Tung Cheehwa. (As with most Chinese, his surname is listed first, so he would be referred to as "Mr. Tung.")
- If many Chinese seem to have similar names, it is because there are only about 400 different surnames in China! However, when these surnames are transcribed into English, there are several possible variations. For example, Wong, Wang, and Huang are all English versions of the same Chinese clan name.
- Most people you meet should be addressed with a title and their name. If a person does not have a professional title (President, Engineer, Doctor), simply use "Mr." or "Madam," "Mrs.," or "Miss," plus the name.

- The Chinese are very sensitive to status and titles, so you should use official titles such as "General," "Committee Member," or "Bureau Chief" when possible. Never call anyone "Comrade" unless you are a Communist also.

Arabic Naming Conventions

- Muslim names are usually derived from Arabic. Translating from Arabic to other alphabets is not an exact science. Arabic names may be spelled several different ways in English. For example, the founder of the Kingdom of Saudi Arabia was King Abdul-Aziz Al-Saud. However, his name is also rendered in English as King Abd-al-Aziz Al Saud. History books tend to render his name as King Ibn Saud.
- Arabic naming traditions are used in many Islamic countries (e.g., Indonesia). In general, names are written in the same order as English names: title, given name, middle name (often a patronymic), and surname (family name). In 2005, the new ruler of Saudi Arabia was King Abdullah Bin-Abd-al-Aziz al Saud; his title was "King," his given name was Abdullah, bin Abd-al-Aziz is a patronymic meaning "son of Abd-Aziz," and al-Saud was his family name. (King Abdullah succeeded the late King Fahd in August of 2005.)
- Many Arab names have specific meanings (e.g., *Amal* means "Hope"), or they are from the Bible (*Ibrahiim* means "Abraham"), or they are based upon the name of God in Arabic. Abd or Abdul are not complete names in themselves; they simply mean "servant of." King Abdul-al-Aziz can be translated as "Servant of the Almighty."
- The term *bin* (sometimes spelled *ibn*) literally means "from" in Arabic, so it is not immediately apparent whether a name like bin Mubarak indicates "son of Mubarak" or "from the town of Mubarak." However, most Saudis use it as a patronymic.
- If an Arab's grandfather is (or was) a famous person, he sometimes adds his grandfather's name. Thus, Dr. Mahmoud bin Sultan bin Hamad Al Muqrin is "Dr. Mahmoud, son of Sultan, grandson of Hamad, of the House (family) of Muqrin."
- Westerners frequently mistake bin for the name Ben, short for Benjamin. Obviously, bin has no meaning by itself, and one cannot address a Saudi as bin.
- The female version of bin is *bint*. Thus, Princess Fatima bint Ibrahim al-Saud is Princess "Fatima, daughter of Ibrahim, of the house of Saud."
- Arabic women generally do not change their names after they marry.
- Another common naming convention is a given name first, then the father's given name second, followed by the family name.
- Most Saudis should be addressed by title and given name (e.g., Prince Khalil), just as you would address a member of the British aristocracy (e.g., Sir John). They can also be addressed as "Your Excellency." In writing, use their full name.
- In Saudi Arabia, the title "Sheikh" (pronounced "shake") is used by any important leader well versed in the Koran, or an individual worthy of great respect; it does not designate membership in the royal family.

- A Muslim male who has completed his pilgrimage to Mecca is addressed as Haji. A woman who has done so would be addressed as Hajjah. Note that these titles are not automatically conferred on spouses; they must be individually earned by making the pilgrimage. However, when in doubt, err on the side of generosity. It is better to give a superfluous title than to omit one.

Indian Naming Conventions

- It is important to note that India's naming conventions are changing. For example, the southern region of India seems to be gradually moving toward the naming customs of the north, and professional females are starting to keep their maiden names.
- Titles are highly valued by Indians. Always use professional titles, such as "Professor" and "Doctor." Do not address someone by his or her first name unless you are asked to do so, or you are close friends; use "Mr.," "Mrs.," or "Miss." (In Hindi, "Mr." is Shri and "Mrs." is Shrimati.)
- Status is determined by age, university degrees, caste, and profession.
- Hindus in the Northern region of India generally have a given name, a middle name, and a family name—written in that order. Female siblings may share a middle name, as may male siblings.
- Because one's name can indicate a caste, Northern Indian families sometimes opt to change their surnames.
- In the southern region, naming conventions differ. Traditionally, Hindus did not have family surnames. A Hindu Indian male may have used the initial of his father's name first, or the town he came from, followed by his own personal name. For example, V. Thiruselvan is "Thiruselvan, son of 'V.'" For legal purposes, both names would be written out with an s/o (for "son of") between the names: Thiruselvan s/o Vijay. In either case, he would be known as Mr. Thiruselvan. However, long Indian names are often shortened. He may prefer to be called either Mr. Thiru or Mr. Selvan.
- Hindu female names follow the same pattern: father's initial plus personal name. When fully written out, d/o (for "daughter of") is used instead of s/o. When an Indian woman married, she usually ceased to use her father's initial; instead, she followed her personal name with her husband's name. For instance, when S. Kamala (female) married V. Thiru (male), she might go by Mrs. Kamala Thiru.
- Some Indians will use Western-style surnames. Christian Indians may have biblical surnames like Abraham or Jacob. Indians from the former Portuguese colony of Goa may have surnames of Portuguese origin, such as Rozario or DeSilva. Such a person could be addressed as Dr. Jacob or Mr. DeSilva.
- Indian Sikhs generally have a given name followed by either Singh (for men) or Kaur (for women). Always address them by a title and first name. While Singh literally means "lion," to refer to a Sikh male as Mr. Singh may be as meaningless as saying "Mr. Man" in English.

Further data on naming conventions can be found on our Web site, *www.kissboworshake hands.com*, or in *Merriam Webster's Guide to International Business Communications*.

Appendix B
Contacts and Resources

Because of the dynamic nature of travel warnings, customs requirements, and so on, we have selected several large Web sites that provide helpful data for international travelers. While every country has its own respective requirements, these U.S. Web sites are a reasonable start for international business contacts, travel advisories, medical information, passports, etc.

Government Sites

Contact your country's embassy when you travel, as it can prove helpful in emergency situations. Many embassies now allow registration of your information online.

Embassies can arrange appointments with local business and government officials; provide counsel on local trade regulations, laws, and customs; and identify importers, buyers, agents, etc. They may also provide economic, political, technological, and labor data. There are many lists of embassies on the Web, such as *http://usembassy.state.gov*. Other helpful government sites include:

www.state.gov/travel
> Provides:
> Travel warnings, consular information sheets, and public announcements
> Passports and visas for U.S. citizens
> Country background notes
> Foreign consular offices in the United States
> Key officers at U.S. foreign service posts

www.customs.ustreas.gov
> Produces a database that can be queried by topic (e.g., travel requirements, importing procedures, etc.), or an individual's status (e.g., importer, traveler, carrier, etc.)

www.cia.gov
> The U.S. Central Intelligence Agency produces several useful documents, including:
> *The World Factbook* (at *www.cia.gov/cia/publications/factbook*)
> The Chiefs of State and Cabinet Members of Foreign Governments (*www.cia.gov/cia/publications/chiefs/index.html*). This directory is updated weekly and includes many governments of the world.

Corruption and Bribery

www.transparency.org
> Transparency International, a worldwide nongovernmental organization, reports on corruption and bribery around the world. They issue an annual "Corruption Perceptions Index," which relates to perceptions of the degree of corruption as seen by businesspeople, academics, and risk analysts. In the "2005 Corruption Perceptions Index," the 5 least

corrupt countries out of 158 were Iceland (number 1), Finland, New Zealand, Denmark, and Singapore. The 5 most highly corrupt were Haiti, Myanmar, Turkmenistan, Bangladesh, and Chad (number 158).

Foreign Language Learning

Whether you are traveling for business or social purposes, learning a foreign language can tremendously increase your success and personal satisfaction. Research has also shown that learning a second language improves students' analytic capacities. Of course, the ability to communicate in another language gives executives a huge advantage in the global market. Even a few words of greeting can make an enormous difference. There are scores of language and translation resources on the Web. On our Web site *www.kissboworshakehands.com* we link to viable options for foreign language programs and translation systems. As a start, try:

> *www.bbc.co.uk/languages*
> The British Broadcasting System's excellent Web site

Medical Information

> *www.cdc.gov/travel*
> The Centers for Disease Control provides an abundance of medical resources for international travelers. It includes everything from health information and vaccinations required for specific destinations, to advice on traveling with children and pets.

Of course, you will want to be thoroughly prepared for your trip, so schedule physical and dental examinations well before leaving. Remember that some vaccinations must be given over a period of time. Also take current medical documentation with you, and list any chronic conditions and current prescription drugs (including dosages). In order to avoid problems at customs, carry all medications in their original containers. Also, take an extra set of glasses, contacts, or prescriptions. In your bags, include the name, address, and phone number of someone to be contacted in case of an emergency.

Prepare a basic medical travel kit, which might include aspirin, a topical antibiotic, bandages, a disinfectant, 0.5 percent hydrocortisone cream (for bites or sunburn), sunblock, a thermometer, and diarrhea medication. Pack the kit in your carry-on luggage.

Also confirm that you have sufficient travel medical insurance. There are two main types of travel insurance: 1) policies that make direct payments for medical care and provide assistance, and 2) policies that reimburse you for emergency expenses. (With the latter option, you might have to pay the doctor or hospital immediately—in local currency—and file a claim once you return home.)

While we do not endorse any specific organizations, the Bureau of Consular Affairs maintains an extensive list of Travel Insurance Companies, as well as Air Ambulance, Med-Evac companies, and Executive Medical Services. A list of these firms is available at:

> *http://travel.state.gov/travel/tips/health/health_1185.html*

Appendix C
Holidays

Every country in the world celebrates holidays, and little or no work is conducted during these celebrations. However, holidays are always subject to change. Governments frequently add, delete, or move certain official holidays. Furthermore, the dates for many holidays do not fall on the same day in the Western (Gregorian) calendar each year. This may be because they are dated using a calendar that does not correspond to the Western calendar (for example, the Arabic Hijra calendar is lunar and is only 354 days long).

Some cultures use lunisolar calendars (for instance, the Hebrew and Chinese calendars—although these two are not similar in other aspects), and some have both the aspects of solar and lunisolar calendars (for example, the Hindu calendar).

Actually, there are over twenty calendars in use around the world! Indonesia is a good example of one country that uses multiple calendars. They include the Gregorian calendar, one which is similar to the Islamic calendar, a calendar used primarily in Java, and several others. In Java, when the fifth day of a month coincides on all the calendars, various celebrations take place (businesses are opened, babies are named, etc.). This is because five is an auspicious number—there are five sacred mountains, five elements, and so forth.

Some holidays are purposefully consecutive, like "Golden Week" in Japan. It allows for Japanese workers to enjoy extended vacations and observe some important holidays together.

The work week may be different in various cultures as well. For example, in the Muslim world, the Sabbath is celebrated on Friday. Some Islamic nations have their "weekend" on Thursday and Friday, so their work week runs Saturday through Wednesday.

Whatever the calendar or work week in use, the only way to be sure your business trip is not interrupted by official or local holidays is to contact reliable, up-to-date sources before your trip. Consult with the country's embassy, call your associates at your destination, or reference our World Holiday Guide at:

www.kissboworshakehands.com

One additional note:

You may see the traditional terms B.C. (before Christ) and A.D. (anno Domini, "the year of the Lord") being used interchangeably or replaced with the terms B.C.E. (before the Common Era) and C.E. (Common Era). The new notation "Common" refers to the most common calendar—the Gregorian, or Western Calendar.

APPENDIX D
International Electrical Adaptors

This data is excerpted from a publication of the U.S. Department of Commerce.

The electricity used in much of the world (220–250 volts) is a different voltage from that used in North America (110–125 volts). Electrical appliances designed for North America may need converters to "step down" this higher voltage to the level required to operate. Some appliances cannot be converted for use elsewhere because they require sixty cycles per second (again, found primarily in North America), or they may have other requirements.

Electrical wall sockets found around the world are also likely to differ in shape from the sockets used in North America. Electrical adaptor plugs are available to slip over the plugs of North American appliances for use in such sockets (see the following charts for graphics of Plugs in Commercial Use, and for the Type of Plug by Country).

Type of Plug by Country

Country Plug	Type	Country Plug	Type	Country Plug	Type
Afghanistan	D	Canary Islands	C, E	France	E
Albania	C	Cape Verde, Rep. of	C, F	Gabon	D, E
Algeria	C, F	Cayman Islands	A, B	Gambia, The	G
Angola	C	Central African Republic	C, E	Germany, Fed. Rep. of	F
Argentina	C, I	Chad	E	Ghana	D, G
Australia	I	Chile	C, F, L	Gibraltar	C, G
Austria	C	China, Peoples Rep. of	C, D, G, H	Greece	C, F
Bahamas	A, B	Colombia	A, B	Greenland	C, K
Bahrain	G	Congo, Dem. Rep of		Grenada	G
Bangladesh	A, C, D	(form. Zaire)	E	Guatemala	A, B, G, H, I
Barbados	A, B, F, H	Congo, Peoples Rep. of	C, E	Guinea	C, F, K
Belarus	C	Costa Rica	A, B	Guinea-Bissau	C
Belgium	A, C, E	Cyprus	G	Guyana	A, H
Belize	A, B, H	Czech Republic	E	Haiti	A, B, H
Benin	D	Denmark	C, K	Honduras	A
Bermuda	A, B	Djibouti, Rep. of	C, E	Hong Kong	H
Bolivia	A, C	Dominican Republic	A	Hungary	C, F
Botswana	C, D, H	Ecuador	A, B, C, D	Iceland	B
Brazil	A, B, C	Egypt	C	India	C, D, G
Brunei	G	El Salvador	A, B, C, D, E, F, G, I, J, L	Indonesia	C, E, F
Bulgaria	F	England	A, C, H	Ireland	G
Burkina Faso	B, E	Equatorial Guinea	C, E	Israel	C, H
Burma	C, D, F	Eritrea	C	Italy	L
Burundi	C, E	Ethiopia	C	Ivory Coast	C, E
Cameroon	C, E	Fiji	I	Jamaica	A, B, C, D
Canada	B	Finland	C, F	Japan	A, B, I

Country Plug	Type	Country Plug	Type	Country Plug	Type
Jordan	C, F, G, L	Nigeria	C, D, H	Sudan	C, D
Kazakstan	C, G, H	Northern Ireland	A, C, H	Suriname	C, F
Kenya	G	Norway	C, F	Swaziland	D
Korea	C	Oman	H	Sweden	C, F
Kuwait	C, G	Pakistan	B, C, D	Switzerland	C, E, J
Laos	A, B, C, E, F	Palau	A, B	Syria	C
Lebanon	A, B, C, D, G	Panama	A, B, I	Tajikistan	C, I
Lesotho	D	Paraguay	C	Tahiti	A
Liberia	A, B	Peru	A, C	Taiwan	A, B
Luxembourg	F	Philippines	A, B, C	Tanzania	D, G
Macedonia.	C, F	Poland	C, E	Thailand	A, B, C, D, E, G, J, K
Madagascar	C, D, E, J, K	Portugal	C, F	Togo	C
Malawi	G	Qatar	D, G	Trinidad and Tobago	A, B
Malaysia	G	Romania	C, F	Tunisia	C, E
Mali, Rep. of	C, E	Russia	C	Turkey	C, F
Malta	G	Rwanda	C, J	Turkmenistan	B, F
Mauritania	C	Saudi Arabia	A, B, G	Uganda	G
Mauritius	G	Scotland	A, C, H	Ukraine	C
Mexico	A, B	Senegal	C, D, E, K	United Arab Emirates	C, D, G
Monaco	C, D, E, F	Serbia-Montenegro	F	Uruguay	C, F, I, L
Morocco	C, E	Seychelles	D	Uzbekistan	C, I
Mozambique	C, D, F	Sierra Leone	D, G	Venezuela	A, B, H
Namibia	C	Singapore	B, H	Wales	A, C, H
Nepal	C, D	Slovak Republic	E	Western Samoa	H
Netherlands	F	Somalia	C	Yemen, Rep. of	A, D, G
New Zealand	H	South Africa	D	Zambia	C, D, G
Nicaragua	A	Spain	C, F	Zimbabwe	D, G
Niger	A, C, E	Sri Lanka	D		

PLUGS IN COMMERCIAL USE

Type A Flat blade attachment plug	**Type B** Flat blades with round grounding pin
Type C Round pin attachment plug	**Type D** Round pins with ground
Type E Round pin plug and receptacle with male grounding pin	**Type F** "Schuko" plug and receptacle with side grounding contacts
Type G Rectangular blade plug	**Type H** Oblique flat blades with ground
Type I Opblique flat blade with ground	**Type J** Round pins with ground
Type K Round pins with ground	**Type L** Round pins with ground

INDEX

About the Authors

Terri Morrison and Wayne A. Conaway have coauthored five books on intercultural communications, hundreds of articles, and several databases—all of which are available at *www .kissboworshakehands.com*. Terri Morrison also offers keynote seminars on intercultural communications, which range from one to three hours. These highly informative, entertaining, and interactive presentations can be customized for specific industries, countries, and regions of the world. A speaker video, biography, and references are available at *www .TerriMorrison.com*.

Their electronic product *Kiss, Bow, or Shake Hands: Expanded Edition* (KBSH:XE) contains up-to-date business and cultural data on over 100 countries. Numerous private and public institutions have found KBSH:XE to be a valuable tool for facilitating globalization. Subscriptions are available for corporate, educational, governmental, and personal usage and contain information on everything from Business Practices (appointments, negotiating, entertaining, etc.) to Intellectual Property Rights and Culturally-Correct Gifts. A demo of KBSH:XE is available at their Web site.

The electronic *World Holiday and Time Zone Guide* contains a useful format of cross-referencing holidays both by the country and by the day of the year. This database is a convenient feature for heavy travelers, meeting planners, and researchers who need current holiday information on 101 countries.

The study of intercultural communication represents a lifelong interest for the authors of *Kiss, Bow, or Shake Hands*. By way of continuing that research, the authors invite your comments. Whether your own experience confirms or diverges from the data in this book, they welcome your perspective. Please contact them at:

TerriMorrison@getcustoms.com
Phone: 610-725-1040

Or via these Web sites:
www.getcustoms.com
www.TerriMorrison.com
www.kissboworshakehands.com

Virtue is bold, and goodness never fearful.
—William Shakespeare